SOCIOLOGY OF FAMILIES

TITLES OF RELATED INTEREST FROM PINE FORGE PRESS

SOCIOLOGY OF FAMILIES

David M. Newman

DePauw University

Visual Essays edited by Shelley Kowalski

University of Oregon

Demographic Essays edited by Jill Grigsby

Pomona College

Pine Forge Press

Thousand Oaks, California • London • New Delhi

For information, address:

Pine Forge Press
A Sage Publications Company
2455 Teller Road
Thousand Oaks, California 91320
(805) 499-4224
E-mail: sales@pfp.sagepub.com

Sage Publications Ltd.
6 Bonhill Street
London EC2A 4PU
United Kingdom

Sage Publications India Pvt. Ltd.
M-32 Market
Greater Kailash I
New Delhi 110 048 India

Production Coordinator: Windy Just
Production Management: Scratchgravel Publishing Services
Copy Editor: Stephanie Prescott
Typesetter: Scratchgravel Publishing Services
Visual Essays Design: Lisa Mirski Devenish
Cover Designer: Ravi Balasuriya
Cover Image: "The Builders" by Jacob Lawrence. Courtesy of the artist and Francine Seders Gallery.

Printed in the United States of America
99 00 01 02 03 10 9 8 7 6 5 4 3 2

Library of Congress Cataloging-in-Publication Data

Newman, David M., 1958–
    Sociology of families / by David M. Newman.
          p.   cm.
      Includes bibliographical references and index.
      ISBN 0-7619-8514-X (cloth)
        1. Family—United States.   2. Family—United States—Public
    opinion.   3. Social problems—United States.   4. Public
    opinion—United States.   5. United States—Social conditions.
    I. Title.
    HQ535.N48   1999
    306.85'0973—ddc21   98-40130
                                                              CIP

ABOUT THE AUTHOR

David M. Newman (Ph.D., University of Washington) is an Associate Professor of Sociology at DePauw University. In addition to the introductory course, he teaches courses in research methods, family, social psychology, and deviance. He has won teaching awards at both the University of Washington and DePauw University.

ABOUT THE PUBLISHER

Pine Forge Press is a new educational publisher, dedicated to publishing innovative books and software throughout the social sciences. On this and any other of our publications, we welcome your comments. Please call or write us at:

Pine Forge Press
A Sage Publications Company
2455 Teller Road
Thousand Oaks, CA 91320
(805) 499-4224
E-mail: sales@pfp.sagepub.com

Visit our new World Wide Web site, your direct link to a multitude of online resources:
http://www.pineforge.com

For my family

BRIEF CONTENTS

CONTENTS

PREFACE

You'd be hard-pressed to find a topic as emotionally compelling and as personally interesting to people as family. It seemed that whenever I told people I was writing this book they'd either start to relate a family anecdote that they thought I should include ("You want to know about families? Just ask me. I'll tell you about *families*. Mine's a doozy!"); express their opinion about society-wide family problems ("Parents aren't disciplining their kids enough, and *that's* why there's so much crime in the streets!"); or ask for my advice on some difficulty they were having ("How can I get my kids to listen to me?!").

I began to think that everybody had something to say or some opinion about families. To probe this issue further, I decided to do some Internet browsing. Not surprisingly, I discovered thousands of sites devoted to different aspects of families. Most are sites related to either the academic research on various aspects of family life (marriage, divorce, children, and so on), political interest groups devoted to some family-related issue, or nonprofit family service organizations. But I also found something unexpected: over 2,500 *personal* family home pages—individual families simply presenting information about, well, *themselves*.

Most of these sites conveyed the sort of information you find in those letters people stuff in their Christmas cards each year. You know, "Fred finally passed the CPA exam"; "Suzie loves her new position as goalkeeper on her soccer team"; "Our trip to Tuscany was breathtaking"; "We're thinking of planting cherry tomatoes instead of Romas this year." Many of them contained elaborate family photo albums with pictures of weddings, christenings, children through various stages of development, beloved pets, redecorated houses, cruise trips, and so on. Some offered even deeper peeks into their lives by providing detailed family trees, religious testimonials, wedding vows, favorite cookie recipes, opinions on controversial issues such as home schooling or gay marriage, or space to submit suggestions for baby names. One woman even broadcast the birth of her child, *live*, over the Internet.

I wondered what would motivate people to open up the private details of their families to the vast, anonymous world of cyberspace. It's not as if there's a critical mass of people out there who need immediate access to information about Joe and Martha Klotzman's passion for Tupperware parties. Instead, people like the Klotzmans are taking this technological opportunity to make a public statement about their commitment to and pride in their families. They're not the only ones. Lately there has been a parade of high-profile people declaring their commitment to their families and their willingness to sacrifice for them. For example:

- A major league baseball player on one of the best teams asks to be traded to an expansion team—and agrees to a large pay *cut*—so he can be closer to his estranged children.
- A powerful member of the presidential Cabinet resigns so that he can focus on the future of his three children.
- Several high-ranking members of Congress give up their seats to spend more time with their families.
- The president and chief executive of one of the largest multinational corporations in the world unexpectedly quits her job because she wants to devote herself to her family.
- A 15-year-old Olympic figure-skating champion decides to turn pro, forgoing a chance to win another gold medal. Her reason? She claims that the rigorous Olympic training regimen had separated her from her family too long.

Family has certainly become fashionable at the end of the millennium. You'd think that a topic that is so central and so deeply interesting to so many people would be the easiest thing in the world to write about, right? Not necessarily. For as long as there have been people ruminating over the human condition, there have been scholars, poets, novelists, musicians, and clergy examining, studying, celebrating, bemoaning, and making predictions and writing about every conceivable aspect of family life. And there is no shortage of contemporary "experts" who are willing to offer their 2 cents about the joys and sorrows of families. So how does one write about something so eternally important without trodding over well-worn ground?

I knew from the beginning that I didn't want this book simply to be an encyclopedia of information that would be useful only in the context of a college course—easily discarded at the end of the semester. I wanted it to be something of a guide as well—not only *informative* in terms of current sociological knowledge of families, but *meaningful* in terms of contemporary family debates, and *applicable* to your everyday family lives. In other words, I wanted the book to connect to your personal experiences while, at the same time, showing you how sociologists understand and explain families.

One of the difficulties I faced in accomplishing this goal was that a student's first course or textbook on family is never a his or her *introduction* to the topic of family. Everybody has grown up in one type of family or another. Consequently, all students bring with them to these courses a lifetime's worth of personal information, data, values, expectations, and assumptions about family life. Many have seen their parents divorce and remarry. Most have some experience with siblings or grandparents or cousins. Some have even formed their own families. Indeed, it's often said that when it comes to a topic like family, everyone is a potential expert.

With this direct knowledge comes some deeply held beliefs about what a family is and how it should work. Such preconceived notions present special challenges to instructors—and, by extension, to textbook authors. Certainly we want our students to be able to apply the course material directly to their own lived experiences. I've discovered in my own classes that students are more attentive and learn more when they find the subject matter immediately relevant to their lives.

But at the same time we want our classes and our textbooks to be more than just an album of personally familiar snippets of family life. That "it-happens-to-me-therefore-it-must-be-true-for-everyone" approach to the material can be a serious obstacle to learning. Discussions that stay at this level become merely exchanges of personal anecdotes, and little is learned about understanding the subject sociologically.

So a course—and a textbook—on the family must go beyond simply telling stories you can relate to. It must show how professional scholars go about understanding the social patterns that underlie those family matters that everyone seems to have some experience with or some opinion about. A textbook must therefore provide you with the intellectual tools you need to *understand* the broader social implications of your own family experiences, *appreciate* the applicability of the sociological perspective to your own life, and critically *evaluate* the social information about families that bombards you every day. In short, it must strike a balance between the personal and emotional relevance of the material on the one hand and the scholarly understanding of it on the other.

One way to accomplish this goal is to teach (and write) "deductively"—starting with an examination of sociological theory and research and then "working down" to the level of personally relevant examples, "real-world" experiences, and controversial issues. This style of teaching often relies on a traditional lecture-style format and an authoritative textbook.

Unfortunately such an approach—especially with a topic like family—runs the serious risk of "losing" you early on. Certainly you should understand the sociological perspective on family. But a perspective that sounds technical and seems scientifically disconnected runs the risk of robbing personally meaningful topics of all their flavor and interest. Many very good, informative textbooks today that aim to be rigorous, scholarly, and thoroughly sociological turn off students before the end of the first chapter. As I've seen in my own teaching, students want the knowledge they acquire in college to be intellectually stimulating, but they also want it to be pertinent, provocative, and timely. I think they have a point.

Thus, I have organized this textbook on family around an "inductive" style of learning, the sort of "active" approach that more and more instructors are using these days. The book begins at the level of personal relevance or controversy with an examination of familiar contemporary issues—topics you are likely to know or feel strongly about. Once this personal connection has been made, we can "work up" to the deeper and more detailed sociological understanding of the issues at hand, using the theories and the data of social science to understand the meaning and broader relevance of those controversies and experiences.

The Design of This Book

Since this book is based on an inductive style of learning, it is organized very differently from most traditional and current family textbooks. It's divided into two parts that are distinct from one another in style, content, and purpose.

Part I—*Private Experiences and Public Issues*—contains eight relatively short essays or "issues" that focus on various controversial topics and questions pertaining to family life. My purpose in these essays is to highlight some crucial and sometimes emotional questions that bear on contemporary family experiences: Who gets to be called a family? How accurate are our popular images of families? How private should families be? Are people's personal interests incompatible with their family obligations? How do race, class, and gender come to bear on people's everyday family experiences? Does a family have to conform to a particular structure in order to be effective? Has family as an institution lost its influence over people's lives?

These essays are meant to provoke critical thought and debate. To that end, each issue concludes with a set of discussion questions. These questions are designed *not* to gauge your ability to recall facts from these essays but to spur classroom debate on the societal and personal implications of the material.

The ultimate teaching value of the issues lies in their connection to the chapters in Part II—*Sociological Dimensions of Family Life*. In these chapters I discuss the sociological concepts, theories, and research that can help you understand the social forces that influence your family experiences, thereby shedding light on the issues introduced in Part I. The specific topics covered in this part of the book closely resemble those you'd find in most family textbooks: attraction and love, marriage and work, parenting and child rearing, intimate violence, divorce and remarriage, old age, death, family policy. But my goal here is to move beyond simple descriptions of these phenomena to an intellectually challenging (and hopefully applicable) examination of the interrelationship between social structural forces and private family experiences that builds on the issues presented in Part I. Particular attention is paid in these chapters to the role of history, culture, economics, politics, and religion in family experiences. Furthermore, issues of race, class, gender, and sexual orientation are woven throughout these chapters.

▲ Look in the margins of the chapters in Part II (or between paragraphs in the issues of Part I) for this symbol, which indicates a "hot link" to a related matter in another chapter or issue.

You will quickly notice that the book is organized around the assumption of interrelatedness among the issues in Part I and the chapters in Part II. One of the greatest difficulties in writing a book on family is that family matters don't align neatly in distinct and conceptually independent chapters. One can't talk about gender in families, for instance, without talking about work issues, power, children and child rearing, domestic violence, and so forth. A topic like divorce is closely related to economics, child rearing, work, social policy, perhaps even intimate violence. So the scholarly information provided in Part II is meant to be applied reflexively to shed some sociological light on the controversial issues raised in Part I. To help you to see these connections, a special feature called *hot links* alerts you to other chapters and issues that discuss related topics. Small triangles in the text mark the statements that can be linked to other sections of the book. ▲

Other Helpful Features

This book contains several other features that are designed to provide useful information in a way that makes teaching more effective. For instance, each chapter in Part II contains a photographic feature called *Windows on Family*. Most textbooks have an abundance of photographic material, but these images often seem to be simply filling up space. I wanted the visual aspect of this book to paint vivid and informative sociological portraits of family life. The multipage *Windows on Family* photo essays will help you "see" many of the concepts and ideas that you will read about in the chapter. As you study the visual essays, you will be practicing the skills of observation that can make you a more astute participant in your family and in your social world.

Each of the Part II chapters also contains a multipage feature called *Demo•Graphic Essay*. These sets of graphs and charts present statistical information on various aspects of families in a way that is easy to understand and visually appealing. The topic of family has been the subject of a vast amount of quantitative research, but a barrage of individual graphs, tables, or charts, like those in a typical textbook, may obscure the overall picture painted by the research. Each *Demo•Graphic Essay* is self-contained, with explanatory text and thought-provoking questions, but it is also tied conceptually to the chapter in which it appears. The purpose of this feature is not only to provide statistical support for the points made in the text but also to help you learn how to go beyond anecdotal understanding to broader sociological perspectives.

Each chapter in Part II also includes a short list of chapter highlights, to clarify the important concepts, and ends with a section called *Your Turn*. This section encourages you to study the "real world," much as professional sociologists do, to get a better understanding of the similarities and differences among families.

Finally, this book comes with a companion volume of short readings—articles, chapters, and excerpts from other sources, edited by sociologist Cheryl Albers. These readings address provocative questions that echo many of the subjects covered in this book. The readings examine common, everyday experiences, controversial issues, or distinct historical events that illustrate the relationship between social forces and individual family life. Many of these pieces show how sociologists gather evidence about families through carefully designed research. An essay at the beginning of each group of readings points up the common threads as well as the discrepancies that make the sociological study of families so endlessly fascinating.

A Word about Words

As a sociologist, I know the power of language in shaping ideas, values, and attitudes. I have tried to be very careful in my choice of terminology. Consider, for instance, the title of this book: *Sociology of Families.* You will notice that I use the word *Families* and not *The Family.* One of the key themes of this book is that families are extremely diverse in form and function. No single family structure can serve as a prototype for all Americans. Hence in the title I have avoided using the term *The Family.* In fact, throughout the book I have opted for the more inclusive (and more accurate) term "families." Only when referring to the *institution* of family or referring to a specific family (for example, "When she became the head of the family . . .") do I use "the family."

A Final Thought

As you've probably noticed, few subjects in today's society carry as much social, political, and emotional freight as "family." Whether spoken of reverently as the moral foundation of the entire society or referred to disparagingly by some rebellious teenager as the greatest obstacle to happiness and freedom, "family" permeates our lives and defines who we are as a culture like no other institution.

Sociologists may have some things in common, but our assumptions, perspectives, and attitudes can be quite different. Some sociologists focus on broad demographic information about large groups of people; others concentrate on the everyday experiences of individuals. Some write from a specific political position or theoretical perspective; others are more pluralistic in the ideologies and theories they use. This book reflects my sociological perspective—one that draws heavily on the interrelationship between the everyday experiences of individuals and the society in which they live. I believe that family is both an individually lived experience and a systematic social institution. So our private lives are always a combination of the idiosyncrasies of the family to which we belong *and* the broader social rules and expectations associated with *families* in general. In that sense, our families are strongly influenced by large-scale social forces like culture, history, economics, politics, religion, the media, and so on. At the same time, however, we, as individuals, are vital contributors to our social structure. As individuals or in groups, we can, through our actions, change, modify, or reinforce existing elements of family life.

I hope you will find the unique organization of this book both informative and provocative. Above all, I hope you will find it useful in helping you understand why and how families have such great significance for all of us.

Good luck,

David M. Newman
Department of Sociology/Anthropology
DePauw University
Greencastle, IN 46135
E-mail: DNEWMAN@DEPAUW.EDU

A Note to the Instructor

One of the chief virtues of the two-part organizational strategy in this book is its flexibility. For instance, an instructor who wants to intersperse discussion of a particular controversy or question from Part I with consideration of related sociological concepts from Part II might ask students to read issues and chapters in the following sequence:

Issue 1	What Is a Family?
Issue 2	How Accurate Are Popular Images of American Families?
Chapter 1	The Link Between Family Life and Social Science
Issue 5	How Do Gender and Power Influence Family Life?
Chapter 2	Intimate Relationships: Love, Sex, and Attraction
Chapter 3	Gender, Marriage, and Work
Issue 6	How Do Race, Ethnicity, and Racism Affect Family Life?
Issue 7	How Do Wealth and Poverty Determine Family Experiences?
Chapter 4	Parenthood and Parenting
Chapter 5	Childhood and Child Rearing

Another organizational strategy might be to use some of the Part I issues at the beginning of the course and some at the end, thereby "bookending" the content-driven chapters of Part II with topics that lend themselves to interesting debate:

The point is that, although the issues and chapters are arranged sequentially, they need not be read in the order in which they appear.

ACKNOWLEDGMENTS

My 9-year old son, Seth, helped me when I packed up the last chapters of this book to send to the publisher. "Wow," he said as he looked at the imposing stack of paper, "it must have taken you *a whole month* to write this book!" I smiled at his naïveté. "Well," I said in that condescending, fatherly tone that we use when we're convinced we know more than the child we're speaking to, "it actually took a *little* longer than that." "What, like two months?" he suggested. "More like two *years*," I replied. He looked astonished. "Two years!?! Boy, you're not very good at this, are you?"

I'm not sure if he's right about that or not. What I do know is that writing a book like this one is an enormously time-consuming endeavor that simultaneously requires total seclusion and utter dependence on others' expertise, guidance, and good will. Although it's my name that appears on the cover, many people contributed their time, suggestions, opinions, emotional support, and sometimes simply a well-timed meal to bring this project to fruition.

First, I'd like to express my heartfelt appreciation to Steve Rutter, publisher and president of Pine Forge Press, for his vision and his wisdom. He pushed hard and demanded a lot, and there were times when I was convinced that he believed there were 36 hours in a day. But he never wavered from his goal of publishing a book that is useful and unique. For that, I will always be grateful.

The staff at Pine Forge—Sherith Pankratz, Jean Skeels, and Windy Just—were invaluable in guiding me through the inevitable obstacles that arose from time to time. My gratitude also goes out to Anne and Greg Draus at Scratchgravel Publishing Services for their efficiency and attention to detail in producing this book. As always, Becky Smith provided impeccable editorial guidance in helping me at the various stages of cutting, revising, and polishing. And Stephanie Prescott did a wonderful job copyediting the final version of the manuscript.

I would like to thank Shelley Kowalski for her work on the visual essays and photographic material in the book and Jill Grigsby and Jillaine Tyson for compiling and producing the Demo•Graphic Essays.

I also appreciate the numerous helpful comments offered by reviewers:

Joan Alway, University of Miami
Trudy Anderson, Texas A&M University, Kingsville

Judith Barker, Ithaca College

Kristin Bates, California State University, San Marcos

Dianne Carmody, Old Dominion University

Cheryl Elman, University of Akron

Kristin Esterberg, University of Massachusetts, Lowell

Betty Farrell, Pitzer College

Carol Gardner, Indiana University Purdue University, Indianapolis

Becky Glass, State University of New York, Geneseo

Elizabeth Grauerholz, Purdue University

Ginger Macheski, Valdosta State University

Jane Nielsen, State University of New York, Oneonta

Susan Roxburgh, Kent State University

Georganne Rundblad, Illinois Wesleyan University

Laura Sanchez, Tulane University

Scott Sernau, Indiana University South Bend

Linda Stephens, Clemson University

Elaine Wethington, Cornell University

I especially want to express my sincere gratitude to the many colleagues and friends who offered cherished pieces of assistance along the way. In particular, I'd like to thank Meryl Altman, Srimati Basu, Istvan Csicsery-Ronay, Nancy Davis, Jodi O'Brien, Eric Silverman, Bruce Stinebrickner, Andrew Williams, Dolores Johnson, Maggie Snow, Carol Jones, and Bizz Steele.

Finally, I want to thank my wife, Elizabeth, and my sons, Zachary and Seth, for their patience and understanding. I know that my frequent bouts with self-doubt, grumpiness, and frustration over deadlines took an enormous toll on them, yet they always remained steadfast in their support.

■　　■　　■

Grateful acknowledgment is also made to the following for permission to reprint photos:

Page 2, *Blended Family* © UPI/Corbis-Bettmann; *Childless Family* © Emily Niebrand; *Intergenerational Family* © Emily Niebrand; *Female-Headed Family* © Annie Popkin; *Two-Woman Family* © Emily Niebrand. **Page 18,** *TV Families* collage by Shelley Kowalski, from *All in the Family* © Corbis-Bettman; *Brady Bunch* © AP/Wide World Photos; *Cosby Show* © AP/Wide World Photos. **Page 34,** *Keep Out!* © Stacey Kowalski. **Page 48,** David and Sharon Schoo © Sue Ogrocki—Reuters/Corbis Bettmann. **Page 62,** *Little Lamb Ad* © Shelley Kowalski. **Page 78,** *White Family Thanksgiving* © Bob Krist—Black Star. **Page 94 (top),** *Washing Family Car* © Rob Nelson—Black Star; **page 94 (bottom),** *Broken Beater Car* © Stacey Kowalski. **Page 112,** *Family Values* © Rob Nelson—Black Star.

Page 131, *With This Ring* © UPI/Corbis Bettman; *Nose Ring* © Stacey Kowalski; *Station Wagon* © Stacey Kowalski; *Sports Car* © Stacey Kowalski. **Page 132,** *Treadmill* © Stacey Kowalski; *Swing set* © Emily Niebrand; *Chuck E. Cheese* © Stacey Kowalski; *Starbucks* © Stacey Kowalski. **Page 133,** *Refrigerator* © Stacey Kowalski; *Brunch Spread* © Stacey Kowalski.

Page 162, *Sexy Mama* © Emily Niebrand; *Large Man* © Emily Niebrand; *Twins* © Emily Niebrand; *Wedding Day* © Emily Niebrand. **Page 163,** *Look Like a Couple* © Emily Niebrand; *Interracial Couple* © Emily Niebrand. **Page 164,** *Office Romance* © Stacey Kowalski; *Marriage Court* © Thom O'Connor—Black Star.

Page 204, *Business Men* © Corbis-Bettmann; *Housewife* © Annie Popkins. **Page 205,** *Bakery Clerk* © Annie Popkins; *Working Mother* © Rob Nelson—Black Star; *Workmate Chat* © Stacey Kowalski. **Page 206,** *Father Cooking Dinner* © Corbis-Bettmann JL002233; *Dinner Alone* © Stacey Kowalski; *Dinner Almost Alone* © Stacey Kowalski. **Page 207,** *Goldman Sach's Day Care* © Lisa Quiones—Black Star; *"Home Office"* © Stacey Kowalski.

Page 248, *Nurturing Mother* © Emily Niebrand; *The Brute and the Lamb* © Corbis-Bettmann; *Baby Duty* © Corbis-Bettmann. **Page 249,** *Sleeping Dad* © Corbis-Bettmann; *Mr. Mom* © Corbis-Bettmann. **Page 250,** *Daughter at Work* © Joseanne Daher—AP/Wide World; *Rollerblading Mom* © Michael Greenier—Black Star.

Page 286, *Baby Shoes* © Emily Niebrand; *Rich Victorian Family* © Brown Brothers B01343; *Dualing Boys* © Brown Brothers B0623. **Page 287,** *Working Toddler* © AP/Wide World Photos; *Driving Toddler* © Emily Niebrand. **Page 288,** *Self-Defense* © Michael Hanulak—Black Star; *Basketball Boys* © Emily Niebrand; *Basketball Girls* © Emily Niebrand. **Page 289,** *Drag Cheerleaders* © Emily Niebrand; *Tea Time* © Emily Niebrand; *All at Play* © Emily Niebrand.

Page 330, *Kid with Gun* © Tyrone Turner—Black Star; *"Replacement Killers"* © Stacey Kowalski. **Page 331,** *Missing Poster* © Shelley Kowalski; *Missing Poster at Grocery Store* © Shelley Kowalski; *Milk Carton* © Corbis-Bettmann; *Breakfast Table* © Stacey Kowalski. **Page 332,** *Hollyhocks* © Stacey Kowalski; *Crying Brother* © Diane Gentry—Black Star; *Television as Parent* © Emily Niebrand. **Page 333,** *Lorena Bobbitt Protest* © Gary Cameron—Corbis Bettmann; *Old Neglected Man* © Bruce Harkness.

Page 374, *Parents' Wedding Day* © Emily Niebrand; *Brothers* © Emily Niebrand. **Page 375,** *Dad* © Emily Niebrand; *Granddad* © Emily Niebrand. **Page 376,** *At the Beach* © Emily Niebrand; *Me and the Guys* © Emily Niebrand. **Page 377,** *Mom Reading* © Emily Niebrand.

Page 420, *Depression-Era School Kids* © Henry Kowalski; *Affluent Elderly* © Nova Development Corporation; *Antiwar Demonstrators* © Corbis; *Boy at FAO Schwarz* © Corbis. **Page 421,** *1974 Baby* © Henry Kowalski; *Partying Twenty-Somethings* © Henry Kowalski; *Marrying Thirty-Somethings* © Henry Kowalski. **Page 422,** *1940s TV Girl* © Corbis; *Pacifier and Computer* © James Sugar—Black Star; *Leave It to Beaver* © AP/Wide World Photos; *Beavis and Butthead* © AP/Wide World Photos. **Page 423,** *Hispanic Family* © Emily Niebrand; *Asian Grocery Store Owners* © Jordana Raiskin. **Page 424,** *Father Cooking* © Robert Footorap—Black Star.

Page 462, *Black Father and Children* © Emily Niebrand; *Gay Wedding* © Corbis—Bettmann. **Page 463,** *Bride Mother* © Emily Niebrand; *Unwed Teens* © Erica Lansner—Black Star. **Page 464,** *Empty Nesters at Graduation* © Henry Kowalski; *Vietnamese Family* © Corbis HD001074.

SOCIOLOGY OF FAMILIES

Private Experiences and Public Issues

Part I of this book examines several controversial issues that make up the social backdrop against which we experience our own families and form our opinions and beliefs about families in general. You will probe questions like, Which arrangements get to be called a family? How accurate are common images of families? Should families be completely private? How do we balance personal interests and needs with family obligations? How do gender, race, and ethnicity affect family life? What is the role of wealth or poverty in our family experiences? Is the institution of family breaking down? The information presented in response to these questions is designed to provoke personal reflection, critical thought, and impassioned discussion.

ISSUE 1

What Is a Family?

On August 13, 1995, Mickey Mantle died. He was a Hall of Fame baseball player for the New York Yankees and idol of millions during the 1950s and 1960s. A network news show that evening ran a videotape of the beginning of the game played at Yankee Stadium earlier in the day. The public address announcer asked the crowd to observe a moment of silence in remembrance of Mickey. "Today is a sad day for the Yankee *family*," he said, "because today we have lost one of our own, and one of the greatest players in the history of baseball."

In the film *Fried Green Tomatoes,* Evelyn Couch—a character played by actress Kathy Bates—becomes quite fond of an old woman named Ninny Threadgoode, whom she meets while visiting a nursing home. Ninny—played by the late Jessica Tandy—inspires Evelyn to take control of her own life. Evelyn decides she would like Ninny to live in her house with her and her husband, Ed. But Ed is unwilling to have a stranger live in their house, and he forcefully shouts, "She's not even *family*!" to which Evelyn quickly replies, "Well, she's *family* to me!"

In a video exhibit in the U.S. Holocaust Memorial Museum in Washington, D.C., one Holocaust survivor after another offers moving testimony of their experiences in German concentration camps during World War II. The survivors reminisce frequently and with great emotion about their *camp families*—those fellow inmates with whom they formed immensely important and powerful relationships in the face of what was surely perceived as certain death. Prior to imprisonment, the people who would become these survivors "parents," "children," "brothers," and "sisters" were complete strangers; many of them came from different countries and spoke different languages.

At the 1996 Democratic National Convention, Christopher Reeve, the actor confined to a wheelchair after a serious horse riding accident, made a speech to the delegates and to a national television audience:

> I know the last few years we have heard a lot about something called "family values." And like many of you, I have struggled to figure out what that means, and since my accident I have found a definition that seems to make sense. I think it means that we are all *family*. And that we all have value. Now if it's true, if America really is a family, then we have to recognize that many members of our family are hurting ... and if you're really committed to this idea of family, we have got to do something about it. (quoted in Democratic National Committee, 1996)

What do these diverse examples have in common? They all illustrate the varied, fluid, and somewhat unexpected ways people use the term *family* and the powerful connotation this term has. In all of these examples, only the word *family* was forceful enough to describe the strength of people's feelings and sense of connection to others. As a symbolic marker of the depth of affection and obligation, the vocabulary of *family* is unparalleled in the English language. No other term would do. The message would have been much less powerful if, say, the Yankee Stadium announcer referred to the grief of *a close-knit organization,* or if Evelyn Couch had tried to make her point by saying, "Well, she's *a real companion* to me!" or if the concentration camp survivors referred to fellow inmates who saved their lives as *good friends.* Could Christopher Reeve have appealed to our collective sense of moral duty if he said we are all *fellow citizens* instead of *family*? Certainly not.

The curious thing, though, is that in none of these examples was *family* used to describe what most of us commonly think of as a family—people related to one another through blood, marriage, or adoption. Instead it was used to describe real and imagined relationships based on love, commitment, sacrifice, and obligation.

Herein lies one of the most provocative but deceptively simple questions facing people who study family: Just exactly what is a family? Who get to be called a family?

In Issue 1, we will begin to look at the various ways *family* is defined. Far from being an obscure issue of linguistic and philosophical debate argued in the hallowed halls of academia, the definition of family—which groups of people get to be called a family and, conversely, which are prohibited from claiming family status—has very real and very critical consequences for all of us. Social policies often reflect prevailing definitions of family (Walters, 1982). A unit defined as a family may be in line to receive such benefits as housing, health care, and sick leave, not to mention legitimate recognition within its community (Popenoe, 1993). Those who fall outside the definition, however, are not only ineligible for such benefits but their relationships may be treated by some as illegitimate, inappropriate, or immoral as well (Hartman, 1994).

At the societal level, our beliefs about what a family *is* determine our beliefs about what it *isn't*. Our ideas about which family forms are acceptable, normal, desirable, and praiseworthy, determine which are considered abnormal, problematic, and in need of fixing or condemnation.

Definitions of Family

It would seem that nothing is more obvious and commonplace than the concept of family. It's something that everyone can relate to. We're all born into a family of some sort or another and will spend at least part of our lives inside one. We're surrounded by influential images of family in books, on television, and in film. If someone asked you to spot the families strolling through a large shopping mall, I would wager that you would have no difficulty doing so.

Yet, as familiar and recognizable as it is, *family* is also a remarkably elusive term that defies agreement or consistent application. Coming up with a universal definition of the family that everyone everywhere would agree on is a little like trying to nail pudding to a wall.

A nationwide poll conducted by the Roper Organization indeed found wide variation in what people consider a family. Although 98 percent of the respondents identified a married couple living with their children as a family, 53 percent also identified an unmarried man and woman who've lived together for a long time as a family; 27 percent felt a lesbian couple raising children was a family; and 20 percent felt two gay men committed to each other and living together constituted a family (cited in Gelles, 1995).

It's often unclear exactly why some arrangements are considered family and others not. Several years ago, for instance, a Cleveland woman was convicted and sentenced to 5 days in jail for failing to comply with the city's local residential zoning laws. Her crime? She resided in a "nonfamily" household in a neighborhood zoned for "families." The ordinance defined family as "a number of individuals related to the nominal head of the household or to the spouse of the nominal head of the household living as a single housekeeping unit in a single dwelling" (Minow, 1993). The woman lived with her son and two grandsons, but since the two boys were first cousins rather than brothers, the arrangement was not considered a family.

Yet in 1990 the New Jersey Supreme Court ruled that a group of ten male college students living in a home in a residential district in the borough of Glassboro could be considered a family. The borough had sought an injunction to prevent the students from using or occupying the home under a zoning ordinance that limited residence in this area to stable and permanent "traditional family units" or their "functional equivalent." The students shared the kitchen as well as household chores, grocery shopping, and yard work. They maintained a common checking account to pay for food and other household bills. They all intended to live there as long as they were enrolled at a nearby college (they were sophomores at the time). The court ruled that these facts reflected a plan by the students to live together for 3 years under conditions that met the requirement of a "stable and permanent living unit" (Thoresen, 1991).

Not only are some people excluded from accepted definitions of family, some family connections are privileged over others. Take adoption laws, for instance. Laws in some states keep adoption records sealed and refuse adoptees access to information about their birth parents. Such laws place biological parents' rights to privacy over adoptees' rights to information about and contact with biological relatives.

Changing Family Forms

One of the most common assessments we hear about current families is that they don't look or function like families of a few decades ago. ▲ Back then, families were assumed to be a married couple with two or more children, a husband who was the sole breadwinner, and a wife who stayed at home and cared for the house and the kids. But significant numbers of families didn't conform to this definition then, and today family forms are even more diverse: dual-earner families, single-parent families, remarried couples, unmarried couples, childless couples, stepfamilies, foster families, ex-

tended or multigenerational families, and so on (Ahlburg & De Vita, 1992). These changes undoubtedly affect our definition of families and our expectations of what goes on inside them. With so much flux and variation in family living, is it possible or even desirable to come up with a single definition of *family*?

▲ *Issue 2 explains why our images of families of the past are often misleading. Comparing current family forms to these images can lead to inaccurate conclusions.*

The "Official" Definition of Family

In the United States, the official definition of *family* comes from the U.S. Census Bureau. This agency distinguishes between *household* and *family*. Households are defined as all persons who occupy a dwelling such as a house, apartment, single room, or other space intended to be living quarters. They can consist of one person who lives alone or several people living together. A family, on the other hand, is defined as two or more persons who are related by blood, marriage, or adoption, and who live together as one household (Ahlburg & De Vita, 1992).

Right away you can see that this definition limits official conceptions of family primarily to what social scientists call the nuclear family—the small unit consisting of a married couple or at least one parent and one child. Although most of us would also consider many other relatives—grandparents, aunts, uncles, and cousins—to be family as well, the nuclear family has received more cultural, political, and scholarly attention than the extended family.

How useful is this official definition of family? Does it describe all American families? Can it be applied universally in all societies? And what do its component parts imply about the nature of people's relationships and responsibilities within families? To address these questions, let's break down the official definition of *family* and examine its component parts.

"Two or More People": Family as Social Group. Sociologically speaking, families contain not only individuals but relationships: husband-wife, parent-child, brother-sister, and so on. These relationships imply connections, bonds, attachments, and obligations *between people,* and they combine to form a type of social group. But the groups we call families are different from other types of social groups, such as friendship groups, social clubs, church groups, and so on (Beutler, Burr, Bahr, & Herrin, 1989). For one thing, the intensity of involvement between family members is stronger than it is in other groups. The range of activities we share with family members is much broader than contacts with friends, co-workers, or other people in groups to which we belong. We do pretty much everything with fellow family members: eating, sleeping, playing, punishing, fighting, convalescing from illness, having sex, and so on. Such close involvement adds a unique emotional element to family relationships.

Another big difference is that families last for a considerably longer period of time than do most other social groups (Klein & White, 1996). We're born into a family that already exists and it endures for our lifetime. Even after we become adults and start our own families, our parents are still our parents and our siblings are still our siblings no matter what we think of them. During the 1997 NCAA Men's Basketball Championships, a great deal of media attention was focused on the strained relationship between Mike Bibby, a star player for the University of Arizona Wildcats, and his estranged father, the former NBA player and current University of Southern California coach, Henry Bibby. Henry had divorced Mike's mother when Mike was quite young and played only a mi-

nor role in his upbringing. Mike clearly bore some animosity toward his father and wanted to downplay the influence he had on his life. But he could not escape the immutable fact that Henry is, and will always be, his father. We can certainly have lifelong relationships with close friends, but families are the only groups that virtually require lifetime membership.

The strong prospect for future interaction gives families a history and tradition rarely found in other groups. Relationships between parents and their children, whether biological or adopted, are not easily severed. Given how common divorce is now—nearly one of every two marriages that begins this year will end in divorce sometime in the future (Cherlin, 1992)—this idea of permanence applied to families may seem hopelessly outdated. ▲ However, we still assume that the people involved don't enter these relationships as temporary arrangements with a foreseeable end.

▲ *As Chapter 7 explains, divorce does not end children's relationships with parents and other relatives, although it may complicate them.*

More than most other social groups, the family is also considered a social institution within the larger society. To be a member of a family group means more than simply being connected to other individuals. It also means having certain legal and culturally recognizable rights and responsibilities, which are spelled out in the formal laws of the state and the informal norms of custom and tradition. Parents, for instance, have legal obligations to provide basic necessities—food, shelter, clothing, nurturance—for their children. If they fail to meet these obligations they may face legal charges of negligence or abuse.

Along with spelling out obligations, the institution of family makes some assumptions about authority—about who has the legitimate right to control or influence the lives of others (Hunter, 1991). In other societies, such authority may be granted to someone outside the nuclear family, such as the father's brother or the community at large. In American society, parents have the legal right to control their children. However, in cases of multiple parents (birth parents, adoptive parents, stepparents, foster parents, and so on) the lines of authority may be murky. Courts must sometimes determine who has legitimate authority over children, as in custody cases where biological parents have attempted to regain custody of children who had been previously put up for adoption.

"Living Together": Family as Household.
Another condition of the official American definition of family is that the family group share a common residence. Indeed, for many social scientists, common residence is *the defining characteristic of family* (for example, Murdock, 1949). It reflects the view that individuals who make up a family constitute a single identifiable entity that is located in a common space.

The belief that members of a nuclear family ought to live together is common but not universal. Among the Kipsigis of Kenya, for instance, the mother and children live in one house while the father lives in another (Stephens, 1963). Among the Thonga of southern Africa, children live with their grandmothers once they stop breastfeeding. They remain there for several years and are then returned to their parents. On the traditional Israeli kibbutz, or commune, children are raised not in the home of their biological parents but in an "infants' house," where they are cared for by a trained nurse (Nanda, 1994). Wealthy European families may send their children away to boarding schools, where they spend the majority of their childhood.

In our own society, there are situations in which members of nuclear families do not oc-cupy a common household. Consider, for instance, the "commuter marriage." A commuter marriage is one in which spouses spend at least several nights a week in separate residences yet are still married and intend to remain so (Gertsel & Gross, 1984). Over a million commuter marriages exist in the United States today. Marriages in which spouses live apart much of the time have always existed. Careers such as the military, the merchant marines, professional sports, and entertainment often require spouses to travel for long periods. Today, however, commuter marriages are likely to be the result of both husband and wife having careers that involve commitments to different locations. ▲ While the difficulties of such arrangements are substantial, no one would deny that they are families.

▲ *Chapter 4 examines commuter marriages as a contemporary adaptation to career demands.*

It's also true that common household residence does not, in and of itself, determine whether a unit is a family. Perhaps you are currently living with a roommate. Not only do you share an address but you are likely to share domestic chores and household expenses as well. You may both even feel very close to one another, sharing personal experiences, helping each other in times of need, and so on. Yet most people wouldn't consider roommates family. Your common residence is assumed to be the result of economic convenience rather than emotional commitment.

The growth of "nonfamily households" (elderly people living with friends, roommates sharing an apartment, cohabiting couples, young single people, and so on) over the past several decades has been dramatic. In 1960, 15 percent of all households were nonfamily; today the figure has more than doubled to over 30 percent (U.S. Bureau of the Census, 1997a).

"Related by Marriage": Family as Legal Entity. Marriage is the legal cornerstone of the official definition of family. The U.S. Supreme Court once declared that marriage is "noble" and "intimate to the degree of being sacred" (Stoddard, 1992, p. 17).

Most of us take for granted that monogamy, the marriage of one man and one woman, is the fundamental building block of the family. Only married people are granted the *culturally legitimate* right to reproduce and therefore create enduring family ties. Some people may have several spouses over their lifetimes, but they are allowed only one at a time (a phenomenon known as serial monogamy). And some families do exist without a married couple. But monogamous marriage continues to be the only adult intimate relationship that is legally recognized, culturally approved, and endorsed by the Internal Revenue Service. It is still the one relationship in which sexual activity is not only acceptable but expected.

Monogamous marriage, like the family in general, is an institution, a patterned way of life that includes a set of commonly known roles, statuses, and expectations: "People know about it; they can describe it; and they have spent a lifetime learning how to react to it. The *idea* of marriage is larger than any individual marriage. The *role* of husband or wife is greater than any individual who takes on that role" (Blumstein & Schwartz, 1983, p. 318). No other intimate relationship has achieved such status. Despite its current state of disrepair and the public concern with its disintegration, monogamous marriage remains the cultural standard against which all other types of intimate relationships are judged.

But even though marriage is undeniably important, not all states agree as to who can and can't marry. Today, some states (such as Pennsylvania) still recognize common-law marriage. These marriages are agreements by which couples who have not had their relationships validated religiously or civilly are considered legally married if they've lived together long enough. Some states allow first cousins to marry, others don't; the minimum legal age for marriage varies from state to state, as does recognition of such contracts across state lines (F. Johnson, 1996).

Despite these variations, it's hard to imagine a society that is not structured around the assumption that the vast majority of adults will live in a monogamous marriage. Yet many cultures around the world allow an individual to have several husbands or wives at the same time (an arrangement known as polygamy). Some anthropologists have estimated that about 75 percent of the world's societies accept some type of polygamy, although few members within those societies actually have the resources to afford more than one spouse (Murdock, 1957; Nanda, 1994). In some parts of northern India, for instance, a woman will sometimes have more than one husband. The husbands are always brothers. The practice stems from economic pressures. This area's terrain is rugged—steep forests and mountains leave only about a quarter of the land suitable for farming. With so little land to support a larger population, having all sons in one family marry the same woman ensures the control of childbirth and keeps the family wealth under one roof (Fan, 1996). It's estimated that roughly 10 out of 100 families in this region still practice polygamy.

A Russian politician recently made headlines worldwide by introducing a bill in the Kremlin that would allow a man to have several wives. There are 9 million more women than men in Russia, and the country is experiencing a dramatic decrease in the size of its population. Fearful of the possibility that ethnic Russians would soon be outnumbered in their own country, this politician advocated polygamy to create a new generation of what he called "Russian wolves."

Even in the United States, certain groups practice polygamy. Between 20,000 and 50,000 members of a dissident Mormon sect in Colorado, Utah, and Arizona live in households made up of a man with two or more wives (Altman & Ginat, 1996; Johnson, 1991). Although this practice is technically illegal, these states have made no arrests for polygamy since the 1950s.

"Related by Blood or Adoption": Family as Kinship Group.   No matter what form it takes, marriage is important in all societies because it serves as the legally sanctioned setting for reproduction. While not all sexual activity in marriage leads to the birth of children and not all children are born to married couples, sexual reproduction in families is the core symbol of kinship (Schneider, 1980).

Even adoption is based symbolically on the biological model of kinship. Adoption approximates reproduction. Once adopted, children are treated and raised just as if they were produced biologically by the adoptive parents. The kinship ties established by adoption are just as powerful and enduring as those established by birth. ▲ As such, adoption presents no challenge to the image of family assembled around a biological core of parent(s) and children (Weston, 1991).

▲ *The issue of transracial adoption, which disturbs some because of kinship implications, is discussed in Chapter 5.*

At birth everyone inherits two separate bloodlines, raising the question of which bloodline—the mother's or the father's—is to be more important for an individual's heredity. These designations are vital because they determine not only names but authority, ownership of property, and inheritance. However, kinship has as much to do with social norms as it does with genetic facts. Definitions of kinship—who is related

to whom across generations—vary from culture to culture.

In some societies, kin are connected by father-child links (called patrilineal descent). In such societies, a woman typically takes her husband's name. Children downplay or ignore their connections with members of their mother's family, showing allegiance and loyalty to kin on the father's side of the family. So, for instance, a mother's sister—whom we'd call an "aunt"—has no culturally recognized role in the family.

In other societies, the family group is made up of people connected by mother-child links (called matrilineal descent). Here a child's status and heritage are traced through his or her mother's lineage, and the father's kin are not considered part of the family. For instance, the Hopi, a Pueblo group in the American Southwest, are a matrilineal society. The relationship a Hopi child maintains with his or her father's relatives may be affectionate, but it involves little direct cooperation or recognized authority.

Finally, in some societies (such as the United States) children trace their descent and define their family relationships through both parents' bloodlines (bilateral descent). Although American women typically take their husbands' names when they marry and children take their fathers' names, descent and inheritance are linked to both parents. We may distinguish between our *paternal* and *maternal* grandparents and even favor one set over the other, but both are equally recognized as kin. Neither side of the family is expected to exert special influence and power over the children.

In bilateral descent societies, the potential for kin relationships can be quite extensive. If you were to map out a family chart of kin on both sides of your family, the size and complexity of your family tree could be immense. But at some point we all stop counting distant kin—for instance, fourth cousins—as family.

Blood Families and Chosen Families

You can see that the official, broad definition of family is not as straightforward as you might expect. In everyday usage, *family* is a significantly more elastic term than implied by the U.S. Bureau of the Census definition: two or more people, living together, who are related by marriage, blood, or adoption.

It seems that today, compared with the 1950s and 1960s, who we consider "family" is increasingly a matter of choice rather than legal obligation. Families can now consist of people who are tied to one another not by law, birth, or blood but by their commitments, love, and ability to confide in one another (Settles, 1987). These relationships form a safety net of significant connections to choose from in case of need. Hence, people today are apt to use the word *family* to describe a group of individuals who have achieved a significant degree of emotional closeness and sharing, even if they're not related. In a national survey, 75 percent of respondents, when asked to define *family,* replied, "a group of people who love and care for each other" (cited in Scanzoni & Marsiglio, 1991).

An approach to defining family that relies more on feelings and less on formal structure is appealing to many family scholars. Compare the following definition from the American Home Economics Association (AHEA) to the Census Bureau definition we examined earlier:

> AHEA defines the family unit as two or more persons who share resources, share responsibility for decisions, share values and goals, and have commitment to one another over time. The family is that climate that one "comes home to" and it is this network of sharing and commitments that most accurately describes the family unit, regardless of blood, legal ties, adoption or marriage. (quoted in Christensen, 1990, p. 36)

Notice that the AHEA definition emphasizes emotional ties, commitment, and cooperation, not formally recognized relationships.

One prominent sociologist defines family as "a unit comprising two or more persons who live together for an extended period of time, and who share in one or more of the following: work (for wages and house), sex, care and feeding of children, and intellectual, spiritual, and recreational activities (D'Antonio, 1983, p. 92). Another author argues that the concept of family should apply to "people who have shared history, who have loved each other . . . lived through major parts of each other's lives together, [and] who share professional interests, economic needs, political views or sexual preference" (Lindsey, 1981, pp. 179–188).

We all know of situations in which *fictive kin*—people other than legal or biological kin—play the family's role in providing for the emotional needs of its members. Sometimes roommates play this role. Or perhaps you have a close family friend whom you've referred to for years as "Uncle So-and-So" or "Aunt So-and-So" even though he or she isn't a sibling of either parent. In some situations, whom you choose to identify as family is left to your discretion. The family status of in-laws and step-relatives, for instance, is often left to the judgment of individual families. The powerful emotional connections we can form with these "chosen relatives" shows that, in practice, family is rarely limited to formally recognized kin relations.

Structural changes in society and changes in contemporary lifestyles (geographic mobility, high rates of divorce and childlessness, kin-group rejection, and so on) compel many people to seek from other groups the kinds of satisfactions that are typically sought from kin (Marciano, 1988). For instance, as life expectancy increases, some elderly people whose children are unable or unwilling to take care of them are turning to longtime friends for companionship, emotional support, and practical assistance.

Fictive kin have historically played an important role in some African-American communities. In her book *All Our Kin,* anthropologist Carol Stack describes "family" relationships in a midwestern black neighborhood called "the Flats." The people in this community used many kinship terms to celebrate relationships based on caring, loving, and close friendship. ▲ These "kin" felt the sort of obligations, responsibilities, and loyalties typically associated with blood relations. Consider the family meanings that one resident bestowed on the people in her life:

> Billy, a young black woman in the Flats, was raised by her mother and her mother's "old man." She has three children of her own by different fathers. Billy says, "Most people kin to me are in this neighborhood, right here in the Flats, but I got people in the South, in Chicago, and in Ohio, too. I couldn't tell most of their names and most of them aren't really kinfolk to me. Starting down the street from here, take my father, he ain't my daddy, he's no father to me. I ain't got but one daddy and that's Jason. The one who raised me. My kids' daddies, that's something else, all their daddies' people really take to them—they always doing things and making a fuss about them. We help each other out and that's what kinfolks are all about. (Stack, 1974, p. 4)

▲ *You can read more about the reasons for such diversity in African-American families in Issue 6.*

Stack found that the community's informal system of parental rights and duties determines who is eligible to be a member of a child's "family." This system often doesn't coincide with the official law of the state concerning parenthood. For instance, a girl who gives birth as a teenager might not raise and nurture the child. While she may live in the same house as the baby, an "othermother"—her mother, aunt, older sister, cousin, or family friend—may do the actual child rearing. Young mothers and their first-born daughters are often raised as sisters. This sort of acquired parenthood lasts throughout the child's lifetime. The child learns to distinguish his or her "mother" and "father" (the biological parents) from his or her "mama" and "daddy" (the people who raised him or her). Most of the time—Stack estimates about 80 percent—the mother and the "mama" are the same person. But in those other cases, the "mama" can be a grandmother, an aunt, or someone else, when relatives conclude that the mother is not emotionally ready to nurture the child and fulfill her parental duties. The "mama's" relatives and their husbands and wives also become a part of the child's extended family.

In sum, Stack found that the people she studied clearly operate within two different family systems: the folk system of their community and the legal system of the courts and welfare offices. People are recognized as family not because they have biological ties but because they assume the recognized responsibilities of kin—they "help each other out." Given the pressures of the economy in these communities, this expanded definition of family and the respect afforded to "othermothers" have served a critical role in people's lives, providing much-needed support.

The Controversy over Gay Families

One of the most contentious debates concerning how elastic the definition of family ought to be is whether gay and lesbian couples should be granted the right to marry and thereby create culturally and legally "legitimate" families. ▲ Traditional heterosexual marriages have long benefited from legal and social recognition. Marriage partners can take part in a spouse's health insurance plan and pension program, share the rights of inheritance and community property, make a claim on a spouse's rent-controlled apartment, receive Social Security and veterans' benefits, including medical and educational services, file joint tax returns, and receive crime victims' recovery benefits (Hunter, 1991; Sherman, 1992). These legal and economic advantages were designed to encourage the stability and interdependence of the traditional family unit.

▲ *Read Chapter 2 for further discussion of sexual orientation and intimate relationships.*

Such benefits have historically been denied to cohabiting heterosexual couples, living arrangements involving long-term platonic roommates, and, of course, homosexual couples—all of which may nevertheless have the same degree of economic and emotional dependence found in heterosexual marriages.

In the past, gay and lesbian couples either had to live with their legally unrecognized status or find ways other than marriage to establish such recognition. One rather creative method of approximating a legal relationship was adoption. In one case, a 22-year-old New York man petitioned to adopt his 26-year-old male partner. The parties testified that "they wish[ed] to establish a legally cognizable relationship in order to facilitate inheritance, the handling of their insurance policies and pension plans, and the acquisition of suitable housing" (quoted in Anderson, 1988, p. 360). They contended that they wanted a "more permanent legal bond" that would provide their relationship with some security. The court approved the petition. This arrangement brought the relationship within the purview of the law and automatically created certain legal rights and duties in both partners (Anderson, 1988).

Recently, many communities have taken a more conventional legal route, enacting "domestic partnership" laws which recognize homosexual unions (as well as heterosexual cohabiting relationships) and grant them some "family-like" legal rights. Couples officially register their relationships and in so doing formally declare that they have "an intimate, committed relationship of mutual caring," that they live together, and that they agree to be responsible for each other's basic living expenses.

Such laws have been enacted in the state of Vermont and in cities such as San Francisco and West Hollywood, California; Ithaca, New York; Minneapolis, Minnesota; Washington, D.C.; Seattle, Washington; and Madison, Wisconsin. The laws extend full spousal rights such as health insurance, life insurance, pension benefits, employee discounts, and health club membership to the domestic partners of city workers. In addition, approximately 500 companies and organizations including Sony, IBM, Walt Disney, Hewlett-Packard, Microsoft, Xerox, Ben & Jerry's, Lotus, Apple Computer, Time Warner, the Democratic National Committee, and the American Sociological Association now grant domestic partners the same benefits traditionally granted to spouses (Griffin, 1993).

The Push to Legalize Gay Marriage

Although domestic partnership laws and policies go a long way in legally recognizing gay and lesbian relationships, many people feel such changes are inadequate. They argue that domestic partnerships are still "not quite" marriages and therefore not quite families in the eyes of the public and the law. Consequently they remain culturally and legally second-class. For instance, in 1991 the governing body of the Presbyterian Church ruled that same-sex union ceremonies could be performed in the denomination's churches by ordained pastors so long as the ceremonies were not considered marriages (Sherman, 1992).

Advocates of gay marriage argue that allowing gay and lesbian individuals to legally marry would result in a more secure, stable, and protective relationship. In 1990 a woman whose lesbian partner had died of cancer charged AT&T (her deceased lover's employer) with discrimination for refusing to pay her the same death benefits it would have paid to a surviving spouse. In her suit she claimed that her relationship was as much a marriage as any heterosexual union. She and her lover had even formalized their relationship in a 1977 ceremony in which they exchanged vows and rings in the company of parents and friends. They bought a house together and raised her children from a previous marriage together. AT&T said its benefits were for legal spouses only, and since the law did not recognize homosexual unions, neither did the company (Lewin, 1990). If the women's relationship had been legally recognized as a marriage, however, the company would have had clear responsibilities and a definite, institutionalized commitment to the surviving partner.

Some advocates argue that legalizing gay marriage would lead to greater public acceptance of homosexual people. Having the right to legally marry and start families would combat the all-too-common belief that gay relationships are only about sexual activity and would force heterosexuals to acknowledge that gay couples can be seriously committed to each other and can take on traditional family responsibilities.

Legalization of gay marriage would therefore show that homosexual men and women could be just as "family oriented" as anybody else. ▲ Far from being a repudiation of family, then, the desire to legally marry acknowledges the ideal of family.

▲ *Chapter 4 examines some of the issues facing gay and lesbian parents.*

Opposition to Legalizing Gay Marriage

Opposition to gay marriage nevertheless remains strong. According to a recent poll, nearly 70 percent of Americans oppose homosexual marriages (cited in "Marriage and divorce," 1996). Gay men and lesbians are typically thought of as individuals, but not as family members, reflecting a pervasive belief that homosexuality and family are mutually exclusive concepts (reported in Allen & Demo, 1995). Indeed, claiming a gay or lesbian identity has typically been considered a rejection of family (reported in Weston, 1991).

To many people, the power and significance of marriage as an institution rest on its uniqueness—the belief that it is not one lifestyle among many but the fundamental intimate arrangement in society. ▲ Their concern is that when relationships that aren't marriages start being treated as if they are, marriage loses its power and significance. One U.S. congressman called homosexual relationships "the most vicious attack on traditional family values that our society has seen in the history of our republic" (quoted in Hunter, 1991, p. 189).

▲ *Issue 2 examines the sources of our image of the "traditional" family.*

Currently, no state legally recognizes same-sex marriage, although in 1996 a circuit court judge in Hawaii ruled that a ban on gay marriage was unconstitutional, a first step toward full legal status. In fact, twelve states have actively banned gay marriage, and another six states are attempting legislative bans. In 1996 President Clinton signed the

Defense of Marriage Act, which formally reaffirmed the definition of marriage as the union of one man and one woman, authorized all states to refuse to accept same-sex marriages from other states (if they ever became legal at the state level), and denied federal pension, health, and other benefits to same-sex couples. However, because each state—not the federal government—has the right to determine who can and cannot legally marry, the bill is primarily a moral statement about the definition of family.

It's important to note that opposition to gay marriage comes not only from people who disapprove of homosexuality and perceive it as a threat to traditional definitions of family but also from some gays and lesbians. These opponents argue that legalizing gay marriage would render gays and lesbians even more invisible to the larger society and undermine the movement to establish a separate and unique gay culture and identity (Ettelbrick, 1992). It would be a civil rights victory, but a subcultural defeat (Johnson, 1996).

Furthermore, they fear that homosexual married couples would be expected to behave just like heterosexual married couples, amounting to an acceptance of a heterosexual standard for what a successful intimate relationship should look like. This sort of arrangement would subsequently diminish the notion that valid and committed relationships can exist outside traditional marriage. In fact, some gay opponents of homosexual marriage argue that the absence of marriage as a dominant, regulating institution in their intimate lives actually gives them the space to define their families in richer ways, to include friends, neighbors, and community (F. Johnson, 1996).

Some gay and lesbian activists take the argument further, contending that having no "marriage" or even "family" should constitute a point of pride for homosexual people (Altman, 1979). Indeed, some gay people look down upon homosexual parents for having failed to "escape" the family and for trying to gain acceptance in mainstream society by approximating the "traditional" family (Lynch, 1982).

In sum, more is at stake in this debate than the emotional rewards of formalizing shared commitment in a loving relationship and the practical rewards of legal recognition of gay and lesbian marriage. This issue is fundamentally about what arrangements we as a culture believe deserve the label "family." These beliefs can ultimately shape the law, public policy, and the contours of our everyday lives.

The Symbolism of Family

Judging from the strong emotions evoked by debates over the definition of family, it's clear that family is important not just for what it looks like but for what it symbolizes. Many people strongly believe that as the family goes, so goes the country. ▲ It stands for what we, as a culture, hold dear. Hence,

> the task of defining what the American family *is* [is] integral to the very task of defining America itself. . . . Obviously more is at stake than a dictionary definition of "the family." The debate actually takes form as a political judgment about the fate of *one particular conception of the family and family life* [emphases in original]. (Hunter, 1991, pp. 177, 180)

▲ *Issue 8 addresses the perceived link between family decline and social decline.*

In American society the idea of family has become a powerful symbol of decency. Disneyland and Disneyworld, for instance, are considered family theme parks because they supposedly emphasize the wholesomeness of the recreational activities they provide. You'll find no bars, strip clubs, or gambling halls there. Likewise, every video rental store has a family section. But the films you'll find in this section aren't necessarily about families. Instead the label "family" presumably identifies films that are devoid of graphic sex and violence, whose themes the entire family can enjoy together.

When politicians rail against policies and practices considered "antifamily" (read indecent and immoral) they are typically signaling their support for "family values" and espousing a view that the American family is being attacked and threatened by dangerous forces of change. Today rivals in elections try to situate themselves as the more "profamily" candidate. Having a smiling spouse and children displayed prominently in photos and television coverage is practically a prerequisite for getting elected. During the 1992 presidential campaign, Vice President Dan Quayle stirred up intense feelings about the definition of family when he criticized the television character Murphy Brown, who had a baby out of wedlock and without any intention of having a husband or father to help raise the child. Quayle directed his attack against those who "seem to think the family is an arbitrary arrangement of people who decided to live under one roof, that fathers are dispensable, and that parents need not be married or even of opposite sexes" (quoted in Quindlen, 1992, p. E19).

Quayle's views reflect a belief, held by many, that an expanded definition of family demeans its symbolic importance. From this perspective, family is a sacred label that should be applied only to the most tradi-tional type of family: married parents and their children. To those who subscribe to this position, family is the very cornerstone upon which the entire foundation of society rests and therefore shouldn't be used casually or taken lightly. People should not have the right to define themselves as family however they see fit. Those who seek to expand the definition of family to apply to all sorts of relationships are believed to be emptying it of its symbolic meaning and power (Gellott, 1985).

But to many others, the rhetoric of family values is little more than a thin cover for a particular political agenda. According to these skeptics, those who deplore the greater visibility of cohabiting and homosexual couples, the increasing numbers of single and working mothers, and high rates of divorce are making a rather explicit judgment about what we ought to define as "appropriate" families. Many people believe, in contrast, that the shape and configuration of a family are less important than the emotional bonds and feelings of mutual obligation that can exist between people. It doesn't matter so much whether a child has two biological parents, a biological parent and a stepparent, a single parent, or two parents of the same sex as long as that child has someone to take care of him or her.

The point here is that there is no agreement among the media, society, and academia about what families are, what they should be, or what the implications of recent social changes will be. These disagreements aren't always politically motivated. They can arise simply and earnestly from people's different perspectives, values, beliefs, and desires.

Something to Think About

One of the issues that most deeply divides American society today is the definition of the term *family* and the privileging of particular family forms over others. You've seen that there's more to family than meets the eye. Some cultures have ideas very different from ours about what sorts of family arrangements are normal and natural. In this society, most people's lives depart in some way from the traditional nuclear family depicted in the official definition of family. This diversity raises some interesting questions:

1. Should the societal recognition of family be limited to blood and legal relations, or should we be able to choose whomever we want to be our family? What is society's interest in controlling which arrangements we call family?

2. As we move toward the twenty-first century, do you think the concept of family will expand to acknowledge the validity of many diverse relationships and living arrangements, or will it contract, reinforcing the legitimacy and desirability of the "traditional" family?

3. Which definition of family do you think ought to provide the basis for official family policy?

ISSUE 2

How Accurate Are Popular Images of American Families?

Media and Families

Historical Ideas about Families

SOMETHING TO THINK ABOUT

On February 13, 1986, a reporter for a newspaper in Stamford, Connecticut, called sociologist Neil Bennett at his Yale University office. The reporter was preparing a Valentine's Day article on love, and she wanted some information on the state of contemporary American marriage (Cherlin, 1990). At the time, Bennett and two colleagues were studying the effects of educational attainment on women's marital probabilities (Bennett, Bloom, & Craig, 1986).

Bennett told the reporter that he had data showing that college-educated women were less likely to marry than women who had never attended college. Furthermore, the marital chances of college-educated women got worse with age: Female college graduates who were still single at age 30 had only a 20 percent chance of ever getting married; women who remained single until they were 35 had only a 5 percent chance of marrying; and those who were 40 and still unmarried had only a 1 percent chance of ever marrying.

The reporter incorporated these predictions into the Valentine's Day article. The next day, the Associated Press picked up the story and dispatched it over the national wire service. Shortly thereafter all hell broke loose:

- *Newsweek* magazine ran a story—complete with an ominous, plummeting graph on the cover—declaring that successful single women in their 30s were more likely "to be killed by a terrorist than find a husband." The magazine said the figures "confirmed what everyone expected all along: that many women who seem to have it all . . . will never have mates" (Salholz, 1986, p. 55).
- *People* magazine ran a feature story about celebrity women in their 40s who were still single, further confirming the reality of this "cultural trend."
- A parade of family experts made its way through daytime talk shows and news

magazine shows addressing the "stark reality" of grim marriage prospects as if it were a newly discovered terminal illness.
- Supermarkets across the country began offering special "singles nights" in an attempt to conquer the statistical trend.
- At professional conferences, social scientists debated the potential implications of low marital probabilities, such as an increase in the number of single women deciding to have children on their own, the future of male-female relationships, and the value of community in the face of shrinking family commitments.
- Conservative critics used the study to support their contention that women's increasing focus on career was having disastrous effects on traditional family life.

It was difficult to find anyone who hadn't heard something about Bennett's statistical predictions, which had caused the sort of collective panic usually reserved for presidential assassinations or approaching hurricanes:

> Her sister had heard about it from a friend who had heard about it on "Phil Donahue" that morning. Her mother got the bad news via a radio talk show later that afternoon. So by the time Harvard graduate Carol Owens, 23, sat down to a family dinner in Boston, the discussion of the man shortage had reached a feverish pitch. With six unmarried daughters, Carol's mother was sounding an alarm. "You've got to get out of the house and meet someone," she insisted. "Now." (Salholz, 1986, p. 55)

Those who weren't sad, depressed, or frightened by the news were angered by the implication that marriage was essential for women's happiness and that women who didn't marry or didn't want to marry were somehow deficient.

Unfortunately, the apparent facts about the future marital chances of educated women may not have been so trustworthy (Cherlin, 1990). Remember that the statistics being cited so frantically were predictions, not hard data. To make such predictions, researchers must assume that when today's 20-year-olds become 30, social conditions will be the same and that they will behave like the current group of 30-year-olds. Such an assumption does not allow for the possibility that unforeseen cultural and historical circumstances can change age-specific marital patterns over time.

Moreover, the percentages may not have been all that accurate in the first place. In fact, researchers at the U.S. Census Bureau, using the same data but different projection formulas, reported that college-educated women in their 30s had a 32 percent to 41 percent chance, and a 40-year-old had a 17 percent to 23 percent chance, of marrying (Moorman, 1987)—not high but certainly not as dire as Bennett's predictions.

Three years after that first newspaper article, when the dust had finally settled, the actual study appeared in a prestigious sociological journal. But the published study bore little resemblance to the statistical predictions that had created such a society-wide panic in 1986. In the journal article, the researchers downplayed the role that education plays in women's marital chances, focusing instead on differences in black and white marriage patterns over the past 25 years.

The damage, to a certain extent, had already been done. But in the process of distorting and misinterpreting Bennett's study, newspapers, television shows, and the media were reaffirming a persistent cultural value: Being married and having a satisfying family life are still an essential part of personal fulfillment, even for women who have successful careers. As is true of many other family-related issues over the years, any inkling of trouble tends to be blown out of proportion in the popular media. And the public typically responds with frantic calls for a return to "traditional family values."

Most of us derive our ideas about families from the media. As we saw in the case of the study on women's marital chances, however, misleading or inaccurate information can take on a highly publicized life of its own in the media, becoming "truth" in people's minds. In this section I will examine the nature of our popular images of families. Where do they come from? Why do we get so upset about possible deviations from the "standard"? And what is the source of the standard against which contemporary families are judged?

Media and Families

Our images of families are often created and generally reinforced by media representations: books, newspapers, magazines, films, and, especially, television. For close to 50 years, television has served as a high-powered cultural lens on American families. Between 1946 and 1990, close to 400 fictional families appeared on prime-time network programming alone (Moore, 1992). Add commercials, daytime soap operas and talk shows, and news stories into the mix, and you get a sense of how pervasive television images of families have been throughout the years.

Whether intended or not, television's portrayal of families serves economic and ideological functions. It's often said that television programs exist to draw viewers to the commercials that punctuate them, and not vice versa. Advertisers cannot offend viewers who are, after all, potential consumers; and producers and writers cannot offend the advertisers, for if a show loses its sponsors, it will no longer be on the air. So, it's not surprising that what eventually gets televised consists, for the most part, of nonthreatening ideals, values, and beliefs—the issues and themes that are acceptable to the majority of viewers and advertisers (Cantor, 1991).

The Role of Television in Everyday Family Life

Television exploded on the cultural scene during the post–World War II years, at a time when society was encouraging people to form large nuclear families with highly structured and predictable roles for men and women and for parents and children (Spigel, 1992). Early on, TV was marketed as a device that would enhance family togetherness. Advertisements invariably depicted Dad, Mom, and the kids huddled around the television, smiling and hugging.

But television has always had its detractors, who feared it could seduce viewers, particularly children, into a state of bug-eyed numbness and could become central to family life. In some ways their fears have been realized. An abrupt change in viewing patterns—for instance, when the family TV breaks down—is likely to have ripple effects on many other areas of family life, such as conversations, eating patterns, and recreational activities (Leichter, Ahmed, Barrios, Bryce, Larsen, & Moe, 1985).

In addition to concerns over television as an intrusion, there have also been fears about its role as a socializing agent. ▲ The famous anthropologist Margaret Mead once wrote, "TV more than any other medium gives models to the American people—models for life as it is, or should, or can be lived" (1978, p. 12). People's perceptions of reality often reflect the skewed versions of social life depicted on television. For instance, individuals who frequently watch soap operas—which, as you know, portray a strikingly wide range of family troubles—dramatically overesti-

mate the real-life number of sexual affairs outside marriage, of divorces, and of illegitimate children (Brown & Bryant, 1990). Adolescent soap-opera viewers also underestimate the problems that most single mothers in the real world face, perceiving them as having good jobs and being relatively well educated and affluent (Larson, 1996).

▲ *Socialization and child rearing are discussed in more detail in Chapter 5.*

Not only do television portrayals of family affect the ways in which people think about their own families, they are also used by people as actual guides to their own family behavior (Douglas & Olson, 1996). For decades, social critics have contended that television undermines harmony in families, fosters dissatisfaction with the family's standard of living, promotes greed and envy, and modifies children's beliefs about proper behavior (Brown & Bryant, 1990).

Television Images of Families

Since the beginning, television programs—particularly prime-time sitcoms—have saturated the culture with idealized images of families (Stacey, 1996). For the most part, these images have tended to be conventional and narrow in scope, fostering a largely inaccurate version of family reality.

A recent study of all long-running prime-time families over the past 4 decades found that the traditional nuclear family predominates. Two-thirds of these shows depicted "conventional" families—that is, families which consist of married couples living together with their children or nuclear families sharing a household with one or more members of their extended families (Moore, 1992). The overwhelming majority of families (88 percent) were middle class or higher. Ninety-four percent of the shows featured white families. Interestingly, at the time of this study there were more white TV families with black members (usually adopted children) than black families. Only 14 percent of the programs featured childless couples.

Of the "nonconventional" television families—defined as one parent living with his or her children, one or both parents living with their adopted children, or one or more adults living with children for which they have assumed guardianship—79 percent featured single-parent households. But, unlike real-life single parents, most single parents on TV had suffered the death of a spouse and not divorce. In only 9 percent of cases was single parenthood the result of divorce.

Why should we care about the way these fictional families are composed? Far from simply being a source of entertainment, television can have an impact on the lifestyles of real-life families by showing how family members are "supposed" to behave and by illustrating desirable family types:

> As the mass media have come to absorb many socializing functions of the family, they have offered us images of the family which may act as touchstones by which we gauge our experiences. The seductively realistic portrayals of family life in the media may be the basis for our most common and pervasive conceptions and beliefs about what is natural and what is right. (Gerbner, Gross, Morgan, & Signorielli, 1980, p. 3)

Yet rarely do television programs reflect the larger social and political contexts in which most Americans live. The more recent programs have addressed the tough problems of everyday life: drugs, poverty, unwanted pregnancy, and so forth. But for most of their history, TV families have rarely tackled real-life problems. Rather, these fictional families act out morality plays about appropriate and inappropriate beliefs and behaviors. The majority of TV programs teach correct (and ideal) social and sexual relationships (Cantor,

1991). We learn to laugh at or dislike unconventional characters who challenge accepted notions about family life.

TV Families over Time

In some ways, media images of families have changed dramatically over the years; in other ways, though, they have remained remarkably similar. In the 1950s and early 1960s, shows like *Leave It to Beaver, Ozzie and Harriet, Make Room for Daddy, Father Knows Best, The Donna Reed Show,* and *The Dick Van Dyke Show* provided optimistic, homogenous images of American families. With some notable exceptions—like the childless, working-class Kramdens in *The Honeymooners* or the urban, interethnic Ricardos in *I Love Lucy*—these early television families were happy, prosperous, suburban, and white. They consisted of husband-father breadwinners and nurturing wives-mothers whose primary task was to look good in an apron and keep peace among the children. In the 1950s one would have been hard-pressed to find on television the sorts of people and families that, in reality, characterized much of American society at the time: the old, the nonwhite, the non–middle class, or people in nontraditional households (Coontz, 1992).

Instead, the viewing audience was presented with nuclear families without serious economic problems or embarrassing histories—households where, aside from minor flare-ups over math homework or prom dates, parents were superpeople whose authority went largely unquestioned. The most pressing problems could be solved in 30 minutes with a piece of Dad's sage advice or a plate of Mom's chocolate chip cookies. The 1950s TV household was a warm and cozy place. It's no wonder that when people today look back on families of the past, they gravitate toward these blissful "good-old-days" TV images. To this day, reruns of these old shows remain a popular fixture on nightly cable syndication.

Even those programs that broke away from the nuclear family model failed to accurately represent reality. For instance, in the 1950s and 1960s several popular prime-time sitcoms featured single parents. However, unlike the real world of single parenthood—predominantly female and poor—these households were overwhelmingly headed by middle-class men. Shows like *My Three Sons*, *Family Affair*, *The Courtship of Eddie's Father*, and *The Andy Griffith Show* featured widowed fathers who were able to raise their children successfully with the help of servants, housekeepers, or female relatives. It wasn't until 1968, when the show *Julia* debuted, that a household headed by a single woman—and an African-American woman at that—appeared on television.

The social upheavals of the late 1960s and early 1970s motivated networks to create shows that were more "relevant" and "realistic." The working-class families on *All in the Family* and *Good Times* demonstrated that family life wasn't always a middle-class haven. Conflict was a part of their day-to-day existence. Television families began making small but significant forays into the uncharted territory of social problems like poverty, violence, drugs, and racism.

TV families were even becoming a little less traditional in their structure. *The Brady Bunch* featured a sugar-coated white, middle-class, suburban family, but the Bradys were a blended family that sometimes had to deal—albeit cheerily—with dilemmas posed by step-siblings and stepparents. The show *One Day at a Time* featured a divorced woman raising two children alone. *Three's Company* consisted of three single adults—one man and two women—living in the same household. Popular shows like *The Mary Tyler Moore Show* and *Laverne and Shirley* featured single women whose emotional nurturing came primarily from close friends rather than family. These characters enjoyed freedoms that had previously been taboo for women on television.

Interestingly, those television shows of the 1970s that did include "traditional" families were often distanced from contemporary concerns by being set in an earlier historical context. *The Waltons*, for instance, depicted a large extended family struggling through the Depression in the 1930s. *Happy Days* featured a traditional middle-class male-breadwinner, female-homemaker, two-child household, but was set in the 1950s.

During the 1980s and early 1990s, however, a time when conservative politics and "family values" became more popular, the nuclear television family reasserted its televised dominance—most notably through shows like *The Cosby Show*, *Family Ties*, and *Home Improvement*—even though the number of people living in intact nuclear families in the real world continued to decline. Although many popular shows—like *Roseanne*, *The Simpsons*, and *Married with Children*—were offering an unsparing portrayal of the ugly side of family life, the tone was humorous and the generally positive emotional interactions that we associate with family relationships remained. These families may have been flawed, but they were still cohesive, especially in the face of crisis.

Television images of families have obviously changed over the years: Women now play a more dominant role than they once did in family shows, gay characters as well as single-parent and minority families are more common, and both mothers and fathers are more frequently seen outside the home (Cantor, 1991; Douglas & Olson, 1996). However, the formulas of contemporary family sitcoms remain quite similar to those aired in the 1950s (Cantor, 1991). Most still feature households with children. The stories often revolve around the trials and tribulations of teen and preteen mischief or parent-child conflict. The content of the conflict has, of course changed. The 1950s argument over kissing and wearing too much makeup has evolved, in the 1990s, into an argument over sleeping with a boyfriend or purchasing contraceptives. But the dynamics of the situations portrayed remain remarkably similar, and parents and children almost always resolve their differences by the end of the show. No matter how "nontraditional" the lifestyle, the central virtue of family togetherness is still depicted as the main source of individual happiness and well-being for adults and children alike.

Historical Ideas about Families

Media depictions reflect a strong tendency to romanticize family life. Underlying a lot of the sitcom jokes about nontraditional families and the news media uproar over stories like the study on women's marital chances is the belief that family life in the past was happier and more stable than it is today. Sociologist William Goode (1971) calls our idealized image "the classical family of Western nostalgia":

> It is a pretty picture of life down on grandma's farm. There are lots of happy children, and many kinfolk live together in a large rambling house. Everyone works hard. Most of the food to be eaten during the winter is grown, preserved, and stored on the farm. . . . The family has many functions; it is the source of economic stability and religious, educational, and vocational training. Father is stern and reserved and has the final decision in all important matters. . . .
> All boys and girls marry, and marry young. . . . After marriage, the couple lives harmoniously, either near the boy's parents or with them. . . . No one divorces. (p. 624)

But this nostalgic image is distorted. The traditional American family of the past never really existed. In truth, from the time of the Puritans to the brink of the twenty-first century, each succeeding generation of Americans has been concerned about some crisis of the family (Hareven, 1992; Skolnick, 1991).

Families have always been diverse in structure and have always had trouble protecting members from economic hardship, internal violence, political upheaval, and social change. By glorifying a mythical past in our media representations, we foster artificial or limited standards of a "normal" family and, in the process, ignore the potential value of other family forms.

Colonial Families

During colonial times, for instance, several distinctly different types of families coexisted. The Iroquois in the Northeast lived in longhouses that accommodated large extended families. Among the more nomadic Native-American tribes, families were smaller. Although marital separation was frequent, it caused no stigma or loss of access to the tribe's resources. African-American slaves—whose nuclear families were routinely and purposely torn apart by their owners—secretly built extended family networks through coparenting, adoption of orphans, and complex naming patterns that preserved family links across time (Coontz, 1996). ▲ White colonial families typically took the form of "little commonwealths," male-dominated institutions ruled by a father who exercised authority over his wife, children, and servants much as a king ruled over his subjects. The colonial family was simultaneously a "school," "vocational institute," "church," "house of correction," and "welfare institution" (Demos, 1970).

▲ *Slave families are discussed in more detail in Issue 6.*

During this era, death was a common occurrence of everyday family life. Almost half of all children died before reaching adulthood; half of those who survived didn't reach 50. Short life expectancies meant that the majority of children spent time in a single-parent family or stepfamily. The average length of an eighteenth-century marriage was less than 12 years (Skolnick, 1991). Even children who were fortunate enough to come from intact families usually left home well before puberty to work as servants or apprentices in other people's homes. Mothers were much less involved in the care of their children than the busiest of working mothers today. Male authority was taken for granted, and slight disobediences by women and children were considered punishable forms of treason. Children were not protected from sexuality, either in action or in discussion.

Colonial America lacked a sophisticated concept of childhood. ▲ Since it was common to send children away from home to work or learn a trade, many children depended more on siblings, neighbors, and masters for their upbringing than on their parents. Such unsentimental treatment derived from a belief that children were inherently corrupt beings. So a key task of parents and other caretakers was to "break the will" of their children and conquer their naturally evil tendencies (Skolnick, 1991). Harsh physical punishment and humiliation were considered legitimate forms of parental authority. Complete obedience and submission were demanded of children:

> In some households [children] were made to stand through meals, eating whatever was handed to them. They were taught it was sinful to complain about food, clothing, or their lot in life. Courtesy of a formal sort was insisted upon. Corporal punishment seems to have been liberally employed. Use was made of birchrods, canes, and [leather straps], and at school dunce stools and caps and placards bearing humiliating names. (Queen & Habenstein, 1974, p. 306)

▲ *See Chapter 5 for a more detailed discussion of changing historical conceptions of childhood.*

Nineteenth-Century Families

At the beginning of the Revolutionary War, small family farms and shops flourished, and a wife's work was valued as highly as her husband's. But by the middle of the nineteenth century, industrialization and wage labor took work (and husbands) away from small family farms and businesses, leaving wives without their former economic partners. ▲ For the first time, men became known as the family breadwinners. By the post–Civil War era, the participation of women in the paid labor force was at an all-time low (Coontz, 1996).

▲ *See Chapter 3 for more detail on the Industrial Revolution and on the changing family roles of men and women.*

But as middle-class women left the workforce, working-class children entered it by the thousands, often toiling in horrible conditions for 10 hours or more a day. In the North, they worked in factories, tenement workshops, and mines. It was estimated that in the early part of the nineteenth century, half the workers in northern factories were children under 11 (Coontz, 1992). In the South, they worked in the fields. Slave children were not exempt from field labor unless they were infants, and even then their mothers were not allowed time off to nurture them.

Middle-class white families depended for their existence on the labor of other families who were too poor and powerless to maintain the nurturing, warm households we typically imagine:

> For every nineteenth-century middle-class family that protected its wife and child within the family circle … there was an Irish or a German girl scrubbing floors in that middle-class home, a Welsh boy mining coal to keep the home-baked goodies warm, a black girl doing the family laundry, a black mother and child picking cotton to be made into

clothes for the family, and a Jewish or an Italian daughter in a sweatshop making "ladies" dresses or artificial flowers for the family to purchase. (Coontz, 1992, pp. 11–12)

At the same time, self-styled "child savers" were defining as unfit parents from the "wrong" religion, race, ethnic group, or social class, thereby justifying the removal of children from their families. These "orphans" were frequently sent to live with farmers in the West who needed extra hands, or they were simply dumped in another town.

People who lived during this period were quite aware that American households were not always particularly nice places. Critics of the time talked about the "great neglect in many parents and masters in training up their children" and expressed grief over the "rising generation" of Americans. Yet when nineteenth-century middle-class families began to withdraw their children from the harsh and dangerous work world, observers were quick to criticize them for raising children who were "too sheltered" (Coontz, 1992).

As is always the case, children were the ones most likely to suffer. Because nineteenth-century adults had a shorter life expectancy than adults today, children at that time were actually more likely to live in a single-parent home, because of the death of a parent, than are children today (Kain, 1990). Although more than 20 percent of American children live in poverty today, about the same proportion lived in orphanages at the turn of the century, and not just because their parents had died. Many were there because their parents simply couldn't afford to raise them. Rates of alcohol abuse, school dropout, and child abuse were all higher a century ago than they are today (cited in Coontz, 1992).

One of the most pervasive myths of nineteenth-century American families is that they were usually large and extended, with a massive and perpetually available support network of grandparents, aunts, uncles, and other relatives living together. Historical research shows, however, that American families have always been fairly small (Goode, 1971; Hareven, 1992). There is no strong tradition in this country of large extended families. In fact, the highest proportion of extended family households ever recorded in this country was only around 20 percent and it occurred between 1850 and 1885 (Hareven, 1978). Even then, these families were large for economic reasons, not emotional ones. "Producing" families depended on the labor of children and others for their survival.

Early Twentieth-Century Families

The early twentieth century brought more changes to American families. Concerned that longer life spans would put a strain on marriages, experts and clergy encouraged people to direct all their emotional, nurturing, and sensual energy into their marriages. While this change introduced new intimacy into marriages, it also created a disturbing trend. People's expectations about what they should get out of their marriages increased, leading more and more married couples to express dissatisfaction over what they weren't getting. Not surprisingly, in the early twentieth century, the United States had the highest divorce rate in the world. ▲ Social commentators bemoaned the fragility of the nuclear family and pined longingly for the "good old days." Birthrates among highly educated Americans dropped, prompting some state legislatures to pass laws prohibiting abortion in order to boost the nation's birthrate.

▲ *For more on historical trends in divorce in this country, read Chapter 7.*

The Great Depression of the 1930s brought further turmoil to American families. Contrary to nostalgic images, the poverty brought about by the Depression didn't bring families closer together. It's true that divorce rates fell during this decade, but they didn't fall because of spouses' strong emotional commitment to each other. With jobs and housing scarce, many couples simply couldn't afford to divorce. Hence, marital unhappiness, domestic violence, and desertion increased dramatically. Economic stress often led to harsh parenting practices, which left many children with emotional as well as physical scars. Murder rates were higher in 1933 than they were in the 1980s (Coontz, 1997). Marriage rates and birthrates plummeted.

The divorce rate rose sharply again right after World War II. In 1946 one out of every three marriages ended in divorce. Such a high rate was due most likely to the brief courtships that took place before the young men shipped out and to the stress of separation when they were overseas. When the soldiers returned home, the disruption of relationships that had occurred during the war was made official. In one study of fathers who returned from the war, four times as many men reported unhappy, even traumatic, reunions as remembered happy ones (Tuttle, 1993).

During World War II, government motivational films convinced women that it was their patriotic duty to enter the labor force and support the war effort (Frank, Ziebarth, & Field, 1982). Thousands entered new jobs, gained new skills, and joined unions. Initially, almost all working women assumed they'd quit their jobs when the war ended. However, an overwhelming majority of working women changed their minds, deciding they didn't want to give up their independence and income by leaving the workforce.

After the war, the government's support and celebration of female patriotism quickly vanished. Women were now being strongly encouraged to return to their "natural" domestic roles. Children needed their mothers at home, they were told. Mothers who continued to work were branded as family villains. The phrase "8-hour orphan" was frequently used in government propaganda to describe the "horrible" experiences to which children of working mothers were subjected. The women who weren't fired found their jobs downgraded to lower-paid, "female" jobs. Not surprisingly, many women grudgingly returned to the homemaker role. But others didn't. The percentage of women in the workforce continued to rise during the late 1940s and 1950s (Reskin & Padavic, 1994). Women were in the workforce to stay. ▲

▲ *Women's participation in the workforce has led to many changes at home, as Chapter 3 explains.*

The Baby Boom of the 1940s and 1950s

By the time the 1950s rolled around, Americans were hungry for financial security and family stability. For people who could recall their family's struggle to make ends meet during the Depression and who had experienced instability and family separation during World War II, the opportunities to buy a home and have a big family represented an attractive promise of security and fulfillment (Acock & Demo, 1994; Mintz & Kellogg, 1988). The result was the "baby boom": Births rose from 18.4 per 1,000 women during the Depression to 25.3 per 1,000 in 1957 (Mintz & Kellogg, 1988).

For many Americans the 1950s still stand out as the "glory days" of families, a reference point against which recent changes in family life can be measured and interpreted. It was the most family-oriented period in U.S. history, dramatically reversing what had been occurring in this country since the turn of the century. For example, half of all women in the 1950s married while they were still teenagers. And the divorce rate steeply declined, to about half what it is today.

For the first time in history the vast majority of American children could expect to live with married biological parents throughout childhood. Although society had some serious problems to deal with—poverty, racial discrimination, lack of educational opportunity—the lives of many white middle- and working-class children were markedly better than they were in the past:

> No longer did children have to be haunted by fears ... that their parents would die, that they would have to live with a stepparent and stepsiblings, or that they would be abandoned. These were the years when the nation confidently boarded up orphanages and closed foundling hospitals, certain that such institutions would never again be needed. In movie theaters across the country parents and children could watch the drama of parental separation and death in the great Disney classics, secure in the knowledge that such nightmare visions as the death of Bambi's mother and the wrenching separation of Dumbo from his mother were only make-believe. (Whitehead, 1993, p. 50)

Economic prosperity further bolstered the pro-family features of this era. Per capita income rose by 35 percent between 1945 and 1960. The increase in ownership of single-family homes between 1946 and 1956 was larger than the increase during the entire preceding 150 years. Eighty-five percent of new homes were built in the suburbs, away from the turmoil of growing cities (Coontz, 1992).

New values regarding families also developed in the 1950s. The belief that all the satisfaction and amusement one needed could be found within the nuclear family had no precedent in history. According to one popular magazine of the time, the defining characteristic of the ideal family was "togetherness," a "new and warmer way of life" in which men and women sought fulfillment not alone, isolated from one another, but as a family sharing a common experience (cited

in Mintz & Kellogg, 1988). Americans consistently reported in surveys that home and family were the primary source of their happiness and esteem. Fewer than one in ten Americans believed that an unmarried person could ever be truly happy. Indeed, people who didn't marry were thought to suffer from "emotional immaturity and infantile fixations," "unwillingness to assume responsibility," the selfish "pursuit of career ambitions," and "deviant physical characteristics" (Ehrenreich, 1983).

It certainly appears as if families of this era were strong, stable, and culturally valued. Unfortunately, the reality of family life was far more painful and complex than television reruns and nostalgic memories of the baby boom era would suggest. Twenty-five percent of Americans were officially poor, and in the absence of food stamps, housing programs, and other forms of government aid, this poverty could literally be deadly. Even at the end of the decade, a third of American children were poor, a figure higher than today's. High school graduation rates were also lower in the 1950s than they are today. Minority families were almost entirely excluded from the gains enjoyed by white, middle-class families. While the vast majority of white middle-class mothers were housewives, close to half of all black women with small children had to work outside the home to support their families (Coontz, 1992). ▲

▲ *Race and class differences in female labor force participation are discussed further in Chapter 3.*

Other mythical ideas about the nuclear families of the 1950s don't hold up under close scrutiny. By 1960, for instance, less than half of American families consisted of traditional single-earner married couples, and nearly one-fourth were dual-earner couples (Masnick & Bane, 1980). Unmarried people were hardly sexually abstinent in the 1950s either. Between 1940 and 1958, the non-marital birthrate tripled (Coontz, 1997).

Even among those families that approximated the middle-class ideal, life was not always so joyous. Beneath the idyllic image of family was an undercurrent of anxiety. Concerns about children's health, safety, and happiness pervaded child care manuals of the 1950s. These fears were very real. Prior to the introduction of the Salk vaccine in 1955, tens of thousands of children were crippled by polio each year. Because of the risk that a minor ailment could grow into a more serious disease, parents were told to be watchful for the tiniest symptoms, such as a sore throat, headache, stomach cramps, fever, neck stiffness, and so on (Mintz & Kellogg, 1988).

Also lurking in the shadows were considerable violence, terror, and misery. While people in white, middle-class suburbs could effectively ignore conflict and turmoil, elsewhere there was tremendous hostility toward people who were defined as somehow different: Jews, African Americans, Puerto Ricans, the poor, and so on. ▲ Blacks in the South faced legally sanctioned segregation and pervasive brutality. Those in the North were systematically excluded from the benefits of economic expansion that their labor helped to create. Harassment and violence awaited blacks who tried to participate in the American family dream. When a black man attempted to move his family into Cicero, Illinois, in 1951, a mob of 4,000 whites spent 4 days tearing his apartment apart while police stood by and joked with them (Coontz, 1992).

▲ *The history of prejudice against several racial and ethnic groups is related in Issue 6.*

Alcoholism, battering, and incest were rampant among all classes but more often than not were swept under the rug. ▲ Researchers in Colorado found 302 battered-

child cases, including 33 deaths, in a single year, although virtually none of them were publicized (cited in Mintz & Kellogg, 1988). When girls or women reported being victimized by incest or sexual abuse, they were frequently told they were "fantasizing" their unconscious desires.

▲ *Chapter 6 exposes the roots of intimate violence in a variety of contemporary cultures.*

Less dramatic, but perhaps more widespread, was a high level of marital unhappiness. Despite the images of family warmth and togetherness, a significant number of people were dissatisfied with their family life. One researcher at the time found that less than a third of the couples she interviewed were happily married (Komarovsky, 1962).

Women who wanted to work—or had to work—were attacked in books and newspapers as seriously ill people or as symbolic castrators of men. Those who didn't want to have children were considered perverted. ▲ *Esquire* magazine called working wives a "menace"; *Life* magazine called female employment a "disease" (cited in Coontz, 1992). The frustration many women felt from being forced into tightly defined domestic roles led to a soaring increase in the incidence of mental illness and the use of tranquilizers and alcohol (Warren, 1987).

▲ *Such "pro-natalist" attitudes have repercussions today, as Chapter 4 discusses.*

Ironically, at the same time women were being labeled as "unnatural" if they didn't seek fulfillment in motherhood and housework, psychologists and psychiatrists were writing that most psychological problems people had could be traced to domineering mothers who spent too much time doting over them as children. As author Betty Friedan noted:

> It was suddenly discovered that the mother could be blamed for everything. In every case history of the troubled child; alcoholic, suicidal, schizophrenic, psychopathic, neurotic adult; impotent, homosexual male; frigid, promiscuous female; ulcerous, asthmatic, and otherwise disturbed American, could be found a mother. A frustrated, repressed, disturbed, martyred, never satisfied, unhappy woman. A demanding, nagging, shrewish wife. A rejecting, overprotecting, dominating mother. (Friedan, 1963, p. 189)

Men were also pressured into accepting family roles. They sometimes lost jobs or promotions because they weren't married. Bachelors were considered "immature," "infantile," or deviant. Those who were married and did have children often expressed discontent over the long, sometimes mindless hours they had to spend at work to support their families. ▲

▲ *Read Chapter 3 for more on how men balance work and family life.*

These stirrings planted the seeds of discontent that drove much of the tumult that characterized the following decade, the 1960s. Many Americans had buried themselves in the private concerns of family, home, and career. Now there were signs of restlessness and change (Skolnick, 1991).

The Sixties and Beyond

People who came of age in the 1940s and 1950s played out a pretty clear life script that escorted them into adulthood rather quickly: they married, had children, and settled into careers all in their early 20s. But by the 1960s

it was becoming increasingly apparent that this life pattern was a poor fit with social reality. The rising educational demands of modern society were keeping young people in school longer and prolonging adolescence (Skolnick, 1991). Americans were being forced to reexamine the previously taken-for-granted foundation of family: sexual norms, gender roles, and marital patterns.

Consequently, since 1960, American families have undergone changes as dramatic and far-reaching as those that took place at the turn of the century. In the 1960s more people began postponing marriage or choosing not to marry at all. Birthrates plummeted as they had during the Depression. The number of divorces in 1966 was three times higher than the number in 1950 (Mintz & Kellogg, 1988). This trend created a sharp increase in the number of female-headed households. New sexual norms allowed people to improvise and experiment with new forms of family, like cohabitation.

To observers in the 1960s and 1970s, the institution of family seemed under fierce attack. But, in many ways, the 1960s marked a resumption of cultural trends that had been put aside since the 1920s. Issues like sexual codes, women's rights, household division of labor, child care, sexual satisfaction in marriage, and so on were merely reemerging.

In part because of women's growing dissatisfaction with and active protest against their roles as housewives and mothers, new family issues began to appear in the 1960s and 1970s that have continued through the 1980s and into the 1990s: the demand for equal work, household, and child care responsibilities for both spouses; the liberalization of divorce laws; paternal and joint custody arrangements after divorce; premarital contracts spelling out marital and economic rights and obligations; cohabitation and singlehood as viable living arrangements; the right of unmarried women to bear and retain custody of their children, and the right of married couples not to have children at all; the legitimacy of homosexual relationships, and so on. ▲ These are the issues that have alarmed those who decry the disappearance of the traditional family (Levine, 1981).

▲ *For more on the role of social movements in changing family life, read Chapter 9.*

In sum, although many of these specific changes are unique to the late twentieth century, family life has experienced serious and sometimes fearsome change throughout our nation's history. When social commentators lament the disappearance of the traditional family, they are invariably referring to a romanticized and idealized image. ▲ Calls for a return to the good old days are, in fact, calls to return to something that has never truly existed outside the realm of prime-time television.

▲ *Two opposing perspectives on the health of American families are considered in Issue 8.*

Something to Think About

We all have two families: the actual one we live in and the imagined one we live by (Gillis, 1996). Popular images of families—whether they come from books, magazines, newspapers, television, word of mouth, or simply our own personal observations (accurate or not)—affect our common-sense notions about how our own families work and what they should look like. But these images also influence social researchers, affecting not only the answers to the questions they ask but their choice of questions in the first place. Suppose, for example, that a researcher is interested in the effects of mothers' work outside the home on their children's well-being. The unstated assumption behind this research question is that working mothers at least have the *potential* to negatively affect their children's well-being. In this sense, even scientific research can never be free of popular images of families. But knowing the pervasiveness of popular images, we can better equip ourselves to truly understand the nature of family life. We can question claims about families that appear in the popular press and keep in mind that families in TV and film reflect a long and complicated social history.

1. On prime-time television, what family form predominates? Have you noticed significant social class or racial variation in TV families? How are "nontraditional" family arrangements (e.g., single-parent households, divorce, gay families, interracial marriage) handled today? What sorts of issues do TV families deal with? How do they solve problems? Make decisions? Deal with crises? How closely do TV families approximate your family experiences?

2. Should there be tighter control over how families are portrayed on television to ensure that the variety of family forms that actually exist are accurately represented?

3. How do media images of family affect people's own family experiences? Do the media (television, in particular) *create* images of family that viewers then use to form their own attitudes about family, or do they simply *reflect* the reality of family life as people experience it?

4. How useful in the search for an accurate image of contemporary American families is information about families of the past? What is the connection, if any, between families of the past and current family forms?

ISSUE 3

How Private Should Family Life Be?

On the evening of October 8, 1977, a 17-year-old St. Paul, Minnesota, high school track star and straight-A student was driving his parents' station wagon when it skidded on some wet leaves and crashed into a tree. The young man was severely injured, went into a coma, and was placed on life support systems and a feeding tube. For several years after the accident, his parents held out hope that he would someday regain consciousness. They consulted various specialists and even considered taking their son to Japan for special treatment.

Eventually the parents made a decision: They wouldn't let their son live longer in his "vegetative" state than he had in his active life. So they elected to disconnect his life-support equipment in 1994, on his thirty-fourth birthday.

But when word of their plans became public, an advocacy group representing disabled people claimed that the young man's rights weren't being adequately represented and filed a last-minute motion to stop his parents from carrying out their wishes. Believing that the parents weren't acting in the best interests of their son, the group contended that he should have a legally appointed guardian before such a life-and-death decision could be made for him. They proposed that a local registered nurse—a woman who did not know the family but who was morally opposed to the removal of patients from life support equipment—be appointed the young man's legal guardian. The parents fought the group in the courts for close to a year to retain the right to make decisions concerning their son. A judge eventually ruled in favor of the family, and their son was taken off the machinery ("Family wins right," 1994).

Dennis and Lorie Nixon had twelve children. Dennis is the pastor of the Faith Tabernacle Congregation in Altoona, Pennsylvania. In 1991 their 8-year-old son died of dehydra-tion and malnutrition when an untreated inner ear infection became worse. The parents did not seek medical attention for the boy. They believe that the Bible is opposed to all means of healing apart from God's intervention and do not use any medical or surgical practices whatsover when they or their children become ill. They pleaded no contest to a charge of involuntary manslaughter and received probation.

In 1996 a second child—a 16-year-old daughter—died of complications resulting from untreated diabetes. She lapsed into a coma after 4 days of severe nausea and dry mouth. Her father attempted to cure her by praying and annointing her head with oil. This time the Nixons were convicted of involuntary manslaughter and child endangerment and sentenced to $2^{1}/_{2}$ to 5 years in a state prison, far longer than the 1-year sentence the district attorney had recommended. The court also ordered social workers to visit the Nixon home every 30 days and instructed County Children and Youth Services to have blood tests performed on the surviving children to see if any of them suffer from diabetes (Mellott, 1997).

What both of these events have in common is that they revolve around the rights of parents to determine the course of their children's lives. In each case the parents believed they were acting in the best interests of their children; and in each case the timing and appropriateness of outsiders' involvement in the private domain of the family became a source of controversy and debate.

In the first instance, a group with no personal ties to the family tried to prevent parents from taking their child off artificial life support. Seeing the issue more as a right-to-life case than a private family matter, they felt it was their duty to step in on behalf of the young man and protect his rights and interests. To most people, however, this group's attempt was insensitive and wrongheaded.

Families, they believe, and not some outside agency, should make such life-and-death decisions. These parents were not acting frivolously. They had agonized over their son's condition for 17 years.

Similarly, in the second case, the privacy rights of a family came into conflict with the physical well-being of their children. These parents, too, adamantly claimed that they would never do anything to harm their child. But, since the family's religious practices and beliefs were not mainstream, most observers felt that the parents sacrificed the right to privately practice their religion when they placed their children's lives in danger.

As you can see, the issue of family privacy, the focus of this section, is a knotty one. When is it appropriate for others to intervene in a family's business? Should there be legal limitations on how family members ought to treat one another? Whether we're talking about children's rights to privacy from their parents, the family's rights to privacy from the larger community, or the state's compelling interest to dictate how families should operate, privacy is one of the most crucial and controversial elements of contemporary family life.

The Ideal of Family Privacy

One of the most powerful values regarding family in American society today is that it is, or should be, a private institution. Within its zone of privacy, a family can exercise its liberty and discretion and be protected from unwanted outside interference. The private family is assumed to be the best judge and guardian of its own interests and needs.

There is nothing "natural" about family privacy. It is created when there is widespread agreement in a society that certain behaviors are legitimately off-limits to others (Nock, 1998). Family privacy therefore is maintained by powerful social norms. For instance, we are advised to "keep our noses out" of other people's family affairs. The violation

of this norm—for instance, when we feel it is necessary to discipline another parent's child—can create profound discomfort in us and extreme anger in others.

Privacy is usually linked to *autonomy*, another important concept, which refers to the family's independence from outside control and its right to make its own decisions about its future or about treatment of its members. In order to protect crucially important intimate relationships, decision making within families is often granted the protection of laws and customs. For instance, in some right-to-die cases, like the one described earlier, courts have ruled that the family should have the right to make such ultimate decisions because it is in the best position to interpret the probable wishes and best interests of a patient in a "persistent vegetative state" (Arras, 1991).

At first blush the question of whether or not family life is—or should be—private and autonomous appears obvious and simple. After all, we decide with whom we will form relationships, what those relationships will look like, if and when to have children, how we will treat other members of our family, and so on. Indeed, few of us would question that these decisions are solely our responsibility.

Many people in our society today feel that what goes on in a family should always be protected from community interference, public scrutiny, and state regulation. Family life, they believe, is best left to families, not the government, courts, or other public agencies (Gubrium & Holstein, 1990). Such privacy is essential to the development of liberty and freedom and protects individual families against the exercise of arbitrary power by the state (Feshbach & Feshbach, 1978; Fraser, 1987).

In 1928 Supreme Court Justice Louis Brandeis stated that privacy is "the most comprehensive of rights, and the right most valued by civilized" people (quoted in Gleick, 1996, p. 130). Justice Brandeis was talking about *individuals'* rights to privacy. But these sentiments are just as powerful when applied to the rights of families. We cringe at the idea of other people or our government telling us how to run a household, how to treat our partners, or how to raise our children.

Unfortunately, the high value that our society places on family privacy has made it difficult for us to recognize the abuses of privacy and the problems it can cause. For instance, the private nature of family often shields domestic violence from public inspection and social control, thereby reducing the risks for the violent family member and making it difficult for his or her victims to seek outside help. ▲

▲ *The relationship between privacy and domestic violence is discussed in detail in Chapter 6.*

The Location of Privacy

Family is an entity that is clearly tied to place—a "home," that is. Although not every family consists of members who live in the same household, the home provides the conceptual as well as the physical boundaries between private and public, between family and nonfamily. ▲ It provides seclusion; anonymity; and security of personal information, opinions, and expressions. Our homes are the places where we most expect to be let alone or to deal with others if and as we choose. Home denotes a place where we can relax, express ourselves candidly, show affection, enjoy sexuality, and reinforce family ties (Allen, 1988).

▲ *Issue 1 examines the relationship between families and households.*

The privacy of the home is protected by a number of constitutional provisions. The Third Amendment prohibits the quartering of soldiers in private homes during peacetime, reflecting the notion of home as a place where people are entitled to undisturbed seclusion. The Fourth Amendment guarantees individuals the right to be secure in their houses against unreasonable searches and seizures. The Omnibus Crime Control and Safe Streets Act of 1986 protects the privacy of the home by placing federal limits on wiretapping and surveillance (Allen, 1988).

To be sure, friends, neighbors, distant relatives, strangers, people selling things or soliciting donations, and various others breach the privacy of our homes from time to time. But allowing their presence is clearly a courtesy we extend. They are visitors, and we expect them to behave as such. Unlike household members, who can use the phone, check what's in the refrigerator, or turn on the TV whenever they want, visitors must seek and receive permission to do these things. I have known my in-laws for 17 years and have slept and eaten in their home many times. Yet despite their clear and sincere invitation to "make myself at home," I am still somewhat reluctant to shed my visitor role and enter without knocking or take food from the refrigerator without asking. Much of the humor of a character like Kramer on the popular television show *Seinfeld* derived from his wanton disregard for this norm when he barged into his neighbor's apartment.

In everyday life, the privacy of the home is useful and valuable in that it gives people a place where they can behave in ways that might be discouraged if such behavior was constantly being watched and evaluated by outsiders. As you're well aware, we all do and say things in the privacy of our own homes and in the company of family members that we wouldn't dream of doing or saying in front of strangers or even close friends.

To some sociologists—most notably, Erving Goffman (1959)—the distinction between private and public behavior is crucial to understanding family life. Goffman argues that social life often requires that we be like actors upon a theatrical stage, performing so that others will see us in a particular way. Think of these people who observe our behavior as the "audience." The "roles" we play are the images of ourselves we are trying to project. And the "dialogue" consists of our communications with others. The overarching goal is to enact a performance that is believable to a particular audience and that allows us to achieve the goals we desire.

Different locations require different sorts of performances. An important consideration is the distinction between public, front stage interaction and private, backstage interaction. In the theater, front stage is where performances take place. These performances are presented for the eyes and ears of the audience and are meant to convey a believable image. The most skilled actors are the ones who portray characters so credible that we forget we're watching actors playing roles. When applied to everyday social interaction, "front stage" is where people carry out interaction performances and maintain appropriate appearances in front of others. For restaurant workers, for instance, front stage would be the dining room where the customers (the audience) are present. Here the servers (the actors) are expected to present themselves as upbeat, happy, competent, and courteous.

In contrast, theatrical backstage refers to the wings and to the dressing rooms where people remove makeup, rehearse lines, rehash performances, and slip "out of character." In social life, "backstage" is synonymous with privacy. It's where people can prepare for upcoming front stage encounters or comment upon those just completed. It's also where people can knowingly and sometimes cynically violate their front stage performances. Going back to the restaurant example, back stage would be the kitchen area where the once-friendly, courteous servers now shout, shove dishes, and even complain about or make fun of the customers.

The distinction between front stage and backstage is crucial to family life. Much of the time we spend with our family members

is spent in front of others—at ice cream shops, Little League games, front porches, school plays, neighborhood parties, and so on—where audiences expect families to present a cohesive and consistent image of themselves. If you've ever seen a married couple fighting in a shopping mall or a parent screaming at a child in a supermarket, you know how disturbing such scenes can be. They violate the unspoken norms that families not "air their dirty laundry" in public. Hence, family members—especially spouses—often feel compelled to hide conflict and criticism of one another when they are on front stage, even if they're in the midst of an ongoing, bitter feud. ▲

▲ *A couple headed for divorce must at some point go public with their dissatisfactions, as Chapter 7 explains in detail.*

Fortunately for society, however, most families do have access to a backstage area in their private households. Think of how utterly unmanageable our family lives would be if there weren't somewhere we could go to escape the prying eyes and expectations of outsiders. We all need a place to relax, where we need not be concerned with how our looks, actions, or statements are received by others. If you've ever had guests stay at your house for a long period of time, you know how disruptive they can be to family life. It's not just that they represent an extra mouth to feed or an extra set of interests and desires that must be taken into account when decisions are made. It's that their presence robs the family of the ability to "go backstage" in its own home.

But the importance of backstage and, more generally, family privacy goes beyond individuals' ability to act comfortably without worrying about the images they present to others. Underlying the distinction between front stage and backstage family behavior is the belief that the most authentic family experiences occur in the privacy of the home (Gubrium & Holstein, 1987). This is where a family's *true* feelings and characteristics emerge. It is widely presumed that the *real* family can only be seen in its private moments, "behind closed doors."

The assumption here is that the public, front stage family is often motivated to conceal its flaws and shortcomings. For example, parents who are harsh and abusive to their children in private may work hard to appear loving and gentle in public. Likewise, the incompatible married couple may maintain a facade of cordiality when with friends. Thus, the backstage aspect of the household is not only intrinsic to family life but is also, at times, camouflaged, hidden, or protected (Gubrium & Holstein, 1990).

This notion has implications for a real understanding of families. We know what our own families are really like because we've seen them backstage. However, despite our interest in other people's family relationships, we usually don't have access to their backstage, so we can only know them in terms of their public presentations and discourse. The gap between public images and private realities may be quite wide (Skolnick, 1979). If, in fact, the "true" nature of family interaction remains hidden from public view, our understandings of families will always be inaccurate or incomplete. ▲ It's ironic that privacy, so essential to family life, is also the cultural value that most obscures our understanding of it.

▲ *The difficulty of researching families while honoring family privacy is discussed in Chapter 1.*

The History of Privacy

Privacy and autonomy, in recent years, have come to symbolize many of the political and cultural struggles over "family values." In our society, we tend to take it for granted that the family is and always was a private, autonomous institution. But according to many family historians, only since the latter part of the nineteenth century and early twentieth century have we begun to perceive family privacy as a basic, inalienable right and made it a rallying cry in political disputes and debates (Laslett, 1973).

Indeed, despite our beliefs about the rugged, independent families of our past, American families have never been completely self-sufficient and autonomous. They've always depended on the government and other social institutions for their survival. Colonial families, for instance, relied on a large network of neighbors, churches, courts, and government officials for their sustenance. Later, prairie farmers and other pioneer families were able to exist because of massive federal land grants, government-funded military expeditions that forced Native Americans off their ancestral land and confiscated half of Mexico, and government-sponsored investment into new territories (Coontz, 1992). Working-class and minority families have always found it difficult to survive without assistance beyond family. Immigrants founded lodges to provide material aid and foster cooperation. Laborers formed funeral aid societies and death or sick benefit associations; they held balls and picnics to raise money for injured workers, widows, or orphans, and took collections at the mills or plant gates nearly every payday (Coontz, 1992, p. 71).

Even 1950s suburban families owed much of their good fortune to government-subsidized programs like the GI Bill, which permitted a whole generation of men to expand their education, improve their job prospects, and own their own homes. Such reliance on outside social institutions, therefore, made complete family privacy and autonomy impossible.

In addition, people's everyday family lives were rarely free of outside scrutiny. In the small, preindustrial societies of the distant past, family privacy was a foreign concept. Every person had to perform essential tasks to ensure community survival. One person's actions had significance for everyone. Such societies depended on close monitoring and supervision to enforce conformity (Nock, 1998). Farm households may have been far apart, but people still had a lot of contact with their neighbors. And more affluent people living in towns and villages frequently interacted with one another as they conducted their business.

Furthermore, norms at the time allowed outsiders—friends, neighbors, customers, and so on—to move freely through others' households, monitoring and observing what went on there. In colonial America, church attendance was practically mandatory, and ministers believed it was their duty to watch the behaviors of their congregants both in and out of church (Nock, 1998). As one social historian put it, at this time "there was no such thing as private life, no refuge from the public gaze and its ceaseless criticism" (quoted in Gleick, 1996, p. 130). Indeed, it was not uncommon for city officials, church elders, and prying neighbors to regularly enter people's homes and tell them with whom to associate, what to wear, and what to teach their children. Families that didn't comply were sometimes punished, or worse, forcibly separated.

In addition, early industrial households typically contained a variety of residents. In working-class homes, the boarding and lodging of strangers and the "doubling up" of families under one roof were common means of helping with financial expenses (Gubrium & Holstein, 1990; Hareven, 1992). Upper-class families could afford to bring servants, distant kin (extended family), and sometimes even employees into the household. Obviously the presence of these other people greatly reduced the degree of privacy that could exist in a home. By just being around, they limited what spouses or parents and children could do without detection. In fact, the key witnesses in eighteenth-century adultery trials were typically servants or other boarders whose curiosity, close proximity, and willingness to peep through key-

holes made sexual privacy nearly impossible (Stone, 1979).

The layout of preindustrial houses also made privacy difficult. Aside from wealthy estates, most homes built in the seventeenth century consisted of a single room. Eating, sleeping, recreating, and procreating all took place in the same area, usually in the company of others. In many cases family members slept in the same bed (Shorter, 1975). Even the great houses of the upper classes were constructed of interlocking suites of rooms without corridors, so that the only way of moving about was by passing through other people's rooms (Stone, 1979). Given such architectural constraints, privacy as we know it today was a luxury most people couldn't comprehend (Gelles & Straus, 1988).

Although we may blanch at the thought of such a lack of privacy in everyday family life, it did have a positive effect: It held social groups together and stabilized society. There was a wholeness and certainty to life that we no longer have. People lived without privacy, to be sure, but they also lived without the sort of social isolation and alienation that characterize contemporary society.

By the mid–nineteenth century, things began to change. New forms of technology and the promise of new financial opportunities and a good living drew people (particularly men) away from the farms and into city factories. For the first time in American history, the family economy was based primarily outside the household. ▲ But the increasing population density brought about by urbanization and industrialization increased the contact people had with strangers. Furthermore, immigrants at the turn of the century, for whom family privacy was likely an alien concept, settled in the close quarters of growing urban areas.

▲ *This change has had many implications for men's and women's family roles, as Chapter 3 explains.*

Amid the clamor of rapidly growing cities, middle-class, urban families began to look to their homes for solace and privacy (Laslett, 1973). An expanding economy eventually gave them the means to move into residences all their own. Domesticity, intimacy, and privacy became desirable characteristics of middle-class family life (Hareven, 1992). Consequently people's family activities became visible to fewer and fewer people (Vanek, 1980). By the end of the nineteenth century, middle-class families were less often taking in boarders and lodgers or joining forces with relatives and more often seeking their own private residence (Hareven, 1992). Married couples were having fewer children. Single-family detached houses became more popular, eventually becoming the ideal setting for American domestic life.

Even the architecture of private middle-class homes changed around this time. Locking doors and a central hallway, with rooms opening to it, permitted a degree of family privacy not previously available (Laslett, 1973). Today we take for granted our homes' separate rooms that accommodate separate functions, freeing family members from even each other's watchful gaze.

The gradual separation of home from public life reflected a technological shift toward family self-sufficiency that continues today (Skolnick, 1987). Innovations in the amenities available within the home (refrigerators, telephones, indoor plumbing, radios, and, more recently, central heating, air conditioning, backyard swimming pools, televisions, and computers) all brought family activities from more visible locations into the private home. ▲ Refrigerators, for instance, have made it unnecessary to visit the market everyday. Air conditioning allows us to spend hot, stuffy summer evenings inside instead of on the front porch or at the local ice cream parlor. Today, with the Internet, fax machines, and home shopping cable networks, a family can practically survive without *ever* leaving the privacy of its home.

▲ *Chapter 9 discusses the link between technological innovation and changes in family life.*

The shift from public to private has not been complete, however. Although the constant, personal surveillance that characterized small, tight-knit communities of the past has largely disappeared, the sort of family surveillance that exists today is likely to be more abstract and carried out by institutions such as schools, courts, hospitals, credit agencies, and so on.

The Paradox of Privacy

So, although we typically think of family as the most private and most intimate of social institutions, complete family privacy is an illusion. Private family decisions are always made within larger societal and cultural boundaries (Burtt, 1994). For instance, cultural expectations, like how we should interact with partners or how much respect parents and children ought to afford one another, provide a normative backdrop against which we live our private family lives.

In addition, there are laws—such as murder laws—that all of us must abide by, even in the privacy of our families. The state cannot be neutral or remain uninvolved in this regard, nor would anyone want it to do so (Olsen, 1993). And even the staunchest supporters of a family's right to privacy will insist that the state needs to reinforce parents' authority over their children from time to time. We may justify state officials returning runaway children to their parents or courts ordering incorrigible children to obey their parents as proper efforts to keep families together. But keep in mind that even in these cases the state is venturing deep into the privacy of family.

Most of us would also agree that the state has the right to intervene in family life when others threaten to interfere. Imagine your reaction if state agencies did nothing to prevent doctors from performing nonemergency surgery on a child without the parents' permission or to prevent neighbors from trying to take a child on their vacation against the parents' wishes. Imagine if the state refused to get involved in nasty child custody battles between divorced parents. Such state intervention is bound to affect other decisions people make, like how families ought to be formed, how power in families ought to be distributed, and how roles ought to be assigned (Olsen, 1993). In short, the state is responsible for the social rules that affect people's family behavior and is deeply implicated in how families form and function. ▲

▲ *Family law and policy is treated further in Chapter 9.*

The state also routinely nullifies privacy rights in situations where behavior is deemed "immoral." In 1986 the U.S. Supreme Court ruled that a Georgia law forbidding married couples, unmarried heterosexual couples, and homosexual couples from participating in oral or anal sex was constitutional. Such a law may be difficult to enforce, but its existence represents a "moral" symbol of what some people in this society will and won't tolerate within other people's private lives.

The legal system, however, is not the main source of outside intervention in private families in today's society. Organizations like the Internal Revenue Service, the Social Security Administration, and local utility companies routinely invade the privacy of families through their access to intimate information. Commercial interests also impinge on family privacy. For example, data sellers market to insurance companies lists of families who have filed medical malpractice suits or workers' compensation claims. Some of these organizations sell lists of renters who have sued landlords.

The workplace can also disturb the privacy of families. Employment actions and policies—such as forced overtime, work schedules, health benefits, transfers, pay cuts, and layoffs—regulate family life far more intimately than the state does.

School officials, too, are beginning to realize that in order to provide an environment conducive to learning, they sometimes must delve into the private lives of their students. For instance, many schools across the country have codes of conduct that control students' *off*-campus behavior, such as smoking or using drugs in their homes (Lewin, 1998a).

In an even more direct sense, other individuals seem to care very much about what goes on in our private lives. If you've ever been the sole single person in a group of couples, you've no doubt felt the subtle, perhaps blatant, pressures people exert on you to "settle down and find someone." Few young married couples are able to escape probing questions from parents and others about if and when they're going to have children. Many divorced couples find they must cope with friends and family who demand explanations for the breakup.

Consider also a common family event we're all familiar with: the wedding ceremony. If you've ever been married or been to a wedding, you know that these ceremonies are not private affairs designed solely for the bride and groom; they exist for the benefit of relatives, friends, and the community. Weddings are traditionally considered the formal beginning of a family, the *public*, *legal*, and sometimes *religious* recognition of a couple's new legal status. Two people traditionally can't declare on their own one day that they're married, without some sort of public ratification.

So families occupy a curious, paradoxical position in today's society. Although many of us may espouse family privacy, our families never really belong exclusively to us. We may resent intrusions into family life, but no family can exist in a vacuum, completely free of external pressures.

Parents and Children

The paradox of family privacy is striking when it comes to parents' rights to raise their children as they see fit. From a societal perspective, the institution of family is important for its role in teaching children habits, patterns, lessons, and values that will eventually make them good citizens. ▲ In order for society to exist at all, it needs loyalty, stability, and achievement from its members—all qualities that families are able to foster (Yoest, 1997). Given the role families play in the very survival of society, it's not surprising that intervening in family life would be considered appropriate, even necessary, under certain conditions. In one sense, then, parents are never allowed to do whatever they want with the children under their care. In earlier times, community elders ensured that children would be raised properly. Today the less personal, more bureaucratic institution of the state sets standards and rules about parental choices in all areas of child rearing (Burtt, 1994).

▲ *For more on the complexities of child rearing, read Chapter 5.*

But there is a growing sentiment that too much state involvement compromises parental authority and family stability. In 1995 a bill was introduced in Congress that would forbid state and local governments from interfering with the right of parents to direct the upbringing and education of their children ("The new 'parental rights' crusade," 1996). This bill would have allowed parents to sue teachers, librarians, school counselors, police officers, and social workers for interfering with parents' ability to control the education, health, discipline, and religious teaching of their children. The bill did not receive full committee approval and never came to the floor of Congress for a vote. Nevertheless, it and similar bills introduced in various states signal a growing concern among some legislators that parents' ability to raise their children as they see fit is being eroded.

Yet when parental behavior clearly violates popular notions of appropriate child rearing, the political winds can shift toward allowing greater intervention and sanctioning. Parents have been tried and convicted of crimes for not exercising appropriate control over their children. Consider, for instance, the story of David and Sharon Schoo. In December of 1992, the Schoos stepped off a plane that had just arrived at Chicago's O'Hare Airport and were promptly arrested by local police. This seemingly average couple from an upper-middle-class neighborhood just outside Chicago had just spent 9 sun-filled days vacationing in Acapulco, Mexico. The problem was, they left their two daughters—ages 9 and 4—at home by themselves with no supervision. The Schoos left a refrigerator full of food and a note full of instructions, but no information on how the children could contact them. The girls were discovered when a smoke alarm in the house accidentally went off and the older girl called the 911 emergency number. The Schoos were charged with multiple felony counts of child abandonment, cruelty to children, and child endangerment. In a plea bargain arrangement, they pleaded guilty to the charge of aggravated battery of a child. The girls were placed under the care of the Illinois Department of Children and Family Services. The Schoos eventually terminated their parental rights and gave their daughters up for adoption (Johnson, 1993).

State intervention in family life is particularly likely when a family's religious or cultural beliefs and values conflict with those of the larger society. For example, in 1996 the U.S. Supreme Court let stand a ruling by the Minnesota Court of Appeals, which awarded $1.5 million to the father of an 11-year-old boy who died after his mother, stepfather, and two Christian Scientist practitioners tried to use prayer to heal his diabetes. In its ruling, the court stated, "Although one is free to believe what one will, religious freedom ends when one's conduct offends the law by, for example, endangering a child's life" (Greenhouse, 1996, p. A12).

The controversy over privacy in parent-child relationships is also apparent when we look at the extent to which children have rights to privacy *from* their parents. Whether a child is granted privacy in any sense—privacy of quarters, of possessions, of thoughts and behaviors, of relationships with others—or whether these things are thought to be open to parents' inspection depends on how parents define themselves and their children (Hess & Handel, 1985). As children mature they begin to demand increasing privacy in their personal lives. As you well know, many adolescents consider their bedrooms to be their impenetrable sanctuaries (Fiene, 1995). It's not uncommon for a teenager today to post a "Keep Out" sign on his or her door or otherwise make it clear to the rest of the family that his or her domain is off limits.

Historically, parents have enjoyed wide discretionary authority over their children's upbringing. But over the past few decades, the nation's courts have held that children do have independent rights that can override parental authority. Some states have struck down laws that give parents an absolute veto over whether a minor girl can obtain an abortion, for instance. Other states have greatly expanded minors' rights, permitting them, in some cases, to seek temporary placement in another home if conflict exists with their parents (Mintz, 1989).

At the same time, however, there seems to be heightened concern about the problems teenagers are getting into and an increased desire to give parents help in monitoring their behavior. Consider these recent innovations:

- Many communities are now forming parenting networks, which often include telephone trees and neighborhood watches, so that parents can help one another keep tabs on their kids.

- Teen curfews have been imposed in cities all across the country.

- Adults can use computer chips and television rating systems to prevent children from watching TV programs parents find objectionable.

- You can now see bumper stickers all across the country that read, "Is my teenager driving safely?" with a toll-free number for anonymous observers to report careless driving (Diamond, 1996).

- A device called DriveRight monitors the speed at which a teenager drives a car. Parents can download data from the device into their home computer and print out driving speeds and rates of acceleration and deceleration.

So strong is the concern over teen behavior and safety (in particular, drug use) that many parents are now monitoring much of their children's private lives. The Psychemedics Corporation of Cambridge, Massachusetts, for instance, is marketing a $75 hair-analysis kit for parents. The kit provides parents with instructions on how to clip a small lock of their child's hair, deposit it in a company-supplied envelope, and send it to the company's chemical lab for drug analysis. The company claims it has a technique that can detect evidence of drug use from no more than four or five dozen strands of hair, although critics warn that such tests aren't always reliable. Within a few weeks, the parents receive a confidential report stating whether or not their child has used drugs within the past 90 days (Frankel, 1996). Concerned parents who don't feel comfortable cutting their children's hair can purchase a kit called DrugAlert, manufactured by Barringer Technologies in New Jersey, which detects traces of up to thirty illicit drugs from a child's room or belongings ("New kit can help," 1995).

Variations in Family Privacy

Every society has some norms protecting family privacy. But the extent and manifestation of these norms varies from culture to culture. In traditional Samoa, for instance, there were no walls in the houses, and only thin mosquito netting separated the sleeping rooms of the married couples, children, and old folks. The processes of birth and death were not hidden from public view; even children were allowed to watch these moments of intimacy. As the famous anthropologist Margaret Mead put it, in the Samoa she studied in the 1930s, "little is mysterious . . . little forbidden" (quoted in Westin, 1984, p. 60).

But even those societies where household entry is fairly free and open typically have rules limiting what a nonfamily visitor can touch or where she or he may go within the house. There may also be norms limiting family acts or topics of conversation while outsiders are present.

In societies that have a tradition of large, extended families and where lots of people live in small, single-room dwellings, privacy is likely to be accomplished through rules of avoidance rather than through architecture. These rules, such as covering the face, averting the eyes, going to one's sleeping mat, or facing the wall, have the effect of ensuring a certain amount of *psychological* privacy even though actual physical privacy is impossible (Westin, 1984). In Java, for instance, virtually all aspects of everyday life occur in the presence of others. But the Javanese are able to "shut people out" with highly developed patterns of etiquette, emotional restraint, and a general lack of openness in speech and behavior.

Families and individuals within the same culture may have different expectations regarding privacy. When my wife and I first began living together, I quickly became aware of a glaring difference in our respective families' attitudes toward privacy. In my family, the bathroom was a place where one was granted automatic, total, and unquestionable privacy. Even though these norms were strong and no one would purposely violate them, locked doors were common. My wife's familial experiences were quite different. For her family, bathroom doors—indeed all doors within the house—remained not only unlocked but wide open. Imagine my surprise the first time she barged in on me while I was using the bathroom. I simply assumed she'd apologize for not knowing it was occupied, show an acceptable amount of repentance, and leave. It soon became clear, though, that she had no intention of leaving and, in fact, intended to stay and chat. Little did I know at the time that, in her family, the bathroom was the preferred location for deep conversations. There one faced few distractions and had, as it were, a captive audience.

More importantly, within American society, privacy is a privilege that not everyone can enjoy equally. A family's class standing has always had a substantial impact on how much privacy its members are accorded. Prior to the mid–nineteenth century, slave families were entitled to no privacy whatsover. ▲ Since slaves were considered property, they had no legal right to make a contract, including a marriage contract. Hence they could not *legally* marry. The slaveowner could decide who lived with whom. Slaves lived in constant fear that their families would be separated (Aulette, 1994).

▲ *Slave families are discussed in detail in Issue 6.*

In today's poor households, dwellings are smaller and more crowded than are those of more affluent households, making privacy structurally difficult to obtain. Thin walls separating cramped apartments hide few secrets. ▲ It's hard for family members to have any semblance of privacy—whether from one another or from neighbors—under such conditions. Privacy is further diminished by mandatory inspections by welfare caseworkers and housing authorities. In addition, poor people must often make use of public facilities (health clinics, laundromats, public transportation, and so on) to carry out the day-to-day tasks that wealthier people can carry out privately. In effect, the need for such facilities forces poor people to share their privacy with strangers.

▲ *Issue 7 addresses other differences between poor and wealthy families.*

Social class also influences broader societal perceptions of "appropriate" environ-ments for children, thereby increasing the state's willingness to step into private matters of poor (and usually minority) families. In 1967, for instance, welfare workers were given the power to remove children from their poor unmarried mothers on the grounds that poverty and lack of marriage, in and of themselves, constituted a potentially harmful environment for children (Coontz, 1992).

In sum, the ideal of family privacy rarely applies to everyday life in its pure form. Furthermore, it is not something that is enjoyed equally by all families.

Something to Think About

One of the most compelling sociological paradoxes is that we have, in family, the most private and protected of all social institutions yet one whose cultural, political, and personal importance provokes unparalleled public attention. Family is both autonomous and regulated, private and public. Most intimate and family behavior occurs away from the watchful eyes of others, and only we have access to our thoughts, desires, and feelings regarding the people with whom we are intimately involved. But whether we like it or not, others do care about what goes on in our families. The people around us, the government, even society as a whole, will always have a keen interest in what happens in our intimate lives.

1. When and under what conditions should a family's privacy and autonomy be tolerated and protected by society? When should it be breached?

2. How can we balance an individual's right to physical and emotional well-being against a family's right to be free from outside intrusion and to make its own decisions? Which of these values should be given top priority?

3. Should children have rights to privacy that protect them from parental intrusion?

4. If family activities are more "honest" when they occur in private, how can we ever accurately study families scientifically? If you were given the task of studying "intimate family communication" or "parental discipline tactics," how would you do it?

Couple Abandon Children for Vacation   David and Sharon Schoo, the Chicago-area couple charged with abandoning their two daughters while they spent the Christmas holidays in Mexico, attempt to cover their faces as they are released on bond from Kane County Jail in Geneva, Illinois, December 31. With them is their attorney, Gerald Kepple (left).

ISSUE 4

How Should Individual Rights and Family Obligations Be Balanced?

SOMETHING TO THINK ABOUT

The 1996 hit film *Shine* is based on the life story of a wildly eccentric but highly talented Australian pianist named David Helfgott, who overcame extreme personal trauma and mental problems to become a successful concert performer. In his early teens, David attracted the attention of a well-known international musician who offered him a scholarship to study piano in America. David was thrilled. But his strict and domineering father couldn't bear the thought of losing David and forbade him from going. In no uncertain terms he told David that his primary loyalty and responsibility must always be to the family. Outsiders, he said, can never be trusted or counted on in times of need as much as family members can. If David left, his father told him, he would surely tear the family apart forever. David grudgingly relented to his father's demands and turned down the scholarship.

Several years later, another opportunity to study abroad arose—this time at the Royal College of Music in London. David finally defied his father's brutal authority and accepted the offer. In doing so, however, he was banished from his home. His father cut off all communication with David while he was in London. David couldn't cope with the separation from his family and the feeling that he had betrayed his father. After one stirring, virtuoso concert performance, he suffered a nervous breakdown and returned to Australia, where for a decade he lived in and out of psychiatric institutions.

The film has a happy ending, though. As an adult, David developed an unlikely romance with a woman who brought stability to his chaotic world. The film concludes with his return to the concert stage in triumph.

Although *Shine* portrays an example of an extreme conflict between individual desire and family obligation, and, to some degree, is fictionalized, it nonetheless raises an important point about the role family loyalty ought to play in our individual lives. People every day face the dilemma of how to balance the pursuit of their personal desires with their responsibilities and obligations to their loved ones. Consider the 18-year-old college student who wants desperately to be an actress but whose parents are counting on her to take over the family dry-cleaning business after graduation. Or what about the 50-year-old son who must turn down a promotion in a different state because he needs to live close to his elderly, ailing parent? When a deep sense of duty and obligation butts up against personal wishes, significant pain and hard feelings can result.

These types of situations raise interesting questions about how group obligations are balanced with individual interests. More specifically, what should be more important, our personal rights or our obligations based on the family roles we occupy? What do people owe one another as members of the same family? Do we need to return to traditional role obligations—parent and child, man and woman—to maintain committed family relationships? These are the issues explored in this section.

Rights and Responsibilities

The tension between individual interests and the collective interests of family can be understood as a difference between personal rights and group responsibilities. Rights are individual entitlements or privileges, which are often protected by law. The right to free speech, to a fair and speedy trial, and to police protection are the sorts of things to which all U.S. citizens are entitled.

Individual rights lie at the very core of U.S. culture. The Declaration of Independence, the Constitution, and the Bill of Rights all declare individual rights to be "inalienable." As children we learn that we have the right to "life, liberty and the pursuit of happiness." The belief that policies ought to emphasize individual rights is deeply ingrained in our collective psyche:

> We believe in the dignity, indeed the sacredness, of the individual. Anything that would violate our right to think for ourselves, judge for ourselves, make our own decisions, live our lives as we see fit, is not only morally wrong, it is sacrilegious. Our highest and noblest aspirations, not only for ourselves, but for those we care about, for our society and for the world, are closely linked to our individualism. (Bellah et al., 1985, p. 142)

On the other hand, we are not so deeply committed as a culture to our responsibilities—our duties and obligations to others. Parents do have an abiding responsibility to provide food, clothing, and shelter for their children. And responsibilities are certainly necessary for a society to exist, and they deserve respect. But we usually don't stand up and cheer for them or fight for their protection as we do for individual rights (Oaks, 1995). Whereas laws exist to *protect* our rights, they exist to *enforce* our responsibilities.

Nevertheless, as the famous sociologist Émile Durkheim (1965) argued, people need clearly defined responsibilities to bind them together in a moral community. He believed that people are inherently selfish and therefore can form lasting relationships with others only if their natural feelings and desires are kept in check by society's rules. Clearly defined family roles and responsibilities thus play a key part in society: They not only sustain the institution of family, they also ensure stable attachments throughout society.

It's worth noting that rights and responsibilities aren't always dissimilar. Parents, for example, may fight for the *right* to child custody, but that right also includes clear responsibilities. Adult children can be both responsible for the care of their elderly parents and, at the same time, exercise their right to protect their

parents from unwanted medical care. My purpose in discussing them as distinct elements is to allow you to see how much of the tension we experience in our family lives can be the result of conflict between what we feel entitled to as individuals and what we feel obligated to do as members of a family.

Culture and Family Obligation

The balance between rights and responsibilities varies from society to society. Scholars often distinguish between *collectivist* and *individualist* cultures. Collectivist cultures are those in which individual goals are subordinated to the goals of the larger group, and obligation to others is emphasized over personal freedom. In contrast, individualist cultures are those in which individual rights, self-realization, personal autonomy, and personal identity take precedence (Dion & Dion, 1996).

Collectivist Cultures

In collectivist societies, such as most Asian countries, it is assumed that family members are interdependent and highly involved in one another's lives. Duty, sacrifice, and compromise are considered desirable traits. Collectivism doesn't mean a complete negation of the individual's well-being or interest, however. Instead, it is assumed that maintaining the group's well-being is ultimately the best guarantee for the individual's well-being (Hofstede, 1984).

Shame is an important sanctioning device in collectivist cultures. Since one person is seen as a reflection of the entire group, his or her singular actions can disgrace everyone in that group. Thus, family members have a great stake in the behavior of other family members. And shame is not limited to living relatives. In China, for instance, an individual's present misbehaviors can dishonor all ancestors as well as all future generations.

In collectivist cultures, personal identity is often subsumed within the family. In India, for instance, feelings of status and prestige derive more from strong identification with the reputation and honor of the family than from individual achievements (Roland, 1988). The tradition of arranged marriages in India fits with this orientation: Personal well-being in marriage is not so much a matter of emotional intimacy as it is in individualistic societies, where marriages are assumed to be based on personal feelings of romantic love (Dion & Dion, 1996).

Japanese society offers another good example of collectivist family ideology. Despite the growing influence of Western culture, the sense of familial responsibility is still strong in Japan. When Japanese men and women reach their mid-20s, pressure to marry—to please parents and peers, and to fulfill one's social obligations—mounts rapidly. Even today, between one-quarter and one-half of Japanese marriages are arranged (Zinsmeister, 1990). In addition, most people have a strong, lifelong commitment to their relatives. Two-thirds of Japanese elderly live with one of their offspring (Zinsmeister, 1990).

Curiously, the Japanese emphasis on family responsibility plays against a societal backdrop of an intense desire for individual social mobility. Workplace pressures are strong, and long hours away from family are the norm—especially for men. On average, Japanese workers put in about 500 more hours on the job a year than their U.S. counterparts. Perhaps we shouldn't be surprised, then, that collectivism appears to be losing some of its influence among younger Japanese. In one study of Japanese attitudes, older people were more likely to hold traditionally collectivist attitudes toward their families and their place in society than younger people, who were found to be more dedicated to improving their own lives and to value their own achievements rather than collective achievements (Ishii-Kuntz, 1989). Even

though their primary loyalty is still unquestionably to their families, many young Japanese report resentment at being forced to subordinate their personal interests to a tightly organized educational and employment system.

Individualist Cultures

In sharp contrast, cultures like those of Western Europe, the United States, Canada, and Australia tend to value individual freedom, autonomy, personal development, and gratification over group obligation and duty. In U.S. society, for instance, we have always admired independent people whose success—usually measured in financial terms—is based on their individual achievement and self-reliance (Bellah et al., 1985).

A key task in "normal" self-development in such an environment is the eventual separation from one's family. We take for granted that some day we will leave the home of our parents and start our own families. Childhood is sometimes seen chiefly as preparation for the crucial event of leaving home. Some people can't wait to "get out of the house" and begin an independent life. Even those who experience significant pain and sadness at the thought of breaking these ties accept that it is a necessary step in growing up. Few people see living with their parents during their 40s and 50s as an attractive option. By contrast, in traditional Japan, people have no such conception. In fact, in Japan the expression "leaving home" is reserved for people entering monasteries, who abandon *all* ties to conventional existence (Bellah et al., 1985).

It should be noted that the value of individualism is not held equally among different segments of U.S. society. For instance, Mexican-American families are often characterized by *familism,* a set of values that favor family solidarity over personal achievement. ▲ Moreover, in poor communities, many people are very loyal to close-knit kinship networks that support the members in times of need.

▲ *The history of Mexican-American families contributes to familism, as Issue 6 explains.*

Cultural Conflict

The differences between collectivist and individualist cultures are all too obvious to individuals who move from one type of culture to the other. Immigrants often expend a great deal of energy trying to maintain their original family ideology in the face of contradictory forces in their new culture. ▲

▲ *For more on immigrants and the maintenance of ethnic identity, read Issue 6.*

Vietnamese immigrants, for example, come from a culture solidly structured around family collectivism (Kibria, 1994a). To them the family is always more important than the individual. It is the center of the individual's life and activities (Tran, 1998). The common practice of ancestor worship among the Vietnamese affirms the sacredness, unity, and permanence of the family group. The individual is transient, but the family is permanent.

At the same time, traditional Vietnamese believe that family is a person's most reliable source of support—something that can always be counted on for help no matter what the circumstances. As an old Vietnamese proverb states, "If your father leaves you, you still have your uncle; if your mother leaves you, you can nurse on your aunt's milk" (quoted in Kibria, 1994b, p. 91).

Vietnamese collectivism encourages cooperative economic behavior, which is essential to the survival of new refugees. The re-

sources potentially available from any one person are limited and unreliable. Pooling wages from several members helps protect the family against economic instability.

The education of young people in Vietnamese families is a collective goal of all members of the household. Schooling is seen as the most effective path by which the whole family can achieve economic mobility in the future, and the academic achievements of young people are a source of family prestige within the ethnic community. Children frequently study together and assist one another with school-related problems. Older siblings play a major role in tutoring younger brothers and sisters.

Not surprisingly, many young Vietnamese Americans feel pressure to sacrifice their true interests—in, say, art or music—to focus on fields of study that will allow them to more effectively meet their economic obligations to the family. Weak students might be persuaded by their families to give up the pursuit of a college degree and find a job that would provide immediate financial contributions so that the family can channel its grander aspirations into a sibling who shows more academic promise.

The challenges of migration and adaptation to American culture have threatened this ideology, however. Families fear that young people will become "Americanized," favoring an individualist rather than a collectivist approach to their future. Indeed, more and more young people are rebelling against the tight constraints family obligation places on them. Consequently there is concern that the "payback" families expect to receive from their investments in the education of the young might not materialize.

Nevertheless, family collectivism among Vietnamese Americans in general remains strong. In a sense, the poverty and uncertainty attending migration have actually reinforced traditional beliefs about the importance of family. Ironically, however, economic success consistent with the American Dream may end up weakening the family's influence on individuals' actions.

Gender and Family Obligation

In the United States, the value of individualism has always varied along gender lines as well as ethnic lines. Independence and self-reliance have traditionally been thought more appropriate for males than females. For instance, research on play patterns shows that girls are rewarded more for remaining close to their parents while boys are encouraged to explore the limits of their play areas (Beal, 1994).

As they get older, men are expected to pursue self-fulfillment, individual achievement, and autonomy. Separation from others (particularly their mothers) is critically tied to their self-image as men (Chodorow, 1986). In other words, cutting attachments is considered normal and necessary for male development.

On the other hand, girls and women have traditionally been encouraged to emphasize relationships, responsibilities, and caring for others (Allen, 1988; Dalley, 1988). Traditionally, female identity tended to develop not by cutting attachments but by developing and maintaining connections to others, particularly spouses and children (Chodorow, 1986). The self-sacrificing woman who subordinates her own desires for the sake of the family has long been the prototype of the ideal wife and mother. The women's movement of the 1960s and 1970s made women aware that they were all too often sacrificing themselves to the demands of family. As one author bluntly put it, "As a group, women have done too much caretaking at the expense of their development as individuals" (Allen, 1988, p. 75). Today, more women than ever before are striving for independence and economic self-reliance. ▲

But the cultural messages women receive still convey the idea that they are responsible for the well-being of other family members. Many contemporary critics charge that the women's movement has focused too much attention on self-development and has encouraged women to place their own interests ahead of their family's. The result, they contend, is that children and, ultimately, society suffer from the inattention.

Those who believe women's individualism hurts society cite a variety of distressing trends. For instance, as work life has replaced family life as a primary source of self-fulfillment for women, couples are having fewer children. And parents are spending less time with the children they do have: The number of hours parents had available to spend with their children dropped 10 hours per week between 1960 and 1986 (Hewlett, 1991). The high value contemporary society places on individual achievement and success sometimes makes social relationships, even close family relationships, expendable. In a recent national poll, 25 percent of Americans surveyed said that for $10 million they'd abandon their entire family (Peterson & Kim, 1991). These trends seem to suggest that American women are less willing than ever before to invest time, money, and energy in their families. To some, the result will inevitably be instability in families and in society.

To others, however, women's increasing independence and self-reliance will, in the end, strengthen families. There is little evidence to suggest that self-reliant women have totally abandoned their familial obligations. Although they may struggle for a sustainable balance between career and family demands, it seems highly unlikely that they will, in the foreseeable future, sacrifice either. ▲ In fact, a mother's career success may serve as a positive model for her own daughters. ▲

▲ *See Chapter 3 for a discussion of trends in female labor force participations.*

▲ *See Chapter 4 for a discussion of the continuing cultural emphasis on motherhood.*

▲ *Issue 8 and Chapter 3 examine, in detail, the effects of maternal employment on children's well-being.*

Costs, Benefits, and Family Decisions

Some critics of individualism note that it implies an economic, cost-benefit, "What's in it for me?" approach to intimacy and family. As in an economic transaction, we're initially attracted to and are more likely to stay with those we think can provide us with the highest "payoff" at the lowest cost. ▲ Our obligations and responsibilities are often not part of the equation. When people ask themselves questions like: "Am I getting what I want from this relationship?" "Am I getting as much as my partner is getting?" "Would I be more satisfied with someone else?" they are implicitly applying a rational calculus to their intimate lives (Bellah, 1995).

▲ *Chapter 2 examines the effect of cost-benefit thinking on the development and maintenance of intimate relationships.*

Such thinking can pervade all stages of family life. Arguments over the distribution of housework chores or imbalances in the expression of affection, for instance, often boil down to one person feeling he or she is doing too much while the partner is doing too little.

Consider also couples' decision making regarding whether or not to have children. The wide availability of contraceptives means that children can be the end result of deliberate planning on the part of parents (Popenoe, 1988). Instead of seeing childbearing as an unquestioned and "natural" family obligation, many married individuals today, when making childbearing decisions, ask themselves whether children will facilitate or inconvenience *their* personal fulfillment, achievement, and success (Nock, 1987). If young

married couples view children as costly— that is, as expensive luxuries or a downright intrusion—they are likely to delay parenthood or avoid it altogether, ultimately creating ambivalence or indifference toward the very idea of having children (Acock & Demo, 1994).

While some degree of cost-benefit thinking in intimacy is inevitable—after all, we're not likely to form a relationship with someone who provides us with *no* desirable or satisfying outcomes—relationships formed only in terms of personal gratification may fail to fulfill their traditional function of providing people with stable relationships that tie them to the larger community (Bellah et al., 1985). Take, for instance, the phenomenon of "mixed" marriage. In a culture that prides itself on the ideal of individual rights and autonomy, marriages between people of different racial, ethnic, or religious backgrounds ought to be perceived as little more than individual people acting on their right to fall in love with whomever they want. ▲ However, for groups whose numbers are declining or are already small, such marriages can be perceived as threats to an entire culture and heritage. Individual decisions to marry outside the faith may have a far-reaching effect on an entire community. The personal cost-benefit calculus, critics of individualism note, is insufficient to protect broader collective interests.

▲ *Chapter 2 examines the role that race, ethnicity, religion, and social class play in mate selection.*

Family Obligation and Social Policy

Some critics argue that when individualism replaces duty as the guiding principle of life, people are inclined to reject the burdens of responsibility not only to the community but even, perhaps, to their own families. Indeed, according to some sociologists, people who live independently before marriage, or who were raised by parents who did so, are less oriented toward family living and are poorly prepared for adult family obligations (Nock, 1998).

As a society becomes more individualistic in general, things like strong emotional interdependence, mutual caring, and a high degree of sensitivity to others' needs and desires begin to crumble. From this perspective, the positive effects of recent societal changes—increasing individual autonomy, choice of lifestyles, material affluence, social power for women as well as men, tolerance of individual and cultural diversity—are far outweighed by the heavy toll they have taken on both family and society (Popenoe, 1995).

Some contemporary family scholars believe that our society will suffer unless family obligation—in particular, parents' obligation to their children—becomes the guiding force in public policy (Bellah et al., 1985; Etzioni, 1993). In families without children, an emphasis on the individual rights of the adults involved may be appropriate. But families with children are engaged in activities with vital social consequences. When parents have children, they enter into an unspoken social contract with the larger society. Hence, many people feel that individual freedoms may need to be restrained in the interests of family obligation (Galston, 1995).

Nowhere is this controversy clearer than in the current debate over existing divorce laws. Critics have argued that the liberalization of divorce laws in the 1970s made it too easy for married couples to abandon their family obligations. ▲ As one columnist put it, "You can divorce someone easier than you can fire a secretary" (quoted in Clark, 1996, p. 416). They feel it may be naive or old-fashioned to celebrate the virtues of individual freedom in the face of the continuing rise in single-parent families or the evidence of the harm to children of "broken" marriages. Hence, in the interests of protecting children's well-being, they feel it would be reasonable to require parents contemplating divorce to at least pause for reflection before proceeding:

> I think we may do more for children by trying to reinforce the responsibilities of parents, natural and adoptive, even when those responsibilities are not legally enforceable. We might start by reducing our enthusiasm for "no-fault" divorces in the case of marriage partners who are parents. In many such cases, we should encourage the parents to keep their marriage together for the sake of interests larger than their own rights, convenience, and desires. (Oaks, 1995, p. 39)

▲ *See Chapter 7 for a detailed discussion of the legal structure of divorce.*

Such sentiment seems to have public support. A recent survey found that 55 percent of Americans favor making it harder to leave a marriage when one partner wants to stay (cited in Leland, 1996). In some states—Iowa, Idaho, Georgia, Michigan, Pennsylvania, and Florida, to name a few—legal measures are being debated that would impose mandatory waiting periods for couples contemplating divorce or restore the old requirement of proving fault in cases where only one spouse is seeking divorce. Such measures are designed to make it more difficult for couples with children to divorce (D. Johnson, 1996).

Such policies reflect a preference for intact, two-parent families. People who support these policies don't necessarily believe that all single-parent families are somehow "dysfunctional" or that all parents seeking divorce are selfish. After all, millions of single parents successfully provide good homes for their children. Nor does the endorsement of two-parent families necessarily imply nostalgia for the traditional male-breadwinner families of the 1950s. Many supporters of divorce law reform simply want to point out that, on balance and all else being equal, two-parent families are best suited to the task of raising children; and that, therefore, family policy ought to focus on strengthening two-parent families (Galston, 1995).

Some social scientists today feel that the problems of families can be reversed simply if we, as a society, abandon our selfish, individualistic pursuits and regain sight of our commitments and responsibilities to those around us. They fear that contemporary marriage has become a "disposable relationship"—much like a rental agreement in which tenants have an escape clause should they desire to move out and seek housing elsewhere (Etzioni, 1994).

To protect the integrity of marriage, one sociologist suggests something called Super Vows (Etzioni, 1993). These would be, in essence, premarital contracts in which those about to be married declare that they are committing more to their marriage than the law requires. They can choose from a menu of items what they wish to include in their voluntary marriage agreement. For instance, the couple may agree that if one partner asks for a divorce, he or she must promise to wait 6 months to see if differences can be worked out. Once the couple arrives at an agreement, the Super Vows would become legal commitments between the spouses. Already, church and synagogue programs are fulfilling a similar social need by encouraging (sometimes requiring) couples to discuss such issues as who will take care of the children, who will control the family finances, and so on *before* they marry.

The crusade to heighten the value of marriage in American society by suggesting programs designed to make people think more about the dynamics of their marriages is an idea few would argue with. The risk, however, is that in trying to promote marriage, more specifically traditional marriage, we will stigmatize other family forms.

A Balance of Individualism and Family Obligation

The suggestion that we should take our family obligations more seriously than we do presently may sound rather simplistic, but it strikes a responsive chord among those who feel the family is in trouble. Given all the negative press about the "decline" of American families, more and more people are buying that argument. The idea that all we have to do to save the institution of family is to return to a bygone sense of responsibility and sacrifice sounds appealing. ▲ But such a position does overlook the historical, social, cultural, and institutional forces that have put us where we are today.

▲ *Issue 2 examines some of the myths surrounding our idealized image of families of the past. Issue 8 is devoted to addressing the question of whether or not American families are in a state of decline.*

Historically, the sacrifice of individuals' rights in favor of family obligations has had a dark side. It gave some members (most notably husbands) power over others (most notably wives), leading to severe forms of exploitation and inequality (Cancian, 1987). Marriage manuals once advised couples that the path to successful marriage was to shed their independent identities and "become one"—a "we" instead of two "I's." Such a perceptual shift, it was believed, was necessary to get people to think of the good of the family first and their personal needs second. Unfortunately for a woman, "becoming one" usually meant subordinating her interests to her husband's and taking on his identity—being known, for instance, as Mrs. John Doe instead of Mary Doe and becoming the wife of, say, an engineer instead of an engineer in her own right. The husband's life, his interests, his identity were dominant. The idealized, "collective" marriage of the 1950s often made women totally economically dependent on their husbands and rendered them incapable of escaping from abusive relationships. More recent marriage manuals have emphasized the importance of two partners giving each other the breathing room to retain their own personalities and some measure of independence. In place of the old norms of self-sacrifice and rigid gender roles are the ideals of self-development and more flexible roles (Cancian & Gordon, 1988).

What the critics of individualism also need to realize is that, just like the work of husbands and fathers, the entry of wives and mothers into the paid labor force is likely to be "for the good of the family." It's rather startling that women's work outside the home is often decried as selfish, while their husbands' work outside the home is perceived as the normal fulfillment of his family duties. Furthermore, women's growing presence in the workforce is a trend that shows no sign of reversing. It is extremely unlikely that we will soon see a massive exodus of mothers—or for that matter, fathers—from the workplace. In a volatile, market-driven economy, few individuals earn enough on their own to support a spouse and children.

Whether we realize it or not, the pursuit of individual interests has become an acceptable part of family life. Even the staunchest critic of individualism would have trouble congratulating a woman who stays with a man who beats her because she agreed to stay married "for better or worse." Few people want to return to an age when it was nearly impossible for women to earn enough money to support themselves or for them to divorce their husbands. And few of us feel that parents should sacrifice *all* their worldly pleasures and personal happiness so that their children or their elderly parents can live a little better (Schwartz, 1987).

So perhaps self-fulfillment isn't necessarily incompatible with family. If you think about it, family obligations are difficult to satisfy unless a person is first personally fulfilled. Can an unhappy person ever be a good, thoughtful spouse? Can a person in a miserable marriage ever be a complete and effective parent to his or her children? Research continually shows that people who are personally satisfied and gratified with their relationships are more committed to seeing them work. In other words, it's easier to remain in a relationship when you're happy than when you're unhappy (Cox, Wexler, Rusbult, & Gaines, 1997).

If all this is true, legal reforms, such as making it more difficult for unhappy spouses to divorce, may in the end do more harm than good to all involved. Sixty-five percent of Americans in a recent survey disagreed with the notion that parents should stay together even if they don't get along (cited in Clark, 1996). People forced to stay in failed marriages against their will often sabotage their relationships, either consciously or unconsciously, through adultery, abuse, or withdrawal. Remaining in loveless or conflict-ridden marriages often costs both the spouses and their children dearly (Riley, 1991).

And what about the argument that parents who devote significant time and energy to work are neglecting their familial obligations? Ironically, such an argument rests on the individualistic assumption that parents alone raise their children. But we all have a stake in the successful development of children, and we all ought to be committed to ensuring their well-being. Other societies protect children not by punishing working parents but by changing the social structure to provide adequate institutional support for children. Sweden, for instance, shows a *societal* commitment to children through prenatal and postnatal medical care and liberal parental leave policies, childhood immunization, adequate nutrition, access to preschool programs and well-funded schools, elimination of child poverty, safe neighborhoods, and the prevention of unwanted pregnancies through sex education and the availability of contraceptives. ▲

▲ *Chapter 5 looks at child care policies across cultures.*

Hence, instead of decrying the reliance on professional day care as the archenemy of family and condemning parents who use it, we could, as a society, work to improve its quality, affordability, and availability:

> The time has come for this nation to regard child care as an infrastructure issue and make the same kind of investment in it that we talk about making in our bridges and roads. . . . To gain insight into the costs, specifically foregone opportunity costs of not endeavoring to improve child care and increase options for families, imagine for a moment an America with the automobile but without paved roads. (Belsky, 1990, p. 11)

Finally, the contention that Americans have completely abandoned all their social, familial obligations and commitments in the pursuit of self-fulfillment is most certainly an overstatement. After all, family—with its enduring emphasis on interdependence and attachment—has survived despite our enormous cultural emphasis on individualism and self-reliance. Couples are still marrying, and interest in having and raising children remains high.

Research evidence also suggests that we haven't become a society of individuals totally isolated from our families. For instance, more Americans than ever have grandparents alive, and the ties between grandparents and grandchildren may be stronger than ever. Today most adults see or talk to a parent on the phone at least once a week (Coontz, 1992), more than half see them at least once a month, and a similar proportion believe that aging parents ought to live with or near their adult children (Orthner, 1990). A majority of Americans stay in contact with family and provide advice, emotional support, and financial help when needed (Cicirelli, 1983). And the vast majority of the elderly who need care receive it from their families. ▲ So even against a cultural backdrop of extreme individualism, collective interests remain strong in American families.

▲ *Chapter 8 examines the degree to which adult children maintain close relationships with their elderly parents.*

Indeed, according to some social observers, we are starting to see an *increasing* commitment to family among some segments of the population (Whitehead, 1993). Ironically, this apparent change is strongest among baby boomers, the generation that defined independent singlehood as a lifestyle. They were at the cutting edge of increasing rates of cohabitation and sexual experimentation. They delayed marriage longer and had fewer children than any previous generation. This generation has now reached a new stage in the life cycle. They've married and become parents. In the process, many have discovered that the attitudes that served them in singlehood don't apply to parenthood.

It would be naive, though, to think that the United States is on its way toward becoming a collectivist culture. I would guess that few of us want a society of isolated individuals who don't know and don't want to know their neighbors and feel no abiding interest in the lives of their fellow citizens or even their fellow family members. However, a heavy emphasis on group obligation and responsibility often requires the sacrifice of individual freedoms that some people have worked long and hard to secure. Most people don't want to return to an era of constraining and oppressive social roles. Furthermore, I'm not sure one can ever be fully removed from concern with personal needs and well-being.

Something to Think About

Being a member of society *and* a member of a family requires a delicate balance between freedom and belonging. Part of being a fully functioning citizen is the ability to choose or guide one's own destiny. Part of being a fully functioning family member is the sense that one belongs to a group of significant others and that he or she matters to them. The problem is that it is difficult to achieve self-fulfillment and, at the same time, meet familial obligations. We all struggle, walking the fine line between what we want to do for ourselves and what we feel we should do for our families.

1. Do you think that individual self-fulfillment is incompatible with family responsibility? Would it be possible or desirable to abandon our cultural emphasis on individual achievement in favor of a more collectivist approach to everyday life?

2. To what extent should society limit individuals' freedom to divorce? What about their freedom to bear children?

3. At what point do individual choices about mixed marriage conflict with or even threaten the larger groups to which people belong? Do we have any compelling obligation to ignore our personal interests and desires and marry only people from similar racial, ethnic, or religious backgrounds?

4. Who do you think feels the power of family obligations more strongly, men or women?

"Mary's like a
LITTLE LAMB
in her all-electric kitchen"

"Just before the war Mary and I moved into a new home equipped with an all-electric kitchen. Mary's whole attitude about kitchens changed immediately. She used to be impatient with the way a kitchen ties a woman to the home. Now she's very happy with her homemaking tasks. Her electric range gives such uniform results that failures and disappointments are a rarity, and the automatic features make cooking much easier. Perhaps her favorite helper is the electric dishwasher. I did a little time-study of her dishwashing and found that the dishwasher saves her about one working day every month. My mechanical mind is fascinated by the garbage disposal unit in the sink. My wife says it's a real convenience—this way we never really have garbage. Well, I could go on a good deal longer about the help she gets from her mixer, juicer, percolator and toaster—and I guess I don't even need to mention her electric refrigerator, for everybody recognizes now that there's no other method of refrigeration that equals the modern, electric way. Boy! Our all-electric kitchen sure has made a difference in our household."

Electric kitchen equipment is not generally available for sale now. Some is being manufactured and distributed. It will be to your advantage to have your name on your electrical dealer's list, so that you will be able to get it at the earliest possible time.

HOW GARBAGE DISPOSAL WORKS

Simply scrape refuse from dishes into disposal unit. It makes no difference whether refuse is soft or hard.

Close cover on disposal unit and turn on motor. Grinder reduces all refuse to a soft pulp in a few seconds.

Water from the tap washes away the finely ground material.

ISSUE 5

How Do Gender and Power Influence Family Life?

Power in Families

Sex, Gender, and Power

Sources of Marital Power

The Consequences of Power

Changing Family Power Relations

SOMETHING TO THINK ABOUT

The president of a feminist research organization in Washington, D.C., calls it a "silent revolution." Some scholars, fearful of scaring men and prematurely declaring the "revolution" won, are more comfortable calling it "gender creep." And some bold journalists have chosen to unabashedly stamp it "the feminization of American culture" (Holmes, 1996a). The "it" that all these people are referring to is the apparent rise in the importance of women and women's concerns in American society. Consider these recent events and trends:

- During the 1996 presidential campaign, "soccer moms" were heralded as the most important political constituency in the country. Public debates over issues like family leave and day care became ubiquitous elements on the political landscape. More women than ever voted in the election and analysts of all political stripes agree that their votes were singularly responsible for President Clinton's reelection.
- The average size of an American home has grown 30 percent over the last few decades, even though the average size of American families has steadily decreased. Most of the size increase has been the result of larger kitchens, bathrooms, and family rooms, features women, not men, demand.
- In the 1970s, when automakers tried to introduce air bags, the mostly male car-buying public rebelled. But women now buy about half of the new cars in this country, prompting car makers to emphasize safety and convenience (what women typically want) and downplay speed (what men typically want). Today air bags are a standard feature on all new cars.
- Seventy-five percent of health care purchasing decisions for families are made by women, motivating large health care providers to develop new programs to train doctors in the art of communication, something many women feel physicians are lacking.
- Women's participation in the paid labor force continues to grow. In response, more and more companies have implemented "family-friendly" work policies like flextime, parental leave, and company-based child care centers. The number of women-owned businesses has grown by almost 50 percent since the late 1980s.

Do societal trends like these mean that women have more power and influence within their families than they used to have? Not necessarily. For instance, new homes may have larger kitchens, bathrooms, and family rooms in response to women's demands, but women are still responsible for most of the workload that takes place in these rooms—even when they are employed and even when they earn more than their husbands. How family roles have changed, particularly the roles of wives and husbands, and what they indicate about power relations within families are the focus of Issue 5.

Power in Families

Much of what happens in families reflects power relationships among members. Within families, power can be defined as the process by which individuals gain the ability to impose their will on others (Lipman-Blumen, 1984). Power can be exercised by using or threatening punishment or by offering or withholding rewards. Power is most obvious when family members desire some sort of changes that, over time, are either realized (because they have the power to put them into effect) or thwarted (because others are able to use their power to create obstacles) (Komter, 1989).

Power can also be quite subtle and difficult to detect. For instance, when a husband anticipates his wife's angry response to his desire for her to do more around the house, he may decide not to voice his concerns in order to avoid conflict. Thus, she has successfully exerted power over him (by preventing him from speaking his mind) without any direct confrontation. Such "invisible" power is important since it can maintain inequality even in those marriages that appear harmonious and conflict free.

Several different family relationships exhibit differences in power: parent and child, husband and wife, older and younger siblings, brother and sister. In some cases, the power differences are obvious and well accepted. For instance, in nuclear families, power is expected to reside mostly with parents—at least until they become enfeebled or incapacitated with age. ▲ Few people would argue that parents shouldn't have the right to make decisions regarding their children's health, education, and morality.

▲ *The transition in parent-child roles that accompanies old age is discussed in Chapter 8.*

But other power relationships in families lack this sort of cultural approval. For instance, if you were to ask a random group of married couples which partner has more power, my guess is that most of them would say "neither of us." Most people would agree that long-term, intimate relationships ought to contain a significant degree of sharing and equality. No one wants to admit to dominating the relationship or, conversely, to being completely subordinate to a partner's desires.

Sociological research has consistently shown, however, that power imbalances are the norm in intimate and family relationships. For instance, as early as 1960, researchers noted that husbands tend to have more power over their wives, particularly when wives are not employed outside the home (Blood & Wolfe, 1960). Social theorists also noted that the family is one of the few groups in contemporary society in which some members (parents) are allowed by law or tradition to use physical force against other members (their children) and in which some members (husbands) have traditionally been allowed to control the lives of others (wives and children). ▲ Power imbalances are even characteristic of many gay and lesbian couples (Blumstein & Schwartz, 1983).

▲ *Chapter 6 takes a closer look at power and violence within families.*

It's tempting to think of power relationships within families as stable and enduring. But power is dynamic and changing. As circumstances change—the loss of a job or a dramatic increase in income, the arrival of children, the physical or mental decline of an elderly parent—so too do power relations.

Furthermore, power is rarely absolute. People in apparently powerless positions are often capable of influencing the behaviors of more powerful others. As much as we parents hate to admit it, there are times when our children can exert considerable control over us. The cries of a newborn infant can easily alter parents' sleep, recreational, and eating patterns. A toddler's supermarket temper tantrum can stop a parent bent on bypassing the ice cream section dead in his or her tracks. An adolescent's volatility can leave even the strongest of parents trembling.

Men's higher status in traditional marriages may grant them the power to exert their will, but their wives often have as much influence as they do (or more) over decisions on running the household, handling finances, organizing child care, orchestrating social life, and so on. Even the most powerless wife—a woman who feels she has absolutely no say in household decisions—may exercise substantial power in the bedroom, where she is able to control sexual access. ▲ Women have also been able to claim significant power in families because of their role as "kinkeeper"—the person who controls those relationships that cross generations or that involve relatives outside the nuclear family (Kranichfeld, 1987). These bonds place women at the very center of family life.

▲ *Chapter 6 describes how sometimes women's attempts to gain power over sexual access can backfire, leading to domestic violence.*

A crucial characteristic of family power is the degree to which it is granted legitimacy by society at large. We allow certain people in the family to exert power over others because of the *positions* they occupy rather than any special or noteworthy characteristics they as individuals might have. The authority of a parent over a child, for instance, is considered legitimate because the norms and traditions of the larger society uphold this power relationship and may even require it.

That people are expected to "obey" the directives of a legitimate authority means that other tactics like coercion or persuasion ought to be unnecessary. Many parents believe that their children should obey them simply *because* they are their parents. Therefore they shouldn't have to resort to rewards, punishments, force, or persuasive argument to get the children to comply. But, as every parent knows, the legitimacy of their power frequently goes unrecognized or ignored by children. Indeed, most parents bargain, cajole, cut deals, manipulate, even plead with their children to get them to behave as they want them to. Nevertheless, because the culture recognizes parents' legitimate power, they are granted the legal right to use other means—such as physical punishment—as they see fit. Nonrelated adults have no such right. If they were to use physical punishment against someone else's child, they would be committing a crime.

Sex, Gender, and Power

Although parent-child power relationships are interesting, the focus here is the relative power of men and women in families. Before examining this issue, we must first distinguish between two important concepts: sex and gender.

Sex is typically used to refer to a person's biological maleness or femaleness: chromosomes (XX for female, XY for male), sex glands (ovaries and testes), hormones (estrogen and testosterone), internal sex organs (uterus and prostate gland), external genitalia (clitoris and penis), reproductive capacities (pregnancy and impregnation), germ cells produced (ova and sperm), and secondary sex characteristics (shape of hips and breasts, amount of facial hair, and pitch of the voice). *Gender*, on the other hand, designates psychological, social, and cultural aspects of maleness and femaleness—that is, masculinity and femininity (Kessler & McKenna, 1978). This distinction is crucial because it reminds us that male-female power differences within families need not spring from biological differences (Lips, 1993).

Nevertheless, every society has ideas about the inherent, biologically based skills and limitations of men and women. To nineteenth-century Americans, for instance, few facts were more incontestable than the notion that women were the products and prisoners of their reproductive systems. Women's place in their families as well as in society was thought to be linked to and controlled by the existence and function of the uterus and ovaries (Scull & Favreau, 1986). Everything about women could be explained by biology: the predominance of the emotional over the rational, the capacity for affection, the love of children and aptitude for child rearing, the preference for domestic work, and so on (Ehrenreich & English, 1979; Scull & Favreau, 1986). Scholars at the time warned that young women who studied too much not only were struggling against nature but would badly damage their reproductive organs and perhaps even go insane in the process (Fausto-Sterling, 1985). The exclusion of women from higher education was thus seen as not only justifiable but necessary for their own health and for the long-term good of society.

Such beliefs about the undesirable effects of women's biological functioning are not just a thing of the distant past. Many physicians and psychiatrists today believe that normal biological processes predispose women to certain personality disorders. Consider, for instance, the menstrual cycle. The Board of Trustees of the American Psychiatric Association continues to debate the merits of including a psychiatric diagnosis called "premenstrual dysphoric disorder" in its official manual of mental disorders. (At the time of this writing, it appears in the manual as a "proposed category in need of further investigation.")

By depicting masculine and feminine social roles as inherent, biological phenomena, sex and gender become confused. ▲ The assumption that sex and gender are natural and unchangeable overlooks the fact that extensive similarities between the sexes and extensive variation within each sex exist. For most personality and behavioral characteristics, the distribution of men and women generally overlaps. For instance, men as a group do tend to be more aggressive than women. Yet some women are much more aggressive than the average man, and some men are much less aggressive than the average woman. Indeed, social circumstances may have a greater impact on aggressive behavior than any innate, biological traits. Some studies show that when women are rewarded for behaving aggressively, they are just as violent as men (Hyde, 1984).

▲ *For information on how children learn about sex and gender, read Chapter 5.*

This assumption also overlooks the power of socialization to shape behavior. In just the past few decades, for example, it has become more socially acceptable for women to be assertive and ambitious. If such traits were purely biological, they would not have become more prevalent so rapidly. Furthermore, the reliance on biology to explain gender differences overlooks the wide cultural and historical variation in conceptions of masculinity and femininity. For instance, every known society has a division of labor based on sex. But what's considered "men's work" and "women's work" is different from society to society. ▲

▲ *Chapter 3 closely examines gender patterns in work.*

The famous anthropologist Margaret Mead (1963) believed that masculine and feminine characteristics are based not on biological sex differences but on cultural conditioning. She set out to support her theory by studying three cultures in New Guinea. Among the mountain-dwelling Arapesh, men and women displayed similar attitudes and actions. They showed traits we would commonly associate with femininity: cooperation, passivity, sensitivity to others. Mead described both men and women as being "maternal." These characteristics were linked to broader cultural beliefs about people's relationship to the environment. The Arapesh didn't have any conception of "ownership" of land, so there were never conflicts over possession of property.

South of the Arapesh were the Mundugumor, a group of cannibals and headhunters. Here, too, males and females were similar. However, both displayed traits that we in the West would associate with masculinity: assertiveness, emotional inexpressiveness, insensitivity to others. Women, according to Mead, were just as violent, just as aggressive, and just as jealous as men. Both were equally virile, without any of the "soft" characteristics we associate with femininity.

Finally, there were the Tchambuli. This group did distinguish between male and female traits. However, their gender expectations were the opposite of ours: Women were the ones who were dominant, shrewd, assertive, and managerial; men were submissive, emotional, and seen as inherently delicate.

Mead's work is important because it shows that definitions of the natural tendencies of men and women vary from culture to culture. Women need not be the nurturers of children; men need not be the aggressors. Nevertheless, as long as people continue to believe that gender-linked roles and societal contributions are determined by nature, they will continue to accept sexual inequality in occupational, political, and family life. Furthermore, we need to remember that even sex differences that are, in fact, biological (for instance, hormonal) aren't completely free from societal influence; nor are they impossible to change. We, as a society, can decide whether certain differences ought to be amplified or ignored.

The Cultural Context of Gender

We obviously cannot begin to understand men and women's power in families without examining the broader cultural perception of gender in the societies in which families exist. Most societies around the world—the United States included—can be characterized as patriarchies, social systems in which men are dominant over women. In these societies, men control most, if not all, of the important social institutions in society: politics, economics, religion, the media, education, and so on. They enjoy privileges, advantages, and benefits that are often denied to women. The power and influence men enjoy in patriarchal societies typically translate into power within the private domain of family. The fact that men are usually the primary breadwinners, for instance, grants

them—in most societies—power and authority within the household. ▲

▲ *As you'll see in more detail in Chapter 3, the uneven distribution of rewards and responsibilities between men and women outside families influences the imbalances that exist inside them.*

In some societies, female powerlessness coincides with a cultural devaluation of women that, in the extreme, can be fatal. According to the World Health Organization, between 85 and 114 million girls and women worldwide have been subjected to female genital mutilation (FGM) (cited in Dugger, 1996a). This practice, often supported by deep historical roots, occurs in some form mostly in Africa and the Middle East (although instances have also been reported in immigrant communities elsewhere, including the United States). Typically the procedure, which entails the removal of the clitoris and/or the destruction of the labia and vulva, is done under highly unsanitary conditions by a midwife using unclean sharp instruments such as razor blades, scissors, knives, or pieces of glass. Anesthesia is generally not used.

This cultural tradition is a reflection of the extreme powerlessness of women in these societies. Where FGM is common, men have traditionally demanded that their wives be virgins when they marry. Indeed, a girl who has not undergone this procedure may be considered "unclean" or a prostitute by local villagers and therefore unmarriageable. The ritual also serves to perpetuate customs that regulate and control the bodies and sexuality of women.

Ironically, it is often women themselves—usually mothers and grandmothers—who enforce the practice (Crossette, 1995). But it is unlikely that such pressure is motivated by cruelty. In fact, these older women may have the girls' best interests in mind. If a young woman's marriageability, and therefore her future economic security, requires that she be subjected to FGM, her very survival is at stake:

> In a culture in which men will not marry you unless you have been mutilated and there is no other work you can do and you are ... considered a prostitute if you are not mutilated, you face a very big problem. Women mutilate their daughters because they really are looking down the road to a time when the daughter will ... marry and at least have a roof ... and food. (Walker & Parmar, 1993, p. 277)

But the relative power of women and men in everyday life can be much more subtle. Iranian women, for instance, cannot shake the hand of a man who is not a close relative. They are forbidden from exposing their heads, necks, and curves of their bodies in public, and from jogging, bicycling, or swimming, except in sexually segregated areas. They cannot become judges or religious leaders. They cannot leave the country without written permission from their husbands (Sciolino, 1997). Still, Iranian women were instrumental in electing a moderate president in 1997. And although they may be subject to tight male control, they can exercise considerable power within the household as mothers and mothers-in-law.

Indeed, in some cultures women actually dominate social life. Among the Naxi of southwestern China, for instance, women have traditionally controlled all aspects of their communities, such as money, farming, religious rites, and so on. Up until this century, marriage was never a part of Naxi customs, and women simply took lovers as they pleased. The Communist government put an end to many of the Naxi practices, but the community still revolves around women (Hessler, 1997).

The relative power of women in rapidly changing cultures is especially complex. In Japan, women have historically occupied a visibly subservient position in families. Some women still walk several steps behind their husbands so as not to offend his dignity by stepping on his shadow (Kristof, 1996a). Wives are legally prohibited from using different surnames than their husbands. Although the 1980s equal rights movement and a booming economy sent many Japanese women surging into the workplace, most became "office flowers"—submissive part-time workers who smile sweetly, talk softly, pour tea, and answer telephones. And the recent economic slump in Japan has forced many women out of the workforce and back into their domestic roles. Those who remain in the workforce suffer discrimination in hiring, salary, and promotion despite an equal opportunity law. One company newsletter advises women who are thinking about getting married to "submit a letter of resignation one month before the wedding" (quoted in WuDunn, 1995, p. 3).

Within Japanese families, however, women's power is very different. Even though women are still expected to clean, cook, and tend to the needs of their husbands, they exercise a surprising degree of authority. Many wives control the household finances, giving their husbands monthly allowances as they see fit. Recent surveys have found that about half of Japanese men are dissatisfied with the amount of their allowances. Many wives refuse to give their husbands cash cards for the family bank account. If he wants to withdraw money from the account, the bank will usually phone the wife to get her approval. Japanese men are even starting to take on some of the housework responsibilities, a development that would have been unthinkable a decade ago. One man summed up the situation this way: "Things go best when the husband is swimming in the palm of his wife's hand" (quoted in Kristof, 1996a, p. A6).

The Devaluation of Women in American Culture

These sorts of cultural contradictions can be found in American society as well. American women's demands for greater autonomy have resulted in significant cultural, political, and economic gains, compared to those of women in other countries. However, American men continue to control most of the important social institutions. They still dominate the upper echelons of business and government while women still bear most of the responsibility for undervalued domestic concerns and household labor.

Women also continue to be devalued by cultural expectations that emphasize superficial appearance over accomplishment. For instance, recent research on images of women in television, films, books, and magazines shows that women are more likely to have their looks commented on or to show concern with their own appearance than are men. Women are significantly less likely than men to be portrayed working but more likely to be shown talking about romantic relationships (Smith, 1997).

In addition, the diversity of American culture yields vastly different conceptions of women's "place" in society and in families. Among certain religious groups (for instance, fundamentalist Protestants) and certain ethnic groups (such as recent immigrants from Latin America), male dominance and authority continue to be the norm. Husbands in these families wield significant power within the household. Among other groups of Americans however—such as Unitarians and Reform Jews—families are more likely to approach gender equality.

Sources of Marital Power

Within families, power emerges from the interactions and personalities of specific individuals. But family power is also affected by broad cultural beliefs as well as people's relative position and resources outside the family.

Occupational status, income, level of education, racial and ethnic history, sexual orientation, and, of course, gender always provide us with varying degrees of *social* privilege that, in turn, exert a subtle or blatant impact on family life. Men's power within families, for example, has traditionally been linked with other sources of power. The average American husband is several years older, has more education, has a higher income, and has a more prestigious occupation than the average wife.

Social Stratification and Family Power

We must not forget that families are embedded in a social system that perpetuates unequal rewards and life chances in society. ▲ In a society stratified along gender, class, and race lines—as ours is—women, members of lower classes, and racial minorities have limited opportunities to claim legitimate power in the larger society.

▲ *Issues 6 and 7 detail the effects of racial and class stratification on family life.*

In "traditional families" in American society, as in other patriarchal cultures, men are assumed to have legitimate power. By virtue of their higher social status in the economic sphere and their roles as husbands and "patriarchs," they can exercise authority over their wives. Imagine a married couple in which the husband works and the wife is a homemaker. She wants to begin taking college courses at night but her husband protests that he wants and needs her at home. She agrees, believing that he has the *right* to demand that she stay at home and that it is her duty to comply. In acceding to his demands, she has reinforced the cultural legitimacy of his power over her. Hence he doesn't have to argue with her or convince her that it would be beneficial if she didn't work; nor does he have to threaten her.

In most American families, however, occupying the position of husband no longer guarantees power in the family. Husbands must prove their worth and therefore their legitimacy by fulfilling the expectations and obligations that go with the position, such as earning a living and supporting the family. Men who fail to meet these expectations—such as those who are chronically unemployed—risk losing the legitimacy of their family authority. ▲

▲ *The relationship among gender, work, and family power is explored in detail in Chapter 3.*

The influence of social stratification is rather complex. For instance, we usually assume that lower- and working-class families are "patriarchal" and "traditional" in structure, whereas middle-class families are more "egalitarian." We typically expect working-class husbands to exert more power and control within their families than middle-class husbands because, in the absence of high wages and prestigious jobs, working-class men have few places other than their families to exercise authority. Middle-class men, on the other hand, typically have more status, wealth, and prestige and therefore more places to exercise power and authority in the larger society. Hence we expect them to have less of a need to exert their masculinity and control within their families. Furthermore, because they are more likely to have more education than working-class men, they're more likely to express beliefs about the importance of equality within families.

In practice, however, things aren't so straightforward. Some research shows that middle-class husbands are actually more concerned with exerting power over their wives than working-class husbands are. These middle-class husbands feel it is their right to translate material resources and professional status into power (Rubin, 1976). Control of material resources often justifies

control over decisions made within the family.

Racial and ethnic stratification can also affect legitimate power relations in families. ▲ Clearly, racial discrimination continues to significantly shape the work lives of many members of racial and ethnic minorities, which inevitably affects the structure and dynamics of their families.

▲ *Issue 6 provides a detailed examination of the influence of race and ethnicity on family life.*

In addition, cultural traditions within certain racial and ethnic groups may affect family power relations. Research over the years seems to indicate that some groups—Asian Americans and Hispanics—are more male dominated, and African-American families less male dominated than white families. Such conclusions tend to be oversimplifications, however. For instance, African-American families may hold more traditional beliefs about family power—that is, that the husband's interests are more important than the wife's—but their actual behavior is significantly more egalitarian. In contrast, white families tend to express more egalitarian beliefs, but are often more traditional in their behavior (Beckett, 1976).

Research also challenges the popular stereotype that Hispanic families operate under the ideal of *machismo,* or male domination. Male dominance in these families is neither universal nor insurmountable. For instance, the balance of power in Mexican-American families is likely to be equal when wives work outside the home (Baca Zinn, 1980).

Conflict over the Control of Resources

In their social relationships, humans are motivated by the same forces that drive economic marketplaces: a desire to maximize rewards and minimize costs. That is, we seek out experiences, people, objects, and so on that we find pleasurable and avoid those we find unpleasurable. ▲

▲ *This theory is explained in more detail in Chapter 1.*

Each person brings certain resources to the family (for example, money and other possessions, status, attractiveness, emotional support, sex and affection). We exchange the resources we have for a desired benefit from our partner. ▲ In general, the more we have to offer, the more we tend to expect in return. Indeed, research has consistently shown that the happiest couples are those in which partners are providing each other with many rewarding experiences and few costly ones (Birchler, Weiss, & Vincent, 1975; Rusbult, 1983; Vincent, Weiss, & Birchler, 1975).

▲ *Chapter 2 describes in more detail the dynamics of social exchange within relationships.*

From this perspective, family power is based on the control of important resources. The more resources individuals believe they contribute to a relationship, relative to their partners, the more power they're likely to believe they are entitled to (Safilios-Rothschild, 1976). If your partner has something that you want or need (money, love and affection, understanding and support, companionship, information, sex, and so on), you'll be motivated to comply with his or her wishes, obey his or her commands, or put up with other undesirable (that is, costly) behaviors in order to get it.

The scarcity of important resources ensures that from time to time there will be competition and conflict over their control. Shortage of money is a common source of arguments in families. Families may also experience conflict over space or territory. Such conflicts are particularly intense in remarriages, where stepparents, sometimes with

children, move into a household formerly occupied by a single-parent family.

Conflict can also exist over less-tangible resources. For instance, siblings often compete for their parents' attention and affection. Children can use another resource, age, to gain advantage over siblings. The oldest child can use success in school or intellectual and social competence to gain his or her parents' attention. On the other hand, the youngest child, "the baby of the family," can use immaturity to gain this advantage (Winton, 1995). Similarly, one spouse may compete with the work setting or friends or even the television for the time and attention of the other spouse.

In this scheme a key factor in power differences is dependence—the degree to which one person relies on the other for important resources. Control over a resource creates power differences only if the resource is highly valued and perceived as essential. Moreover, it must be something that can't be obtained elsewhere. So if you don't care about sex or financial security or if you have other prospects for sex or for acquiring financial security, you won't depend on your partner to provide these things. Therefore, he or she will not be able to exercise much power over you.

When we depend on people to provide resources that we desperately want but that are unavailable elsewhere, we find ourselves in a position of powerlessness. Power and dependence are *inversely* related. That is, the more dependent a person is on a relationship to meet his or her needs, the less power he or she is likely to have. This is as true for emotional resources as it is for financial ones. For instance, a partner who loves more is more dependent and therefore more likely to be submissive. ▲ Such submission can be used as a means of keeping the other partner happy, thereby maintaining the stability of the relationship (Winton, 1995).

▲ *Imbalances in love and affection are discussed further in Chapter 2.*

Since men and women tend to control different types of resources, dependence and power in families are inherently based on gender (Howard & Hollander, 1997). Men's higher earnings and greater access to more prestigious occupations have historically given them more power and privilege inside their families. Women who don't work outside the home or who are burdened with the care of young children have considerably fewer opportunities to earn money and are particularly likely to be dependent on their partners economically.

But control of money alone is not sufficient to provide people with power in their family relationships. Even traditional male breadwinners, who can use their economic wherewithal as power over their wives, still may depend on their wives to provide the physical, psychological, and emotional support necessary to maintain their ability to work. In short, they can be as emotionally dependent on their wives as their wives are economically dependent on them (Hertz, 1986).

Cultural ideology can also overshadow the effect of monetary resources on family power. It's highly unlikely that, if there were a sudden redistribution of income so that women began earning more than men, women would be able to claim the lion's share of power and influence in families. Conceptions of power and family that are deeply embedded in our society would impede such a shift. Indeed, sexual inequality has persisted in American society despite women's movement into the labor force in the past few decades and their increasing representation in male-dominated occupations (Ridgeway, 1997).

One example of a cultural ideology that can affect power is the belief that promoting the husband's career rather than the wife's is the most efficient way to serve the interests of all family members (Pyke, 1996). Such a belief justifies the contention that "a women's place is in the home" on the grounds that it is a natural family arrangement which maxi-

mizes family resources and efficiency. Unfortunately, it also undermines women's long-term economic interests and limits their claims to family power (Blumberg & Coleman, 1989).

Women's economic gains may also be offset by cultural ideologies that value women primarily for the noneconomic resources they provide. In Korea, for example, research has found that wives who work outside the home actually *lose* power in their marriages (Balswick & Balswick, 1995). Since Korean wives already have responsibility and authority to spend the family's money, they gain little personal power from increasing their own financial resources. Furthermore, when they work outside the home, wives *lose* the emotional power they had. The nurturing resources— such as showering husbands with care and attention after a day's work—are highly valued in Korean society, more so than any extra income wives provide to their families.

What is also crucial in the development of power relations in families, then, is the *meaning* that couples attach to resources (Pyke, 1994). The effect that a resource like money has on marital power depends on whether couples consider it a gift or a burden. For instance, a woman married to a man who sees her employment as a threat to him rather than as a contribution to the household will derive less power from her wage earning. This is particularly true when the husband is chronically unemployed or works in a low-status, menial job that exacerbates his dependency on his wife's wages. A woman's employment in these situations may be such a sore spot for her husband that she is actually expected to compensate for it by perhaps doing more work around the house or by deferring to his authority. Sensitive to her husband's feelings of failure, a woman may feel the need to soothe his threatened ego by consciously downplaying her own employment status (Hochschild & Machung, 1989).

On the other hand, a nonemployed woman married to a man who sees tremendous value and importance in her domestic work may actually derive more power from that role. She may be grateful to him for enabling her not to work for pay, and he may value her choice to stay home, especially when children are present. If her nonparticipation is perceived as her choice, staying out of the workforce may actually reflect her power and the ability to make decisions on her own behalf.

The Consequences of Power

In some settings, the consequences of power are clear. The schoolyard bully who threatens to beat up smaller classmates if they don't turn over their lunch money is gaining financial rewards from his or her use of power. But in families, the consequences of power are sometimes not so tangible.

Usually power outcomes in families are defined in terms of which person gets his or her way. Family life requires many decisions and choices. When two people fall in love and want to spend their lives together, they must choose whether to maintain separate residences or live together (whether married or not). If they decide to live together, they must figure out where to live, how to decorate the home, and who's going to be responsible for certain domestic tasks. They must make decisions on how their respective careers will influence family life, whether to have children, how to discipline them, and so on. The way they make all these decisions—from the trivial ones like what to have for dinner to the important ones like whether to accept a job transfer to another state—depends on the way relationships of power and authority have been structured.

In traditional, male-breadwinner/female-homemaker families, it is taken for granted that husbands have the final say in all important decisions. But research consistently shows that when women enter the workforce,

they participate more forcefully in family decision making than when they are not employed (Blumstein & Schwartz, 1983; Rubin 1994). ▲ It should be noted that working women may still defer to their husbands in many situations, and working women still retain primary responsibility over domestic work. Even so, employed women, in general, are more likely to feel they have the right to have their say at home and contradict their husbands than nonemployed women. One wife, who oversees a large laboratory, explaining why working women often play a more forceful role at home, says, "I think we share in the decision-making. I make decisions at the office from nine to five and I think it would be a little strange if I came home and was treated like a pussycat" (quoted in Blumstein & Schwartz, 1983, p. 141).

▲ *Family equality as a consequence of women's labor force participation is discussed in detail in Chapter 3.*

Conversely, women who drop out of the paid labor force often experience a perceptible decrease in their ability to make family decisions at home: "We don't get along as well as we used to when I was working because then he used to listen to me more than he does now. He tends to boss me around the way he tends to boss his students" (quoted in Blumstein & Schwartz, 1983, p. 142).

But decision making is not a perfect indicator of power. Indeed, it's difficult to determine who has power in a relationship simply by observing who makes the most decisions. Obviously, having the power to make trivial decisions is not the same as having power over the more important ones (Hood, 1983). Put another way, who gets to decide how decisions will be made? Sociologists distinguish between *orchestration power*, making decisions about what will be done, from *implementation power*, making decisions about how it will get done (Safilios-Rothschild,

1976). If a wife decides the family will take a trip and tells her husband that he will make all the decisions concerning travel arrangements and accommodations, who really has the decision-making power?

In many fundamentalist Christian families, for instance, most family decisions are apparently made by the wife. But upon closer inspection, you would find that she is simply implementing what has been delegated to her by her husband. Although she is in charge of the household and looks quite powerful, the husband typically claims final authority in decision making (Ammerman, 1987; Balswick & Balswick, 1995).

Furthermore, power differences can affect family decisions even when couples claim their decisions are "mutual" and "egalitarian." In a recent study, sixty-one married couples who had faced important work and family choices were interviewed to determine what factors influenced their decisions (Zvonkovic, Greaves, Schmiege, & Hall, 1996). Most of the decisions they had to make revolved around the adjustments the wife should make—namely, whether she should either increase or decrease the number of hours she spent at work. These issues were usually related to constraints (such as having a young child) or opportunities (children reaching an age where they could more easily look after themselves) that traditionally affect women. When the decisions did concern the husband's job, the couples tended to focus on whether he ought to switch jobs rather than on changes in the amount of time he spent at work instead of at home.

When the husband's job was the focus of attention, both partners tended to know what the other wanted and both spouses tended to want the same thing from the decision. But when the decision revolved around the wife's job, there was significant disagreement about the most favorable outcome and a general lack of understanding of the other spouse's desires. The researchers attributed this dis-

agreement and uncertainty to ambivalence about the wife's participation in the labor force in the first place. For example, in one couple, the wife enjoyed her part-time job and believed it had beneficial effects on her and on the marriage. Yet her husband viewed her job as just one in a series of rather unimportant temporary jobs.

Interestingly, most couples maintained that the decisions they made were "joint" or "mutual." However, the picture of couples openly expressing opinions and making decisions together that these terms imply belies the fact that most of the time the husband's preferences prevailed. Husbands' unspoken power over work and family decisions was reflected in one wife's description of how she and her husband make important decisions: "We usually talk and come to full agreement, or I give in and do what he wants on . . . [a] majority of things. I love him, and minor disagreements are a part of life" (quoted in Zvonkovic et al., 1996, p. 98). Clearly, such outcomes serve to further marginalize women economically, especially when their labor force participation is constrained by household responsibilities.

Changing Family Power Relations

Gender and power relations in our society and, by extension, in American families are slowly but noticeably changing. ▲ In one national survey, 79 percent of men and 74 percent of women agreed that the status of women has improved over the last 25 years (Boxer, 1997). Women have increased their participation in the paid labor force, and, as a consequence, are making greater financial contributions to their families.

▲ *See Chapter 9 for a more thorough exploration of the sources and outcomes of such change.*

Likewise, women have become a political and cultural force that can no longer be ignored. The greater societal awareness of sexual exploitation and violence has reduced—although not yet eliminated—our culture's traditional tolerance for sexual harassment, rape, and spouse abuse. To an increasing degree, the public and the media now support women's desire for more sharing and emotional expressiveness from their partners.

Consequently, family arrangements that were once taken for granted—like who's going to sacrifice a career to stay at home and raise children—are now more likely than ever to be the product of *decisions* arrived at by partners through open negotiation. At the very least, people entering into long-term relationships are starting to acknowledge that not every woman wants or expects to have children and take care of the household and not every man wants to be a primary breadwinner. More and more women are in the paid labor force and are therefore less dependent economically on their husbands than they once were. In addition, an increasing number of employed wives are now earning more than their husbands. Most importantly, gender norms are changing. Hence more and more couples today are trying to establish relationships in which power is balanced (Schwartz, 1994).

But this process isn't always easy. For one thing, male power is still considered more acceptable *to both men and women* than female power. The traditional power structure is so ingrained in cultural ideology that couples seem more comfortable when the balance is tilted in the male direction than when it is tilted in the female direction. Research on marital satisfaction, for instance, has consistently found that women as well as men are less satisfied in female-dominated relationships than in either egalitarian or male-dominated ones (cited in Brehm, 1992).

Furthermore, people in positions of power are typically reluctant to sacrifice their privilege (Goode, 1981). American men have long benefited from living in a society where language, identity, intimacy, history, culture, and institutions are built on gender distinctions, even if individual men themselves do not support such inequality. Most men do not see sexual inequality—either in their families or in society at large—as their fault or their problem; it's a "woman's issue." Like most people whose interests are being served by the system, men are largely unaware of the small and large advantages that the social structure and prevailing family ideology provide them (Goode, 1981). Because of their historical position in society, men are less likely to see sexual inequality as unjust or to see change as necessary. Therefore, an important step toward complete sexual equality inside and outside families is that men will have to come to understand their role in the process.

Something to Think About

Power remains an important feature of family relationships. It can be expressed to varying degrees and in varying styles: It may be shared equally or belong more to one partner than the other. But whatever its shape, it is always there. To say that there is no power in a family is like saying there is no weather.

1. To what extent are our lives determined by biological sex? Do you feel that biology is an insurmountable obstacle to full equality between men and women? Is full gender equality in society and in families even a desirable goal?

2. When you were a child, in what ways did you exert power and control over your parents? How much power should children have within their families? Should they be under the complete legal control of their parents?

3. To what extent do other social institutions—education, politics, economics, religion, the media—reinforce men's and women's power positions within families?

4. Do you think that earning a higher wage than one's partner entitles a person to certain privileges within a family?

5. As women gain more power and influence in the larger society, will they begin to exert more power within families? If this does occur, how will specific aspects of family life (sexuality, communication, childbearing, child rearing, household labor, etc.) be affected?

6. Imagine that we lived in a *matriarchal* rather than a *patriarchal* society. What differences would you expect in our common, taken-for-granted assumptions about family life?

ISSUE 6

How Do Race, Ethnicity, and Racism Affect Family Life?

Racial and Ethnic Identity

African-American Families

Asian-American Families

Hispanic Families

SOMETHING TO THINK ABOUT

Gregory Williams is currently the dean of the College of Law at The Ohio State University. He was born in Virginia in the late 1940s, a time when racial segregation was part of the natural order of life in the United States. He led a typical white, middle-class life. He had many black friends when he was young but understood that their "place" was separate from his white world. He went to "whites-only" schools, "whites-only" movie theaters, and "whites-only" swimming pools.

When he was 10 years old, his parents divorced. His father decided to move back to his hometown of Muncie, Indiana, with Gregory and his brother Mike. On the bus ride there, Mr. Williams gave his sons some startling news: Once they reached Indiana, he told them sternly, they could no longer be white. It turned out that their paternal grandmother was black and this, therefore, made them black too. "Life is going to be different from now on," he told them. "In Virginia you were white boys. In Indiana you're going to be colored boys. I want you to remember that you're the same today that you were yesterday. But people in Indiana will treat you differently" (Williams, 1995, p. 33).

Stunned by the revelation, the boys initially interpreted their new identities in terms of the restrictions that would be imposed on their lives. Gregory's brother shouted, "I don't wanta be colored. We can't go swimmin' or skatin' " (Williams, 1995, p. 33).

While Gregory initially refused to believe his father's news, his perceptions quickly began to shift:

> I didn't understand Dad. I knew I wasn't colored, and neither was he. My skin was white. All of us are white, I said to myself. But for the first time, I had to admit Dad didn't exactly look white. His deeply tanned skin puzzled me as I sat there trying to classify my own father. Goose bumps covered my arms as I realized that whatever he was, I was. I took a deep breath. I couldn't make any mistakes. I looked closer. His heavy lips and dark brown eyes didn't make him colored, I concluded. His black, wavy hair was different from Negroes' hair, but it was different from most white folks' hair, too. He was darker than most whites, but Mom said he was Italian. That was why my baby brother had such dark skin and curly hair. Mom told us to be proud of our Italian heritage! That's it, I decided. He was Italian.... [But when] I glanced across the aisle to where he sat ... I saw my father as I never had seen him before.... Before my eyes he was transformed from a swarthy Italian to his true self—a high-yellow mulatto. My father was a Negro! We were colored! After ten years in Virginia on the white side of the color line, I knew what that meant. (Williams, 1995, pp. 33–34)

Much of Gregory's life from that moment on was a struggle to learn to be black. It was never easy. He was rejected by black and white children alike. Even his aunts, uncles, and cousins resented him because he looked white. In junior high school, Gregory realized that straddling the color line made everyone uncomfortable because it shattered too many racial taboos. Each day, it seemed, brought a new dilemma about his "proper place." Dating was particularly problematic. Because he was considered black he wasn't supposed to date white girls. But because he *appeared* white, the community couldn't tolerate seeing him with black girls either.

Despite all the obstacles, Gregory managed to excel in academics and sports. He went on to a successful career as a lawyer and a professor. In the process, he came to accept and embrace his multiracial identity. He learned the importance of race in everyday life by living under the simultaneous influence of two different racial labels.

Gregory Williams's story provides an interesting example of the fluid nature of race, the role families play in shaping racial identity, and people's need to categorize others by well-defined racial groupings. The racial conflicts and tensions of an entire nation played themselves out inside this one individual. Of course, one doesn't have to "change" racial identities to know that in this country distinctions among large groups of people are made primarily on the bases of race and ethnicity. We all know the powerful role of race and minority status in American society.

Clearly it would be silly, if not downright misleading, to ignore racial and ethnic variation and talk about *the* American family as if it represented a monolithic, universal form. And yet focusing on diversity—talking about European-American families and African-American families and Hispanic families and Asian-American families and Native-American families and Jewish families and other racial or ethnic types of families as distinctly different—raises other difficult issues.

Recently I have noticed that students of color in my own courses are becoming increasingly uncomfortable with compartmentalized treatments of racial/ethnic family types. They worry that the family diversity that exists *within* a particular racial or ethnic group or the similarities that exist *between* groups will be overlooked and slighted. After all, they claim, it's as misleading and erroneous to talk about *the* African-American family, *the* Hispanic family, or *the* Asian-American family as it is to talk about *the* white family. They also fear that as long as family patterns that differ markedly from the idealized image of the white, middle-class family—whether based on race, ethnicity, religion, class, or something else—are considered "variations," chances are they will be viewed either as curiosities that need to be examined, "dysfunctional" barriers to a minority group's success that must be overcome, or "shortcomings" upon which blame for many social ills ought to be heaped.

In this section I will examine the role of race and ethnicity in family structure, paying attention to the commonalities as well as the differences across groups. You'll discover that framing this issue simply as a matter of "racial differences" is woefully inadequate when we consider some of the historical complexities involved in forming racial and ethnic identities.

Racial and Ethnic Identity

Race is an elusive term to define. In common usage, *race* refers to a category of people labeled and treated as similar because of common biological traits, including skin color; color and texture of hair; and shape of eyes, nose, or head. Most people think of race as a fixed and immutable biological characteristic that can easily be used to separate people into distinct groups.

But the idea that races are pure biological categories with clear boundaries is a myth. Scholars can't even agree on how many human races exist—estimates range from four to more than forty.

From one race to another, genetic differences are minuscule. Despite obvious differences in physical appearance, Swedes, New Guineans, Japanese, and Navajo are far more similar genetically than they are different (Diamond, 1994). Furthermore, most people are a mixture of races. Some genetic surveys estimate that as many as 80 percent of American blacks have some white ancestry (cited in Taylor Haizlip, 1995). All ethnic groups have mixed gene pools. According to one geneticist, modern Europeans (ancestors of America's "white" immigrants) have long been a mixed population whose genetic ancestry is actually 65 percent Asian and 35 percent African (Cavalli-Sforza, 1994). There has never been a pure "Caucasian" gene. In short, there is no such creature as a "pure" white—or for that matter "pure" black—American.

The diversity of physical traits *within* a racial group is sometimes as great as the diversity *between* groups. People who consider themselves white may actually have darker skin and curlier hair than some people who consider themselves black.

Indeed, there is so much physical overlap between presumed races that race is a more meaningful *social* category than it is a *biological* one. That is, the characteristics selected to distinguish one group from another have less to do with physical or genetic differences than with what that particular culture defines as socially significant. In Brazil, for instance, people are classified into one of many possible races on the basis of physical appearance and class standing, not genetic ancestry. The designation of race is so fluid that members of the same biological family—parents, children, brothers, and sisters—are sometimes accepted as representatives of very different races (Harris, 1964). As Brazilians climb the class ladder by educational and economic success, their racial classification often changes.

Race is even more complex because of its connection to *ethnicity*—the history, values, language, tastes, and habits that you learned from your family and your community as you were growing up. Indeed, ethnicity may be a more important indicator of your identity than your skin color or other anatomical features (Williams, 1991).

Race and ethnicity need not coincide. For example, although their skin color may be similar, Caribbean-American blacks are quite different ethnically from African-American blacks and often take great pains to avoid being identified as "black" (Gladwell, 1996).

Multiracial Identity

Despite the complexities of race, Americans still tend to see it in simple color terms: black, white, red, yellow, brown. As Gregory Williams learned, people even try to force mixed-race children into specific racial categories.

The United States has traditionally adhered to the *one-drop rule* in determining race (F. J. Davis, 1991). The term comes from a common law in the South during slavery that a "single drop of black blood" made a person black. According to the U.S. Census, anyone who has any known African black ancestry is officially considered black. Anthropologists call this a *hypodescent* rule, meaning that racially mixed people are always assigned the status of the minority group (F. J. Davis, 1991). Hence a person with seven out of eight great-grandparents who are white and only one who is black could still be considered black.

Many ethnic groups informally establish identity using the hypodescent rule in one form or another. Among older Japanese Americans, for instance, a child who is predominantly Japanese with some white blood is considered white by the rest of the community and not fully admitted into the ethnic group. Not surprisingly, a recent study of 1,500 offspring of Asian-Anglo couples found that the majority of these children (52 percent) identified themselves as Anglo. The rest viewed themselves as Asian (38 percent) or a combination of the two (10 percent) (Saenz, Hwang, Aguirre, & Anderson, 1995). Among Orthodox Jews, a child born to one Jewish and one non-Jewish parent is forbidden to claim a Jewish identity (Spickard, 1989).

The dramatic growth in the number of multiracial and multiethnic children is beginning to upset traditional views of racial identity. In 1992 the U.S. Census Bureau reported that for the first time in history, the number of biracial babies increased at a faster rate than the number of single-race babies (Marmor, 1996). More and more people are rebelling against the "one-drop rule" and refusing to identify themselves as one race or another. They are claiming multiple ethnic identities, a trend that may someday render our traditional racial vocabulary obsolete. People have come up with some rather creative ways of expressing their racial identity, such as "Korgentinian" (for Korean and Argentinian), "China-Latina," or "Blackanese" (Leland & Beals, 1997). In short, the traditional ethnic and racial boundaries that once served as primary societal determinants in everyday life seem to be eroding (Stephan & Stephan, 1989).

Most individuals who have multiracial backgrounds have experienced being arbitrarily assigned a racial identity by a school principal or an employer that may differ from the identity of other members of their families or may differ from their identity in other settings. And people who don't feel they fit into one of the present categories on official forms—white, black, Asian, native Hawaiian and other Pacific Islander, or American Indian—are currently forced to check the unflattering and ambiguous "other" category. (Since Hispanic origin is considered an ethnic, not a racial distinction, a Hispanic category does not appear.) Thus multiracial and multiethnic individuals recently lobbied Congress and the Census Bureau to add a multiracial category to the next census. Changing the census questionnaire may not solve all their problems, but it would add visibility and legitimacy to a racial identity that has heretofore been ignored. Some even argue that a multiracial category has the potential to soften the racial lines that divide the country. For people who are biological blends of several races and ethnicities, race is a meaningless concept; therefore they represent a biological solution to the problem of racial justice (White, 1997).

But not everyone thinks such a change is a good idea. Many civil rights organizations object to the inclusion of a "multiracial" category. They worry that it would reduce the number of Americans claiming to belong to long-recognized minority groups, dilute the culture and political power of those groups, and make it more difficult to enforce civil rights laws (Mathews, 1996). Lawsuits that assert job discrimination, affirmative action policies, and federal programs that assist mi-

nority businesses or that protect minority communities from environmental hazards all depend on official racial population data from the census. Furthermore, people who identify themselves as "biracial" or "multiracial" are sometimes perceived by members of racial groups as sellouts who avoid discrimination by taking advantage of the confusion their mixed identity creates (Graham, 1995).

Recent evidence suggests that these concerns might be somewhat premature. A 1997 Census Bureau study found that relatively few people would opt to characterize themselves as multiracial if given the chance on the census form (cited in Holmes, 1997a). Thus few racial groups would see their numbers significantly diminished. Among blacks, for instance, only between 0.7 percent and 2.7 percent considered themselves anything but African American, depending on how the question was asked. Among Asian Americans, though, as many as 11.8 percent considered themselves as belonging to more than one race and about 3 percent of these respondents would choose to describe themselves as multiracial.

In 1997, after 3 years of study, the government decided not to add a "multiracial" category to official forms. However, it did adopt a policy allowing people, for the first time, to identify themselves on the census form as members of more than one race (although at the time of this writing it had not been determined how people who selected this option would be counted). Members of a task force studying this issue felt that creating a separate multiracial category would add to racial tensions and further fragment the population (Holmes, 1997b).

Differences and Similarities

One of the bedrock goals of the American value system has been the ultimate assimilation of racial and ethnic minority groups into mainstream society. Assimilation is the process by which members of minority groups change their ways to conform to those of the dominant culture. Many immigrants believe that if they gradually lose their differences and adopt the lifestyle of the majority, they can get high-paying, stable jobs and become accepted members of mainstream society.

However, assimilation has an inherent trap: The only way for a group to conform to the dominant—in our society, Anglo-American—way of life is to abandon many of the traditions of the culture it left behind (Murray, 1994). Furthermore, assimilation has often been systematically forced upon certain groups. Native Americans, for instance, were forced to abandon their traditional family lifestyle by whites who could not accept their different values. When blacks were brought to America as slaves, they were forced to take new names and forbidden to practice any of the family and social traditions of their native cultures.

Thus some members of minority groups consider assimilation an undesirable goal. Instead they promote multiculturalism, a society made up of groups that maintain not only their ethnic identities but also their own languages, arts, music, foods, literature, religions, and family forms. ▲ They believe that multiculturalism enriches the society. With the massive influx of foreign-born, non–English-speaking people into this country in recent years, it has indeed become difficult to think of the United States as one culture and Americans as one people.

▲ *The role of immigration in shaping American families of the future is referred to in Chapter 9.*

Whether we espouse assimilation or multiculturalism, we must be cautious not to overgeneralize. Often the variation within an identified racial/ethnic category is significant. For instance, although they all are considered "Hispanic" or "Latino," Mexicans, Domini-

cans, Puerto Ricans, Cubans, Nicaraguans, Colombians, and other groups have very different histories, dialects, and immigration and citizenship experiences, and they have settled in different regions of the country (Bean & Tienda, 1987; Chilman, 1995). The same can be said for people considered "Asian." Filipinos, Chinese, Laotians, and Japanese differ markedly in cultural expectations and behaviors. Among recent Asian immigrants, some (for example, Chinese, Japanese, and Korean) arrived in this country as educated middle-class professionals with highly valued skills. But others (like Laotians, Cambodians, Indonesians, and Vietnamese) were likely to arrive uneducated and impoverished. Japanese Americans have an extremely low unemployment rate (about 3.4 percent) whereas the unemployment rate for Hmong immigrants from Laos is a staggering 62 percent (U.S. Bureau of the Census, 1993).

Race, Racism, and Class

The historical conditions under which any group enters American society are crucial in determining the degree of economic success and achievement it will experience as well as the nature of its family and community life. Those groups that most closely approximate the national ideal in language (English), religion (Protestant), cultural heritage (northern European), and physical appearance (light Caucasian) have historically had an easier time being accepted than groups that were further from these norms. Not surprisingly, those groups whose skin color and traditions were very different from the white majority faced harsher obstacles. Some were simply treated with derision and suspicion; others were persecuted. Slavery was the most dramatic example, but many other immigrant groups have struggled to find a place in American society. Jews, for instance, were refused admission to many of the best American universities until the middle of the twentieth century. Limits on Greek and Italian immigration lasted from 1924 until the 1960s. Help-wanted ads in late nineteenth-century newspapers routinely carried the message "No Irish need apply."

Social and economic exclusion has forced racial/ethnic minority groups to adapt their families to deal with hardships imposed by the larger society. Extended families, single parenthood, dual-earner couples, and many other deviations from the mainstream culture's family ideal have often been means of adapting to demanding societal circumstances. ▲ Even though these patterns are the products of historical conditions, they are often blamed for a particular group's social and economic difficulties:

> Latinos, among whom extended family networks play a crucial role in integrating family and community, [are] criticized for being too "familistic"—their lack of social progress ... blamed on family values which [keep] them tied to family rather than economic advancement. African-American families [are] criticized as "matriarchal" because of the strong role grandmothers [play] in extended family networks. (Dill, Baca Zinn, & Patton, 1994, p. 16)

▲ *See Issue 7 for a detailed discussion of the relationship between social class and family life.*

This general discussion leaves us with interesting questions to ponder: Are the family patterns found in racial and ethnic minority groups really all that different from the mainstream? If so, what were the social and historical conditions that created these differences?

African-American Families

Of all racial minorities in the United States today, African-American families are the most negatively portrayed. The stereotypical image projects marital violence; broken homes; large numbers of children; and a resulting cycle of poverty, illegitimacy, crime, welfare, unemployment, and so on. Black men, in particular, are typically portrayed as being on the outer fringe, either uninterested in or incapable of participating in the lives of their families. How accurate are these images, and how have they developed throughout history?

Slavery, Racism, and Blocked Opportunities

The experiences of African-American families have been unique among ethnic groups in this country because of the direct and indirect effects of slavery. Although accurate, reliable information on slave families has been difficult to obtain, certain aspects of slave life are clear. Because slaves were not allowed to enter into binding legal contracts, there was no legal basis for marriage between slaves. Slave owners determined which slaves could (or even had to) marry and which marriages would be dissolved. Children had economic value since they represented future slaves (Burnham, 1993; Staples, 1992). Slave owners had an interest in keeping slave families intact because married slaves were thought to be more docile and less inclined to rebel or escape. However, when economic troubles forced the sale of slaves to raise capital, many slave owners were not averse to separating the very slave families they had once advocated. The threat of separation "hung like a dark cloud over every slave couple family" (Burnham, 1993, p. 146). Even a "kind" and "sympathetic" master was no assurance of family stability and security.

In this environment, African-American families showed a remarkable capacity to adapt and endure. And the family was an important means of survival. It was within families that slaves received sustaining affection, companionship, love, and support. It was here that they learned to cooperate with one another to avoid punishment and retained some degree of self-esteem.

Even when individual families were destroyed, the values of marriage and two-parent households persevered. Sociologist Herbert Gutman (1978) examined marriage licenses, birth records, and census data from 1855 to 1880 and found that two-parent, intact black families prevailed both during slavery and after emancipation. In counties and towns in Virginia, Mississippi, South Carolina, and Alabama, between 70 and 85 percent of black households contained both a mother and a father.

After slavery, blacks had the freedom to legally marry, and they did so in large numbers. Children were of special value to emancipated slaves, who could easily remember having their children sold away during slavery. Indeed, by 1917, 90 percent of all black children were born into existing marriages (Staples, 1992).

During the late nineteenth century, the strong role of women in black families emerged. Because a working woman was seen as a reminder of slavery, many black men preferred that their wives not work. But racism and legal, social, and economic exclusion made it extremely difficult for black men to find employment adequate to support their families. Survival dictated that black women enter the labor force. In 1900, 41 percent of black women were in the labor force compared to 16 percent of white women (cited in Staples, 1992).

Despite the difficulties left over from slavery, African Americans were able to create impressive norms of family life over the years. At the same time, though, their family structures were widely disparaged by whites. Negative images received a sort of official legitimacy in 1965, when Daniel Patrick Moynihan, then an assistant secretary of labor, wrote a report titled *The Negro Family: The Case for National Action*. At the time, the South was still highly segregated, and blacks were at the bottom of all relevant social categories.

Moynihan argued that the root of the problems blacks experienced was not economic but instead was the inherent weakness and deterioration of black families. He described black families as a "tangled pathology," whose key feature was the absence of the father and the unusually large amount of power held by women. Moynihan felt that this "variant" family structure resulted in, among other things, low self-image, low IQ, high rates of school dropouts, delinquency, unemployment, violent crime, drug abuse, and so on—especially among sons.

To add fuel to the fire, the conditions Moynihan originally described with such alarm seemed to get worse over the ensuing 3 decades. Black families, it seems, experienced broad family trends and changes more rapidly and with greater intensity than other sectors of society (Tucker & Mitchell-Kernan, 1995). ▲ For instance, blacks have a lower marriage rate than whites and wait longer to marry (Cherlin, 1992). Yet, despite the increasing tendency for both blacks and whites to delay marriage, blacks begin sexual activity and childbearing earlier. This combination has resulted in a dramatic racial difference in nonmarital births.

▲ *Many of these trends fuel the debate over the stability of the American family, which is the subject of Issue 8.*

It would be impossible to discuss these features of African-American families without examining the broader economic effects of racism, which continue to impede educational advancement and block access to high-paying jobs. African Americans as a group have one of the highest unemployment rates in the country and are heavily marginalized into low-paying jobs. For those who are employed, there's a greater chance of underemployment, inconsistent employment, and lower wages. As a result, three times as many black children as white children live below the poverty line (Duncan, Brooks-Gunn, & Klebanov, 1994).

When men don't work or don't earn sufficient wages, they become less interested in becoming husbands, since they are constrained in their ability to perform the provider role in marriage (Dickson, 1993; Wilson, 1987). Black single men who are in stable employment are twice as likely to marry as single men who are sporadically employed or unemployed (Testa & Krogh, 1995). In addition, black men's anxiety about being able to provide for their families also increases the likelihood of marital difficulties and divorce, particularly in early marriage (Hatchett, Veroff, & Douvan, 1995). ▲ This argument, of course, assumes that male employment is perceived to be a necessary requirement for marriage (Raley, 1996).

▲ *The causes, processes, and consequences of divorce are discussed in greater detail in Chapter 7.*

While black men have historically had limited employment opportunities, black women have seen their opportunities increase. More black women than men go to and graduate from college and more work as professionals. In 1994, about 900,000 black women were enrolled in undergraduate and graduate programs at American colleges and universities compared to 550,000 black men (Cose, 1996). Black college-educated women are much more likely than white college-educated women to marry men without degrees (Cose, 1995). Hence, there is less of a financial incentive to marry (Farley & Bianchi, 1991).

In short, black families have good reason for their long tradition of relying on women's income to survive. You can see that policies advocating marriage for poor single mothers are questionable because the men who compose the eligible marriage market would have difficulty supporting a family (Eggebeen & Lichter, 1991). Movements like the Million Man March in 1995 and programs like Operation Fatherhood, designed to help absent fathers of children on welfare become financially and emotionally involved in the lives of their children (Peterson, 1992), may be more effective, because they are attempting to restore the dignity and increase the presence of black men within their families. ▲

▲ *American ideals of fatherhood are sketched in Chapter 4.*

African-American Family Diversity

The pervasive image of black family collapse ignores the diversity of African-American family life. The "African-American community" consists of families with widely different histories and experiences. Not all have ancestors who entered the country enslaved. Some came to the Americas as freemen; others came as indentured servants who worked off their indebtedness and went on to lead free lives. Today, African-American families come from different classes, different religions, and different geographical areas. While most have had to deal with racism, discrimination, and oppression, their family structures are quite varied. The despair of poverty, single parenthood, underemployment and unemployment, and lack of opportunity are not uniformly experienced among all African-American families.

In short, the image of black families as "pathological" overlooks the large number of families that don't fit this negative stereotype. One-third of African Americans have incomes, educations, and lifestyles that place them in the middle class. The median income of black married couples living in the northeastern part of the country is the same as that of white couples in that area. In 1996 the poverty rate among black families fell below 30 percent for the first time since the U.S. Census Bureau began keeping track in 1959 (all statistics from Holmes, 1996c).

In over half of black families, two parents are present (U.S. Bureau of the Census, 1997a). In these two-parent families 52 percent of the fathers work full-time, and another 32.7 percent work part-time (McAdoo, 1998). It's true that fewer than half of all African-American adults are married. But contrary to the contention that all black men are averse to marriage, approximately 90 percent of those who are college-educated with annual incomes over $25,000 are married and live with their spouses. The black teenage birth rate has fallen 17 percent since 1991, and the proportion of black babies born out of wedlock dropped in 1995 for the first time since 1969 (Holmes, 1996b).

In fact, in some ways African-American families are stronger than other families. Family relationships remain a crucial form of emotional and economic support. A recent survey of African Americans found that over 90 percent considered themselves close to their families (Hatchett & Jackson, 1993). Extended families tend to be large, often including both blood-related kin and people informally adopted into the family system (McAdoo, 1998). ▲ Furthermore, loyalty and responsibility to others in one's family are highly valued. Interestingly, this value is strengthened by the belief that everything a person does reflects not only on his or her family but on other African Americans as well.

▲ *Issue 1 examines the important role of "fictive kin" in African-American families.*

Asian-American Families

When examining the difficulties faced by racial and ethnic minority groups in America, Asians are often considered to be the "excep-

tion" because of their well-publicized educational, occupational, and economic success. Japanese Americans, for instance, are often labeled the "model minority" because they show respect for cherished values such as hard work, achievement, self-control, dependability, manners, thrift, and diligence (Kitano, 1976). However, such stereotypes tend to overlook the growing class of inner-city Chinese, Vietnamese, and Laotians for whom desperate economic conditions have spawned gangs, violence, alienation, and family dysfunction.

Immigration and Racism

Like other ethnic minority groups, Asian Americans have endured a history of prejudice and discrimination that has had a noteworthy impact on the structure of their families. For instance, in the second half of the nineteenth century, Chinese immigrants were recruited by industrialists in the western United States to perform the arduous work of extracting wealth from the mines and building the transcontinental railroad. But from the outset they were treated with hostility. The image of the "yellow peril" was fostered by fears that hordes of Chinese would take scarce jobs and eventually overrun the white race.

Initially, working in this country was a means of gaining financial support for one's family back in China. The end goal was to earn enough money to return to China and purchase land there. So most workers assumed they were here temporarily. Indeed, U.S. law in the late nineteenth century prevented Chinese laborers from becoming permanent citizens.

In addition, those who arrived before 1882 were not allowed to bring their wives and were prevented by law from marrying whites (Dill, 1995). Thus, for many years, the predominant family form among the Chinese in the United States was a *split household,* where financial support was accomplished by one member (the father) who lived far from the rest of the family. ▲ Everything else—consumption, reproduction, socialization—was carried out by the wife and other relatives in the home village (Dill, 1995). This arrangement required considerable sacrifice—men were separated from their families sometimes for up to 20 years. Many children grew up never knowing their fathers. Wives who remained in China were forced to raise children and care for in-laws on the meager earnings their husbands sporadically sent them. These families became interdependent economic units that spanned two continents (Glenn & Yap, 1994).

▲ *Commuter marriage—a contemporary manifestation of the split household—is discussed in Chapter 3.*

Even when they were able to have intact families here, prejudice, violence, and discrimination kept Chinese people poor and segregated. By necessity, Chinese-American communities—which would eventually become the "Chinatowns" we can see in many large cities today—were tightly structured and insulated against the threats from white American society. In these close communities people learned to become self-reliant, creating their own businesses, organizing their own social clubs, and so on.

Because of the collectivist nature of Chinese culture, traditional family life required the sacrifice of individual needs and desires in favor of the overall welfare of the family unit (Collins & Coltrane, 1995). In traditional Chinese families, children were taught to be loyal and obedient and to value educational achievement. Although many Chinese wives were more or less equal producers in family businesses, gender roles at home were rigidly defined. ▲ They were expected to assume major responsibility for the household and child care (Wong, 1998). Fathers tended to have final authority and wielded unquestioned power; others—wives and children—

were expected to be obedient (Kitano & Daniels, 1988).

▲ *American working women have faced the same dilemma, as Chapter 3 explains, although the trends are toward greater gender equity.*

Early Japanese immigrants, who arrived around the turn of the century, were much like the Chinese. In response to prejudice and discrimination, they created separate, insulated communities where children were taught the Japanese language and culture in schools established by their parents. They learned the importance of hard work, obedience to authority, and self-sacrifice. Tight families and a strong work ethic enabled many Japanese families to pool money and resources and achieve relative success.

However, this perceived success motivated lawmakers to enact legislation that limited Japanese people's ability to own or lease land. Fearing a rapid growth in the Japanese population, the National Origins Act of 1924 barred all further Japanese immigration (Takagi, 1994).

Hostility toward Japanese reached its peak in 1941 following Japan's attack on Pearl Harbor. Vocal special-interest groups, influential members of Congress, and the military held the Japanese-American community responsible for the surprise attack. The military used suspicion, fear, and racial prejudice to successfully pressure the government to suspend Japanese-American citizens' constitutional rights. The government authorized extensive searches of private residences and businesses. Japanese books, newspapers, and magazines made ordinary families the object of further surveillance. Eventually President Franklin Roosevelt signed an executive order authorizing the relocation and internment of Japanese immigrants and American citizens of Japanese descent in camps surrounded by barbed wire and watchtowers.

Since economics and family were so connected, internment had a devastating impact on the Japanese-American community. As part of the registration process, internees were forced to express their loyalty to the United States and renounce their ties to Japan. Many second-generation Japanese (those born here) felt more American than Japanese and thus could easily express loyalty to the United States. When they did so, Japanese-born parents felt their children were betraying their heritage. Hence, internment marked a shift away from traditional family organization. Children became more independent. By the time the Supreme Court ruled in 1945 that internment was unconstitutional, young Japanese Americans had become significantly more "American" than their elders.

Both Chinese-American and Japanese-American family structures emerged as adaptive strategies for survival in a racially hostile environment. For the most part, because people were forced to turn to their relatives for support, families took on an important economic as well as emotional role in their lives. With such a strong familial foundation, it is not surprising that many Asian-American families have achieved high levels of educational and professional attainment and earnings exceeding those of the rest of the population.

Contemporary Asian-American Families

In contemporary Asian-American families—as in other ethnic groups that were originally immigrants—tensions often arise between younger and older generations over the extent to which tradition ought to determine people's lives. As Asian families adapt to the dominant culture, they are more likely to adopt family behaviors characteristic of other American families. For instance, young Asian-American women's dissatisfaction with traditional gender attitudes has made

them much more likely than men or older generations of women to marry non-Asians.

The traditional cohesiveness of Asian families has also given way to societywide trends. For instance, the divorce rate—which at one time was lower than that of any other group—is increasing for Asians as it is for other groups. ▲ Because Asian Americans tend to come from cultures in which relatively few women work outside the home, the contemporary need for two earners in a household has created further tension and conflict between generations.

▲ *Divorce is the topic of Chapter 7.*

Nevertheless, Asian Americans are twice as likely as whites to live in extended families and half as likely to live alone. More workers in a family mean more earnings, which may explain why household income is higher among Asian Americans than any other group (U.S. Bureau of the Census, 1997a).

Yet we must be aware of the variation *within* the Asian-American population. For instance, families of Chinese, Japanese, and Korean descent are significantly smaller than Vietnamese, Cambodian, Laotian, and Hmong families. Those Asian groups that have been here the longest—most notably Chinese and Japanese Americans—have a higher proportion of native-born individuals and are less culturally distinct than groups that are more recent arrivals (such as Southeast Asians). The more recent arrivals are more likely to use new conditions to recreate the traditional family structure of their homeland. ▲ Recently arrived Vietnamese families, for instance, have vigorously tried to reconstruct their traditional complex, extended family networks in the face of disruption caused by the migration process. In doing so they have had to adopt a more fluid, inclusive conception of family, which has allowed for the incorporation of people (such as friends and neighbors) into the extended kin network who may not have been part of it in Vietnam (Kibria, 1994a).

▲ *A detailed discussion of the adjustment of immigrant Vietnamese families appears in Issue 4.*

Hispanic Families

One of the fastest-growing segments of the American population is that of Spanish-speaking people who have migrated from Mexico, the Caribbean, Central America, and South America. By the year 2030, it's estimated that people of Hispanic origin will compose close to 20 percent of the U.S. population. But, as is true of Asian Americans, there is tremendous cultural and familial diversity among groups considered Hispanic.

Early Immigrant Families

This diversity stems from distinctly different immigration histories. For instance, when Fidel Castro came to power in Cuba in the late 1950s, Cuban immigrants poured into this country. Since they were fleeing a Communist political regime at odds with American political ideals, their initial entry into this country was met with enthusiasm (Suarez, 1998). Many of the early immigrants were wealthy executives and business owners who were able to set up lucrative businesses, particularly in Florida. Today, Cuban-American families have the highest median income of any Hispanic group.

The immigration experience of people of Mexican descent is much different. In 1848, following war with the United States, Mexico lost more than half its territory, giving up all claims to Texas and ceding much of what is now Arizona, New Mexico, Utah, Nevada, and California (Dill, 1995). Although Mexicans who had been living on the American side of the new border were supposed to be granted all the rights of U.S. citizens, their property

rights were routinely violated, and they lost control of mining, ranching, and farming industries. The American takeover resulted in the gradual displacement of Mexicans from their ancestral lands. In the early twentieth century, life continued to be a daily struggle for survival. Frequently, workers had to house their families in primitive shacks with no electricity or plumbing for months on end while they did their seasonal labor (Rico & Mano, 1991).

Family roles were strongly defined by gender. Women were valued first and foremost for their household skills. In rural areas they might also be responsible for tending gardens and looking after animals. But high rates of widowhood—due to the hazardous nature of the work available to men—and temporary abandonment by men in search of employment created sharp increases in female-headed households during the mid-nineteenth to the early twentieth century (Griswold del Castillo, 1979). Women (and children) began joining the labor force primarily as maids, servants, laundresses, garment workers, cooks, and dishwashers.

Eventually entire families were participating in the labor market, particularly in seasonal, itinerant farm labor. This occupation was a way of increasing earnings and of keeping the family together. Mexican Americans in extended families fared better economically and experienced less downward mobility than people in smaller, nuclear families (Dill, 1995). Extended families could assist immigrating relatives in finding housing and employment and could pool their resources to pay for food, housing, transportation, and schooling (Gelles, 1995).

Contemporary Hispanic Families

The consistent decline in white family size over the years has not been mirrored in the Hispanic population (Frisbie & Bean, 1995). Because of higher fertility, the influx of immigrants with large families, and religious (Catholic) proscriptions against birth control, Hispanic families tend to be relatively large and stable in structure compared to families of other ethnic groups. ▲ Although Hispanic families have been affected by rising divorce rates, just like any other group in American society, their rate tends to be lower or comparable to other groups. ▲ In 1996, for instance, 7.7 percent of the Hispanic population was divorced, compared to 11.5 percent of blacks and 9.3 percent of whites (U.S. Bureau of the Census, 1997a). And despite a greater percentage of single-parent families among Hispanics than among whites, a lower percentage of them are due to divorce.

▲ *Pro-natalist ideologies are discussed in Chapter 4.*

▲ *Chapter 7 discusses divorce in greater detail.*

Furthermore, a sense of familial responsibility and mutual obligation continues to play a prominent role in Hispanic families (Hines, Garcia-Preto, McGoldrick, Almeida, & Weltman, 1997). Their large kinship networks can best be described as "expanded families" (Horowitz, 1997). Relatives tend to live in the same neighborhood and interact on a regular basis, even though each household comprises a nuclear family. Within expanded families, members are able to exchange important services such as babysitting, meals, personal advice, and emotional support (cited in Becerra, 1992). Feelings of mutual obligation strengthen relationships. Rather than being labeled a freeloader, a person who can survive without money for a long period of time by going from relative to relative is considered to have a strong, cohesive family (Horowitz, 1997). But, in recent years, fulfilling familial obliga-

tions has become especially difficult in light of the rapidly growing elderly Hispanic population. ▲

▲ *Read Chapter 8 for more on the link between culture and treatment of the elderly.*

Of all the popular stereotypes surrounding Hispanic families, one of the most prevalent is the concept of *machismo*. Machismo is frequently equated with male dominance, pride in masculinity, honor in being the economic provider, and a belief in a sexual double standard. The father is considered the head of the household, the major decision maker, and the absolute power holder in the family (Becerra, 1992). Manhood is expressed through independence, strength, control, and domination.

For women, motherhood was traditionally seen as the most culturally acceptable identity available to women. The gender stereotypes surrounding Hispanic families imply that women are self-sacrificing and passive caretakers of the entire family.

But the ideals of the patriarchal tradition of machismo are frequently contradicted by the demands of contemporary life, and most scholars agree that the degree of male dominance associated with machismo has been exaggerated. ▲ Economic conditions and the types of jobs available to many Hispanic men have often kept them away from their families for long periods of time. Over time, more and more women have become heads of households and entered the job market. And Hispanic men appear to share child care, decision making, and household tasks as much as white men do (Ybarra, 1982).

▲ *The complexities of gender roles in contemporary families are the subject of Chapter 3.*

Something to Think About

American society—especially the economic opportunities it provides and the obstacles it sets in place—can look quite different to people from different racial and ethnic groups. It should come as no surprise, then, that different groups have created unique family adaptations. Despite the desire among some people to brand certain minority families as dysfunctional or even dangerous to society, these families—particularly African-American, Asian-American, and Hispanic-American families—are more often than not a source of strength for their members, providing crucial support and nurturing.

1. When it comes to family, should we emphasize the similarities that exist across racial/ethnic groups or the differences? As a society, should we aspire to assimilation or multiculturalism? Do you think we will ever reach a point when racial/ethnic categories become irrelevant?

2. How has your race or ethnicity influenced your own family experiences? In what ways do you think your family life would be different if you were a member of another race or ethnic group?

3. Should people be allowed to formally identify themselves as "multiracial"? How might official recognition of this category affect family dynamics in the future?

4. Do you think that legislation forbidding discrimination would have a noticeable effect in the family life of racial minorities?

How Do Wealth and Poverty Determine Family Experiences?

Class Stratification

Poverty and Family Life

SOMETHING TO THINK ABOUT

Many of us grew up in middle-class or working-class families. We may not have been wealthy enough to enjoy unlimited freedom and opportunity, but we probably had enough resources to enjoy a level of security and stability far above the circumstances of the impoverished family illustrated in the following paragraphs.

> One of my sons was diagnosed as having a high lead level in his blood. The Welfare Department placed my son under protective services and told me that I would have to find another place to live or they would put [him] into a foster home. With six children on a welfare budget, it's not easy to find an apartment. And I had to find one within thirty days! To keep the state from taking my son, I was forced to move into the first available housing I could find.
>
> Since I was an emergency case and eligible for a housing subsidy, my name was placed at the top of the list. I had to take the first available unit offered by the Housing Authority. The offer: a brand new town-house-type apartment *fifty miles away* in a white, middle-class suburb!
>
> I knew this move would devastate my family because we would be so far away from our relatives and friends. When you're poor, you have to depend on your family and friends to help you through when you don't have the money to help yourself. At least two or three times every month I take my children to my mother's house to eat. How would we ever be able to get to her house from fifty miles away?
>
> I also knew my neighbors wouldn't welcome me and my children: a black single woman with six children. I imagined the sneers of the merchants as I paid for my groceries with food stamps and the grunts of the doctors as I pulled out my Medicaid card.
>
> I thought about the problems of transportation that were sure to crop up. How would I get my children to school? What if they got sick; how far was the nearest hospital? I envisioned the seven of us walking for miles with grocery bags....
>
> We now live in a totally hostile environment severed from our family and friends. And although we live in a physically beautiful development, life for us is hard. A poor family with no transportation is lost in the suburbs. We are as isolated as if we lived on a remote island in the Pacific. (quoted in Dujon, Gradford, & Stevens, 1995, p. 282)

It doesn't take much of an imagination to see how very difficult family life can be for poor families. Poverty brings hardship, even when something good happens—like placement into a nice apartment.

Of course, the relationship between wealth (or lack of it) and family life is not always so straightforward. Wealthy families are not immune from despair, disappointment, and pain. The lives of children in extremely wealthy families are often tightly monitored and controlled by their parents to avoid any damage to the family's fortune and reputation. Such restrictions can create resentment and rebellion. At the other end of the spectrum, some poor families experience a great deal of trouble and heartbreak, but others are strong, supportive, and emotionally gratifying. Many successful adults who grew up in abject poverty have prospered from the love and guidance of their parents.

Nevertheless, wealth and, by extension, socioeconomic standing are an important backdrop to family life. Much of the heated criticism of family we hear these days focuses on those families at the low end of the economic spectrum. In this section, I will examine the influence of broad economic forces on family dynamics and structure.

Class Stratification

Contemporary industrialized societies are likely to be stratified on the basis of social class, that is, people's economic position in society. Social class distinguishes one group's pattern of behavior from another's and determines access to important resources and life chances. We live in a society that is solidly structured along class distinctions.

People's positions in the class system affect virtually every aspect of their lives, including political preferences, sexual behavior, church membership, diet, health, life expectancy, place of residence, fashion, access to education, dating and marital patterns, child rearing, and treatment by the criminal justice system (Della Fave, 1980; Mantsios, 1995; Reiman, 1998). For instance, working-class and poor people are significantly more likely to get arrested, get convicted, go to prison, and receive the death penalty than are upper-class people (Reiman, 1998). Poor two-parent families are approximately twice as likely to break up as are two-parent families that aren't poor (Rank, 1994). ▲

▲ *Other correlates of divorce are discussed in Chapter 7.*

Those at lower levels of the stratification system are more likely to die prematurely as a result of homicide, accidents, or inadequate health care than are people at higher levels (Kearl, 1989). With each step down the income ladder comes an increased risk of headaches, varicose veins, respiratory infection, hypertension, emotional distress, heart disease, and early death (Shweder, 1997). The death rate for Americans with family incomes of less than $9,000 a year is three times higher than that of people with family incomes of more than $25,000 a year (Pear, 1993). Lack of adequate health care causes three times more deaths than does AIDS each year (Navarro, 1992).

Theoretically, class systems are different from other systems of stratification—such as the Indian *caste system,* which bases social position on heredity—in that there are no legal barriers to social mobility. In practice, however, mobility between classes may be quite difficult. As much as we'd like to believe otherwise, the opportunities to move from one class up to another are not available to all members of society.

To rank families on the basis of class, contemporary sociologists usually compile information on quantifiable factors like household income, wealth, occupational status, and educational attainment. But the boundaries between classes still tend to be rather fuzzy. Some have argued that there are no discrete classes with clearly defined boundaries, but only a socioeconomic continuum on which individuals are ranked (Blau & Duncan, 1967).

Nevertheless, class designations remain a part of both everyday thinking and social research:

- The "upper" class is usually thought to include owners of vast amounts of property and other forms of wealth, owners of large corporations, top financiers, and members of prestigious families.
- The "middle" class is likely to include managers, supervisors, executives, small business owners, and professionals (for example, lawyers, doctors, teachers, engineers).
- The "working" class includes those who earn modest wages, such as industrial and factory workers, office workers, clerks, and farm and manual laborers.
- The "poor" consist of people who work for minimum wages or are chronically unemployed. These are the people who do society's dirty work and whose lives are the most precarious (Walton, 1990; Wright, Costello, Hachen, & Sprague, 1982).

But class is about more than income and type of occupation; it defines an entire way of life. Thus when we talk about social class, we are making broad generalizations about large groups of people regarding what they look like and how they live. But keep in mind that families within the same social category—whether based on race, ethnicity, religion, or class—do not represent a monolithic group. There is often as much diversity *within* a category as *between* categories.

Upper-Class Families

Members of upper-class families tend to be born into wealth gained by earlier generations (Langman, 1988). Their formidable wealth provides political and economic power as well as insulation from the rest of society. A definition of the upper class formulated 40 years ago, which still rings true today, identifies this class as

> a group of families whose members are descendants of successful individuals of one, two, three or more generations ago . . . the top of the social class hierarchy. They are brought up together and they are friends. They intermarry and have a distinctive style of life. There is a primary group solidarity that sets them apart from the rest of the population. (Baltzell, 1958, p. 60)

An important feature of upper-class families is the rather traditional role that women play (Ostrander, 1984). Many wives, for instance, believe they should put their husbands' interests ahead of their own:

> He's the brain in the family and it's my role to see that he's at his best. I've subjugated everything to that. When he comes home in the evening, this house must be perfectly quiet. . . . He wants me to be pleasant, pretty, and relaxed. I never bring a problem to him, except during forty-five minutes set aside on Sunday mornings for that purpose. (quoted in Ostrander, 1984, p. 39)

Such an attitude seems out-of-date as we approach the twenty-first century. However, as was the case in many nineteenth-century families, these women see such supportive behavior as their essential contribution to their families. They take for granted that their job—their part of the bargain in exchange for a life of luxury—is to "run the house." ▲ They rarely do the actual cooking, laundry, and cleaning themselves, but they make decisions about how other people—whose labor they have purchased—perform the housework.

▲ *This traditional division of labor is gradually disappearing in most other segments of American society, as Chapter 3 explains.*

Many upper-class women also tend to have a rather traditional perspective on the mother role. ▲ Children's preschool years are typically spent at home in the presence of mothers and nannies, nurses, or other private, in-home caretakers. From kindergarten through college, these upper-class children are usually enrolled in private schools (Domhoff, 1983). There they are set apart from children of other classes or, as one upper-class mother called them, "ordinary people" (quoted in Ostrander, 1984, p. 85). Because inheritance and pedigree in extremely wealthy families are passed down through the children, it is crucial that they be raised to value their social position and understand the responsibilities that come with it. Mothers play a dominant role in enforcing these high standards of behavior and structuring the child's participation in "appropriate" activities and organizations.

▲ *For more on the influence of social class on child rearing practices, read Chapter 5.*

The popular belief that upper-class women leave the raising of their children to nannies, au pairs, or other hired caretakers may therefore be largely mythical. Many of these women feel it is important to be present in their children's lives, particularly when they are young, even if these other caretakers do take over much of the hands-on, day-to-day care. Upper-class women often arrange their own activities, particularly volunteer work, so they can be home for their children.

What many upper-class parents seem to want *most* for their children as they get older is a "compatible marriage"—that is, a marriage to someone of equal class standing. To that end, they are concerned that their children engage in class-exclusive recreational activities and join organizations whose membership is by invitation only. Social clubs are places where "acceptable" people of "the same kind" can meet, ultimately resulting in "acceptable" marriages (Ostrander, 1984). Though marital choices are technically "free," there is a high degree of scrutiny and surveillance of dating and courtship among upper-class youth. ▲ Marriage between cousins is often encouraged to ensure proper lineage. Marrying someone of a different social class—or "marrying down"—means not only accepting that person as an equal partner but also blurring the class distinctions that currently exist in the next generation, should the couple have children (Kalmijn, 1991).

▲ *Chapter 2 describes the influence of social class on dating and mate-selection patterns.*

The "New Rich"

Unlike those elite families in which vast amounts of wealth are inherited, other affluent families experience a rapid increase of wealth and social mobility through personal achievements. They are headed by high-level managers in large corporations, successful entrepreneurs, lawyers, doctors, scientists, entertainers, and professional athletes. They are the "new rich," people who have made, not inherited, their fortunes. Some executives

and professionals were born into poor or working-class families or belong to a disadvantaged racial or ethnic group, but they have been able to climb the social ladder and create a comfortable life for themselves and their families.

Personal effort and achievement are such crucial components of their identities that many of these newly rich families are opposed to leaving their children huge inheritances. They feel that inherited wealth can corrupt and spoil young people. For example, Microsoft owner Bill Gates, currently one of the richest men in the world, says, "One thing is for sure. I won't leave a lot of money to my heirs because I don't think it would be good for them" (quoted in Linden & Machan, 1997, pp. 152, 154).

It should be noted, however, that the children of such wealthy individuals will never be left destitute. Gates will leave his baby daughter and any of her future siblings $10 million each. This is a tiny piece of a vast estate, but a substantial amount of money in its own right. Furthermore, we must also keep in mind that inheritance involves more than money or property. Children inherit a recognized family name and the respect and privilege that goes along with it. Hence, they are likely to have access to opportunities and social advantages that are beyond the grasp of most.

Since they owe their economic position to their occupational achievements, newly rich professionals tend to make their careers the focal point of their lives. Gender plays a key role here. Husbands in particular are likely to work long hours and travel on business frequently. While upper-class wives work to maintain class boundaries in current and future generations, wives in newly rich families tend to be concerned with keeping their husbands in the occupations that put them where they are (Kanter, 1986).

Although they may themselves be trained professionals and are more likely to be employed than upper-class wives, these women for the most part support their husbands by playing an adjunct role in the family. For instance, a wealthy doctor's wife may help run the business by decorating the office or managing the staff of nurses and office personnel (Fowlkes, 1987). In this way she does work that would otherwise be done by a paid employee. Likewise, she provides indirect support by hosting social events such as dinners with colleagues or potential clients. However, as women increase their representation in high-paying professions like medicine and law, we will surely see adjustments in these trends. ▲

▲ *Chapter 3 looks at the relationships among employment, income, and domestic responsibilities.*

Working-Class Families

Toward the other end of the economic spectrum are those families that struggle financially. Because working-class individuals depend on wage work for their income, they are particularly susceptible to downturns in the economy, which can lead to layoffs, plant closings, and unemployment.

Historically, working-class people have always tended to marry younger—often because of a desire to leave home and become independent—and have children earlier than members of higher classes, creating further economic pressures. ▲ Most working-class women are employed before they marry, and so young couples may expect that two incomes will enable them to maintain a home. But early pregnancy—in one study, half of the working-class wives in the sample had given birth by the time they had been married 7 months (Rubin, 1976)—quickly takes these women out of the labor force, making it difficult to pay for day-to-day expenses. The demands of the baby make matters worse. Instead of the happy life they imagined, young couples may begin to feel trapped. Because of the resulting anxiety, conflict, and

perhaps hostility, many young working-class couples divorce. Others are forced to move back in with their parents, which leads to even more stress.

▲ *Variations in mate selection and marriage that are correlated with social class are discussed further in Chapter 2.*

Another characteristic of many working-class families is a severe split between masculine and feminine cultures. Working-class couples tend to be traditional in their perceptions of gender roles. Working-class wives—like upper-class wives—seem willing to grant legitimacy to their husbands' authority.

Communication between working-class husbands and wives regarding personal or emotional matters is difficult. In one comparative study, middle-class and working-class wives were asked what they valued most in their husbands. The middle-class subjects tended to focus on such issues as intimacy, sharing, communication, and the comforts and prestige that their husbands' occupations provided them. Working-class wives were more dismal in their assessments, focusing on the *absence* of such problems as unemployment, alcoholism, and violence. ▲ As one 33-year-old housewife put it, "I guess I can't complain. He's a steady worker; he doesn't drink; he doesn't hit me. That's a lot more than my mother had, and she didn't sit around complaining and feeling sorry for herself, so I sure haven't got the right" (Rubin, 1976, p. 93).

▲ *Chapter 6 explains the relationship between social class and other forms of inequality, gender and power within the family, and violence against spouses and children.*

Sociologist Lillian Rubin (1995) held in-depth interviews with working-class families to examine how the economic downturn of the 1980s and early 1990s had influenced their families and their dreams. The title of her book, *Families on the Fault Line,* suggests a precarious life on the edge of disaster. The families she studied aren't considered officially "poor." Nevertheless, the hope that sustained working-class people through bad times two decades ago—the belief that if they just worked hard and played by the rules, they'd eventually grab a piece of the American Dream—no longer existed. It's not so much the possibility of falling into poverty that worries them, it's the fear that there's no possibility of ever moving upward.

As a consequence of the harsh economic landscape, many working-class young people continue to need their parents' help well after becoming adults. Twenty years ago working-class women and men were significantly more likely than their middle-class counterparts to marry young and leave home. More affluent young people, in contrast, delayed marriage to attend college and enhance their employment prospects. Today, however, more and more working-class men and women in their 20s, 30s, and 40s are postponing leaving their parents' home or are returning after a period of absence. ▲

▲ *Chapter 8 provides more detailed information on the tendency of adult children to remain at home.*

To psychologically survive in a world of economic instability and powerlessness, many working-class parents begin to define their jobs as meaningless and irrelevant to their core identity. But instead of focusing on the dreariness or the insignificance of their work, they come to view it as a noble act of sacrifice. A bricklayer put it simply: "My job is to work for my family" (Sennett & Cobb, 1972, p. 135).

Defining a job as sacrifice solves the problem of powerlessness in two ways. First, in return for their sacrifice, working-class parents—especially men—can demand a position of power within their own families. Second, framing degrading work as sacrifice

allows them to slip the bonds of the disappointing present and orient their lives toward their children's and grandchildren's future, something that gives them a sense of control they can't get through their jobs.

Ironically, framing work as sacrifice causes other hidden injuries within the family. ▲ On the one hand, working-class parents want to spend time with their children and show concern for them. On the other hand, they know that the only way they can provide a "good home" for their family is to work longer hours at an unfulfilling job and be absent from home more frequently. Unfortunately, from the perspective of the child, this absence is precisely what constitutes a "bad home."

▲ *Other complexities of child rearing are discussed in Chapter 5.*

In addition, it is more difficult for working-class parents to sacrifice "successfully." Upper-class and middle-class parents make sacrifices so that their children will have a life *like* theirs. Working-class parents sacrifice so that their children will *not* have a life like theirs. Their lives are not a "model" but a "warning." Hence, the sacrifice does not end the conditions that made the parents prey to feelings of shame and inadequacy in the first place. The danger of this type of sacrifice is that if the children do fulfill the parents' wishes and rise above their quality of life, the parents may eventually become a burden or an embarrassment to them. Thus, people who struggle to make ends meet are caught in a vicious trap.

Downwardly Mobile Families

Another group of people whose families are affected by economic insecurities have somewhat different experiences than working-class families. These are the people who have fallen out of the middle class. Once successful, financially stable models of the "American

Dream," they have seen their jobs disappear or their salaries drastically reduced and have fallen hard.

A rapid reduction in income has far-reaching consequences. It often means moving to inferior housing and leaving behind familiar routines. It means drastically less money for recreation and leisure and more pressures due to inadequate time and finances. The sudden financial strain also causes social dislocation through the loss of familiar friendships and emotional support networks.

Women are particularly vulnerable to downward mobility. Some plunge when they or their partner lose a job. But for most women, the main cause of downward mobility is divorce. ▲ Handicapped by a gender-stratified labor market, divorced women rarely have an income equal to that of their former husbands. They are also hurt by a lack of affordable and high-quality child care services and by disproportionate responsibility for child rearing expenses. ▲ What divorced women do earn is thus often not adequate to support a family (Grella, 1990).

▲ *Chapter 7 examines the economic consequences of divorce for women.*

▲ *Child care issues are discussed in Chapter 5.*

Children are hard hit by downward mobility, too. Not only are their values and future plans threatened, but their perception of their parents is also affected. The parental authority that sprang from financial control disappears. A 15-year-old girl describes the sad transformation of the father she once idolized after he lost his job as a successful show business promoter:

> He just seemed to be getting irrational. He would walk around the house talking to himself and stay up all night, smoking cigarettes in the dark.... All I perceived

is that somebody who used to be a figure of strength was behaving strangely: starting to cry at odd times ... hanging around the house unshaven in his underwear when I would bring dates home.... In the absence of any understanding of what was going on, my attitude was one of anger and disgust, like "Why don't you get your act together? What's the matter with you?" (Newman, 1988, p. 96)

Some children of downwardly mobile families never escape the feeling that failure may be lurking around the corner: "The higher they climb, the more urgently they sense they are about to fall" (Newman, 1988, p. 142).

Poverty and Family Life

The economic woes of working-class or downwardly mobile families are difficult, but nowhere are the stresses of class stratification on family life more apparent than among the poorest of American families. Despair and insecurity are everyday features in families at the bottom of the class structure. Acquiring and keeping basic necessities—food, clothing, and shelter—are daily struggles. They face tremendous difficulty accomplishing the day-to-day tasks that most of us take for granted. Instead, their daily chores, and frustrations, might include

> having to take one's dirty clothing on the bus to the nearest laundromat with three children in tow; being unable to afford to go to the dentist even though the pain is excruciating; not purchasing a simple meal at a restaurant for fear it will disrupt the budget; never being able to go to a movie; having no credit, which in turn makes getting a future credit rating difficult; lacking a typewriter or personal computer on which to improve secretarial skills for a job interview. The list could go on and on. (Rank, 1994, p. 60)

Large supermarket chains rarely open stores in very poor neighborhoods because of security fears. Hence, residents who are without transportation must rely on small neighborhood grocery stores that charge higher prices for food than larger supermarkets do. Poor people may also pay more for winter utility bills because of the lack of insulation in poor-quality homes. Nearly half of poor working people in this country have no health insurance, meaning that any sustained illness can turn into a financial catastrophe (Kilborn, 1997c).

Growing up in poverty has been linked to a variety of problems in children, such as dropping out of school, low academic achievement, teen pregnancy and childbearing, poor mental and physical health, delinquent behavior and unemployment in adolescence and early adulthood (Harris & Marmer, 1996). In addition, the longer children live in poverty, the worse their cognitive, social, and emotional functioning.

Of course, not all poor children suffer from these conditions. ▲ Clearly the individual home environment can play an important role. Close, positive supervision and emotional support can actually improve social and emotional development, school performance, and self-worth even among the poorest children (Parcel & Menaghan, 1994).

▲ *Chapter 5 discusses social class and child rearing in more detail.*

But, in general, life on the edge of financial survival is dangerous. When nothing out of the ordinary happens, people are able to manage. But an unexpected event—a sickness, an injury, the breakdown of a major appliance or automobile—can set off a "domino effect" that imperils everything else. When such events occur, families must make difficult decisions. Imagine being a poor single mother with a sick child. One trip to the doctor might cost an entire week's food budget or a month of rent. Dental work or an

eye examination is easily sacrificed when other pressing bills need to be paid. If you depend on a car to get to work and it breaks down, a few hundred dollars to fix it might mean not paying the electric bill that month and having less money for other necessities.

One of the most painful choices facing poor households is sometimes called the "heat-or-eat" dilemma: having to choose between paying the heating bill and buying food. A 3-year study in a Boston hospital found that emergency room visits by malnourished children under the age of 6 increased 30 percent after the coldest months of the year. According to one of the researchers, "parents well know that children freeze before they starve, and in winter some families have to divert their already inadequate food budget to buy fuel to keep the children warm.... When we say, 'You have to buy more milk for Johnny,' they say, 'But I've got to pay the bills'" ("Study of poor children," 1992, p. A17).

The Debate over Welfare

In 1935 the federal government developed a social welfare system to help people in need—the aged, the poor, the unemployed, the disabled, and the sick. The system is actually divided into two segments. One segment consists of programs that provide benefits that are "earned" through employment: Social Security, disability insurance, unemployment insurance, worker's compensation, Medicare, and so on. Recipients in these programs are predominantly working and middle class, and, therefore, benefits are neither stigmatizing nor degrading. When it comes time for the budget cuts to be made, these programs are usually spared.

In contrast, the second segment of the welfare system consists primarily of aid to the poor. This second segment is most commonly associated with the term *welfare,* which is today the object of much hostility. When budgets need to be trimmed, these programs are typically the first to be affected. Entitlement programs for the poor constitute only about 23 percent of all federal entitlement programs but accounted for 93 percent of the entitlement budget cuts enacted by Congress in 1996 ("Harper's index," 1997).

Sixty years after its inception, no one is particularly happy with the nation's welfare system—not the social workers who must administer it, not the politicians who try to fix it, not the poor people themselves who must live under it, and not the working taxpayers who must support it (DiNitto & Dye, 1987). The American public has a deep, underlying fear that welfare for the poor contributes to the breakdown of family by encouraging families to dissolve, women to have more children, extended families to break apart, dependency to be handed down to future generations, single mothers not to marry, and so on. ▲ But the conclusion that welfare *causes* such problems is not supported by the social scientific evidence. For instance, if it were true that welfare *causes* or at least perpetuates poverty, you'd expect that increasing welfare payments would lower the incentive to work and lengthen the time it takes to escape poverty. Recent research, however, points out that higher welfare payments actually hasten the escape from poverty for some single-parent families (Butler, 1996). Even prior to recent reforms, which sharply limit the amount of time people can be on welfare, only 30 percent of recipients stayed on for more than 2 years and only 7 percent stayed on for more than 8 years (Gans, 1995).

▲ *Read Issue 8 for contrasting views on the causes and consequences of such trends.*

What about family breakdown? Welfare spending increased between 1960 and 1970 and decreased between 1972 and 1984, yet there were no accompanying changes in family-composition trends during these periods. For instance, the number of households headed by women increased steadily between 1968 and 1983, showing no fluctuation as a result of changes in welfare benefits (Baca Zinn, 1997). Furthermore, differences in welfare benefits from state to state don't produce corresponding differences in family breakdown. In fact, states with *higher* welfare benefits have lower rates of female-headed households and welfare participation (Darity & Meyers, 1984).

Does drawing welfare benefits encourage single women to have more babies? The common perception is that it does. However, the birthrate of women on welfare is actually considerably *lower* than that of the general population (Rank, 1994). In fact, the longer a woman remains on welfare, the less likely she is to give birth. The economic, social, and psychological situations in which women on welfare find themselves are not particularly conducive to desiring or having more children. Becoming pregnant and having a child are perceived as making the situation worse, not better, by making it more difficult to ultimately get off welfare—something most welfare recipients want. A study by the National Academy of Sciences found that the overwhelming majority of births to never-married women in general (70 percent) and to unmarried teenagers in particular (over 85 percent) were unintended (cited in Sandefur, 1996), suggesting that most welfare pregnancies are not based on conscious decisions to increase financial benefits.

Family Life on Welfare. The strain and stress of public assistance inevitably influence family relationships. Each benefit—housing subsidies, food stamps, Medicaid, and so on—comes with its own set of rules and regulations that must be followed if participants wish to remain eligible (Dujon et al., 1995). A welfare recipient can be removed from the rolls if she is found to be living with a man without being married to him. If welfare recipients fail to observe child care norms or are believed to use more physical punishment than social workers deem desirable, they can be charged with child neglect or abuse and lose their children to foster care (Gans, 1995).

To add insult to injury, welfare payments are usually not sufficient to cover ordinary family expenditures. A study of single mothers on welfare in four American cities (Boston, Chicago, Charleston, and San Antonio) found that welfare payments fall short of providing enough money to pay for household expenses by an average of $200 to $400 a month (Edin & Lein, 1996). The average maximum benefit amount for a family of three is less than $400 a month ("Tough love index," 1996). After covering all other expenses, one 51-year-old divorced mother of two teenage daughters had to provide food, toiletries, and clothing for her family on what amounted to $4 per person per day. She sums up her life:

> This is probably about the lowest point in my life, and I hope I never reach it again. Because this is where you're just up against a wall. You can't make a move. You can't buy anything that you want for your home. You can't go on a vacation. You can't take a weekend off and go and see things because it costs too much. And it's just such a waste of a life. (quoted in Rank, 1994, p. 52)

Contrary to the popular image that welfare parents are neglectful of their children, many of the fifty people that sociologist Mark Rank (1994) studied spoke fondly of the way their children have enriched their lives and the pride they take in their children's accomplishments, their worries about their children's well-being, and their efforts to do what is best for them. They try to teach their children the importance of education as a means of becoming independent so they won't have to rely on public assistance when they become adults. Of course, most of the parents Rank interviewed felt a tremendous amount of frustration over not being able to meet their children's physical, social, and educational needs.

Clearly, trying to lead a "normal life" while on welfare is extremely difficult. Recipients often have to depend on family and friends, boyfriends, or absent fathers to help make ends meet. Some cut back on their own food intake so they can buy shoes for their children; others hire professional shoplifters to get coats so their children can go to school in the winter (DeParle, 1997a). One study of fifty welfare mothers in Chicago found that all of them supplemented their welfare checks fraudulently, with either under-the-table work or money from friends and relatives, and none reported this income to the welfare office as they are required to do (Edin & Jencks, 1992). As one such welfare recipient put it, "We weren't trying to beat the system. We were just trying to make it" (quoted in Penner, 1995, p. 11). The irony of these practices, of course, is that contrary to popular stereotypes, women on welfare are not isolated from the world of work. They're often already working but not earning enough to survive.

So it's not that people on welfare don't want to work. It's that the available jobs often pay too little, demand too much, and offer few opportunities for advancement (Oliker, 1995). ▲ What's more, the costs of *going* to work—for transportation, clothes, and above all child care—are so high that the income of a poor single mother who works full-time is likely to be the same as or less than the income of a mother on welfare (Edin & Lein, 1996).

▲ *Women at the lower end of the occupational scale are especially likely to be shunted into low-paying "female ghettos," as Chapter 3 explains.*

Work income is also less stable than welfare income—employers who offer low-wage jobs can seldom guarantee their workers full-time hours. Furthermore, these jobs are often incompatible with parenting. Workers must leave their children in care that may be untrustworthy. ▲ Since these jobs rarely offer sick leave or paid vacation days, it is next to impossible to take time off to care for sick children who can't go to school.

▲ *The child care system in this country is discussed in Chapter 5.*

Although the road to gainful employment is littered with obstacles, most welfare recipients have worked in the past and want to work in the future. They recognize the stigma that their friends, their community, and the larger society imposes on welfare recipients, and they anticipate a boost in self-esteem and social standing from working.

Welfare Reform. In 1996 President Clinton signed into law an unprecedented welfare-reform bill designed to reduce poor people's reliance on government aid and "end welfare as we know it." The new welfare system includes a mandatory work requirement, dubbed "workfare," after 2 years of receiving assistance (or enrollment in vocational training or community service), a 5-year lifetime limit on benefits for any family, a transformation of welfare from an entitlement to a "block grant" that each state decides how to spend, a massive reduction in food stamps, and other cuts that concentrate on legal immigrants, the disabled, and the elderly poor (McCrate & Smith, 1998; Shalala, 1996). The law also requires states to provide child care and health care for working mothers, but doesn't specify how long states must offer such support to each recipient (Harris, 1996a). This new system is expected to reduce government spending by $54 billion over 6 years.

The assumption behind welfare reform is that making work mandatory will teach welfare recipients important work values and habits, make poor single mothers models of these values for their children, and cut the nation's welfare rolls. Hard work will lead to the moral and financial rewards of family self-reliance. It will cure poverty and welfare dependence and ensure that new generations of children from single-parent families will be able to enter the American mainstream.

However, the current welfare system can work only if there are viable employment opportunities for people on welfare and if those opportunities provide a sufficient wage to lift them out of poverty (McCrate & Smith, 1998). Many studies of state-run welfare-to-work programs show little or no change at all in unemployment rates and only small increases in earnings, which are due primarily to working longer hours, not earning higher wages (Oliker, 1995). One study found that people in workfare programs started out at very low wages and increased their salaries by only an average of 6 cents an hour every year (cited in Sexton, 1997). More than half of the women who leave the welfare rolls when they can support themselves with jobs eventually return to welfare because their jobs end or because they aren't earning enough to make ends meet (Harris, 1996b).

Welfare reform has also had some unforeseen consequences. For instance, although across the country thousands of former welfare recipients are going to work, for the most part, they're not entering new jobs created for them, as President Clinton had envisioned when he signed the reform bill into law. Instead, many of them are taking over jobs previously occupied by regular employees. Each state is required to meet annual workfare quotas or risk losing some of its federal money for welfare. So there is pressure upon employers to hire workfare participants. Furthermore, employers are able to pay workfare participants lower wages than they would pay to regular employees because they are partially subsidized by the government. In Baltimore, for example, several school districts hired welfare recipients at $1.50 an hour rather than renew contracts with agencies that supplied cleaning people at $6 an hour (Uchitelle, 1997).

How do workfare programs influence the personal lives and parenting strategies of the poor single mothers involved in them? Sociologist Stacey Oliker (1995) observed several state-run workfare programs and interviewed both participants and providers over a 5-year period. Even though program leaders encouraged the women to "go for it" and find the kinds of jobs they would enjoy, all of the women interviewed found only low-wage work as cashiers, clerks, kitchen workers, nurse's aides, home health aides, waitpersons, baby-sitters, and factory assemblers. Most of them initially were strongly oriented toward improving the financial well-being of their children and were willing to work long hours and be away from home to do so. Hence, they saw the shift from welfare to work as a positive change in their lives. But forced to choose between *insufficient* work and *insufficient* family care, many chose to emphasize caregiving and stopped working.

Interestingly, the women Oliker interviewed spoke of their moral duty to be home with their children in the same way that affluent mothers speak of their role in the upbringing of their children. However, their accounts focused not on the general notion that mothers ought to play a dominant role in enforcing high standards of behavior and maintaining class standing, but on the concrete importance of protecting their children's well-being in a threatening environment. In fact, the leaders of the workfare programs that Oliker studied reported that many women dropped out of the program shortly after being victims of or witnesses to burglaries or assaults, when concerns over their children's safety became most urgent.

It's still too early to tell what the effects of welfare reform will be. Many critics doubt that the majority of previous welfare recipients will be able to support their families on the low wages they are able to earn. But there is some positive news. The economic prosperity of the late 1990s has meant that fewer people are in need of welfare. Since the welfare reform law went into effect, 2.2 million people have dropped from the rolls (Pear, 1998). Some states are taking the money they're saving and are spending it on transportation, job placement, and programs that let welfare recipients keep more of their benefits even while earning paychecks (DeParle, 1997b). Some states are paying women—often welfare recipients themselves—to set up family day care centers in their homes. In allowing women to earn a living by caring for the children of others, the states both create jobs for welfare mothers and pave the way for the mothers of the children they care for to go to work (Kilborn, 1997b).

Poverty and Housing

It is hard to overestimate the importance of safe, decent, affordable housing in the lives of families. It keeps children in school and adults on the job. It allows upwardly mobile families to save money so they can someday buy a house of their own and keeps downwardly mobile families from having to turn to foster care or homeless shelters (DeParle, 1996). The cost of housing breaks the budgets of low-income families or crowds them into unsafe, dilapidated, and sometimes violent ghettos, which are usually some distance from good schools and good jobs.

Despite the critical importance of good housing to family life, President Clinton signed a housing appropriations bill in 1996 which essentially cut off government rent subsidies. Coincidentally, at the same time, a government report noted that 5 million needy families now pay more than half of their pretax income on housing, meaning that other necessities, like food, are probably being crowded out. (Incidentally, the government defines housing as "affordable" if rent and utilities cost no more than 30 percent of a household's income.) By comparison, the average middle-class home owner spends only 23 percent of his or her after-tax income on house payments.

Unstable housing is particularly hard on children. Poor children whose families do not receive government rent subsidies are more likely to be malnourished and underweight than other children. Some poor families are displaced so often that their children attend half a dozen schools in a single year. The head of foster care in the District of Columbia estimates that as many as half the city's foster children could be reunited with their parents if their families had stable housing (cited in DeParle, 1996).

In 1997 Congress placed further disadvantages on the poorest Americans by passing a bill which cut the number of government-subsidized housing units available to very poor families and increased the number available to "working poor"—those earning up to 80 percent of the median income in a particular area (Alvarez, 1997; Pader, 1997). Supporters of the bill argued that raising the proportion of tenants with jobs would improve the social environment in most housing projects. If tenants are able to pay more rent, local housing authorities could afford to better maintain the buildings. Furthermore, the mixing of working and unemployed people would provide needed role models to children in public housing. Others, however, worry that these changes will shut the poorest people out of the only housing they can afford, thereby forcing them to "double up" with relatives or, worse yet, forcing them out into the streets.

Homeless Families

When we think of homelessness, most of us conjure up images of single, isolated individuals, cut off from any and all family relationships, drinking cheap wine out of a paper bag and begging for money from passersby.

In truth, however, the majority of homeless people are married and unmarried couples, single mothers and their children, and intact families (Seltser & Miller, 1993). Families with children, constituting about 43 percent of the entire homeless population, now represent the fastest-growing segment of the homeless (cited in Anderson & Koblinsky, 1995). Ninety percent of homeless families with children are female-headed households, and three-quarters of these families are members of racial and ethnic minority groups (Kondratas, 1991).

In addition to the "official" homeless, countless thousands of other families are one catastrophe away from homelessness—one fire, one broken water pipe, one collapsed roof, one injury, or one job loss. And the families living doubled or tripled up with strained relatives or friends in cramped apartments are always an argument, fight, or ill-conceived comment away from being kicked back out to the streets.

Many families become homeless because of a specific crisis, like the loss of a job, divorce or desertion, or loss of a house due to fire, flood, or some other catastrophe. Others become homeless when a mother takes her children and moves out of an abusive relationship. ▲ What they all have in common, though, is that their move into homelessness is less of a fall than a sidestep. These are families already living on the edge of survival. Most homeless families are poor well before they become homeless, often living month-to-month until they can no longer sustain a residence.

▲ *Poor women in abusive relationships have few options, as Chapter 6 explains.*

Homeless parents must deal with a double crisis: They must deal with the disruptive and traumatizing effects of losing a home while acknowledging that their capacity to provide protection and support and to respond to their children's needs has been eroded. Studies of homeless parents living in shelters have found that most of them feel that living in the shelter seriously hurts their children. The loss of privacy that comes from parenting in public erodes a parent's confidence, not to mention his or her relationship with the children. In shelters that are noisy, chaotic, and stressful, there is a lot of wasted time, unsupervised activity, and little opportunity to establish a family routine. One observer described the shelter experience as divided into "time that is mealtime and time that is not mealtime" (quoted in Hausman & Hammen, 1993, p. 360). However, in those shelters that are small, quiet, and orderly, there can be a lot of nurturing, safety, and support, making effective parenting less difficult.

Whatever the condition, when parenting is visible and public, it becomes open to criticism, particularly in the emotionally fragile environment of a homeless shelter. ▲ Conflict between mothers is a common characteristic of most homeless shelters (Hausman & Hammen, 1993). Mothers may begin to distance themselves from the unruly behaviors of their children in an attempt to avoid blame from other adults. Under such conditions, parents, and ultimately children, can become irritable and demoralized.

▲ *Issue 3 examines the relationship between social class and family privacy.*

Homeless families tend to lack the emotional resources that might be drawn upon in bad times (Bassuk, Rubin, & Lauriat, 1986). Indeed, a lifetime of disappointing, harmful, and traumatic experiences has taught many homeless mothers to be suspicious of everyone—strangers, acquaintances, and relatives—and reluctant to trust anyone, particularly with the care of children (Browne, 1993). Such isolation contributes to the lonely strain of homelessness and interferes with healthy parent-child relationships.

The result of all this is that homeless children suffer higher rates of depression, anxiety, behavioral problems, and academic difficulties than other children. In a comparative study of homeless and housed children, researchers estimate that half of all homeless children demonstrate at least one developmental problem (maladaptive behavior, academic deficiency, emotional problems, and so on), compared to 16 percent of housed children (Rafferty & Rollins, 1989). Not surprisingly, many homeless children either are not enrolled in school or attend sporadically. A few children are able to succeed despite their desperate conditions. But the vast majority of homeless children will suffer well into their adulthood.

Something to Think About

Economic factors—from the amount of money coming in to the day-to-day management of finances and major purchasing decisions—are involved in virtually every aspect of family life. When a family doesn't know how it will pay this month's rent or where its next meal is coming from or whether there will be a warm place to sleep that night, that family will have a difficult time being comfortable, happy, and satisfied. When economic foundations are weak, the emotional bonds that tie a family together can easily crumble.

1. In what way would your life be different if you had been born into a different social class? What might your childhood have been like? What type and amount of education would you have received? What would your occupational opportunities be like? How would your personality and outlook on life be different? What would your family look like?

2. Do you think that a more equal distribution of wealth in society is possible? If so, how could such a redistribution be accomplished? Do you think it alone would be enough to help impoverished families?

3. What social policy do you think would be the most effective way to help poor families? How do you think recent welfare reform will ultimately affect families?

ISSUE 8

Is the Institution of Family Breaking Down— and Society with It?

The Family Decline Perspective

The Family Transformation Perspective

Examining Cross-Cultural Evidence of Family Decline

SOMETHING TO THINK ABOUT

On May 19, 1992, then Vice President Dan Quayle gave a speech at the Commonwealth Club in San Francisco, California. Although the speech began as an assessment of United States–Japan relations and trade, it quickly turned to the Los Angeles riots, which had occurred about $2^1/_2$ weeks earlier following the verdict in the Rodney King case. In trying to make sense out of the violence many of us had witnessed on television, the vice president minced no words. He placed blame for the riots squarely at the doorstep of troubled families:

> I believe the lawless social anarchy which we saw is directly related to the breakdown of family structure, personal responsibility, and social order in too many areas of our society. For the poor the situation is compounded by a welfare ethos that impedes individual efforts to move ahead in society.... The failure of our families is hurting America deeply. When families fail, society fails. The ... lack of structure in our inner cities [is] testament to how quickly civilization falls apart when the family foundation cracks. Children need love and discipline. They need mothers and fathers. A welfare check is not a husband. The state is not a father. It is from parents that children learn how to behave in society; it is from parents above all that children come to understand values and themselves as men and women, mothers and fathers. And for those concerned about children growing up in poverty, we should know this: marriage is probably the best anti-poverty program of all.... Where there are no mature, responsible men around to teach boys how to be good men, gangs serve in their place.... Marriage is a moral issue that requires cultural consensus, and the use of social sanctions. Bearing babies irresponsibly is, simply, wrong. Failing to support children one

has fathered is wrong.... It doesn't help matters when prime time TV has Murphy Brown—a character who supposedly epitomizes today's intelligent, highly paid, professional woman—mocking the importance of fathers by bearing a child alone, and calling it just another "lifestyle choice." ... It's time to talk again about family, hard work, integrity and personal responsibility. We cannot be embarrassed out of our belief that two parents, married to each other, are better in most cases for children than one. (Quayle, 1992, pp. 517–519)

Quayle's speech was highly controversial at the time, but it echoed a concern held by many Americans: "Alarming" trends and changes in the family have robbed it of its traditional influence over people's everyday lives and its importance as a vital societal institution. The result is a fraying of America's social fiber symbolized by disturbing media stories about violent crime, school shootings, drugs, poverty, homelessness, and so forth. Journalists, politicians, and social commentators use the rhetoric of "moral panic" (Stacey, 1996a)—words like *endangered, vulnerable, dying, disappearing, declining,* and *doomed*—to assess the current health and future prospects of American families.

As popular as these sentiments seem to be, not everyone agrees that families are in such dire straits. Some scholars argue that as an institution, the family is as strong as ever. Consider its ability to change form and process in response to shifting economic, political, and cultural forces. Although today's families may bear little resemblance to the traditional families of our nostalgic past, they still work for the most part and hence are here to stay. ▲

▲ *Issue 2 provides a detailed examination historical images of family.*

Who's right? Is the institution of family weak and on the verge of collapse, or is it strong in its ability to adapt to changing social circumstances? Does family "breakdown" cause the problems that plague society today, or is it a consequence of those problems? My purpose in this section is to examine the current state of American families and attempt to assess just how much trouble they are in.

The Family Decline Perspective

In the United States and other Western societies, there has been a strong movement in recent years toward more diverse family arrangements. The result, many believe, is an erosion in the family's overall importance as a social institution. They support what we can call the *family decline perspective*. Over time, they argue, the institution of family has lost many, if not all, of its traditional functions (Lasch, 1977).

The Declining Influence of Family

Historically, the family has been the center of many important activities. ▲ It is in the family that children have received most of their education and religious training; that both children and adults could expect emotional nurturing and support; and that sexual activity and reproduction have been regulated. And the family has also been the economic center of society, where family members worked together to earn a living and support one another financially.

▲ *For more on the history of American family life, read Issue 2.*

But as our economy has shifted so has the role of the family. ▲ When economic production moved from the home to the factory, the teaching of skills and values that were once a part of everyday home life began to take place in schools. A large part of the his-

tory of childhood and adolescence in the twentieth century has been a steady decline of parental authority and influence and an accompanying increase in the influence of peer groups and the mass media.

▲ *Chapter 3 provides a detailed discussion of historical changes in the economics of family life.*

Families have also lost much of their ability to regulate the sexual behavior of members, as witnessed by high rates of premarital and extramarital sex. ▲ And more recently, the family's role as a source of emotional security and nurturing has disappeared as it has become less able to shield its members from the harsh realities of modern life (Lasch, 1977). The absenteeism rate of fathers, the decline in the amount of time parents spend with their children, and the increasing proportion of a child's life spent alone, with peers, or in day care attest to the loss of this function (Popenoe, 1993).

▲ *Sexuality is discussed in greater detail in Chapter 2 and, in regard to adolescents, in Chapter 5.*

The strength (or weakness) of family as an institution is seen not just in how well (or poorly) it performs important social functions but in the hold it has over its individual members. Strong families are those that maintain close coordination over the relationships between members and direct their activities toward collective goals. But today individuals have become increasingly more autonomous, less bound by their family, and less committed to its norms and values (Popenoe, 1993). Those who maintain that the family is in steep decline cite the steady erosion of the belief in mutual assistance among family members, of a strong sense of family loyalty, of concern for the perpetuation of the family as a unit, and of the subordination of individual interests to the interests and welfare of the family as a group (Popenoe, 1993). ▲

▲ *Issue 4 examines the conflict between individual interests and family obligation.*

The past several decades have also seen a dramatic and pervasive weakening of the normative imperative to marry, to remain married, to have children, to restrict intimate relations to marriage, and to maintain separate roles for males and females. The result has been a loosening of the controls that traditionally maintained family and social structure. The transition from singlehood to marriage no longer carries the strong sense of obligation and commitment it once did. The blurring of rights and duties has destroyed the boundaries among childhood, adolescence, adulthood, and old age; between parents and children; between male and female; and so on (Farber, 1987).

Social Change and Family Structure

In addition to believing that the family is weakening as a social institution, those who ascribe to the family decline perspective note that its fundamental form—the nuclear family—is becoming less common. Family structure in modern industrialized societies has indeed undergone greater change, and at a more accelerated rate, in the past several decades than in any previous period of human history (Popenoe, 1988, 1993). According to a report by the Population Council, similar trends are occurring worldwide (Lewin, 1995a). For instance, in many industrialized countries (such as Canada, France, the United States, and Denmark) divorce rates doubled between 1970 and the mid-1980s and have remained high. In less-developed countries, about 25 percent of first marriages end by the time women are in their 40s.

Likewise, unwed motherhood is increasing everywhere. In northern Europe, for example, as many as a third of all births occur to unwed mothers. Mothers worldwide are carrying increasing economic responsibility for their children, too. Nor, according to the report, do fathers in any society provide as much child care as mothers and in very few societies do fathers have regular, close relationships with their children.

We should note that since the beginning of recorded history, family has always been changing. But, according to family decline theorists, recent changes—beginning in the 1960s—have been unique and much more serious. ▲

▲ *The accuracy of our images of what family life should be is assessed in Issue 2.*

The Shrinking American Family. One of the chief concerns of the family decline perspective is the shrinking size of American families. In the 1950s the average American woman had 3.7 children over the span of her life. By the early 1990s, that figure had dropped to a little less than 2.0, where it remains today (Popenoe, 1993).

Why are people having fewer children? Certainly economic pressures have forced many married couples to limit the number of children they produce. But equally important are changes in the timing of marriage and childbearing. Increasing numbers of women are getting married later and delaying childbearing until after they've graduated from college and established careers. When couples wait to marry and begin childbearing, the number of children they eventually have is inevitably reduced.

In addition to having fewer children, more and more married couples are choosing not to have children at all. Whereas nearly half of American households contained children in 1970, just over a third did in 1995 (De Vita, 1996).

Changes in the size of American families have been accompanied by what some see as a troubling decrease in positive attitudes toward parenthood. Although a majority of American teenagers expect to become parents when they get older (Goldscheider & Waite, 1991), adults are becoming less enamored with the thought of having children. When asked to name the two or three most enjoyable things about being a woman, 53 percent of respondents in 1970 answered "being a mother, raising a family"; in 1983 only 26 percent chose that response (Dowd, 1983, p. 66). Between 1962 and 1980, the proportion of American mothers who stated that all couples should have children declined from 84 to 43 percent (Thornton, 1989). Such figures seem to show that childlessness is more acceptable than it once was. ▲

▲ *Voluntary childlessness is discussed further in Chapter 4.*

A reduction in the size of families is not proof, in and of itself, of family decline. Strength is not always in numbers. But shrinking families can be problematic. The American fertility rate is currently below the level necessary to replace the current population in the next generation. In parts of Western Europe and Scandinavia the deficit is even greater (Goldscheider & Waite, 1991). In Italy, which has the world's lowest fertility rate, alarmed government officials are looking for ways to make it easier for women to have careers and children simultaneously. Furthermore, some fear that smaller families may make children a lower priority politically and less important in the overall scheme of life (Popenoe, 1993).

A decrease in the number of children being born has long-term consequences for individual families as well, especially in their ability to care for needy members. The past several decades have witnessed a dramatic shift in the age structure of American society. More people are living into their 80s and 90s than ever before. Hence, families are expanding *vertically* (more generations living per family) at the same time they're shrinking

horizontally (fewer individuals per generation). The consequence may be a shortage of family members to share in caring for elderly parents in the future (Sherman, Ward, & LaGory, 1988). With few or no siblings to help them, many people—particularly women—in their 40s, 50s, and even 60s will have to cope with the burden of caring for elderly parents on their own in addition to the usual demands of work and family, adding further strain to family relationships. ▲

▲ *Gender and ethnic differences in the obligation to care for elderly parents are discussed in Chapter 8.*

Changing Marital Roles. Other changes having a powerful impact on family are those breaking down the traditional separation between male and female family roles (Goldscheider & Waite, 1991). ▲ In the past several decades, the women's movement has encouraged large numbers of women to reject the idea that motherhood and family are their primary destiny and to strive for success, independence, and occupational achievement (Nock, 1987). Today mothers participate in the labor force as much as nonmothers. In fact, the fastest increase in female labor force participation has been among mothers of children under the age of 2 (U.S. Bureau of the Census, 1997a).

▲ *The interplay of gender, work, and family life is discussed in Chapter 3.*

Similar changes in the gender-based division of labor are occurring worldwide. In the Philippines, for instance, a country that retains many traditional views on gender, women contribute 55 percent of the household finances (Lewin, 1995b). Although the reasons for entering the labor force vary from country to country and from family to family within the same country, women worldwide are finding that in order to provide their children an adequate life they must earn more money (Lewin, 1995b). In short, women are contributing more to the economic well-being of their families than ever before.

To those who feel the institution of family is in decline, such a change is cause for alarm. With more women entering the paid labor force, wives are becoming less dependent on their husbands for economic support. Indeed, the higher a wife's income relative to her husband's, the greater the likelihood of separation or divorce (Cherlin, 1992). Furthermore, families in which both parents work can experience serious internal conflict over the balance between work and family responsibilities. ▲ Many working women have come to expect complete equality in their relationships and therefore feel disillusioned when they face the day-to-day task of juggling household chores, child care and spousal responsibilities, and career. Given these forces, the concern is that husbands and children will cease being the most important part of women's lives and that the family will relinquish even more of its nurturing functions to day care centers and others outside the family.

▲ *See Chapter 3 for more detail on the relationship between work and family.*

Some observers see a link between a lack of parental presence at home and rising rates of teenage suicide, growing juvenile arrest rates, more and earlier drug use and sexual activity, and falling SAT scores. According to one developmental psychologist, early and extended day care for children constitutes a "risk factor" for the development of insecure infant-parent attachments and contributes to the development of aggressiveness and noncompliance (Belsky, 1988). Another researcher has found that so-called latchkey children—those who are unsupervised by adults after school is out for the day—suffer from heightened rates of psychological dis-

turbance, delinquency, and drug use (Galambos & Maggs, 1991).

Burgeoning Divorce Rates. For most of the history of human civilization, the death of a parent was the most common form of family disruption. Separation and divorce were kept rare by social, religious, and legal restrictions. But separation and divorce have become increasingly common experiences for American families. Consequently, a growing number of children are experiencing a significant period without one parent (usually the father) present. In 1960, 9 percent of children under 18 lived with a single parent; by 1994, the figure had increased to 31 percent. The rate is even higher for African-American children (around 65 percent) and Hispanic children (36 percent) (U.S. Bureau of the Census, 1995).

The causes of the high divorce rate include things like the weakening of the family's traditional economic bonds, higher expectations for marriage, a reduction in the influence of religion, and the stress of shifting gender roles (Popenoe, 1993). ▲ Moreover, divorce tends to feed upon itself. The more normal it becomes, the less stigmatizing it is.

▲ *Chapter 7 examines the causes and consequences of divorce.*

Although divorce can be traumatic for adults, most recover and are able to get on with their lives after a while. Children, however, have a more difficult time adjusting. For them, divorce sets a series of changes in motion, each with the potential to disrupt their lives. They may have to move to a new home in a new neighborhood, make new friends, and go to a new school. Because the overwhelming majority of divorced children live with their mothers, their standard of living may also decline because of the lower earning capacity of women and the all-too-common failure of noncustodial fathers to pay child support.

In addition, the relationship children have with their noncustodial parent diminishes over time. One study found that only 40 percent of children living with their mothers had seen their fathers in the past month. Thirty-five percent of them hadn't seen their fathers in over 5 years (cited in Brody, 1991). To some sociologists, the disappearance of fathers is one of the most serious changes that has taken place in American families (White, 1987). Children who grow up in divorced, fatherless households are more likely than other children to:

- Earn poorer grades in school and perform worse on standardized tests
- Be absent from school
- Drop out of school
- Commit violent crime and engage in drug and alcohol abuse
- Be victims of child abuse and neglect
- Suffer from eating disorders and depression
- Be poor and, when they reach adulthood, have lower earnings
- Marry early, have children early, and divorce (McLanahan & Booth, 1991; Popenoe, 1996).

From the family decline perspective, the high divorce rate doesn't affect only divorced couples and their children, it affects the institution of family as well. Once considered an event to be avoided unless absolutely necessary, marital separation has come to be seen as morally neutral or even positive in some cases. Few people today feel that a couple in a troubled marriage should stay together "for the sake of the children" (Adelson, 1996). Given these prevailing societal attitudes, couples have increasing difficulty committing themselves wholeheartedly to their marriage. As a result, many couples take protective steps, such as prenuptial agreements, that may undermine the quality of the relationship and predispose it to failure (Gill, 1991). Not surprisingly, there has been a steady erosion of the expectation that marriage is permanent. Furthermore, children of divorce may grow up expecting that their own future marriages will not last. A high divorce rate, therefore, can have cumulative and long-lasting effects on the cultural perceptions of marriage.

The "Flight" from Marriage. Traditionally, marriage has been perceived as a *social obligation*—a relationship designed to promote economic security and procreation. But today people are likely to see marriage as a path toward self-fulfillment. ▲ Hence, it has become a voluntary relationship that people can make or break at will (Popenoe, 1993). Even for couples who don't end up divorcing, marital quality has taken a turn for the worse. An increasing proportion of people who have never married report being happy, while a decreasing proportion of married people report being happy (Glenn & Weaver, 1988).

▲ *Issue 4 examines the tension between self-fulfillment and family responsibility.*

The last several decades have witnessed a dramatic increase in nonmarital cohabitation. In 1960 the United States had 439,000 cohabiting couples, representing 1.1 percent of the total of married and cohabiting couples. In 1993 there were 3.5 million such couples, constituting over 6 percent of all couples (Farley, 1996). In the past, cohabiting couples were likely to be poor people who couldn't afford to get married. Today, cohabiting couples come from all classes and all age, ethnic, and racial groups. Interestingly, the largest increase in cohabiting couples is not among young people in their 20s but among people over 35 (Steinhauer, 1995).

Social policies may be motivating many people's decision to "live together" rather than marry (Martin, 1996). For instance, marriage reduces welfare eligibility. Also, the standard tax deduction is often lower for working married couples than for two singles.

Despite its growing popularity, cohabitation has some built-in difficulties. For one thing, it lacks the predictability, normative expectations, cultural support, and social recognition that marriage has. This lack of institutionalization may explain why cohabitors express lower levels of commitment to their relationships, report lower levels of happiness, and have poorer relationships with parents compared to married individuals (Nock, 1995). Some research shows that people who cohabit prior to marriage actually have higher divorce rates—regardless of whether they marry their cohabiting partner or somebody else—than people who don't cohabit before marriage (DeMaris & Rao, 1992).

Another sign of the reduced importance of marriage in people's lives is the increasing number of women who are bearing children while unmarried (Cherlin, 1992). The proportion of out-of-wedlock births increased from 38 per 1,000 in 1940 to 310 per 1,000 in 1993 (Hollander, 1996).

Contrary to popular belief, these single mothers aren't just teenagers. Only 30 percent of out-of-wedlock births occur to women under the age of 20 (Dornbusch, Herman, & Lin, 1996). In fact, between 1980 and 1993, births to teenage mothers as a percentage of all births actually decreased, from 15.6 percent to 12.8 percent (U.S. Bureau of the Census, 1996). And over the past 5 years, the teenage birth rate has decreased substantially for all racial groups (Lewin, 1998c).

At the same time there has been a dramatic increase in the number of older, never-married single mothers (Gringlas & Weinraub, 1995). Between 1982 and 1992, the birthrate doubled among never-married, college-educated women and almost tripled among never-married women who work in a

professional or managerial capacity (Siegel, 1995). Like married mothers, these women accept motherhood as a fundamental part of their womanhood. However, they don't feel the need to become a spouse in order to become a parent.

This so-called flight from marriage is troubling to family decline theorists because they feel that marriage provides people—and ultimately the larger society—with significant benefits. For instance, there is some evidence to suggest that married individuals—especially men—are physically healthier, live longer, show higher rates of overall satisfaction, and have more money than single or cohabiting individuals (Waite, 1995). Hence, they fear that a decline in marriage rates will create an overall drop in people's well-being.

The Family Transformation Perspective

These trends are understandably cause for concern. But many social scientists oppose the notion that the institution of family is in steep, perhaps irreversible, decline. They disagree that a family's structure is more important than the relationships and processes that take place within it. So, for instance, parental supervision, control, involvement, and sensitivity to the needs of children are better predictors of a child's well-being than whether the child lives with one parent or two, whether the child's mother works or not, or whether the parents are biological parents or stepparents (Acock & Demo, 1994). In addition, by accepting the notion that the idealized, "traditional" family is something to be preserved, the family decline perspective misses the crucial sociological point that historical changes influence family structures and create new arrangements.

This perspective, what we'll call the *family transformation perspective*, maintains that the family—both as a living arrangement and as a social institution—is not disappearing at all but instead is becoming more diverse and complex as it adapts to changing social circumstances (Kain, 1990). ▲ Although changes in work, family, and sexual opportunities for men and women can create significant instability and uncertainty in people's lives, these changes also have the potential of introducing greater democracy, equality, and choice into our family relationships (Stacey, 1996a). In short, just because many families today aren't "traditional" in form doesn't mean that the institution of family itself is disappearing or in some sort of danger.

▲ *For more on transformations in family structure, read Issue 2 and Chapter 9.*

Supporters of the family transformation perspective ask us to rethink our traditional ideas about what family is or should be (Sjoberg, Williams, Gill, & Himmel, 1995; Stacey, 1994). "Nontraditional" family forms like dual-earner families, childless couples, single-parent families, and heterosexual and homosexual cohabiting couples are viable alternatives. The difficulties that all families face today may be as much a matter of rapid demographic, economic, and political change as a matter of family decline, more a failure of social policy than a failure of individual families (Elkind, 1994).

Those who support the notion of family transformation also take issue with the argument that the collapse of the traditional family is the prime cause of social decay. They believe that the losses in real earnings and high-paying jobs due to the decline in industrial manufacturing, the persistence of low-wage work for women, and global restructuring which exports jobs to other countries, have wreaked far more havoc on families and on society than the effects of feminism, sexual revolution, divorce, cohabitation, and

individualism. When significant economic changes take place, it's inevitable that families will feel their effects. ▲

▲ *Issue 7 provides more detail on how economic status affects family life.*

For instance, because of corporate restructuring, the average wage for full-time male workers dropped from $34,048 in 1973 to $30,407 in 1993 (in constant dollars). About a third of all American men between the ages of 25 and 34 don't earn enough today to keep a family of four out of poverty (Thurow, 1995). In addition, many contemporary economists say that we as a nation must "tolerate" a certain amount of unemployment to boost productivity, cut costs, and ultimately sustain a viable national economy (see Lekachman, 1991). Although this policy may make good economic sense, it says nothing about the lives of those people who lose their jobs and are without sufficient income to support their families.

At the global level, the competitive pressures of the international capitalist marketplace have forced many businesses and industries to make greater use of so-called disposable workers—those who work part-time or on temporary contract—in order to maintain profits. These jobs offer no benefits and no security and therefore import instability directly into family life (Kilborn, 1993; Uchitelle, 1993).

In short, the belief that we just need to return to the good old nuclear family and everything will be fine allows the public and the government to avoid responsibility for intervening in destitute neighborhoods, creating affordable housing, ensuring that all young people have access to quality education, and creating needed jobs. Focusing on the personal and moral failings of individuals as the source of family and social problems hinders the discussion of improvements that could be made in other social institutions to alleviate the current strains on family life. ▲ As a society, we have two choices, according to family transformation theorists:

> We can come to grips with the [contemporary] family condition by accepting the end of a singular ideal family and begin to promote better living and spiritual conditions for the diverse array of real families we actually inhabit and desire. Or we can continue to engage in denial, resistance, displacement, and bad faith, by cleaving to a moralistic ideology of *the family* at the same time that we fail to provide social and economic conditions that make life for the modern family or any other kind of family viable, let alone dignified and secure. (Stacey, 1996a, p. 11)

▲ *Family policy is discussed in more detail in Chapter 9.*

Rebutting the Notion of Family Decline

The statistics on family problems are very compelling. But is it possible that a high divorce rate, falling marriage rate, shrinking family size, and so on are not as harmful as the family decline perspective leads us to believe? Let's take another look at the evidence.

Marriage and Divorce.   Although family expectations have shifted somewhat over the past three decades, overall our feelings about intimacy and family seem to be quite stable. The majority of Americans still want the love, affection, companionship, and emotional security that go with long-term relationships. ▲ And most Americans who marry are still committed to the idea of having healthy and happy children (Barich & Bielby, 1996). ▲ The stability of these feelings suggests that

our family expectations are highly institutionalized and embedded in the culture.

▲ *Chapter 2 demonstrates the persistence of interest in intimate relationships and explains their development.*

▲ *Cultural attitudes toward childbearing are discussed in Chapter 4.*

For instance, even though cohabitation has become more popular in recent years, it does not threaten marriage. Most cohabiting relationships either end or move into legal marriage within a few years (Macklin, 1980). Hence, the most notable effect of cohabitation is that it delays marriage for people who live together first. Also, the older people are prior to marriage, the less likely they are to divorce, so cohabitation, for some, may actually have a stabilizing effect on marriage.

What about divorce? Divorce undeniably creates serious problems for families and for society. But some social scientists argue that the negative impact of divorce has been exaggerated. Throughout history, significant numbers of people have been involved in intact but miserable marriages. Just because people weren't divorcing in large numbers—for religious or social or financial reasons—didn't mean their marriages were solid and satisfying. Indeed, many of those intact families of the past were filled with emotional and physical abuse or irresponsible behavior (Coontz, 1992).

Despite the high rate of divorce—and growing rates of cohabitation and voluntary singlehood—marriage still remains the living arrangement of choice for the overwhelming majority of American adults. In 1990, for example, 95 percent of women and 94 percent of men aged 45 to 54 had been married at some point in their lives (Ahlburg & De Vita, 1992); and a consistent 96 percent of the American population over the past several decades has expressed a personal desire for marriage. Even individuals whose own parents had divorced show a rather strong commitment to marriage (Landis-Kleine, Foley, Nall, Padgett, & Walters-Palmer, 1995).

Divorce itself doesn't seem to diminish people's desire to marry again either. ▲ Half of all marriages today involve at least one partner who was previously married (Bumpass, Sweet, & Castro Martin, 1990). Overall, about 70 percent of divorced individuals in this country are likely to remarry, and many more will enter cohabiting relationships (Cherlin & Furstenberg, 1994). Most remarried couples feel that their second marriages are happier and more satisfying than their first (Kain, 1990). The high rate of remarriage indicates that people who are unhappy with their spouses do not necessarily become disillusioned with the institution of marriage. People still value marriage and will seek long-term, fulfilling relationships with others in the aftermath of divorce.

▲ *For more details about remarriage and stepfamilies, read Chapter 7.*

Another concern raised by divorce is the effect it has on children. ▲ The problems that children with divorced parents experience are typically attributed to factors such as the absence of a father, increased strain on the custodial parent to keep the household running, or the emotional stress and anger associated with the separation. But many factors that create the most serious problems for children can also be found in two-parent, "intact" families: low income, poor living conditions, and lack of parental supervision (Cherlin, 1992).

▲ *The effects of divorce on children are discussed in Chapter 7.*

Furthermore, some research suggests that children's behavioral problems—particularly those of younger children—are caused not by the divorce per se, but by exposure to conflict between parents, both before and after the divorce (Stewart, Copeland, Chester, Malley, & Barenbaum, 1997). If we look at those kids whose parents are unhappily married or display a great deal of conflict, we find that differences in the frequency of problems between children of divorce and children in intact families virtually disappear (Furstenberg & Cherlin, 1991). In fact, children who grow up in intact families where there is frequent parental conflict may actually have *more* problems. In short, the simple fact of being exposed to a breakup may not be as important in the development of a child as the way parents relate to one another and to the child. It seems that a stable, conflict-free family with at least one responsible, caring, nurturing adult is a child's best path to becoming a well-rounded adult (Furstenberg & Cherlin, 1991).

From the family transformation perspective, single-parent families—whether the result of divorce or nonmarital birth—may even have some benefits. Children in these settings tend to have more autonomy, make more decisions, and have more control over their lives than children in two-parent families. In addition, children in single-parent families tend to be less stereotypically masculine or feminine than children in two-parent households (Amato, 1987). Boys learn to cook and do laundry; girls learn to do household repairs.

In sum, even though single-parent families have been vilified in the media and by politicians, the problems that children experience in them cannot all be attributed to "poor" child rearing values, lack of rules, or low expectations for children. Instead, the disadvantages of single-parent families tend to stem from sustained economic hardship—a factor that can impede children's development in two-parent households just as easily (Acock & Demo, 1994).

Marital Roles. Another area of concern for the family decline perspective is the entry of married women, particularly mothers, into the paid labor force. Some feminist sociologists (for example, Stacey, 1994) have argued for years that the traditional breadwinner-homemaker marriage makes women economically dependent, reduces their influence in the family, and makes their survival in the case of divorce difficult. Thus, family transformation theorists would argue that the dual-earner family is an important development in making marriages more equitable. ▲ Furthermore, the argument that parents' (particularly mothers') decision to enter the paid labor force is motivated by the selfish pursuit of career ambitions ignores the economic realities facing many families which require both parents to work to support the household.

▲ *Issue 5 and Chapter 3 examine the issue of fairness in marital relationships.*

Yet an important question remains: Is mothers' employment outside the home in fact detrimental to the well-being of children? Although working women spend less time with their children than nonemployed women, and although stress on the job can sometimes spill over into family relations, research suggests that maternal employment itself has few adverse effects (Acock & Demo, 1994; Bianchi & Spain, 1986; Gottfried, 1991; Rodman, Pratto, & Nelson, 1985). In fact, maternal employment may even have positive consequences. For instance, daughters of employed mothers show higher levels of independence and more egalitarian sex role attitudes than daughters of nonemployed women (Spitze, 1988). One study found that children who have mothers with high-paying, complex jobs show greater verbal and cognitive abilities than other children (Parcel & Menaghan, 1990).

Some social scientists argue that *more* time together is not always *better* time to-

gether. In some cases, higher levels of interaction between nonemployed mothers and their children become strenuous and stressful. Indeed, rates of child abuse are higher among housewives who spend all day with preschool children than among full-time employed mothers who see their children less frequently (Gelles, 1987).

The belief that working mothers create problems for their children is not so much a conclusion based on a body of research as it is a function of broader cultural attitudes. According to several prominent sociologists who fall into the family transformation camp, we could easily solve the "problems" created by working mothers if we, as a society, had the will to provide more government-supported child care services, workplace day care, after-school programs, longer school days, and flexible work schedules for parents (Gerson, 1985; Skolnick, 1991). To that end, in 1998 President Clinton proposed a $21 billion package of federal grants and tax breaks to address the shortage of qualified and affordable child care. Among other things, the money would be used to increase the number of licensed child care centers, boost wages of child care workers, and improve safety and training (Schmitt, 1998).

Family Size. The contention that shrinking family size can adversely affect the institution of family may also be overstated. With all the talk we hear these days about the perils of overpopulation, it would seem that smaller families would be beneficial to society. A smaller population would not deplete limited resources. Furthermore, with fewer children, parents could invest more time, energy, supervision, and enrichment in each child.

The sheer number of people in a family should not be used as a barometer of its quality. In the latter half of the nineteenth century, urbanization and industrialization combined to reduce the size of nuclear families. Some scholars have argued that because children were beginning to be seen for their emotional value and not so much for their economic contributions, this reduction enabled families to do more emotionally for each child (Zelizer, 1985).

The view that the drop in family size is a harbinger of doom (see Popenoe, 1993) may be based on an unfair and historically misleading comparison. Certainly, compared to the 1950s, American families today are quite small. But the 1950s was a decade of *abnormally large* families. ▲ People were having more babies then than at any period in the twentieth century, both before or since. Aside from this anomalous era, the size of American families has been declining since around 1800.

▲ *The 1950s was an abnormal era for families in other ways too, as Issue 2 explains.*

Examining Cross-Cultural Evidence of Family Decline

Many studies have attempted to link specific indicators of family decline (divorce, single-parent households, stepfamilies, and so on) to negative well-being in children, but few social scientists have attempted to examine the impact of multifaceted, societal-level decline. An exception is a study by sociologists Sharon Houseknecht and Jaya Sastry (1996). They ranked four countries (Sweden, United States, Germany, and Italy) on several indicators that supposedly measure family decline: median age at first marriage, percentage of the population never married, marital and nonmarital birthrates, divorce rate, percentage of single-parent households, percentage of working mothers, and average household size. They found that Sweden, by far, ranked highest in overall "family decline" based on these factors, followed, in order, by the United States, Germany, and Italy. They then compared these countries on various measures that are typically associated with the well-being of children: average reading and writing proficiency, percentage of children in poverty, rate of child abuse deaths, teen suicide rates, juvenile crime rates, and rates of juvenile drug offenses.

The comparisons across countries showed mixed results. The situation for Italian children supports the family decline perspective. Italy, the country that showed the lowest levels of family decline, also showed the most positive levels of child well-being on four indicators (lowest child abuse death rate, lowest teen suicide rate, lowest juvenile crime rate, and lowest drug offense rate). And children in the United States—second only to Sweden in the severity of family decline—were the least well off of the four countries on four of the six indicators of well-being (highest percentage of children in poverty, highest child abuse death rate, highest teen suicide rate, and highest juvenile drug offense rate).

Sweden represents an interesting exception. One sociologist has described Sweden as the world leader in family decline (Popenoe, 1988). But Swedes take pride in the fact that they are a nation of individuals, and their family policies reflect that attitude. Married couples receive no tax benefits and cannot file joint income tax returns. There is no tax deduction for children. Swedes aren't particularly religious, and without financial incentives, it's not surprising that many couples don't bother to marry. About half the babies in Sweden are born to unwed mothers, though very few are born to teenagers ("Home sweet home," 1995). Half of Swedish marriages end in divorce, and unmarried parents separate three times as often as married ones. As of 1991, 18 percent of Swedish families were single-parent.

Despite all these "problems," the Swedish birth rate has increased steadily since 1970 ("Home sweet home," 1995), and children rarely suffer. Sweden has several generous state-supported policies that assist children—such as parental leave, subsidized day care, and leave for sick children. Consequently, fewer than 7 percent of Swedish children live in families with less than half the average income. Perhaps as a result, Swedish children showed the highest educational performance, the lowest percentage in poverty, and nearly the lowest child-abuse death rate of the four countries in the study.

These findings may alarm some, but they are also cause for hope. It's hard to imagine a society *without* some type of family. As one prominent historian notes, "For at least 150 years there have been periods of fear that 'the family'—meaning a popular image of what families were supposed to be like, by no means a correct recollection of any actual 'traditional' family—was in decline; and these fears tended to escalate in periods of social stress" (Gordon, 1988, p. 3). It seems that as long as people need other people in their lives and are willing to form long-term, committed, interdependent relationships with them, there will always be family. It may not look much like a family looked 30 years ago, and it may have vocal detractors with very real and legitimate concerns, but it will still be a family to those within it.

Something to Think About

You can see that there is no clear answer to the question of whether the institution of family is falling apart or undergoing a metamorphosis. Both sides of the issue have compelling arguments. And scholars on both sides genuinely care about the state of American families. Certainly, we shouldn't ignore or trivialize the very real problems that things like unwed parenthood or divorce can create. On the whole, children usually do better with two parents than one. And many people are suffering because of the breakdown of their families. But at the same time, we shouldn't condemn single mothers, divorced parents, or voluntarily childless couples as the culprits behind the destruction of society. Some unwed parents are incapable of taking on the slightest parental responsibilities, but others do a splendid job in raising their children. Some divorces do irrevocable harm, but others create better situations for everyone involved. Some married couples do decide not to have children for selfish reasons, but others are motivated by a real concern for society and find other ways to contribute to its perpetuation. In short, there is no formula that can predict which family forms are most likely to keep society functioning smoothly.

1. Do you think that American families are in decline, or are they simply adjusting to shifting social circumstances?

2. Why do you think there's such a pervasive tendency in the media to focus only on the problems facing American families?

3. Do you believe that voluntary childlessness, cohabitation, working mothers, divorce, and so on are dangerous trends in American society?

4. Imagine that you've been given the responsibility of designing a set of federal policies that will help families in the twenty-first century. What would be your top two or three priorities? Why?

PART II

Sociological Dimensions of Family Life

In Part II of this book we will explore how sociologists study families and what they have to say about them. You will see how family relationships are formed, how couples balance the demands of marriage and work, how people become parents and raise children, why intimate violence is so pervasive, what factors affect divorce and remarriage, and how people make the transition into adulthood and beyond. The final chapter will peek into the future to see how families might change and how they might stay the same in the twenty-first century.

CHAPTER 1

The Link Between Family Life and Social Science

Social research is all around us. Throughout our lives we are flooded with a sea of statistics that are supposedly the result of scientific research: which detergents make clothes brighter, which soft drinks are preferred by most people, which chewing gum four out of five dentists recommended. Many of the important decisions we make, from purchasing a car to voting for a political candidate, are supported by some sort of research.

Of all the topics that scholars research, none is more popular or has more immediate personal relevance than family. You can hardly pick up a newspaper or turn on the television without someone making a claim about how families are changing, the problems they will face in the twenty-first century, or the problems that some types of families are causing now. Answers to questions about families are not just important to sociologists and other researchers. A variety of professionals deal directly with family issues, including counselors, social workers, psychologists, psychiatrists, lawyers and judges, teachers, doctors and nurses, police officers, and politicians. Indeed, anyone who runs a business must be attuned to the family lives of employees.

At the same time, the general public wants to understand how families are formed, why people act the way they do within them, why some succeed and others fail, how best to raise children, and so on. In fact, I would guess that one of the reasons you are taking this course in family sociology right now is that you want some answers to questions about families in general that you can apply to your own family.

In this chapter I will provide a broad overview of theory and research as it applies to family. I will describe how sociologists and other social scientists go about answering questions regarding family experiences, and I will identify some factors that may help us evaluate the trustworthiness of social research. This knowledge is critical, for it provides a grounding not only for understanding what research findings mean and how they're generated but for assessing whether they're credible as well. Because we are exposed to so many statistical claims regarding family, it is important that we be critical, informed consumers of this information.

Family Matters: A Sociological Quiz

In this society, we associate certain common objects with families.
Below are a series of matched situations, places, or things.
Which one of each pair is something you'd expect to find in a family,
and which is something you think comes with single life?

1.

2.

3.

4.

5.

ANSWERS

1. Wedding rings imply a transition from single to married life; for many this transition marks the start of family living. The nose ring belongs to the father of a 3-year-old boy.

2. The owners of both the sports car and the station wagon are single.

3. The swing set is in the backyard of a single mom, whereas the treadmill is in the community gym of an apartment complex for low- to moderate-income families.

4. The birthday party at Chuck E. Cheese's was for a single man turning 30, whereas the people in Starbucks are high school students still living with their parents.

5. The open refrigerator belongs to a couple of 20-something, single guys. The Sunday brunch table was set at a co-op housing unit for single people.

So, how did you do?

Are these the answers you gave or expected? What do they imply about our conceptions and misconceptions about family life?

If anything, this quiz should make it apparent that the sociological study of families is interesting and engaging, but not necessarily easy!

Everyday Research

Whether you realize it or not, you spend a significant proportion of your life doing research. Every time you seek out the opinions of others, try to gauge the attitude of a group of friends, or draw conclusions about an event, you are engaging in a form of research. Say, for example, that you thought your score on the next exam would improve if you studied with others. You then formed a study group. After the exam you compared your grade with the grade you received on the previous exam. If you noticed any significant improvement, you'd likely attribute your better performance to the study group. This is the essence of research: You had an idea about some social process, and you went out and tested it to see if you were correct.

While useful, such casual, everyday "research" can be fraught with problems. We may make inaccurate or selective observations, overgeneralize on the basis of a limited number of observations, or draw conclusions that protect our own interests (Babbie, 1992).

In contrast, the research that social scientists perform helps answer questions through a systematic, careful, and controlled process of collecting information, interpreting that information, and drawing conclusions. To that end, researchers do the following:

- Methodically record observations across a variety of situations.
- Design and choose questions in advance, and ask them in a consistent way of a large number of people.
- Use sophisticated techniques to ensure that the characteristics of the people in a study are similar to those of the population at large.
- Use computers to generate statistics from which confident conclusions can be drawn.

Furthermore, published social research is subjected to the scrutiny of colleagues who will point out any mistakes and shortcomings. Researchers are obligated to report not only their results but also the methods they used to collect data and the conditions surrounding the study. Such detailed explanation allows **replication** of the study—that is, it allows other researchers to perform a similar study themselves to see if the same results are obtained. The more a particular research result is replicated, the greater its acceptance as fact in the scholarly community.

Social scientific research, then, is a more sophisticated and structured form of the sort of individual inquiry we use every day. However, the results of social scientific research cannot always be trusted. Since published research tends to be couched in scientific and highly sophisticated terms, the general public is likely to assume that the information is accurate and credible. Unfortunately, the tendency to believe the veracity of research findings just because they appear in print can sometimes get us into trouble.

In 1996 several news reports announced that traditional families were making a comeback (Coontz, 1997). These reports were based on the fact that the total number of married couples with children had increased over the previous 5 years. Was this conclusion warranted? Probably not. Rather, a rise in the number of people of marrying age accounted for the rise in the number of marriages. True, more people were getting married and having children, but increases were also occurring in the number of people who married but remained childless, who lived together without getting married, who had children without getting married, who lived alone, and so on.

Thus, the proportion of married couples with children relative to all types of other family forms had not really changed.

A week later, another story appeared, proclaiming the opposite—that marriage, as an institution, was eroding. This report was based on the fact that the ratio of cohabiting couples to married couples was 7 times higher in 1994 (7 per 100 couples) than in 1970 (1 per 100 couples) (cited in Coontz, 1997). But drawing conclusions from this piece of information was also questionable. The apparently dramatic increase in cohabitation obscured the continuing importance of marriage. If we look at the data in another way, they show that in 1994, of every 100 couples living together, 93 were married and only 7 were not. That's hardly a sign that the institution of marriage is about to collapse. ▲ Indeed, even though cohabiting couples and single-parent families are growing at a faster rate than married-couple families, they still constitute a small percentage of all families (see Exhibit 1.1).

▲ For an analysis of whether or not American families are in decline, read Issue 8.

You can see that it's impossible to separate what we know about families from how that knowledge is acquired. So to be informed consumers of social research—and to form accurate conclusions about family life—we must always ask ourselves: How accurate is this information? And how well does information about a specific case generalize to the entire society?

Exhibit 1.1

American Families: 1980–1995

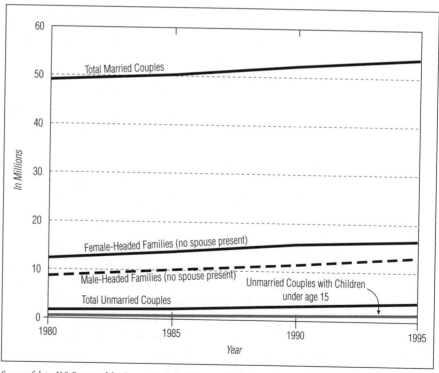

Source of data: U.S. Bureau of the Census, *Statistical Abstract of the United States: 1997* (117th edition). Washington, DC, 1997.

Theory and Research

Unlike our personal quest for answers, which may be motivated by a hunch, whim, or immediate need, most social research is guided by a particular theory. A **theory** is a set of statements or propositions that seek to explain or predict a particular aspect of social life (Chafetz, 1978). Theory does not mean, as is popularly thought, conjecture or speculation. Furthermore, theories ideally concern phenomena as they exist, not morality or ideological preference—that is, they deal with the way things are, not the way they ought to be.

Research and theory closely depend on one another. Research without any underlying theoretical reasoning is simply a string of meaningless bits of information (Mills, 1959); theory without research is abstract and speculative.

Theoretical Perspectives on Family

Sociologists use a variety of theories to explain the structure and dynamics of families. These theories make very different assumptions about human nature. Yet they are not necessarily mutually exclusive. Some are broad frameworks that attempt to explain the origin of families and the existence of family as a social institution. Others are more narrowly conceived, focusing on specific family issues such as mate selection, interpersonal communication, power relations, conflict, and so on.

Sociobiology   Some theorists focus on the biological imperatives that underlie human family relationships. They assume that some features of families are the natural end products of a long evolutionary process. This perspective, known as **sociobiology**, seeks to understand human behavior by integrating relevant insight from the natural sciences into traditional sociological thinking. This perspective doesn't posit any ultimate causes of human behavior. Rather it suggests that biology always interacts with culture in creating certain family forms (Walsh & Gordon, 1995). Some features of human behavior are shared with other species; some are unique to humans; and some vary from culture to culture or even person to person within the same culture. But all are believed to be influenced to some degree by strong biological forces.

Several brands of sociobiology exist: Some argue that cultural influence is minimal and that underlying physical states determine *all* human behavior; others acknowledge the strong effect of social experience and the environment. However, the fundamental assertion of the sociobiological perspective, no matter what its emphasis, is that we are endowed by nature with a desire to ensure that our genetic material is passed on to future generations (Lindsey, 1997).

According to this perspective, human families reflect the biological characteristics of our species' mating and reproductive system (van den Berghe, 1979). Family patterns in humans, sociobiologists argue, evolved over millions of years to ensure that mothers and infants remain closely attached and that adults mate and reproduce healthy offspring who will survive to adulthood, when they too will reproduce. ▲ The dominant family forms that exist today—most notably, the nuclear family—are those that have proved to be the most effective in ensuring species survival (Buss, 1994).

▲ Chapter 4 discusses the tendency in our culture to place great value on parenthood.

Structural Functionalism   Other sociologists see families as essential for survival not because they ensure genetic fitness but because they serve as an individual's primary source of emotional and practical training in society. Such an image of family derives from a theoretical perspective in sociology called **structural functionalism**.

This perspective emphasizes how a society is structured to maintain its stability. Societies are thought of as massive organisms, with the various social institutions working together to keep society alive, maintain order, and allow individuals to live together relatively harmoniously. According to this perspective, all societies require certain things in order to survive. They need to ensure that the goods and services people need are produced and distributed; they must provide ways of dealing with conflict and maintaining order; they must provide ways to ensure that individuals are trained appropriately into the existing culture.

When examined from this framework, family becomes not simply a place in which people live out their intimate lives but an important—even necessary—institution for the very survival of the larger society (Parsons & Bales, 1955). This perspective forces us to look at the family in terms of its contribution to society.

Structural functionalists identify several important social functions that are best performed by the family. One such function is the control and regulation of reproduction. All societies need to have a system by which new members are produced and trained. Obviously, children can be, and with more frequency are, born outside of "conventional" families. But most societies do not encourage and in many cases strongly discourage reproduction outside the family setting. One of the issues that is at the forefront of contemporary public debate over the state of the family concerns the increasing likelihood that children will be born *outside* of what is traditionally

▲ This debate rests on assumptions about what a family is (see Issue 1) and on popular images of what American families should be and have been (see Issue 2).

thought of as the family. ▲

Another important function served by families is socialization—the process by which individuals learn the values, attitudes, and behaviors appropriate for them in a given society. Families provide members with a sense of self and identity, as well as a set of beliefs and attitudes. It is within families that we get our first sense of our own worth in the eyes of others and our first taste of what's expected of us as males or females. ▲

▲ Gender socialization is discussed in Chapter 5.

But some family sociologists argue that this important function has been lost to other institutions. In the distant past, for instance, families controlled the practical and moral training of members until they reached adulthood and formed families of their own. In recent years, however, families have surrendered much of this responsibility to religious and educational institutions. Schools, for example, transmit the skills and values we believe are necessary to being a good citizen in society.

Balancing the relative influence of schools and families is not always without conflict. Although some families are glad to relinquish all responsibility for education to schools, others want to retain control. When parents protest against the teaching of certain subjects in school or the reading of certain books, or when they fight for the right to choose the schools their children attend, they are attempting to reclaim the family's right to train their children.

Although the family plays a less prominent role in educating children than it did in the past, it continues to serve the necessary function of providing affection and emotional security. To some, a family's most useful service to society is to be a "haven in a heartless world" (Lasch, 1977) where one can find safety and protection and escape the stresses and strains of public life. Families are supposed to provide intimacy, warmth, and trust, an antidote to the dehumanizing and alienating forces of modern society.

▲ Issue 2 presents
popular and historical
images of family roles.
In Chapter 6 we see
that families are often
the settings for
enormous brutality.

This image became popular in the late nineteenth century, when the tenderness of the family (presided over by a genteel and understanding wife) stood in opposition to the harshness of the urban, industrial world of commerce (inhabited almost exclusively by men). The family's task, indeed its economic obligation, was to protect the father/husband against the ravages of the outside world, to soothe him enough so he could go out the next day to support his family, not to mention the economy. ▲

The Conflict Perspective   Structural functionalism was the dominant theoretical tradition in sociology for most of the twentieth century. Prior to the 1970s, much about families was simply taken for granted: that they're pretty much the same everywhere, that they're generally harmonious, that men's and women's roles within them are necessary and inevitable, and that the daily realities of family life correspond to norms about the ways families are *supposed* to work (Skolnick, 1996).

Within the past 3 decades, however, such assumptions about families have been challenged. Structural functionalism, in particular, has been criticized for emphasizing the usefulness of existing social arrangements without examining how those arrangements are created and maintained and how they might exploit or otherwise disadvantage certain groups or individuals.

In contrast, the **conflict perspective** examines society not in terms of stability and agreement but in terms of conflict and struggle. The focus is not on how all the elements of society contribute to its smooth operation and continued existence but on how social structure promotes divisions and inequalities between groups. Social order, then, arises not from the societal pursuit of harmony but from dominance and coercion. Political, religious, educational, and economic institutions foster and legitimate the power and privilege of some individuals or groups at the expense of others. The key question that the conflict perspective asks is, Who benefits from and who is disadvantaged by particular social arrangements?

The famous political philosopher Karl Marx felt that in modern societies, two classes of people emerge: *capitalists*, who own the means of production (land, commercial enterprises, factories, and other forms of wealth) and can purchase the labor of others; and *workers*, who neither own the means of production nor have the ability to purchase the labor of others. Instead, the workers must sell their own labor to survive. In such a structure, capitalists inevitably tend to use their power to create more wealth for themselves, to act in ways that will protect their interests and positions in society, and to exploit the workers to meet those ends.

Conflict sociologists see families as a small version of such a society in which relationships and expectations benefit some members more than others. They are particularly likely to focus on the link between families and larger systems of political and economic inequality. ▲ For instance, how does racial discrimination in politics, education, and employment affect family life? How does a family's position in the class structure affect its ability to act on its own behalf? How do economic trends like corporate downsizing, falling wages, and the globalization of economic marketplaces change the power structure in families?

▲ The effects of social
inequality on family life
are addressed in Issues
5, 6, and 7.

Inequality can also exist *within* a particular family. The well-being of one family member sometimes results from the oppression and exploitation of another. Because families are organized principally around age and gender, parents and children, women and men, boys and girls do not derive benefits from their families in the same way (Thorne & Yalom, 1982). Family relations can be characterized by a competitive struggle to control scarce social, emotional, and economic resources within the family. Members often have different interests and desire different outcomes as they go about trying to get their way. Conflict can arise over a wide range of issues—from how loud the stereo ought to be to whether or not the family should relocate to another city. Every parent knows what it's like when his or her desire to have a child go to bed comes into conflict with the child's desire to stay up late. Indeed, it's the rare parent who is able to avoid battling with his or her children over meals, homework, fashion, hygiene, and sibling conflicts. Likewise, spouses commonly compete with one another over how to spend money, where to go on vacations, and how to raise children. Sometimes the competition occurs through bargaining and negotiation; other times, through force and aggression.

One particularly noteworthy and influential version of conflict theory is **feminist theory**. This approach attempts to explain women's subordination in families by arguing that men's dominance within families is part of a wider system of male domination. ▲ The way gender is defined and expressed in families is linked to the way it's defined and expressed in the larger society. For instance, women have traditionally been encouraged to perform unpaid household labor and child care duties while men have been free to devote their energy and attention to earning money and power in the economic marketplace. Women's lower wages when they do work are often justified by the assumption that their paid labor is secondary to that of their husbands.

▲ Gender and family power are the subject of Issue 5.

But the oppression of women exists not just in specific household arrangements but in the *ideology* of family. In the distant past women were considered the sexual property of men, and the marriage contract legally obligated women to abide by the wishes and desires of their husbands. Although such formal contractual obligations no longer characterize marriages, overall male dominance in society and general beliefs about women's "proper place" are still closely linked to gender inequality in families.

The conflict perspective paints a rather pessimistic picture of family life. Its emphasis on conflict and coercion tends to overlook the cooperation, agreement, and stability that exist in many families. Nevertheless, it sensitizes us to the reality that people in families often have conflicting needs, and with limited resources, some will get what they want and others won't. And it has provided the intellectual framework for social movements designed to alter the male authority structure of families and to challenge women's economic dependence and exclusive responsibility for nurturing.

Social Exchange Theory   Like the conflict perspective, **social exchange theory** uses the principles of economics to explain family experiences. But it pays special attention to the way people make decisions and choices. In particular, it focuses on why we are attracted to some people and not others and why we pursue and remain in some relationships and avoid or leave others. ▲

▲ Chapter 2 includes a more detailed discussion of how social exchange shapes intimate relationships.

This theory assumes that humans are motivated by the same forces that drive economic marketplaces: a desire to maximize rewards. Rewards can assume many forms: money, desired goods and services, attention, status, prestige, approval by others, and so on. At the same time we are also motivated by a desire to minimize our costs—to avoid unpleasant, undesirable, or painful experiences. Humans will choose a particular line of action over other alternative lines of action because it produces the best profit (rewards minus costs).

When applied to intimacy, this fundamental premise implies that those relationships that are the most "profitable" to both partners will be the most satisfying and the most likely to last. Intimate relationships provide obvious rewards—like love, sexual gratification, warmth, desirable characteristics of the partner, companionship, and so on. But they present certain costs as well—time and effort spent trying to maintain the relationship, undesirable characteristics of one's partner, bickering, and so on. Research has consistently shown that the couples who indicate high levels of happiness are those in which partners are providing one another with many rewarding experiences and few costly ones (Birchler, Weiss, & Vincent, 1975; Rusbult, 1983; Vincent, Weiss, & Birchler, 1975).

Unlike purely economic exchanges, whose rewards and costs are objective and defined in terms of money, the rewards and costs in an intimate, family context are likely to be matters of subjective definition. A characteristic that one person may define as sensitivity and finds rewarding, another may define as wimpiness and find costly. Even so, such preferences are, in many ways, embedded within the larger society's definitions of desirability. As long as we have generally agreed-upon standards of a person's worth, our preferences and our relationships will share some features of the economic marketplace (Rubin, 1973).

Social exchange theory also directs our attention to people's expectations. These expectations are derived from past experiences. We judge the attractiveness of the outcomes we receive in present relationships by comparing them to outcomes we've received in previous ones. If our present relationship exceeds our expectations—that is, it is "better" than any relationship in which we've been involved before—satisfaction is likely to be high. On the other hand, if our present relationship doesn't provide us with what we have come to expect, we probably won't be very happy.

We also compare the attractiveness of a present relationship to the kinds of profits we think are available in an alternative relationship (Thibaut & Kelley, 1959). If an individual perceives that available alternatives would be more rewarding than the present relationship, he or she will be less likely to remain. But when people feel that they have few or no alternatives, they tend to stay in their relationship, even if it is far from satisfying.

Symbolic Interactionism   A final sociological perspective on family is **symbolic interactionism**. This perspective attempts to understand society and social structure through an examination of the personal day-to-day interactions of people as individuals, pairs, or groups. These forms of interaction take place within a world of symbolic communication. The symbols we use—language, gestures, posture, and so on—are influenced by the larger group or society to which we belong. When we interact with others, we constantly attempt to interpret what they mean and what they're up to. Most human behavior, then, is determined not by the objective facts of a given situation but by the subjective meanings people attach to it.

▲ Issue 2 examines the effect of media images on how individuals interpret their own family experiences.

This perspective presents an image of family as a reality that must be negotiated. ▲ *Family* is not a "thing" that is self-evident. If you think about it, you can't really "see" a family. You can only see people and infer from the way they live, treat one another, and resemble one another whether or not they can be considered a family.

In everyday life we use language to refer to many objects that we can't see: feelings, attitudes, nations, and so on. We come to know these "things" through our experiences with them. We learn the shape of and give meaning to these "things" when we speak of them, act toward them, and respond to them (Gubrium & Holstein, 1990). For instance, when I refer to the "Newman family," I'm describing something that has an identifiable "inside" and "outside." I can describe the characteristics of the people in it and their feelings for and relationships to one another. I can also talk about its structure, its geographical location, its financial wherewithal, and its quirky traditions. In doing so, I give shape and meaning to this "thing" called the Newman family.

Simple enough, right? But is the Newman family I describe the same one my wife describes? According to some sociologists (e.g., Bernard, 1982), it can never be. Every marriage contains two marriages: "his" and "hers." These different definitions depend on everyday experiences like housework, leisure time, financial and physical well-being, and so on. Two spouses are unlikely to "see" the same family that they are both a part of. ▲

▲ Issue 5 and Chapter 2 examine how gender influences the way people perceive their family experiences.

What about the Newman family that my sons see? Certainly children have very different family experiences than parents and therefore are likely to define family differently. Take, for example, a child's perception of a "single-parent family." If a divorced parent remarries, does that automatically turn the "single-parent family" into a "married-couple family"? It probably would to the parent who now has another adult with whom to share parenting responsibilities. But it may not be perceived that way by the child, who may rebel against considering his or her parent's new spouse a parent. Hence the child may still "see" a single-parent family even though two adults are present (Trost, 1988).

And how do those people at the edges of a particular family—grandparents, aunts, uncles, cousins, close friends, and so on—see it? Conceivably my uncle's description of the Newman family may bear little resemblance to mine. And even if all of us could agree on a definition of the Newman family, it may bear little resemblance to the Nguyen family or the Garcia family or, for that matter, the vast majority of families that exist in the world today.

In sum, although all families consist of identifiable statuses, roles, and norms, each individual family adapts these structural features to its own everyday experiences. The reality of family life is not fixed and inevitable. It is created, sustained, and changed through the day-to-day interactions that take place among members.

Variables and Hypotheses

The concepts that are the basis of family theories are usually abstract and not amenable to empirical observation. You can't directly observe concepts like "marital satisfaction," "gender expectations," or "attachments to parents." So researchers must translate these concepts into measurable entities called variables. A **variable** is any characteristic, attitude, behavior, or event that can take on two or more values or attributes. For example, the variable "sex" has two categories: male and female. The variable "attitudes toward divorce" has categories ranging from very favorable to very unfavorable. The variable "social class" ranges from upper to lower.

Sociologists distinguish between independent and dependent variables. An **independent variable** is the factor that is presumed to cause or influence another variable. The **dependent variable** is the one assumed to depend on, be caused by, or change as a result of the independent variable. If you believe that a person's gender affects his or her attitude toward abortion (for instance, women will hold more favorable attitudes than men), then "gender" would be the independent variable and "attitudes toward abortion" the dependent variable.

To test theories, sociologists must translate abstract theoretical propositions into testable hypotheses. A **hypothesis** is a researchable prediction that specifies the relationship between two or more variables. If you suspected that household income was related to marital happiness, you might hypothesize that as income increases, marital happiness would also increase. To test this hypothesis, you would figure out a way to measure the independent variable (income) and the dependent variable (marital happiness) and compare them statistically.

The Modes of Research

Although the answers to important sociological questions are not always simple or clear, the techniques sociologists use to collect and examine data allow them to draw informed and reliable conclusions about human behavior and social life. The most common techniques are experiments, field research, unobtrusive research, and surveys.

Experiments

An **experiment** is typically a research situation designed to elicit some sort of behavior and is conducted under closely controlled laboratory circumstances. In its ideal form, the experimenter randomly places subjects in two groups and then deliberately manipulates or introduces changes into the environment of one group of subjects (called the "experimental group") and not the other (called the "control group"). The experimenter takes care to ensure that the groups are relatively identical except for the variable that he or she manipulates. Any observed or measured differences between the groups can then be attributed to the effects of the experimental manipulation (Singleton, Straits, & Straits, 1993).

Experiments have a significant advantage over other types of research because the researcher can directly control all the relevant variables. Thus, conclusions about one factor causing changes in another can be made more convincingly. The artificial nature of laboratory experiments, however, may make subjects behave differently than they would in their natural settings, leading some people to argue that experimentation in sociology—and, in particular, in family research—is practically impossible.

To overcome this difficulty, some sociologists have created experimental situations outside the laboratory. In 1974 two social psychologists, Donald Dutton and Arthur Aron, devised an experiment to determine the degree to which physiological arousal influenced people's feelings of sexual attraction for others. In the experimental condition, the researchers had an attractive female assistant stand in the middle of a fear-inducing suspension bridge—a 450-foot wobbly footbridge that swung in the wind 250 feet above the raging Capilano River in British Columbia. When she saw a lone male hiker walking along the bridge who appeared to be between the ages of 18 and 40, she would approach him and ask if he would be interested in participating in a study she was doing on "creativity in scenic places." If he agreed, she'd ask him to write some brief stories based on a picture she'd show him. When the man was done writing the stories, she would tell him, "I'm sorry I can't tell you any more about the study until it is over, but it will be over tonight, and if you want you can phone me to learn more about it." She would then give him her name and phone number.

For the control condition, the researchers found another bridge upriver, built of heavy cedar beams and only 10 feet above a shallow rivulet. There, the female assistant followed exactly the same procedure.

Dutton and Aron believed that those men on the rickety footbridge would perceive their state of arousal (which was actually fear) as attraction to the female researcher. Therefore, they would be more likely to call her later that day than those on the safe bridge, who had no physiological basis for making an attribution of attraction.

In the experimental condition on the rickety bridge, nine out of eighteen subjects called the interviewer later that day; in the control condition on the more solid bridge, only two out of sixteen called her. In addition, the stories the subjects in the experimental condition wrote contained significantly more sexual imagery than those written by the control subjects. The researchers concluded that physiological arousal is indeed linked to the level of sexual attraction people feel for others. ▲

▲ Attraction is discussed in more detail in Chapter 2.

Field Research

In **field research**, sociologists observe events as they actually occur, without selecting experimental and control groups or purposely introducing any changes into the subjects' environment. In field studies, researchers typically seek to obtain in-depth information about some issue or question by observing it firsthand. Such research involves spending a significant amount of time with subjects, observing the context of their lives to gain familiarity with their everyday experiences. It relies less on quantitative data than other forms of social research do. Findings are typically presented with long quotes of and stories about real people as opposed to sets of statistics, tables, charts, and so on.

Field research often involves unstructured, in-depth interviews with subjects. For her book *Families on the Fault Line*, sociologist Lillian Rubin visited the homes of 162 working-class and lower-middle-class families who lived in a variety of cities all across the country. Twenty years earlier she had interviewed some of these families as part of a previous study. She had kept in touch with some of them over those 20 years, playing the role of friendly adviser when needed. Whenever possible, she spent time with wives, husbands, and teenage children—eating meals, sitting in living rooms, and so on. Because of the nature of the topics Rubin was studying, it wasn't always easy to get people to cooperate. So she devised a strategy:

> Experience long ago taught me that my best chance for getting cooperation is to approach the woman in the family first. If I could convince her, she almost always became my ally in helping to persuade the other family members. So I phoned the woman, introduced myself, and explained what I was doing and why it was important for me to talk with her. . . . Some of the women were able to secure the promise of cooperation from their husbands and, where they had any, their teenage children, even before I arrived on the scene. In other families, it had to wait until afterward, by which time I had become something of a family event, provoking the curiosity of other family members sufficiently so that they didn't need much convincing to talk to me. (Rubin, 1994, pp. 14–15)

Through her close observations, Rubin was able to go directly to the experiences of ordinary people and show how social, political, and economic changes influence the ways families organize and reorganize themselves.

Fieldwork is a useful method of doing research on families because it allows the researcher to observe the subtle attitudes and behaviors that can't be seen in paper-and-pencil questionnaires or structured interviews. Rubin's vivid accounts of working-class people's frustrations, anger, fears, hopes, and dreams could not have been obtained through any other research method. ▲ As a general rule, it's always better to observe people interacting than to ask them questions about their interactions because their answers may be inaccurate or biased to give a good impression of themselves or their families. For instance, observing a parent disciplining a child usually produces more accurate information than asking that parent how she or he has disciplined the child in the past.

But field research does have its drawbacks. For one thing, it usually requires a significant investment of time. Arlie Russell Hochschild's (1997b) examination of how people balance their work and family lives involved in-depth observations and interviews of employees at a single corporation over 3 years. ▲ Conceivably she could have mailed the employees questionnaires, thereby gathering data—albeit less trustworthy data—in only a fraction of the time.

Furthermore, because fieldwork is so time-consuming, researchers can conduct only a limited number of interviews and can observe only a limited number of people. Hochschild may have collected rich information about people's work/family trade-offs, but she studied only one corporation. It's rather risky to generalize from the experiences of a small group of workers in one company to all workers in all sorts of work environments.

The possibility also arises that the researcher will unwittingly change people's behavior simply by being there. As you well know, people act differently when they know they are being watched. However conscientious researchers are in minimizing their influence on subjects, the fact remains that their presence changes things.

Surveys

When carrying out field observations or setting up a controlled experimental situation is impossible or impractical, social researchers use the survey. **Surveys** require that the researcher pose a series of questions either orally or on paper. Survey researchers typically use standardized formats to ask subjects the same questions in roughly the same way, and large samples of the target population are used as subjects. The questions should be understood by respondents the way the researcher wants them to be understood and measure what the researcher wants them to measure. In addition, respondents are expected to answer the questions honestly and thoughtfully.

All of us have had experience with surveys of one form or another. Every 10 years we are required to fill out questionnaires for the U.S. Census Bureau, the source of most statistical data on families. At the end of some college courses you have probably filled out a form whereby you can evaluate your instructor and the course. Or perhaps you've been interviewed in a shopping mall or answered questions during a telephone survey on your favorite pizza or computer software.

Surveys are the most common approach to studying marriage and family life. Sociologists Philip Blumstein and Pepper Schwartz (1983) undertook a massive study of intimate couples in

▲ Issue 7 presents some specific findings of Rubin's study.

▲ For more detail on Hochschild's study read Chapter 3.

▲ For more on
Blumstein and Schwartz's
findings, read Chapter 2.

America using survey research. ▲ They sent questionnaires to people from every income level, age group, religion, political ideology, and educational background. Some of their respondents were not married but lived together, others were married. Some had children, others were childless. Some were heterosexual, others homosexual. All couples filled out a thirty-eight-page questionnaire that asked questions about their leisure activities, emotional support, housework, finances, sexual relations, satisfaction, relations with children, and so forth. More than 6,000 couples participated. From these surveys Blumstein and Schwartz were able to draw conclusions about the importance of money, work, sexuality, power, and gender in couples' lives.

The major advantage of surveys is that they typically require less time and money than field research does. Information can be collected from large numbers of people in a relatively short period of time. But the disadvantages of surveys are equally obvious. Can a researcher gain an understanding of the rich nuances of family life through a highly structured questionnaire? Certainly not. At best, surveys provide a quick, somewhat shallow glimpse into family life. Consequently, survey research may oversimplify complex issues. Furthermore, through surveys researchers learn about what people say they do, not what people may actually do (Gelles, 1995). Nevertheless, surveys remain useful for research on certain areas of family life that, for ethical or practical reasons, are simply not amenable to direct observation or experimental manipulation (sexual intercourse, violence, and so on).

Unobtrusive Research

All the research methods I've discussed so far require the researcher to have some contact with the people being studied: asking them questions, giving them tasks to do in an experiment, or watching them. The problem with these techniques is that the very act of intruding into people's lives may influence the phenomenon being studied. Asking people questions about their voting intentions prior to an election, for instance, may actually affect their eventual voting behavior. So sociologists sometimes make use of another research technique, unobtrusive research, which requires no contact with people at all. **Unobtrusive research** is an examination of the evidence of social behavior that people create or leave behind. Several types of unobtrusive research exist, including analysis of existing statistics, content analysis, and historical analysis.

Analysis of Existing Statistics   One type of unobtrusive research is the analysis of statistical data that have already been collected by others. As I mentioned earlier, one of the most popular and convenient sources of data on families is the U.S. Census, which collects demographic information on all Americans every 10 years. Most family studies that examine broad, nationwide trends (for instance, marriage, divorce, or premarital childbearing rates) use existing census data.

Another existing source of data that provides the basis for much family research is the National Survey on Families and Households. This survey, conducted in the late 1980s, includes information derived from interviews with over 13,000 respondents. A second wave of the survey, conducted between 1992 and 1994, includes interviews with surviving members of the original sample. The sample comprises a diverse array of households, including single-parent families, families with stepchildren, cohabiting couples, and recently married persons. A great deal of family information was collected from each respondent, including family arrangements in childhood, dating experiences, experiences of leaving home, marital and cohabitation experiences, contact with kin, and economic well-being, as well as education, childbearing, and employment histories. Much of the research discussed in this book is based on an analysis of data collected from this survey.

Content Analysis   Another form of unobtrusive research is called content analysis. **Content analysis** is the study of recorded communication—books, speeches, poems, songs, television commercials, and the like. ▲ Suppose you were interested in whether or not the women's movement has improved the status of women in American society. Perhaps a good indicator of how well or poorly women are thought of in society is the nature of their images in the popular media. You could identify several influential magazines (*Time, Life, Newsweek*) and examine changes in the depiction of women in ads in these magazines over the last 10 or 20 years. Or, if you had access to television archives, you could ascertain whether or not there have been any changes in the way women have been portrayed in TV commercials or prime-time sitcoms over the years.

▲ Issue 2 examines the role of popular media in shaping our images of American families.

Historical Analysis   Related to content analysis is a third type of unobtrusive research: historical analysis. **Historical analysis** relies on existing historical documents as a source of information. Family is not a static entity. Not only do families change over the life course of individual members but the social definition of family also changes over time within a given society. ▲ Charting those changes and reconstructing the lives of past families requires a detective-like examination of what people in the past left behind.

▲ For more on historical images of American families, read Issue 2.

Historian Lawrence Stone (1979) was interested in how massive shifts in worldviews and value systems between 1500 and 1800 affected British families. Obviously he could not observe or survey people who have been dead for centuries. And existing statistics from the distant past often prove unreliable. So Stone examined every possible type of evidence to pick up hints about how these changes were being incorporated into people's everyday lives. He studied personal documents, diaries, autobiographies, memoirs, letters, wills, marriage contracts, and divorce decrees. He sifted through birth, marriage, and death records of towns, villages, and cities. He studied the architectural designs of homes to see how the physical properties of the household affected family interaction. Realizing that accounts of social phenomena can usually be found in the informational and entertainment media of the time, he also examined newspaper columns, novels, plays, poems, and popular art of the day.

The key problem encountered in historical analysis is interpretation of these records. Historical researchers have no way to check the accuracy of diaries, memoirs, autobiographies, and letters, for instance, and therefore must treat these records with a high level of critical scrutiny. Many of these documents are often quirky and idiosyncratic. A letter cannot "tell us more than what the author of the document thought—what he thought happened, what he thought ought to happen or would happen, or perhaps only what he wanted others to think he thought, or even only what he himself thought he thought" (quoted in Stone, 1979, p. 25). The best way to overcome these problems, Stone felt, was to examine as many documents as possible, not to rely on a single person's unique interpretation of events.

Furthermore, the reliance on written records necessarily limits any study of the past to the people who were literate and articulate and who had sufficient leisure time to write detailed accounts of their experiences. This requirement, of course, excludes the majority of people, particularly in the distant past, who could not write a word, let alone keep detailed, thoughtful, and frank diaries of their family life. Women, too, tended to be excluded from the world of literacy. Hence, most written records reflected a distinctly male perspective on events.

Nevertheless, despite the built-in limitations of historical information, historical analyses like Stone's are able to provide a compelling account of at least some people's experiences with marriage, birth, death, lineage, sexuality, child rearing, and the role of gender in family life.

The Trustworthiness of Family Research

Most family sociologists see research not only as personally valuable but as central to human knowledge and understanding. But we, as consumers of this information, must always ask ourselves how accurate it is. As I mentioned earlier, much of what we see is either inaccurate or misleading. To evaluate the results of family research, we must examine the researcher's units of analysis, samples, indicators, values, and interests.

Units of Analysis

Families are made up of individuals, but they have a structural reality larger than the sum of those individuals. Some family researchers focus on individual family members, some on families as a whole, and some on the institution of family as a part of society's structure. With so much possible variation in who or what is being studied, family researchers must be careful to specify whether the units they wish to study—called **units of analysis**—are individuals, pairs of individuals, nuclear families, households, extended families, or the institution of family (see Demo•Graphic Essay, "Households versus Families," at the end of this chapter).

Studying individuals in families is not the same as studying families themselves. For instance, if you are interested in whether children from rich families are more likely to attend college than children from poor families, the units of analysis are individuals. On the other hand, if you are interested in whether families with higher incomes contain fewer children than families with lower incomes, the units of analysis would be individual families.

The identification of the appropriate units of analysis is not always straightforward. For instance, much research on "families" relies on information acquired from one family member, who reports on the characteristics of the entire family. This strategy is easier and less time-consuming than surveying all members of a family, but it assumes that each family member sees the same reality. If you were interested in determining whether rich and poor families differ in the way household tasks are divided, would you be comfortable assuming that the one person from each household you surveyed would have the same perspective as all other members about who does what around the house?

Such an assumption can be dubious. Family members have been known to disagree on even the most fundamental facts, such as how many people are in the family. One study of children whose parents had divorced found disagreement about the number of people considered to be in the family. ▲ The children were listing absent parents as family members, but the custodial parents were not (Furstenberg & Nord, 1985).

▲ Chapter 7 includes children's perspectives on divorce and remarriage.

Nor can husbands and wives always provide valid data on their partner's attitudes or perceptions (Deal, 1995). Spouses have been known to disagree on the most obvious facts about their relationship: how they met, how long they've been married, how often they see friends, and so on. In fact, according to one prominent sociologist, even happily married husbands and wives disagree on three out of four questions regarding their marriage (Bernard, 1982). Data on socially disapproved or sensitive family issues like marital violence, marital conflict, and sexuality are especially likely to produce disagreement among partners (Szinovacz & Egley, 1995).

How trustworthy are our beliefs about the nature of American families if the data fluctuate depending on which member of a family happens to be providing information? One way around this problem is to acquire information from both members of a couple. Then the researcher can compare partners' answers to the same question and discern systematic differences in their perceptions of the relationship. In the case of marital violence, gathering data from couples as opposed to only one partner provides a way of estimating the extent to which violence is underreported. In one study, the estimated marital violence rate when data were gathered from only one partner was 50 percent to 80 percent lower than the violence rate indicated by couple data, where violence is taken to exist in the couple if *either* partner reports it (Szinovacz & Egley, 1995). ▲ Similarly, estimates of the amount of injury to wives caused by marital violence are substantially higher when wives' reports or couple data is used rather than husbands' reports.

▲ Additional data on marital violence are presented in Chapter 6.

Samples

In determining the accuracy of published research, we must also be aware of the people who participated as subjects in the study. Frequently, researchers are interested in the attitudes, behaviors, or characteristics of certain groups—college students, women, Americans, and so on. But directly interviewing, surveying, or observing all the people in these categories would be impossible. Hence researchers must select from the larger population a smaller **sample**, or subgroup, of respondents for study.

Ideally, the characteristics of the sample approximate the characteristics of the entire population of interest. A **representative sample** is a small subgroup typical of the population as a whole. For instance, a sample of 100 divorced people should include roughly the same proportion of men and women that characterizes the entire adult population. Techniques for selecting a representative sample have become highly sophisticated, as illustrated by the accuracy of polls conducted to predict election results.

In the physical sciences, sampling is not an issue. Certain physical or chemical elements are assumed to be identical. One need only study a small quantity of nitrogen because one sample of nitrogen is exactly the same as any other of the same size. Human beings, however, vary widely on every imaginable characteristic. One could not make a general statement about all

American families on the basis of interviewing one family. For that matter, one could not draw conclusions about all families from observing a sample consisting only of white families, working-class families, or families with small children. Samples that are not representative can obviously lead to inaccurate and misleading conclusions.

As a consumer of research findings, you also need to know not only who constitutes the sample of subjects in a research report but how they were selected. Recently, psychologist Benjamin Karney (Karney, Davila, Cohan, Sullivan, Johnson, & Bradbury, 1995) conducted several studies to determine if different sampling procedures could actually produce different results. In one study he recruited sixty newlywed couples to participate in a long-term, longitudinal study of marriage by placing a classified newspaper advertisement that offered $50 in compensation. Another sixty couples, selected through a review of marriage licenses in a large urban county, were sent a letter inviting them to earn $75 for participating in the study. The eligibility requirements and the testing procedure were identical for both samples.

Karney and colleagues found that couples contacted through newspaper advertisements differed from the preselected couples contacted by letter in several important ways. The ones who responded to the newspaper ads were younger, had lower incomes, were more likely to have lived together before marriage, were less likely to have participated in premarital counseling, showed more depressive and neurotic symptoms, and had generally poorer-quality marriages than the preselected couples. All of these factors are associated with greater risk for marital distress and divorce. Karney and his colleagues speculated that the newspaper ads required couples to be taking some kind of action (that is, looking through the classified advertisements) before they could become aware of the research. The mailed invitations required no such action. Hence, the couples who responded to the newspaper ads may have chosen to participate because they were seeking some guidance or experience that could help their marriage.

You may also consider samples unrepresentative if you have reason to believe that the people who chose to participate in the study are different in important ways from the people who chose not to participate. For instance, the people who choose not to participate in a voluntary survey of domestic violence are more likely than volunteers to have something to hide. Hence, the data derived from a sample of volunteer respondents will, in all probability, underestimate the rate of violence.

To examine the possibility that self-selected respondents differ significantly from those who decline to participate, Karney and his colleagues compared couples in his survey who responded to the mailed invitation to the couples who were contacted but didn't respond. The researchers found that these two groups differed on almost every variable for which marriage licenses included information. Couples who expressed an interest in the research project had received more education, were employed in higher-status jobs, and were more likely to have cohabited premaritally than couples who didn't express an interest. In addition, among couples who responded, wives were less likely to be housewives. In short, the couples who responded were less traditional and of higher status than couples who didn't respond. The fact that couples who wanted to participate in the research differed systematically from couples who didn't want to participate severely limits the generalizability of the researchers' findings. All studies that rely on voluntary participation have the same potential problem.

Indicators

Another problem sociologists face when doing research on families is that the variables they are interested in studying are usually difficult to observe and measure. What does powerlessness look like? How can you "see" marital dissatisfaction? How would you recognize social class? None of these concepts can be observed directly. So sociologists resign themselves to measuring **indicators** of things that cannot be measured directly. Researchers measure events and behaviors commonly thought to accompany a particular variable, hoping that what they are measuring is a valid indicator of the concept they are interested in.

Suppose you believed that people's attitudes toward divorce are influenced by the strength of their religious beliefs, or "religiosity." You might hypothesize that the more religious someone is, the less accepting he or she will be of divorce. To test this hypothesis you must first figure out what you mean by "religious." What might be an indicator of the strength of one's religious beliefs? You could determine if the subjects of your study identify themselves as members of some organized religion. Would this measure how religious they are? Probably not, because many people identify themselves as, say, Catholic or Jewish but are not religious at all. Likewise some people consider themselves quite religious but don't identify with any organized religion. So this measure would highlight group differences but would fail to capture the intensity of a person's beliefs or the degree of religious interest.

Perhaps a better indicator would be some observable behavior, like the frequency of attendance at formal religious services. Arguably, the more one attends church or synagogue, the more religious he or she is. But here too we run into problems. Regular church attendance may reflect things other than the depth of one's religious commitment, such as family pressure, habit, or the desire to socialize with others. Furthermore, many very religious people are unable to attend organized religious services because they are too frail or disabled.

Frequency of prayer might be a better indicator. People who pray a lot are presumably more religious than people who don't pray at all. But some nonreligious people pray for things all the time.

Surveys are particularly susceptible to inaccurate indicators. A loaded phrase or an unfamiliar word on a survey question can dramatically affect people's responses in ways unintended by the researcher. The National Opinion Research Center asked in an annual survey of public attitudes if the United States was spending too much, too little, or about the right amount of money on "assistance to the poor." Two-thirds of the respondents said the country was spending too little. But when the word *welfare* was substituted for "assistance to the poor," nearly half of the respondents said the country was spending too much money (Kagay & Elder, 1992).

If a subject misinterprets what the researcher intended to ask, then the researcher will inevitably misinterpret the subject's response. For instance, people often comprehend terms referring to sexual behavior differently. To some people, a "virgin" is someone who has never had penile-vaginal intercourse. But to others, a "virgin" is someone who has never experienced an orgasm—manually, orally, or otherwise—in the company of someone else. Using a question like "Are you a virgin?" as an indicator of sexual activity can create an inaccurate estimate if subjects are interpreting the term differently.

Another problem associated with indicators is the **social desirability bias**—the tendency for subjects to report or present characteristics or behaviors they believe are the most socially acceptable or appropriate (Larzelere & Klein, 1987). Even on anonymous surveys, people want to depict themselves in a favorable light. Hence, they will often accentuate positive attributes and downplay or hide negative ones. In research on marital satisfaction, for instance, couples have a tendency to report more satisfaction and happiness than actually exists. Similarly, in research on marital power, some studies have found a "powerlessness bias"—with each partner claiming the other is more powerful—because claiming power is perceived to be socially undesirable (Brehm, 1992).

You can see that, for most sociological variables of interest, indicators seldom perfectly reflect the concepts they are intended to measure. Hence, as you read published research findings, you should determine whether the questions people are being asked truly reflect what the researchers intend them to reflect or whether the indicators are likely to elicit socially desirable—and not necessarily truthful—responses.

Values and Interests

In addition to units of analysis, samples, and indicators, the researcher's own values and interests can influence the conclusions drawn from social research and thereby influence sociological information about families. Ideally, research is objective and nonbiased and measures what *is* and not what *should be*. The study of social events, however, always takes place in a particular cultural, political, and ideological context (Ballard, 1987; Denzin, 1989).

In fact, because family is such a politically charged topic, research in the area is sometimes designed to support narrowly defined political interests. You can be reasonably certain that research supported by conservative political organizations like the Institute for American Values will uncover the harmful effects of working mothers. But it's equally likely that research supported by more liberal organizations like the Institute for Women's Policy Research will find less damaging, even positive effects.

We must also remember that sociologists are people too, with their own biases, preconceptions, and expectations. Our values always determine from which vantage point information about a particular social phenomenon will be gathered. In fact, values can influence the questions that researchers find important enough to address in the first place (Reinharz, 1992). For instance, family research has historically reflected the interests of men by viewing the female-headed household as deficient or dysfunctional (Thorne & Yalom, 1982). Similarly, the male bias affects the questions that are researched in the study of women's work (Acker, 1978). The term *labor force* has traditionally referred to those working for pay and has excluded those doing unpaid work, such as housework and volunteer jobs—areas that are predominantly female. Thus findings on labor force participation are more likely to reflect the significant elements of men's lives than of women's lives.

Family Privacy and Research Ethics

To produce trustworthy information, researchers must choose an appropriate research method, focus on appropriate units of analysis, select a representative sample, design valid indicators, and avoid the incorporation of personal biases and interests. They must also take seriously the ethical dilemmas posed by their research. Since most social research represents an intrusion into people's lives, it can disrupt their ordinary activities and often requires them to reveal personal information about themselves. Research on families often deals with sensitive topics and activities. The most compelling and interesting elements of family life occur beyond the watchful eyes of others. ▲ Most sexual acts, for instance, occur in the privacy of the home and aren't amenable to observation. Indeed, unless the researcher uses a hidden camera, the very fact of observing people changes the nature of the phenomenon being studied. Private family life immediately ceases to be private once people are aware that they are being studied.

▲ Issue 3 offers a detailed examination of the role that privacy plays in family life.

Even paper-and-pencil surveys sometimes involve the disclosure of very personal information—like sexual satisfaction or marital conflict—which can be embarrassing or damaging to the self-esteem of subjects. To a person who has just lost his or her job, answering a simple question like "What is your annual income?" can be a devastating blow.

For my doctoral dissertation, I surveyed eighty-two married and cohabiting couples to analyze the effects that gender and power have on the ways people think about, speak about, and explain events in their intimate relationships. One particular question I wanted to answer was whether relative power has an impact on the ways people perceive conflict in their relationships. Are powerless people more or less likely than powerful people to blame themselves for problems? Are powerless people more sensitive to potentially problematic situations? I designed a series of questionnaire items to generate the necessary data.

I followed all the appropriate procedures (securing approval of the university's human subjects review committee, informing subjects of the nature of the study, and obtaining signed consent forms). But right from the start it was painfully clear to me that I was entering potentially dangerous territory. I was asking people to indicate things about their partners and their relationships that caused problems. If I had been a family therapist eliciting this information so I could offer them helpful advice, I could easily justify the intrusion into their privacy. But I was just some researcher they didn't know who was asking them very intimate questions to add to my discipline's collective understanding of the dynamics of intimacy. In fact, not only were they doing me a favor by participating, they were doing it for free (as a poor graduate student, I couldn't even pay them anything for their trouble).

I worried terribly about the possibility that in answering my questions about conflict, some of the respondents might become aware of a level of unhappiness they hadn't been aware of before. I had nightmares about couples fighting—and eventually divorcing—over an item on my questionnaire. Such is the risk we take when we attempt to peer into the private lives of families in order to explain them.

Family researchers, therefore, must take special care to balance the risks posed to participants by procedures that could be seen as intrusive and threatening with the benefits to society of studying something we all have an interest in: the intimate aspects of family life (Bussell, 1994). Family researchers must try to protect the rights of subjects and minimize the amount of harm or disruption they may experience as a result of being part of a study. Consequently, most researchers agree that no one should be forced to participate in research, that those who do participate ought to be fully informed of the possible risks involved, and that every precaution ought to be taken to protect the confidentiality and anonymity of subjects.

At the same time, however, researchers must attempt to secure the most accurate information possible. Sometimes this requirement conflicts with ethical considerations. Consider sociologist Laud Humphreys' 1970 study called *The Tearoom Trade*, a study many sociologists found ethically indefensible. Humphreys was interested in studying homosexuality. In particular, he was interested in anonymous and casual homosexual encounters among strangers. He decided to study such interactions in "tearooms"—places, like public restrooms, where male homosexuals go for anonymous sex. (This study was done well before the AIDS epidemic significantly curtailed such activity.)

Because of the secretive and potentially stigmatizing nature of the phenomenon he was interested in, Humphreys couldn't just come right out and ask people about their actions, nor could he openly observe them. So he decided to engage in a secretive form of field research. He posed as a lookout, called a "watchqueen," whose job was to warn of intruders as homosexual men engaged in sexual acts in public restrooms. By misrepresenting his identity, Humphreys was able to conduct very detailed observations of these encounters.

But he also wanted to know about the regular lives of these men. Whenever possible he wrote down the license numbers of the participants' cars and tracked down their names and addresses with the help of a friend in the local police department. About a year later he arranged for these individuals to be part of a simple medical survey being conducted by some of his colleagues. He then disguised himself and visited their homes, supposedly to conduct interviews for the medical survey. He found that most of the men were heterosexual, had families, and were rather respected members of their communities. In short, they led altogether conventional lives.

Although this information shed a great deal of light on the nature of anonymous homosexual acts, some critics argued that Humphreys had violated the ethics of research by deceiving his unsuspecting subjects and violating their privacy rights. Others, however, supported Humphreys, arguing that he could have studied this topic in no other way. In fact, his book won a prestigious award. But close to 30 years later, the ethical controversy surrounding this study still persists.

In sum, despite all the potential problems, social research remains an effective and efficient way of providing us with information about families. We just have to be careful and critical consumers of such information, questioning how and from whom it was collected.

Conclusion

I hope that you now have a good sense of what family research is, how it is related to theory, how it is done, and what some of its potential pitfalls are. The development of a body of knowledge about families depends on solid research techniques. Thus we must maintain a healthy skepticism and curiosity as we critically examine the family claims made by scholars, social critics, politicians, pundits, and talk show hosts.

CHAPTER HIGHLIGHTS

- To some degree, everyone is an expert on families. That expertise is based on personal experiences with our own families. However, such information is inevitably biased and

idiosyncratic. Systematic social scientific research provides a more sophisticated understanding of family experiences and patterns.

- Sociological research is grounded in a handful of theoretical perspectives: sociobiology, structural functionalism, the conflict perspective, social exchange theory, and symbolic interactionism. Each perspective has something to offer in the effort to understand families and the institution of family; each has shortcomings.

- Sociologists provide useful information about families through a variety of research techniques: experiments, field research, surveys, and unobtrusive research.

- Although systematic research is more trustworthy than informal observation, we still must be careful consumers of published research information about families. The nature of the people being studied, the way certain phenomena are measured, and the values and interests of the researcher can all skew the results of a study, rendering our beliefs about family life inaccurate.

DEMO•GRAPHIC ESSAY

Households versus Families

One of the most useful sources of data on families is the U.S. Bureau of the Census. As mandated by the U.S. Constitution, the Census Bureau compiles a complete count of the U.S. population every 10 years, called the decennial census. The most recent count was done in 1990, and the next one takes place in the year 2000. The Census Bureau sends a survey form to every household, as well as to institutions such as prisons, college dormitories, and nursing homes.

According to the Census Bureau, a household consists of a group of one or more persons who live and eat together in a residence with its own access to the outside or to a common hallway. Households consisting of only one person are called single-person households. Another type of household is a family household, a group of two or more persons living together who are related by birth, marriage, or adoption. (See Issue 1.) Nonfamily households include single-person households and households with two or more persons who are not related. By these definitions, a married couple without children is a family household, but two friends who live together are a nonfamily household. Extended kin who do not live in the same residence are not considered part of a single family, according to the U.S. Census. These definitions have important ramifications for both theory and research on families.

Exhibit 1-A uses the Census Bureau's definition of families and households. It shows that in 1996, 70 percent of all households were family households and 30 percent were nonfamily households.

Exhibit 1-A

Types of
Households

United States: 1996

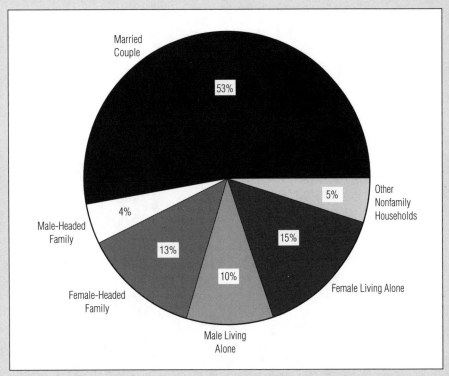

Source of data: U.S. Bureau of the Census, *Statistical Abstract of the United States: 1997* (117th edition). Washington, DC, 1997.

Exhibit 1-B

Average Size of
Families and
Households

*United States:
1790–1995*

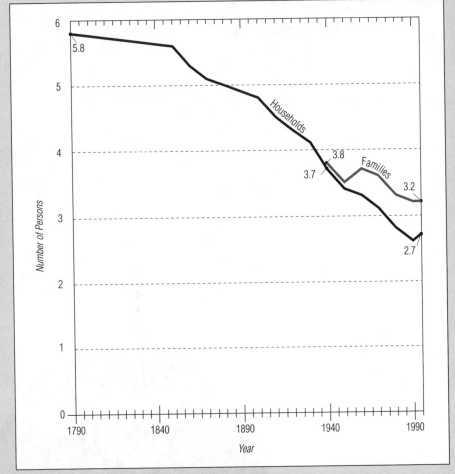

Sources of data: 1790–1970: U.S. Bureau of the Census, *Historical Statistics of the United States, Colonial Times to 1970.*
Washington, DC, 1975. 1980–1990: U.S. Bureau of the Census, *Statistical Abstract of the United States: 1997* (117th
edition). Washington, DC, 1997.

Although some researchers use different definitions, all would agree that the average size of households
and families has been declining. Exhibit 1-B charts the decline in household size beginning with the first census in 1790. Since 1940, the Census Bureau has also collected information about the average size of families
in the United States. Why might the trends for the size of households be different than the trend for the size of
families? One way to answer this question is to look at the composition of households over time. Exhibit 1-C
reveals two trends: Since 1940, the proportion of family households has declined steadily, while the percentage of single-person households has been rising. Because more and more households consist of persons living alone, the average size of households has declined more steeply than has the average size of families.

Exhibit 1-C

Types of Households

*United States:
1940–1995*

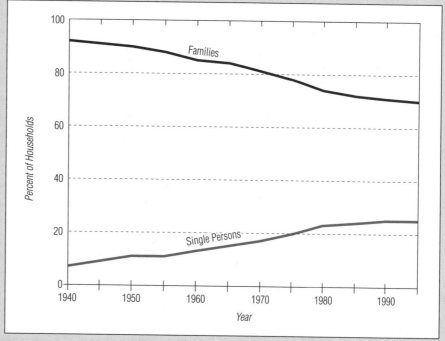

Sources of data: 1940–1965: U.S. Bureau of the Census, *Historical Statistics of the United States, Colonial Times to 1970.* Washington, DC, 1975. 1970–1995: U.S. Bureau of the Census, *Statistical Abstract of the United States: 1997* (117th edition). Washington, DC, 1997.

Questions for Further Study

1. **In what ways are the Census Bureau's definitions of "family" and "household" useful for research? In what ways might they be too constraining?**

2. **Have you heard the expression "lying with statistics"? Explain how the information in Exhibit 1-A could be used to tell two opposite stories about "family values" in the United States today.**

3. **What factors could account for the historical decrease in the average size of families? Put more simply, why do you think that families are smaller today than they were in 1940? The *Statistical Abstract of the United States* contains tables that may provide clues to this question.**

4. **What might be some of the reasons for the increase in single-person households in the United States? What characteristics might be typical of persons who live alone in their own household? Consider such variables as age, gender, marital status, ethnicity, income, and education. Try to come up with hypotheses that could predict who is likely to be living alone.**

YOUR TURN

In this chapter I have outlined some of the basic ways sociologists go about understanding families—from the theories that shape their thinking to the methods they use to collect data. But one of the key themes has been that you can be an informed consumer of sociological information on families even if you are not a trained researcher. You just need to understand the ways that research can be biased.

Over the span of 2 weeks, collect all the articles you can find in newspapers and weekly news magazines that deal with some aspect of families. (You can expand your comparisons by including an assessment of coverage in local and national television news shows.) Try to examine a local newspaper as well as a major national newspaper (*USA Today*, the *New York Times*, the *Washington Post*). Pay particular attention to the information that is presented in these articles as "fact" (census statistics, academic research findings, informal interview results, and so on). How are these "facts" presented? Do the authors provide any information about the way the "facts" were collected or the way subjects were recruited? Does a particular theoretical framework or political ideology seem to guide the article? What is missing from the account that would have allowed a more comprehensive understanding of the "facts" that were presented?

Was a particular event (for instance, a high-profile divorce or custody case) covered in all the sources you looked at? If so, how did their coverage of this event differ? That is, did news magazines cover it differently from newspapers? How did local coverage differ from national coverage? How can you explain the differences that you've identified?

What can you conclude about the "trustworthiness" of family information as presented in the popular press? Are some press sources more "objective" than others? How do you think this coverage affects our "knowledge" of families?

CHAPTER 2

Intimate Relationships: Love, Sex, and Attraction

All of the following appeared on the same day in the "Style" section of a recent edition of my local newspaper:

- Two letters to a column called "Single File": one from a love-starved widower who wanted to know how to find a companion and another from a woman who was distressed over the fact that her lover wanted a friendship more than a serious relationship.
- An article on how larger single women can find ways to look more attractive without losing weight.
- An ad for a matchmaking service designed exclusively for busy professionals. The company's motto was "Life, love & dessert."
- An article on a company that is marketing a product called Boyfriend-in-a-Box. For $14.95 you receive a kit which includes a 5" x 7" portrait and a matching wallet-sized photo of an attractive, successful man (you have six "Mr. Rights" to choose from); several letters from "him" expressing everlasting love and devotion; several "I'm sorry" cards; a stack of pink phone message slips to prove he can't stop calling; and a summary of all pertinent physical, biographical, financial, and personality information. Of course, the man doesn't exist. The company hopes that many unattached women want to convince people that they have a boyfriend, even when they don't. ("Perfect boyfriend," 1997)

Newspapers all over the country commonly devote considerable space to these and other aspects of intimate relationships. You'd be hard-pressed to find a single issue of a supermarket tabloid or glamour magazine that didn't have an article about the joys and anxieties of love, romance, and sex. Internet sites, television talk shows, and self-help books provide us with advice, warnings, and pseudoscientific analyses about every conceivable aspect of intimacy.

Our colossal cultural preoccupation with intimacy has given rise to a thriving industry devoted to bringing people together and keeping them together. Singles' bars, singles' apartment complexes, church-based singles groups, and computer and video dating services serve as modern-day matchmakers. International dating services—often in the form of "mail-order catalogs"—are becoming increasingly popular, and thousands of American men each year search for potential brides in distant countries like Russia, Korea, or the Philippines (Egan, 1996).

What's all the fuss about? Why do we devote so much attention to these matters? It no doubt has a great deal to do with the importance of intimate relationships in our everyday lives. We learn early on that these relationships are the standard against which we judge the quality and happiness of our entire lives. Cultural and media images tell us that we can't be truly fulfilled without falling in love, being sexually satisfied, and having a long-term relationship with someone, although our attitudes toward intimacy can be somewhat ambivalent (see Exhibit 2.1).

But while the need for intimacy continues to occupy a lofty position in the culture, dramatic social changes over the past few decades have made relationships confusing. Young people today become sexually active and involved in intimate relationships earlier than ever before. Heretofore unacceptable forms of intimacy—heterosexual and homosexual cohabitation, for example—are becoming more commonplace and acceptable. At the same time, marriages and other long-term relationships continue to be far from permanent. More people are choosing not to marry or are waiting longer to get married (see Demo•Graphic Essay, "Trends in Marriage," at the end of this chapter). And the darker side of intimacy—physical abuse, sexual violence, AIDS and other sexually transmitted diseases—is now impossible to ignore.

Exhibit 2.1

Conflicting Values Regarding Marriage

United States: 1994 and 1996

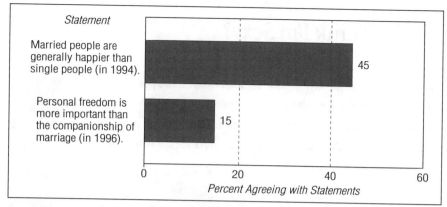

Sources of data: National Opinion Research Center, University of Chicago, *General Social Survey, 1994* and *1996.*

The intense need for intimacy, coupled with all these difficulties, has increased the demands we make on our intimate partners. We have come to expect our partners to fulfill *all* our sexual, emotional, social, intellectual, and economic needs. Under the weight of such a burden, it's not surprising that so many people spend so much time thinking about—and will pay good money to find out—how to attract and keep the right person; how to add spice, vigor, and longevity to a sagging relationship; or how to end a relationship that's not working so the search for a more fulfilling one can begin.

One thing remains constant, however: Close, intimate relationships provide people with a great deal of happiness, often serve as a prelude to marriage, and are the fundamental building blocks of all family forms (see Exhibit 2.2). To understand their role in family life you need to examine how these relationships develop and what personal and social factors influence them. This chapter looks at the process through which relationships unfold, paying particular attention to dating, courtship, and mate selection. But first it examines the broader cultural contexts of love, romance, and sexuality—the defining characteristics of intimate relationships.

Exhibit 2.2

The Nature of Romantic Relationships: Survey of 320 Unmarried Men and Women

United States: 1996

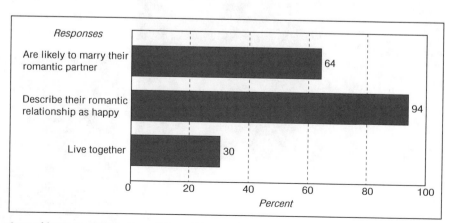

Source of data: National Opinion Research Center, University of Chicago, *General Social Survey, 1996.*

Do You Think I'm Sexy?

Fools fall in love, as the saying goes, but what compels two people to become involved with each other? For most people it starts with finding someone they consider attractive and desirable. Attractiveness often begins with a glance. As much as we hate to admit it, looks are the initial and foremost indicator of attractiveness.

We may agree that this man lacks the traditional characteristics of attractiveness, but what exactly is he lacking? This woman is also not the supermodel type, but she seems to see herself as attractive. More than just lacking physical prowess and classical beauty, the man doesn't demonstrate the self-confidence and allure we find so compelling. But what is attractive? Is it the same for everyone? At what point are we able to move beyond physical appearance in assessing another person's attractiveness?

Ideas about who is attractive are certainly more than a matter of genetics. Take these twins. The one in the photo on the left has recently gotten married. The one below certainly has a love interest, but her taste is very different from her twin sister's—she is a lesbian.

Some sociologists maintain that we look for partners who are similar to us in attitudes, values, beliefs, and educational attainment. These two people are so closely matched that they even dress somewhat alike.

Other sociologists believe in an "opposites attract" philosophy—that we're drawn to people who are different from us. As race relations improve, younger generations are not maintaining the imperative that previous generations felt to date and marry within their religion, ethnic group, or race. But coming from different social backgrounds means that these individuals are likely to bring different perspectives, socialization experiences, and tastes with them into their relationship.

More importantly, people are drawn to those they are in close proximity to. Most of the time we can become involved only with someone we come into contact with, which may explain the prevalence of office romances. As the old song says, "If you can't be with the one you love, love the one you're with."

In the end, despite our idealistic dreams, relationship formation exists in the real world, which is often anything but sexy and romantic.

The Cultural Context of Intimacy

Intimacy is the state of being emotionally and affectionately close to another person. It exists in all sorts of relationships, such as those between friends or between parents and children. But here we will focus primarily on romantic and sexual relationships.

Romantic Love

To most of us, love is a magical emotion that defies logical explanation. We don't really know how or why we fall in love. Most of us would have a difficult time describing the point in time when we knew we were in love. And for the most part we don't want those things explained. Many people feel that too much analysis would defile the wonderful and mysterious essence of the love experience. Nevertheless, a scholarly examination of love provides us with important insight into common patterns as well as the role social forces play in its definition and experience.

Webster's Unabridged Dictionary defines love as "attraction or desire for a person who arouses delight or admiration and elicits feelings of tenderness or sympathy." In everyday life, we typically don't use such concepts when we describe love. Indeed, common descriptions of love often include a variety of physical sensations that sometimes seem more like pain and discomfort than an enjoyable emotional experience, as we see in this characterization: "I have trouble concentrating. . . . I experience heart palpitations and rapid breathing. . . . I experience physical sensations—cold hands, butterflies in my stomach, tingling spine. I have insomnia. I can't think of anyone else but my lover" (quoted in Carr, 1988, p. 53).

Sociologists tend to use a more "sophisticated" definition of **love**:

> Love is a relatively enduring bond where a small number of people are affectionate and emotionally committed to each other, define their collective well-being as a major goal, and feel obliged to provide care and practical assistance for each other. People who love each other also usually share physical contact; they talk to each other frequently and cooperate in some routine tasks of daily life. (Cancian, 1993, p. 205)

What is it that makes one situation between two people who care for each other and revel in each other's company a "friendly relationship" and another a "love relationship"? Of course, at one level, the people involved define their own relationship. According to the symbolic interactionist perspective, one's interpretation of a specific relationship defines it as friendship or love. ▲ Maybe you know two people who like to do things together, confide in each other constantly, and are very affectionate toward one another in public. They look, for all intents and purposes, as if they're in love. Yet they say that they aren't—that they're just very close friends. On the other hand, you may know of two people who always seem to be at each other's throats—constantly arguing, fighting, and insulting each other. Yet they maintain that they are very deeply in love and couldn't live without each other.

▲ See Chapter 1 for an overview of symbolic interactionism.

The people involved might themselves experience this sort of definitional ambiguity. I'm sure you know of situations in which the two people involved have vastly different definitions of their relationship.

You can see that love relationships don't develop smoothly. Instead they "ebb and flow, with false starts and continual negotiations and renegotiations" (Kollock & Blumstein, 1988, p. 481).

In the early stages of a relationship, when a clear definition has yet to emerge, a little uncertainty may be tolerable or even enticing. Later on, however, ambiguity can become frustrating. Some may tackle the matter boldly and directly by simply asking, "How do you feel about me?" or "What exactly is going on here?" Others are less direct, looking for signs and clues of the other person's affections, seeking out the opinions of third parties, or dropping subtle hints in an attempt to draw the other person's feelings into the open.

Cultural Variation in Love   Conceptions of love and of its importance in relationships varies across cultures. One question that has interested anthropologists and sociologists is whether or not romantic love is a universal emotion. Anthropologists William Jankowiak and Edward Fischer (1992) examined cultural folklore and anthropologists' accounts of 166 societies around the world, seeking indicators of the existence of romantic love. ▲ They looked for stories of personal longing, use of love songs in romantic involvement, elopement due to mutual affection, and native accounts of passionate love.

▲ This is an example of unobtrusive research, which is discussed in Chapter 1.

On the basis of these indicators, they found that an overwhelming majority of the societies they studied (about 88 percent) recognized romantic love as a component in the formation of intimate relationships, although they point out that societies vary a lot in how common such passionate feelings are. One woman who lived in a hunting and gathering society in the Kalahari Desert of Africa differentiated between companionship and romantic love by contrasting her relationship with her husband and her lover. She used terms like "rich, warm and secure" to describe her marriage. But in describing her lover she said, "When two people come together their hearts are on fire and their passion is very great" (quoted in Jankowiak & Fischer, 1992, p. 152).

In another study, college students from ten countries were asked this question: "Would you marry someone with all the right qualities if you didn't love them?" (Levine, 1993). The researcher assumed that individuals from cultures that emphasized romantic love would be likely to answer "no" to such a question. Indeed, 86 percent of the American respondents said they wouldn't consider marrying without love; a similar percentage of Brazilian students also said "no." But three-quarters of Pakistani and Indian students said they would have no problem marrying someone they didn't love.

In Pakistan and India, of course, arranged marriages based on family and economic considerations are still commonplace. To people from these countries, the reason Western marriages frequently fail is the inevitable disappointment that sets in after romantic love wears off (Bumiller, 1992). In response to a question about whether she loved her husband, a 20-year-old married Indian woman once replied:

> That's a very difficult question. I don't know. This whole concept of love is very alien to us. We're more practical. I don't see stars, I don't hear little bells. But he's a very nice guy, I get along with him fine and I think I'm going to enjoy spending my life with him. Is that love? (quoted in Bumiller, 1992, p. 123)

You can see in this comment that this woman is fully aware of the ideal of romantic love—equating it with frivolous experiences like "seeing stars" and "hearing bells." Her perspective is not that romantic love doesn't exist but that it is not and shouldn't be the most important force behind a successful marriage.

▲ See Issue 4 for an examination of the balance between individual rights and family obligations in different cultures.

According to some scholars, the presence and importance of romantic love are determined by the broader values and traditions of a given culture. ▲ Psychologists Karen Dion and Kenneth Dion (1996) found that romantic love is much more important as a basis for intimate relationships in **individualist societies** than **collectivist societies**, which emphasize group obligations. When a society celebrates individual freedom, people's intimate choices are likely to be driven by personal feelings and emotions.

In collectivist societies where romantic love is not a crucial aspect of relationships, people's intimate expectations can seem quite low to us. For example, Japan has what appears to be a strong family institution. The Japanese divorce rate is half that of the United States. Yet in many cases intimate relationships in Japan are structured on a very different emotional foundation than we in the West would expect in our marriages. To some Japanese, the strength of their marriages is a matter of patience and low emotional expectations. When asked if he loved his wife of 33 years, one man said, "Yeah, so-so, I guess. She's like air or water. You couldn't live without it, but most of the time, you're not conscious of its existence" (quoted in Kristof, 1996b, p. A1). Low expectations function to prevent marital breakups. If a couple discovers that they don't love each other or have nothing in common, they really don't have much reason for divorce, because low emotional involvement is par for the course. Although the Japanese tend to oppose divorce, only about a third of them would marry the same person if they had it to do over again, according to one study (cited in Kristof, 1996b).

▲ Issue 5 presents a detailed examination of gender and power in families.

Feminization of Love   In this society, how people define love relationships and how they express affection are often influenced by the different power positions of men and women. ▲ Certainly men and women are more similar than they are different when it comes to intimacy. But the differences that do exist are worth noting. For instance, research suggests that women generally scrutinize their experiences of love more than men do, leading to more sensitivity and responsiveness to what is going on in their relationships (Holtzworth-Munroe & Jacobson, 1985). Men, on the other hand, tend to be less reflective, falling in love more quickly and less intentionally than women. They are more likely to believe in "love at first sight" and less likely to "work" on their love relationships than women (Hochschild, 1983).

Within the context of marriage, research consistently shows that wives disclose more emotional intimacy to their partner than husbands do (Thompson & Walker, 1989). Women also usually experience and express a wider range of emotions in marriage, such as tenderness, fear, and sadness. In short, wives generally seem to be more expressive and affectionate than husbands—a difference that upsets many wives:

> Women tend to complain that their husbands do not care about their emotional lives and do not express their own feelings and thoughts. Women often say that they have to pull things out of their husbands and push them to open up. Men tend to respond either that they are open or that they do not understand what it is their wives want from them. Men often protest that no matter how much they talk it is never enough for their wives. (Thompson & Walker, 1989, p. 846)

The emotion of love has itself become *feminized*. The **feminization of love** means that love is culturally defined in terms of emotional expression, verbal disclosure, vulnerability, warmth, and affection—tendencies typically considered "feminine" in American society (Cancian, 1993). Expressing tender feelings, being gentle, and being aware of others' feelings—things we would all agree ought to be present in love relationships—are ideal qualities we stereotypically associate with women, not men. Desirable qualities for men, on the other hand, usually include being independent, strong, competent, assertive, and unemotional, characteristics that run counter to common conceptions of love.

In heterosexual relationships, feminized conceptions of love reinforce men's power over women. The emotional dependence on women that many men do experience remains, for the most part, culturally unrecognized. But women's economic dependence on men is overt and exaggerated (Cancian, 1987). Furthermore, the intimate talk about personal troubles that appeals to women requires a willingness to see oneself as weak and in need of support. Being responsive to the needs of others—another feature of women's love—leads to giving up some control and, in a sense, being "on call" to provide care whenever it's required (Cancian, 1993). Hence, the power that women can have—controlling such resources as understanding, sex, or, in traditional couples, homemaking—remains largely hidden because men's dependence on these abilities is not something we hear much about. ▲

▲ For more on the devaluation of women in American society, read Issue 5.

According to sociologist Francesca Cancian (1987), love became feminized with the rise of capitalism and the shift from an agrarian to an industrial economy in the nineteenth century. As economic production separated from the home and from personal relationships, women's and men's roles became more polarized. ▲ Women became responsible for the "emotional management" of the family relationships. Men took on duties in the larger world of work and became defined by the responsibilities they held there. The masculine ideal in a capitalist economy was to be an independent, self-made man with virtues like self-control, economic success, courage, and an upright character. Intimacy, emotional expression, and other feminine qualities had no place in the work world and therefore became devalued. Love was what women did in the home; it had nothing to do with what men did at work. In fact, women's "superior" ability to love was seen as enabling them to more effectively comfort and care for their children and husbands.

▲ Additional detail on the history of American family life appears in Issue 2.

Cancian (1987, 1993) argues that men today tend to have a distinctive style of love that focuses on practical help, shared physical activities, time spent together, and sex. She describes an interview with a 29-year-old man who said that he feels especially close to his wife after they have had sex: "I don't talk to her very often, I guess, but somehow I feel we have really communicated after we have made love" (quoted in Cancian, 1987, p. 77). There is no doubt in this man's mind that he shows his wife how much he loves her every time they have sex. For many women, of course, such an attitude is precisely the problem. To them, the only real communication is verbal communication. If sexual behavior were widely regarded in the culture as the primary means of expressing love, the way talking about feelings currently is, then we would be reading all sorts of books and articles about the problem of *men* wanting love "too much" and women not wanting it enough. But for men today, love is defined not by constant verbal expressions of affection but by the things they do with and for their partner.

Given the feminization of love, we should not be surprised to find that many studies show women to be more interested and more skilled in love than men are (Cancian, 1987). For one thing, during adolescence girls acquire more cultural knowledge about romantic love, including

▲ The gender sociali-
zation of children and
adolescents is discussed
in Chapter 5.

the social norms that guide the expression of those feelings, than adolescent boys do (Simon, Eder, & Evans, 1992). ▲ In addition, researchers who study love, friendship, and intimacy often use indicators of love that reflect "feminine" styles. These studies tend to examine such activities as verbal self-disclosure and emotional expressiveness. When less-biased measures are used, the differences in men's and women's ability to love are slight. In one study, for example, women were much more likely than men to *say* that their loved ones (including parents and relatives) were very important to them. However, when actual contact with loved ones was measured, the differences disappeared (Adams, 1968).

In sum, the fact that women have more close relationships, appear to care about those relationships more, and seem more skilled at expressing feelings doesn't mean that men are distant and unconcerned about love relationships. In national surveys, men and women alike rank family bonds as the most important element of their lives. The feminized perspective on love, however, leads us to believe that women *need* love more than men do, even though research on the effect of love relationships on physical and psychological well-being shows that men need it at least as much as, if not more, than women do (Gove, Style, & Hughes, 1990; Umberson, Chen, House, Hopkins, & Slaten, 1996).

Sexuality

Sexuality is another crucial element of intimate relationships. America, as I'm sure you know, is preoccupied with sex, overflowing with media images and cultural traditions that emphasize sexuality. As sociologist Lillian Rubin describes it:

> In the public arena, sex screams at us at every turn—from our television and movie screens, from the billboards on our roadways, from the pages of our magazines, from the advertisements for goods, whether they seek to sell automobiles, soap, or undergarments. Bookstore shelves bulge with volumes about sex, all of them dedicated to telling us what to do and how to do it. TV talk shows feature solemn discussions of pornography, impotence, premarital sex, marital sex, extramarital sex, group sex, swinging, sadomasochism, and as many other variations of sexual behavior their producers can think of, whether the ordinary or the bizarre. (Rubin, 1990, p. 9)

The publication of the independent counsel's report on President Clinton's affair with a White House intern in 1998 created unprecedented traffic on the Internet as citizens hurried to read about the explicit details of their sexual encounters.

All this attention is a far cry from the late nineteenth century, when sex was something people spoke about only in hushed, secret tones. So disagreeable was the discussion of sex then that any topic remotely sexual was to be avoided. For instance, the terms "white meat" and "dark meat" used to describe poultry emerged to avoid names of body parts like thighs and breasts (Coontz, 1992).

Yet Americans are reluctant to acknowledge the role of these cultural images on our own sexual attitudes and behaviors (Schur, 1988). Instead, we tend to see sexuality as a "natural" phenomenon that we develop into. Admittedly, our expression of affection for another person has obvious biological components. And human genital equipment is pretty much the same world-wide. Consequently, many people simply assume that we are born with sexual drives that play themselves out at the appropriate stage of development.

But if human sexuality were purely biological, it would fall under strict hormonal control much like the sexual behavior of other animals. The majority of animals engage in no sexual behavior at all during most of the year. Mating occurs only when the male and female are fertile and such activity can lead to pregnancy. This period of time, known as *estrus,* instinctually drives sexual urges. If you've ever had a pet dog "in heat," you know how profoundly its behavior can change during this season.

In humans, as in other mammals, the production of sperm and eggs is controlled by hormones. But human sexuality does not fall under complete hormonal control. We have no limited period of estrus. The average human female is able to conceive about once a month, and the average human adult male is more or less constantly fertile. Furthermore, humans regularly have sex at times when conception is not possible and indeed not desired. Sexual activity thus has symbolic as well as physical significance. We have sex for fun, as a way of telling another how much we care for him or her, as a way to satisfy our egos, or for any number of other reasons. Our advanced cognitive abilities allow us to become sexually aroused by vivid mental imagery or simply by the sound of a lover's voice.

If sexuality were a universal biological drive, we'd also expect to see vast similarities across time and space in the ways people experience sexuality. But sexual diversity is the rule, not the exception. People differ dramatically in what they find attractive and arousing. Some people's sexual appetites are insatiable and indiscriminant; others' are highly particular and selective. For some, sex is a pleasurable physical activity that need not be connected to deep emotions; for others, sex is enjoyable only if it occurs within the context of a long-term love relationship.

The meaning of sex can even change over the course of a relationship. In general, couples who are satisfied with their overall relationship tend also to be satisfied with their sex life (Blumstein & Schwartz, 1983). Married people tend to have sex more often than single people (though not as often as cohabitors), but sexual interest and activity tend to decrease as the relationship progresses. They are at their height during dating and courtship, drop when people begin to live together, fall further after marriage, and show the steepest decline after the birth of the first child (Rubin, 1990).

Culture and Sexuality   You can see that exclusive reliance on biological drives as an explanation for human sexuality falls short. Individual preferences play a big role. So does culture. Every society has its own rules and expectations for sexual behavior. Most people in a given society follow the rules; some break them; but none can forget about them (Schwartz & Rutter, 1997).

Throughout your life you've been receiving messages telling you which sexual desires and behaviors were "normal" and which were "abnormal." These sexual customs and values are passed on by example, through informal and formal teaching, and indirectly through media images.

Within the same culture, however, different families have their own values and therefore teach widely divergent sexual lessons. A teenager growing up in our permissive culture but in a family in which sex outside of marriage is considered reprehensible may have to suppress feelings of arousal or channel them into "appropriate" pursuits like competitive sports. Teens raised in a home environment that encourages them to celebrate their sexuality will likely have a much different experience. But neither the culture's nor the family's values unequivocally influence sexuality. Siblings raised in the same environment can sometimes express their sexuality quite differently.

Cultural expectations regarding sexuality are most notable for their diversity. In some cultures, sexual contact between people of the same sex is considered a heinous crime punishable by death. In many others, however, it is socially acceptable, at least for certain people at certain times. Among the Sambia of Papua New Guinea, for example, every adolescent male is expected to engage in sexual relationships with other men as part of his initiation into adulthood; as an adult he's expected to enter a heterosexual marriage. In Sweden and the Netherlands, premarital sex is accepted as normal, and both men and women are expected to be sexually experienced when they marry. But in most Islamic societies, virginity at the time of marriage is the norm, especially for women. In some societies, women have no concept of orgasm; in other societies, they become intensely aroused during sex (Schwartz & Rutter, 1997).

Even our ideas about sexual dysfunction are culturally determined. Take, for instance, the problem of "abnormal" sexual desire. It is the number one complaint bringing American clients to sex therapists (Rosellini, 1992). On one end of the spectrum of "abnormality" is *hypoactive sexual desire disorder*, which the American Psychiatric Association identifies as a deficiency or absence of desire for sexual activity. The afflicted individual is not motivated to seek sexual stimuli and doesn't feel frustrated when deprived of the opportunity for sexual expression; she or he rarely initiates sexual activity and may only engage in it reluctantly when it is initiated by a partner. This "disorder" is believed to be about twice as common in women as in men. At the other end of the spectrum are people who engage in *compulsive sexual behavior*. Their sexual desire is considered too strong. Some people with this "condition" feel as if they're addicted to sexual activity. Although no one knows for sure how many people suffer from this problem, experts estimate the prevalence to be roughly 5 percent of the adult population (Rosellini, 1992).

Here we have two identifiable sexual disorders that affect millions of people. But what do "too much" and "too little" desire mean? How much sex should a "normal" person want? Of course what is considered normal sexual behavior varies widely from culture to culture. A "normal" amount of sexual activity among Chinese married couples, for example, is generally lower than that among couples in the West, even though approval of pre- and extramarital sex is substantially higher in China (cited in Hatfield & Rapson, 1993).

Even within the same culture, one person's idea of normal sexual desire could easily contrast with another's. Researchers of marriage and family have repeatedly found disagreement between spouses about the frequency and duration of sexual activity (Rubin, 1990). The partner who wishes for more tends to have lower estimates of sexual activity than the one who does not. In a scene from the 1977 film *Annie Hall* a split screen shows Alvie Singer (Woody Allen) and Annie (Diane Keaton) as unhappy lovers, each discussing the relationship with their respective therapists. Alvie complains that the couple "hardly ever" has sex anymore—maybe *only* three times a week. On the opposite side of the screen, Annie complains that she feels like they're having sex "constantly"—*as often as* three times per week (Schwartz & Rutter, 1997).

Ideals regarding normal sexual desire change over time as well. In the nineteenth century, low sexual desire was considered a good thing, at least in women; sexuality for purposes other than procreation and outside of marriage was considered evil. In 1907, Dr. John Harvey Kellogg developed the popular corn flake cereal that bears his name in an unsuccessful attempt to curb sexual desire (Rosellini, 1992).

Another common sexual problem that is highly influenced by culture is *premature ejaculation*, defined by the American Psychiatric Association as male orgasm with minimal sexual stimulation before or shortly after penetration and before the person wishes it. Notice that this definition implies heterosexual intercourse. So it can be considered a problem only within a narrowly defined realm of sexuality. In addition, premature ejaculation can only be considered a problem in a culture that contains some conception of female sexual desire, needs, and pleasure. The idea that a man can achieve an orgasm "too quickly" implies that it occurs before his partner has been satisfied. In cultures where only male sexuality matters or is defined as legitimate, it wouldn't make any difference when the man achieved an orgasm. In fact, in some countries where women's sexuality is of secondary importance, a man who ejaculates quickly is considered healthy, even virile (Schwartz & Rutter, 1997).

So you see that sexuality—from what we want to what we do—is more than just biology. Human beings are constantly involved in complex interactions with others. We all develop our own sexual scripts out of the range of experiences we've had. These scripts are limited by what we're taught, what we expect, and what we believe to be permissible and correct.

Sexual Orientation   Many people believe homosexuality is a choice, a preference, which is not influenced at all by a person's biological inheritance. Such a view has been popular for decades. Psychiatrists in the 1950s and 1960s wrote extensively about homosexuals as perverts and degenerates who, with the appropriate therapy, could overcome their pathological choices and "learn" to be heterosexual.

Recently, however, a growing body of literature is providing evidence in support of the argument that homosexuality—indeed, sexual orientation in general—is anatomically or genetically determined. In 1995 two scientists at the National Institutes of Health transplanted a single gene into the bodies of male fruit flies that caused them to display "courtship" behaviors with other male fruit flies (Zhang & Odenwald, 1995). Granted, the notion that a fruit fly could *be* "homosexual" in the same sense that a human could be is an overstatement, because sexual orientation is a human construction that includes not only physical desires but also psychological imagery and self-identity. Nevertheless, this research added to the mounting body of evidence that sexual orientation is rooted in biology.

In 1991 a California neuroscientist performed autopsies on the brains of men and women of known sexual orientation (LeVay, 1991). He found that a tiny region in the center of the brain was substantially smaller among the gay men he examined than among the heterosexual men. Despite the researcher's plea for caution in drawing quick conclusions from his findings—he pointed out that his research couldn't determine whether the observed brain differences were the cause or a consequence of sexual orientation—this study became a catalyst for scholarly and not-so-scholarly debate on the origins of human sexual orientation.

Another study found that the male relatives of known gay men were substantially more likely to also be homosexual (13.5 percent) than were the entire sample studied (2 percent). Indeed, the researcher discovered more gay relatives on the maternal side, fueling the contention that homosexuality is passed from generation to generation through women (Hamer & Coupland, 1994). Some researchers contend that studies like this one point toward a "gay gene."

As compelling as findings like these are, however, we must interpret them with caution. To date, there is no scientific agreement on the meaning of any of these findings.

The popular rhetoric surrounding genetic explanations of human behavior supposes that genes represent an unchangeable unit of human identity. Yet genes always interact with other genes and with the environment. A single gene is unlikely to be responsible for any complex human trait. We know, for instance, that genes are responsible for the development of our lungs, larynx, mouth, and the areas of the brain associated with speech. But such complexity can't be collapsed into a single "talking" gene. Likewise, genes determine the development of our penises, vaginas, and brains. But that's a far step from the contention that a single gene determines sexual orientation. Indeed, that "high" rate (13.5 percent) of homosexuality among relatives of gay men, for example, means that in over 86 percent of the cases these relatives were not gay. In short, variation in any trait is influenced by genes, family, wider life experiences, and the interaction between one or more genes and one or more environmental variables. A genetic factor may be one factor among many that help us to understand sexual orientation.

In this sense, genetic predispositions are hard to disentangle from the cultural vehicles of expression and identification. How do our genes get us from the biochemistry of cell proteins to the complex and unpredictable interplay of fantasy, courtship, arousal, and sexual selection that constitute "sexuality" (Horton, 1995)? Your genes may enable you to act in certain ways, but since we are all influenced by culture, these actions necessarily take on specific cultural forms. Terms like "heterosexuality" or "homosexuality" are thus inadequate and in some ways inaccurate. In fact, in some other cultures "sexual orientation" is not a variable with only two attributes; some cultures have three to five categories or even more.

Moreover, these studies really aren't examining the origins of sexual orientation. They're examining the origins of one type of sexual orientation: homosexuality. None of these researchers seem interested in explaining the origins of heterosexuality or bisexuality. For instance, if a certain structure in the brain is small in homosexual men and large in heterosexual men, is it somewhere in between among bisexual men? Furthermore, no data exist to prove a genetic link or a link based on brain structure with *female* sexual orientation, whether heterosexual or homosexual.

Consequently, none of these studies bothers to define just exactly what homosexuality is or how homosexuals are distinguished from heterosexuals. Classifying sexuality into homosexual and heterosexual categories doesn't really fit real-world experiences. Sexual behavior and lifestyles among men and women vary from day to day or year to year. Whether or not a sexual experience is characterized as homosexual depends on the definition one uses (Johnson, 1992). For instance, men in prisons who engage in sex acts with other men typically don't identify themselves as homosexual. Likewise, many people who consider themselves homosexual have never had an actual homosexual experience. In a national survey, many more people reported homosexual desire and behavior than reported homosexuality or bisexuality as their main sexual identity (Michael, Gagnon, Laumann, & Kolata, 1994).

We use terms like *lesbian, gay, bisexual*, and *straight* to refer to the ways in which people classify themselves. But these taken-for-granted sexual categories are, to some degree, cultural constructions. At the time of Plato, for instance, people didn't have a notion of two distinct sexual appetites allotted to different individuals or at odds with each other in the same individual. They simply saw two ways of enjoying one's pleasure (Foucault, 1990). Concepts like "the homosexual" and "the heterosexual" originated only toward the end of the nineteenth century when certain behaviors stopped being attributed to particular individuals and came to define certain groups of people. Those who had sexual relations with members of their own sex were now "homosexuals." Those who had sexual relations with people of the opposite sex were a different type of person, "a heterosexual."

Such categories emphasized inherent differences between groups of people based on sexual feelings. Medical writers eventually applied these categories to stigmatize same-sex relations as a form of sexual perversion. Men and women could no longer write of their affectionate desire for a loved one of the same gender—as was heretofore commonplace—without causing suspicion (D'Emilio & Freedman, 1988).

Our culture's fondness for dichotomous sexual categories has been questioned since the 1950s, when Alfred Kinsey published a report which argued that sexual orientation is not an "either-or" proposition but in fact lies along a continuum with "complete heterosexuality" at one end of the scale and "complete homosexuality" at the other. In between there are various gradations of sexuality, suggesting that people could be "bisexual" or "predominantly" heterosexual or homosexual. People's desire to code themselves as "one or the other" is in part influenced by the social costs of doing otherwise.

But let's suppose that sexual orientation is, in fact, biologically determined. What would be the social implications of such a contention? Some people argue that when individuals understand that being gay or lesbian is an innate characteristic beyond personal control, like hair or eye color, they will be more open minded about equality and the civil rights of gay Americans. For instance, the long-standing concern that homosexuals shouldn't work in occupations involving children (Boy Scout leader, elementary school teacher, child care worker, and so on) because of their potentially corrupting influence would disappear, because environmental influence on children's sexuality would no longer be considered a factor. ▲

▲ For more on the complexities of sexual orientation and childhood, read Chapter 5.

A 1992 *New York Times/CBS News* poll found that 71 percent of people who believe homosexuality is "something people choose to be" said they'd object to having a homosexual as a child's elementary school teacher. But only 39 percent of those who believe homosexuality is "something people cannot change" said they'd object (cited in LeVay, 1996). Incidentally, such negative feelings extended beyond those occupations that offer an opportunity to influence children. People who believe homosexuality is a choice were four times more likely to object to gay airplane pilots than people who believe it isn't a choice.

On the other hand, information about the genetic origins of sexual orientation might be used to perpetuate the belief that homosexuality is a "defect" that needs to be fixed, thereby further stigmatizing gays and lesbians. Ideas about biological determinism inevitably carry the threat of trying to manipulate genes, the brain, hormones, or whatever the purported biological cause to adapt to prevailing social norms. For instance, some scientists have argued that exposure to certain levels of testosterone at certain times in fetal development is a crucial factor in the development of "sex centers" in the brain. If so, prenatal tests like amniocentesis could, perhaps, "predict" homosexuality. And if this "condition" can be predicted, "prevention" is but a short step away. So alarming are the possibilities that eleven states currently have laws preventing information derived from genetic testing to be used in a discriminatory fashion (Horton, 1995).

Gender and Sexuality   Although contemporary research indicates that the female sex drive is just as strong as the male sex drive, common everyday beliefs still emphasize the "heightened" nature of male sexuality. For the first 60 years of this century, sex manuals portrayed female sexuality as either nonexistent, weak, or dormant compared to that of males. Even today people assume that men have stronger sexual appetites than women. Women, on the other hand, are assumed to "want" sex primarily within the context of an intimate relationship or within the security of married life and motherhood (Hollway, 1993).

These sorts of attitudes are particularly apparent in the kind of sexual possessiveness that characterizes American marriages. In our society, marriage is a contract for exclusive rights to sexual access between two spouses (Collins, 1992). Marriages are created by establishing sexual ties; thus the first act of sexual intercourse on the wedding night has traditionally been thought to symbolically ratify the marriage. If a couple who is legally married never has sexual intercourse, they are said not to have "consummated" the marriage. Such a situation used to be grounds for annulment, since a key term of the marriage contract had not been put into effect.

In traditional societies a woman's body was the exclusive sexual property of her husband (which explains why more emphasis was placed on the bride being a virgin at marriage than the husband). A husband's property rights over his wife were threatened if she had intercourse with another man. Under English common law, a man was legally incapable of committing adultery except as an accomplice to an errant wife. Indeed, the offense of adultery was not the sexual betrayal of one partner by the other, but the wife's engaging in acts that could taint the husband's bloodlines (Stoddard, 1992).

Gender differences in sexuality are further illustrated by comparing lesbian and gay male couples. Like their heterosexual counterparts, homosexuals grow up exposed to distinct male and female sexual norms. ▲ But unlike heterosexuals, homosexual partners bring similar, rather than different, sexual expectations into their relationships. Just as norms for heterosexual males and females differ, so too do the norms for gay men and lesbians (Schwartz & Rutter, 1997).

In the 1970s and early 1980s, the gay male community advocated a stereotypically male approach to sexuality: **recreational sex** (sexual pleasure for its own sake) over **relational sex** (sex within the context of ongoing relationships). By the mid-1980s, however, the spectre of AIDS brought a noticeable shift toward couplehood. Nevertheless, a significant number of gay men still approve of recreational sex and nonmonogamy, even if they are currently in lifetime relationships.

Lesbians, like heterosexual women in general, tend to prefer sex in the context of ongoing, committed relationships. Despite the growth in recent years of "lesbian sex clubs," which celebrate anonymous sex, few lesbians approve of recreational or nonmonogamous sex. As a group, lesbians have sex less frequently than married, cohabiting heterosexual or gay male couples. They also tend to prize nongenital physical contact—cuddling, touching, hugging—more than

▲ Differences between heterosexual couples and homosexual couples—and between lesbian and gay male couples—are discussed further in Chapter 3 and Chapter 6.

other couples. Whereas heterosexual women, having to adapt to male sexuality, come to see snuggling and touching as a prelude to intercourse, lesbians are likely to consider these activities as ends in themselves (Blumstein & Schwartz, 1983).

We must be careful, therefore, in assuming that "having sex" means the same thing to people of all sexual orientations. ▲ Does the fact that lesbians indicate a lower frequency of sex than heterosexuals or gay men indicate that they "have less sex"? Perhaps not. The average duration of a heterosexual sexual encounter is approximately 8 minutes, punctuated by one partner (typically the man) or both partners achieving orgasm. The average duration of a lesbian sexual episode is quite a bit longer—30 to 60 minutes on average—and may not result in orgasm on either partner's part (Frye, 1992). How many instances of "having sex" are included in an entire evening's worth of cuddling and hugging? To the extent that a standard heterosexual and male definition is used by everyone, the frequency of "having sex" among lesbians will be underestimated. Indeed, if we simply use achieving orgasm as the punctuating event that determines whether an encounter is or isn't "having sex," then most lesbian couples (and many heterosexual women) *never* "have sex."

▲ Chapter 1 examines the importance of accurate indicators in social research on families.

Dating and Courtship

Against the cultural backdrop of love and sexuality, we can now examine the institutional mechanisms through which people meet potential partners. Every society has its own acceptable means of bringing people together, although the process varies markedly from society to society.

In American society, **dating** is the recognized means by which most people move from being single to being coupled. Dating is a somewhat ambiguous phenomenon, blurred by different uses of vocabulary. Terms like "dating," "going out," "going around," "hanging out," "going steady," and "being involved" often lack clear definition and agreement.

One day my elder son (he was 10 at the time) came home from school and happily proclaimed that a girl in his class wanted to "go out" with him. But he was in a quandary. It seems he was already "going out" with someone else. What I couldn't figure out was where fifth graders who were going out with each other actually went. So I asked him.

"Oh, we don't go anywhere," he said, matter-of-factly. Nor did he spend any time at school with the girl or talk to her.

"How do you even know you like each other?" I asked.

"Well . . . if she likes me one of her friends will tell one of my friends who'll tell me. If I like her, one of my friends will tell one of her friends who'll tell her."

"And that's when the two of you are 'going out'?" I asked, hoping to have finally gotten it.

"I dunno," he said, a little surprised that I'd even ask such a question, "I have no idea what she thinks."

Such a conception of "going out" is a far cry from what I or most people my age would consider dating. Although it's difficult to come up with a definition that would apply across situations—first dates, blind dates, double dates, group dates, formal courtship, dating among divorced or widowed people, and so on—all dating seems to involve some degree of companionship, communication, good times, mutual sharing, romantic overtones, and perhaps sexual contact (Laner, 1989). It is these last two features—romance and sex—that typically distinguish "dating" from casual social outings that take place between people who consider themselves "just friends."

The Purposes of Dating

Some sociologists (for instance, Waller, 1937) have long argued that one of the key functions of dating in American society—particularly high school dating—is that it serves as a way of gaining social status among one's peers.

▲ This view is consistent with structural functionalism, whose uses and shortcomings are discussed in Chapter 1.

According to other sociologists, a more important social function of dating—at least in a heterosexual context—is that it allows males and females to interact with and learn about one another. ▲ It provides an opportunity for exploring romantic intimacy without requiring a rapid escalation toward marriage. It lets individuals learn about the types of people to whom they're attracted. Dating, then, can be seen as a sort of rehearsal for future serious relationships.

Indeed, the American dating culture is based on an assumption that dating provides important experiences and valuable lessons that will eventually help people select mates and construct happy marriages. But what exactly is the relationship between dating experiences and future marital success and happiness? Sociologist Martin King Whyte (1990) interviewed 459 women in the greater Detroit area to answer this question. The women, from diverse racial and ethnic backgrounds, ranged in age from 18 to 75. All had been married at least once.

Whyte asked them to recall their dating and premarital experiences. Contrary to common perceptions, he found that neither dating variety, length of dating, length of courtship or engagement, or degree of premarital intimacy with a future husband were related to marital success. The amount and type of dating didn't seem to make a difference one way or the other. Women who married their first loves were just as likely to have long-lasting and satisfying marriages as women who had dated a lot before marrying. Similarly, women who married after only a short acquaintance were equally likely to have successful marriages as women who knew their husbands-to-be for years. Marital quality was the same for women who were virgins upon marriage as it was for women who had a variety of sexual partners before marriage.

So apparently dating doesn't really serve as a training ground for marriage. And if you think about it, we really don't have any reason to expect it to. The behaviors that tend to characterize dating—fun, recreation, erotic teasing, and so forth—are not the sorts of activities that necessarily prepare one for the everyday demands of married life.

A Brief History of Dating in America

Even in my son's rather hazy conception of dating is a taken-for-granted assumption that the participants involved are solely responsible for deciding whether or not to "go out" with each other. Parents, relatives, or peers may influence these decisions, but they usually don't directly arrange dating relationships.

Americans have never had a tradition of "arranged relationships." Eligible males and females, even as early as colonial times, have always taken the initiative to get to know each other, and the decision to marry was always left to them, even if that decision was ultimately subject to parental approval (Whyte, 1992).

Although not all relationships were closely supervised, up until the late nineteenth century, much of dating and courtship in North America—especially among the middle and upper classes—was based on a ritualized system known as *calling.* Young people could initially meet in a variety of ways—community or church socials, fairs and dances, informally on the street or in school, or through introductions from friends or relatives (Whyte, 1992).

When one or both people wanted a relationship to develop, the male suitor would visit the young woman at her home, usually during daylight hours. Although the process varied by region and social class, the following general guidelines were involved:

> When a girl reached the proper age or had her first "season" (depending on her family's social level), she became eligible to receive male callers. At first her mother or guardian invited young men to call; in subsequent seasons the young lady . . . could bestow an invitation to call upon any unmarried man to whom she had been properly introduced. . . . Other young men . . . could be brought to call by friends or relatives of the girl's family, subject to her prior permission. . . . The call itself was a complicated event. A myriad of rules governed everything: the proper amount of time between invitation and visit (two weeks or less); whether or not refreshments should be served . . . ; chaperonage (the first call must be made on mother and daughter . . .); appropriate topics of conversation (the man's interests, but never too personal); how leave should be taken (on no account should the woman accompany [her caller] to the door nor stand talking while he struggles with his coat). (Bailey, 1988, pp. 15–16)

The supervision was so tight—during initial visits the mother remained present in the room at all times; later on she might hover in an adjacent room—that anything resembling recreational enjoyment or romance was next to impossible.

Everyone involved understood that calling was a means by which potential marriage partners could be examined. The practice of calling maintained the social class structure by serving as a test of suitability, breeding, and background (Bailey, 1988). Calling enabled the middle and upper classes to protect themselves from what many at the time considered the "intrusions" of urban life and to screen out the effects of social and geographical mobility that were reaching unprecedented levels at the turn of the century. It also allowed parents to exert some degree of control over their children's relationships, without going so far as to actually arrange them.

But the courtship process didn't end with calling. If the relationship deepened sufficiently, it might progress to *keeping company,* an early version of *going steady* (Whyte, 1992). Visits would still take place in the young woman's home, but now those visits were limited to one man rather than a host of suitors, they more frequently took place at night rather than in the afternoon, and they sometimes continued after the young woman's parents had retired to bed.

Contrary to popular belief, young people a century ago did find time to be alone. Premarital sex and premarital births were not uncommon. According to one study, 13 percent of American women born before 1890 and 26 percent born between 1890 and 1899 engaged in premarital intercourse (Terman, 1938). The premarital pregnancy rate increased from 10 percent in the mid-nineteenth century to 23 percent in the decades between 1880 and 1910 (D'Emilio & Freedman, 1988).

The formal tradition of calling began to disappear in the early 1900s. Economic and educational innovations enabled young people to interact with the opposite sex away from the watchful eyes of parents (Coontz, 1992). The expansion of commercial recreation in the form of movie theaters, dance halls, amusement parks, and so on gave young people new places in which to meet and congregate. Compulsory schooling in public, coeducational institutions provided an arena where young people could see each other daily.

In addition, the growing affluence of America and the shift from an agriculture-based economy to an industry-based economy meant that more and more young people had leisure time on their hands. These trends coincided with part-time and after-school employment, which provided young people with spending money that didn't have to be turned over to the family. By the 1920s and 1930s autonomous dating among young people had become a common feature of America's interpersonal landscape (Gordon, 1981).

Technology also played a prominent role in the growth of the institution of dating. The innovation that perhaps had the most direct and long-lasting effect was the automobile. Cars were not only a means of transportation away from the home, they also provided a somewhat private space for romantic and sexual activity (Whyte, 1992). The growth of drive-in movie theaters coincided with the growing role cars played in young people's intimate lives. In later years, the borrowed family car was replaced by cars (and then vans) owned by young people themselves.

By the 1930s dating had pretty much moved out of the home and into the public world. In the process, family surveillance was replaced with peer supervision and judgment. Dating now involved activities and places that were virtually off-limits to adults, such as private parties and dance halls. In most communities young people identified secluded areas (sometimes referred to as "lovers' lanes") where they could escape the supervision of peers as well as adults.

The gender roles of dating and courtship changed too. For one thing, the initiative shifted from the woman to the man. He asked her out rather than waiting for an invitation to call, as had been the practice at the turn of the century. Finances and transportation were his responsibility. In exchange, she was expected to provide the pleasure of her company and maybe some romance and intimacy. Although women could withhold affection and thereby exercise some control over the event, the absence of parental oversight and absence from the safe confines of their home placed women in a more vulnerable position than they had occupied during the era of calling.

Greater privacy and autonomy promoted romantic and sexual experimentation, perpetuating this sexual double standard. Men were expected to be the sexual aggressors, and the "success" or "failure" of their date could often be measured by how much intimacy they were able to achieve. Women who "went too far," however, risked destroying their reputations and their ability to attract other desirable men. Women bore the responsibility of setting limits and therefore had to walk a fine line between being too unfriendly and too friendly (Whyte, 1992).

One of the key features of the modern form of dating, which emerged during the 1930s and 1940s and continues today, is a primary concern with enjoyment rather than selection of a marital partner. Both young men and young women are encouraged to "play the field" and, as I mentioned earlier, the frequency of dating is often used as an indicator of popularity. Dating is still viewed as a necessary first step toward marriage, but that need not be its primary purpose.

By the 1950s an intermediate phase between dating and marriage developed: *going steady*. It was considerably different from the turn-of-the-century notion of "keeping steady company," which was a preliminary to engagement. Going steady simply entailed a recognizable commitment on the part of both people to date each other exclusively. Few steady couples expected to marry each other, although they often *acted* as if they were married. Not surprisingly, many adults feared that going steady would inevitably lead to more serious sexuality between young people. Some dating manuals of the 1950s even argued that a young woman was better off dating a series of strangers than having a steady boyfriend (Bailey, 1988). Teenagers, on the other hand, simply viewed going steady as a form of "social security"—guaranteeing a date to major school functions and for most weekend nights.

Contemporary Dating

Contemporary culture gives popular approval to young people pairing off with various romantic partners, without adult supervision and without defining their dating partners as potential mates (Whyte, 1990). In contrast to earlier generations, teenagers today feel entitled to make their own choices about sex and tolerate all kinds of sexual behaviors, as long as they meet the norms of peers. Dating is defined more in terms of immediate gratification than the goal of choosing a life-long partner.

▲ Chapter 9 further discusses the trend toward greater sexual freedom.

Not surprisingly, one of the things that most distinguishes modern dating from its predecessors is the increasing prevalence of sexual activity in dating relationships. ▲ One survey found that approximately 28 percent of sixth graders, 50 percent of eighth graders, and 67 percent of tenth graders had already had sexual intercourse (Barone, Ickovics, Ayers, Katz, Voyce, & Weissberg, 1996). The average age at first intercourse today is about 16.6 for boys and 17.4 for girls (cited in Ingrassia, 1994).

Parental Influence   Even though they don't "arrange" their children's relationships, parents today do exert influence over their children's romantic lives. They always indirectly influence their children's dating choices by their financial status and lifestyle, their decision to live in a particular neighborhood, and the general values and beliefs they instill in their children from early childhood. But they can go to great lengths to more directly influence their children's dating choices as well. Parents sometimes "threaten, cajole, wheedle, bribe, and persuade their children to 'go with the right people,' during both the early love and later courtship phases" of relationships (Goode, 1959, p. 45).

In a world of interpersonal relationships that seems to get more dangerous with each passing day, more and more parents are opting for greater control over their teenage children's dating patterns and choices. But the strategies can be quite varied. At one extreme is complete prohibition—those parents who simply refuse to allow their teenage children to date at all. Here's how one family dispenses with the dating game:

If a young man wants to date a young woman, he contacts her father to ask permission. During that first meeting or phone call, the father explains that the family believes in courtship, which means that the young man must be spiritually and financially prepared to marry the young woman if they fall in love—otherwise, he shouldn't even bother to start a relationship. (As for our sons, they know they must meet the same requirements before they can begin courting a young woman.) This means, in effect, that there will be no courtship or dating during the high school years, and perhaps not until after college graduation. . . .

Courtship . . . brings practical benefits. For one thing, bringing Dad into the picture takes the responsibility for saying yes or no to a relationship off a daughter's shoulders. . . . Courtship includes time spent with the entire family. In our home, a young man interested in Heather or our youngest daughter, Catharine, is apt to find himself playing basketball with our . . . sons . . . or helping out in the kitchen after dinner. (Ryun & Ryun, 1997, pp. 28–29)

At the other extreme is the "if you can't beat them, join them" strategy. These are parents who allow their teenage children (primarily sons) to sleep with their dates—as long as they stay in the parents' home. Frightened by the spectre of AIDS, drugs, street crime, and other realities of teenage life today, these parents are deciding that acknowledging their children's sexuality and providing them a "safe" environment is better than pretending the sexuality doesn't exist. However, these parents sometimes find themselves torn between the desire to protect their children from harm and the nagging fear that they are encouraging their children to engage in sex. As one mother of a 17-year-old son put it, "It's not that I think it's wonderful. But I don't want my son and his girlfriend hiding in basements or the back seat of a car, getting mugged. I feel better knowing where my child is, so I decided that his room is his territory, his privacy" (quoted in Lawson, 1991, p. C1).

Most parents fall between these two extremes, trying to gradually loosen the reins over their children's sexual behavior while still promoting their own values. But parental influence varies by social class; the higher the class, the more control parents try to have over the dating behaviors of their children. ▲ Exclusive neighborhoods, private schools and clubs, and supervised functions help affluent parents ensure that their children will come into contact with "suitable" dating partners. Lower-class young people are less likely to use structured activities like dances and formal parties as settings for their dates. They are more likely to "hang out" in popular gathering spots like parks, parking lots, shopping malls, and fast food restaurants to meet other people. Such areas are usually far removed from the watchful eyes of parents or other adults.

▲ Issue 7 explains why upper- and middle-class parents have and seek more control than working-class and poor parents over their children's dating behavior.

Gender and Dating in Contemporary America   The sexual double standard so prevalent in the first half of the twentieth century—"real" men have lots of sex with lots of women, "good" women have no sex outside of marriages—seems to have weakened somewhat in recent years. Clearly women today are more likely to initiate dates and share expenses than they ever were in the past. And women have greater cultural "permission" to be sexually active than they once had. These changes, coupled with the informality and absence of clear norms that characterize contemporary dating, can cause tremendous anxiety and confusion among young people. Rules are constantly being defined and redefined.

Given what we already know about gender differences in sexuality, we shouldn't be surprised that men and women may evaluate dating experiences differently too. For instance, men tend to perceive sexually suggestive behavior on the part of a dating partner (for example, leaning close when sitting together, repeated touching) as an indicator that things are moving toward more intense sexual activity, whereas women are more likely to be uncomfortable with sexually suggestive behavior. Men also tend to see rejection of *their* sexual advances as a sign of a "bad date" (Alksnis, Desmarais, & Wood, 1996).

▲ Such disagreement, as Chapter 6 explains, can increase the risk of rape and other forms of sexual assault.

Disagreement over signals of sexual desire is one of the most notable problems in contemporary dating. ▲ One study found that 53 percent of female high school students had been in a dating situation in which they believed a boy *over*estimated the level of sexual intimacy the young women desired; while 45 percent of male students had been in situations where they felt girls *under*estimated the boy's level of desired sexual intimacy (Patton & Mannison, 1995). As you can see, the old double standard may have weakened, but it still plays havoc with people's attempts to get together with the opposite sex.

The Influence of Social Structure in Mate Selection

The participant-driven nature of the American dating system implies that we can become attracted to, fall in love with, and eventually choose as lifelong mates whomever we want. Theoretically, we are attracted to certain people and not others solely on the basis of our assessment of their personal qualities as well as sexual and emotional compatibility. But just how free are we to form long-term intimate relationships with whomever we want? "Freedom of choice" regarding mates is substantially limited by social structure. In most societies, for instance, marriage is an economic arrangement, a contract, between families. Marriages are important not because they are personally fulfilling to partners but because they provide economic links between kin groups. ▲ In societies that have an elaborate and highly structured stratification system, such as India and Pakistan, a family's social status is extremely important in determining who is eligible to marry whom. Marriages are usually arranged from within the same caste, although the ideal situation is that the man's family be of slightly higher status than the woman's. Under such circumstances little thought is given to the desires or shared affections of the partners.

▲ For more on arranged marriages, read Issue 4.

Many of us would view arranged marriage as an anachronism and a violation of personal freedoms. However, it can provide people with significant benefits. For instance, arranged marriages tend to be very stable. Although romantic love is not a consideration, love often grows as the partners get to know each other. Arranged marriage also strengthens ties with other families, which in turn strengthens the social order of the community (Lee & Stone, 1980).

We also must realize that our own intimate choices in this society are far from free and private. The choices we make regarding whom to date, live with, or marry are governed by two important social rules that limit the field of eligible partners: exogamy and endogamy.

Exogamy requires that an individual marry outside certain social groups to which he or she belongs. In almost all societies, exogamy rules prohibit people from marrying members of their own nuclear family—siblings, parents, and children. Rules of exogamy usually extend to certain people outside the nuclear family, to include cousins, grandparents, and, in some societies, stepsiblings. In South Korea, people are strongly discouraged from marrying someone with the same surname, not a trivial rule considering that 55 percent of the population are named Kim,

Park, Lee, Choi, or Chong (WuDunn, 1996). One of the advantages of exogamy rules is that they encourage alliances between groups larger than the primary family.

Less obvious, but just as powerful, are the rules of **endogamy**, which limit marital choices to people *within* one's social group, however that group is defined. Royal families of the past often encouraged members to marry blood relations to keep the power and wealth of the group intact. As I mentioned, in India and Pakistan people usually marry someone within their caste.

▲ Issues 2 and 6 also look at the broad social pressures to form relationships within one's racial, ethnic, or religious group.

Although American society doesn't have such formal endogamy rules, the vast majority of marriages occur between people from the same religion, race, and social class. ▲ These similar backgrounds increase the likelihood that the two people will share common beliefs, values, and experiences. But more importantly from a sociological point of view, rules of endogamy reflect our society's traditional distaste for relationships that cross group boundaries.

Religion

Marrying outside one's religion isn't as uncommon as it once was. Today, about one-quarter of all marriages occur between people of different religions (Glenn, 1982).

Although the traditional norms that once obligated people to marry within their faith have diminished, most religions still actively discourage interfaith marriages. Their concern is that such marriages may weaken people's religious beliefs and values, lead to the raising of children in a different faith, or may take religion out of the family entirely. Religious leaders often worry about the bigger problem of maintaining their ethnic identity within a diverse and complex society (Gordon, 1964).

According to recent figures, the percentage of Jews in the American population has declined from 4 percent to 2.3 percent in the last 50 years (Safire, 1995). While one Jew in ten married a non-Jew in 1945, one in two does so today. A lower birthrate coupled with the propensity to *not* raise children Jewish can explain, in part, why the Jewish population is dropping so precipitously. A statement issued in 1973 by Reform Judaism's Central Conference of American Rabbis (the most liberal, and therefore the most tolerant, branch of American Judaism) defined interfaith marriage as "contrary to Jewish tradition" and discouraged rabbis from officiating at them (Niebuhr, 1996). Indeed, most American rabbis today refuse to perform interfaith weddings, even though there is some evidence that interfaith couples who have been married by rabbis are likely to raise their children as Jews.

Many Jewish leaders fear that the outcome of this growing trend will be not only the shrinking of the Jewish population but also the erosion and perhaps extinction of an entire way of life. They believe that the survival of American Jewry itself depends on maintaining the integrity of traditional Jewish values and institutions. Young people who decide to marry outside the faith "are threatening to transform Judaism into a religion of half-remembered rituals, forgotten ancestors and buried beliefs" (Rosen, 1997, p. 7).

Race and Ethnicity

▲ For more on intermarriage, read Issue 6.

Even though marriages that cross racial and ethnic lines have become more common—they've tripled over the past 30 years—they still remain rare relative to marriages between people of the same race or ethnic group (see Exhibit 2.3). ▲ In 1970 there were 310,000 interracial couples;

Exhibit 2.3

Interracial Married
Couples

*United States:
1980–1996*

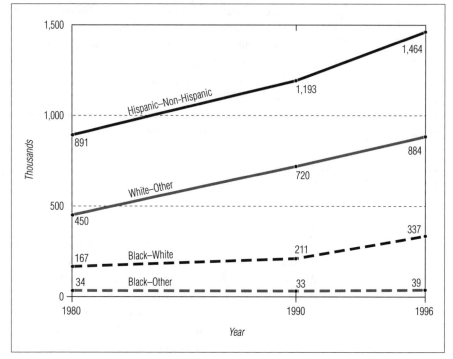

Source of data: U.S. Bureau of the Census, *Statistical Abstract of the United States: 1997* (117th edition). Washington, DC, 1997.

by 1994 there were 1.3 million. Still, this figure constitutes only 2.3 percent of all U.S. marriages. Twenty-three percent of interracial marriages are black-white unions, accounting for just 0.5 percent of all marriages (U.S. Bureau of the Census, 1996).

The strength of racial and ethnic endogamy varies from group to group. Historian Paul Spickard (1989) compared the intermarriage experiences of three ethnic/racial groups: Japanese Americans, Jews, and African Americans. The patterns of intermarriage for Jews and Japanese Americans have followed a common sequence: with each succeeding generation, intermarriage becomes more prevalent. Less than 2 percent of eastern-European Jews who immigrated to the United States in the early twentieth century married non-Jews; between 5 and 10 percent of their children married outside the faith, and upwards of 30 percent of their grandchildren married non-Jews. The same generational pattern holds for Japanese Americans. ▲ First-generation immigrants tended to maintain their Old World identities and were mindful of traditional prohibitions against intermarriage. Following generations tended to be more ambivalent about their minority ethnic heritage and more enthusiastic about "being" American.

Today, compared to other racial and ethnic groups, Asian Americans have fairly high rates of intermarriage—23 percent versus about 2 percent for the general population (Lee & Yamanaka, 1990). Most scholars have attributed this high rate of intermarriage to the process of assimilation, whereby minority identity gradually dissolves as individuals adjust to the practices of the

▲ For a historical discussion of Japanese-American families, see Issue 6.

dominant culture. For some, the assimilation of Asians through intermarriage is a positive development, given America's past history of racism and mistreatment of Asians. But for others such assimilation comes with a hefty price. They are concerned about the survival of their ethnic traditions. According to one study, if their rate of intermarriage should continue to escalate rapidly, "Japanese Americans, given a generation or two, could well disappear as a distinct ethnic group unless the offspring of intermarried couples consciously choose to . . . solve their identity problem in a Japanese direction" (Levine & Rhodes, 1981, p. 65).

Black patterns of endogamy are distinctive among U.S. ethnic minorities (Tucker & Mitchell-Kernan, 1990). African Americans are the least likely of all racial and ethnic groups to marry someone from another race. Furthermore, unlike every other group, African-American men are more likely to marry outside the race (3.6 percent) than African-American women (1.2 percent).

Note, however, that intermarriage rates for all groups are affected by structural factors and are not uniform from one region to another. For instance, rates for African Americans are highest in the West (12.3 percent for black males and 3.1 percent for black females), where attitudes toward interracial relationships and race in general are more permissive and tolerant than in other parts of the country, and lowest in the South (1.6 percent for males, 0.6 percent for females) where attitudes are the least tolerant (Tucker & Mitchell-Kernan, 1990).

Where ethnic communities are strong and concentrated, rules of endogamy tend to be powerful impediments to intermarriage. For Jews, intermarriage has traditionally been lower in eastern cities with large Jewish populations and has been higher in the South and West where the Jewish population tends to be smaller. Intermarriage among Chinese Americans and Korean Americans is significantly higher in Hawaii, which has no large Chinese or Korean communities exerting control over marital choice, than it is in Los Angeles, where ethnic communities are strong (Kitano, Yeung, Chai, & Hatanaka, 1984).

In short, the strength of the ethnic community is crucial in determining how much the rules of endogamy will influence mate selection. These communities provide a large supply of ethnically similar marital candidates. Ethnic institutions in these communities (fraternal organizations, churches, synagogues, and so on) often actively discourage intermarriage. Gossip and ostracism from within the community can sometimes be enough to dissuade people from choosing a mate from outside the group. But where these community structures and social networks are weak, personal interests and desires can easily override group constraints. ▲

▲ For more on the tension between personal desires and group obligations, see Issue 4.

The issue of racial endogamy is an especially emotional one in American society. Fear and condemnation of interracial relationships have been a part of American culture, politics, and law since the first European settlers arrived here close to 400 years ago. The first law against interracial marriage was enacted in Maryland in 1661, prohibiting whites from marrying Native Americans or African Americans. Over the next 300 years or so, thirty-eight more states put such laws on the books, expanding their coverage to include Chinese, Japanese, and Filipino Americans. These laws were supported by biological and evolution-based theories of race, which spelled out essential differences (and therefore implied superiority or inferiority) between the races. Laws were enacted to prevent a mixing of the races (referred to as "mongrelization") that would destroy the racial purity (and superiority) of whites. The irony, of course, is that racial mixing had been taking place since the nation's very beginning, much of it through coercive sexual activity between white slave owners and black slaves.

The gruesome murder in 1955 of Emmett Till, a black youth thought to be overly friendly with a white woman, and the subsequent acquittals of his murderers became powerful symbols of the civil rights movement. The case brought to light the deep-seated feelings that some people harbored over even the suggestion of interracial intimacy. In 1958, when white Richard Loving and his new wife, black Mildred Jeter, moved to their new home in Virginia, a sheriff arrived to arrest them for violating a state law that prohibited interracial marriages. The Lovings were sentenced to 1 year in jail but then learned that the judge would suspend the sentence if they left the state and promised not to return for 25 years. They agreed but, after leaving town, filed suit. Nine years later, in 1967, the U.S. Supreme Court ruled in their favor, concluding that using racial classifications to restrict freedom to marry was unconstitutional.

Some 40 years later people are no longer murdered or banished for expressing intimate feelings for people of a different race. But some Americans still experience discomfort over the thought of interracial relationships. People involved in interracial relationships state that the most important problem they face, both before and after marriage, is racism (Rosenblatt, Karis, & Powell, 1995). Some interracial couples, fearful of family ostracism, never tell their own parents that they are married and have children. Others suffer blatant indignities, such as being spat on or refused services. One in five whites still believes interracial marriage should be illegal. Sixty-six percent say they would oppose a close relative's marriage to a black person. Only 4 percent say they would favor it (Wilkerson, 1991). So pervasive are these feelings that many couples involved in interracial homosexual relationships report finding it more difficult being an interracial couple in American society than being a gay couple (Gillings, 1996).

Social Class

If we were to base our ideas about the formation of romantic relationships on what we see in movies, we might be tempted to conclude that divisions based on **social class**—that is, people's economic position in society—don't matter or perhaps don't exist at all. Recent films like *Titanic, Good Will Hunting, Fools Rush In,* and *Inventing the Abbotts,* as well as older ones like *Pretty Woman, White Palace,* and *Pretty in Pink,* send the message that when it comes to love, we're all really alike. In these stories the power of love is strong enough to blow away differences in education, pedigree, resources, and tastes. When it comes to love, Hollywood's America is a classless society.

In reality, however, class is a powerful factor in mate selection. People face strong pressures to choose marital partners of similar social standing (Carter & Glick, 1976; Kalmijn, 1994). Even if two individuals from different races or religions marry, chances are they will have similar socioeconomic backgrounds. Certainly some people do marry a person from a different social class, but the class tends to be an adjacent one—for instance, an upper-class woman marrying a middle-class man. Marriages between people of vastly different class rankings are quite rare. The reason is that individuals from similar social classes are more likely to come into contact and to share values, tastes, goals, expectations, and educational backgrounds.

Our education system plays a particularly important role in bringing people from similar class backgrounds together. Neighborhoods—and thus neighborhood schools—tend to be homogeneous in social class. College continues class segregation. People from upper-class backgrounds are considerably more likely to attend costly private schools, whereas those from the middle class are most likely to enroll in state universities and those from the working class are most likely to enroll in community colleges. These structural conditions increase the odds that the people whom college students meet and form intimate relationships with will come from a similar class background.

Social Theories of Intimate Relationships

Within the norms and constraints of social structure, just how do people form intimate relationships? Social theorists have developed several ways of describing why and how long-term, intimate relationships develop. Three of them will be presented here: the sociobiological model, the stage model, and the social exchange model. Unfortunately, their cold, scientific language contradicts our culture's deeply held and romantic visions of how intimate relationships grow. And certainly not every relationship follows the same pattern. But they provide some important insights into the possible ways relationships develop.

A Sociobiological Model of Mate Selection

To some scholars—most notably sociobiologists—mate selection is less a matter of choice than a matter of fulfilling our genetic destiny. They argue that all species must evolve efficient ways to

▲ An overview of the sociobiological perspective is provided in Chapter 1.

pass on their genetic material through successful reproduction (van den Berghe, 1979). ▲

Different strategies require different levels of **parental investment**—the relative contribution parents make to the fitness of offspring. Some species, like most fish, have evolved a strategy in which parental investment in the reproduction of offspring is quite low. Female fish produce and lay thousands of eggs at a time. Males produce billions of sperm, which they spread over the eggs that have been laid. In this strategy, males and females don't have to "pair up" to raise their offspring. Thousands of eggs are fertilized during the process, but most are eaten by predators or otherwise die. Only a tiny percentage survive and grow to adulthood. But even a small percentage of survivors allows the species to continue. Other species, like humans, use a strategy that invests a great deal more effort in each fertilized egg. Both men and women gain an evolutionary advantage—as does the entire species—from producing as many healthy offspring as possible and ensuring that enough of them live long enough to perpetuate the gene pool.

Some sociobiologists also hypothesize that to maximize the chances of species survival, men and women have evolved different mate-selection strategies, based on biological differences in the reproductive process. Compared to some other animals, human females make an enormously high investment in the reproduction process. They produce very few eggs, perhaps between twelve and fifteen a year. A single act of sexual intercourse can close off the woman's other mating opportunities for at least 9 months. While pregnant, she can't become pregnant again (Buss, 1994). Women also bear exclusive responsibility for lactation—which can last up to 3 or 4 years after the child is born.

Human offspring also take a long time to mature in the mother's womb and are completely helpless at birth. Because of the large size of human babies' heads and the small size of the mother's pelvis (a consequence of walking upright), human babies are born at a much earlier stage of development than other animal babies. A day-old human baby can't get up and gallop away like a newborn colt. Human babies need a great deal of supervision and care—mostly by their mothers—to ensure their survival until they are independent enough to survive on their own—which may take 20 years or more! From the perspective of species survival, babies are a scarce and precious resource. ▲ As a result, women in our evolutionary past may have had to be extremely selective in their mating and "stingy" in offering their reproductive resources. Their taste for sex within the context of an ongoing relationship and the greater significance for women than men of each sexual act are thought to be consistent with women's high reproductive investment.

▲ From a sociological perspective, the value of childbearing varies from culture to culture, as Chapter 4 explains.

The picture is strikingly different for men. They have just as much interest in species survival as women do, but their investment in the process is not that much higher than that of a male flounder. To put it crudely, sperm are plentiful and cheap relative to eggs. One man can fertilize as many eggs as his stamina and the sexual availability of ovulating women will allow. The most prolific human parent, according to *The Guinness Book of World Records*, was an eighteenth-century emperor of Morocco who reportedly fathered more than 1,000 children. A single act of sexual intercourse for a man requires minimal investment. Once he "deposits" his sperm, he is free—in a physiological sense—to do anything he wants, even impregnate other women. If so inclined, he could walk away from a casual coupling without any *biologically necessary* obligations. ▲

▲ Fortunately, our society expects more than biological involvement from fathers, as Chapters 4 and 7 point out.

According to some sociobiologists, men's apparent "fondness" for recreational sex and their desire for a variety of partners are consistent with their evolved reproductive strategy. Their sexual interest is more easily aroused than women's because sex has fewer biological costs to them. Some sociobiologists cite the fact that prostitution is a service overwhelmingly sought by males around the world as evidence of men's biologically based sexual strategies.

Some sociobiologists also argue that because of gender differences in reproductive investment, men and women are genetically programmed to desire different traits in a mate. They claim that women's reproductive need for protection and stability means they have evolved a preference for mates who can make a commitment, who are willing and able to invest resources in them and their children, and who are willing and able to protect them from harm (Hatfield & Rapson, 1993). Following this logic, men can afford to be less choosy. Because of their low level of investment in the reproductive process, they have evolved a powerful desire for engaging in sexual encounters with a wide array of partners. In the interests of reproducing offspring with the highest likelihood of survival, they are attracted to women who show signs of reproductive fitness: physical appearance, health, and youth.

In sum, according to this sociobiological argument, mate-selection tendencies in humans evolved because a certain kind of sexual partnership and division of labor maximized the probability of survival for individuals, groups, and ultimately the species. However, we have no way of proving unequivocally that these tendencies stem exclusively or even primarily from biological imperatives. These differences between men and women are just as likely due to social and cultural norms regarding men's and women's sexuality. Historically, norms and laws were designed to protect men's sexual property—namely, women. Even today, sexually promiscuous women are substantially more likely to be called derogatory names (slut, whore, and so forth) than sexually promiscuous men. Given such a cultural context, we should expect men and women to show different mate-selection proclivities. Thus the role of biology in mate selection is still a question mark.

A Stage Model of Relationship Formation

Most sociologists still argue that mate selection is less a matter of innate biological drives than of social and interpersonal processes. One approach suggests that relationships form in a series of stages. For instance, a series of filters may progressively limit the field of eligible partners (Kerckhoff & Davis, 1962). Early on, a first filter screens for cultural variables such as age, race, religion, and social class. This initial filter increases the likelihood of endogamy. As the relationship progresses, a second filter screens out those who cannot meet the person's specific needs or who don't share the person's unique values.

Sociologist Ira Reiss (1960) also uses a stage model to explain mate selection. He focuses on the development of emotional attachment that occurs after initial attraction. According to Reiss, we proceed through the stages of rapport, self-disclosure, and mutual dependency and need fulfillment in order. For instance, before we will disclose intimate information about ourselves, we must first achieve a certain level of rapport and compatibility with that person.

Rapport   When two people first meet, their interactions tend to be somewhat superficial. Nevertheless, they are attempting to establish **rapport**—a general sense of compatibility (for example, "My favorite ice cream flavor is Vanilla Swiss Almond, I like to play tennis, and my favorite group is Smashing Pumpkins").

At this stage, interaction may be complicated by deliberate attempts to manipulate information about oneself. Individuals may try to present values, opinions, and biographical information that they think the other person will find appealing. They don't want to say or do things that will upset, anger, or repel the other person. They want to present idealized images of themselves and at the same time accept the idealized image of the other person.

Intimate Self-Disclosure   However, as people grow more comfortable and trusting of each other, the disclosures become more intimate and revealing—and therefore more risky. This next stage of relationship development is characterized by **intimate self-disclosure,** a willingness to go beyond providing basic background information to reveal some very personal facts, thoughts, and feelings. These disclosures can include problematic events in our past, the depth of our feelings toward the other person, our fears and vulnerabilities, and so on. They not only convey information, they are symbolic gestures meant to tell the other person, "I feel close enough to you to share this with you. I trust you not to laugh, belittle, devalue, or fear what I am going to tell you." Research has shown that the greater the level of self-disclosure between partners, the greater their satisfaction in the relationship (Altman & Taylor, 1973; Hendrick, 1981).

Self-disclosure is governed by a clear set of social norms and expectations. One important, but often unspoken, expectation is that the intimate self-disclosure should be reciprocated

(Derlega, Harris, & Chaikin, 1973). We provide more and more intimate facts about ourselves in hopes that our partner will do the same. When people complain about communication problems in their relationships, they are usually referring to an imbalance in the nature and amount of information that partners are sharing.

Reciprocity is particularly important in the disclosure of the depth of one's affection. Often we go through a great deal of strategic maneuvering before first disclosing to our partners how we feel about them. But once we do, we expect similar levels of disclosure from our partners (Cunningham, Strassberg, & Haan, 1986). When they don't reciprocate, we are forced to acknowledge that our definition of the relationship does not conform to theirs.

So you can see that self-disclosure is a potentially hazardous stage in a relationship. When our partners do not disclose enough, we don't know what they are truly feeling. But we don't want to appear pushy by constantly asking for feelings and reassurances, so we sometimes resign ourselves to quiet suffering. In the absence of clear information, we frequently let our imaginations run wild. We find ourselves attributing feelings we *think* our partner has. We scrutinize every sentence, every gesture for some tiny morsel of information—some shred of evidence that will tell us what this other person is feeling.

On the other hand, disclosing too much, too quickly can also be problematic (Altman & Taylor, 1973). Those who tell everyone, even complete strangers, every intimate detail of their lives and feelings have not learned about the importance of timing self-disclosure. The recipient of prematurely personal disclosures usually feels quite uncomfortable in the role.

Mutual Dependency and Need Fulfillment　When a relationship endures beyond the point of shared self-disclosures and partners begin to interpret as serious their level of commitment to the relationship, they enter the next stage: **mutual dependency and need fulfillment** (Reiss, 1960). Eventually the everyday lives of the partners become intertwined. We get used to doing things that require the other person—an audience for our jokes, a confidante for the expression of our fears and wishes, a partner for our sexual experiences, and so on (Reiss & Lee, 1988). As a relationship progresses to this point, we begin to rely on our partner to satisfy our psychological and physical needs. These needs can be as basic as sexual appetites but may also include the desire for someone with whom we can share feelings, someone who can take care of us and whom we can take care of, and someone who will reinforce our own sense of worth and identity (Brehm, 1992).

One of the clearest signs that partners in a relationship have become mutually dependent comes from outside the relationship, when others define the two individuals as a "couple." Often partners don't even consider themselves a couple until they are publicly recognized as such by their friends and peers. Then the couple is bound by a new and complex set of expectations: They might be issued joint invitations to social gatherings, be expected to accompany each other ▲ The couple's "face" in to public events, or be assumed to know each other's whereabouts at all times. ▲

The power that these expectations have over how we act and think reinforces the contention that personal relationships develop within a social context. As much as we would like to believe otherwise, intimacy—even love—is not just a phenomenon that occurs between the two people involved. Other people react to the relationship and can either validate it ("You two make a lovely couple") or disapprove of it ("I think you can do better").

▲ The couple's "face" in social interaction is discussed further in Issue 3 and Chapter 7.

The Social Exchange Model

▲ Social exchange
theory is explained
further in Chapter 1.

The social exchange perspective is also useful in understanding the development of intimate relationships (Blau, 1964; Emerson, 1962; Homans, 1961; Rubin, 1973; Thibaut & Kelley, 1959). ▲ Reiss's stage model simply identified the steps in a process of relationship development. The exchange approach tries to explain why we are attracted to some people and not others. People evaluate their own qualities (for instance, economic standing, attractiveness, and so on) and seek partners whose assets match their own.

The exchange approach also explains why we pursue and remain in some relationships and avoid or leave others. Intimate relationships provide obvious rewards—like love, sexual gratification, warmth, desirable characteristics of the partner, companionship, and so on. But they present certain costs as well—time and effort spent trying to maintain the relationship, undesirable characteristics of one's partner, conflict, and so on. Long-term relationships, including marriage, occur only if they offer positive outcomes and the partners believe they would be better off together than single (Becker, 1981).

The recent decline in the marriage rate for women can be explained in these terms. The increasing availability of employment opportunities has enabled many more women than in previous eras to be economically independent and therefore has eroded one of the key factors that motivated women to marry in the past: economic protection. In other words, the costs of remaining single no longer clearly outweigh the benefits.

▲ The effects of race on
family life are also
discussed in Issue 6.

Social exchange theory may also explain racial differences in marriage rates. ▲ Historically, the percentage of African-American women in the paid labor force has been higher than the percentage of white women, and the wage gap between men and women has been smaller for blacks than whites (Lichter & Costanzo, 1987). The fact that African-American women have less economic incentive to marry than white women do may explain why they have lower marriage rates.

The Role of Expectations   In addition to taking into account costs and benefits, social exchange theory also considers people's preferences and expectations. These go a long way in shedding light on the curious and sometimes inexplicable things people do in their intimate relationships. I'm sure you've seen people who remain in relationships that to outside observers seem undesirable or unrewarding. Why would they stay if, as social exchange theorists argue, people form and maintain relationships only if they are profitable?

The person's expectations and perceptions of alternatives may play a role. For example, if a woman receives certain necessary resources (such as financial support) from her obnoxious, beer-swilling partner and feels that she can't get those resources elsewhere, she may stay in the relationship out of necessity. If a man has had a history of bad relationships, his expectations may be quite low to begin with; hence, it wouldn't take much to exceed them. So he may be satisfied in a relationship that others would find intolerable.

Availability of Partners   The comparisons we make regarding our relationships are also influenced by larger social or "market" conditions. Marital opportunities vary by age, race, and educational attainment (South & Lloyd, 1992). Even where you live can influence your chances of finding a partner.

You must have some contact with someone before you can fall in love and begin a relationship. Clearly where you live will determine whom you come into contact with on a regular basis and ultimately the pool of prospective marital partners (Lichter, LeClere, & McLaughlin, 1991). People who end up marrying usually—but, of course, not always—meet where they spend most of their time: in their neighborhood, in school, at work, at a friend's house. Many people are involved in "long distance" relationships, but even those require some sort of contact at the outset to take shape at all.

In addition, marriage rates can be affected by the overall supply of men and women of marriageable age and, to be more precise, the number of potential mates with desirable economic and other social characteristics (Lichter et al., 1991). Thus the shortage of marriageable, well-educated, and employed black men may have driven down the marriage rate among African Americans. Such an explanation of mate selection is important because it suggests that improving the socioeconomic status of black men could increase the number of "marriageable" men and thus have a stabilizing effect on black families.

Perhaps you disagree with this contention. Don't people who face a shortage of attractive potential partners simply lower their standards a bit? This question was addressed by sociologist Dan Lichter and his colleagues (Lichter, Anderson, & Hayward, 1995). They found that a favorable marriage market—that is, lots of possibilities—indeed increases the likelihood of marrying someone with a good education and a good job. However, they found that people will forgo marriage altogether in an unfavorable market—that is, when no "suitable" mates are available.

Equity and Investment in Intimate Relationships   Judgments of how much "profit" is to be derived from a relationship and how well it compares to past experiences and perceived alternatives are not made by one partner and one partner alone. Being in a relationship means that another person is also interested in maximizing rewards and minimizing costs. Relationships work best when the exchange is fair or *equitable*—when both partners are deriving benefits from the relationship that are *proportional* to what they are investing in it. ▲ The presence or absence of such **interpersonal equity** has profound effects on the satisfaction felt by individuals as well as the stability of the relationship itself (Hatfield, Traupmann, Sprecher, Utne, & Hay, 1985; Utne, Hatfield, Traupmann, & Greenberger, 1984).

▲ Issue 5 shows how the principles of social exchange can explain power differences in families, and Chapter 3 applies them to the household division of labor.

An **interpersonal investment** is anything one has to offer to the relationship, such as time, money, interest, or personal characteristics, like good looks or a sense of humor (Brown, 1986). Investments are important because they create feelings of entitlement or deservedness. When a friend says to you, "You deserve better than her," or "You're entitled to some happiness," an implicit statement of equity is involved: "Given what you have invested or what you have to offer, in all fairness you should be receiving greater benefits." As you might suspect, not every relationship is perfectly equitable. When things become disproportional, feelings of unfairness result.

There are two types of inequity: **underbenefitted inequity** (that is, you feel you are not getting out of the relationship what you feel you deserve) and **overbenefitted inequity** (that is, you feel you are getting too much for what you have to offer). Each kind of inequity threatens the stability of the relationship.

Social psychologist Elaine Hatfield and her colleagues (Hatfield, Walster, & Traupmann, 1978) interviewed 537 college men and women who were dating someone. She asked them whether they expected to be with their partners in 1 year and in 5 years. Those who felt their relationships were perfectly equitable were much more likely than others to think the relationships would last. Interestingly, the overbenefitted subjects were just as doubtful as underbenefitted subjects about the future prospects of their relationships. Presumably, the underbenefitted individuals felt they would do better in the future, and the overbenefitted individuals didn't expect their luck to last. Incidentally, a follow-up study 3 months later indicated that the equitable relationships were, in fact, more likely to still be intact.

Both types of inequity are uncomfortable and motivate individuals to restore either actual or psychological equity (Brehm, 1992). Underbenefitted partners may attempt to restore equity by reducing their investments in the relationship or by demanding more from their partner. For example, if I feel I am being underbenefitted, I may decide not to do as many favors for my partner or I may stop showing affection. If that fails, I may start to demand more benefits or more investments from my partner: "Do you think you could start showing some appreciation for all that I do for you!?" Overbenefitted partners, on the other hand, may come to feel guilty for getting *more* than they feel is deserved. They may try to increase their contributions (such as taking more responsibility for planning social events) or increase the benefits they offer their partner (such as showering the partner with gifts).

The problems with these strategies is that they may backfire. For instance, my reduction of contributions to the relationship may be met by a similar reduction on the part of my partner. Or my partner may take advantage of my attempts to increase his or her benefits. Hence, individuals will often resort to attempts to restore equity psychologically—to convince themselves that, although it seems otherwise, equity does in fact exist (Brehm, 1992). I may talk myself into believing that my partner is a special person who deserves more than I do. Perhaps she has had terrible experiences in the past and deserves to be treated well in this relationship. On the other hand, if I am the overbenefitted partner, I may convince myself that, because of some particularly noble quality I possess, I truly deserve the favorable inequity.

Inequity is fairly obvious when the imbalances are in financial contributions to the relationship or in the performance of certain chores around the house. But an imbalance in feelings—in *emotional* investment—is more difficult to identify. We all know of relationships in which one partner seems to be more in love than the other partner. Such imbalances in emotional attachment have the potential of creating serious and potentially dangerous power differences in relationships. ▲ The person who loves *less* or does not express unconditional affection has the upper hand in the relationship, because the other person will presumably suffer more if the relationship should end (Blau, 1964). Hence, the individual who loves less can dictate the terms of the relationship and can, if so inclined, exploit the other by making heavy demands. The partner who loves more has greater interest in maintaining the relationship and may be forced to put up with a lot to do so.

▲ Issue 5 takes a closer look at the relationship between emotional attachment and power.

Such a situation implies a rather depressing reality about intimate relationships. The less-dependent partner—that is, the one who has more alternatives outside the relationship—has the greatest power in it because that person can more easily abandon the relationship. This phenomenon—referred to as the **principle of least interest**—suggests that control over the relationship rests with the partner who has the least interest in continuing it. This person is able to dictate the conditions of the relationship, make demands of the other, and even exploit that person's dependence if he or she is so inclined. I'm sure you've seen relationships in which one partner is so much more "in love" than the other that he or she is willing to tolerate a lot of pain and nastiness in hopes that the relationship will continue.

Conclusion

Trying to shed intellectual light on something so precious and so personal as love relationships has several inherent dangers. One is that upon close inspection the dark side of intimacy will appear. You have seen in this chapter that intimacy often involves conflict and even exploitation. Such facts fly in the face of popular images of intimacy and therefore shake the foundation of that which is so culturally and personally valuable: our love relationships.

Another danger is that the attempt to intellectually examine intimacy will appear too cold and emotionless. Who among us wants to equate love with a marketplace where people seek to maximize benefits and minimize costs through negotiation, bargaining, and comparison shopping? These concepts conflict with our deeply held, romantic visions of what love relationships are or should be. The fact that we desire, establish, and maintain intimacy with others only because we find it profitable to do so or that nonromantic factors like race, class, religion, and geography determine, to some degree, who we find attractive is a bitter pill most of us would prefer not to swallow. The idealized image of love we have in American culture largely denies control and rationality. We "fall" in love; we're "swept off our feet"; or we're "carried away." In short, love "puts a spell on us."

And yet we're all aware, at least at some level, that these nonromantic factors are important, that many of them influence our intimate choices. We secretly express doubt over the staying power of a relationship between two people who love each other very much but who have no visible means of support and no future prospects. "Starry-eyed romance" may make for enjoyable novels, but it may not be enough to sustain a relationship through the practical demands of day-to-day family life.

CHAPTER HIGHLIGHTS

- Although love exists everywhere, it is not experienced in the same way in all cultures. The role that love plays in people's intimate lives is determined by the nature of the culture in which they live.
- In this society, love has become a "feminized" emotion, making it incompatible with such socially valued traits as power, independence, and control. Consequently, men and women tend to express love differently.
- Human sexuality is more than just a biological drive. Its expression is subject to strong societal norms. Hence, the way it is experienced by individuals varies from culture to culture and among different groups within the same culture.
- Unlike societies in which relationships are arranged by families, American society recognizes dating as the means by which most people move from being single to being coupled.

- Dating is not a matter of completely free choice, however. Parental influence, cultural conceptions of gender, concerns over social class, and other societal constraints may determine who dates whom. Over the years the nature of dating has been changed by economic, educational, and technological changes in society.
- Mate selection is strongly influenced by cultural rules of endogamy and exogamy. Although we are sanctioned against mating with close relatives, we tend to find partners among people of the same religion, social class, and race and ethnicity.
- Attempts to identify the biological underpinnings of our intimate relationships remain controversial. More useful at this point are the stage model and the social exchange model. They attempt to explain how people become attracted to each other and why they stay together. Relationships appear to develop in stages, and they are influenced by partners' expectations, availability, and perceptions of fairness.

DEMO•GRAPHIC ESSAY

Trends in Marriage

The popular media have made much of the large numbers of unmarried persons, suggesting that Americans are rejecting the institution of marriage. Data like those in Exhibit 2-A show how marriage in the United States has changed over the last generation. Exhibit 2-A shows a pronounced decline between 1970 and 1996 in the percentage of Americans who are married, along with a pronounced increase in the never-married and divorced populations. Although the widowed population outnumbered the divorced population 3 to 1 in 1970, by 1996, the percentage of divorced persons exceeded that of widowed persons.

Why did the proportion of the population never married and the proportion divorced increase while the proportion married and the proportion widowed decreased? One explanation could be changes in marriage behavior. For example, more individuals in 1996 could be postponing marriage or resorting to divorce. Another explanation could be changes in the composition of the adult population between 1970 and 1996. The big story in the American population between 1970 and 1996 has been the aging of the baby boom generation, the huge cohort of persons born between 1946 and 1964. In 1970 older baby boomers were just beginning to enter the young-adult years, although most baby boomers were still children and adolescents. By 1996, however, all of the baby boomers had reached young adulthood, and the older ones were beginning to

Exhibit 2-A

Marital Status
Ages 18 and Older

*United States:
1970 and 1996*

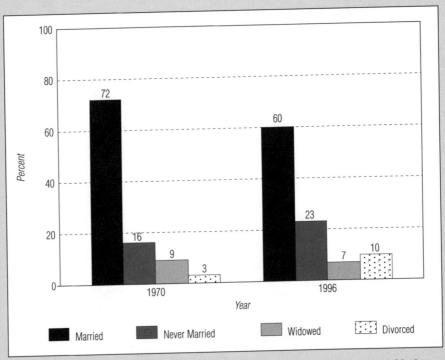

Sources of data: 1970: Arlene Saluter, "Marital Status and Living Arrangements: March 1994." U.S. Bureau of the Census, *Current Population Reports Series P20-484.* Washington, DC, 1996. 1996: U.S. Bureau of the Census, *Statistical Abstract of the United States: 1997* (117th edition). Washington, DC, 1997.

turn 50. The widowed population may have dropped so dramatically because the adult population became dominated by baby boomers, most of whom were still too young to experience widowhood. Similarly, the 1996 adult population could have had a greater proportion of never-married persons than the 1970 adult population did because more of the 1996 adult population were in the younger adult years.

The proportion of married adults is not the only noticeable change in marriage behavior. Median age at first marriage has also been rising in recent years. But what many people may not realize is that the levels in 1990 represent a return to the median age at first marriage around the turn of the century (see Exhibit 2-B). What is unusual, therefore, is not the current high age at marriage but rather the relatively low age at marriage of the 1950s and early 1960s. Not surprisingly, the baby boom occurred at the same time.

Another interesting aspect of Exhibit 2-B is the gender gap in median age at marriage. At every year, men, on average, marry women who are several years younger than they are. The age gap has shrunk, however, from 4.1 years in 1890 to 2.2 years in 1990.

Age is not the only significant variable in marriage behavior. Both the popular media and social science research note the lower levels of marriage among black persons in the United States. Exhibit 2-C indicates differences among ethnic groups in the proportion of never-married adults ages 45–54 in 1994. Persons in this age group are likely to have completed childbearing, one of the traditional reasons for a couple to marry. For both men and women, black persons are the most likely group to have never married, followed by Hispanic persons, then whites. Within each ethnic group, women are more likely than men to ever marry.

Exhibit 2-B

Median Age at
First Marriage

*United States:
1890–1990*

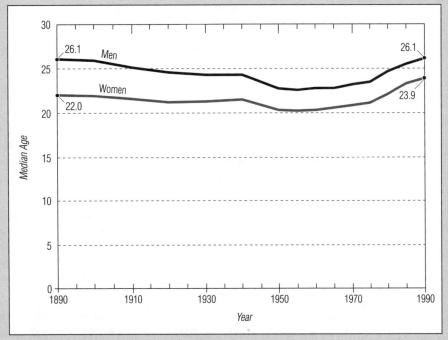

Source of data: Arlene Saluter, "Marital Status and Living Arrangements: March 1994." U.S. Bureau of the Census, *Current Population Reports Series P20-484.* Washington, DC, 1996.

Exhibit 2-C

Never-Married
Adults Ages 45–54
(by gender and
ethnicity)

United States: 1994

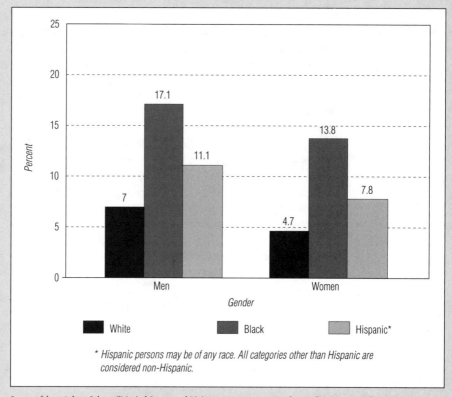

* Hispanic persons may be of any race. All categories other than Hispanic are considered non-Hispanic.

Source of data: Arlene Saluter, "Marital Status and Living Arrangements: March 1994." U.S. Bureau of the Census, *Current Population Reports Series P20-484.* Washington, DC, 1996.

Questions for Further Study

1. Why might young adults today be marrying later than people did in the 1950s and 1960s? Consider the kinds of social and economic experiences that three cohorts—persons born during the 1920s and 1930s, the baby boomers, and generation X (born during the late 1970s) had during significant points in their lives, such as childhood, adolescence, young adulthood.

2. What could account for the narrowing over the last century of the gender gap in median age at first marriage? What kind of changes have occurred in the ways men and women meet one another that could be related to their ages? If we consider age to be an indicator of social power, with older persons typically having more power than younger persons, how might the changing gender gap affect the power relationship between husbands and wives?

3. Social scientists attempt to look for commonalities among several groups of people as well as significant differences. What does Exhibit 2-C say about the shared experiences of whites, blacks, and Hispanic persons in the United States? What does it say about ethnic differences? What are the implications of these similarities and differences for the social meaning of marriage in the United States?

YOUR TURN

The formal purpose of colleges is to provide students with a quality education. But they also informally provide students with countless lessons about friendship, intimacy, sexuality, and so on. To delve deeper into the role that colleges play in creating or reinforcing gendered expectations regarding intimacy, consider *all* the ways people meet others and establish intimate relationships *on your campus*. Distinguish between informal mechanisms (meeting someone in class or at the library) and *institutional* mechanisms that are designed explicitly to bring people together, such as university-sponsored social events, fraternity and sorority parties, and so on. Have some places in the surrounding community (bars, clubs, etc.) gained a reputation for being good spots to "meet people"? What proportion of students use computer or video dating services? Does the campus newspaper or local newspaper have a "personals" section? Does your campus have programs in place to help students deal with the problems of intimacy (for example, information about sexually transmitted diseases, sexual assault support networks, pregnancy testing, and/or abortion information)? Roughly how many students use these services in a given month?

Describe how each of the institutional mechanisms you've identified incorporates broader beliefs about gender and intimacy. Do they tend to reinforce or contradict traditional gender expectations? What does each tell us about the pervasiveness of gender ideologies in everyday campus life?

Now think about other social factors at work. For instance, did you notice any variations attributable to age, race or ethnicity, social class, or sexual orientation in the amount and type of student use of these mechanisms? Do any of these events or services segregate students? Do they actively seek to integrate students from varied social backgrounds?

More generally, what should be the college's role in creating or enhancing intimate relationships among students? Should it be liable for any harm that these relationships might cause (for example, sexual violence)?

CHAPTER 3

Gender, Marriage, and Work

Forty-one years ago a 14-year-old Albanian woman named Sema Brahimi decided to become a man. Sema's father had recently died, leaving a widow, four daughters, and an infant son to survive on their own. In Albania's heavily male-dominated society, such a task would have been hard enough. But in the isolated, mountainous, rural area in which the family lived, it was inconceivable that they could run a household without a man in charge. So Sema, the eldest daughter, decided to take the job (Demick, 1996).

She cut her hair short, put on men's clothes, and went to work in the fields. She changed her name from Sema to Selman (the masculine equivalent). Her mother and siblings began to use male pronouns when they referred to her. Gradually Selman assumed responsibility for tending the family's crops and making the regular 3-hour trips by mule to the nearest city to sell them. Later on, as the head of the household, Selman took responsibility for selecting a wife for her brother and wore a suit and tie to his wedding, taking the role of father of the groom.

Looking back on the decision, Selman, now 55, has no regrets:

> I've lived my whole life as a man. I've got the habits of a man.... If anyone has a problem with it, I've got my gun to deal with them.... Until I was 18 to 20, I had proposals of marriage. My brother was old enough to work, and my mother said that I should follow the fate of my sisters and get married. But once something is decided, you can't undo it, and I already thought of myself as a man.... I've had to work very hard to earn bread for the family and to be honest and correct in my relations with others. But, no, I have never regretted the decision. I've not had a bad life as a man. (Demick, 1996, p. C8)

Interestingly, nobody *does* have a problem with it. Selman has long been accepted by men in the village as a man among equals. Under local law, women have few legal protections. They can be beaten or chained if they disobey their husbands and have no property or inheritance rights whatsoever. The only path to self-determination is to assume the life of a man. In fact, even in a country like Albania, where the expectations of men and women are sharply delineated, such a practice is actually part of an age-old tradition. The folklore of northern Albania is filled with stories of women who took an oath never to marry so they could fill voids left by a shortage of males. As "men" they often became fierce warriors and village leaders.

All over the world, gender plays a crucial role in the organization of family life. All societies have clear conceptions about what men and women are obligated to do or what they're entitled to, particularly when it comes to meeting the financial needs of the family. Gender and economics are tightly intertwined. In her male-dominated society, the only way Selman could support her mother and siblings and acquire some degree of authority in her community was to "become" a man. With no older brothers and a widowed mother, such an extreme step was the only viable solution.

In American society, earning capacity and professional credibility have always been linked in some way to gender. In the past, women had few opportunities to enter prestigious occupations, own property, or be financially independent. Today much has changed, and the traditional barriers to financial stability are no longer as impenetrable as they once were.

Yet despite advances, American women still lag behind men economically and politically and continue to encounter frustrating cultural barriers and closed doors. While not "becoming" men in the literal sense that Selman did, women have nonetheless attained economic stability and social power only by drifting away from their traditional family roles and entering historically male realms of occupational life. In the 1996 film *The Associate*, Whoopi Goldberg plays a bright Wall Street stock analyst whose insightful ideas are repeatedly trivialized because she's a woman. So she quits her job in disgust, opens her own firm, and creates a fictitious, invisible male partner to whom she gives credit for all her best ideas. Her business thrives, and "he" soon becomes one of the best-known, most successful advisers on Wall Street. The message of the film is clear and not all that different from that conveyed by the experience of the young Sema Brahimi halfway across the world: It's easier to achieve economic power as a man than as a woman.

In this chapter we will examine the intersection of gender, work, and family. We will pay particular attention to how marriage and family life are influenced by the different work experiences and expectations of men and women both inside and outside the home.

Colliding Spheres

"Women's world"

"A women's place is in the home"

"Private, family life"

Traditionally, women's place has been in the domestic sphere, an area of life removed, for the most part, from the stress and scrutiny of the "dog-eat-dog" world of the larger society. The public sphere has traditionally been male domain, with men doing most of the social planning and policy making.

This dichotomy has been breaking down over the past 25 years. As inflation hit in the mid-1970s, many women who once stayed home to raise children used their traditional skills of cooking and sewing to make money.

Some of the jobs women occupy reflect traditional assumptions about "women's work." But whether they're cooking in the kitchen or serving doughnuts for minimum wage, women who work outside the home are trying to gain a measure of economic security. In doing so, they have helped redefine men's and women's adult roles.

This phenomenon has created serious workplace issues and some problems in the traditional family structure. As women have earned their spot beside men in the workplace, they feel entitled to a redistribution of household duties. Studies show, however, that in families with working wives, women still do more housework than men do.

On the surface, work seems like something separate from family life. But as technology and machinery advance, we are witnessing not only an erasure of occupational gender distinctions, but a blurring of traditional boundaries between family and work.

More and more people are finding their emotional and social needs met not by family members, but by colleagues and work mates.

Traditional ideas about family have changed, too. Although men are more likely to cook family meals than they were in the past, many families are finding that the notion of a family dinner hour is fast becoming a nostalgic memory.

Although family relationships continue to be important, more and more people are engaging in everyday activities by themselves. Many dine alone. Even fixing a meal at home may be a solitary activity as other family members are doing their own thing.

Ironically, when men are able to engage in family life, they often do so at work. Here we see a man playing with his kids at the corporate day care center in his office building.

For many women, the idea of bringing office work home is becoming increasingly popular. The term *home office* has rapidly become part of our everyday vocabulary.

So what is family life as distinct from work life? Will this be a relevant question in the twenty-first century? What do you think your work and family arrangements will look like?

The Transition to Married Life

▲ Chapter 2 examines the process by which relationships are developed and maintained.

Most adults experience the change from being single to being "coupled." Such a transition requires some major adjustments, such as learning to live with someone else in the same house, pooling financial resources, changing insurance coverage, and so forth. It also requires a dramatic shift in identity. Becoming a spouse is more complicated and time-consuming than signing the appropriate papers and saying "I do" during a wedding ceremony. Spouses must learn to act and think like married people in a way that conforms to cultural expectations. ▲ The husband and the wife are now a social unit in others' eyes; they must think of themselves as a couple and organize their activities accordingly (Berger & Kellner, 1964).

Because marriage is an *institutionalized* form of intimacy, we can anticipate what it will be like long before we actually marry. We come equipped with information from our parents' marriage, the marriages of people we know, and the images of marriage we see in the media. But the unique qualities and expectations both partners bring with them means that each marriage will be experienced differently. Spouses must create a new identity for themselves as a *couple* and, through interaction with one another, reinforce this identity (Berger & Kellner, 1964).

▲ Issue 3 provides a more detailed analysis of the role of privacy in family life.

Eventually couples create a consistent pattern of interaction—a set of habits, rules, and shared reality. They develop a sort of **private culture**—their own unique way of dealing with the demands of everyday married life (Blumstein & Kollock, 1988). ▲ The private culture includes things as mundane as a weekly dinner schedule or a Sunday morning ritual of breakfast and newspaper reading in bed, or as serious as the distribution of power and the handling of household finances. Some rituals and habits disappear as the composition of the family changes (for instance, with the arrival of children); others persist and are passed on to future generations. But one of the key elements of the private marital culture—and the one that is the focus of this chapter—concerns decisions about how work and family obligations are balanced.

Two Worlds: Work and Family

▲ For more on historical changes in family structure, see Issue 2.

Up until the mid-nineteenth century, the nation's economy was primarily agricultural. ▲ People's lives centered around the farm, where husbands and wives were partners not only in making a home but in making a living (Vanek, 1980). The word *housework*—distinct from work done in other places—was not even part of the language. Men and women performed different tasks, to be sure. But they worked together. Although the relationship between husbands and wives on the farm was never entirely equal—wives did most if not all of the housekeeping, child care, and care of the sick, in addition to producing many of the family's basic necessities (Bernard, 1981)—complete male dominance was offset by women's indispensable contributions to the household economy (Vanek, 1980).

With the advent of industrialization, though, things began to change. New forms of technology and the promise of new financial opportunities and a good living drew people away from the farms and into cities and factories where they could earn wages for their work. Many of the first factory workers were actually women. But as factory work came to be seen less as a peripheral activity and more as the primary feature of the new economy, men took control of this new source of income, power, and prestige (Haas, 1995). For the first time in American history, the family economy was based outside the household, and the majority of families depended on wage labor for their financial support.

Industrialization relieved men of much of their domestic labor duties. And women no longer found themselves involved in the day-to-day supervision of the family's business as they had once been. Instead, they were consigned to the only domestic responsibilities that remained: the care and nurturing of children and the maintenance of the household. Since this work was unpaid and since visible goods were no longer being produced at home, women quickly found their work devalued in the emerging industrial economy (Hareven, 1992).

These historical changes reveal that the common notion of men as "good providers" did not always exist. It's been estimated that in hunting and gathering societies thousands of years ago, men provided only about a fifth of human subsistence (Boulding, 1976). In colonial times, women were viewed as performing a providing role in families. They ran inns and taverns, managed shops and stores, and sometimes even worked in the fields (Bernard, 1981). The good provider as a specialized male role emerged around the 1830s with the rise of the market-based industrial economy and "officially" ended in 1980 when the U.S. Census declared that a male was not automatically assumed to be the head of the household (Bernard, 1981).

The Ideology of Separate Spheres

In the first decades of industrialization, the divergence between men's and women's labor resulted in the ideology of **separate spheres**. Women's place was in the home (the "private" sphere); men's was in the work world outside the home (the "public" sphere). ▲ This ideal fostered the belief that men and women were *naturally* predisposed to different pursuits. Women were assumed to be inherently nurturing, demure, and sacrificial—a perfect fit for their restricted domestic roles. Women's "natural" weakness and frailty made them ill suited to the dog-eat-dog life of the competitive labor force and justified their limited job opportunities. The ideal image of men, on the other hand, was that of the rugged individual whose virtue came from self-reliance, power, and mastery of his job and family. Men were thought to be *naturally* strict, aggressive, calculating, rational, and bold—a perfect fit for the demands of the marketplace.

▲ The implications this ideology has for power relations in contemporary marriages is discussed in Issue 5.

What's ironic about the power of the ideology of separate spheres is that the reality of American family life has never quite fit this image. Even in the late nineteenth century, well after the advent of industrialization, men weren't the only ones who left their homes each day to work in factories. Many children worked long hours to help support their families. At the turn of the century, for example, 120,000 children—some as young as 11—worked in Pennsylvania coal mines and factories; and children made up close to one-quarter of all workers in southern textile mills (Coontz, 1992).

Many women, too, entered the industrial labor force. By 1900, one-fifth of American women worked outside the home (Staggenborg, 1998). But the experiences of working women varied along class and race lines. For middle- and upper-class white women, few professions other than teaching and nursing were available to them, and these jobs paid poorly. Most entered and exited the labor force in response to family demands or took up volunteer work to fill up their free time.

In contrast, poor women worked mostly in unskilled jobs in clothing factories, canning plants, or other industries where working conditions were often dangerous and exploitive. Female factory workers often faced exhausting paces and serious health risks, sometimes for 14 hours a day. Some were even forced to pay "rental fees" for the machines and equipment they used on the job (Staggenborg, 1998).

The conditions for women of color were especially bad. Black domestic servants, for instance, were often forced to leave their own families and live in their employer's home, where they were expected to work around the clock. But most had little choice. Throughout history, black women have rarely had the luxury of being stay-at-home spouses and parents. In 1880, 73 percent of black single women and 35 percent of black married women reported paid jobs. Only 23 percent of white single women and 7 percent of white married women reported being in the paid labor force at that time (cited in Kessler-Harris, 1982).

Immigrant women, especially from southern and eastern Europe, rarely worked outside the home and would therefore seem to support the ideal of separate spheres. However, they contributed significantly to the family income by taking in boarders, sewing, making paper flowers and cigars, or taking on a variety of other money-earning tasks that could be done in the home. Italian men routinely employed their wives and sisters as helpers, though they weren't officially considered employees.

But despite these discrepancies, the ideology of separate spheres became a powerful force. Its imagery was used to justify restrictions on women's involvements in economic and political activity and men's lack of involvement in family and community. The majority of women were excluded from full participation in the emerging industrial economy. Those who did work outside the home were paid significantly less than men and were confined to "female" jobs (Cowan, 1987).

At the same time, the unpaid work that most women did in the home was accorded little social value. This devaluation was the result of the difference in power between the public and private spheres (Sidel, 1990). As long as men controlled the public sphere, they could wield greater economic and political power within society and translate that power into authority at home. ▲

▲ For more on the economic basis of family power, see Issue 5.

The belief in separate spheres for men and women was the basis for creating a very popular national holiday: Mother's Day. Most of us, when we think of Mother's Day, think of a day for celebrating each mother's devotion to her own family. However, a look at history reveals quite a different story.

The original proposal for a day for mothers occurred in 1858. Mothers' (plural) Day was to be a day to celebrate women's roles as community organizers and activists. These were women who acted on behalf of the entire generation of children, not just their own (Coontz, 1992). Later versions also stressed that Mothers' Day ought to be a vehicle for organized social and political action by all mothers.

But the eventual adoption of Mother's (singular) Day by Congress in 1914 represented a reversal of everything nineteenth-century mothers' days stood for. Politicians now made speeches linking Mother's Day to domestic life. They repudiated mothers' roles outside the household. Merchants hung testimonials to their own mothers in their stores, hoping to entice others to buy things for their mothers. What was once an occasion for activism and controversial causes in the community was reduced to an occasion for sales pitches and marketing, all cloaked in the image of mother as a domestic servant to her family.

The doctrine of separate spheres has been weakened from time to time by larger historical, political, and economic necessities. During World War II, for example, the government initiated a massive public relations program designed to lure women out of the homes and into factories where they would take up the productive work of men who had gone off to fight in the war. ▲ Government motivational films depicted child care centers as nurturing environments where children would flourish while their mothers worked. Between 1940 and 1945 the female labor force increased by over 50 percent. Three-fourths of these new workers were married, and a majority had children (Coontz, 1992).

After the war ended, however, the message was very different. Women were encouraged to return to their "natural" domestic roles, and child care centers were depicted as horrible, dangerous places. Working mothers were labeled as selfish and irresponsible. Women were laid off in droves, despite the fact that the overwhelming majority wanted to continue working. Practically overnight, the political atmosphere had changed and with it the perception of women's appropriate place in the family and in the economy.

The years right after the war represented the heyday of the separate spheres ideology. Media messages heavily emphasized women's obligations to take their rightful position on the domestic front. Few women entered college during this era, and of those who did, two out of three dropped out before graduating. Most women left because they feared that a college education would hurt their marriage chances (Mintz & Kellogg, 1988).

But since the 1950s, the boundary separating men's and women's spheres has steadily eroded. Prior to 1960, about a third of female high school graduates enrolled in college (compared to over 50 percent of male graduates). By 1994, the percentage of women going on to college was 63 percent, slightly higher than for males (61 percent) (Bianchi & Spain, 1996). In 1950 a little over 30 percent of adult women were in the paid labor force; today, almost 75 percent of women between 25 and 34 work in the paid labor force (Haas, 1995). At the same time, men's labor force participation has declined from about 87 percent in 1950 to a little over 70 percent today. About 46 percent of all people in the paid labor force today are women, compared to a little under 32 percent in 1950. Furthermore, 60 percent of American mothers with children under 6 are employed (Ahlburg & De Vita, 1992; Reskin & Padavic, 1994; U.S. Bureau of the Census, 1995). (The Demo•Graphic Essay, "Patterns of Labor Force Participation for Women and Men," at the end of this chapter, explores this trend further.)

Yet despite these trends, Americans still tend to perceive domestic work as women's sphere and outside employment as men's sphere:

> Few Americans admit that job discrimination against women is acceptable, yet most feel uncomfortable when confronted with a female mechanic or a CEO in a dress. . . . When it comes to marriage and family life, Americans are even more ambivalent about women's roles, wanting them to be generous self-sacrificing mothers even if they are also expected to be dedicated professionals. Although women are encouraged to go to college and pursue their careers as never before, they are still held accountable for what was once called

▲ This historical trend is also discussed in Issue 2.

"women's work." If their houses are a mess, or if their children are unkempt, women . . . are still subject to blame. . . . Although eight out of ten Americans believe it is OK for women to work, half still think that men should be the real breadwinners. Americans want fathers to be more involved with their children, but most feel uncomfortable if a man takes time off work "just" to be with his kids. (Coltrane, 1996b, p. 26)

Indeed, in some corners of American society, calls can still be heard for a return to the traditional male breadwinner–female homemaker division of labor. ▲ A statement of beliefs issued at the 1998 national convention of Southern Baptists included a declaration that a woman should "submit herself graciously to the servant leadership of her husband," while a husband should "provide for, protect and lead his family" (quoted in Niebuhr, 1998, p. 1). She has the God-given responsibility to respect her husband and serve as his helper. A women's organization called "Heritage Keepers"—an offshoot of the large men's organization "Promise Keepers"—teaches women how to "let go of the reins" of family control. Their credo is "Submission is a place of honor" ("The Promise Keepettes," 1997, p. 15).

But how likely is it that vast numbers of American women will willingly withdraw from paid employment and happily return to the domestic sphere? A growing number of women are now the primary source of financial support in their families. And it's not just the money. A recent national poll found that only about a third of working women said they'd prefer to stay home, even if money were no object, because of the respect, esteem, and friendship networks their jobs provide (cited in Coontz, 1997). Furthermore, women are just as likely as men to feel successful in their work lives as well as their family lives (see Exhibit 3.1).

 ▲ Issue 8 explores the impact of working wives and mothers on the institution of family.

Exhibit 3.1

Success in Family and Work Life: Survey of 973 Married Men and Women

United States: 1996

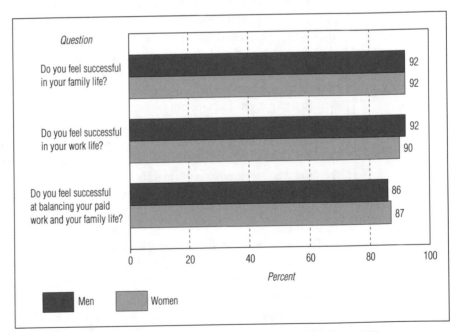

Source of data: National Opinion Research Center, University of Chicago, *General Social Survey, 1996.*

Gender Ideology in the Workplace

Although women and men are now both in the workplace, traditional gender ideologies still affect their experiences there. **Gender ideologies** refer to the ways people identify themselves regarding the work, marital, and family roles that are traditionally linked to gender (Greenstein, 1996a). ▲ Gender ideology is what distinguishes the man who believes that breadwinning is "men's work" and housework is "women's work" from the man who believes that "being male" means sharing breadwinning and cooperating with household chores. Employers as well as the public at large still believe women and men are naturally inclined to do certain jobs in the paid labor force (Reskin & Hartmann, 1986).

▲ Issue 5 looks at the role of gender ideology in shaping power relations between husbands and wives.

To measure the power of beliefs about gender-appropriate work, sociologist Richard Levinson (1975) had male and female undergraduate sociology students make job inquiries in response to 256 classified advertisements. The jobs were categorized as "male" (security guard, truck driver, car sales, etc.) or "female" (receptionist, hostess, cosmetic sales, etc.). Working in male-female pairs, one partner made a telephone inquiry about a "sex-inappropriate" job—for example, the male would ask about a receptionist position, and the female would ask about a truck driver job. About 30 minutes later, the "sex-appropriate" partner called about the same job: The woman called about the receptionist job, the man about the truck driver opening. The students were instructed to be polite and to use identical words in their inquiries.

Levinson found clear-cut discrimination in 35 percent of the cases. The sex-inappropriate caller might be told that the person doing the hiring was out of town or that the position had already been filled. However, when the sex-appropriate caller phoned a half-hour later, he or she might be told that the position was still open or was even encouraged to come in for an interview. Ambiguous discrimination was found in another 27 percent of the cases. This type of discrimination ranged from expressions of surprise to subtle attempts on the part of employers to discourage the sex-inappropriate caller from applying for the job. A more recent replication of this study found that these forms of sex discrimination, while not as common as they were in Levinson's study, still exist (Winston, 1988).

The standard assumptions that drive the typical workplace usually disadvantage women. Think for a moment about what you have to do to be considered a good worker by your boss. Obviously you have to show competence and a deep, serious commitment to the company. Evidence of such commitment might include working extra hours, traveling to faraway business meetings or professional conferences, attending training programs, working unpopular shifts, entertaining out-of-town clients on weekends, and so on. Such activities are possible only if your household setup allows you the time to place your job above other considerations, such as family. Because women, especially mothers, still tend to have the lion's share of responsibility at home, they have more difficulty making time for these activities and therefore are less able to "prove" to their bosses that they are good, committed employees.

Assumptions about what constitutes an "ideal" worker can run deep. Imagine for a moment that you're a boss who's just been told that your most valuable employee, Chris, is engaged to be married. How will you respond?

If Chris is a man, chances are his impending marriage will be seen as a "stabilizing" influence. His carefree days of bachelorhood will soon give way to the serious responsibilities of family life. Job security will now be extremely important to him, perhaps making him a more committed and dependable worker. He might even need a raise, since fatherhood is probably looming not far down the road. You'd be unlikely to think that these new family responsibilities will somehow prevent Chris from devoting himself entirely to his job. On the contrary, it's likely that they'll motivate him to work even harder so he can support his family.

Now suppose Chris is a woman. How might your response to the nuptial news change? Chances are that the impending marriage will now be seen as a potential impediment to career mobility. You might begin to question whether she'll be able to remain fully committed to the job. Will she move if her husband finds a good job somewhere else? Perhaps you begin to wonder how long it will be before Chris becomes pregnant and seeks maternity leave or quits altogether. Rather than making her a more dependable worker, marriage may actually make her less dependable, less stable, and less invested in the company.

In the real-life workplace, these gender-based expectations can play a decisive role in hiring and promotion decisions (Reskin & Hartmann, 1986). In addition, research consistently shows that mothers earn lower wages than women without children. This "wage penalty" doesn't disappear even when different levels of work experience are taken into consideration (Waldfogel, 1997). Not surprisingly, about 90 percent of male executives but only 35 percent of female executives have children by the time they turn 40 (cited in Schwartz, 1989). Notice, however, that these differences are not the result of outright sexism and overt discrimination but a more subtle consequence of a pervasive ideology that underlies our beliefs about gender, family, and the workplace.

The "Mommy Track"   In recent years, many companies have attempted to accommodate larger numbers of women on their payrolls by developing alternative work arrangements, such as part-time positions, reduced workloads, temporary positions, flextime, irregular shifts, or jobs that can be performed from home. These innovations—sometimes referred to collectively as the **mommy track**—have provided many employed women with less demanding career paths that enable them to continue meeting their family obligations. The mommy track represents an important institutional recognition that many female workers take their domestic responsibilities very seriously. Not surprisingly, more than two-thirds of temporary and part-time workers in this country are women ("Ten facts about women workers," 1997).

However, these "irregular" jobs are not without problems. For one thing, they tend to be more insecure than "regular" ones. Because their jobs are the most expendable, these workers are the first ones pushed out of employment during hard times. They also tend to be paid less and lack the benefits that typically accompany full-time, regular employment.

Moreover, women in "mommy track" positions are often regarded as less committed to the profession and therefore are excluded from opportunities that might lead to monetary rewards and promotions (Barker, 1993). Career advancement can be permanently slowed by the belief that mothers' commitment to their children interferes with workplace efficiency (Schwartz, 1989). For instance, female lawyers in part-time positions are often given the lowest-status projects to work on, which are not only less interesting but also lead to a professional dead end. Clearly, the lawyer most likely to have a bright future in the profession is the one who can be totally committed to the firm and who has no family at home or a family with a spouse at home to care for it ("Why law firms," 1996).

The Wage Gap　In the United States women have made remarkable progress in overcoming traditional obstacles to employment. Over the past several decades, women have increased their representation dramatically in male-dominated fields like engineering, medicine, law, and administration (Reskin & Hartmann, 1986). The representation of women in skilled trades has increased by over 80 percent (Sidel, 1986). One-third of all U.S. businesses, employing over 13 million people, are owned by women (U.S. Bureau of the Census, 1996).

Although these figures are encouraging, women still face disadvantages when it comes to wages, promotions, and authority (Reskin & Padavic, 1994). In particular, women still face a **wage gap**: Their earning power—and thus their ability to financially support their families—lags behind men's. In 1995 the average income for all men working full-time year-round was $31,496 per year. All women working full-time year-round earned an average salary of $22,497 per year (U.S. Bureau of the Census, 1997a). To put it another way, for every dollar a man earns, a woman earns approximately 71 cents. The differences are even more pronounced for African-American and Hispanic women, who earn 65 and 55 cents, respectively, for every dollar a man earns. In addition, 61 percent of employed women have little or no ability to advance in their jobs, 40 percent of those over 55 have no pension plan, and 34 percent have no health insurance ("Working women's woes," 1994).

These figures are clearly an improvement over past wage differences. In 1973, for instance, all women earned only 56.6 cents for every dollar a man earned. Advances in work experience and job-related skills have enabled some women—particularly middle- and upper-class women—to improve their income levels relative to men's. However, some sociologists argue that the wage gap has narrowed somewhat not because women's earning power has improved but because men's has worsened (Bernhardt, Morris, & Handcock, 1995). Also, the discrepancy between men's pay and women's pay has proved remarkably resilient over the years, despite the 1963 Equal Pay Act, which guaranteed equal pay for equal work, and Title VII of the 1964 Civil Rights Act, which banned job discrimination on the basis of sex (as well as race, religion, and national origin).

I should point out that the wage gap is not an exclusively American phenomenon. To varying degrees in every country around the world, men earn more than women. In the developing countries of Latin America, Africa, and Asia, women commonly earn 25 percent or less of what men earn (Tiano, 1987). In some countries, however, such as France, Sweden, Australia, and Denmark, the wage gap is narrower than it is here, with women earning 80 to 90 percent of what men earn (Reskin & Padavic, 1994).

Why does the American wage gap continue to exist? Some economists and policy makers argue that the wage gap is an institutional by-product of men's generally higher levels of work experience, training, and education. The U.S. Bureau of the Census, however, reports that gender differences in education, labor force experience, and seniority—factors that might justify discrepancies in salary—account for less than 15 percent of the wage gap between men and women (cited in National Committee on Pay Equity, 1995). For instance, the average income of full-time female workers is significantly lower than men's with the same level of educational training. In fact, women with a bachelor's degree can expect to earn about the same as men with only a high school diploma (median annual income of $26,841 for college-educated women compared to $26,333 for high school–educated men) (U.S. Bureau of the Census, 1997a). Hence, the continuing gap seems to have little to do with men's and women's different abilities or credentials.

A more likely reason for the wage gap is the types of jobs women typically have. The majority of employed women work in jobs, such as nursing, social work, and teaching, that are extensions of their traditional family roles. These jobs not only lack social prestige, they are usually on the low end of the pay scale. For the five "most female" job positions (that is, those more than 96 percent female) of secretary, receptionist, licensed practical nurse, private household worker, and child care worker, the average weekly salary is $219. By contrast, the average weekly salary for the five "most male" job positions (those less than 3 percent female) of airplane pilot, construction worker, truck driver, firefighter, and miner is $506 (adapted from Barrett, 1987).

Dual-Earner Families

Despite the wage gap, women remain committed to the idea of participating in the workforce. One obvious reason is that the financial strains of modern living—shrinking incomes, increasing cost of housing, and so on—have made it virtually impossible for most couples today to survive on one income. In 1990, 54 percent of families with at least one child under the age of 6 had two working parents. That figure is up from 32 percent in 1976. Of those families with children between the ages of 6 and 10, 68 percent consist of an employed mother and father (U.S. Bureau of the Census, 1991). The dual-earner family is now the single most common American family type. Even so, controlling for inflation, median incomes for American families have risen quite slowly over the past several decades—from $32,229 in 1970 to $34,076 in 1995 (both figures in 1995 dollars) (U.S. Bureau of the Census, 1997a). ▲ Some types of families have been more successful than others, however. Hispanic families have seen their median income drop substantially between 1970 and 1995. Families with children have seen only a 2.4 percent increase in income, and the incomes of a subset of these families, single mothers, have not changed at all since the mid-1970s. At the same time, childless families have enjoyed a 19.6 percent increase in income (Peterson, 1994).

▲ Issue 7 takes a closer look at the role that economics plays in family life.

The image of the traditional family, in which Mom stays home to raise the kids, simply cannot work for most people given the economic realities of modern society. Nevertheless, social institutions, for the most part, are still built around the outdated belief that only one partner (typically the father) in a couple should be working. Historically, such beliefs have created serious burdens for working parents. Consider the case of a 32-year-old Minnesota woman. She was fired from her job as an accounting clerk at a computer company because she had to stay home from work frequently to care for her sick baby, who had a series of illnesses including pneumonia, influenza, and pinkeye. The company stated that she missed almost half the work time from January to May of 1990. The state commissioner of jobs and training said she was not eligible for unemployment benefits because she had "voluntarily" put family interests ahead of her employer's interests, which amounted to misconduct (Lewin, 1991). However, her husband was unable to care for the child, and all her nearby relatives worked. In addition, she said, most day care providers do not accept sick children, and bringing somebody into the home to care for the child was far too expensive. Eventually an appeals court overturned the denial of benefits, ruling that her absenteeism was beyond her control and therefore did not amount to misconduct.

Many couples find they must make career trade-offs to try to balance their work and family lives. A survey of more than 6,000 employees of a major chemical company found that, at the managerial and professional level, 47 percent of women and 41 percent of men had told their supervisors they would not be available for relocation; 32 percent of the women and 19 percent of the men told their bosses they wouldn't take a job that required extensive traveling; and 7 percent of women and 11 percent of men turned down a promotion. Among those in manufacturing jobs, 45 percent of women and 39 percent of men refused to work overtime, and 12 percent of women and 15 percent of men had turned down a promotion (cited in Lewin, 1995b).

▲ Issue 8 and Chapter 5 examine the state of child care in American society.

Some experts feel that the single most important step our society could take to help dual-earner families would be to help them deal with child care demands. ▲ As recently as 1990, only 52 percent of the nation's largest companies had some form of maternity leave guaranteeing that an employee can use 6 weeks of vacation or sick time and not lose her job (Aldous & Dumon, 1990). However, in 1993 President Clinton signed into law the Family and Medical Leave Act, which guarantees some workers up to 12 weeks of unpaid sick leave per year for the birth or adoption of a child or to care for a sick child, parent, or spouse.

This law represents a noteworthy shift in the government's recognition of the needs of dual-earner families, but it has some important qualifications that seriously limit its applicability to a significant proportion of the working population:

■ The law covers only workers who have been employed continuously for at least 1 year and who work at least 25 hours a week. As a result, temporary contract or part-time workers—who, as we've seen, are predominantly female—are not eligible.

■ The law is of no value to parents who can't afford to take unpaid leave.

■ The law exempts companies with fewer than fifty workers; hence, only about 40 percent of the full-time workforce is covered.

■ The law allows an employer to deny leave to any employee who is in the highest paid 10 percent of its workforce if allowing that person to take the leave would create "substantial and grievous injury" to the business operations.

Between 1994 and 1995, less than 4 percent of employees in companies covered by this law actually took leave from their jobs ("Impact of the family," 1997).

While this law represents an improvement over past conditions, the United States still lags behind other countries. According to a recent United Nations survey of 152 countries, the United States is one of only 6—along with Australia, New Zealand, Lesotho, Swaziland, and Papua New Guinea—that does not have a national policy requiring paid maternity leave (cited in Olson, 1998). By comparison, consider the policies of other industrialized nations:

■ Both Germany and Japan guarantee a minimum of 3 months of *paid* family leave to all employees regardless of the size of their employer. Additional unpaid leave is available if it is needed (Shanker, 1990).

- In Canada, mothers can take up to 41 weeks off and be paid 60 percent of their salary for 15 of those weeks (Reskin & Padavic, 1994).
- In Sweden, pregnant women are given 8 weeks of full paid leave *before* the baby is born, and either parent can remain at home for up to 9 months after the child is born while drawing 90 percent of his or her salary (Kamerman, 1985; Sidel, 1986). Swedish parents can take 60 days off a year with 80 percent pay to care for sick children or to visit children at day care or school. Both fathers and mothers also have the right to reduce the workday to 6 hours or the workweek to 4 days in order to care for children (Haas, 1995).

The Disappearing Boundary Between "Home" and "Work"

Many American families, especially those with young children, still struggle with lack of support from employers, government, and businesses. They face difficulty trying to fit in all the tasks that used to be performed by housewives, trying to find dependable day care, having to call in sick themselves in order to care for a sick child, having to use vacation time as maternity leave, and so on. But each year the number of employers who offer "family friendly" work policies grows. In some large companies you can now choose to work part-time, share a job with another worker, work some of your hours at home, or work on a flexible schedule.

Given the rhetoric about the importance of spending time with family, you'd expect workers to be rushing to take advantage of these opportunities. But relatively few employees appear to use them. A recent study of 188 companies found that, when available, less than 5 percent of employees made use of part-time shifts and less than 3 percent chose to work some hours at home. A Bureau of Labor Statistics survey asked a national sample of workers if they would prefer a shorter workweek, a longer workweek, or their present schedule. About 62 percent preferred their present schedule; 28 percent wanted to work *longer* hours; less than 10 percent wanted to work a shorter schedule (cited in Hochschild, 1997b).

In other words, while many working parents say they want to spend more time with their families and less time at work, relatively few are taking advantage of opportunities to reduce their work time. To explain why, sociologist Arlie Russell Hochschild (1997b) interviewed 130 employees at a large public relations company she called "Amerco" over a period of 3 years. At Amerco, only 53 of 21,000 employees—all of them women—chose to switch to a part-time schedule in response to the arrival of a new baby. Less than 1 percent of the employees share a job or work at home, even though the company permits it.

From the information she gathered, Hochschild dismissed some widely held explanations for why people would forgo family-friendly policies:

- *They can't afford to work shorter hours.* If this were true, you'd expect workers at the lowest end of the pay scale to be the most reluctant to voluntarily cut their hours. But at Amerco, the highest-paid employees were actually the least interested in using these opportunities.
- *They are afraid that working part-time or asking for time off would make them vulnerable to layoffs.* Hardly any of the workers Hochschild interviewed worked longer hours because they were afraid of being laid off. Indeed, she found that most layoffs had nothing to do with work schedules.

■ *They don't know such policies exist.* The vast majority of employees were fully aware of the options available to them. In fact, many of them were quite proud to work for a company that had such an enlightened approach.

So why were these workers so unwilling to change their work lives to spend more time with their families? Hochschild believes the explanation can be found in the meanings people attach to their jobs and their families. ▲ For many Americans, work has become a form of "home," and home has become "work." Home has traditionally been defined as a soothing place where people should feel secure, relaxed, and comforted. Work, on the other hand, has traditionally been defined as a harried and insecure place where people often feel dehumanized ("just a cog in a machine") and where their worth is judged not by who they are but by how much they produce. But things have changed.

▲ Symbolic interactionism, described in Chapter 1, emphasizes the role of subjective meaning in everyday family life.

New management techniques have transformed many workplaces into more appreciative, personal sorts of places. Ironically, according to observers, the increased presence of women in the workplace has led to a greater emphasis on cooperation and support.

At the same time, the home has become a frenzied place where efficiency is the overriding concern. When both partners have busy work schedules, their opportunities to spend time with one another or with children are reduced, making it particularly difficult to sustain emotionally gratifying family relationships (Kingston & Nock, 1987). Technological innovations like cellular phones, beepers, faxes, and electronic mail intrude even further into family life, making many workers accessible 24 hours a day. In the interests of getting things done, children are often subjected to factory-style "speedups," hurried from one place to the next. Dinner must take 10 minutes or there won't be enough time to get the kids to soccer or violin lessons. Like business meetings, each family event must be planned in advance and entered in the time schedule. People are forced to cram all their emotional needs into the 30 or 45 minutes they spend with each other before bed.

Because people aren't getting what they want and need at home, things there are messy. Children become sullen, spouses become resentful. To make things even more stressful, in addition to the traditional needs of children and spouses, there are now the needs of elderly parents as well as the blending and reblending of stepparents, stepchildren, ex-spouses, and former in-laws. ▲

▲ Chapter 7 examines the unique demands of stepfamilies; Chapter 8 describes the dilemmas associated with adult children caring for their elderly parents.

And so for many people work has become a sort of refuge. Some of the workers Hochschild interviewed told her that they come to work early and stay late just to get away from the house. At work they can relax, have a cup of coffee, and share jokes and stories with friends without the hectic anxiety that characterizes modern home life. They use terms like *fun, carefree,* and *emotionally supportive* to describe their work. Not surprisingly, they are perfectly willing to flee a world of unrelenting demands, unresolved quarrels, and unwashed laundry for a world of relative harmony, companionship, and understanding. Work has become their main source of pleasure and personal satisfaction.

The tendency to see home as work and work as home is, of course, not something that characterizes everyone or even most people. And Hochschild's study looked at only one company. But the tension between work and home is a growing reality that must be faced. Increasing numbers of female workers are discovering what men have known all along: that work can be an escape from the pressures of home.

The unfortunate consequence, according to Hochschild, is that people "downsize" their ideas about how much care a child or a partner really needs from them. At the same time, families learn to make do with less time, less attention, and less support at home than they once imagined possible. Where couples once "needed" time with each other, they are now fine without it. Where parents once felt cheated if they couldn't spend the entire weekend with their kids, they are now content with an hour or less each evening. In sum, neither men nor women are going to take advantage of family-friendly policies as long as the current realities of work and family remain as they are.

The Guilt Gap

Because of the lingering notion of separate spheres, men have historically been able to feel they are fulfilling their family obligations by simply being financial providers. A man may have to explain to people why he's chosen a particular career, but he rarely, if ever, has to explain or justify *why he is working*. Most people would interpret his long hours at work as an understandable sacrifice for his family's sake. In contrast, women's employment is usually perceived as optional or, more seriously, potentially damaging to family life. Women have traditionally had to justify why their working outside the home is not an abandonment of their family duties. You'd be hard-pressed to find many journalists and scholars fearfully describing the perilous effects of men's outside employment on the family. But the mountain of articles and editorials in popular magazines, newspapers, and academic journals focusing on the difficulties women have in juggling the demands of work and family and on the negative effects of employed mothers on their children's well-being perpetuates the idea that their labor force choices are potentially dangerous (Faludi, 1991).

▲ Issue 8 assesses the evidence concerning the effect of maternal employment on family relationships.

Despite these concerns, research shows that wives' and mothers' employment actually has very little negative impact on their family's well-being (Greenstein, 1995). ▲ And most Americans believe that working mothers are just as capable of establishing warm relationships with their children as mothers who don't work outside the home (see Exhibit 3.2). Nevertheless, popular images die hard, and so it's not surprising that few married women with children feel completely self-confident in the choice they make to enter or remain in the paid labor force. They agonize over whether their gains in financial well-being and personal independence are being purchased at the cost of their family relationships (Coontz, 1992).

Men, on the other hand, rarely spend as much time worrying about the effect their work will have on their children as mothers do. This gender difference in worrying is referred to by some as the **guilt gap** (Hays, 1996).

The Dilemma for Working Women   Sociologist Kathleen Gerson wrote a book in 1985 titled *Hard Choices: How Women Decide About Work, Career and Motherhood*. The book, a classic in the sociology of work and family, focuses on how women make the difficult choices between work and family commitments. Drawing on the life histories of working- and middle-class women, Gerson paints a vivid picture of the complex and competing forces women face: their aspirations, their commitment to motherhood, their beliefs about children, their perception of their place in their families and in society.

Exhibit 3.2

Adults Who Agree or Strongly Agree that a Mother in the Labor Force Can Establish as Warm and Secure a Relationship with Her Children as a Mother Not in the Labor Force

United States: 1977–1996

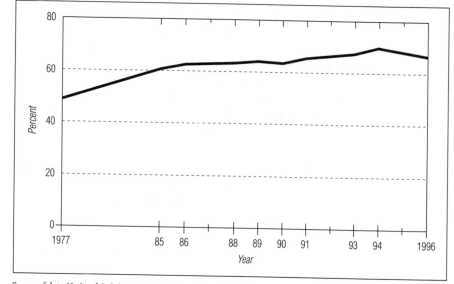

Source of data: National Opinion Research Center, University of Chicago, *General Social Survey, 1977–1996.*

The experiences of Gerson's subjects were quite diverse. Some of these women entered adulthood wanting to become mothers and homemakers; others began adulthood with ambivalence or downright animosity toward motherhood. Some continued on these early paths; others veered off, experiencing a dramatic change in their family plans and desires. But all of them faced tough decisions on how to balance work and family. More than a decade later, the choices for women remain hard.

Such difficulty stems from powerful and sometimes conflicting social pressures. We seem to have a profound cultural ambivalence regarding how mothers ought to behave. At one extreme is the image of the traditional mother who stays at home with the kids and devotes all her energy to her family. At the other extreme is the image of the "supermom," effortlessly juggling the demands of home and work. She has a briefcase under one arm, a cell phone in one hand, a baby in the other, and a smile on her face.

The ambivalence comes from the fact that although both images are considered socially acceptable, both are also indicted for their failings. Add to the mix the fact that American culture also seems unwilling to embrace childless career women, and you can see how an adult woman faces a no-win situation (Hays, 1996). ▲ If she voluntarily remains childless, some will accuse her of being cold, selfish, and unfulfilled as a woman. If she is a mother who works hard at her job, some will accuse her of neglecting her children. If she has children, is employed, but puts her kids before her job, some will judge her to be uncommitted and place her on the "mommy track." And if she is a full-time homemaker, some will call her an unproductive throwback to the 1950s, content with her subordinate family status.

These images lead many women to *feel* less than adequate. It's difficult for a stay-at-home mother to feel happy and fulfilled when she keeps hearing that she is mindless and bored. It's

▲ Chapter 4 examines gender differences in the cultural emphasis on parenthood.

difficult for the working mother to ably juggle her roles when she hears that she must dedicate *all* her energy in *both* directions to be considered successful.

Under these circumstances, it's not surprising that many employed mothers feel guilty and many stay-at-home mothers feel isolated and invisible to the larger society. Nor is it surprising that both spend a great deal of time making sense of and justifying their position. Employed mothers can come up with lots of compelling reasons why it's good and right to have a job and career, and traditional mothers can come up with equally compelling reasons why it's good and right to stay home (Hays, 1996).

Separate Spheres for Working Men   The point here is that while many men make sacrifices regarding their careers or their families, in general they don't face the same kind of cultural ambivalence and hard choices that women face. In fact, men's choice, for the most part, is no choice at all. Since men are still expected to attach primary importance to their careers, they seldom feel stress over sacrificing family time for their jobs. The stress some men do feel over balancing their careers and their family commitments can be tempered by the knowledge that they are conforming to cultural expectations if they devote most of their time to work. Indeed, men have historically been more able than women to keep family commitments from intruding on their work time and have used job demands to justify limiting their family time. In short, while women's family obligations and work aspirations have always been tightly intertwined, since the nineteenth century men have typically been able to maintain separate spheres.

In fact, evidence suggests that fathers who are freed of the burden of family obligations— that is, whose wives stay home to take care of the house and children—actually earn 20 percent more and get higher raises than fathers whose wives work. Such differences hold even after taking into consideration the effects of the number of hours each group of men works, their experience and training, and their field of employment (cited in Lewin, 1994a).

Some argue that these differences exist because men who are the sole breadwinners in their families work longer, produce more, and push harder for raises. In other words, without having to spend time on child care and housework, these men are freed up to pursue their careers with their full attention and energy. Others suggest that the higher salaries of men with nonworking wives simply reflect the fact that highly paid husbands can afford stay-at-home wives. Still others argue that a sort of "daddy penalty" is at work—that employers are prejudiced against men with "nontraditional," working wives.

We have no way to definitively determine which of these explanations is correct. However, some men with working wives do report feeling that they are being judged more harshly by their employers:

> I do think my boss is very aware that my face time is a little bit less than some of the men who feel like they can work as late as they like because their wives are at home with the kids. I'm as productive as those guys. I work smarter now that I have kids. I take work home. I don't do all the meaningless social stuff that can take up a lot of hours. But I do worry that it's going to slow down my promotions. (quoted in Lewin, 1994a, p. A15)

But another man whose wife stopped working to be at home with their children, looks at his job differently:

Knowing a parent is with the kids all day long removes the terrible sense of conflict and guilt if I have to work late. I leave the house at 6:10 in the morning, before the kids are awake and if I don't get home before they go to bed at 8:30 I miss them, and that's hard for me, but I don't feel as worried as I used to that they're not getting enough parent time.... Now that my job is our sole source of income, striving to keep it secure and maximize it is more important than ever. (quoted in Lewin, 1994a, p. A15)

Work Expectations in Same-Sex Couples

How does the gender-skewed approach to examining the interconnections between work and family apply to those situations in which there are no gender distinctions, that is, with same-sex couples? Gay and lesbian households can transcend the limitations and inequalities of sex-based "husband" and "wife" roles. Family work and breadwinning responsibilities cannot be automatically based on sex. They must be negotiated.

For same-sex couples, the issue is not who has the right to work or, conversely, the obligation not to work. Instead, the issue is how can the relationship and the household be kept together given the career demands on *both* partners? The vast majority of same-sex couples emphasize sharing and fairness and believe that both partners in the relationship should work (Blumstein & Schwartz, 1983). ▲ Few consider either not working or supporting someone who chooses not to work. But the reasons for their feelings about this issue provide insight into the meaning of work for both men and women, regardless of sexual orientation.

▲ Power imbalances can exist in all types of relationships, as Issue 5 explains.

For gay men, work remains a key aspect of male self-respect. Unlike many heterosexual men, they don't feel obligated to support their partners financially. Instead, each partner is expected to work because that is what it means to be a man (Blumstein & Schwartz, 1983). Hence, there is little interest in being a full-time homemaker. Housework in gay male households tends to be shared or is performed by outside hired help.

For lesbians, work means the ability to avoid being dependent on others and being cast into the stereotypical homemaker role. While they understand the importance of earning their own living, rarely do these women think they will have to support, or be supported by, another person. Lesbians don't expect to be the head of a household in the same way a husband expects to enter the breadwinner role in a heterosexual marriage. They are likely to see themselves as "workers," not "providers" or "dependents."

Men's Changing Commitments to Work and Family

In contemporary heterosexual households, too, the two partners' work responsibilities are more a matter of negotiation than they were in the days when husbands were expected to be the primary breadwinners. Working wives today make a substantial contribution to their household's income. For instance, in 45 percent of dual-earner households, women earn about half or more of the income (cited in Ingrassia & Wingert, 1995). By 1990, the percentage of American households that consisted of a married couple dependent on a sole male breadwinner had dropped to less than 14 percent, from a high of almost 60 percent in 1950 (Gerson, 1993). The heretofore unchallenged belief in the superiority of the male "good provider" has been replaced by uncertainty over men's proper place in society. It's no longer obvious what goals men should pursue and how much energy they should devote to pursuing them. At a more philosophical level, it is no longer clear what it means to be a man. Because women are becoming just as likely as men to bear the responsibility for supporting a family, it has become harder for men to justify advantages based simply on being male. ▲

▲ How such uncertainty affects traditional power relations in families is addressed in Issue 5.

Along with such uncertainty, men today are facing new choices about how to structure their lives. Sociologist Kathleen Gerson (1993) interviewed 138 men ranging in age from the late 20s to the mid-40s. These men came from diverse social and occupational backgrounds. Less than half of them remained committed to the traditional male breadwinner role and expected women to occupy the traditional female homemaker role. However, these men felt that changes in women's lives had not—or should not—change men's traditional status as dominant breadwinner.

The remainder of the men Gerson interviewed rejected the traditional male breadwinner role. Of these men, the largest group—about 46 percent (or 24 percent of the total sample)—cited freedom from the breadwinner role as a reason to renounce marriage and parenthood. To these men, marriage always seemed more like a trap than a reward. They felt they had much to lose and little to gain by getting married. Many had negative experiences with other people's children, which convinced them that parenthood was not something they wished to pursue either. Fearing that becoming responsible for a family would rob them of the option to pursue unpredictable careers or nontraditional jobs, these men rejected the whole package of domestic and work commitments that constituted the traditional definition of male success. Freed from the social obligation to financially support a wife and children, these men turned away from family alto-

▲ For more detail on the father role after divorce, see Chapter 7.

gether. Those who had already fathered children were quite uninvolved in their lives. ▲

Another group of men Gerson interviewed—about 30 percent of those who turned away from the breadwinner role (17 percent of the total sample)—didn't consciously oppose marriage, parenthood, or steady work. They simply didn't think about the future at all. Such passivity, according to Gerson, came from two different and contradictory assumptions. One was that men had the luxury of not having to plan. Some of these men simply believed that everything would work out fine with or without planning. They tended to come from comfortable middle-class backgrounds, which they felt guaranteed them a good start in life. A second, more pessimistic, assumption was held mostly by working-class men. They felt that their restricted economic opportunities would take away any future "choices" anyway. They simply resigned themselves to the fact that nothing they could plan would work out, so why bother.

A small segment of men who rejected the breadwinner role (9 percent, or about 4 percent of the total sample) exhibited a more extreme version of this sort of pessimism. They expected to succumb to the dangers of being an adult long before they had a chance to face adult challenges and responsibilities. Future planning seemed, to them, irrational because they didn't expect to live that long. Such men turned to risky or dangerous pursuits like drugs, violence, or military service.

Finally, about 15 percent of this nontraditional group saw the decrease in breadwinning responsibilities as an opportunity to embrace a more nurturing parent role and construct a marriage based on equality and fairness. These men believed that a working wife would make a happier, more fulfilled companion than a homemaker. As one man put it, "I just could not see myself being attracted to somebody who was not gonna have their own career, and have the same kind of interest and passion about what they want to do as I had about my career" (quoted in Gerson, 1993, pp. 65–66). They hoped that an employed spouse would lessen their own economic burden and give them the freedom to seek personal fulfillment and not just job security at work. They wouldn't have to worry about earning a big paycheck. These men also showed a deep emotional attachment to their children and devoted much of their time at home to their care. They showed a willingness to parent not seen in their fathers' or grandfathers' generations.

Although statistically rare among Gerson's subjects, such attachment is becoming more and more socially acceptable. Shortly after the 1996 presidential election, then Secretary of Labor Robert Reich wrote a letter to the *New York Times* lamenting the difficulty he faced in balancing his career and his family. Unable to strike the kind of balance he wanted, he made the tough choice to resign from his powerful cabinet position so he could spend more time with his family:

> I have the best job I've ever had and probably ever will. No topping it. Can't get enough of it. I also have the best family I'll ever have, and I can't get enough of them. Finding a better balance? I've been kidding myself into thinking there is one. The metaphor doesn't fit. I had to choose. I told the boss I'll be leaving, and explained why. (Reich, 1996, p. A33)

Mr. Reich's story was a poignant one. Unfortunately, the best solution to his problem—and the problem of millions of other workers—lies not in personal decisions made by individuals but in a shift in structural arrangements. Few people have the economic wherewithal that Mr. Reich has to leave their jobs and devote more time to their families. A working-class father, for example, isn't about to "resign" from his job to relax and frolic with his children. In fact, recent reforms in welfare laws may actually prevent him from doing so. Ironically, Mr. Reich, as labor secretary, was the person responsible for federal guidelines concerning workplace policy. He was the very person who could have helped to change the workplace culture to be more conducive to family obligations so that such difficult sacrifices wouldn't have to be made in the first place.

Equality in Dual-Career Marriages

Sociologist Rosanna Hertz (1986) examined a smaller subset of dual-earner couples: middle- and upper-middle-class working couples in the corporate world. In these couples, not only are both partners employed, they are both professionals, committed to their careers. These individuals are, for the most part, economic equals.

Hertz points out that dual-career couples tend not to be politically or socially motivated individuals consciously pursuing an agenda of gender equality. Their desire for equal careers is not driven by any sort of ideology. Instead, they are the by-products of a shifting economy, where the expansion of white-collar employment coupled with the growth of career opportunities for female college graduates combined to make two careers—not just two jobs—in one family a popular option. Their unique position as marital equals is more behavioral than attitudinal. Labor market trends have made them advocates of gender equality, even if they weren't initially supporters of this cause.

How does such equality play itself out in family life? Hertz found important shifts in the roles of these husbands and wives. They understand each other's situation and tend to relate to each other as partners with similar goals, aspirations, and pressures.

The traditional "separate spheres" boundary, between "breadwinner" and "homemaker," dissolves when neither spouse can claim greater power and influence due to working outside the home or earning more money. The marriage can no longer respond entirely to the demands of only one spouse or only one spouse's career. Similar work schedules and employer demands muddy questions about whose work commitments should take precedence.

Indeed, the emergence of new and more complex forms of breadwinning—which typically emphasize greater sharing in the division of family responsibilities—have served to blur traditional gender boundaries in families. Breadwinners vary in terms of the amount of financial support they provide as well as the importance of their jobs in the experiences of other family members. For instance, some wives who earn significant income in their careers consider themselves employed homemakers, define their financial contributions to the family as supplementary, or stake a claim to the breadwinner role only with significant reluctance. Others, however, are highly committed to their careers. Because they believe that providing for one's family ought to be as much the responsibility of women as of men, they consider themselves "cobreadwinners" (Potuchek, 1997).

Couples trying to make their new reality fit an old, traditional family model often feel frustrated. They constantly struggle not to fall back on the old rules and roles they witnessed as children, when any conflict over work and family was resolved by letting one person's career atrophy.

Hertz found that the dominant mechanism couples used to negotiate these potential conflicts was to view their marriage as a third, shared career that requires commitment, attention, and hard work *from both partners*. Marital equality in this "third career" is not taken for granted; it takes substantial time and energy. As one husband states, "I certainly don't think this is a gloriously equal marriage marching off into the sunset. I think we struggle for equality all the time. And we remind each other when we are not getting it" (quoted in Hertz, 1986, p. 55). In "reminding each other" of inequalities—keeping each other in check so that neither spouse's career becomes favored—partners in dual-career marriages try to strike a livable balance.

▲ The weighing of costs and benefits to determine fairness in relationships is a central feature of the social exchange perspective, described in Chapter 1.

Most of the dual-career couples in this study reported having to be very explicit about fairness in the relationship, adopting a "bookkeeping mentality." ▲ They often instituted clear rules about job choices or relocation decisions should one spouse face transfer. For instance, one couple decided that if one spouse received a job offer that required a move to another city, the other spouse always had veto power, retaining the right to reject the city. This agreement operated as a constraint on the pursuit of one career to the possible disadvantage of the other person. Such rules may sound unromantic, but they serve to ensure fairness in the marriage.

Despite moments of doubt, ambivalence, or conflict, dual-career couples often create a communication style quite different from traditional marriages. Their lives outside the home, although rarely in the same profession, share a rhythm and structure. Such a situation is far different from the gulf that can sometimes separate the worlds of working and nonworking spouses. Dual-career couples have a deep understanding of each other's lives that is at once intimate and empathetic. They both understand, for example, that a last-minute crisis in the office can mean a late night at work, or that one or the other will periodically need to travel out of town on business, or that going out for a drink with colleagues after a particularly rough day can be important. Furthermore, they can both understand inevitable bad moods and therefore can correctly attribute them to job tension and not to the individual. As one man put it, "She has a sense of what I'm doing because she's out there doing the same damn thing every day" (quoted in Hertz, 1986, p. 77). An advantage of this kind of situation is the increased potential for mutual respect stemming from the heightened understanding of each other's lives.

Hertz's research offers compelling insight into the ways couples strike satisfying balances between work and family. But it's important to note that this balance is still rare among less-affluent dual-earner couples. Furthermore, it is always a struggle. For one thing, these couples still must cope with a culture that assumes male and female roles in the family ought to be divided into separate spheres of influence and responsibility, with one partner (usually the husband) given final authority. Hence, they are likely to go through periods in which they worry about their futures and the futures of their children. Partners who've made compromises in their careers, for example, must face parents, in-laws, and fast-track friends who frown upon those who don't try to maximize potential financial success. As one sociologist puts it, "Forgoing income is almost a cardinal sin in this country" (Schwartz, 1994, p. 186).

While the marriage of two careers brings a level of autonomy and financial freedom unavailable to most families that rely on a single source of income or on two modest incomes, such arrangements are always contingent upon the availability of careers in the labor market, people to help with housework and child care, and the ability of couples to adapt to competing employer demands. In other words, dual-career couples are always dependent upon others outside the relationship. Lack of adequate day care or a sudden downsizing at one's place of employment can destroy the delicate balance a couple may have achieved.

Nontraditional Lifestyles of Dual-Earner Couples

Clearly, couples who want to work and remain committed to their families are subject, to some degree, to the whims of the workplace. For instance, nearly one in five full-time workers finds him- or herself working long, nonstandard, or erratic hours and struggling to find a family arrangement that will match (Hays, 1995). As the economy has become more global, more companies require around-the-clock shifts to meet the demands of international customers in different time zones. Therefore, many dual-earner and dual-career couples have had to construct nontraditional lifestyles in order to adapt to the demands they experience.

Shift Work   Among dual-earner couples in the United States, approximately one-third consist of one spouse employed during the day and the other employed during the evening, at night, or on some form of rotating schedule (Presser, 1994). According to the Department of Labor, 60 percent of women with children under 6 and 78 percent of women with school-age children work nonstandard hours (cited in Hays, 1995).

▲ Social class variations in family experiences and recent welfare reforms are discussed more fully in Issue 7.

The perception of shift work can vary along class lines. ▲ Young, middle-class couples might perceive it as an attractive alternative for the flexibility it offers. For working-class families, however, shift work is likely to be an arrangement over which workers have little control. Parents earning the lowest incomes are the ones who are more likely to be assigned to work weekends and on unstable or rotating schedules. As political pressures to get people off welfare and into the workforce increase, more parents may be forced to take undesirable jobs with nonstandard hours, further complicating their family lives.

Although shift work is attractive to some couples, for most it is a source of tension. It can reduce marital happiness and the amount of interaction that occurs between partners, increase sexual and household problems, and ultimately increase the likelihood of divorce (White & Keith, 1990). Irregular work arrangements are particularly difficult for parents of very young children. Few child care centers operate 24 hours a day or on weekends. (By one estimate, only about a dozen 24-hour day care centers exist in the country.) So most parents of young children must either rely on friends and relatives or work opposite shifts, sacrificing time together so that one of them can be with the children (Hays, 1995).

Commuter Couples Another nontraditional solution to the problem of balancing work and family is to live apart. Over a million married couples living in separate residences—so-called **commuter couples**—are estimated to exist in the United States today (Baca Zinn & Eitzen, 1996). It is often difficult to pursue two careers in the same geographic area. The conventional solution, of course, is that one spouse—usually the wife—takes a less desirable job or chooses not to work at all. But more dual-career couples are choosing to meet the incompatible demands of work and family by adopting a commuting lifestyle, living apart for at least 3 nights a week.

Living apart is not unique to dual-career couples. Some occupations—like sales or politics—and some circumstances—like war, immigration, imprisonment, and seasonal work—have always required some marital separation. However, the husband has historically been the one to leave for some period of time (Anderson & Spruill, 1993).

Research shows that today's commuter couples tend to be well-educated professionals in their mid-30s. But their commuting characteristics vary widely. The time that separate residences are maintained can range anywhere from a few months to a dozen years or more. The distance between the residences may be short (40 or 50 miles) or span the entire country. Some couples reunite every weekend; others don't see each other for months at a time. Some have children; others don't (Anderson & Spruill, 1993). What they all have in common, though, is that the separation is motivated not by problems in the relationship but by both partners' desire to maximize success in their demanding careers. And it is perceived not as a freely chosen, perfect arrangement but as a necessary, temporary, accommodation (Gertsel & Gross, 1987).

Nevertheless, the commuting situation can *create* problems in the relationship. It is a lonely, inconvenient, and expensive lifestyle that takes tremendous effort. Communication, sexual activity, and the economics of maintaining a marriage are issues that must be worked out during infrequent visits.

Yet despite the potential problems, most commuters maintain that the career benefits outweigh the strains of separate living. Spouses report satisfaction with the freedom they have to continue working in their chosen occupations. They can devote long, uninterrupted hours to their jobs without worrying about missing dinners or social events at home. Furthermore, as in long-distance dating relationships, the time spouses in commuter marriages do spend together can be intensely arousing.

Women tend to be more positive about their commuting arrangements than men. Their gains in independence and professional mobility may counteract the costs of reduced emotional

▲ To some critics, women's increasing emphasis on independence has reduced their commitment to family obligations, a topic addressed in Issue 4.

closeness. ▲ The arrangement can validate the belief that their career is as important as their husband's. Consider the highly positive comments of two commuter wives:

> I was really unprepared for the fierce joy I have felt at being my own woman, being able to concentrate on my own activities, my own thoughts, and my own desires. It's a completely selfish, self-centered existence. It's almost a religious experience when you're fifty years old and have never felt that before.

> Every night I bring work home. If he was here, I'd have to let it go. I would have prepared real meals, made sure the house was neat, had more laundry to do. Oh, you know, the whole list. But, being alone, it's just easy to do my work. I'm kinda lured into it. (quoted in Gertsel & Gross, 1987, pp. 427–428)

The Domestic Division of Labor

In the pursuit of equal relationships, men have had a much easier time relinquishing some responsibility for the traditional breadwinner role than taking on more of the responsibility for the traditional homemaker role. Men's involvement in family work (defined here as doing household chores, caring for children, tending to others' emotional needs, keeping up relationships with kin, and so on) has not kept pace with women's increasing commitment to paid employment. Some sociologists have referred to this situation as a "stalled revolution" (Hochschild & Machung, 1989). That is, American families are indeed changing, but men are dragging their feet (Hunt & Hunt, 1987).

Even in dual-career couples where wives have prestigious careers, domestic matters are typically assumed to be outside the repertoire of male responsibilities. Consider the swirl of controversy that enveloped the 1993 confirmation hearings of the first two female nominees for U.S. Attorney General, Zoe Baird and Kimba Wood. These two women, both highly successful professionals, had employed undocumented immigrants as nannies for their children and thereby avoided paying Social Security taxes. These practices, while technically illegal, were commonplace among middle-class and upper-middle-class working parents. Nevertheless, the news was enough to sink the nominations of both women. Up to that point no male nominee for any Cabinet post had ever had his household so thoroughly scrutinized, even though such scrutiny would have no doubt found similar transgressions. Questions about nannies would have been considered completely irrelevant to his capacity to perform as a member of the presidential Cabinet. Clearly the assumption regarding these two women was that, despite their professional stature, they were the ones accountable for what went on in their homes. Interestingly, the woman who eventually was confirmed for the post of attorney general, Janet Reno, is single with no children.

Many conflict sociologists explain this sort of lingering bias as a by-product of patriarchy
▲ The basic assumptions of conflict theory are described in Chapter 1.
and our capitalist economic systems. ▲ Family work is invaluable to the entire economic system. However, the people who perform the majority of family work—that is to say, women— earn no money for providing services like cooking, cleaning, and caring for the needs of others. Mothers also provide an important service to society by physically and emotionally nurturing the next generation of workers. If a woman were to be paid the minimum going rate for all her

labor as mother and housekeeper—child care, transportation, errands, cleaning, laundry, cooking, bill paying, grocery shopping, and so on—her yearly salary would be over $35,000, more than the average salary of male full-time workers ("Mom's market value," 1998). In 1990 unpaid household work was equal to about 44 percent of the gross national product, or over $1 trillion (Strong & DeVault, 1992).

▲ Issue 5 describes the pivotal role that money plays in determining power relations in families.

Such work does not afford women the prestige it might if it were paid labor because societal and family power are usually a function of who earns the money. ▲ It's not that homemakers don't work, it's that they work invisibly outside the mainstream economy, in which work is strictly defined as something one is paid to do (Ciancanelli & Berch, 1987; Voyandoff, 1990). Furthermore, defining unpaid household labor and child rearing as women's responsibilities upholds male privilege in society. Free from such obligations, men are able to enjoy more leisure time and take advantage of the opportunity to pursue their own careers and interests. Women burdened with domestic responsibilities have less time and energy to devote to their careers. Hence, the division of labor in the home reinforces the division of labor in the workforce, further solidifying the gender-based power structure of American society.

Debate over the devalued perception of housework created a national controversy in Canada a few years back. In 1991 a Canadian housewife took issue with a question on her census questionnaire that asked, "How many hours did you work in the last week, *not including volunteer work, housework, [home] maintenance or repairs*?" (Smith, 1996). She had run her household for 19 years, raising three children in the process, and she was furious that her hard work was considered irrelevant. So she refused to fill out the questionnaire, a crime according to Canadian law. Under threat of prosecution, she embarked on a protest campaign, which eventually drew in women from all over the country. She formed a group called the Canadian Alliance for Home Managers, which threatened to boycott the next census if unpaid work remained uncounted. Five years later, Canada became the first country in the world to count the hours spent performing household labor and child care without pay on its national census.

Women's Work, Men's Help

It's true that men do more around the house than did their counterparts 30 years ago and that they play a more prominent role in the raising of children. And it's also true that women, because they are more likely to be in the paid labor force than in the past, are doing less. But despite these changes, family work responsibility continues to be predominantly female (Brines, 1994).

Research consistently shows that women spend on average about 50 hours a week doing family work, while men contribute a maximum of about 11 hours (Cowan, 1991; Levant, Slatter, & Loiselle, 1987). On average, men are responsible for between 20 and 35 percent of the domestic work (Shelton & John, 1996). The average American wife puts in about 15 hours more each week than her husband on all types of work—paid and unpaid—amounting to an extra month of 24-hour workdays a year (Hochschild & Machung, 1989).

Moreover, the housework men do tends to be quite different from the work their wives do. Their chores are typically infrequent, irregular, or optional:

> They take out the garbage, they mow the lawns, they play with children, they occasionally
> go to the supermarket or shop for household durables, they paint the attic or fix the faucet;

but by and large, they do not launder, clean, or cook, nor do they feed, clothe, bathe, or transport children. These . . . most time-consuming activities . . . are exclusively the domain of women. (Cowan, 1991, p. 207)

From a structural functionalist perspective, traditional gender disparities in household responsibilities may actually reflect an equitable, functional, interdependent division of labor that maximizes benefits for the entire family. ▲ Families work most efficiently when people are responsible for the tasks for which they are best suited: men caring for the family's economic needs and women caring for its emotional needs.

▲ The structural functionalist perspective is introduced in Chapter 1.

If this were the case, you would expect family work to be shared equally if both partners work full-time, right? There is some evidence that husbands perform more of the mundane household tasks traditionally performed by wives when their wives have a long history of extensive work in the paid labor force (Pittman & Blanchard, 1996). However, in general, the gender discrepancy in household responsibilities does not diminish all that much as a result of women's full-time employment.

Several national studies have found that, on average, employed women spend over 33 hours a week on housework, compared to 18 hours a week for husbands (Lennon & Rosenfield, 1994; South & Spitze, 1994). Other studies place the figure for men closer to 7 hours a week (Brines, 1994). Women employed outside the home continue to be primarily responsible for the upkeep of the household and end up working what amounts to two full-time jobs (Demo & Acock, 1993). Interestingly, this discrepancy holds even among couples who profess egalitarian, non-sexist values. Husbands who say that all the housework should be shared equally still spend significantly less time doing it than their wives do (Blumstein & Schwartz, 1983).

▲ Racial and ethnic variation in a wide variety of family experiences is addressed in Issue 6.

Race and ethnicity play an important role in the domestic division of labor. ▲ For instance, Asian and Hispanic men tend to do less family work than other men. This is particularly true in ethnic neighborhoods, where the high proportion of recent immigrants ensures a steady flow of people with traditional, patriarchal values. According to one study, despite stereotypes about black men abandoning their families, they are actually *more* likely than white, Asian, or Hispanic men to be intimately involved in family work and child rearing (Rubin, 1994). Indeed, black men employed full-time may actually spend *more* time doing household labor than unemployed black men, indicating that when men are attached to the provider role they are also committed to their family obligations (Shelton & John, 1993).

▲ Social class does, however, account for differences in other family matters, which you can read about in Issue 7.

On the other hand, social class appears to have little impact on the gender-based division of domestic labor. ▲ The common assumption is that working-class men are less "enlightened" and therefore do proportionately less family work than middle-class men. Stereotypically, the macho factory worker whose masculinity is threatened by doing laundry and cleaning the bathroom is contrasted with the "yuppie" father happily cooking meals and pushing a stroller in the park. But research shows that class has little to do with how much housework husbands perform (Wright, Shire, Hwang, Dolan, & Baxter, 1992).

However, men's economic standing *relative to their spouse's* does have an effect. When men earn more than their wives, the fulfillment of traditional gender roles fits well with the exchange of resources: his financial support for her domestic services. But when women earn more, couples sometimes resort to a traditional division of family power in order to reinforce the gender differences that could be undermined by the switching of traditional economic roles. To shore up their threatened masculinity, men who earn less than their wives may try to avoid "feminine" household chores and thus do less of the housework than other men. Men who have suffered through prolonged joblessness are prone to entirely disavow housework, the performance of which would be further evidence of their "failure" at the male provider role (Brines, 1994).

For those couples who do share household tasks, imbalances still exist. For instance, the arrival of children often signals a return to a more traditional division of household labor (Cowan & Cowan, 1992). In fact, employed men may actually *increase* their time at work upon becoming parents while women significantly decrease theirs (Shelton, 1992). ▲ In other words, having children often means more work *inside* the house for women and more work *outside* the house for men.

▲ Chapter 4 provides a more detailed examination of motherhood and fatherhood in American society.

Many women whose husbands make significant contributions to household work and child care report frustration over the fact that they are still "household managers" who are ultimately responsible for planning and initiating household activities. They complain that they must instruct and remind their husbands before the men begin to notice and take care of the tasks necessary to run a home (Coltrane, 1996a). Some women have found that if they want their husbands to do certain household tasks, they must prepare itemized lists every time they leave the house, spelling out exactly what needs to be done (Hays, 1996). Others complain that men seem so blind to what needs to be done that it is often easier just to do the job themselves.

Men's literal and figurative distance from family work is also reflected in the ways they define their domestic contributions. Some men distance themselves from the activity by indicating to others that it is not the sort of thing they typically do. Rather than defining the work they do around the house as an ordinary, expected aspect of their family responsibilities, they may define it as "help"—implying that they're assisting the person who's usually responsible for such tasks.

Even men who assume major responsibility for planning and initiating housework and child care tend to define their role as "helper" (Coltrane, 1989). The tendency of many fathers to refer to their child care behavior as "babysitting" verbally aligns them not with the general category of parents for whom taking care of children is a taken-for-granted element of their family role, but with outsiders who periodically care for other people's children. Mothers rarely refer to the time they spend with their own children as "babysitting."

A key social element of "help"—as distinct from "work"—is that it requires expressions of gratitude or at least some acknowledgment on the part of the person "receiving" the assistance (Hochschild & Machung, 1989). Compared to his father or perhaps other men in his community, a husband who does the laundry, dusts the furniture, and washes the dishes may feel that he is providing more help than his wife could reasonably expect from a man. Given such a frame of reference, his domestic tasks are something extra—a helpful gift. And his wife should feel grateful.

But she has a different frame of reference. If, in addition to her full-time job, she is still responsible for 70 to 80 percent of the family work, her husband's contribution might be perceived as little more than what she deserves—not something extra and certainly not a gift.

Hence, he may see her failure to thank him for watching the baby a few hours each afternoon as a lack of appreciation for "all he's done." She, on the other hand, thinks he's just done what he should do as a parent and therefore she's not obliged to express any special gratitude. She may even resent him for demanding that she acknowledge his domestic contributions, which, relative to her ordinary responsibilities, are quite small.

Perceptions of Inequity

Imbalances and inequalities exist in most families. However, actual, objective inequality in domestic responsibilities is less important than the *perception* of inequity and unfairness. As you might expect, men in general are less likely than women to perceive the unequal distribution of household labor as unfair (see Exhibit 3.3), although their perceptions of fairness may vary across racial lines. Since, as we've already seen, African-American men tend to spend more time on housework than white men, they are less likely to view the household division of labor as unfair to their wives. When comparing their household labor to other men's, African-American men may conclude that they're contributing their fair share more than other men (John, Shelton, & Luschen, 1995). What's striking is that relatively few wives (estimates range from one-third to one-fourth) regard the unequal division of labor as unfair. White, African-American and Hispanic women are equally unlikely to report unfairness (John, Shelton, & Luschen, 1995).

Research indicates that men and women in general agree that wives should do about twice as much family work as husbands do (Lennon & Rosenfield, 1994). Even among professional wives in dual-career marriages, only a small percentage say their husbands do *too little* work around the house (Yogev, 1981). In a study of couples of relatively equal economic and professional status, 62 percent of wives said their husbands did a satisfactory amount of domestic work, and 13 percent actually felt their husbands did *too much* (Biernat & Wortman, 1991).

Gender Ideology and Family Work Some people do feel an unbalanced household division of labor is unfair to women (Hochschild & Machung, 1989). But under what circumstances do

Exhibit 3.3

Division of Household Labor: Survey of 759 Adults

United States: 1996

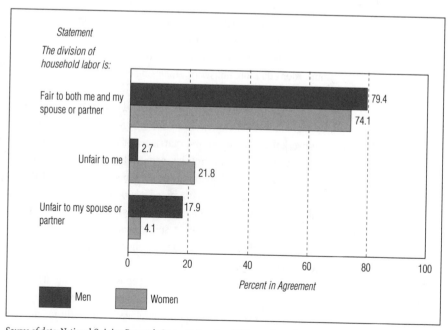

Source of data: National Opinion Research Center, University of Chicago, *General Social Survey, 1996.*

these perceptions arise? People's perceptions are, in part, contingent on their beliefs and ideologies about gender. In general, husbands with egalitarian gender ideologies tend to see the typically gender-based division of family work responsibilities as more unfair to their wives than husbands with traditional ideologies (DeMaris & Longmore, 1996), even though there's no evidence that egalitarian husbands are particularly motivated to increase their contribution to domestic labor.

Women's perceptions are somewhat different. Wives with a "traditional" gender ideology are likely to value stability and harmony in their relationships, but "egalitarian" wives might be more concerned with independence and autonomy (Greenstein, 1996b). If a wife truly believes that married women—no matter what their employment status—are *supposed* to do most of the housework, she will probably view inequalities as legitimate and not see them as unjust. On the other hand, a wife who enters marriage expecting her husband to share in the household work will perceive the inequalities as unfair because her expectations are being violated. Such unmet expectations are likely to decrease marital stability and marital happiness.

It should be noted that gender differences in family work don't just reflect a culturally learned pattern. Women don't do most of the household chores just because they are taught that doing the family work is part of their gender identity. If women believed that doing household chores was part of being a woman, gender differences in family work responsibilities would be noticeable at all stages of family life, including singlehood, cohabitation, and remarriage. But research indicates otherwise. Although the amount of family work that men do is quite similar across different marital statuses, the amount that women do fluctuates considerably (South & Spitze, 1994). Single women do about the same amount of housework as single men. Significant differences between women and men exist only among married and cohabiting couples and are especially pronounced among couples with children.

Differences in contributions to family work based on marital status apparently reflect different expectations of how one "does gender" (West & Zimmerman, 1991). Perhaps women believe that doing the housework is a means of displaying their love of or subordination to men. Single women don't do more housework than single men because they don't feel any pressure to do so (Perkins & DeMeis, 1996).

A recent comparison of first-married and remarried couples offered some support for this explanation. Women in their second live-in relationship contribute significantly less time to housework than women in first marriages or first cohabiting relationships. Men's housework time, predictably, was uniformly low across all situations (Sullivan, 1997). The women in second relationships may have had lower rates of housework because they started their first marriage under one set of norms and reexamined it later under a different one. In another study, a majority of previously divorced women did in fact say they'd left their first marriage because of inequitable treatment (Schwartz, 1994). So a woman who perceived the domestic division of labor in her first live-in relationship to be unfair might be inclined to seek a more equal division in subsequent relationships.

Because family work is a feature of *all* households, no family type is exempt from facing decisions about how it ought to be divided. As in heterosexual couples, lesbians and gay men do more housework if they are not fully employed (Blumstein & Schwartz, 1983). But since same-sex couples cannot assign housework on the basis of who is male and who is female, the division of household labor can be quite complex. A study of gay male couples, for instance, showed that the handling of household chores varied by the stage of the relationship (McWhirter & Mattison, 1984). In the early years, partners make a conscious effort to share all household chores. As the relationship progresses, however, tasks are assigned primarily on the basis of skill or work schedule.

Compared to both married and gay male couples, lesbians are more likely to espouse an ideology of equality and share household tasks evenly (Kurdek, 1993; Sullivan, 1996). Some researchers have found that lesbian couples tend to be more egalitarian than heterosexual couples both ideologically and behaviorally (Blumstein & Schwartz, 1983). Any inequalities that do exist are attributed to differences in the resources each partner controls. When children are present, lesbian parents seem to divide their domestic duties such that neither partner assumes a disproportionate share of the work load nor is rendered economically dependent on her partner. Such an approach reflects explicit, self-conscious commitments to equity that extend beyond the tight proscriptions of gender ideology (Sullivan, 1996).

Social Exchange and Household Inequity   The social exchange perspective can also shed some light on how men and women perceive domestic arrangements. ▲ This perspective argues that people can feel deprived without feeling dissatisfied if they conclude that they are getting what they deserve out of their relationships. People with few outside alternatives tend to have lower expectations of a relationship because they stand to lose more from its disruption than people who have more options available to them (Lennon & Rosenfield, 1994).

▲ Issue 5 and Chapter 2 provide further discussion and application of the social exchange perspective.

Thus, the women who have fewer alternatives to marriage and fewer available economic resources are more likely to view an unequal division of family work as fair. If wives have low wages and sense a high risk of divorce in their marriages, they may lower their expectations and feel grateful for whatever household chores their husbands do (Hochschild and Machung, 1989). On the other hand, women who are self-sufficient and who perceive available alternatives to their marriage are less dependent on their spouses and are less fearful of divorce. Hence, they are more likely to view unequal family work as unfair. These women tend to be more distressed and depressed by an unequal division of household labor than women who accept inequality as fair (Lennon & Rosenfield, 1994).

According to psychologist Brenda Major (1993), feelings of entitlement and deservedness can come from several sources:

- *Gender differences in comparison standards.* Husbands and wives typically compare their situation to others of the same sex (Hochschild & Machung, 1989). So wives will compare themselves to other wives (perhaps including their own mothers), and husbands will compare their situations to those of other men (perhaps including their own fathers). Given the social changes that have occurred over the past generation, men may see their contributions to the household as quite extensive compared to those of their fathers, who lived in an era when men did virtually nothing around the house.
- *Social norms governing married life.* Norms about the priority of motherhood and homemaker roles for women or breadwinner roles for men can be deeply ingrained. If women define household work as "women's work," the unequal distribution of household labor will

not violate their sense of entitlement or lead to perceptions of injustice—even if they are employed and still do three times as much housework as their husbands. Some research has shown that the greater a wife's income relative to her husband's, the worse she feels about her performance as a spouse, presumably because she thinks she is falling short of social expectations regarding women's traditional family roles. In contrast, the more the husband earns, the better a spouse and parent he perceives himself to be, presumably because he is meeting or even exceeding expectations regarding men's family roles (Biernat & Wortman, 1991).

■ *Perceived availability and attractiveness of alternative arrangements.* If a working wife with a heavy load of housework, for example, compares her situation to the alternative of *not being employed*—rather than the alternative of being employed with an equal division of household labor—she may conclude that things aren't so bad after all. Moreover, many women feel that they are highly unlikely to obtain a better division of labor in another relationship. Under these circumstances, as Major (1993) puts it, "Doing 60 percent of the family work seems better than the alternative of doing it all" (p. 152).

Women may also see imbalances in the household division of labor as justifiable if they earn significantly less than their partners. They may come to believe—or believe based on prior socialization—that they are exchanging their responsibility for family work for their husband's more substantial income. Even though members of the same household have the same standard of living, the question of who earns the family's income and how it is shared has a great deal to do with the distribution of power and influence within families (Okin, 1989). Perceived responsibility for the "breadwinner" role, then, can be a critical justification for the unequal distribution of domestic labor (Ferree, 1991). But as you know from the statistics on household labor presented earlier, earning more money excuses men from housework, but not women. In fact, some studies show that, as women's income increases, they actually perform *more* household tasks (Biernat & Wortman, 1991).

In short, what's important is not just the income difference but the meaning attached to that difference. A wife may earn more than her husband, but her earning power won't have an impact on her household responsibilities if she and he don't perceive her as being *responsible* for breadwinning (Potuchek, 1997). One study found that only 16 percent of American working wives are "willing breadwinners" who believe that their primary responsibility is to support the family financially (Haas, 1986). But those wives who do believe they are the family breadwinner are likely to feel entitled to more assistance around the house.

Manufactured Equity

Inequity in relationships can be uncomfortable for all involved. In an effort to create the *appearance* of equity in inherently inequitable relationships, some couples engage in a process of "family mythmaking."

Sociologist Arlie Russell Hochschild's qualitative study of gender and family work employs detailed case studies to provide insight into the mechanisms couples use to artificially create feelings of equity (Hochschild & Machung, 1989). She describes one couple, Nancy and Evan Holt, who struggled for years over the wife's desire for a more equitable division of labor and the husband's continual opposition to sharing housework. At one point, an exasperated Nancy offered to split the responsibility for cooking dinner so that each would cook 3 days a week and they would go out or cook together on Sundays. Evan's response was that he didn't like "rigid schedules" but he'd try it anyway. The first week he forgot his cooking responsibility 2 out of his 3 scheduled days.

As the pattern continued, Nancy became more frustrated. When the conflict became so great that it began to threaten the marriage, Nancy and Evan created the myth that their marriage would be equitable if Nancy would shift her work hours from full- to part-time and do all the "inside" housework while Evan would be responsible for "outside" work, like cleaning the garage and feeding the dog. Nancy convinced herself that taking care of the dog was an onerous task she wanted nothing to do with. In doing so, she elevated this task to a level of importance akin to that of her career—which she was willing, in part, to sacrifice. The solution further "allowed Nancy to continue thinking of herself as the sort of woman whose husband didn't abuse her—a self-conception that mattered a great deal to her. And it avoided the hard truth that, in his stolid, passive way, Evan had refused to share" (p. 44).

Such intricate "solutions" highlight a growing problem facing American households at the close of the twentieth century. Increasing numbers of couples find themselves negotiating the complex dilemma that arises from the clash of the changing cultural perceptions of fair relationships and the actual gender-based division of labor in their own households. The complexity of trying to "create" equity in inequitable situations results in elaborate perceptual shifts and justifications. These solutions also show, as has much of the research, that women and men similarly view men's housework as critical to fairness (Sanchez, 1994), despite the fact that, by and large, men still don't see family work as "their issue" (Coltrane, 1996b).

In sum, men's participation in household tasks has increased only slightly over the years, despite their growing attachment to fatherhood and the dramatic increase in employment outside the home among married women. But as the gender attitudes of men and women gradually become more egalitarian, both sexes may be predisposed to expect men to do more family work in the future. Whether these expectations eventually translate into actual behavior may depend on such factors as the relative power of partners, as indicated by differences in resources like education and earnings. Furthermore, as more and more people turn to irregular work shifts and couples thus find little overlap in their work schedules, housework and child care may become more equally shared by necessity.

One study, for instance, found that the more hours husbands are not employed during times when their spouses are employed, the more likely they are to do housework traditionally performed by women (Presser, 1994). Thus, for example, day-shift husbands whose wives work night shifts are in a situation bind: They're the only ones around to cook dinner or put the kids to bed.

Conclusion

What seems quite clear is that, both in fact and as an ideal, the division of labor that assigned wage-earning responsibilities to men and unpaid family work to women is breaking down, and it will likely never return to the form it occupied a century ago. Women are in the labor force to stay. Yet as we approach the end of the millennium, women still aren't able to share equally in providing the family income because of persistent inequalities in the labor market and men's persistent lack of interest and full participation in domestic work.

Nevertheless, men's and women's interests are beginning to converge. Women, in some respects, have become more career oriented but remain committed to family; men, in some respects, have become more family oriented yet still find their primary source of identity in their careers.

Unfortunately, these changes have not been matched by changes in the workplace. Many employers continue to value a workaholic ethic that leaves little time for a family life. Couples who equitably share work and domestic responsibilities continue to face a culture that doesn't quite know what to do with them. These couples may shrug off or angrily reject others' disapproval, but they still are called on to justify their nontraditional division of labor. Why is he in the grocery store or in the park with his 3-year-old in the middle of the day? Why are they moving to another city to accommodate her career?

As the twenty-first century approaches, we face the crucial task of integrating family and work as smoothly and effectively as possible without sacrificing too much of either. We can resist the social changes that are uniting the once "separate" spheres of work and family—or we can accept these changes and work with them. We can encourage men to sacrifice their family lives to fit into the rigid structure of the conventional workplace and encourage women to sacrifice their careers to meet their family responsibilities—or we can learn to value family caretaking and economic productivity in equal degrees. Piecemeal adjustments on the part of individual workers and couples will not be enough. What are needed are adjustments in institutional support systems so men can feel free to act on their emerging parenting values without fearing a risk to their careers and women can feel free to pursue their careers without fearing they are placing their families at risk.

CHAPTER HIGHLIGHTS

- The contemporary belief that work life and family life are separate spheres emerged with industrialization in the nineteenth century. Along with this shift came an expectation that family life was women's domain and work life was men's domain. However, the notion of "separate spheres" has never applied equally to members of different classes and different ethnic groups.

- Work and family are never completely separate. Nevertheless, the ideology of separate spheres was, and continues to be, a powerful force in economics and politics. Consequently, women's experiences in the labor force—from the jobs they occupy to the wages they earn—are still tied to broader cultural assumptions about gender.

- Lingering notions of separate spheres shape the way men and women today perceive the balance between their family lives and their work lives.

- Recent decades have witnessed a dramatic increase in dual-earner families. This change has placed unprecedented demands on the workplace to accommodate employees with family obligations and on families to find ways of tending to their needs when time at home is limited.

- Couples in which both partners have careers challenge the principles that have traditionally guided married life.
- The growing presence of women in the paid labor force has not been accompanied by an increase in the responsibility men take for household work. An inequitable division of household labor continues to be a source of strain for many families.

DEMO•GRAPHIC ESSAY

Patterns of Labor Force Participation for Women and Men

It is widely known that since 1960, the labor force participation rates for married women have increased. Surprisingly, however, as Exhibit 3-A shows, the labor force participation rates for men have *decreased*. What do these trends indicate about the relationship between work and family in the late twentieth century?

Notice in Exhibit 3-A that the increasing labor force participation among married women has been especially great among those with children under age 6. Furthermore, the labor force participation rates of married women with children ages 6–17 are greater than the participation rates of married women in general. One possible explanation is that mothers of school-age children tend to be younger than married women in general. Indeed, Exhibit 3-B shows that in 1996 age was more important than marital status in determining labor force participation rates of women. Women ages 25–34 and ages 35–44—the likely ages of mothers

Exhibit 3-A

Labor Force
Participation Rates
of Married Men and
Married Women
(by age of children
for women)

*United States:
1960–1995*

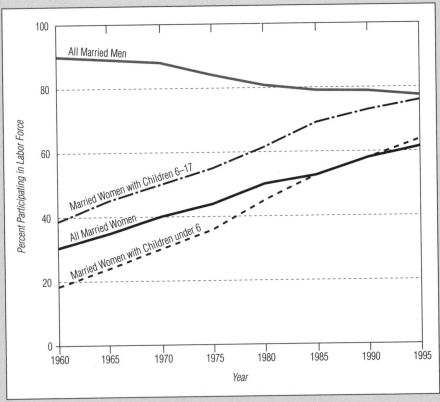

Source of data: U.S. Bureau of the Census, *Statistical Abstract of the United States: 1997* (117th edition). Washington, DC, 1997.

Exhibit 3-B

Female Labor Force
Participation
(by marital status
and age)

United States: 1996

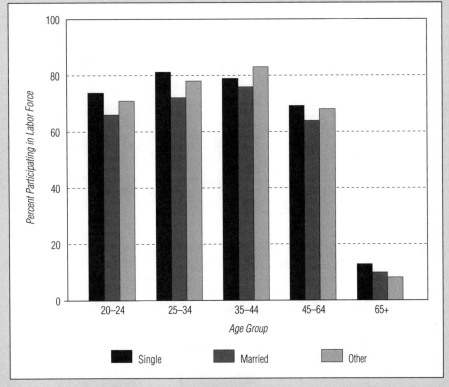

Source of data: U.S. Bureau of the Census, *Statistical Abstract of the United States: 1997* (117th edition). Washington, DC, 1997.

with school-age children—tend to have higher labor force participation rates than women in younger or older age groups. Even though married women have lower labor force participation rates than other women at most ages, married women ages 25–44 have higher labor force participation rates than all women ages 45 and older.

Now let's turn to the declining labor force participation rates for married men. A key contributor to this trend has been rising unemployment rates. However, unemployment does not threaten all men equally. As Exhibit 3-C shows, black and Hispanic men are significantly more likely than white men to be unemployed. In general, taking on the role of husband (and father) requires being able to earn an income. One reason for the relatively low rates of marriage among black and Hispanic men (shown in Exhibit 3-D) could be their relatively high unemployment rates. To the extent that a job is a prerequisite for a man to marry, ethnic differences in unemployment rates can help to explain ethnic differences in marital status among men in the United States.

Exhibit 3-C

Unemployment
Rates by Ethnicity
Men Ages 18 Years
and Older

United States: 1996

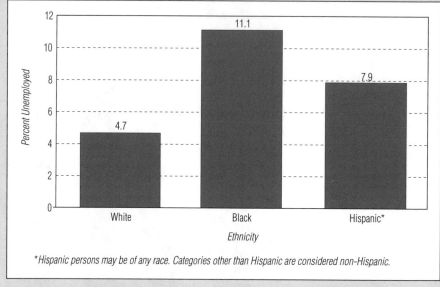

*Hispanic persons may be of any race. Categories other than Hispanic are considered non-Hispanic.

Source of data: U.S. Bureau of the Census, *Statistical Abstract of the United States: 1997* (117th edition). Washington, DC, 1997.

Exhibit 3-D

Marital Status by
Ethnicity
Men Ages 18 Years
and Older

United States: 1996

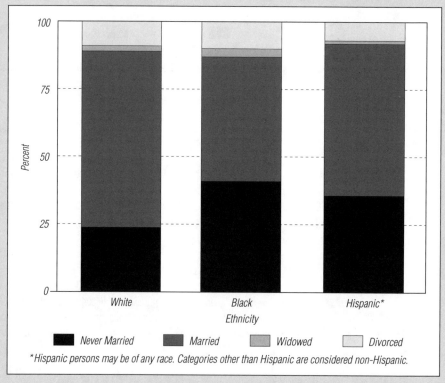

*Hispanic persons may be of any race. Categories other than Hispanic are considered non-Hispanic.

Source of data: U.S. Bureau of the Census, *Statistical Abstract of the United States: 1997* (117th edition). Washington, DC, 1997.

Questions for Further Study

1. What explanations other than age can account for the relatively greater labor force participation rates of married women with school-age children? Can you think of other reasons that could explain the age patterns of female labor force participation?

2. What might be some reasons that white men have lower unemployment rates than black or Hispanic men? What characteristics other than unemployment could explain ethnic differences in marital status?

3. Are ethnic differences in marital status and unemployment for women similar to those for men? Look in the *Statistical Abstract of the United States* for the data. Then speculate on some of the reasons for the patterns.

YOUR TURN

The intersection of gender, family, and work is where we see most clearly how expectations and beliefs can be translated into action. Locate at least one of each of the following types of couples in which both partners work full-time outside the home:

- Cohabiting heterosexual
- Cohabiting homosexual
- Newly married without children (married less than 1 year)
- Married with at least one child living at home
- Married without children (married 10 years or more)
- Stepfamily

Ask each person in each couple (partners must not be in each other's presence when answering these questions) to make a list of all the household chores that need to be done during the course of a week. Ask them to be as specific and exhaustive as possible (for example, "cleaning windows" rather than "cleaning the house"). After the lists are completed, ask each person to indicate which of these tasks he or she is primarily responsible for, which his or her partner is responsible for, and which are shared. Ask the participants also to estimate the total amount of time spent each week on all these tasks combined. Finally, ask them about how many hours they work outside the home during a typical week.

Compare responses of the following to see if you can find any differences in time each partner spends doing housework and the number of tasks for which each is responsible:

- Partners in the same couple
- Men and women
- Younger and older couples
- Married and cohabiting couples
- Couples with and without children at home
- Married and remarried couples
- Heterosexual and homosexual couples

Do the women still bear the primary responsibility for housework? Are household responsibilities more equitably split by certain types of couples? If partners within the same couple had different ideas about housework responsibilities, to what can you attribute this lack of agreement? Describe the tensions men and women experience when trying to balance work and home responsibilities.

CHAPTER 4

Parenthood and Parenting

If a Hmong woman in Laos experiences problems becoming pregnant, she will resort to a variety of remedies commonly used by her people. She may consult a shaman, who will ask the couple to sacrifice a dog, cat, chicken, or sheep. After the animal's throat is cut, the shaman strings a rope bridge from the doorpost to the bed, over which the soul of the couple's future baby, who, it is believed, has been detained by a malevolent spirit, can now freely travel to earth. A Hmong woman can also take precautions to avoid becoming infertile in the first place. For instance, she will never set foot in a cave because evil spirits who dwell there can make a woman sterile by having intercourse with her.

Once pregnant, the Hmong woman can ensure the health of her baby by paying close attention to what she eats. If she craves ginger but doesn't eat any, the child will be born with an extra finger or toe. If she craves chicken but doesn't eat it, the child will be born with a blemish near its ear. If she craves eggs but doesn't eat them, the child will be born with a lumpy head.

A long or painful labor can be eased by drinking water in which a key has been boiled, in order to unlock the birth canal. If she attributes her labor difficulty to not having treated an elder member of the family with sufficient respect, she can alleviate the problem by washing the offended relative's fingertips and apologizing profusely (Fadiman, 1997).

When a Hmong woman gives birth, she squats on the dirt floor in the center of her one-room house. But the newborn doesn't get dirty since the mother never lets it actually touch the floor. Instead, she delivers the baby into her own hands, reaching between her legs to ease out the head and then letting the rest of the body slip out onto her forearms (Fadiman, 1997). No birth attendant is present. If she becomes thirsty during labor, her husband can bring her a cup of hot water. But he is forbidden to look at her body. Since the Hmong believe that moaning and screaming can disrupt the birth, she labors in silence, except for an occasional prayer to her ancestors. Chances are that she is so quiet that her other children, sleeping in the same room, will only wake up when they hear the cry of the newborn.

Soon after the birth, the father digs a 2-foot-deep hole in the floor and buries the placenta. If the infant is a girl, the placenta is buried under the parents' bed; if it's a boy, the placenta is buried in a place of greater honor, near a central wooden pillar that holds up the roof of the house. The placenta is always buried with the smooth side, the side that faced the baby in the womb, upward. If it's buried upside down, the baby will vomit after nursing. If the baby develops spots on its face, that means that ants are attacking the placenta, and so boiling water is poured down the hole (Fadiman, 1997).

To most Americans, these practices and rituals seem quite bizarre, even unhealthy—can the parents have the baby's best interests in mind by allowing it to be born into such an unsterile and medically unsupervised environment? But Hmong parents take their parenting responsibilities extremely seriously. To the Hmong, becoming a parent is the most treasured human experience. Although most Hmong families are extremely impoverished, the amount of love, care, and attention Hmong parents heap on their infants is, by Western standards, astounding. A newborn baby is *never* apart from its mother, sleeping in her arms all night and riding on her back all day. Hmong children are almost never beaten, since it's believed that an evil spirit who witnesses the mistreatment might take the child, assuming it's not wanted. Research indicates that Hmong mothers are more sensitive, more accepting, and more responsive to their children's signals than are American parents. They hold and touch their babies much more frequently (cited in Fadiman, 1997). So, although their childbirth practices strike the Western observer as somewhat dangerous, the Hmong actually seem to be better parents than we are.

In this chapter I will discuss some of the important issues associated with parenthood. It's hard to imagine an experience more innate and universal than having children. Reproduction is the essence of life—human and otherwise. Yet, as you can see from this description of Hmong childbirth and parenting, parenthood is a phenomenon that, although clearly biological, cannot be separated from cultural norms, values, and definitions. Furthermore, although we live in a society that places enormous value on children and in which the vast majority of adults want to have children, *becoming* and *being* a parent are seldom problem-free experiences.

Familiarizing Father

"Wait till your father gets home!" is an utterance that has sent shivers down the spine of many a misbehaving youngster over the years. Fathers have traditionally been perceived as the distant disciplinarians—the family member least seen but most feared. Mothers, on the other hand, have usually been the ones expected to provide emotional nurturing.

Images like this one of children being beaten would elicit immediate calls to the police today, but the idea of stay-at-home dads is only slowly becoming socially acceptable.

While mothers were entering the workforce in the 1940s in record numbers, more fathers were *not* deciding to stay home with their children. The very idea of a dad caring for the kids was met with dismissive humor, as this 1954 photograph of a father "minding the baby" shows.

Mothers raised children, and fathers occasionally "babysat" when their wives went away to evening functions. These men may have realized what an exhausting task child rearing was, but they were still reluctant to contribute their full share at home.

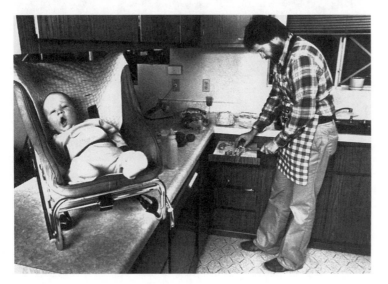

Things have changed since the 1950s. In response to myriad social, economic, and personal pressures, including rising divorce rates, fathers began taking more interest in the upbringing of their children during the late 1970s and 1980s. Today, fathers are often fully capable of, and very willing to, undertake all the chores associated with child rearing.

Conversely, many women have negotiated the dual responsibilities of work and parenting by emphasizing their careers. On "Bring Your Daughter to Work Day," working mothers are encouraged to take their daughters to work, not only to show them what to do but to provide them with what many consider positive female role models.

As men have begun to make changes in the way they relate to fatherhood, they are seeking social support for those changes. With high divorce rates, growing single-parent status, and bitter custody battles, more and more men are demanding the chance to show they can be nurturing parents.

Mothers are also developing new relationships with their children, encouraging them in physical, public, and professional realms as never before.

Adapting to social change, some parents are fostering new and closer ties with their children. How fathers and mothers relate to children in the future will be determined in part by what parents want and what society expects of them.

Pronatalism

Sociologists often characterize the United States as a **pronatalist society**—one in which it is believed that all married couples should reproduce or should *want* to reproduce. Although most people don't believe the main purpose of marriage is to have children, they do tend to believe that people who want children ought to marry (see Exhibit 4.1). Having children is portrayed as essential to self-fulfillment and necessary for the future survival of the society. ▲

▲ To family scholars who feel that the institution of family is in trouble, a dropping birth rate is cause for alarm, as described in Issue 8.

Our cultural commitment to parenthood stems from a Judeo-Christian tradition that depicts children as "blessings" and childlessness as a curse or punishment (Miall, 1989). The Bible encourages people to "be fruitful and multiply." These norms—coupled with pro-birth governmental policies, such as income tax deductions for each child—encourage reproduction and reinforce the belief that parenthood is a vital feature of society.

The value that a society places on having children is often influenced by broader political or economic issues. For instance, because of the heavy loss of young men during World War I, the French government in the 1920s promised medals of honor to women who produced eight or more children. Nazi Germany in the 1930s and 1940s strongly encouraged Aryan families to procreate, at the same time actively and viciously preventing other ethnic groups from doing so. In France today, concern over the growing population of nonwhite immigrants has led some extreme right wing politicians to advocate financial awards and other incentives for white, native-born French women who reproduce.

One of the most dramatic examples of governmental childbearing policy took place in Romania 3 decades ago. In 1966, Romanian dictator Nicolae Ceauşescu instituted a plan to increase the country's population from 23 million to 30 million by the year 2000. Ceauşescu declared that "the fetus is the property of the entire society. Anyone who avoids having children is a deserter who abandons the laws of national continuity" (quoted in Breslau, 1990). He outlawed sex education, classifying books on sexuality and reproduction as state secrets (Breslau, 1990). A

Exhibit 4.1

The Relationship Between Marriage and Children: Survey of 1,406 Adults

United States: 1994

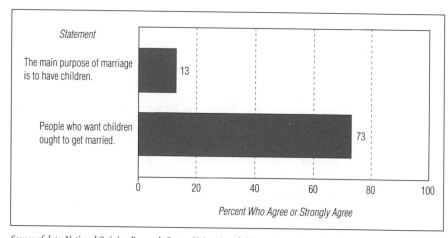

Source of data: National Opinion Research Center, University of Chicago, *General Social Survey, 1994.*

pregnant woman who had a miscarriage would automatically be suspected of arranging an illegal abortion and could be summoned for questioning. If a child died in a doctor's district, that doctor could lose 10 percent to 25 percent of his or her salary. The world was given its first glimpse of this policy when Ceauşescu was overthrown in December of 1989. The consequences of his "program" have been tragic. Not only have thousands, perhaps millions of women suffered through unwanted pregnancies and self-induced illegal abortions, but the country's orphanages are bulging today with unwanted and unhealthy children.

Sometimes a society takes a firm *anti-natalist* posture. For instance, in order to reduce family size among the poor, the Peruvian government promises peasant women cash incentives or gifts of food and clothing if they undergo surgical sterilization (Sims, 1998). Similarly, China's leadership has been struggling for decades to reduce family size because its limited resources cannot support a population of more than 1.2 billion people. Since the 1970s the Chinese government has actively *discouraged* couples from having babies, imposing strict waiting periods, yearly provincial birth quotas, local oversight of contraceptive use and women's menstrual cycles, and forced sterilization (Ignatius, 1988; Kristof, 1993b). Couples who have more than one child may be fined as much as a year's salary, lose access to apartments, schools, and free education, or be fired from their jobs. The average number of births per Chinese woman decreased from more than seven in the 1960s to fewer than two in 1992 (Kennedy, 1993; Kristof, 1993a).

In American society, most people marry with the expectation that they will have children; and they become parents because parenthood brings social approval and because all relevant social structures deem parenting to be a good thing (Denny, 1994). Having children is not only considered desirable, it is seen as normal and is taken for granted. It's often said that weddings create couples, but it's birth that makes a family (Gillis, 1996). People learn that having children proves their worth and gives them the status of "mature adults."

Because having children is expected and normal, people with children have a common ground: They can talk about their children to other parents, who will understand them and relate to their experiences. Parents often relate to each other through their children and feel more acceptable to others once they have children. Consequently, people who don't have, can't have, or don't want to have children are often made to feel like outsiders and cultural outcasts.

Adoption and the Primacy of Genetic Parenthood

In this culture, the biological bond between parents and children is considered by most people to be of paramount importance. One of the most powerful cultural lessons we learn is that parenthood gives us genetic identity and immortality (Nelkin & Lindee, 1995). Many of the common questions and comments made to new parents reflect the deep-seated importance of this bond: "He's got your eyes," or "She has your Uncle Ed's mouth" are the sorts of things most new parents hear as friends and relatives try to establish genetic links and physical resemblances. Without thinking, people often ask adoptive mothers of newborns about pregnancy, labor and delivery, breast-feeding, and so on. Physicians who are seeing an adopted child for the first time might ask about family health history.

▲ Debate over groupings that get to be called "real" families is the topic addressed in Issue 1.

In some people's minds, the adoption of a child may provide the experience of being a parent, but it can never provide the biological connection upon which "real" or "natural" families are assumed to be based. ▲ Because parenthood tends to be associated with procreation and blood links, adoption is often considered a "debased form of parenting" (Bartholet, 1993a). A recent nationwide survey found that although nine out of ten respondents considered adoptive parents both lucky and unselfish, half believed that adopting was "not quite as good as having one's own child" (cited in Lewin, 1997c). In a society like ours, which extols the virtues of having children, adoption is usually a second choice. Most young people don't imagine their life script will consist of growing up, getting married, and adopting a child. They typically expect to grow up, get married, and have kids of their own.

▲ This concern is particularly strong in cases of transracial adoption, as discussed in Chapter 5.

▲ The role of media portrayals of family in shaping cultural beliefs is discussed in Issue 2.

Consequently, some fear that adopted children will always lack a crucial piece of their identity. ▲ Indeed, this theme provides the backdrop for the many moving stories we hear about adoptees searching for their biological roots. A recent book describes adoptees as people with "a hole at the center of their being" or "people without selves," who can only become whole, functional adults when they find out who their biological parents are (Lifton, 1994).

Media images reinforce this notion. ▲ One researcher found that one in five television characters who are adopted choose to track down birth parents, a percentage that is eighteen times higher than the real-life percentage (cited in "Tune in," 1988). Stories like these are framed as holy quests, transformative journeys in search of one's self. Such images appeal to the cultural notion that adopted individuals are missing an essential element of identity and that one's "real" identity is somehow linked to shared genes.

Recent court cases in which biological parents have been granted custody of children they had earlier put up for adoption reinforces the cultural primacy of biological over adoptive parents. Indeed, groups opposing the sealing of adoption records have grown in recent years. These groups—with names like Operation Identity, Adoptees Liberty Movement, and Concerned United Birthparents—argue that genetics is the primary basis of identity and that adoptees have the same rights as anyone to know their roots and their heredity.

Fears about unknown inherited flaws accompany anxiety about genetic continuity (Nelkin & Lindee, 1995). Psychologists use the term "adopted child syndrome" to explain the antisocial acts of adoptees, which are said to include "pathological lying, stealing, truancy, underachievement, firesetting, promiscuity, running away, and learning problems" (Kirschner, 1992, p. 325). Unfortunately, this preoccupation with genetic relationships can stigmatize the adoption experience. When people comment about how "good" or "wonderful" a couple is for adopting they send the implicit message that adoptive parenting lacks the joyous quality characteristic of "true" parenting. Similarly, comments about how "lucky" a child is for being adopted can be unintentionally insulting to the child. When adoptees first tell friends of their adoptive status, the most common reaction is a sympathetic "I'm sorry" (Bartholet, 1993a).

The fact that conscious choice is the defining feature of adoptive parenting is unnerving to those conditioned to believe that biological and genetic connections are what parenting is all about. But this element of choice ought to make adoption all the more valuable and praiseworthy. Most adoptive parents devote a great deal of effort to becoming parents. They *want* to be parents. By contrast, many biological parents conceive by accident and may see parenthood as the least bad of the various bad options available to them (Bartholet, 1993a).

Infertility

The ideal of pronatalism is clearly illustrated in the societal response to couples who want genetically related children but are unable to have them. Between one in five and one in ten American couples experience infertility (Miall, 1989; Whiteford & Gonzalez, 1995). Involuntary childlessness, as it is sometimes called, is typically considered a multidimensional disability:

- *Medical disability.* Most cases of infertility are medically diagnosed as the consequence of some form of physical impairment—although a small percentage may be related to psychological factors.
- *Social disability.* Infertility prevents couples from reproducing—a social role expectation that is extremely powerful in a pronatalist society such as ours.
- *Legal disability.* Many adoption agencies require documented proof of infertility before they will accept adoption applications for infants (Miall, 1989).

Infertility manifests itself as an acute life crisis (Whiteford & Gonzalez, 1995). It is often unanticipated and unexplained, has no identifiable onset, and lasts for an indeterminate amount of time. It can create overwhelming stress and feelings of guilt and grief. Unlike other stigmatizing disabilities, such as blindness or paraplegia, infertile individuals display no visible stigmatizing features; only their own knowledge of their condition distinguishes them from others (Greil, 1991). Because of its invisibility, infertile couples can easily "pass as normal" (Goffman, 1959). Nevertheless, people feel the stigma of infertility as deeply as they would feel the stigma of any other "abnormal" condition:

> I feel like I'm isolated in a prison; I have no one who understands how horrible this is. People don't know what to say to you . . . I think I'm alternatively dealt with as either someone who has died or that [I] have a handicap. And I think people approach it like that because they don't understand death; they don't understand handicaps; and they don't understand infertility. (quoted in Whiteford & Gonzalez, 1995, p. 29)

Although infertility can have devastating effects on both men and women, it is especially difficult for women, whose socialization experiences have traditionally placed greater importance on becoming a parent than men's. Sociologist Charlene Miall interviewed or surveyed approximately seventy involuntarily childless women between the ages of 25 and 45. Nearly all of the respondents characterized infertility as something negative, and nearly all experienced feelings of anxiety, isolation, and conflict.

Many of these women felt that to admit their infertility publicly was in some way an admission of failure. As one woman put it, publicly acknowledging problems with reproduction was "an admission that you're not a whole person . . . either sexually or anatomically or both. That there's something wrong, and I guess reproduction, the ability to reproduce, strikes at the very essence of one's being" (quoted in Miall, 1989, p. 392).

Another woman was concerned that people's awareness of her infertility would cause them to view her as abnormal: "I do believe it lessens you in some people's eyes, makes you different and possibly even morally suspect, like God is punishing you or something. Somehow infertility lessens your accomplishments for some people" (Miall, 1989, p. 392).

Not surprisingly, these women often engaged in some form of information control. Many of them simply concealed their infertility from everyone except their physicians and counselors. Others used the medical nature of the problem as a way of distancing themselves from blame, saying essentially, "It's beyond my control." Others disclosed the information only to people they knew would not think ill of them. No matter what the strategy, all were motivated by the knowledge that information about their infertility would be judged negatively.

Technological "Cures" for Infertility   Until the 1950s, the cause of infertility was often considered to be emotional rather than medical. Not until the 1960s and 1970s—with advances in drugs that controlled ovulatory cycles and scoping technologies that allowed physicians to see internal reproductive organs—did infertility become medicalized. It is now considered a medical disorder that can be diagnosed, treated, and, with increasing frequency, cured.

Today, infertile couples are faced with a variety of medical interventions. Despite the availability of these procedures, the choices can mean undergoing years of costly and painful treatment and continuing the stigma and loss of personal identity felt by infertile people. These interventions fail more often than they succeed. Nevertheless, the hope they provide allows infertile couples to define themselves not as "childless" but as "not yet pregnant" (Whiteford & Gonzalez, 1995, p. 27).

In recent years, there has been dramatic growth of new reproductive methods such as fertility drugs, artificial insemination, in vitro fertilization, embryo transfer, and surrogate motherhood. ▲ Although access is limited primarily to the affluent—some procedures can cost as much as $20,000—these techniques have the potential of increasing the reproductive choices and opportunities available to infertile couples (Rothman, 1987; Rowland, 1990).

▲ Chapter 9 explores the possible effects of these technological advances on future families.

Because of the cultural value placed on children, infertility research has faced virtually no criticism and has been allowed to expand with little community debate (Rowland, 1990). After all, who would oppose research that could provide infertile couples with the miracle of a baby? Consequently, the field of high-tech infertility treatment is flourishing. In only a decade it grew from 30 clinics to more than 300 (Gabriel, 1996). Each year more than 1 million patients seek help from fertility clinics in this country (Nelkin & Lindee, 1995). These clinics are largely exempt from government regulation and immune to the downward pressure on costs that insurance companies exert (Gabriel, 1996). At some hospitals, fertility doctors earn more than the top hospital administrators.

Most infertility research focuses on women's reproductive difficulties. Women are the ones who must face the physical and emotional risks, which may include infection, painful side effects, permanent physical injury, and the heartbreak of failure. Their bodies become "alternative reproductive vehicles," "human incubators," or "uterine environments" within which "harvested" eggs can be planted (Raymond, 1993).

Pregnancies that result from infertility treatment are often high risk. You may recall the Iowa woman who gave birth to septuplets in 1997. She had been taking a fertility drug to heighten her chances of becoming pregnant. All seven babies survived. The pregnancy and birth captivated the nation and became the "feel good" story of the year. Unfortunately, the story for most parents of multiple births is much more painful. As more and more couples try infertility treatments, births of triplets, quadruplets, and quintuplets are becoming more common. But the health risks of such pregnancies—to mother and babies—are great. The human uterus is simply not built to carry that many bodies. A mother who carries multiple babies for 20 weeks—about half the length of a normal pregnancy—is five times more likely to lose them before birth. Of those who are born, 92 percent are premature and below normal weight, increasing the likelihood of developmental problems. In fact, between 1980 and 1994, nearly one out of every ten babies born in a multiple birth (triplets or more) died in their first year (cited in Belluck, 1998).

Surrogate motherhood is perhaps the most controversial infertility treatment. It involves the agreement of a woman to conceive artificially, to carry the fetus for the full gestational period (9 months), and to relinquish the child at birth to the genetic parent (Robinson, 1993). The most common method is artificial insemination of the surrogate with the genetic father's sperm. In such a situation, the surrogate is genetically related to the child since her egg is being used. In the less common embryo-transfer procedure, however, the child is genetically unrelated to the surrogate, who is simply carrying out the role of "gestational environment."

 Issue 3 examines other controversies surrounding family privacy and autonomy.

Surrogate motherhood pits our pronatalist values against individual liberties and against state interest. ▲ The Supreme Court decided years ago that individuals have the right to be free from government intervention in decisions that involve reproduction—rights frequently called "procreative liberty" (Robinson, 1993). And the majority of adults feel surrogacy ought to be available to infertile couples (see Exhibit 4.2). However, the state *can* intervene if certain other societal rights are threatened. For instance, surrogate motherhood may violate several compelling state interests, such as protection against the possible exploitation of poor women as surrogates. Many critics of reproductive technology fear that poor women may be coerced into be-

Exhibit 4.2

Attitudes Toward Use of Surrogacy by Infertile Married Couples, by Sex and Race

United States: 1996

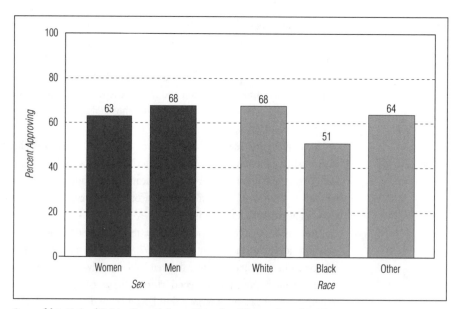

Source of data: National Opinion Research Center, University of Chicago, *General Social Survey, 1996.*

coming surrogates by financial necessity. Compensation sometimes totals $15,000 or more in addition to payment for all pregnancy-related expenses.

Compensation for surrogate motherhood, itself, may justify state control and intervention. Many critics are concerned about the "commercialization of reproduction" (Robinson, 1993). Indeed, every state has a law banning the sale of children or limiting the transfer of money in connection with private adoptions. The state has a compelling interest in preventing individuals from being bought and sold as property, and such laws exist to prevent what to some might be considered "baby selling" (Robinson, 1993).

The state also has an interest in protecting the institution of family, whose definition is complex and varied. ▲ It can be loose and somewhat vague at the individual level, but we have an urgent need for clarity at the institutional level. Surrogate motherhood might undermine the structure of the traditional nuclear family by introducing a new member—the surrogate mother—resulting in a new form of extended family (Robinson, 1993).

▲ The difficulties in defining *family* are analyzed in Issue 1; the effect of technology on such definitions is revisited in Chapter 9.

Reproductive technology also calls into question the very nature of the parent role, especially that of the mother. Certainly parental responsibilities and the nature of the parent-child relationship continually change over time. But surrogate motherhood raises the possibility that a child might be born with three mothers: a genetic mother, a gestational mother, and a social mother (Robinson, 1993). Until recently, other than in cases of adoption and remarriage, these three roles were occupied by the same person. Surrogate motherhood thus challenges the traditional legal definition of a mother as the woman who gives birth to the child.

Moreover, the technology has advanced more quickly than consideration of ethical and legal issues. Recently in California, a judge ruled that a 2-year-old girl, who had been conceived in a laboratory with donor sperm and egg and who had been carried and delivered by a surrogate, had *no parents* in the eyes of the law. The infertile couple divorced a month before she was born. When her mother sought child-support payments, the father claimed he was under no legal obligation to support the child since he had no genetic ties to her. The judge agreed and went even further, ruling that the mother—also with no genetic ties to the child—wasn't "entitled" to be declared a legal mother either (Foote, 1998). Indeed, the only parties with genetic ties to the child were the anonymous donors.

Changing Conceptions of Infertility　　The very fact that an entire professional discipline has organized around the task of enhancing people's fertility indicates not only the central place reproduction occupies in this culture but also the fact that it is becoming an increasingly public phenomenon. Not long ago, infertility was an invisible, private tragedy—a topic avoided by the couple in question and spoken about by concerned friends and relatives only in hushed tones. Today, however, considerable attention is focused on the difficulties of those defined as "infertile" (Scritchfield, 1995).

Yet infertility does not seem to have become a more prevalent problem in this country. In fact, the rate of infertility has been quite stable over the past 25 years. What has increased is the public's interest in the problem (Scritchfield, 1995). This increase tells us a great deal about the influence of broad social changes on the private experiences of individual people.

The recent medical and public attention devoted to infertility reveals a process of social redefinition. Expectations and definitions of normal patterns of fertility have changed so that couples today are more likely to suspect problems, seek assistance, and expect solutions than previous generations. Several social factors have contributed to the redefinition of infertility (Scritchfield, 1995):

- *Improved knowledge about contraception.* Although methods of birth control have been around throughout history, only recently have they become sufficiently effective to enable couples to exert some control over their reproduction. Hence, most couples today feel that the questions of whether they're going to have children, when, and how many are issues that they will decide for themselves. However, not all couples who plan their family size are successful. Few couples can produce children "on demand." Nevertheless, the vast majority of couples assume that having children is a matter of deciding when. So the inability to have children is met with shock and a marked sense of loss of control (Greil, 1991).

▲ The overall trend toward delayed child-bearing is discussed in Issue 8.

- *Demographic trend of postponed parenthood.* Women—particularly well-employed, college-educated women—are delaying their childbearing. ▲ Today, about a quarter of all first-time births are to women 30 to 44 years old (Maranto, 1995). The desire to establish oneself professionally and personally is a key reason behind postponing childbearing. The relatively advantaged position of people who postpone childbearing gives them a pretty strong sense of control over all parts of their lives (Scritchfield, 1995). Hence, they tend to plan their pregnancies carefully, often around important professional events (for instance, taking a bar exam), business cycles, or teaching schedules (as is often the case for college professors and teachers). But the older women get, the more difficult it becomes to conceive. Well-to-do, achievement-oriented couples who have difficulty conceiving are likely to aggressively pursue treatment for infertility at all costs (Scritchfield, 1995).

- *Overall drop in the birth rate.* In 1957 the average number of births per American woman was 3.6. Since 1976 it has fluctuated between 1.7 and 2.1 (Scritchfield, 1995). With couples having fewer children, the need for standard childbirth services has diminished considerably. Hence, a substantial proportion of obstetricians and gynecologists have shifted their focus toward the more lucrative and high-demand market of infertility services. Furthermore, because the lower birth rate is particularly characteristic of white, financially secure, and well-educated couples, and because these couples are more likely to seek expensive medical solutions to their reproductive difficulties, "infertility" has become a medical problem of the affluent. Concern about the fertility patterns of poor people and racial minorities tends to focus not on *in*fertility but on family planning and sterilization—that is, efforts to *reduce* rather than enhance their childbearing.

- *Technological innovations in diagnostic and treatment procedures.* The very availability of these techniques has helped to center public attention on infertility treatments. Furthermore, they are presented in the popular press as miraculous innovations, granting the gift of parenthood to couples who would have otherwise had to "suffer" the "tragedy" of childlessness. Hence, not only can the source of infertility be identified but there is the strong perception that it can be successfully treated. And if one technique doesn't work, the affluent couple is usually willing to try another, perhaps even more expensive, one. Ironically, the *perception* that these methods are effective is not matched by their actual effectiveness. For instance, it's estimated that less than 15 percent of in vitro fertilization treatments result in a viable pregnancy (cited in Scritchfield, 1995).

In sum, infertility has been transformed from an irreversible private agony that was accepted as fate into a public medical condition for which costly but frequently unfulfilled hopes of rescue exist (Whiteford & Gonzalez, 1995). Stories of happy, beaming parents who have spent upwards of $50,000 (perhaps going deeply into debt) for the treatments that helped them have a baby support the powerful cultural idea that the ultimate prize is worth any struggle, any pain, and any cost.

Not even the ticking of the biological clock can stand in the way of our faith that medical technology can "cure" infertility. In 1997, a 63-year-old woman gave birth to a healthy girl. She was being treated in a Los Angeles infertility clinic and had received a donated egg from a much younger woman. This woman wanted to bear a child so badly that she lied about her age in order to be accepted as a patient by the clinic (Kolata, 1997a). And so it seems that with eggs donated by younger women and fertilized in laboratories, practically any woman with a uterus has the potential to become pregnant.

Four decades ago infertile couples had limited choices: They could simply resign themselves to the fact that they would forever be childless, or they could adopt. Some would meet their desire to parent by becoming their nieces' and nephews' favorite aunt and uncle. Today, however, it is difficult for couples to choose *not* to have children. So powerful is the pronatalist expectation that those who do not try every conceivable method for overcoming infertility are often considered cultural traitors or objects of pity.

The Stigma of Voluntary Childlessness

▲ The shrinking size of American families is examined in Issue 8.

Even though having children is still considered the desirable, expected consequence of being married, and the vast majority of married couples have children, more and more people are willfully violating these cultural expectations and *choosing* to remain childless. While nearly half of American households contained children in 1970, just over one-third had at least one child in 1995 (DeVita, 1996). ▲ In 1960, 47.5 percent of women between the ages of 20 and 24 were childless; in 1992, that figure rose to 67 percent. During this same time period, the proportion of women in all other age groups who were childless doubled (cited in Maranto, 1995). The U.S. Census Bureau predicts that somewhere between 7 and 24 percent of women 18 to 24 will never have children (cited in Nemy, 1995).

Couples who are childless *in*voluntarily due to infertility may feel stigmatized by others, but they pose no threat to the pronatalist values of society because their *desire* for children remains strong and intact. Voluntarily childless couples, however, directly challenge the commonly held assumption that childbearing is the appropriate course of action in marriage. They must explain to others not only why they don't have kids but why they don't *want* them. Even though voluntarily child-free couples report being significantly more satisfied with all aspects of their marriage than couples with children, they still perceive that they are viewed negatively by others (Somers, 1993). Often these couples are maligned for "selfishly" putting their personal needs ahead of the social obligation of parenthood:

> There has been a very strong attitude that the child represents an obstacle to achievement. Not just that the child is something desirable that you add further down the line . . . but that the child is an obstacle to a lifestyle that will include the yacht and weekend skiing. . . .

A great many couples are opting not to have any children at all because of the portrayal of the child as an obstacle, especially to a woman's career and a two-salary family. (quoted in Luker, 1997, p. 370)

Research suggests, however, that voluntary childlessness is more complicated. Sociologist Jean Veevers (1980) interviewed 156 married men and women who had deliberately avoided having children to determine how they arrived at their decision. Veevers found that couples followed either of two paths in their decision making. About a third of the couples decided before marriage that they didn't want to have children. For whatever reason—the dislike of children, the desire to remain free and unfettered, the demands of their careers—these couples knew from the start that their marriage would not include children. The agreement to remain childless was part of their marriage "contract."

The rest of the couples, however, were "chronic postponers." They didn't reject parenthood in the beginning, but eventually, through a series of postponements, found the option of having children less and less possible. Their postponement of childbearing is a four-stage process:

1. *Deferring childbearing for a specific period of time.* At this stage, these couples are indistinguishable from couples who will eventually have children but are waiting to achieve certain goals first, such as finishing graduate school, buying a house, or getting established in their careers.

2. *Postponing childbearing for an indefinite period of time.* The couple at this stage has become more vague as to when pregnancy will happen. They say they'll have children "when they can afford it" or "when they are emotionally ready." The open-endedness of these comments illustrates a growing ambivalence toward future parenthood, although these couples are reluctant to close the door on childbearing completely.

3. *Acknowledging a very real possibility of permanent childlessness.* At this critical stage, the couple deliberates the pros and cons of parenthood. They may express admiration for childless couples they know, focusing in particular on the advantages of their lifestyle. At the same time, they may be inclined to notice the disadvantages suffered by the couples they know who do have children.

4. *Accepting childlessness as permanent.* The couple's realization that they will not have children is often formalized when one or both partners chooses surgical sterilization to ensure their childless status.

Veevers's research shows that most voluntarily childless couples are influenced by the powerful norms of pronatalism. They start off their marriages assuming they will have children. But through a series of postponements—often for legitimate, credible reasons—they reach a point where having children is either impractical or, because of age, too risky.

Pronatalism and Public Policy

Although the cultural value of parenthood is dominant, not everyone in this society is expected or encouraged to have children. In 1996 the journal *Society* published a symposium on the question of whether parents should be licensed. The underlying rationale used by several authors to argue in favor of licensing was that incompetent parenting is the most important factor associated with costly social problems such as poverty, child abuse, and violent crime (Westman, 1996). The argument is that people should be discouraged—and perhaps even legally prevented—from becoming parents if they do not meet certain basic requirements, such as pledging to protect the well-being of their children or completing some sort of course that provides basic parenting knowledge and skills. Licenses could be revoked if parents show an inability or unwillingness to care for their children.

Such policy recommendations are unlikely to ever be implemented. However, they illustrate that many people are coming to the conclusion that, although having children is normative and natural, it is also a privilege that should be and sometimes is, restricted.

Pronatalism and the Poor

▲ The structure of poor families is discussed in more detail in Issue 7.

Opponents of such proposed policies worry either about too much governmental intrusion into family lives or about yet another form of discrimination against poor people and racial minorities (Jencks & Edin, 1995). But many policies already in place are designed to limit the childbearing of poor people. ▲ The debate over whether welfare benefits should be reduced for mothers who have additional children is a case in point. Some might argue that preventing mothers on welfare from having additional children will reduce negative consequences both for society and for the children themselves. Nevertheless, underlying such a position is the perception that poor mothers—especially unwed poor mothers—are being too fruitful and multiplying too much.

In some situations, women have been forced to give up their ability to have children, through court-ordered contraceptive use, as a form of punishment for crimes they've committed. In 1991, for example, a 27-year-old mother of four was sentenced to 3 years on Norplant—a contraceptive device that consists of small rods implanted under the skin of a woman's arm—after being convicted of several counts of felony child abuse. She was given a choice: 1 year in prison and 3 years on probation or 4 months in prison and 3 years on probation using Norplant. Without her lawyer present, she chose the latter option. Although her lawyer later requested that the order be rescinded, the judge stuck to the sentence.

Since then, several similar cases have come to light. Politicians have been eager to exploit Norplant as a means of dealing with "problem mothers." Some legislators have considered mandating Norplant use for *all* poor women convicted of serious drug offenses. Others have proposed it as a solution to what they consider to be the problem of excessive family size of welfare mothers (Young, 1995).

When that Iowa couple had their septuplets, people from all over the country responded with great generosity, sending boxes of diapers, baby-care products, and groceries. Locally, the parents were given a fifteen-seat van, free college tuition for the children, even a house. No one suggested that they were freeloaders; no one suggested that they put a couple of the children up for adoption, advice commonly given to poor pregnant women who already have many children. It's hard to imagine that the admiration and generosity afforded this family would have been forthcoming had the parents been on welfare. Indeed, a working-class black couple who produced six babies a few months earlier (five survived) received no publicity and no help until the preferential treatment afforded the Iowa family became too obvious to ignore.

▲ Chapter 5 examines
child rearing in homo-
sexual households.

Gay and Lesbian Parents   Another segment of the population that is frequently discouraged and sometimes prevented from becoming parents are gay and lesbian couples. ▲ An estimated 20 percent of gay men and 33 percent of lesbians have previously been in heterosexual marriages; over half of these individuals have at least one biological child (Harry, 1983). Other homosexual men and women have become parents through reproductive technology. And some have become parents through adoption, despite significant societal disapproval.

The oft-heard argument that homosexuality is a threat to the institution of family focuses on the notion that the *capacity* to reproduce (though not necessarily the desire or the success) is a fundamental cornerstone of "family" and, by extension, society. After all, for a society to survive, there must be a flow of new members to replace those who die. Since gay men and lesbians don't procreate in the traditional biological sense, they are also assumed to be incapable of parenting and establishing kinship ties.

However, such an argument inevitably falls short. Many heterosexual couples are either incapable of reproducing or are committed to not doing so. Yet the state does not ask prospective heterosexual spouses if they intend to have children and the law grants childless married couples the same rights and benefits as married couples with children (F. Johnson, 1996).

The Process of Becoming Parents

The biological facts of parenthood—sexual intercourse, pregnancy, birth, lactation—are, of course, universal. But much more is involved in becoming a parent than biologically creating a child. In every society, the conceiving, bearing, and rearing of children are shaped by cultural and historical beliefs, expectations, and norms.

The Social Construction of Childbirth

Even something as seemingly natural as giving birth is profoundly influenced by social forces. What are considered normal, healthy childbirth practices in one era, one culture, or even one social class can be seen as dangerous and barbaric in others. What is considered a technological improvement for one age often turns out to be a problem for the next.

Early Attitudes Toward Childbirth   In the seventeenth and eighteenth centuries, pregnancy and childbirth were seen simply as normal events in a woman's life, not as the beginning of an all-encompassing career of parenthood (Gillis, 1996). They were described as an activity—"breeding"—which was no more or less important than a woman's other family activities. The elaborate ritualized attention that many of today's pregnant women receive—regular doctor's visits, baby showers, medicalized deliveries, and so on—was unknown. Instead pregnancy was represented as something that happened *to* a woman, an episode in her life in which she was merely the object of natural—and perhaps supernatural—forces.

Since childbirth was not considered a special event, there was little advance preparation for it. In fact, prior to the nineteenth century, births were hardly anticipated at all. Some people considered it unlucky to interfere with nature or God by preparing for birth too overtly. Most women continued their normal routines right up to the moment of labor. Anything resembling prenatal care was quite rare. Unlike contemporary childbirth, for which labor is sometimes chemically induced, no effort was made to hasten nature.

Up until the nineteenth century, male doctors were almost completely absent from the birthing process. Female midwives and other women in the family or in the community commonly attended women during and after childbirth. Birth was considered a woman's affair. Only in extremely wealthy families or when the mother's life was in danger was a male doctor consulted (Ulrich, 1990). Indeed, well into the twentieth century, few poor, minority pregnant women had access to doctors and hospitals when they gave birth.

Every effort was made to keep the husbands as far away from the painful and sometimes lethal process as possible. They typically awaited news of the baby's arrival in the company of male friends.

The Medicalization of Childbirth

By the early twentieth century, more and more well-to-do American women chose hospitals as the site of their child's birth. In 1900 only 5 percent of American births took place in hospitals; by 1939 over 50 percent of all births and 75 percent of urban births occurred there. The overwhelming consideration for these expectant mothers was the minimization of pain (Mitford, 1993). Obviously, pain has always been an element of childbirth. But with advances in medical technology, affluent women were beginning to believe that they had a right to avoid pain if at all possible. Initially, women were put to sleep with chloroform or ether throughout labor and delivery. Eventually, localized anesthetics—drugs that alleviated pain but allowed women to remain conscious throughout the delivery—became popular.

The medicalization and hospitalization of childbirth increased women's dependence on the male medical profession. Little interest was given to the mother's well-being or self-esteem. Typically she was placed in a position with her legs widespread in the air and her genitals totally exposed. Once labor began, doctors commonly resorted to invasive procedures such as the use of forceps and suction. Episiotomies—incisions that increase the size of the vaginal opening to give the baby more room to emerge—became a common part of the birthing process. Today episiotomies are used in 90 percent of all American births, and cesarean sections are performed in almost 25 percent of births (Gillis, 1996). Clearly medicalization means that the doctor, not the mother, delivers the child.

By the 1950s, however, concern was growing over the possibility that babies might be harmed in some way by the use of drugs and other invasive procedures during delivery. In addition, some women were beginning to complain about the dehumanizing conditions of hospital delivery wards. As one mother of three in the 1950s wrote:

> Women are herded like sheep through the obstetrical assembly line, are drugged and strapped on tables while their babies are forceps-delivered. Obstetricians today are businessmen who run baby factories. Modern painkillers and methods are used for the convenience of the doctor, not to spare the mother. (quoted in Gillis, 1996, p. 173)

Hence, "natural" childbirth, without the aid of anesthetics, became popular in the 1960s and 1970s. It restored women to a central role in the birth process. Expectant mothers, and their sometimes reluctant husbands, were encouraged to attend childbirth classes to learn special breathing techniques that could ease the delivery without resorting to drugs.

One of the major changes in the process of childbirth that has occurred over the past 30 years is the growing role of fathers. In the past, a father's participation in the event was usually confined to driving his expectant wife to the hospital and pacing the floor in a nearby waiting room until someone came to tell him his baby had been born. Today, however, fathers are expected to be present during the delivery—about 90 percent of fathers attend the birth of their child (Griswold, 1993)—though most are passive, sometimes queasy witnesses or cameramen, not active participants. Indeed, their presence in the birthing room is more likely to provide emotional support for the mother than to receive the child as their own. Nevertheless, fathers who choose not to be involved risk being labeled as insensitive and uncaring.

The popularity of "natural" childbirth—less medical intervention, more maternal contact with the newborn right after birth, and so on—has been accompanied in recent years by a nostalgic desire to return to a simpler, less technological childbirth experience. Many hospitals today are turning their cold and sterile "delivery" rooms into homelike, reassuring "birthing" suites. The goal is to re-create the benefits of the cozy home birth of the nineteenth century in a safe hospital setting. Most of these rooms are large enough so that the baby and the father can sleep there as well. In addition, more expectant couples are choosing to give birth at home, with the aid of a trained nurse-midwife and with relatives, friends, and other children in attendance.

The Transition to Parenthood

Becoming a parent involves more than giving birth. It involves entry into a social role that represents a significant shift in a person's life and identity. Whether the parent is single or married, rich or poor, heterosexual or homosexual, or the birth is planned or unplanned, no transition is more life altering than that from nonparent to parent.

Few role transitions can be as enriching and fulfilling as becoming a parent. For many parents a child is a tangible symbol of the love they share for each other (Neal, Groat, & Wicks, 1989). Children often give parents a sense of meaning and purpose in their lives. Watching children grow and accomplish things can give parents an enormous feeling of pride. Most parents are genuinely thrilled that they have had children and clearly would make the same decision if they were starting over (Cowan & Cowan, 1992). In addition, children expand parents' interaction network by connecting them to other family members—aunts, uncles, grandparents, cousins—as well as the larger community—neighbors, schools, churches, recreational facilities, and so on.

But the transition to parenthood does not come without a fair amount of difficulty:

> As they bring their first baby home from the hospital, new mothers and fathers find themselves crossing the great divide. After months of anticipation, their transition from couple to family becomes a reality. Entering this new and unfamiliar family territory, men and women find themselves on different timetables and different trails of a journey they envisioned completing together. (Cowan & Cowan, 1992, p. 75)

What makes the transition to parenthood so difficult? For one thing, it is a transition that is irrevocable (Rossi, 1968). Unlike a marriage that you can dissolve if it is no longer working or a job that you can quit if you no longer like it, once you are a parent, you are always a parent. You can have an ex-spouse or an ex-boss or even an ex-friend, but you can't have an ex-child. Parents who try to become ex-parents through abandonment or neglect face prosecution for child endangerment or abuse. Some—like the 18-year-old couple in 1996 who killed their newborn son and left his body in a motel trash bin—have been charged with murder.

In addition, the transition to parenthood is one that most people are ill prepared to make. Although nowadays most people who are expecting children take classes, what they learn mostly touches on the birthing process, not the day-to-day parenting that follows. Spending time with other people's babies prior to the birth may help somewhat in navigating the terrain of an infant's anatomy. But most of the learning parents experience is "on-the-job" training. Despite 9 months of anticipation, when the baby arrives, it arrives abruptly. A person really can't *gradually* become a parent or be a "parent-in-training" until he or she feels more comfortable in the role. The immediate demands of parenthood are especially difficult for single parents, who might not have someone around with whom to share the parent role.

All of these things occur within a framework of ambiguity. The goal of parenthood, of course, is to raise competent, well-rounded individuals who will become successful adults. But few guidelines are available to parents on how to reach this goal. Little is known about the long-term outcomes of various child rearing styles—that is, what works and what doesn't. Hence, parents have no way of knowing whether the things they do with, for, and to their children will ultimately create the sorts of beings they want them to be in 15 or 20 years.

Societal changes over the past several decades have made the transition to parenthood even more difficult (Cowan & Cowan, 1992). Nuclear families have become smaller and are likely to live more isolated lives, often far away from their extended kin. In addition, many young parents today are trying to create families based on a relatively new egalitarian ideology, in which both partners work and both are expected to care for the child. ▲ These changes require new arrangements to accommodate the increasing demands on parents of young children (Cowan & Cowan, 1992).

▲ Chapter 3 looks at how couples balance the demands of work and child rearing.

The Stress of Having Children

Given the difficulties associated with the transition to parenthood, it's not surprising that some couples perceive parenthood as a "crisis" that increases stress and decreases marital happiness. Children—as wonderful as they are—represent a substantial drain on time, energy, privacy, and money. Those quiet, intimate, spontaneous moments of passion that spouses once had quickly become hazy relics of a past life. Over half of the couples with new children surveyed in one study experienced either a severe or moderate decline in the quality of their marriage after the child arrived. For example:

> [New parents] find themselves riding the same roller coaster of elation, despair, and bafflement. . . . [They approached] parenthood full of high hopes and soaring dreams . . .

[but] six months or a year after the child's birth they . . . find themselves wondering "What's happening to us?" (Belsky & Kelly, 1994, p. 4)

Parents are pretty much on call 24 hours a day for 18 years—at least. The infant's demands for food eventually become the toddler's demands for attention, which inevitably become the teenager's demands for autonomy and the car keys. Not surprisingly, married couples tend to report being happiest before the arrival of their first child and after the last one has left home (Spanier, Lewis, & Cole, 1975).

About 10 years ago, researchers asked 1,100 women across the country about their experiences as mothers. About 25 percent of the women said the experience had been mostly positive, and 20 percent said the experience had been mostly negative. The majority (55 percent) had ambivalent feelings about being a parent: Although they acknowledged wonderful aspects of having a child, they also experienced disillusionment over the fact that it wasn't at all what they'd expected (Genevie & Margolies, 1987).

Research on new parents has also found that, although most of them had believed having a child would bring them closer together, the new child in fact represents a significant source of tension (Cowan & Cowan, 1992). Parenthood can sometimes increase feelings of anger, especially for women (Ross & Van Willigen, 1996). Issues of equity become paramount as parents fight over whose turn it is to change the diaper or put the baby to sleep.

Gender and Parenthood

Because of the obvious biological elements associated with bearing children, we could easily conclude that the relationship between parents and their children is an unalterable fact of nature. Parenthood may look quite different in different societies, but underlying these differences is an essential, universal drive.

According to the sociobiological perspective, because males and females are physically and genetically different, they logically have different biologically determined roles in raising children. ▲ Since women are better equipped anatomically to take care of infant children, the survival of the species depends on their doing so. They are the ones who get pregnant, give birth, and breast-feed. Consequently, they are guided by a different set of parenting expectations than men.

▲ For an overview of sociobiology, see Chapter 1.

Sociologist Alice Rossi (1977) argues that biological sex differences exist and affect parental behavior not only during pregnancy but also after birth. Much of mothering, she feels, is instinctual. For instance, the cry of an infant is sufficient to stimulate the secretion of the hormone oxytocin in the mother, which triggers nipple erection in preparation for nursing. Rossi also notes that the vast majority of women instinctually cradle their infants in their left arm, regardless of handedness, where the infants can be closer to the soothing sounds of the mother's heartbeat.

But are these observations sufficient to support the claim that mothering is instinctual? The oxytocin secretion is experienced by mothers as a "milk letdown"—that is, the milk rushes to the nipple and sometimes even leaks out. But milk leaks in response not only to hearing the infant cry but also to being sexually or emotionally aroused, running up or down stairs, or simply leaning over (Rothman, 1987). Over time, the let-down response becomes less immediate, eventually taking several minutes of actual sucking to activate. Hence, mothers aren't really responding instinctually to the sound of their infant crying but to the social meaning they attach to it. That is, letdown is a social as well as physiological phenomenon.

Likewise, mothers who hold their infants on the left, over their hearts, may be responding not to instinct but to something they've learned: Infants do calm down when they are held over a human heartbeat. For that matter, babies calm down when they hear *any* heartbeat—even one that is taped. In short, mothers hold babies this way because it works; it feels right because the baby settles down.

Furthermore, many of the original causes of differences between male and female parenting roles have been done away with by advances in technology. Children's survival no longer depends on a mother's constant care. With day care, infant formula, and so forth, children can survive quite well without a constant maternal presence. Cultural shifts have also made it more acceptable and even desirable for men to take a more active role in parenting. In fact, men who find themselves single parents can successfully raise children from infancy (Risman, 1989).

So the key question is not whether parenting behaviors are biologically programmed but what the social consequences of parenting are. Whether they are instinctual or learned, biological or social, the pregnancy and birth experiences are culturally and personally significant to women. In a culture that places such a high premium on parenthood—and, in particular, motherhood—people have come to believe that women are uniquely, biologically suited to the task. But even in such a culture, not all women want to be mothers. These decisions are influenced by a variety of social factors and experiences and not by some biological predisposition (Gerson, 1985). If having children were solely the result of a biological instinct, we wouldn't see variation in birth rates over time, across cultures, and between different social groups within the same culture (see Demo•Graphic Essay, "Trends in Motherhood," at the end of this chapter).

In addition, not all women who give birth form nurturant bonds with their infants. Some are indifferent to their children's needs; others are abusive. ▲ And while mothers all over the world are similarly equipped to nurse their infants, not all are the exclusive caretakers of children after infancy in many of the world's societies (Epstein, 1988).

▲ Child abuse is discussed in more detail in Chapter 6.

Nevertheless, the belief in the primacy of the mother-child bond remains strong (see Exhibit 4.3). Even our vocabulary reflects gender-based expectations regarding the different parenting responsibilities of mothers and fathers. Consider the verbs *to mother* and *to father*. In common usage, to *mother* a child is to care for, cherish, or protect that child. *Mothering* is associated with nurturant parenting. On the other hand, to *father* a child is to engage in the physical act of procreation, requiring little more than the fertilization of an egg. In common usage, *fathering* has nothing to do with a man's parental behavior.

▲ Chapter 3 takes a more detailed look at the domestic division of labor.

Despite significant advances in their societal well-being, women still bear a disproportionately high degree of responsibility for domestic labor and child care. ▲ Regardless of children's ages, mothers typically are more invested and involved in the day-to-day lives of their children than are fathers. They also do more of the "emotional" work with children and worry more about their well-being. As a result, women are called upon, far more than men, to sacrifice interests and identities outside the family—such as career and education—in order to devote more time to raising the children.

Exhibit 4.3

Attitudes Toward
Women as
Caretakers of
Children, by Sex

United States: 1996

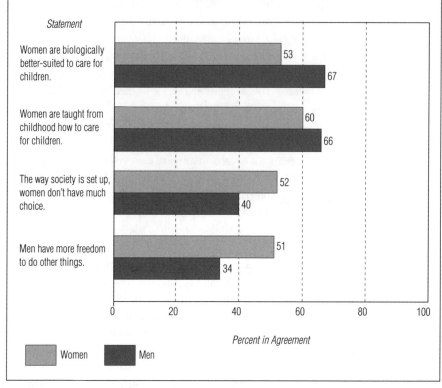

Source of data: National Opinion Research Center, University of Chicago, *General Social Survey, 1996.*

Active, hands-on parenting is required of mothers but is optional for fathers, whose contribution to parenting—although more visible and more acceptable than ever before—still tends to be defined as "helping" (Thompson & Walker, 1989). As one author put it, "fathers are volunteer providers; mothers are the staff" (Barry, 1993, p. 70). Even the physical separation of home and work has not created psychological distance for women in the same way it has for men. Mothers never cease being mothers. They are expected to be "mentally at home" in ways fathers are not. Men's increased involvement in pregnancy and childbirth has not resulted in equal responsibility for child care *after* the baby is born (Lorber, 1994). Even in households where other forms of housework and breadwinning are shared equally, child care responsibilities still tend to be divided along traditionally unequal gender lines.

Images of Motherhood

Women are still socialized to value the rewards of motherhood and to believe that having children is a primary source of self-identity:

Motherhood is inevitable; every woman will or should be a mother. A woman's identity is tenuous and trivial without motherhood. A woman enjoys and intuitively knows what to do for her child; she cares for her child without ambivalence or awkwardness.... Within the "magic circle" of mother and child, the mother devotes herself to her child's needs and holds her child's fate in her hands. (Thompson & Walker, 1989, p. 860)

▲ Gender socialization is explored in more detail in Chapter 5.

These lessons begin early in a girl's life. ▲ Girls' toys often reinforce the expectation that they will, or should, someday become mothers. For example, My Bundle Baby, manufactured by Mattel, is a 10-inch infant doll in a padded pouch that can be worn around a child's abdomen. By pressing a button hidden inside the pouch, the child can feel the baby inside "kick" and can hear its heartbeat (Lawson, 1992). The Judy doll, manufactured by the Judith Corporation, looks like any other 11-inch doll except that she is pregnant. She comes with a distended tummy that, when removed, reveals the presence of a cute baby nestled comfortably inside the doll's plastic uterus. The baby can be bloodlessly removed and a flat, nonpregnant tummy inserted in its place. The advertisement reads, "Judy is more than a toy, she's a natural way for your child to learn while playing." Clearly these toys teach young girls the cultural value of motherhood.

Having a baby is thought to be essential if a woman is to be whole, for the experiences of pregnancy and motherhood are "the core of women's being" (quoted in Nelkin & Lindee, 1995). As one journalist described it, the unpleasantness of pregnancy is a minor price to pay for the self-validation and social rewards it provides:

Even though I hated the sweating, the heartburn and the funny underpants I wore when I was pregnant, I liked the feeling that being pregnant was something. SOMETHING! I stuck out and waddled, and society smiled at me and gave me seats on busses . . . I felt queenly and grateful. (Marzollo, 1981, p. 47)

Women who downplay the importance of motherhood have always been the object of community or family concern. In the late nineteenth century, physicians feared that too much thinking would lead to a degeneration of a woman's uterus and ovaries. Thus, young women were often prevented from entering college to ensure their reproductive health.

Today, women who pursue intellectual and professional interests and thereby postpone childbearing are similarly led to believe that they might experience reproductive difficulty. Ominous cultural images of ticking "biological clocks" reinforce the idea that working women who have postponed pregnancy are running out of time in what should be their urgent need to reproduce. This idea is no longer based on some alleged connection between brain use and ovarian development but on modern scientific understanding of the link between infertility and maternal age. Yet the underlying notion is eerily similar: Nonparental interests and pursuits harm female reproductive capacity (Nelkin & Lindee, 1995). As one author gravely put it, too many women "have continued to put off childbearing without fully understanding the possible consequences of that choice" (Maranto, 1995, p. 56).

Motherhood and Maternity   To most people, the centrality of maternity (the state of being pregnant and the physical act of giving birth) gives women not only the ability but also the desire to nurture—in other words, maternity fosters motherhood. So it's not surprising that when we hear of mothers abusing or murdering their children we are stunned. When Susan Smith drowned her two young sons by pushing the car in which they were strapped into a South

Carolina pond in the early 1990s, people around the country asked, "How could a *mother* do that to her children?" The fact that she was their biological mother rendered her act even more unfathomable and unforgivable. In 1997, when a Miami man who was angry at his wife killed two of his young sons in a similar fashion, the media paid scant attention.

Although we take the equation of maternity with motherhood to be universal and timeless, it is, in fact, a relatively recent development. Indeed, until the nineteenth century, anyone who raised a child was addressed as "Mother" regardless of her biological connection to the child. The term was applied to the proprietors of brothels and to innkeepers. In colonial New England all older women—whether they had children or not—were called mothers (cited in Gillis, 1996).

The distinction between maternity and motherhood in the eighteenth century is particularly evident in what typically took place moments after the birth. ▲ Mothers may have had a central role in the physical act of giving birth, but once the child was delivered they became peripheral. Instead of being placed at the mother's breast, the newborn was usually taken to the hearth, symbolically identifying it with the household rather than the mother (Gillis, 1996). It was then swaddled and brought to the father to show to friends and other neighbors. The relative neglect of the mother immediately after the birth was a result of a belief that she wasn't supposed to show too much affection toward the child. Mothers were usually isolated for days, even weeks after the birth. They were rarely present at the church when their children were baptized and played little part in the child's life in the weeks after its birth. The deep love of a mother that is so celebrated today was regarded with suspicion.

Giving birth and giving nurture were often incompatible for demographic reasons (Gillis, 1996). Because birthrates and death rates were so high in Europe and North America up until the mid–nineteenth century, there was no way that all mothers who gave birth could mother all their children. Only about half of all babies born lived to the age of 21, and mothers were likely to die before all their children had left home. Intensive involvements with each individual child were simply impossible. ▲ Consequently, maternity and motherhood were understood to be separable, much as paternity (creating a child) and fatherhood (nurturing a child) are separable today.

But children in these eras didn't lack a maternal presence. Wet nurses—women who would breast-feed other women's children for extended periods—were commonly employed not only by upper-class women, who found breast-feeding distasteful and unfashionable, but also by working-class women, who had neither the time nor the energy to feed their infants. Of the 21,000 babies born in 1780 in Paris, 17,000 were sent to wet nurses (deMause, 1975). But wet nurses commonly took on too many babies in order to make more money. Frequently they ran out of milk, so many babies had to be sent to a series of different nurses, depriving them of a single "mother" figure (McCoy, 1981).

Eventually, the very idea of an infant being breast-fed by someone other than its mother became incompatible with cultural definitions of good motherhood. By the late nineteenth and early twentieth centuries, wet nursing had become a thing of the past, associated with primitive, unenlightened times. Mothers either suckled their infants themselves or bottle-fed them.

But intense, continual contact between mothers and their children was rare in the nineteenth century. It was still common for pre-teenage children to be informally adopted by relatives. When kin lived nearby, children often ate meals and slept apart from their biological par-

▲ Other historical images of family life are explored in Issue 2.

▲ See Chapter 5 for a discussion of how these demographic realities shaped definitions of childhood.

ents. When families had many children, older ones were frequently sent to live permanently with distant relatives. Girls from poor families were likely to be sent away to work in domestic service. ▲ Foundling hospitals and orphanages were common fixtures on the social landscape; parents often placed their children in these institutions because they couldn't afford to raise them. For a mother to give up her children "to the kindness of strangers" was considered neither immoral nor unnatural (Gillis, 1996, p. 155). Not until the 1920s could parents expect most if not all of their children to be their responsibility until the children were married.

▲ *Shifting conceptions of childhood are explored in Chapter 5.*

Fetal Rights versus Mothers' Rights   One of the great ironies of our cultural conception of motherhood is that while women are believed to be naturally endowed to nurture their children and are expected to place their children's well-being above all else, they are also seen as the greatest threat to their children *before* they're born. Pregnant women in American society often find that their rights are considered secondary to those of the babies they're carrying. The contemporary debate that pits **fetal rights** against women's rights illustrates a growing public desire to place women's reproductive capacities under governmental control. ▲ Such control denies pregnant women the rights of bodily integrity and self-determination that all competent adults in this society are supposed to be granted (Tavris, 1992).

▲ *Issue 3 takes a broader look at the tension between family privacy and outside intervention.*

Today a vast array of policies, laws, and practices protect fetal rights over women's rights. The fetus is often granted an individual identity, which gives it equality with (and perhaps, according to some, superiority over) the mother and establishes its independent relationship with society that bypasses the mother (Roth, 1993). These measures gained popularity in the 1980s and 1990s, when employers, hospitals, and local, state, and federal governments increasingly imposed limits on pregnant women (Daniels, 1993).

Today pregnant women are usually assumed to have a moral, societal, and legal responsibility to ensure a healthy birth, even perhaps at the cost of their own health. Consider the story of Angela Carder. In 1987, 25 weeks into her pregnancy, doctors discovered an inoperable tumor in Carder's right lung. Carder and her doctors decided that when she reached 28 weeks she would undergo a cesarean section. At this point the fetus would have a strong chance at survival. But when Carder's condition worsened prior to 28 weeks, the hospital administration was granted a court order to intervene and perform the cesarean section at 26 weeks in order to save the fetus. The baby died within 2 hours; Carder died 2 days later (Roth, 1993).

Often judges will subject pregnant women who commit crimes to harsher sentences than men or nonpregnant women. For instance, several years ago a 29-year-old pregnant Maryland woman was sentenced to 6 months in jail for forging $722 in checks. It was her first offense, which typically would have resulted in probation. The judge acknowledged her differential treatment:

> It is true that the defendant has not been treated the same as if she were a man in this case. But then a man who is a convicted rapist is treated differently from a woman. She has also not been treated the same as a nonpregnant woman. But [she] became pregnant and chose to bear the baby who, like most criminal defendants the court sees so frequently, will start life with one other severe strike against it—no father is around. Arguably, [she] should have demonstrated even greater responsibility toward her child. (quoted in Roth, 1993, p. 126)

Concern with the harm mothers pose to their fetuses is particularly strong with regard to the use of drugs and alcohol. Cigarette packs come with a warning that smoking while pregnant poses health risks to the baby. Restaurants in some states are required to post signs warning pregnant mothers that the ingestion of alcohol can jeopardize their babies' health. This concern is certainly warranted, but the question is what interest the state has in a pregnant woman's behavior.

The problems caused by substance abuse during pregnancy are growing (Burtt, 1994). An estimated 11 percent of all babies born in this country each year have been exposed to street drugs while they were in the uterus (cited in Roth, 1993). The health risks to fetuses posed by the pregnant mother's ingestion of certain drugs are widely known. Four thousand babies each year are born with fetal alcohol syndrome and another 11,000 with fetal alcohol effect. These conditions are associated with, among other things, congenital heart defects, defective joints, and mental deficiencies. Fetal exposure to cocaine has been known to cause neurological problems, poor attention, and impaired social interaction (Chasnoff, 1989).

Increasingly, society's response (other than the printed warnings, which are designed more to relieve companies of liability than to protect the health of babies) has been to prosecute and incarcerate pregnant women who use drugs. Consider the following cases:

■   A pregnant woman in Wyoming was arrested for endangering her unborn child when she arrived drunk at a hospital for treatment of injuries inflicted by her abusive husband. The charges were dropped but were to be reinstated if the child was born with any alcohol-caused defects. No charges were filed against the husband (Pollitt, 1991).

■   A Florida woman was convicted of "delivering drugs to a minor." To avoid the debate over when the fetus becomes a person, the prosecutor contended that she delivered drugs to her baby through her umbilical cord after the baby had been born but before the cord had been cut.

■   A Kentucky woman who gave birth to three children during her 17-year addiction to drugs was sentenced to 5 years in prison for criminal child abuse (Hoffman, 1990).

■   A South Carolina woman was convicted of child abuse and sentenced to 8 years in prison for using cocaine while pregnant. In upholding this decision upon appeal, the South Carolina Supreme Court ruled that a viable fetus is a "person" who is covered by the state's existing child abuse laws (Lewin, 1997b; "Prenatal drug use," 1996).

■   A Wisconsin woman was charged with attempted murder for giving birth to a baby with a blood alcohol level twice the threshold for a legal finding of intoxication. The mother had a history of problem drinking and had been drinking heavily the night of the birth (Terry, 1996).

■   Also in Wisconsin, a pregnant woman was forcibly detained in a county sheriff's department and later in a hospital when a juvenile court directed that her fetus be taken into protective custody because of her use of cocaine and other drugs. The Wisconsin Supreme Court eventually struck down the ruling (Lewin, 1997a).

Since the late 1980s, over 200 women in thirty states have been prosecuted for behavior while pregnant that posed danger to their fetuses, the vast majority involving the use of illegal drugs

(Terry, 1996). Even more have been deprived of custody of their children or jailed during pregnancy (referred to as "protective incarceration") (Roberts, 1991).

Mothers' behavior has become the most urgent political target in the fight to protect children. While the motivation to protect the health of fetuses is understandable, the societal response is often unjust. Most of the women prosecuted for giving birth to infants who test positive for drugs are poor and black (Roberts, 1991). These women are the least likely to obtain adequate prenatal care. Also, because poor women are generally under greater government supervision—through public hospitals, welfare agencies, and probation officers—their drug use is more likely to be detected and reported than more affluent expectant mothers. Indeed, the government's main source of information about prenatal drug use is hospitals' reporting of infant drug exposure to child welfare authorities. Private physicians, who serve more affluent women, perform fewer drug-screening procedures. One study found that, despite similar rates of substance abuse, pregnant black women are ten times more likely than pregnant white women to be reported to public health authorities (Chasnoff, Landress, & Barrett, 1990).

But far from deterring dangerous drug use, prosecution of drug-addicted mothers often deters pregnant women from using available health and counseling services—out of fear they will be reported to government authorities and charged with a crime. To make matters worse, such mothers can obtain alcohol- or drug-dependency treatment only with extreme difficulty. Most substance-abuse programs will not accept pregnant women because they fear liability. Withdrawal from some drugs can actually do more harm or even kill a fetus (Roth, 1993).

Advances in prenatal technology have made the debate over fetal rights versus mothers' rights even more complex and contentious. Over the past several decades, we have seen an expansion of prenatal diagnostic techniques (such as amniocentesis, chorionic villus sampling, and ultrasound) that identify fetal anomalies. An estimated one-third or more of all pregnant women in the United States undergo ultrasound alone (Blank, 1993).

As these techniques become less dangerous and more accessible, courts are extending their idea of prenatal injury to include acts of omission as well as acts of commission (Blank, 1993). That is, mothers will find themselves increasingly obligated to use available diagnostic techniques. To not make use of a technique prescribed by a physician is to risk being labeled irresponsible, negligent, or, ultimately, criminal. In 1983 a Michigan court recognized the right of a child to sue his or her mother for failure to monitor the pregnancy and identify and correct threats to his or her health during gestation.

Everyone would agree that babies should receive the best possible start in life. However, focusing solely on pregnant women allows us to ignore other threats to the well-being of children that lie outside the mother's body: poverty, inadequate health care, poor housing, environmental hazards, racism, and so on—not to mention fathers' unhealthy sperm (Blakeslee, 1991). One in five pregnant women today lack access to any sort of prenatal health care (Pollitt, 1991), yet such facts are overlooked in the pursuit of fetal rights. Controlling the behavior of mothers allows the government to appear concerned about babies without having to spend any money, change any priorities, or challenge any vested interests (Pollitt, 1991). But as we become more obsessed with pregnant women's behavior, the health and well-being of American children continues to decline. ▲

▲ Issue 7 examines the effect of poverty on children.

Like poverty, homelessness, and crime, the health of children is construed as a matter of freely chosen individual behavior: "We have crime because we have lots of bad people, poverty because we have lots of lazy people ... and tiny, sickly, impaired babies because we have lots of women who just don't give a damn" (Pollitt, 1991, p. 243). Once a problem is defined this way, state intervention, coercion, and punishment come to be seen as justifiable and necessary responses. I'm not suggesting that using drugs or smoking cigarettes while pregnant is a good thing to do. But the problem of infant sickness must be placed in the larger institutional context:

> The concept of fetal rights ... posits a world in which women will be held accountable, on sketchy or no evidence, for birth defects; ... in which courts, employers, social workers and doctors—not to mention nosy neighbors and vengeful male partners—will monitor women's behavior. It imposes responsibilities without giving women the wherewithal to fulfill them, and places upon women alone duties that belong to both parents and to the community. (Pollitt, 1991, p. 251)

Images of Fatherhood

▲ The primacy of fatherhood in the past had a strong impact on how custody issues were decided, as you can read about in Chapter 7.

Images of fatherhood have also changed over time. In the eighteenth century, fathers rather than mothers were considered the primary parents. ▲ Fathers were active in all the major nurturing and educational functions we now associate with motherhood (Gillis, 1996). They oversaw wet nurses and carried on the bulk of family correspondence.

The Industrial Revolution of the nineteenth century sent a shock wave through the domestic world that fathers ruled. The male family role became defined primarily as that of the breadwinner. ▲ This role, of course, has always varied by social class. The search for work commonly sent poor men away from their families; and aristocratic fathers were typically away in the military or civil service. Men who could do much of their work in the house—artisans, farmers, businessmen—tended to be the ones who took on a more active father role.

▲ The historical development of the notion of "separate spheres" for men and women is examined in Chapter 3.

Since then, common conceptions of fatherhood have lacked the emotional pull of motherhood. Symbolically, fathers are never quite at the center of everyday family life in the same way that mothers are (Gillis, 1996). But the percentage of American households that consisted of a married couple dependent on a sole male breadwinner dropped from 60 percent in 1950 to 14 percent in 1990 (Gerson, 1993). ▲ As men have escaped from the excessive burdens of the good-provider role, they have been freed to participate more fully in their families (Furstenberg, 1997).

▲ Issue 5 and Chapter 3 examine the role of economics in marital power relations, with particular attention to the changing nature of the male breadwinner role.

Men's involvement in their families is a relatively new topic of concern for researchers. Indeed, scholars paid very little attention to fathering prior to the 1970s. Most assumed that fathers were peripheral to their families, even if their presence was desirable. Even today, the U.S. Census Bureau can document the 70 million or so mothers age 15 or over in the United States but has little idea how many fathers there are (Gibbs, 1993). With greater access to in vitro fertilization, artificial insemination, and other reproductive technologies, more and more women are now able to become pregnant and raise children without a man (Ludtke, 1997).

In general, though, fathers appear to be increasingly involved in raising their children. According to U.S. Census figures, fathers are taking care of one in every five preschool children while mothers work, the first increase in more than 10 years. This increase is likely due to increased unemployment, the high cost of professional child care, the growing number of parents who work part-time or night shifts, and changing public attitudes (cited in Chira, 1993).

In some circles, fathers are assuming an active role in the care of their children whether or not the mother's employment forces them to. Since the 1970s, a new, but not yet dominant, culture of fatherhood has emerged. A "good father" is expected to be "an active participant in the details of day-to-day child care. He involves himself in a more expressive and intimate way with his children, and he plays a larger part in the socialization process that his male forebears had long since abandoned to their wives" (Rotundo, 1985, p. 17).

In 1974 Dr. Benjamin Spock's famous advice book, *Baby and Child Care*, advised mothers not to force fathers to participate too much in child care, suggesting that he be asked, perhaps, to change a diaper every once in a while. The most recent edition, however, states that fathers should be involved, just as much as mothers, in the day-to-day care of their children (Gibbs, 1993b).

Indeed, recent research suggests that, if given the opportunity, fathers can interact with and care for their children just as well as mothers can. For example, although the proportion of children living in father-only families is rather rare—they constitute about 4 percent of all children—such living arrangements have increased dramatically over the last 20 years (Eggebeen, Snyder, & Manning, 1996). Because of the immediate demands of their circumstances, single fathers respond to the nontraditional role of single parent with strategies that could be considered stereotypically feminine (cuddling, nurturing, expressing intimacy, and so on). With no wife to depend on, men can be effective "mothers" (Risman, 1989).

Thus, you can see that modern fathering is no longer just about procreation and bread-winning. For many men today, becoming a father means making a commitment to emotionally and physically caring for children (Coltrane, 1996b; Furstenberg, 1997). In fact, more men are taking time off work to care for their children than ever before. ▲ At AT&T, for example, the ratio of women to men on parental leave dropped from 400 to 1 in the 1980s to 18 to 1 today (cited in "Workplace experts say," 1997). Notice how this father's experience belies the image of the cold, aloof breadwinner-father:

▲ The dilemmas both men and women face in balancing work and family responsibilities is examined more closely in Chapter 3.

> It was real hard to sit down and hold them when they were sick. I had to keep telling myself that this is important, you need to be here with them doing nothing. Which is the feeling I had—I'm not doing anything—but I was. Eventually those things really paid off with the trust the kids developed in me. (quoted in Coltrane, 1996b, p. 12)

Such participation in children's lives certainly has its benefits. Most child development experts agree that children do better when their fathers take an active, supportive role in their lives. As one sociologist put it, "When men and women share family work, the entire society benefits" (Coltrane, 1996b, p. 199).

But many scholars continue to express doubts about the willingness of most men to become fully involved in their families (Bernard, 1981; Ehrenreich, 1983). The recent stampede of fathers into delivery rooms to witness the *births* of their children has not been accompanied by increased participation in ongoing daily care and rearing (Cowan & Cowan, 1992). One study found that, in two-parent families with employed mothers, fathers spend about 33 percent as much time as mothers actually engaged in one-to-one interaction with their child. In addition, they spend about 65 percent as much time as mothers being accessible—that is, ready or available to tend to a child if needed. Finally, mothers carry over 90 percent of the responsibility for their children (making sure they have clothes to wear, get to activities on time, go to the pediatrician, and so on) (Lamb, 1987). This imbalance in hands-on parenting has led some experts to conclude that the *culture* of fatherhood—our beliefs about what fathers should do or what we'd like them to do—has changed more rapidly than the *conduct* of fatherhood—what fathers actually do (LaRossa, 1992). ▲

▲ Chapter 3 provides further evidence showing that men still take on substantially less child care at home than women do.

▲ For more detail on why noncustodial fathers don't have much contact with their children see Chapter 7.

Moreover, more fathers than ever before are absent from their children's lives. A growing proportion either deny paternity or shirk parental obligations. In divorced families, contact between children and their noncustodial fathers drops off sharply with the length of time since the parents separated—although it's not altogether clear if the problem is fathers' unwillingness to get involved or mothers' effectiveness at preventing them from doing so (Furstenberg, 1997). ▲

Even fathers who want to be involved in their children's lives often feel that their contributions to child rearing are less significant and less necessary than the mothers'. As one new father stated, "[My wife] has the kid on her breast every two hours. And then, for ten minutes, I get to clean up the poop and diaper him and put him back to sleep. What's the point? I might as well be out bringing in some more money" (quoted in Cowan & Cowan, 1992, p. 103). Fathers who feel this way are likely to retreat from active child rearing and make their way back to their work, where they know they can make an essential, measurable contribution to their family's welfare.

And so breadwinning, despite all its disadvantages and harmful possibilities, remains the unifying element in the lives of most American fathers (Griswold, 1993). Certainly many men say they want to take a more active role in raising their children. One poll found that 39 percent of fathers would quit their jobs to spend more time with their children; another found that 74 percent of men would welcome a scaled-down job, off the fast track (cited in Gibbs, 1993b). ▲

▲ Chapter 3 addresses this issue as well.

However, the workplace still discourages men from completely abandoning the breadwinner role. A man who wants to work part-time or not at all in order to care for his children is still likely to be looked on with suspicion, disappointment, or amusement by an employer. As one father who took a leave of absence from work when his two children were born put it, "[My boss] was very generous with the time, but he never let me forget it. . . . You don't get a lot of points at the office for wanting to have a healthy family life" (quoted in Gibbs, 1993b, p. 55). In short, while contemporary fathers are now likely to take substantial pride in their role as nurturer, the breadwinner ideal retains its association with maturity, respectability, and masculinity.

Conclusion

Parenthood occupies a formidable place in American society. Despite the increasing proportion of the population that is choosing to remain childless or delaying childbearing in the interests of achieving other goals, becoming a parent remains this culture's pinnacle of family commitment and maturity. Societal expectations are powerful. Parenthood, as both a social role and a procreative accomplishment, is so deeply ingrained in the culture that its absence in married life still evokes curiosity, pity, or condemnation.

As we've seen throughout this chapter, the cultural ideal of parenthood sometimes doesn't match its ambivalent reality:

■ The cultural primacy of biological parenthood persists despite the growing recognition that emotional bonds can be just as strong as genetic ones.

■ Parenthood itself continues to be presented as a joyous, valuable, and, of course, normal experience even though it frequently causes unexpected stress, strain, and unhappiness in people's lives and is looked upon with ambivalence in the world of work.

■ Women are still expected to place motherhood at the top of their list of priorities, even though more and more women consider it a potentially oppressive role and are rejecting the notion that becoming a mother is necessary for their emotional fulfillment.

■ A new definition of fatherhood is taking hold in the culture even though men's contributions to parenting continue to lag behind women's and they are still drawn by the unambiguous rewards of the traditional breadwinner role.

Perhaps it's not so strange that such discrepancies exist. Certainly the stability of society depends on people seeing parenthood in the most positive light possible. Research on the downside of becoming or being a parent usually remains safely hidden in academic journals, rarely entering the societal discourse on parenthood. As a society, we have much at stake when couples contemplate having children. Indeed, it's hard to imagine a society in which parenthood is not actively promoted and encouraged. Is it any wonder, then, that the dominant cultural messages we receive about parenting emphasize its advantages and downplay its problems?

CHAPTER HIGHLIGHTS

■ Some sociologists characterize the United States as a pronatalist society—one in which married couples are expected to reproduce. Having children is seen as essential to self-fulfillment. Other societies have even stronger pronatalist values, sometimes enacting policies that require people to try to have children.

■ The ideal of pronatalism affects the societal response to infertility, which in turn affects infertile couples' feelings of stigma. Because of the value placed on parenthood, medical treatments for infertility have become a booming business.

■ Even though having children is still expected of married couples, more and more Americans are choosing to remain childless.

■ Even the universal, biological experience of giving birth is profoundly influenced by cultural and historical forces. What is considered normal and healthy in one society or in one era can be considered barbaric in another.

■ Although parenthood can be an extremely rewarding experience, the transition from nonparent to parent can be stressful.

■ Images of motherhood and fatherhood are often influenced by beliefs about the natural, innate tendencies of mothers and fathers. However, gender differences in parenting behavior are clearly linked to broader cultural expectations.

DEMO•GRAPHIC ESSAY

Trends in Motherhood

Becoming a parent is one of the most important transitions an individual can make. For biological mothers, pregnancy and childbirth are significant experiences that are difficult to forget. It is possible, however, for men to be the biological fathers of children they do not even know exist. For this reason, both vital statistics and the U.S. Bureau of the Census include data on the experience of childbearing for women rather than men.

Birthrates in the United States have been decreasing over the past century, except for the period of the post–World War II baby boom, from 1946 to 1964. Exhibit 4-A shows the number of children born to U.S. women ages 40–44, who at the time were either married, separated, widowed, or divorced. Because most women ages 40–44 have completed their childbearing, these numbers are estimates of the total number of children these women will bear over their lifetime, in other words, their completed family size. The graph shows that completed family size dipped in the 1950s and then rose to a peak in 1975. The completed family size per woman has declined continuously since then.

At first, the dip in the 1950s may seem to contradict what we know about the baby boom. Remember, however, that the data refer to women in their 40s, most of whose children were born some 15–25 years earlier. The baby boom, therefore, which occurred between 1946 and 1964, with a peak in 1957, shows up in Exhibit 4-A approximately 20 years later.

Along with this trend toward smaller families among married women is the trend toward increased childbearing outside of marriage. Since 1970, births to unmarried women in the United States have tripled. This trend in the United States echoes a general trend in Europe, as Exhibit 4-B shows, demonstrating evolving definitions of parenthood and family in many places across the world. Contrast these changes in the percentage of births to unmarried women with trends in Japan. Not coincidentally, Japan's culture is quite different from the culture of the other countries shown in Exhibit 4-B.

Exhibit 4-A

Total Number of Children Ever Born to Ever-Married Women Ages 40–44

United States: 1940–1995

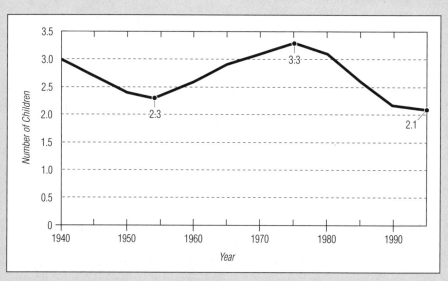

Source of data: U.S. Bureau of the Census, *Statistical Abstract of the United States,* for 1947, 1984, 1988, 1992, 1995, 1997.

Exhibit 4-B

Births to Unmarried
Women

*United States and
Selected Countries:
1970–1994*

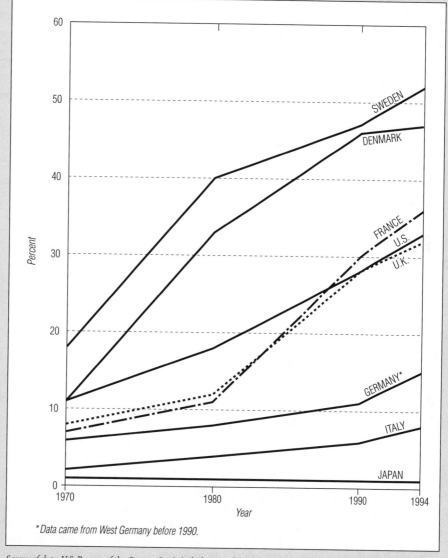

*Data came from West Germany before 1990.

Source of data: U.S. Bureau of the Census, *Statistical Abstract of the United States: 1997* (117th edition). Washington, DC, 1997.

Cultural differences are a force within the United States as well. For example, Exhibit 4-C shows the percentage of women with one or more children by age, race, and marital status. As expected, the proportion of women who have made the transition to motherhood increases by age for the women who have been married, but not so clearly for single (never-married) women. The differences between never-married women and women who have been married demonstrate that one of the social norms of marriage in the United States is

Exhibit 4-C

Women with One or
More Children

United States: 1995

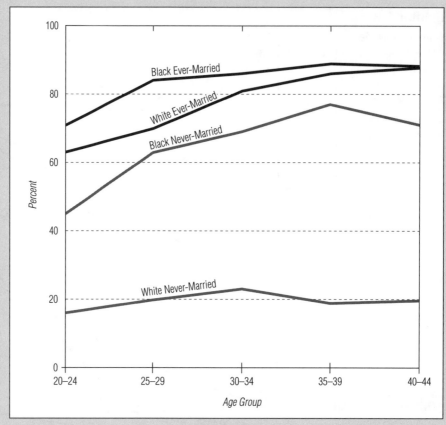

Source of data: U.S. Bureau of the Census, *Statistical Abstract of the United States: 1997* (117th edition). Washington, DC, 1997.

childbearing, although certainly marriage is not an absolute prerequisite for parenthood, nor do all marriages necessarily lead to procreation.

One of the most striking things about Exhibit 4-C is that by ages 40–44, approximately the same percentage of black women and white women have become mothers. Race differences in fertility, therefore, are not in the total number of children women have, but rather the timing of those births. At younger ages black women are more likely than white women to become mothers.

Questions for Further Study

1. **What are some of the biases involved in asking women ages 40–44 to state the total number of children they have ever borne? Which women might overstate their total number of births? How could some women omit some births from their total count (i.e., understate the total number of children they have ever borne)? After considering these potential discrepancies, do you believe that this question can elicit valid responses?**

2. What do the countries with the highest rates of unmarried fertility have in common? What else would you like to know about these countries that could explain these trends?

3. According to Exhibit 4-C, does marital status or race make more of a difference in fertility? Which group has the smallest difference by age? How could you interpret this finding? What variables beside race and marital status could affect the age pattern of the transition to motherhood?

YOUR TURN

We've seen in this chapter that the transition to parenthood can simultaneously be a wonderful and a frightening experience. Although most couples look forward to the transition with great anticipation, many experience a sense of dread or general anxiety. Fortunately, prospective parents today have many options available to them to ease the transition: parenting magazines, books, and web sites; childbirth classes; videos; and so on. These sources of information can relieve some of the tension associated with entering a new world of responsibilities, but they can also inadvertently create an idealized image of parenthood that can lead to unreasonable expectations and worries.

See if you can get permission to sit in on a local childbirth class. Most hospitals offer some sort of program for prospective parents. What sorts of information are these soon-to-be parents provided? What is the balance between the positive and negative elements of the transition to parenthood? How are men incorporated into the lessons? Are they treated as "outside observers" or as "equal participants"? It might be useful to talk to some of the fathers to see what their expectations are with regard to their role in the birth and subsequent care of the child.

To get a deeper understanding of the cultural and historical context of the transition to parenthood, see if your library has back issues of a magazine that's devoted to parenting, such as *Parents* magazine. Analyze the contents of a sample of these magazines from the past 3 or 4 decades. Pay particular attention to articles devoted to childbirth, the mother role, and the father role. Such articles serve as a valuable barometer of changing attitudes and expectations regarding mothers and fathers. Do you notice any interesting changes in the type of guidance given to parents? How have society's expectations of parents changed over time? To what do you attribute these changes?

CHAPTER 5

Childhood and Child Rearing

On a brisk spring day in 1997, a Danish tourist was arrested in New York City for leaving her 14-month-old daughter unattended in a stroller on a busy sidewalk while she ate inside a restaurant. Passersby notified the police, who, after some discussion, apprehended the woman. She was charged with child neglect and endangering the welfare of a child and spent 2 days in jail. Her baby was placed in foster care for 4 days.

The charges against the mother were eventually dropped on the condition that she leave the country and return to her native Denmark. She was able to convince authorities that, in Danish society, such acts are considered perfectly appropriate. If you were to stroll along the streets of Copenhagen, even in the dead of winter, you'd likely see scores of baby carriages—with babies snuggled in them—parked outside apartment buildings, supermarkets, and cafés (Dyssegaard, 1997). On the relatively crime-free streets of Denmark, parents do not worry about their children's safety. The Danes also have an almost religious conviction that fresh, preferably cold, air is good for children. All Danish babies take naps outside, even in freezing weather, tucked under warm blankets.

But such a cultural explanation did little to assuage the anger that many people felt toward this woman. While news of her *arrest* was met with shock waves of disbelief in Denmark, news of her *actions* were met with outrage here. As one journalist put it, even a place like New York City "turns into a small town and reacts with a vengeance against parents who behave badly" (Ojito, 1997, p. E3). To Americans, leaving such a small child alone scales the heights of parental irresponsibility. And leaving it alone in New York, of all places—with its infamous crime rate and likelihood of abduction—is perceived not only as irresponsible but as criminally negligent.

On the day after Christmas in 1996, the bound and beaten body of 6-year-old JonBenet Ramsey was found in the basement of her Boulder, Colorado, home. The death of a child is always a tragedy. But as the shocking details of her murder made their way across the nation, we quickly learned that JonBenet was not just an ordinary 6-year-old. She was a beauty pageant veteran and a star of some repute—the reigning Little Miss Colorado.

Television news shows and supermarket tabloids were saturated with images of this little girl wearing false eyelashes and high heels, preening for audiences with coy expressions and vaguely sexual poses. One pageant publication had described JonBenet as a "natural . . . who could win the cars and the cash"; a photographer marveled at her maturity, noting that she could "hold a pose forever" (quoted in "The strange world," 1997, p. 44).

Many people in this country immediately implicated JonBenet's parents—not necessarily for murdering her but for selfishly robbing their daughter of her innocent childhood in pursuit of fame, recognition, and fortune:

> In photographs, her characteristic expression is a fixed smile of concentration, earnest and studied. It could be perky, coy or sweet, although the only sure way to tell is by her costume. Strapless ball gown, sailor suit, swimsuit—JonBenet Ramsey . . . worked hard at winning beauty contests, but her mother must have worked even harder. And her father paid for her portfolio of professional photographs, a world beyond the artless family-album snapshots we are accustomed to seeing when a child is killed. But the effect is distancing rather than illuminating: in all the miles of film that were lavished on JonBenet it is hard to find one frame that captures her soul. ("The strange world," 1997, p. 43)

This case exposed a massive beauty pageant culture that few of us knew existed—a world that enlists thousands of girls under 12 and their parents and grandparents in about 500 contests a year. They support a billion-dollar industry of contest promoters, costume designers, grooming consultants, and publishers. A hand-sewn gown can cost $1,000.

The contestants in these beauty pageants are "child-women," whose anxious childhoods are spent trying to attain just the right balance of poise, charm, and good looks. Although parents stress the long-term benefits of participating (greater self-esteem and confidence), the financial stakes are undeniably tempting. Modeling contracts await the best performers. One 6-year-old pageant star has already won enough money to pay for her college education.

Of course, the beauty pageant culture is not the only place where we can find pushy parents and pushed children. Just spend a few hours at your local youth league baseball or soccer fields, and you will spot moms and dads breeding hypercompetitive kids.

Nevertheless, the sight of JonBenet showing off her body as a competitive activity outraged many people, who liken these pageants to child pornography. Child development experts warn that such activities create hollow children and narcissistic parents and send the message to these girls that all they need to do to get attention is look pretty. Unlike competitive sports, where skills are clear and success is measurable, girls who excel in beauty pageants are learning simply how to perform for and please other people.

Although the cases of the Danish tourist and the JonBenet Ramsey murder are markedly different, they both show how quickly the public condemns child rearing practices that don't match the general public's sense of propriety. The public's response in these cases was predictably swift and passionate. Although our culture values family privacy and parents' right to raise their children as they see fit, such ideals are easily sacrificed when our conceptions of childhood and our beliefs about "appropriate" child rearing are violated. ▲

▲ Issue 3 examines the controversy over family privacy.

Fundamental to our powerful image of family is its role as producer and socializer of children. As a society, we consider the bond between parents and children sacred. We like to say that the fate of the nation lies in the well-being of our children. So we shouldn't be surprised that the perception that parents are "irresponsibly" exposing their children to danger or exploiting them for personal gain produces hostile accusations. However, as this chapter explains, not everybody has, or has had, the same ideas about appropriate child rearing techniques.

Free to Be You and Me?

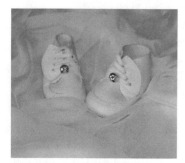

Before we have even learned to walk, we are being socialized to fit into society. In many senses, race, class, and gender help form the shoes we will walk in for the rest of our lives.

Throughout the ages, upper-class children have had the benefits that typically come to those in wealthy families: beautiful clothes, top-notch private instruction, musical and cultural lessons, and so on. In the past, through this training, upper-class children were taught to act and see themselves as different from less affluent children. They were trained from day one to be economic, political, and social leaders. Notice how in the pursuit of upper-class respectability, individuality and spontaneity are lacking: The boy and the girl are not only rigidly placed beside their mother, they are dressed nearly identically.

Working-class and poor children, free to roam the streets without much supervision, had to improvise toys out of garbage can lids and sticks.

Some urban areas have deprived children of their exuberance and innocence. Violence and poverty have created structures of pain, not play, causing children to grow up quickly. In some areas both abroad and in the United States, even young children are forced to work simply to survive.

Class, race, and ethnicity are not the only social factors that influence how children play and develop. Gender is a crucial status that is reinforced in children from their first moments after birth, when boys are swaddled in blue blankets and girls in pink. Boys and girls are taught in countless ways, both subtle and overt, how to be boys and girls.

Boys have traditionally been taught to assert dominance at the expense of expressing their feelings. This 2-year-old boy, donning a dark blue baseball cap, is already being positioned behind the wheel in the driver's seat.

Since the 1960s, however, gender roles have been changing. Here we see young girls being taught how to defend themselves from assault by adults and older children.

But patterns of socialization are hard to break. Subtle forms of gender discrimination exist despite our best efforts. For the most part, the popular, well-liked boys in high school are still the ones who play sports, and the popular, well-liked girls are cheerleaders.

Women's sports have grown in the past few years, with many young girls taking athletic competition as seriously as boys.

However, the idea of boys cheer-leading—that is, taking on typically feminine activities—may still be considered an absurdity.

The very youngest, however—those who have not been completely gender socialized—are beginning to embrace all types of play and activity. Here we see a young boy pretending to serve tea and cookies.

It will take many more societal changes before children of all social classes, racial and ethnic groups, and genders have the same opportunities and goals.

The Historical Construction of Childhood

Childhood is such a universal feature of human life that it is easily considered a natural stage of development. After all, doesn't every society, current or past, include some people that can clearly be identified as "children"? Aren't children everywhere younger, smaller, weaker, and generally less experienced than adults? As obvious as the answers to these questions are, "childhood," as a special phase of life, has not always been defined the way we define it today. Western societies at the end of the twentieth century take for granted that children are qualitatively and quantitatively different from adults. It seems inconceivable to us that our laws, customs, and values regarding children—for instance, that they are dependent and innocent and therefore require and deserve guidance and protection—haven't always been the cornerstone of a "civilized" society. However, current attitudes about the welfare, rights, and requirements of children are, for the most part, relatively new (Aries, 1962).

Images of childhood don't spring from nature; ideas about childhood and child rearing are tightly connected to a society's culture and organization (Corsaro, 1997). That is, these ideas are socially and historically constructed, emerging from the prevalent attitudes, beliefs, and values of particular societies at particular times (Archer, 1985; Hays, 1996). Thus, notions of parental responsibility, investment, neglect, and abuse vary as cultural and historical definitions of childhood change. ▲

▲ Issue 4 also addresses the notion of parental responsibility.

For instance, if we think of children as autonomous, rational beings who can make decisions for themselves, then parents will be inclined to grant them considerable freedom and negotiate with them as they would with fellow adults. If we define children as property or as beings who are born with natural trouble-making tendencies, the appropriate parental course of action would be to direct and control them. And if we see children as naturally innocent, parents will be inclined to shelter and protect them as much as possible (Ribbens, 1994).

Throughout history all of these conceptions of childhood have existed. However, these models are not mutually exclusive. Even within a given society, several different conceptions may exist simultaneously. Indeed, all of them exist, to some degree, in contemporary American society, where conceptions of childhood vary across geographic, racial/ethnic, and class lines.

Children as Miniature Adults

According to some historians, the notion of childhood as a distinct phase of life didn't develop in Western culture until the sixteenth and seventeenth centuries (Aries, 1962). Before then, childhood wasn't considered a unique and crucial phase of life that required special treatment and protection. Instead, children were viewed as little more than miniature versions of adults. The evidence for this idea comes from examinations of medieval artwork and family portraits, in which children, if shown at all, are depicted as shrunken replicas of adults (Snow, 1997). Their clothes and bodily proportions are the same as those of their elders.

Other historians disagree with the idea that children were not considered any different from adults, pointing out that some illustrations as early as the thirteenth century show children playing with balls and puppets (Gies & Gies, 1989). In the fourteenth century children appeared in artwork in a way that is recognizably "childlike" to modern observers. Parents were sometimes depicted playing with their children and showing affection. These historians also note that in medieval encyclopedias, separate medical sections on children expressed the need for special care to ensure children's proper physical development.

Despite this disagreement, it's clear that children at the time were defined quite differently than they are today. Many—though certainly not all—parents, it seems, were indifferent to the fate of their children. Between the fourteenth and seventeenth centuries, parents' references to children in diaries, correspondence, and other documents was sparse (Demos, 1986).

Moreover, children were sometimes expected to participate in all aspects of social life right alongside adults (Archer, 1985). According to the diaries of aristocratic children in sixteenth- and seventeenth-century Europe, everything was permitted in their presence: foul language, sexual acts and situations, death, and so on. Adults commonly played with or fondled children's genitals. Children were valued for their role in inheritance and procreation, but they clearly didn't elicit the kind of sentiment that we in the late twentieth century simply assume they are entitled to.

In the colonial period in this country, children often worked alongside adults, doing the same work. Sons were considered miniature versions of their farmer fathers, and girls were models of their mothers (Demos, 1986). But although they were subjected to adult expectations, children were in no way considered equal to adults. They were morally and physically inferior and so were given certain tasks considered "children's work." But they were not seen as a group with their own needs and interests.

Such "unsentimental" treatment of children probably had something to do with the demographic realities of the time. Fatal disease during this era was quite prevalent, and infant mortality rates were extremely high. Young children were not expected to live for very long. In seventeenth-century France, for instance, between 20 and 50 percent of all infants died within the first year after birth (McCoy, 1981). It was commonly believed, therefore, that if one wanted only a few children, it was necessary to have many, because some inevitably wouldn't survive.

Since children were so often lost, parents couldn't allow themselves to get too emotionally attached to them. Many parents of the time referred to a child as "it" until he or she reached an age at which survival was likely. Children were not individuals with their own identities. In some countries, they were considered interchangeable and frequently were given the same name as a sibling who had recently died.

The death of a baby, although considered unfortunate, was certainly not the long-term, emotional tragedy that it is now. Today, we take for granted that no experience could be more painful or sorrowful than the death of a child. Even parents who experience a miscarriage or a stillbirth are expected to mourn the loss of the fetus as if it were once a living child (Fein, 1998). In contrast, parents 300 or 400 years ago seldom attended their children's funerals. In some sections of France, when an infant died he or she was likely to be buried almost anywhere on the premises, like a pet cat or dog. At death, even the children of the rich were treated as paupers, their bodies sewn into sacks and thrown into big, common graves (cited in Zelizer, 1985).

Children weren't seen as deserving of special treatment when they were alive either. Until the late 1800s, child labor was commonly practiced and accepted (Archer, 1985). Like adults, children were expected to "earn their keep." In poor rural families; children worked on the farm as long and as hard as adults simply to help the family survive. In poor urban families, children often engaged in scavenging and street peddling. Prior to child labor laws, children were sometimes given difficult and hazardous jobs, like cleaning out the insides of narrow factory chimneys or operating heavy machinery in paper mills.

In addition, abandoned children were sometimes recruited by unscrupulous adults for use in robbery and prostitution. Some of them were physically mutilated so they could elicit more sympathy as beggars (Stone, 1979). We have little evidence that society completely approved of or tolerated these kinds of practices, but clearly they weren't severely sanctioned either:

> Some [children] had their teeth torn out to serve as artificial teeth for the rich; others were deliberately maimed by beggars to arouse compassion.... Even this latter crime was one upon which the law looked with a remarkably tolerant eye. In 1761 a beggar woman, convicted of deliberately "putting out the eyes of children with whom she went about the country" in order to attract pity and alms, was sentenced to no more than two years' imprisonment. (Stone, 1979, p. 298)

But concern over the mistreatment of children grew throughout the nineteenth century. In 1825 the first House of Refuge in America was founded, an institution whose purpose was to provide sanctuary to children who had been abused or neglected. In subsequent years many similar institutions were established.

Even these, however, were not totally sensitive to the welfare of children. Upon close inspection, their purpose was not to protect children but to prevent them from becoming economic burdens and threats to society. It was widely believed at the time that children who had bad childhoods would grow up to be bad adults. The value of removing children from their homes, then, was not to focus on abuse or neglect but to decrease the likelihood that negative parental influence would be transferred to the next generation. The House of Refuge sought to prevent the potential criminal tendencies of poor urban youths from ever surfacing by removing them from abusive environments and placing them in institutions. Here they would share a "proper growing up" with other abandoned and neglected youths as well as delinquents who had violated the law (Pfohl, 1977).

Children as Little Monsters

Another conception of childhood that emerged several centuries ago is the idea that children have naturally evil tendencies. In medieval Europe, for instance, infants were often considered inherently corrupt, occasionally referred to as unformed animals or "exasperating parasites" (McCoy, 1981, p. 62). Some parents considered them uncontrollable monsters whose arrival threatened to destroy a heretofore peaceful home. Educators of the time felt it was their duty to continually remind parents of children's natural propensity for evil. In the Christian world, children were believed to be marked by original sin at birth and therefore dangerously prone to evil. If left to their own devices, these creatures would harm not only other people but themselves as well (Hays, 1996). One widespread popular fear, for instance, was that if not restrained by tight swaddling clothes, an infant might "tear off its ears, scratch out its eyes, or break its legs" (Stone, 1979, p. 115). Swaddled babies were often hung on a peg on a wall where they couldn't get into trouble.

In Puritan New England, children were subjected to early obedience training to overcome their sinful nature. Any sign of independent thinking on the part of the child was considered blasphemous and therefore punishable. Only when the child's sinful nature was quashed forever could that child become appropriately obedient to God and family.

The task of responsible parents was to stamp out the beast in their children. The old saying, "Spare the rod and spoil the child," reflected this view. Whippings and beatings of children, to "beat the devil out of them, were common" (Straus, 1994). Opium was often used to keep them sedated throughout the day (Beekman, 1977). The Puritans sometimes also used psychological terror to overcome their children's sinful nature, locking rambunctious children in dark closets for an entire day or telling them tales of death and hell to purge the sin (McCoy, 1981). In seventeenth-century Europe, children were sometimes forced to inspect the rotting corpses of people who had been executed so they would be reminded of what happens to bad children when they grow up (deMause, 1975).

Not all attempts to overcome children's "natural tendencies" toward evil and monstrous behavior were this harsh. For instance, baptism and other religious sacraments were often used to gently expunge the child's sinful nature (Hays, 1996).

Today, of course, most popular images of children depict them as cute, lovable, and cuddly members of the family. But still, just below the surface, lurks a nagging fear about their monstrous potential. The contemporary image of the "little monster" is likely to refer not so much to natural sin but to the possibilities of children disrupting social life with their animalistic tendencies. People talk of the "terrible twos" as if it were an inevitable stage of development in which the "demonic" impulses that have been lying dormant in the child finally bloom in all their tantrum-throwing, food-spilling fury.

Media portrayals of children often reinforce the idea that they are potentially destructive. An entire genre of horror films—like *The Exorcist*, *The Omen*, *Firestarter*, *Children of the Corn*, and *The Bad Seed*—and comedies like *Problem Child* and *Home Alone* depict children as precocious and powerful beings who are especially threatening and dangerous to adults (Steinberg & Kincheloe, 1997). Indeed, adults in these films are often depicted as dimwitted buffoons who deserve the havoc these dangerous children offer up. Characters like Kevin in the *Home Alone* films and television's Bart Simpson never hesitate in devilishly taking advantage of the disorder created by incompetent adults.

Such a conception of childhood is also likely to be associated with negative attitudes toward "permissive" parenting. Parents who allow their children significant freedom from restriction are "asking for trouble" or "playing with fire." Such responses reflect a belief that if left unrestrained, children's inherent lawlessness might be unleashed. As one mother put it, "[If] you just give in to them all the time . . . as soon as you start doing that they just push you, and push you, and push you, until they're doing the most awful outrageous things, and you're not able to control them at all." (quoted in Ribbens, 1994, p. 150)

Children as Natural Innocents

By the mid–nineteenth century, reformers and child advocates had achieved some success in convincing people that children were neither miniature adults nor naturally evil. On the contrary, they argued persuasively that children, if anything, are naturally weak and need to be treated with care and compassion; that they should be sheltered from the harsh realities of adult life.

This more sympathetic belief in childhood innocence, though, had a darker side: It implied that children's inherent innocence makes them susceptible to temptation. It wasn't that they were inherently evil, it was that they were easily influenced. Without adequate oversight, they might easily succumb and get into trouble. Thus, most parents continued to believe that only through harsh discipline could they properly shape their children. Children were often beaten, not to subdue the devil inside them but to teach them right from wrong and give them the strength to avoid temptation. Such beatings of children in the nineteenth century were particularly cruel, although they were usually justified on religious grounds. ▲ One theologian offered a theory that God had formed the human buttocks so that they could be severely beaten without incurring serious bodily injury (Stone, 1979).

▲ Read Chapter 6 for more on the thin line between discipline and child abuse.

A century later, the dominant model of childhood is that children's "natural" innocence is to be cherished. It must be protected for as long as possible because once it is gone, it is gone forever. We now take for granted that childhood ought to be carefree and full of fun, play, and creativity (Ribbens, 1994). Children are given license to act in ways that are unacceptable for adults. A child can talk to him- or herself in public, play with imaginary mates, throw tantrums, wear mismatched clothes, or simply do nothing and be scarcely noticed by others. Their inherent "silliness" is a counterweight to the rationality and responsibility that awaits them in adulthood. Indeed, we don't expect, nor do we want, children to worry about paying bills, or impressing bosses, or any of the other multitude of concerns that adults fret about.

We still believe that parents have an abiding duty to guard their children against the corrupting and tempting influences of society (Aries, 1962; Lee, 1982). But most parents are likely to consider this duty in terms of protection and shelter rather than harsh, punitive discipline. For instance, in Western cultures, people simply assume that children should not be exposed to potentially disturbing images of sexuality and death. Discussion of these topics awaits a time (usually adolescence) when, it is generally believed, they have the cognitive ability to appreciate the gravity of such topics.

Indeed, we often think of society as an overwhelmingly dangerous placed filled with constant threats to children's innocence and well-being: child abuse, child pornography, incest, child molestation, harmful rock lyrics, child abductors, and so on (Best, 1993). The concern over childhood innocence has evolved into a powerful belief that all children are potential victims.

Childhood innocence also implies that small children are incapable of making rational decisions for themselves (and, therefore, are not responsible for their acts). Hence, we have made parents liable for their children's transgressions. Several states have enacted laws allowing parents to be cited for failure to reasonably care for their children or for somehow contributing to their children's unlawful behavior. In West Virginia, for example, parents of a child caught defacing a public building can be liable for up to $5,000 in fines. In Louisiana, parents can be found guilty of "improper supervision of a minor" and fined up to $1,000 and imprisoned for up to

6 months if their child associates with a convicted felon, drug dealer, or members of a street gang (Applebome, 1996a). In 1996 a couple from St. Clair Shores, Michigan, was convicted of violating a city ordinance that requires parents "to exercise reasonable parental control" over children after their son repeatedly defied them in public, smoked marijuana, and stole $3,500 from his church. The parents were fined $100 each and ordered to pay $1,000 in court costs (Applebome, 1996b). Implicit in such laws is the belief that parents must be forced, under threat of punishment by the state, to take more seriously their obligation to protect the innocence of their children.

In one sense, the value of childhood innocence reflects a societal concern that letting children become adults too soon is harmful. The collective worries we have about the effects of divorce on children, for instance, are worries that innocent children will be forced to deal with the sort of pain, seriousness, and inconvenience that many people believe children shouldn't have to deal with. You often hear people say that children of divorce are forced to grow up too soon.

Yet at the same time our conception of childhood as a time of innocence and dependency has been undermined in recent years by children's access to adult knowledge about the world (Meyrowitz, 1984; Steinberg & Kincheloe, 1997). Children today are exposed to events, devices, and ideas that would have been inconceivable a generation ago. The cultural "secrets" of adulthood—death, illness, violence, sexuality—are revealed to them in their homes, in their schools, on television, and over the Internet. As a result, children speak more like adults, dress more like adults, and act more like adults than they used to (Meyrowitz, 1984).

Furthermore, childhood has become a dangerous time again. We hear of 12-year-olds getting pregnant, of 7-year-olds being tried for such crimes as rape, assault, and drug smuggling. A spate of schoolyard shooting sprees has made victims and mass murderers of scores of children over the past few years. Children today have to worry about such things as AIDS, drive-by shootings, unemployment, the national debt, the deteriorating environment, and so on. To some observers, the idea of childhood as a sheltered, innocent time has become a nostalgic luxury (Darnton, 1991).

But the loss of childhood innocence is not just the result of exposure to serious social problems and adult issues. Pressures to perform and succeed—often from parents themselves—rob childhood of its anxiety-free state. At increasingly younger ages, children are being asked to "put away their childish things" and get on with the serious task of growing up and measuring up. To get into one of the most prestigious preschools in Manhattan, for example, children must first take a standardized intelligence test. Those who score in the 98th percentile (an IQ of 132) go through a second round of screening in which they are observed by teachers in a classroom. Less than 4 percent of the initial applicants make it through this "cut" and are eventually accepted into the preschool. Although parents are advised that no practice or training technique will help their children pass this screening, many frenetically search for expensive "enrichment" programs that will give their toddler an advantage (Hartocollis, 1997).

The pressure increases when the achievements of American children are compared to those of children in other countries. A recent international comparison of schooling found that students in other countries consistently outperform American students in fields like mathematics and science. The author of the study bleakly proclaimed, "Our best students in mathematics and science are simply not world class" (quoted in Bronner, 1998, p. A1).

Such findings are cause for alarm among many educational experts and political leaders. They point out that American children spend an average of 180 days a year in school, compared to 210 in Germany, 211 in Russia, 222 in Korea, and 243 in Japan (Applebaum & Chambliss, 1995). Japanese schools, in particular, are famous for producing high achievers. Three-year-olds may spend hours a day memorizing stories, learning vocabulary, making calendars, and taking achievement tests so that they can pass the grueling entrance exams to get into the best elementary schools, which in turn serve as gateways into the top high schools and universities (WuDunn, 1996).

Few people would argue that we should emulate the pressurized Japanese educational model. In fact, some critics feel that our society already places far too much emphasis on performance and achievement (Mannon, 1997a). Nevertheless, concern over our ability to compete in the global marketplace has led to nationwide calls for various educational reforms: heavier emphasis on math and science, more time spent on foundational skills like reading and writing, increased computer literacy, and training in political geography and international relations. Some school districts have even done away with recess, a period of the day for relaxation and play. In the end, changes like these—and the concerns and worries that spawn them—are eroding the belief that childhood ought to be a time of playful innocence.

Children as Property

Another common conception of childhood that has existed to greater and lesser degrees throughout history is that children are a form of "property." In the distant past, children literally belonged to their parents. In ancient Rome, for instance, a father could punish his children any way he saw fit, even put them to death if he wished. As late as the seventeenth century, they were considered possessions with no individual rights. They sometimes ended up as security for their parents' debts, as marriage partners for their father to use in expanding his business alliances and property holdings, even as slaves sold for profit (McCoy, 1981).

▲ These rights are often thought to be a matter of family privacy, which is the topic of Issue 3.

Today in our society we don't think of parents as *owning* their children. Nevertheless, parents do retain certain rights over them and often act vigorously to defend those rights. ▲ Parents have the power to keep children in the parents' house, send them to school, or take them places the parents want them to go. Parents can direct children's behavior in many respects, determining how they dress, who they spend time with, what their religion (if any) is, and so on (Collins, 1992).

Related to the notion of property is the idea that children represent economic assets. Not so long ago, children were expected to help support their families financially by working without pay in the family business or on the farm or by going out and getting a job. Even today, children's incomes are legally the property of their parents until the children reach the age of majority.

In this country, the shift from a predominantly agricultural economy to an industrialized one in the nineteenth century revolutionized the "property value" of children. Children were a crucial source of labor in the family economy, and they were a source of financial support in old age (LeVine & White, 1992). Consequently, the birth of a child was hailed as the arrival of a future laborer who would contribute to the financial security of the family (Zelizer, 1985).

By the middle of the twentieth century, however, children were no longer seen primarily as economic necessities. In most families, the main source of income was now the parents, or more accurately the father, working outside the home. As a result, children became economically useless. In fact, people began to see them as downright costly to raise (LeVine & White, 1992). At the same time, though, the culture was beginning to recognize their emotional value. Today's parents are more likely to look to their children for intimacy and less likely to expect anything tangible in return, such as economic support in old age. The contemporary "property" value of children is determined not by their labor potential but by their emotional worth (Zelizer, 1985).

We can see the strength of the emotional value of children when parent-child ties are threatened. In contemporary divorce, for instance, one of the key points of conflict is custody of the children. Some noncustodial parents have gone so far as to defy court orders and kidnap their children. The fact that parents are willing to commit a felony to "have" their children and that courts are willing to prosecute such cases with so much vigor shows how important emotional property rights over children can be (Collins, 1992).

As you can see, childhood is not simply a biological stage of development. Rather it is a social category subject to changing definitions and expectations. Consequently, parental investment in children is less a function of instinct than it is a function of parents' perceptions of their responsibilities toward their children. Cultural notions of appropriate parenting—or, for that matter, of child exploitation, neglect, and abuse—are fluid and varied.

Adolescence

Like childhood, the definition of **adolescence**—that gut-wrenching, noisy, awkward, tumultuous, ill-defined but recognizable stage of life that hovers somewhere between childhood and adulthood—varies in different eras and different cultures. Adolescence is usually thought to be synonymous with puberty. But, as you'll see, the two aren't necessarily the same.

The Social Construction of Puberty

Certainly people throughout human history and all over the world experience the physical changes of **puberty**: the maturing of the genital organs and the development of secondary sex characteristics (for example, breasts and hips in girls; facial hair and deepening of the voice in boys). For both sexes, the onset of puberty often coincides with society's first acknowledgment of the sexual capacity of the youth.

But the physiological changes marking sexual maturation and the changes in social status and cultural meaning that may or may not accompany them are two different things. The physical changes themselves are not solely responsible for what happens to young people during and after puberty. Much more critical are the social reactions to these changes and the meanings that are assigned to them.

Consider, for instance, the different meanings attached to the dramatic biological events that mark the onset of puberty for males and females. For males, that event is the ability to ejaculate. Most adolescent males have their first orgasm while they are asleep, having erotic dreams. *Nocturnal emissions* or *wet dreams* are quite common for young males who have no other sexual outlet. Eventually, they realize that they can bring about the pleasurable experience of orgasm through masturbation. Despite the guilt and anxiety that can surround this activity, virtually *all* males are thought to have masturbated to orgasm before their first sexual experience of any kind with another person (LoPresto, Sherman, & Sherman, 1985; Rubin, 1990).

Now think of the social characteristics of masturbation: Its *only* motive is sexual pleasure; it is gratification for its own sake. And it is something over which the individual has complete control. It isn't tied to romance nor is it dependent on the availability and willingness of sexual partners.

For females, the signifying physical event that marks puberty is menstruation. Menstruation is neither sexually stimulating nor controllable. It is associated with the ability to become pregnant, not sexual pleasure. Hence, unlike males, adolescent females are not provided with the same physical incentive to begin active sexual behavior.

Indeed, the social meaning attached to menstruation has always been somewhat ambivalent. Historically, the onset of menstruation was seen as a serious threat to a girl's emotional and physical well-being. In 1900 the president of the American Gynecological Society stated that "many a young [girl's] life is battered and forever crippled on the breakers of puberty" (quoted in Ehrenreich & English, 1979, p. 110). Physicians advised mothers to do whatever they could to delay the beginning of menstruation in their daughters.

Today, although girls generally equate menstruation with growing up and being normal, many still find it an anxiety-producing event. A survey of adolescent girls found that many of them consider menstruation embarrassing, disgusting, and annoying or dislike the idea of its not being controllable. The vast majority felt that it was a subject that should never be discussed with males (Golub, 1992).

▲ A more extensive discussion of sexuality appears in Chapter 2.

Certainly adolescent girls do become sexually active in their early teens, and the long-standing sexual double standard is beginning to crumble. ▲ But for teenage girls, puberty marks a time when parents and peers perceive them as someone for whom dating and relationships are now appropriate, not necessarily a time when they may pursue sexual pleasure for its own sake (Golub, 1992).

In sum, the cultural focus on ejaculation (for males) and menstruation (for females) as the key biological events associated with puberty serves to reinforce cultural attitudes toward male and female sexuality in adolescence and beyond. For young men, puberty is associated with sexual pleasure for its own sake. For young women, however, sexual pleasure is a small part of their experience with puberty.

Not surprisingly, adolescent girls consistently show lower levels of masturbation than boys, and they are less aroused by explicit sexual material. Their entry into sexual activity is usually associated with romance, love, and affection rather than simple physical desire (Rubin, 1990). These differences—male adolescent desire for sex and female adolescent desire for affection—set the stage for the conflicts and awkwardness that characterize adolescent heterosexual relationships.

The Culture and History of Adolescence

The meaning and significance of puberty vary across societies too. Some societies take no note of the physical changes of puberty, and the transition from childhood to adulthood takes place without social recognition. Among the Rungus of Borneo, for instance, the onset of menstruation does not constitute a recognized stage in a girl's development. Indeed, the Rungus have no institutionalized rites of passage for either males or females upon reaching puberty. Instead, sometime between age 12 and 15, girls and boys have their teeth filed and blackened in an attempt to make themselves more attractive to the opposite sex (Appell, 1988).

Other societies have elaborate initiation rituals that serve to publicly declare that a child is now an adult. The ritual may require that the child undergo a difficult and dangerous task, such as going off alone into the wilderness to hunt an animal, or it may consist of a painful alteration of his or her body. Among the Temne of Sierra Leone, the initiation of a girl into womanhood can last for 1 year. The girls are first taken into the forest for a genital operation and 2 weeks of healing. Then they must move to a special house where they are enclosed for the remainder of the year, hidden from the eyes of men except for brief trips to fetch water. The ritual is so secret that it is considered a serious crime for an initiated girl to discuss the details of what happens to her with a prepubescent, uninitiated girl (Lamp, 1988).

In other cases, the ritual may simply consist of a festive, happy celebration. Among the Asante of Ghana, a girl who reaches puberty sits in public view under an umbrella (a symbol usually reserved for kings and other dignitaries). There she receives gifts and congratulations and observes singing and dancing performed in her honor. When the festivities are over, she is eligible for marriage (Buckley & Gottlieb, 1988).

Sometimes the ritual isn't tied to biological changes at all. In traditional, historical Jewish culture, for instance, a boy became a man when he turned 13, the day of his *bar mitzvah* ceremony. (The female equivalent, *bat mitzvah*, is a recent development that doesn't carry the same developmental meaning as the bar mitzvah.) During the ceremony, he would read from the sacred Torah, something that only adults—and until recently, only men—were allowed to do. He needn't have reached puberty to have a bar mitzvah ceremony. But from that day forward, he would occupy adult status within the community. Today such a ritual is largely symbolic and festive and doesn't carry the same legal significance within the community.

For the most part in the United States, elaborate rituals have not been a part of the arrival of puberty or the entry into adulthood. Prior to the second half of the nineteenth century, youth was an ill-defined category (Skolnick, 1991). Puberty didn't mark any particularly significant status change or life experience. For the vast majority of young people who lived on farms, life as a worker began early—say, around age 7 or 8. As they grew older, they were given more responsibility, and they would gradually move toward maturity. Where occupations were passed down from parent to child, each generation quietly merged into the next.

Adolescence as we know it today appears to have evolved in the late nineteenth century, a consequence of social and economic changes that extended childhood dependency into the teen years. As industrialization gradually moved paid labor away from the home, the gap between adult responsibilities and children's activities widened. As young people were removed from the labor market, child labor laws went into effect. The movement to regulate working conditions and set a minimum age at which children were allowed to work outside their own families helped segregate teenagers from the rest of society and extend their dependence on their parents.

Furthermore, compulsory education became necessary as young people's free time increased. School attendance was required, and truancy became defined as a punishable act. The age-graded school system created separate worlds for children and youth. High schools separated young people from the rest of society and helped create a youth culture.

These social changes helped make adolescence a legally and psychologically recognizable stage of life. It became known as the period between puberty and the ages specified by the law for the end of compulsory education and the beginning of employment. Soon people began writing about the *adolescent experience*, which included the urge to be independent of the family, the search for personal and sexual identity, and the questioning of adult values.

As adolescence emerged as a recognizable stage of life, family ties between parents and their teenage children intensified. Adolescents began depending more completely and for a longer time on their parents than they had in the past. ▲ At the same time, as family size decreased, mothers were encouraged to devote themselves to the nurturing of their children.

▲ "Delayed adulthood" is one of the family transitions discussed in Chapter 8.

But the growing intensity of family life increased the emotional strains of adolescence. A young person's awakening sexuality—particularly that of young men—was likely to have been more disturbing to everyone in the household than it was when young men lived away from home, a common practice before industrialization. Not surprisingly, fear of adolescent sexuality became intense and widespread. Medical books of the late nineteenth century identified masturbation as one of the most destructive and evil of sins.

By the beginning of the twentieth century, *adolescence* had become a household word and part of the social structure of modern society. It also became an important stage in an individual's biography—a recognized, intermediate period of being neither a child nor an adult.

But this socially recognized stage of life is notoriously problematic for young people. We've all heard the horror stories: uncontrollable, awkward, hormone-drenched adolescents getting into trouble, disrespecting their parents, locking themselves in their bedrooms, and swooping around on their emotional roller coasters.

Adolescent girls may have a particularly difficult time. In 1990 the American Association of University Women polled 3,000 boys and girls between the ages of 9 and 15 on their attitudes toward self, school, family, and friends. They found that for the average American girl, adolescence is marked by a loss of confidence in her abilities, especially in math and science; a scathingly critical attitude toward her body; and a growing sense of personal inadequacy (cited in Orenstein, 1994). Although all children experience confusion and a faltering sense of self during adolescence, girls' self-regard drops further than boys' and for many never recovers.

This decrease in esteem is particularly true for white and Latina girls. Between the ages of 9 and 15, the number of girls who are "happy with the way I am" decreases by 38 percent for Latinas and drops 33 percent for whites. But it drops only 7 percent for African-American girls, perhaps because of the more influential role African-American women play in their communities and families and the lower emphasis placed on weight and body shape (Molloy & Hertzberger, 1998).

In many areas of the country, the teen years have become an exceedingly dangerous time. Three-quarters of the deaths of young people between the ages of 10 and 24—about 30,000 a year—occur not from disease but from preventable causes (Foster, 1994). Among youths between the ages of 15 and 19, the risk of being shot to death has more than doubled in the past decade. Any way you measure it, adolescents today are in trouble. They face escalating rates of depression, suicide, substance abuse, delinquency, early sexual activity, and health problems.

But the picture of adolescence as a universally tumultuous time of extreme rebellion and rejection of parents is overstated. For most young people, adolescence is marked by mild rebelliousness and moodiness. Although it is difficult time for everyone involved, it is not one of deep alienation from conventional values for most youth (Skolnick, 1991). One national poll found that the majority of adolescents trust their government, admire their parents, and believe in God (cited in Goodstein & Connelly, 1998).

In fact, parents may suffer more during adolescence than the adolescents themselves. Some research has found that when children reach puberty, parents themselves experience tremendous changes, and their attitudes toward their children change. Marital satisfaction—which typically declines over the course of a marriage—reaches its lowest point when the oldest child reaches adolescence (Rutter, 1995).

Adolescent Sexuality

One of the central societal concerns regarding adolescence is young people's entry into sexual activity. In 1970, 4.6 percent of female 15-year-olds were sexually active; by 1988 the figure had increased to 26 percent (cited in Scott-Jones, 1997). The average age at first intercourse has been decreasing steadily for males and females of all races since the 1950s (Michael, Gagnon, Laumann, & Kolata, 1994). By the time they reach the age of 20, about 70 percent of girls and 80 percent of boys have had a sexual experience outside of marriage.

The increase is particularly apparent among adolescent girls, who are becoming sexually active at younger ages than ever before and are showing levels of sexual frequency that approach male levels. Among sexually active adolescent girls, over 60 percent have had more than one partner, up from 38 percent 2 decades ago (cited in Gibbs, 1993a). However, their reasons for having sex can be quite different from those of boys. One national survey found that close to half of all women cited affection for their partner as the reason for having sex the first time. In contrast, more than half of the men said they were motivated by curiosity and their "readiness" for sex; only a quarter said they had sexual intercourse for the first time out of affection for their partner. In fact, most men said they were not in love with their first sexual partner, but the vast majority of women said they were (Michael et al., 1994).

Peer Pressure and Sexuality   The transformation into a responsible adult is not easy under current social conditions. The caution that should be inspired by news of the health-threatening nature of AIDS and other sexually transmitted diseases is overshadowed by the sexual images and messages bombarding adolescents in movies, television, rock videos, and product advertisements. ▲ At the same time that their sexuality is coming into focus, adolescents encounter stories of sexual harassment and sexual violence in virtually every social location (the workplace, the school, the military, the government, and so on). As a result, they have few role models for positive, responsible adult sexual behavior and lack clear standards for accepting themselves as sexually mature individuals (Scott-Jones, 1997).

Adolescents struggling to establish an identity distinct from their families turn to **peer groups** for a reference point against which to measure themselves and express their "new self"

▲ For more on how culture affects sexuality, read Chapter 2.

(Harris, 1998; Rubin, 1990). But like the family, the peer group has its own demands for conformity and its own requirements for acceptance. Although the adolescent's relationship with a peer group is essential in facilitating separation from the family, the restrictions and expectations it imposes influence behavior in powerful ways.

Adolescent sexual behavior is influenced not just by the need to belong but also by the need to know:

> A member of the peer group is the first to take the plunge and talk about it. It's news; it's consequential. For those who have not yet had the experience, it's riveting. Someone close has actually done it, can describe it, can say what it feels like. The veil of silence is pierced. But for the uninitiated, the mystery deepens; the pressure to know grows. (Rubin, 1990, p. 66)

Sometimes the pressure to become sexually active is direct and specific. But more often the pressure resides in the heightened sexual atmosphere that permeates every facet of adolescent life: fashion, language, music, not to mention daily conversation. Of course, some adolescents are able to resist the pressure. For most, however, even though they may never have any conscious awareness of the pressure, the peer culture in which they reside powerfully influences their sexual decision making (Rubin, 1990).

Teen Pregnancy Young people in our society are becoming biologically mature earlier and earlier. For instance, the average age of menarche (a girl's first menstrual period) has gradually lowered from about 14 years of age a century ago to 12.5 today (Darton, 1991; Skolnick, 1991). Yet we haven't responded by socially accepting young people as adults at earlier ages. In fact, the opposite has occurred: Adolescence has been prolonged and adulthood delayed, with a resulting trend toward later marriage. ▲ Thus, on average, American girls and boys face over a decade of their lives during which they are sexually mature *and* single.

▲ See Issue 8 for a further discussion of this trend.

Many teenagers, almost by definition, are disqualified as "too young" to get serious about a relationship. The kinds of sexuality they are eligible for—for pleasure rather than reproduction, in relationships that are short-term rather than marriage bound—challenge the values about sexuality of many adults (Luker, 1994). Thus, at the same time that young people are biologically ready to have sex (and bear children), society expects them to wait until they are much older before they behave as adults (see Exhibit 5.1). ▲

▲ See Chapter 8 for further discussion of this trend.

Not surprisingly, teens aren't waiting to become sexually active. However, although more adolescents are having sexual intercourse at younger ages than ever before, a recent government report found that the proportion of American teens who've had sexual intercourse actually dropped for the first time in more than 20 years ("Sexual activity," 1997). In addition, the report also found that adolescents today are more likely to use contraceptives than they were in the past.

Furthermore, contrary to popular belief, even with high rates of adolescent sexuality, the number of adolescents having children has actually *decreased* since the 1950s, and the decrease has been sharpest among African Americans. Still, by the time they turn 18, about 7 percent of all whites, 14 percent of all Hispanics, and 26 percent of all African-American women will have given birth (Baca Zinn & Eitzen, 1996).

Exhibit 5.1

Sex Between
Unmarried
Teenagers,
14 to 16, Is
Always Wrong:
Survey of Adults

United States:
1986–1996

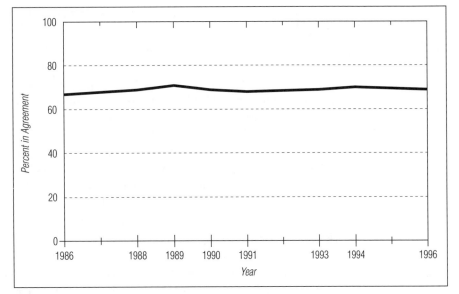

Source of data: National Opinion Research Center, University of Chicago, *General Social Survey, 1986–1996.*

▲ This is one of the
social changes prompting
concern about the
breakdown of American
families, as Issue 8
explains.

What's changed is that young parents today are less likely to be married—or to get married—than their counterparts several decades ago. ▲ In 1970 babies born out of wedlock represented about a third of all babies born to teen mothers (Luker, 1994). In the late 1980s and early 1990s two-thirds of first births to white teenagers and 97 percent of first births to African-American teenagers were conceived out of wedlock.

Out-of-wedlock births among adolescents must be placed in the larger context of non-marital childbearing among all women in this society. In 1993 about 1.2 million infants were born to unmarried American women, nearly fourteen times the 1940 total of 89,500 (Hollander, 1996). Contrary to popular belief, the largest increases in rates of childbearing among single women over the past few years has occurred among older women who are college educated and employed. In 1970 teen mothers were responsible for almost half of all out-of-wedlock births in America; today they account for a little less than a third (Luker, 1994).

Why do we have such strident public outcry against adolescent sexuality and childbearing? Conventional thinking presumes that teen parenthood is associated with a variety of harmful conditions, including disrupted education; fewer job opportunities; an increased likelihood of living in poverty; and an increased likelihood of health, psychological, and educational problems for the children of teen parents. Conservative and liberal politicians alike speak mournfully of the problems caused by "babies having babies." One national poll showed that 80 percent of Americans thought teen pregnancy was a "serious problem" facing the nation (cited in Luker, 1994).

By framing the issue this way, Americans can shift responsibility for many serious social problems to adolescents who are too impulsive or too ignorant to postpone sexual activity, use contraceptives, seek abortion, or, failing all that, give their babies up for adoption to "better" parents (Luker, 1994). In truth, the causes for such problems as poverty are complex and costly to overcome through changes in the minimum wage or the education system, for instance. A more politically expedient solution to reducing poverty and other social problems, some people believe, is to reduce teen birthrates, either by encouraging or even demanding chastity (the politically conservative approach) or by making abortion, contraception, and sex education more readily available (the politically liberal approach).

Reducing teen pregnancy would no doubt be a good thing. After all, the United States has a higher teen pregnancy rate than any other industrialized, democratic country in the world, even though its rate of adolescent sexuality is not higher. But the link between adolescent pregnancy and social problems—especially poverty—is not so straightforward. Many of the adverse conditions associated with adolescent childbearing—educational failure, fewer employment opportunities, lower self-esteem—contribute both to the likelihood of early pregnancy and to the disadvantages that follow from it.

Since poor and minority youth tend to become sexually active earlier than more "advantaged" young people, they are "at risk" of pregnancy for a longer time. Among youngsters who become pregnant, abortions are more common if they are white, affluent, urban, of higher socioeconomic status, get good grades, and come from two-parent families. And a young woman who has other troubles—such as not doing well in school or lacking high aspirations for herself—is also more likely to become pregnant. Hence, many, if not most, teenage unwed mothers are already both disadvantaged and discouraged *before* they get pregnant. No wonder they experience difficulties later in life. As one sociologist put it:

> Teen pregnancy is less about young women and their sex lives than it is about restricted horizons and the boundaries of hope. It is about race and class and how those realities limit opportunities for young people. Most centrally, however, it is typically about being young, female, poor, and non-white and about how having a child seems to be one of the few avenues of satisfaction, fulfillment, and self-esteem. It would be a tragedy to stop worrying about these young women—and their partners—because their behavior is the measure rather than the cause of their blighted hopes. (Luker, 1994, p. 177)

The Social Complexities of Child Rearing

Despite the growing influence of peer groups later on, parents, because of their continuous interaction with their young children, have a crucial effect on their social and emotional development. Parents typically provide children with emotional attachments, communication skills, a sense of right and wrong, and the skills to eventually become functioning adults in the social world.

These things are accomplished through the process of child rearing. **Child rearing** refers to the actions parents take that enable their children to develop a sense of personal identity, learn what people in their particular culture believe, and learn how people are expected to behave. Through support, control, modeling, moral lessons, and direct instruction, parents socialize their children so that they can be transformed from helpless infants into more-or-less knowledgeable members of society.

▲ Chapter 4 focuses on the effects of child rearing on parents.

Child rearing is a developmental process for all involved. We often assume that a child grows, changes, and interacts with a fixed entity: the adult. But parents grow and change too. ▲ And children are not just passive recipients of parental influence. They are energetic actors who frequently exert as much influence on their parents' outlooks, attitudes, and behaviors as parents exert on theirs. Indeed, a being from another planet might very well conclude that a newborn infant is the most influential and powerful member of the family, judging from its ability to train the parent to respond to an elaborate array of cries and squeals.

Parental influence over child rearing is also limited by the fact that many of the socializing functions that families provided in the past now commonly occur in other social settings: in school, with peers and friends, in front of the television. These **agents of socialization** typically become more influential as children get older and are exposed to forces that discourage conformity to parents' wishes. Indeed, as children mature and spend more and more of their time in school, they collectively construct a "peer culture"—a set of shared activities, routines, artifacts, and values—that becomes significantly more influential than their parents in guiding their behavior (Corsaro, 1997).

To make matters more complex, child rearing practices are always shaped by a variety of other factors, including the birth order of siblings, child spacing, family structure, overall family size, neighborhood, the unique personalities of parents and children, and so on. But of particular sociological interest are broad, societal factors, such as culture, social class, race and ethnicity, and gender, which can exert enormous influence on parents' values and expectations regarding their children's development.

Culture and Child Rearing

You have seen how notions of childhood and conceptions of children can change over time. Parents form attitudes about how to raise their children based on cultural definitions of appropriate child rearing strategies. The diversity of cultures in the world naturally supports a wide variety of beliefs and values about child rearing.

In most cultures, child rearing means looking after small children until they reach an age at which they are considered able to participate in some aspects of the adult world (Hays, 1996). Usually, child rearing consists minimally of protecting the child from physical harm and providing enough food and clothing to ensure survival. When environmental, economic, medical, or cultural conditions make survival uncertain, many cultures develop strategies that provide for the well-being of some family members at the expense of others, such as selective neglect, abandonment, even infanticide.

But whether minimal care is provided for every child or not, all cultures seem to acknowledge that early child rearing means more than just ensuring survival. And all societies develop child rearing practices designed to produce individuals who can fit well into that particular society. Yet different cultures have developed different ideas about who children are, what they need and deserve, what their development entails, and who should raise them. No culture's approach stems automatically from a universal definition of the needs of children (see Exhibit 5.2).

Exhibit 5.2

Importance of
Teaching
Independence
to Children in
the Home:
Cross-Cultural
Survey

*Selected Countries:
1998*

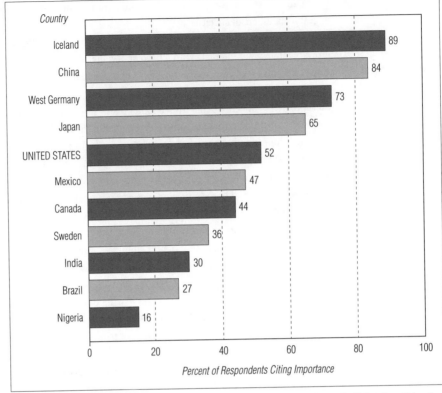

Source of data: Ronald Inglehart, Miguel Basañez, and Alejandro Moreno, *Human Values and Beliefs: A Cross-Cultural Sourcebook.* Ann Arbor: University of Michigan, 1998.

As you know, most Americans feel that children are innocent and priceless and that their upbringing ought to be primarily the responsibility of individual parents and should be centered on the child's needs (Hays, 1996). We assume that if parents attend to the child's drives and desires with consistency and affection, that child will learn to trust them, adopt their values, develop a sturdy self-concept, and turn out to be a well-rounded, normal individual. Exhibit 5.3 gives us a sense of what American parents feel is important to teach children.

In contrast, Japanese parents are likely to view the young infant not as dependent and helpless but as a willful creature whose natural instincts need to be tamed (Kagan, 1976). Any excitement on the part of the child must be suppressed. In the highlands of Guatemala, parents believe that their child's personality is determined by the date of birth. The parents are almost entirely uninvolved in the child's life, standing aside so he or she can grow as nature intended. In many societies—Nigeria, Russia, Haiti, the Dominican Republic, and Mexico, to name a few—many parents think the best way to teach children to be respectful and studious is to beat them. In contrast, most American child development experts believe that hitting a child can deaden his or her spirit and lead to violence later in life (Dugger, 1996b).

Exhibit 5.3

Most Important
Lesson Imparted
to Children:
Survey of Parents

United States: 1996

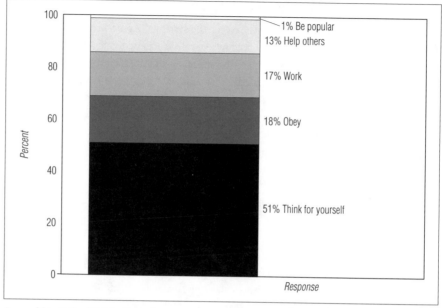

Source of data: National Opinion Research Center, University of Chicago, *General Social Survey, 1996.*

Culture often combines with social standing to produce unique child rearing philosophies. Among the somewhat wealthy Rajput caste in northern India, for example, child rearing practices are directed toward training the child to function within the structure of his or her family, caste, and village (Hitchcock & Minturn, 1963). From infancy, Rajput infants are trained to be emotionally unresponsive. Although they are attended to when they are hungry or fussy and are never left alone, babies are not the center of attention. They spend most of the time lying on their cots, wrapped in blankets to keep off insects. Adult interaction with babies is more likely to be aimed at stopping a response (for example, crying) rather than stimulating one (for example, laughing). Children aren't praised by their parents, who feel such behavior would spoil them and make them disobedient. But they receive little pressure to become self-reliant either and, hence, no encouragement for toilet training, walking, or talking. This lack of self-reliance is consistent with the caste culture, which emphasizes group orientation over individual achievement. ▲

▲ Issue 4 compares
family orientation in
collectivist and
individualist cultures.

In addition, the Rajputs have little feeling that children should be given chores to do simply to teach them "responsibility." This lack of responsibility training is consistent with the Rajputs' caste values. Manual work is considered degrading and spiritually unclean. Most Rajputs are wealthy enough to employ servants to do the menial tasks that would otherwise be done by children.

Despite these dramatic differences in what people believe to be the "appropriate" way to raise a child, most children in all cultures grow up equally well adapted to their particular society.

Social Class and Child Rearing

▲ Issue 7 examines the role of wealth and poverty in family life.

Although we don't have a caste system, the process of raising a child within American society can also be influenced by a family's socioeconomic standing. ▲ Parents from all social classes want what's best for their children and want their children to have a sense of accomplishment, self-satisfaction, and self-confidence. But the values and orientations that children learn as they're growing up are influenced by their family's class standing. Imagine how the experiences of the child of a CEO of a large corporation would differ from those of the child of a single parent on welfare. What sorts of values would the upper-class parent instill in his or her child? What would the welfare parent teach his or her child about how to survive in American society?

Sociologist Melvin Kohn (1979) provides evidence to support the contention that children from different classes are socialized by their parents to have different values and outlooks on life. He interviewed 200 working-class and 200 middle-class couples who had at least one child of fifth-grade age. He found that the middle-class parents were more likely to value characteristics that promote self-direction, independence, and curiosity than were the working-class parents. Conversely, working-class parents were more likely to value characteristics that emphasize conformity to external authority. They want their children to be neat and clean and to follow the rules.

These differences may be related to the conditions that working-class and middle-class parents experience in their jobs. Middle-class occupations are likely to involve considerable task complexity, flexibility, discretion, and freedom from supervision. Working-class occupations, on the other hand, typically involve standardized tasks, rigid schedules, and closer supervision. These conditions can readily be translated into conceptions of social life that parents instill in their children.

Of course, not every middle-class or working-class parent raises children the same way. Nevertheless, Kohn felt these general tendencies were consistent regardless of the sex of the child or the size and composition of the family. Moreover, such differences are directly related to future goals. Working-class parents tended to believe that eventual occupational success and survival depend on their children's ability to conform to and obey authority. Middle-class parents saw future success as stemming from assertiveness and initiative. Hence, middle-class children were much more likely than working-class children to feel that they had control over their own destiny.

▲ For a more detailed discussion of poor families in American society, see Issue 7.

Poor parents have their own values and outlook on life, which exert similar influences on their children's socialization. Perhaps more basically, however, poverty itself is a serious obstacle to successful child rearing. ▲ The proportion of children under the age of 6 who live in poverty has been growing steadily over the past 2 decades. Poverty poses significant health risks for these children; infant mortality, malnutrition, and homelessness are all higher among poor children than others. Poverty also hinders children's development of a strong sense of self-worth and self-confidence. According to the Children's Defense Fund, unlike most Western industrialized nations, the United States lacks federal policies that could help poor parents raise their children. Such policies might include free or inexpensive medical care for all workers and their dependents, guaranteed prenatal care for poor pregnant women, federally funded child care facilities, and guaranteed paid maternity/paternity leave programs for all workers (cited in Aulette, 1994). Such help would at least ensure America's children a healthy start in life, regardless of social class.

Race, Ethnicity, and Child Rearing

The American educational system is designed to socialize children from various racial, ethnic, and religious backgrounds into the dominant culture. Thus, the family remains the primary institution for passing along ethnic traditions and for instilling in children a sense of group identity (Klaff, 1995). ▲ When parents downplay, ignore, or conceal racial or ethnic traditions, their children typically adopt more "mainstream" views and may lose touch with their heritage. (See the Demo•Graphics Essay, "Effects of Race and Ethnicity on Child Rearing Practices," at the end of this chapter).

▲ Issue 6 contains a more detailed discussion of the influence of race and ethnicity on family life.

Child Rearing among Racial Minorities   The day after the Los Angeles riots in May 1992, students in one of my classes became embroiled in a heated discussion of the incident. One student, who was white, expressed concern that young children of all races would now grow up mistrusting or even hating the police. As a child, she had been taught that the role of the police was to help people and that if she were ever in trouble or lost, she could approach an officer for help. She never questioned whether or not the police could be trusted. She then speculated how awful life would become for kids without the sense of safety and certainty she had been socialized to take for granted.

A few of the African-American students in class immediately pointed out to her that their childhood experiences had been quite different. Parents and others in their neighborhoods had taught them never to trust the police because officers were just as likely to exploit and harass them as to help them. They were taught to turn to neighbors if they ever needed help. To them, the police were not knights in shining armor but bullies with badges (see Exhibit 5.4).

Exhibit 5.4

Attitudes Toward Police Officers Striking Adult Males in Certain Situations: Survey of Adults

United States: 1996

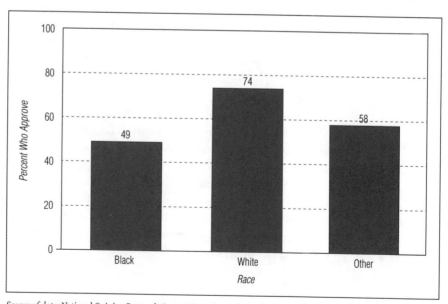

Source of data: National Opinion Research Center, University of Chicago, *General Social Survey, 1996.*

Although the two perspectives of my students are not representative of every white person or every African-American person in this country, the interchange illustrates the powerful impact that race can have on the lessons parents teach their children. The values taught to white children are likely to mirror those of the wider society. Chances are that schools and religious institutions will reinforce the messages expressed to them in their families—for example, that "hard work will pay off in the long run."

For racial minorities, however, child rearing occurs within a more complex social environment (Taylor, Chatters, Tucker, & Lewis, 1990). In 1947 psychologists Kenneth Clark and Mamie Clark conducted an experiment that showed how much black children were internalizing the prejudice that society was directing toward their race. Two hundred and fifty black children were shown two black and two white dolls and were asked to choose the one they preferred. Two-thirds preferred the white dolls (Clark & Clark, 1947). Forty years later, a psychologist replicated this experiment and obtained virtually identical results: 65 percent of the black children preferred white dolls (Powell-Hopson & Hopson, 1988). Society's message, it seems, was still just as powerful in the 1980s.

From such findings we can see that minority children live simultaneously in two different worlds: their ethnic community and "mainstream" society. To simply survive, they must become knowledgeable of the dominant, "white culture" as well as their own. Parents have to teach their children to deal with the realities of racism they will encounter every day (Staples, 1992). Childhood training frequently involves preparation for living in a society that has been and still is set up to ignore or perhaps actively exclude them. Even minority children from affluent homes in integrated neighborhoods need reassurances about the racial issues they will encounter (Comer & Poussaint, 1992). They are more likely than white children from affluent homes to be taught that "hard work" alone might not be enough to get ahead in this society.

However, significant differences may exist within the same ethnic group. Middle-class African-American parents, for instance, are likely to have high educational and occupational expectations for their children. So they try to teach them to have positive attitudes toward hard work, thriftiness, and property ownership (Blackwell, 1985). Many poor African Americans, on the other hand, are so disillusioned and alienated that they see little chance of breaking out of their economic circumstances. These parents are likely to be somewhat limited in their ability to provide guidance for their children and have difficulty controlling their children's behavior (Willie, 1981). Yet not all low-income African-American families are the same. They too have diverse beliefs about desirable child rearing values, goals, and practices (Abell, Clawson, Washington, Bost, & Vaughn, 1996).

Even with these differences, some aspects of child rearing are similar across all groups of American parents. One study of parenting styles, for instance, found that white, African-American, Hispanic, and Asian-American parents are more similar than different in their parenting attitudes, their parenting behaviors, and their involvement with their children (Julian, McKenry, & McKelvey, 1994).

Transracial Adoption   The importance of race in child rearing is clearly illustrated in the contentious debate over transracial adoption. The key issue is whether or not children adopted by parents of a different race should and can receive the cultural training of their racial group. In the 1995 film *Losing Isaiah*, a black lawyer representing a black mother who abandoned her infant son argues during a custody trial that the child should be removed from his white adoptive parents and returned to his birth mother, a recovered crack addict. He states simply, "Black babies belong with black mothers." At one point he asks the white adoptive mother, an affluent pediatrician, whether any of the bedtime stories she reads her son have black characters. She replies that the stories contain characters of all colors. The lawyer responds, "So who is this child to identify with? The yellow 'muppet'"?

The answer to this question is not easy. Experts in child psychology and racial identity differ widely on whether children of color—particularly African-American children—are harmed by being adopted by white families (Williams, 1995). The practice of families adopting children from a different racial group has generated heated debate between those who feel a child's racial and cultural identity are essential to the development of a positive self-image and those who feel race is irrelevant and ought to be minimized or ignored in the interests of finding a solid and loving home for a child. ▲

▲ Identity issues may affect adopted children of any race, as Chapter 4 explains.

Those who support transracial adoption assume that the minority child, who likely comes from a financially depressed and deprived background, will have new and precious opportunities in a more "advantaged" environment. Advocates also argue that transracial adoption has the potential to transform a racially divided society into a racially integrated one. Most important, as the National Committee for Adoption has formally stated, because so many minority children are waiting for adoption, a permanent home rather than racial matching should be of paramount consideration (Adamec & Pierce, 1991). If the child doesn't get love, education, discipline, and so on, no amount of ethnic culture is going to make that child a functioning, successful adult. One African-American author raised by white adoptive parents noted that "kids need love, not cultural models" (McBride, 1996).

But transracial adoption has not been without its critics. In 1972 the National Association of Black Social Workers (NABSW) passed a resolution, still in effect today, against the adoption of black children by white parents:

> Black children should be placed only with black families whether in foster care or for adoption. Black children belong, physically, psychologically and culturally in black families in order that they receive the total sense of themselves and develop a sound projection of their future. Human beings are products of their environment and develop their sense of values, attitudes and self-concept within their family structures. Black children in white homes are cut off from the healthy development of themselves as black people. (quoted in Bartholet, 1993b, p. 72)

In 1971—the year before this policy statement was issued—there were 2,574 transracial adoptions. By 1975—the last year in which such statistics were systematically generated—there were 831 (Bartholet, 1993b). By the early 1990s, 43 states had laws that encouraged public adoption agencies to match a child with prospective parents of the same race (Holmes, 1995).

The standard procedure in most adoption agencies today is to separate children and prospective parents into racial classifications and subclassifications. Children who are classified as black are further categorized by skin tone and sometimes by nationality, ethnicity, or other cultural characteristics. The goal is to place children with parents of the same racial, ethnic, and cultural background. Transracial adoption is a last resort.

These sorts of matching systems have several important implications for adoption agencies. First, adoption workers may actively recruit black families interested in adopting through churches and the media, or offer minority families financial subsidies to encourage them to adopt minority children. In addition, to increase the number of black prospective parents, agencies reach out to include people who would likely be excluded from the white parent pool: singles, older people in their 50s and 60s, and people living on welfare or Social Security (Bartholet, 1993b). Despite these efforts, there continues to be a shortage of black adoptive families. As a result, black children are often "held" in foster or institutional care rather than placed with available white families.

Feeling that such policies do serious harm to minority children who are denied placement, Congress in 1994 passed the Multiethnic Placement Act. It prohibits states and adoption agencies that receive federal money from delaying or denying the placement of a child solely on the basis of race, color, or national origin. This law makes it easier for couples to adopt children with different racial backgrounds ("Black or white," 1994).

Nevertheless, opponents continue to argue that transracial adoptions are harmful to black heritage. They point out that white parents can never provide a black child with sufficient information about what it is like to be black in a predominantly white society. Even well-meaning white parents may not receive the necessary preparation. Agencies with transracial adoption programs typically don't offer parents adequate literature on racial awareness, training sessions, or support systems, and they don't encourage families to live in integrated neighborhoods (Kallgren & Caudill, 1993).

Considering the larger historical and political context, it is understandable that some groups fear transracial adoption. In Australia, as many as 100,000 Aboriginal children were forcibly removed from their families between 1910 and the early 1970s and given to white families to be raised. Motivated by the belief that dark-skinned people were simply incapable of raising a family, government programs attempted to assimilate Aborigines into Australia's white culture, claiming that it was in the best interests of these children to grow up in white society (Farnsworth, 1997; Shenon, 1995).

Similarly, in this country in the 1960s and 1970s, nearly 30 percent of all Native-American children were removed from their families and put up for adoption. Social workers deemed thousands of parents unfit because of poverty, alcoholism, and other problems. So devastating was the removal of these children that the Indian Child Welfare Act was passed in 1978, giving tribes special preference in adopting children of Native-American heritage (Egan, 1993). Recently, however, this law has come under attack. Some children with only a minute trace of Indian ancestry have had their adoption by white parents contested by the tribe. An adoption bill is pending in Congress that would limit a tribal court's jurisdiction in adoption proceedings involving children whose biological parents do not maintain "significant social, cultural or political affiliation with the tribe" (Schmitt, 1996, p. C18).

▲ For a historical view of black family life, read Issue 6.

The civil rights movement of the 1960s instilled in African Americans an unprecedented sense of pride in their racial identity. ▲ At a time when broad-based political power seemed to be within reach, the possibility that some black children were being raised as white was difficult to tolerate. If it was true that black children adopted by white parents had difficulty identifying with the black culture, then they would be less likely to support black political issues. In this sense, the potential loss of culture and racial identity could not be separated from broader political concerns.

Have the fears that children would lose their racial identities been borne out? Research on this issue is mixed. Some studies have shown that a relatively low percentage of young black children adopted by white families have problems with racial identity (Feigelman & Silverman, 1984). Several studies have found that preschool children involved in transracial adoptions are as well adjusted as children from same-race adoptions (Shireman & Johnson, 1986; Zastrow, 1977). Studies that have followed transracially adopted children from infancy to beyond adolescence have found that, despite periodic racial taunts at school and in other public situations, these individuals do not have problems identifying themselves as black Americans, are well adjusted for the most part, and show high self-esteem (Simon, Alstein, & Melli, 1994; Vroegh, 1997).

Beyond the level of individual adjustment, though, the broader problem of cultural heritage remains. There is some evidence that white adoptive parents are likely to minimize or ignore the racial identity of their children, considering parenthood and family more important than race (Ladner, 1978). In a study of thirty adolescent black children adopted by white parents, only ten of them identified themselves as black, six said they were "mixed," and the rest tried to avoid a racial identity altogether by saying they were "human" or "American" (McRoy & Zurcher, 1983).

Gender and Child Rearing

An examination of child rearing would be incomplete without looking at the process by which children develop a sense of gender, which, along with race and ethnicity, is one of the key aspects of our social being. Everything we do—our behavior, our tastes and desires, our intimate relationships, our health and well-being, and our career choices—is linked directly or indirectly to gender. Although our conceptions of gender are constantly being reaffirmed or modified in interactions with others throughout our lives, the early gender lessons we learn in childhood can have a lasting impact.

Sex and Gender In this society, learning gender requires identification as male or female. Sociologists make a distinction between **sex**—a person's biological maleness or femaleness—and **gender**—the psychological, social, and cultural aspects of *being* male or female. ▲ Most people take for granted, of course, that we have only two sex categories and that children are socialized into one or the other:

▲ Issue 5 examines the relationships among sex, gender, and power.

> People are either one or the other, zero or 100 percent. We may modify our decision ("He is an effeminate man"), but we do not usually qualify it ("Maybe he is a man"). If we should have to qualify it, then we seek further information until the qualification is no longer necessary. (Kessler & McKenna, 1978, p. 2)

Yet things aren't always so clear-cut. Not every society subscribes to the biological "fact" that there are two and only two sexes. In traditional Navajo culture, one could be male, female, or *nadle*—a third sex assigned to those whose sex-typed anatomical characteristics were unclear at birth (Martin & Voorhies, 1975). Physically normal individuals also had the opportunity to choose to become nadle if they so desired. Nadle were allowed to perform the tasks of both men and women.

The *hijras* in India are neither men nor women. They are born as men, but they live as women—dressing, standing, walking, and sitting as women. They undergo an operation in which their genitals are surgically removed, but this transforms them into hijras, not women. There are many figures in Hindu mythology that are neither male nor female, hence Indian culture not only accommodates the hijras but views them as meaningful, even powerful beings (Nanda, 1990).

Even in this society, the male/female categorization is not always sufficient. **Hermaphrodites**, for instance, are individuals in whom sexual differentiation is either incomplete or ambiguous. Experts estimate that 1 baby in 2,000 is born with sex organs that don't fit either of the standard categories (Cowley, 1997). Hermaphrodites may have the chromosomal pattern of a female but have the external genitalia of a male; or they may have both ovaries and testicles. These individuals don't fall neatly into either sex category. Indeed, according to one prominent biologist, instead of two sexes, we have many gradations of sex running from female to male, and along that spectrum lie at least *five* sexes (Fausto-Sterling, 1993). In addition to males and females, we have "true hermaphrodites," people who possess one testis and one ovary; "male pseudohermaphrodites," people who have testes and some aspects of female genitalia but no ovaries; and "female pseudohermaphrodites," people who have ovaries and some aspects of male genitalia but no testes.

Debate over clinical responses to cases of babies with "ambiguous genitalia" has become more heated recently. In 1973, researchers published an account of an infant boy whose penis had been accidentally cut off by a surgeon who was trying to repair a fused foreskin. Convinced that a boy couldn't adjust to the loss, the doctors recommended to the parents that he be reared as a girl even though he had a twin brother. The parents agreed.

The infant's testicles were removed, and a preliminary attempt to construct a vagina was made. The parents treated their genetically male child as a daughter, choosing feminine clothes, toys, and activities. The child appeared to have accepted the new identity and to be content with life as a female. The case was publicized worldwide and entered the scholarly literature as proof that sexual identification has more to do with socialization and exposure to the cultural world of boys and girls than with anatomy or genetics.

In 1997, however, a follow-up study refuted the initial reports of glowing success. The authors reexamined the child's life through adolescence and into adulthood and concluded that the female identity never took. During the elementary school years, the child tore off dresses, rejected dolls, and sought out male friends. Instead of imitating her mother putting on makeup, she mimicked her father shaving. At age 12, she began receiving estrogen treatments so that breasts would grow during puberty, but she disliked the effects and stopped taking treatments. At age 14 she renounced her female identity and chose to live as a man, even undergoing surgery to attempt a reconstruction of the male genitalia. At 25 "he" married a woman and adopted children (cited in Angier, 1997a).

The researchers used this information to underscore the importance of prenatal events like exposure to hormones in building sexual identity. An editorial accompanying their report stated, "Despite everyone telling him constantly that he was a girl and despite his being treated with female hormones, his brain knew he was a male. It refused to take on what it was being told" (quoted in Angier, 1997a, p. A10). Indeed, according to his twin brother, "There was *nothing* feminine about [her]. She walked like a guy. She talked about guy things, didn't [care] about cleaning house, getting married, wearing makeup.... We both wanted to play with guys, build forts and have snowball fights and play army" (quoted in Colapinto, 1997, pp. 64–65).

This case study is being used to call for changes in the treatment of babies born with ambiguous genitalia. Every month dozens of sexually ambiguous newborns are "assigned" a gender and undergo surgery to confirm the designation (Cowley, 1997). About 90 percent of such infants are designated female, because creating a vagina is considered surgically easier than creating a penis (Angier, 1997b). But the authors of this case study proposed that many of these "constructed females" may not be happy with their enforced identity and may be better off being reared as boys.

Not everyone agrees, however. For instance, an increasingly vocal group of "intersexuals"— people who fall between unambiguous males and unambiguous females on the sexual continuum—protest that many of the surgical techniques used to "correct" the problem of anomalous genitalia are mutilating and potentially harmful. They cite cases of people with ambiguous genitals being robbed of any sexual sensation in the attempt to surgically "normalize" them— that is, give them the physical appearance of either a male or a female. They fear that the earlier case will motivate doctors not to reduce the overall number of surgical interventions but to treat more hermaphrodites as males and try to construct a penis from a small amount of tissue. The founder of the Intersex Society of North America eloquently summed up her organization's frustration: "They can't conceive of leaving someone alone" (quoted in Angier, 1997a, p. A10).

The medical profession can't leave these individuals alone because to do so would undermine our *cultural understanding* of sex. Cases of hermaphroditism are usually defined by biologists as some variation on the two existing categories and not as a third, fourth, or fifth category unto itself. Furthermore, upon the diagnosis, a decision is always made to define the child as either male or female. The drastic surgical intervention that ensues is undertaken not because the infant's life is threatened but because our entire social structure is organized around having two and only two sexes (Lorber, 1989). The male-female dichotomy in our culture is so essential to our way of life that those who challenge it are considered either crazy people or cultural heretics who are being disloyal to the most fundamental of biological "facts." To suggest that the labels "male" and "female" are not sufficient to categorize everyone is to threaten a basic organizing principle of social life.

The Acquisition of Gender   The male/female sexual dichotomy that we take for granted in this society influences how children learn gender. One's identity as boy or girl, man or woman has a profound impact on his or her self-development, determining paths chosen, decisions made, and treatment received at the hands of others. ▲ Gender distinctions can have serious educational, political, and economic implications.

▲ Issue 5 discusses how gender affects roles within the family; the intersection of gender, work, and family life is also discussed in Chapter 3.

How do children come to understand their gender in a way that is consistent with larger cultural dictates? The gender socialization process begins the moment a child is born. A physician, nurse, or midwife immediately starts that infant on a career as a male or female by authoritatively declaring whether it is a boy or girl. In most hospitals the infant boy is wrapped in a blue blanket, the infant girl in a pink one. From that point on, the developmental paths of males and females diverge. The subsequent messages that children receive from families, books, television, and schools not only teach and reinforce gender-typed expectations but also influence the formation of their self-concepts.

Parents are their children's first source of information about gender. If you asked parents whether they treated sons any differently from daughters, most would probably say no. Yet considerable evidence shows that what parents do and what they say they do are two different things (Lips, 1993; Lytton & Romney, 1991; Renzetti & Curran, 1989). Gender-typed expectations are so ingrained in American parents that they are often unaware that they are behaving in accordance with them (Goldberg & Lewis, 1969; Will, Self, & Datan, 1976).

In one study, when thirty first-time parents were asked to describe their newborn infants (less than 24 hours old), they frequently used common gender stereotypes. Those with daughters described them as "tiny," "soft," "fine-featured," and "delicate." Sons were seen as "strong," "alert," "hardy," and "coordinated" (Rubin, Provenzano, & Luria, 1974). A replication of this study 2 decades later found that today's parents continue to perceive their infants in gender-stereotyped ways, although to a lesser degree than in the 1970s. In addition, mothers are more emotionally responsive to girls and encourage more independence with boys. Fathers spend more time with their sons and engage in more physical play than with their daughters (Karraker, Vogel, & Lake, 1995). Parents also use different subtle tones of voice and pet names for their female and male children, like "Sweetie" for girls and "Tiger" for boys (MacDonald & Parke, 1986; Tauber, 1979).

New parents, understandably proud of their new parental status, can be very sensitive about the correct identification of their child's sex. Even parents who claim to consider sex and gender irrelevant nevertheless spend a great deal of time ensuring that their child has the culturally appropriate physical appearance of a boy or girl. This sensitivity is not surprising given the centrality of sex and gender in our culture and its distaste for ambiguity. Misidentifying the sex of their baby can be an embarrassing, even painful experience for some parents, which may explain why parents of a girl baby who has yet to grow hair (a visible sign of sex in this culture) will often tape pink ribbons to the bald baby's head. In many Latin American countries, families have baby girls' ears pierced shortly after birth, providing an obvious visual indicator of the child's sex.

Both boys and girls learn at a very young age to adopt gender as an organizing principle for themselves and the social world in which they live (Howard & Hollander, 1997). They begin to distinguish the female role from the male role, learn to see a broad range of activities as exclusively "appropriate" for only one sex or the other, and come to identify themselves accordingly. Most developmental psychologists believe that by the age of 3 or so most children can accurately answer the question "Are you a boy or a girl?" (Kohlberg, 1966). But to a very young child, being a boy or a girl means no more than being named Bobby instead of Betty. It is simply another characteristic, like having brown hair or ten fingers. The child at this age has no conception that gender is a category into which every human can be placed (Kessler & McKenna, 1978).

At around age 5 the child begins to see gender as an invariant characteristic of the social world—something that is fixed and permanent. Likewise, children exhibit a high degree of gender typing in their preferences for particular activities (Kohlberg, 1966). Children at this age express statements such as "men are doctors" and "women are nurses" as inflexible, objective "truths." Only later are they able to realize that gender roles are more flexible than they once believed.

Parents, siblings, and other significant people in the child's immediate environment provide these early lessons of gender. Often these individuals serve as observational models with whom the child can identify and whom the child can ultimately imitate. Other times the lessons are more purposive and direct—as when parents provide their children with explicit instructions on proper gender behavior, like "Big boys don't cry" or "Act like a young lady."

Evidence suggests that the instructions for boys are particularly rigid and restrictive in our culture and the social costs for their gender-inappropriate behavior are disproportionately severe (Franklin, 1988). The "sissy" has much more difficulty during childhood than the "tomboy." This difference is clearly linked to the different social value ascribed to men and women.

As children grow older, parents tend to encourage more gender-typed activities. Research consistently shows that children's household tasks differ along gender lines (Antill, Goodnow, Russell, & Cotton, 1996). For instance, boys are more likely to mow the lawn, shovel snow, take out the garbage, and do the yardwork, whereas girls tend to clean the house, wash dishes, cook, and babysit the younger children (White & Brinkerhoff, 1981).

Parents also influence their children's gender through the things they routinely purchase for them, such as clothing. Not only do clothes inform others about the sex of an individual, they also send messages about how that person ought to be treated. Clothes direct behavior along traditional gender lines (Shakin, Shakin, & Sternglanz, 1985) and encourage or discourage certain gender-typed actions. Frilly dresses do not lend themselves easily to rough and dirty play. Likewise, it is difficult to walk quickly or assertively in high heels and tight miniskirts. Clothes for boys and men rarely restrict physical movement in this way.

Toys, too, serve to distinguish between the sexes. The toy industry has been built on a solid foundation of sex stereotypes. War toys, competitive games of strategy, and sports paraphernalia have been long-standing staples of the toy industry's boy market. The words *hero, warrior, battle,* and *speed* characterize boys' toys. Dolls, makeup kits, and toy kitchens continue to be profitable items for girls. The vocabulary of girls' toys consists of terms like *nurturing, love,* and *magic* (Lawson, 1993). Sex-specific toys foster different traits and skills in children and thereby serve to further segregate the two sexes into different patterns of social development. Boys' toys encourage invention, exploration, competition, and aggression. Girls' toys encourage creativity, caregiving, and physical attractiveness (C. L. Miller, 1987).

Many people today, concerned with the overemphasis on male/female distinctions and sex segregation in social institutions and occupations, are pushing for less restrictive conceptions of gender (Lips, 1993). To achieve this goal, some espouse **androgynous socialization**—bringing up children to develop both male and female traits and behaviors (Bem, 1974). Advocates for androgynous socialization see no reason, except for a few anatomical and reproductive differences, to differentiate males from females. In fact, modern parents are probably more likely than their predecessors to be concerned about gender stereotypes and to attempt to overcome them in the raising of their children.

Yet parents' ability to carry out androgynous socialization may be somewhat limited (Sedney, 1987). Four- and five-year-old children often engage in strongly gender-stereotypical play, regardless of the attitudes and beliefs expressed by their parents (O'Brien & Huston, 1985). As they get older, children, particularly boys, tend to resist nonstereotypical gender models (Katz, 1986). Findings like these have led some researchers to suggest that the effects of nongender-typed socialization are more likely to show up in adulthood rather than in childhood, after individuals have developed the cognitive maturity and the confidence to incorporate nontraditional gender attitudes and beliefs into their everyday lives (Sedney, 1987).

The Sexual Orientation of Parents Between 6 and 14 million American children are believed to live with gay male or lesbian parents (Patterson, 1992). Given our society's reluctance to acknowledge the legitimacy of gay families, it's not surprising that some people worry about the ability of gay parents to successfully raise children. Some people are concerned that these children will become gay or lesbian themselves. Others feel that these children will be less psychologically healthy and exhibit more adjustment and behavioral problems than children growing up in heterosexual homes. Finally, some people worry that children raised by homosexuals will experience teasing, ostracism, or traumatization by peers and the public at large (Patterson, 1992).

Are these beliefs about the dangers of growing up in a gay or lesbian household warranted? Can a parent's sexual orientation impose undue burdens on a child? Over the past 20 years, numerous studies have compared children growing up with homosexual parents (usually lesbian mothers) with those of other parents. Researchers have consistently found few or no differences between the two groups of children in the development of gender identity, gender role behavior, or sexual orientation (Gartrell et al., 1996; Golombok & Tasker, 1996; Gottman, 1990; Patterson, 1992). Studies have also found no deficits in self-concept, intelligence, or moral judgment among children of lesbian mothers (Patterson, 1994). Furthermore, children raised by lesbian mothers have normal, healthy relationships with other children as well as adults (Golombok, Spencer, & Rutter, 1983). In fact, some studies show that lesbian mothers are more child oriented (Miller, Jacobsen, & Bigner, 1981) and self-confident (Greene, Mandel, Hotvedt, Gray, & Smith, 1986) than heterosexual parents.

In sum, we have no evidence to suggest that the psychosocial development of children growing up with homosexual parents is compromised. In fact, a review of all the research on this issue reveals not a single study that has found children of lesbian or gay male parents to be disadvantaged in any significant respect. In short, "homosexual" home environments are just as likely to support and enable children's psychosocial growth as "heterosexual" homes are (Patterson, 1992). ▲

▲ For more on gay and lesbian families, read Issue 1.

The Issue of Child Care

Because so many families these days consist of two working parents or a single parent who works, more and more families are finding that they must look to people outside the home for assistance in raising their children. More than half the preschool-age children with working mothers in this society are in some form of day care, whether it's a private babysitter, day care center, or preschool. The rest are cared for by relatives (Lubeck & Garrett, 1990).

Often parents feel great guilt about using outside child care and worry about the effects that such arrangements will have on the child. Some social critics question whether working parents can possibly devote sufficient time to their children's needs. Research has found that parents in dual-earner families do spend less time with their children than parents in single-earner, "traditional" families (Nock & Kingston, 1988). A recent national survey found that employed women devote, on average, less than 1 hour a day to undivided child care; for employed men the figure is $2^1/_2$ hours a week (Robinson & Godbey, 1995). Some researchers have found a relationship between day care and later behavior problems like noncompliance and aggression (Howes, 1990).

But most research suggests that the simple fact that a child spends time each day with a caretaker other than his or her parents is not sufficient to cause harm. Instead, the child's development is affected by the quality of care both inside and outside the home. A long-term study by the National Institute of Child Health and Human Development found that children who receive good care and a lot of attention at home seem unaffected by day care (cited in "Child care caste system," 1998). And regardless of the quality of the care and the age when the child enters it, the emotional attachments between parent and child do not appear to be damaged by the experience (Vobejda, 1996). Only those children who don't get good parenting at home are less securely attached to their parents. Indeed, high-quality child care offered by sensitive and committed providers can actually enhance a child's development.

What makes the situation particularly stressful for American parents, though, is the lack of a coherent national policy regarding child care. Virtually all western European countries have a policy of universal but voluntary preschool for children from age 2 to when they begin compulsory education (Kamerman & Kahn, 1995). The preschools tend to be heavily subsidized by the governments and so cost little to parents who want their children to attend. These programs are seen as part of the overall education system and are therefore designed to enhance children's development and prepare them for school. They are so highly valued for the cognitive stimulation they are believed to offer that even parents who aren't employed send their children to preschool. In Germany, Denmark, Finland, and Sweden the vast majority of children between the ages of 3 and 5 attend preschool; in France, Belgium, and Italy over 90 percent of children attend (Kamerman & Kahn, 1995).

In contrast, most American child care providers fall under private auspices, both nonprofit and for-profit. Some are licensed, many are not. We have a hodgepodge of providers that includes nannies, au pairs, relatives, day care centers, and private homes. Their quality tends to be uneven, forcing parents to "shop around" for the best—or for many families, least expensive—situation. A full-time nanny may provide the most personal and attentive care but can cost from $250 to $2,000 per week. The average day care center costs considerably less—about $90 per week—but often day care centers have a high child-to-adult ratio, and they are frequently staffed by untrained and underpaid workers. The average child care worker in this country earns about $6 an hour, which is less than the wage earned by the average parking lot attendant. Moreover, federal changes in welfare laws—which force women with young children to work after a period of time—have increased the demand for jobs that require little education or job training. Consequently, more and more child care centers are hiring untrained welfare recipients to whom they can pay minimum wage (Lewin, 1998d).

Unlike child care in Europe, American child care is typically seen as separate from the formal education system. Consequently, most organized facilities are perceived merely as places where working parents can send their children so the children won't go unsupervised.

The relative inattention to child care in this country is beginning to disappear. Most Americans today have begun to see child care as an inevitable feature of modern family life. ▲ Other changes in society—in particular, recent welfare reforms that require most recipients to start working within 2 years of receiving benefits—have crippled the argument that all mothers should stay at home with their children. New welfare laws provide a year of transitional child care assistance for women who leave welfare to work. And some states provide child care assistance to low-income families even if they haven't been on welfare. In 1998 President Clinton proposed a major child care initiative, including increased subsidies for low-income families and expanded tax credits for child care expenses. If such legislation passes, children of all social classes will benefit.

▲ The dual-earner family, whose stresses and adaptations are discussed in Chapter 3, is probably here to stay, as Issue 8 and Chapter 9 discuss.

Conclusion

As a society, we express great love for children. They occupy a hallowed place in our culture, and it is upon their tiny shoulders that we place our most precious hopes and dreams for the future. On a personal level, most parents today tend to regard their children with deep pleasure. To many parents, there is no greater delight than seeing the first sign of recognition on an infant child's face or coming home to children's hugs after a tough day at work. These are the gifts that sustain us as parents.

But our cultural and personal ideals regarding children don't always match the reality of their lives. Many children today face a miserable life filled with poverty, ill health, and violence. Others face a life of parental indifference or worse. Even those children who are fortunate enough to have parents who love them or to be born into a family with the economic means to sustain a comfortable life can sometimes bear the heavy burden of unrealistic expectations and excessive pressures to grow up and measure up.

Such societal ambivalence is made even more complex by the inherent irony of child rearing: We never really know what the long-term effects of our parenting will be. As I watch my own children develop, I can't help but wonder if the way I'm raising them is the "right" way. I think most parents have gnawing worries that they'll say something or do something to their children that will somehow tarnish them for life.

What makes child rearing all the more unsettling is the knowledge that we can never completely determine and control the course of our children's lives. Much as some parents would like to believe otherwise, powerful forces over which they have absolutely no control will profoundly affect the way they raise their children. Societywide economic conditions, for instance, can place extraordinary financial and emotional strains on parents, which spill over into the relationship they have with their kids. Even more directly, much of parents' influence over their children stops at the front door. Children easily forget lessons about the virtues of nonviolence in the throes of playing a friend's shoot-'em-up video game. To be part of the group out in the schoolyard, they blithely ignore our pleas to judge other children as individuals, not on the basis of their gender or other social attributes.

In short, it's worth remembering that childhood and adolescence are not just universal stages of growth and that child rearing is not simply a preprogrammed skill. They always take place within a particular cultural and historical context. And they are always influenced by prevailing values, social forces, and cultural definitions. These things can either markedly enhance or drastically impede even the most loving and competent parents' ability to raise their children "successfully."

CHAPTER HIGHLIGHTS

- The experience of being a child is influenced, to a large degree, by broader social definitions of childhood. Throughout history, children have been seen as miniature adults who deserve no special treatment, little monsters that need to be tamed, innocent beings who deserve nurturance and love, and parental property with no special rights. Childhood is not merely a biological stage of development. It is a social category, subject to changing definitions and expectations.

- Like childhood, adolescence is a socially defined stage of life. It marks the transition between childhood and adulthood. Adolescence, as we know it, emerged in the late nineteenth century as a product of social, economic, and educational changes that extended childhood dependency into the teen years.

- In some societies, the change from child to adult is marked by an elaborate rite of passage. In other societies, as in ours, the change is much less explicit and much more gradual.

- Broad gender ideologies affect the ways males and females experience adolescence, especially regarding sexuality.

- The ways that children are raised depends on cultural definitions of appropriate child rearing, social class, and race and ethnicity.

- We learn our gender and the social expectations that go with it through socialization, especially within families. Whereas sex refers to biological characteristics, gender refers to the psychological, social, and cultural aspects of being male or female. The different ways male and female children are raised have serious educational, political, and economic implications. Gender socialization begins from the moment we're born and continues throughout our lives.

- Institutional child care has become a common feature of American family life. Its quality, though, still remains uneven; and despite some recent high-level attention, it remains a low political priority.

DEMO•GRAPHIC ESSAY

Effects of Race and Ethnicity on Child Rearing Practices

One of the chief determinants of childhood experiences in the United States is race or ethnicity. Children face somewhat different opportunities and family structures because of the social inequities that may be closely related to race or ethnicity in the United States. For example, Exhibit 5-A demonstrates the correlation between ethnicity and the number of parents in a household. The great majority of white children live with two parents. In contrast, over half of black households with children are headed by a mother only. Among all three ethnic groups shown in the exhibit, father-only households represent small proportions of the total, although the largest proportion is among black households, contrary to popular myths about the lack of participation by black fathers with their children.

Exhibit 5-A

Family Household
with Children Under
18 (by ethnicity)
United States: 1996

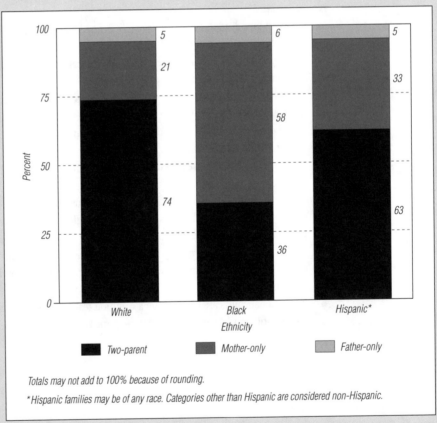

Totals may not add to 100% because of rounding.

*Hispanic families may be of any race. Categories other than Hispanic are considered non-Hispanic.

Source of data: U.S. Bureau of the Census, *Statistical Abstract of the United States: 1997* (117th edition). Washington, DC, 1997.

Compare Exhibit 5-A with Exhibit 5-B, which shows trends in the percent of U.S. children living below the poverty level. White children, the most likely to be living with two parents, have been the least likely to live in poverty. Both black and Hispanic children have been much more likely than white children to live in poverty, although somewhat higher percentages of black children live in poverty. Across time, the rates of poverty have increased steadily for both white and Hispanic children. But for black children, poverty rates declined slightly between 1990 and 1995.

The economic data in Exhibit 5-B have implications for the kinds of child care arrangements parents use, as shown in Exhibit 5-C, although cultural factors can also affect the kinds of choices parents make. For example, Hispanic children are most likely to be cared for only by parents. White children are most likely to receive child care from nonrelatives; and black children are most likely to receive child care from relatives. These differences probably reflect the costs of each kind of care, as well as cultural preferences. In addition, language barriers in institutional settings might explain why black children and white children are more likely than Hispanic and other children to receive child care in a center-based program.

Exhibit 5-B

Children Living below Poverty Level (by race and Hispanic origin)

United States: 1970–1995

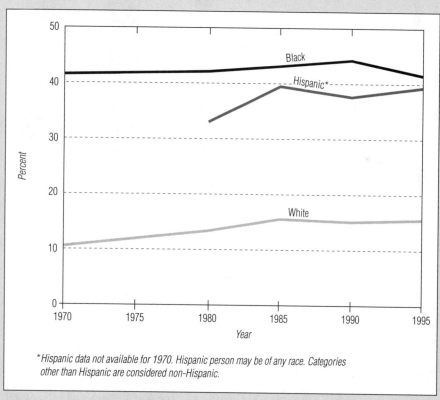

Hispanic data not available for 1970. Hispanic person may be of any race. Categories other than Hispanic are considered non-Hispanic.

Source of data: U.S. Bureau of the Census, *Statistical Abstract of the United States: 1997* (117th edition). Washington, DC, 1997.

Exhibit 5-C

Regular Child Care
Arrangements for
Children Under 6
Years Old

United States: 1995

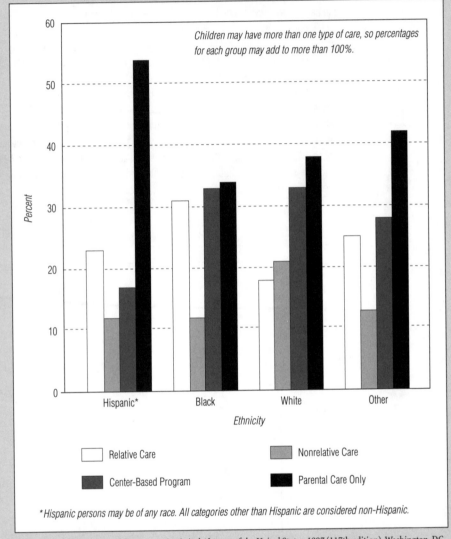

Children may have more than one type of care, so percentages for each group may add to more than 100%.

Relative Care   Nonrelative Care

Center-Based Program   Parental Care Only

Hispanic persons may be of any race. All categories other than Hispanic are considered non-Hispanic.

Source of data: U.S. Bureau of the Census, *Statistical Abstract of the United States: 1997* (117th edition). Washington, DC, 1997.

Questions for Further Study

1. **Children who live with only one parent, instead of both, do not necessarily have only one adult for social and economic support. How could the single-parent households in Exhibit 5-A be separated into several categories to include other adults along with the single mother or single father? For example, one possible single-parent household cat-**

egory could be a father and child living with one or more of the child's grandparents. Try to define two other categories of households that include at least one other adult in addition to the single parent.

2. The poverty rates for white children increased more between 1970 and 1980 than in any other period shown in Exhibit 5-B. What might be the reason? Hispanic children, however, experienced a greater increase than either black or white children in poverty rates between 1980 and 1990. What might be the reason for this difference?

3. The quantitative data in Exhibit 5-C could be supplemented with qualitative data gathered in various child care settings. What further questions does Exhibit 5-C suggest that could be answered by doing field research or carrying out interviews? Suppose your school wanted to study the child care options for students and employees. What items would be important to include in a survey questionnaire?

YOUR TURN

Being a child or *being* an adolescent is not simply a biological stage of development. It is a social identity. People's experiences in these identities emerge from a particular cultural and historical context as well as the process of socialization that takes place within their families. But many other social institutions assist in the process of socialization in ways that are sometimes not immediately apparent.

To see firsthand how this sort of socialization works, visit a local shopping mall. Most malls today have a children's clothing store. If yours doesn't, go to one of the large department stores and find the children's clothing section. Start with the infant clothes. Note the differences in the style, color, and texture of boys' clothes versus girls' clothes. Collect the same information regarding clothes for toddlers, preschool children, and school-age children. Now find a store that specializes in the clothes of "teens" or "preteens." How do clothing styles differ along gender lines at this age level?

After collecting your data, try to interpret the differences you noticed. Why do they exist? What do these differences say about the kinds of activities in which boys and girls are expected and encouraged to engage? For instance, whose clothes are "dainty"? Whose are "rugged"? How do these clothing differences reinforce our cultural conceptions of masculinity and femininity? How do clothing styles popular among teens encourage sexuality?

The next stop on your sociological shopping trip is the toy store. See if you can tell when you've entered the "boy" section or the "girl" section. How do you know? How do the toys differ? Note the differences in color, sound, and type of material used in the store fixtures and displays.

What sorts of interactions with other children do the toys encourage? Competition? Cooperation? Which sex's toys are designed for active play? Which encourage passive play? For what sorts of adult roles do the toys prepare children?

Finally, find a bookstore that has a children's book section. Are there "boy" books and "girl" books? How can you tell? What are the differences in the sorts of characters and plots that are portrayed? Does the bookstore have a section that contains books designed to help adolescents through puberty? If so, do these books offer different advice to adolescent boys and girls?

Use your findings to discuss the role that consumer products play in socializing children into "appropriate" gender roles. Why is there so much sex-typing in these products? What are the "gender lessons" that preteens and teens receive? Is there more or less gender segregation as children get older? Do you think manufacturers are simply responding to market demands (that is, do they make sex specific products because that's what people want), or do manufacturers play a role in creating those demands?

CHAPTER 6

Intimate Violence

The 1990s has been a decade awash in highly publicized cases of intimate violence. Names such as Menendez, Bobbitt, and Simpson have become synonymous with child abuse, sexual assault, victim retaliation, mayhem, and murder. Hardly a week goes by without some famous actor, musician, or athlete being accused of beating his wife or girlfriend. But what is perhaps even more disturbing than these high-profile cases is the sheer volume of incidents that few of us ever hear about—those local stories that never make the national news and remain tucked away in the back sections of newspapers. The following is just a sampling of domestic violence incidents reported in one newspaper, the *New York Times*, during the first 4 months of 1997. All occurred in New York City. None was considered newsworthy enough to appear as front-page headlines:

- January 1: A 38-year-old mother of three was charged with reckless endangerment in the death of her 10-month-old daughter who was found with a fractured skull, fractured leg, and multiple blunt-force traumas.
- January 5: A 49-year-old man was charged with assault and attempted murder after he threw rubbing alcohol on his wife and set her on fire.
- January 6: A 22-year-old mother was arrested and charged with murder for throwing her newborn girl out of a third-story window into an alley.
- February 12: A 35-year-old man who spent 16 months in prison for killing a baby in 1985 was taken into custody on charges that he fractured the skull of his girlfriend's 5-month-old son.
- February 22: A pregnant mother and her boyfriend were each charged with seven counts of aggravated assault and endangering the welfare of a child after all seven of her children were found with bruises and welts.
- March 7: A 26-year-old man was arrested after a rampage in which he beat his five young children. Two of the children—ages 3 and 4—suffered broken legs.
- March 27: A 23-year-old man was charged with kidnapping and murdering his fiancee just days after she had obtained a court order of protection against him.
- March 31: A 27-year-old woman was charged with murder after taking her 5-year-old son— his bruised body already lifeless from weeks of starvation and abuse—to a nearby hospital.
- April 2: A 33-year-old woman was arrested on charges that she severely burned her 7-year-old daughter by forcing her to sit on a radiator as punishment for fighting with her siblings.
- April 10: A 28-year-old woman was charged with attempted murder for trying to strangle her 8-year-old daughter on a busy sidewalk while another woman tried to shield them from view.
- April 11: A 22-year-old man was charged in the beating death of his girlfriend's 3-year-old son. The boy died from stomach wounds, blunt trauma, and internal bleeding.
- April 21: A 33-year-old man was charged with attempted murder for beating his girlfriend's 14-month-old son into unconsciousness.

We can only imagine how many other cases took place during that period which either didn't result in debilitating injury or death, or simply never came to the attention of the police or the press. Had I examined a different 4-month period or looked at newspapers from a different major city there's a good chance I would have found a similar array of tragic stories.

In this chapter I will take a close look at the nature, prevalence, causes, and consequences of intimate violence and abuse. With such a broad and emotionally volatile topic, it is impossible to cover every aspect or acknowledge every opinion. Hence, I will limit my focus primarily to three types of violence: dating violence, spouse or partner abuse, and child abuse. Furthermore, although intimate violence usually includes emotional, psychological, and sometimes financial abuse as well, I will pay particular attention to physical battering. Finally, I will use terms like *intimate violence, domestic violence,* and *family violence* interchangeably to refer to acts of violence and aggression that take place between people related by blood or involved romantically.

Signs of Violence

From global terrorism to gang-related drive-bys to schoolyard slayings, violence is increasingly invading American families.

Acts as horrific as the recent spate of school shootings may shock us, but signs of violence exist all around us. Entertainment and leisure are fraught with violence as the gratuitous carnage of Hollywood blockbusters all too closely mirror some children's reality.

MISSING

Elisabeth Ann Huster
DOB: 09-26-86, 11 yrs. old
Description as of August 1996:
4'6", 100 pounds
Medium to heavy build
Brown hair / blue eyes
LNU #M022693537
NIC #M9962977045

ELISABETH ANN HUSTER was taken by her mother, Karen Lee Huster, from Beaverton, Oregon, in August 1996. Karen Huster has been located and arrested for Custodial Interference First Degree. When arrested, Elisabeth was not with her mother. Elisabeth has Attention Deficit Disorder and has been prescribed Ritalin. The Washington County Sheriff's Office is the investigating agency.

If you have any information, please contact:

Detective Stratford
Washington County Sheriff's Office
Case #9622355
(503) 648-8731

OR

Oregon State Police
Missing Children Clearinghouse
(503) 378-3720 or 1-800-282-7155

MCC 97-04

Clipboards with FBI wanted posters appear in virtually every post office in the country. Images of missing children line the entrances of most grocery stores.

Representations of violence inflicted on the young can find their way even onto the breakfast table.

Even the tall and lovely hollyhocks are not able to cover up the protective bars on these windows.

Abuse plays out in families in a wide range of acts and situations. We can see the pain and terror of physical child abuse, but what about the "benign" neglect by busy executive parents who leave their children to be brought up by television?

Cases of women retaliating against domestic abuse—such as Lorena Bobbit, who cut off her husband's penis after he had raped her—have received national attention. In this awareness has come the realization that society must take active measures to protect women and children, who constitute the overwhelming majority of domestic violence victims.

At the same time, however, few have spoken loudly enough to bring attention to the suffering of other victims of family abuse and neglect, such as the elderly.

The Roots of Intimate Violence in the United States

No one would deny that the United States is a violent society. Rates of violent crime here—although decreasing in recent years—still exceed those of any other industrialized nation. Americans have long been committed to the use of violence to achieve desirable changes and resolve interpersonal problems. It is in our streets, our schools, our movies, our television shows, our toy stores, our spectator sports, and our government. It's even in our everyday language: we *assault* problems, *conquer* fears, *beat* others to the punch, *pound* home ideas, and *shoot down* opinions (Ewing, 1992).

While there's no denying the violent nature of American society, it is surprising to many that the majority of violent acts occur between people who know one another (see Exhibit 6.1). Certainly most of us are reluctant to label American families as violent. "Violence" and "families" don't seem to naturally go together. One of the most enduring popular images of family is that it is a "safe haven"—the one place in society to which we ought to be able to escape when life becomes overwhelming. Family is not a place where you'd expect to get screamed at, emotionally belittled, punched in the face, raped, or have your life threatened simply because you came home too late, got a C on a calculus test, said the wrong thing at the wrong time, or just happened to be there. But that is precisely what awaits a large number of people, especially children and women, in this country.

The tragic truth is that, outside of wars and riots, the home is the most violent location in a violent society. Americans are more likely to be killed, beaten up, sexually victimized, hit,

Exhibit 6.1

Relationship of
Murder Victim
to Offender

United States: 1996

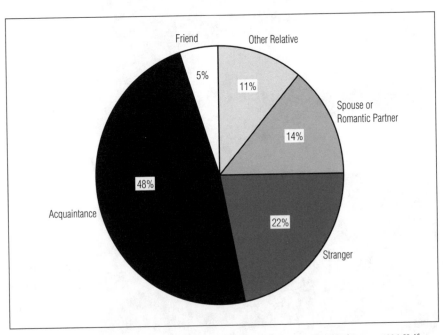

Source of data: U.S. Department of Justice, Federal Bureau of Investigation, *Crime in the United States—1996: Uniform Crime Reports.* Washington, DC, 1997.

slapped, or spanked in their homes by fellow family members than in any other location or by any other person in this society. The likelihood that a man will be assaulted by someone in his own family is 20 times higher than the odds he will be assaulted by a stranger. Women are 200 times more likely to be assaulted by a family member than by an outsider (Straus, 1991). Intimate violence happens in rich homes and poor homes, black homes and white homes, heterosexual and homosexual homes, rural and urban homes.

As recently as 40 years ago, most Americans saw intimate violence as an unfortunate, but nonetheless "normal" part of family life. In the popular 1950s sitcom *The Honeymooners*, Ralph Kramden (played by Jackie Gleason) would routinely threaten to hit his wife so hard he would send her "to the moon." Such scenes never failed to elicit laughs from the audience.

At the same time, though, intimate violence wasn't something a family wanted to publicize. It was considered a secret that was better kept out of sight. Because it remained so well hidden—particularly among the middle and upper classes—the public didn't believe such behaviors constituted a serious social problem. Instead, family violence was thought to be characteristic of those segments of the population unable to keep their private lives private, such as poor and minority families. ▲

▲ Class and race differences in family privacy are addressed in Issue 3.

The hidden nature of domestic violence prevented the vast majority of victims from getting help. They had little choice but to keep their experiences to themselves. They couldn't call for help because there wasn't any help available.

Between the 1970s and the 1990s, however, we have witnessed a marked change in public conceptions of domestic violence. Child abuse, spouse abuse, and other forms of intimate violence have been publicly redefined. While still cloaked in secrecy, domestic violence no longer has the sort of tacit approval and look-the-other-way tolerance it once enjoyed from police, courts, and the public at large. Every major city now has shelters for battered women and self-help groups for victims and former abusers. Hospitals sponsor special treatment programs concerned with abused and neglected children.

▲ Issue 2 presents more detail on older notions of family roles, as does Issue 8.

Families themselves are no longer the harsh little kingdoms they once were, where fathers ruled with iron fists. ▲ Children now have recognized rights and are not expected to submit to their parents' will with unquestioned obedience. Women are no longer expected to be docile and subservient. They are now likely to enter marriage assuming they will have a high degree of autonomy and sufficient opportunity to assert themselves educationally and professionally (Pleck, 1987).

Public perceptions have also changed. Intimate violence is more likely to be reported and prosecuted than it once was, which has, ironically, produced what appears to be a rising incidence of intimate violence. College students today overwhelmingly oppose the use of violence and coercion in dating situations (Cook, 1995). Few people would dare argue that wife battering is justifiable when wives disobey their husbands or that regular beatings are the best way to raise a child.

And yet, despite the dramatic changes that have taken place in this society, old attitudes and expectations die hard. A few years ago, after his team had barely beaten a much weaker team, star basketball player Charles Barkley said, "This is a game that, if you lose, you go home and beat your wife and kids." That same year, after his college football team lost a heartbreaking game, Penn State head coach Joe Paterno "jokingly" told reporters, "I'm going to go home and beat my wife" (both quoted in Nack & Munson, 1995). To my knowledge, neither of these men did, in fact, go home and beat their wives or children. But such statements do show that those old attitudes toward domestic violence are far from extinct.

Perceptions of family violence are always influenced by broader historical and political conditions. Our ideas about what constitutes unacceptable intimate violence and how we should respond to it are linked to the political moods that characterize our historical era. For instance, over the past century the women's rights movement has been most influential in confronting and publicizing family violence and demanding that action be taken against it. Historically, concern with family violence has grown when feminism was strong and has receded when feminism was weak (Gordon, 1988). Similarly, during conservative periods, intimate violence tends to be explained in terms of the individual psychologies of batterers and victims. When progressive political attitudes prevail, explanations tend to revolve around broader social conditions, such as economic uncertainty and changing power relationships in families or in society as a whole.

Violence in Dating Relationships

When we think of violence between intimates, we usually think of violence that occurs within nuclear families. But a great deal of intimate violence occurs even before relationships become serious. Recent research has shown that as many as three-quarters of all college students may have experienced violence in a current or past dating situation (Carlson, 1996). Dating violence crosses lines of race, ethnicity, age, class, and sexual orientation (Levy, 1991).

You'd expect violent episodes to shatter the romantic images held by dating partners and signal the end of the relationship. However, in many cases the violence seems to enhance rather than destroy the illusions of romance. According to one study, one out of four victims and one out of three offenders interpret dating violence as a sign of love (Henton, Cate, Koval, Lloyd, & Scott, 1983).

When sociologist Jan Stets (1992) examined dating violence, she found several patterns of aggression, each with a different cause. A one-time-only violent outburst is likely to be caused by a disagreement over some sensitive issue (spending habits, sex, future plans, and so on). Such an act is likely to come as a surprise to both partners. But aggression that happens many times may be due to a more persistent, long-term issue such as basic and repeated value conflicts in the relationship. For instance, a person who tends to neglect the partner's needs, concerns, and wishes and to put his or her desires first may repeatedly act aggressively.

▲ The symbolic interactionist perspective, outlined in Chapter 1, emphasizes the importance of people's definitions and interpretations in constructing the reality of family life.

What's important about these different patterns of dating aggression is that they elicit different interpretations. ▲ When violence is a single instance, the partners are likely to interpret it as an instantaneous means of expressing feelings. If the aggression is immediately challenged, chances are it won't happen again.

When a person is violent more than once, however, it may not be so much a spontaneous expression of feelings as an instrument to get what he or she wants. Repeated aggression may be deliberate, calculated, and planned (Stets, 1992). If the conduct is not challenged, it can become part of a person's behavioral repertoire and become solidly embedded in the relationship.

Sexual Coercion

Young women consistently report that the thing they dislike most about dating situations is unwanted pressure to have sex. The prevalence of **sexual coercion** in dating relationships is well documented (Reinholtz, Muehlenhard, Phelps, & Satterfield, 1995). Studies have found that as many as one in three women engage in unwanted sexual activities because of pressure from dating partners. ▲

▲ Other links between gender and sexuality are explored in Chapter 2.

Still more women—perhaps more than half the population—engage in unwanted sexual activity for reasons other than pressure from a partner, such as general peer pressure; fear of appearing shy or afraid, unfeminine, or inexperienced; and a desire to be more popular. This sort of pressure doesn't come from a partner but from one's own expectations about how one should behave sexually (Reinholtz et al., 1995). About a quarter of both men and women cite peer pressure as one of the main reasons they had intercourse for the first time when they didn't want it (Laumann, Gagnon, Michael, & Michaels, 1994).

Although not as violent in a direct, physical way as rape and sexual assault are, sexual coercion is often the precursor to these crimes.

"Date Rape"

Although the number of rape victims appears to have fallen over the past few years (Butterfield, 1997), forcible rape remains the most frequently committed but least reported violent crime in America today. A study funded by the U.S. Department of Health and Human Services found that 683,000 women had been raped in 1990, a figure more than five times as high as the 130,260 sexual assaults officially reported to the police that same year (D. Johnson, 1992). Studies consistently show that close to 60 percent of college-aged women have been sexually assaulted after the age of 14 (Abbey, Ross, McDuffie, & McAuslan, 1996). Most incidents of forced, nonconsensual sex involve acquaintances or dating partners (see Exhibit 6.2). In one oft-cited study from the late 1980s, 84 percent of college women who had been the victims of rape or attempted rape knew their attackers, and 57 percent were dating their attackers at the time (Koss, Gidycz, & Wisniewski, 1987).

Cultural beliefs about gender, sexuality, and intimacy influence societal and legal responses to rape. In fifteen Latin American countries, for instance, a man who rapes a woman—whether he knows her or not—can be absolved of all charges if he offers to marry her. As one Peruvian man put it, "Marriage is the right and proper thing to do after a rape. A raped woman is a used item. No one wants her. At least with this law the woman will get a husband" (quoted in Sims, 1997, p. A8).

In the United States we have a somewhat more sympathetic response to rape victims. Even so, rape has one of the lowest conviction rates of any violent crime: Only about 1 in 150 suspected rapists is ever found guilty (Renzetti & Curran, 1989). Unlike any other crime, rape trials typically require the victims to prove their innocence rather than requiring the state to prove the guilt of the rapist. This state of affairs stems partly from a definition of rape that is based on a traditional model of sexual intercourse—penile-vaginal penetration—rather than the violent context within which the act takes place. In other words, rape, especially in dating situations, is

Exhibit 6.2

Relationship of
Victim to Offender
in Cases of Rape
or Sexual Assault

United States: 1996

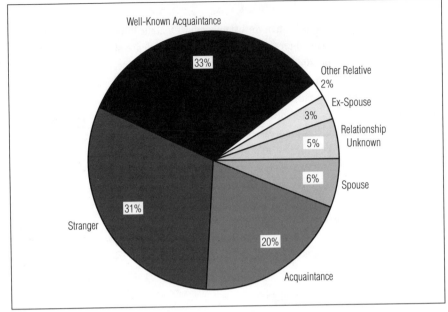

Source of data: U.S. Department of Justice, Federal Bureau of Investigation, *Crime in the United States—1996: Uniform Crime Reports.* Washington, DC, 1997.

still largely viewed in terms of women's sexuality rather than men's coercion (Sheffield, 1987). The notion that sex is synonymous with penile-vaginal intercourse also means that forced oral sex, nonconsensual fondling, or same-sex coercion may not be considered rape (Reinholtz et al., 1995).

The exclusive focus on the sexual component of the crime requires that information about the social circumstances around the act and about the relationship between the people involved be taken into consideration. Victims must provide some evidence that they were "unwilling" and tried to resist. No other crime requires that the victim prove lack of consent. People aren't asked if they agreed to having their car stolen or if they did something to provoke being robbed.

If women cannot prove that they resisted or cannot find someone to corroborate their story, consent is often presumed. Even in cases of stranger rape, anything short of vigorous and repeated resistance calls the victim's motives into question. In 1992 in Austin, Texas, a man forcibly entered a woman's apartment. The woman fled and locked herself in the bathroom. He broke down the door, held a knife to her, and demanded sex. Fearing for her life, not only because of the knife but also because of the chances of contracting a sexually transmitted disease, she begged the man to put on a condom. He agreed and went on to assault her for over an hour. The next day he was arrested for burglary with intent to commit sexual assault. In a sworn deposition he admitted that he had held a knife to her and had sex with her. But the grand jury originally refused to indict the man on the rape charge because the victim's act of providing a condom was taken to mean consent. Only after widespread public outrage was the man tried, convicted, and sentenced to 40 years in prison.

Excusing the Rapist   Cultural norms and beliefs about male sexuality also influence our understanding of sexual coercion and rape in dating relationships. One such belief is that men's sexual urges are uncontrollable. Men are frequently portrayed as overwhelmingly sexual beings who, once aroused, are compelled by forces beyond their control to seek sexual gratification. Thus, sexual coercion and violence are rendered inevitable.

In 1993 a group of teenage boys in Lakewood, California, who called themselves the "Spur Posse" made national headlines for their practice of keeping a tally of the many girls with whom they had sex. These boys were predominantly well-known athletes from middle-class families. Nine of the boys—aged 15 to 18—were arrested and charged with various crimes, including forcible rape, rape by intimidation, unlawful intercourse, oral copulation, and child molestation. Within a week all but one were set free. The district attorney's office explained that it does not file charges in sexual assault cases if the perpetrator and the victim are of roughly the same age and social experience (Allen, 1993). You can see in one father's response the belief that these behaviors were an inevitable product of male sexual nature: "Nothing my boy did was anything that any red-blooded American boy wouldn't do at his age" (quoted in "The body counters," 1993, p. 36).

Rape in dating situations thus becomes less an act of deviance and more an act of overconformity to cultural expectations; less an act by abnormally brutal individuals and more an act by "normal" men behaving in ways they think are appropriate. As one author wrote, rape is the "all-American crime," involving precisely those characteristics traditionally regarded as desirable in men: strength, power, domination, and control (Griffin, 1989).

Blaming the Victim   Related to this belief in uncontrollable male sexuality is the belief that women are ultimately responsible for men's sexual behavior. ▲ That is, women "do something to" men that arouses their sexuality, and men cannot resist. A woman who is raped is therefore held responsible for failing to control the man's behavior (Reinholtz et al., 1995).

▲ This is another aspect of gender and sexuality discussed in Chapter 2.

Many people also regard women as partly or wholly responsible for being victimized when they purportedly place themselves at risk by acting seductively, wearing provocative clothing, or telling dirty jokes. Accused rapists have been acquitted in cases in which the victims had been raped during beer drinking parties, had willingly entered a car with several men, had hitchhiked, or had gone dancing with the men who ultimately assaulted them (Wood, 1975).

Research indicates that the cultural belief that women provoke rape is pervasive. One survey of 400 teens (Goodchilds, Zellman, Johnson, & Giarusso, 1988) found that approximately half of the boys and about 30 percent of the girls felt it was acceptable for a man to force sex on a woman when:

■ She is going to have sex with him and changes her mind.
■ She has "led" him on.
■ She gets him sexually excited.
■ They have dated for a long time.
■ She lets him touch her above the waist.

In another study, male and female high school students were given a list of statements and asked to indicate the extent to which they agreed with them (Kershner, 1996). Fifty-two percent agreed that most women fantasize about being raped by a man. Forty-six percent felt that women encourage rape by the way they dress, and 53 percent said they felt that some women provoke men into raping them. Thirty-one percent agreed that many women falsely report rapes. Thirty-five percent felt that the victim should be required to prove her innocence during a rape trial.

The important sociological point of these findings is that many men and even some women don't always define violent sexual assault within dating relationships as wrong, and that they think it is what men are expected to do under certain circumstances. These views have become so entrenched in this culture's view of rape that many women have internalized the message, blaming themselves for not doing enough to prevent their own victimization. Outside of fear, self-blame is the most common reaction to rape; it is more frequent than anger (Janoff-Bulman, 1979).

The crucial consequence of these attitudes is that women must bear most if not all of the responsibility for preventing rape. I frequently pose this question to students in my classes: What can people do to stop rape? Their responses always include things like: Don't hitchhike. Don't walk alone at night. Don't get drunk at parties where men are present. Don't initiate sex play. Don't engage in foreplay if you have no intention of "going all the way." Don't miscommunicate your intentions. Don't wear provocative clothing. Don't accept invitations from strangers. But note that these suggestions focus exclusively on things that women should avoid in order to prevent rape and say nothing about the things men can do to stop it.

I don't mean to imply that women ought to ignore this advice. Certainly, given the violent nature of today's society, women should communicate their intentions clearly and not put themselves in dangerous situations. The implication of such instructions, however, speaks volumes about the nature of rape, expectations in intimate relationships, and the place of women in this society. Confining discussions of rape prevention to women's behavior suggests that a woman cannot dress the way she wants, walk where and when she wants, talk to whom she wants, enjoy "partying," or change her mind about having sex.

Remedies for Sexual Violence in Dating Relationships

Without a fundamental restructuring of society, it may seem, no significant reduction in sexual violence in dating situations is likely to occur. We would have to transform male-female relationships and childhood socialization, override the cultural beliefs and images that perpetuate certain sexual attitudes, and institute a more equitable sharing of political and economic power.

Until that time arrives, the most practical response may be to clarify the fuzzy boundary between seduction and coercion, helping men and women understand the conflicting values and expectations they bring to dating relationships. The most noteworthy example of such clarification came a few years ago when tiny Antioch College in Yellow Springs, Ohio, implemented a formal set of rules for intimate interaction. The policy instantly made national headlines.

Disturbed by the frequency of intimate violence on their campus, Antioch students tried to eliminate the gray area between consent and rape in sexual situations by mandating verbal permission at each step of a sexual encounter:

- If sexual contact and/or conduct is not mutually and simultaneously initiated, then the person who initiates sexual contact/conduct is responsible for getting the verbal consent of the other individual(s) involved.

- Obtaining consent is an ongoing process in any sexual interaction. Verbal consent should be obtained with each new level of physical and/or sexual contact/conduct in any given interaction, regardless of who initiates it. Asking, "Do you want to have sex with me?" is not enough. The request for consent must be specific to each act.

- The person with whom sexual contact/conduct is initiated is responsible to express verbally and/or physically his/her willingness or lack of willingness when reasonably possible.

- If someone has initially consented but then stops consenting during a sexual interaction, she/he should communicate withdrawal verbally and/or through physical resistance. The other individual(s) must stop immediately.

- To knowingly take advantage of someone who is under the influence of alcohol, drugs, and/or prescribed medication is not acceptable behavior in the Antioch community. ("Excerpt from the Antioch College," 1995, p. 287)

Fundamental to this policy is the need for "prior consent." Silence can no longer be construed as consent. The formality of the policy certainly threatens to undermine the pleasurable spontaneity of mutually desired sexual encounters. And its "one-size-fits-all" approach to relationships overlooks the wide variation in people's sexual tastes, desires, and patterns.

But for all the criticism and ridicule it generated, the policy was a student response to the fact that sexual interactions on campus—with their characteristic set of vague, implicit rules—weren't working very well. Far from establishing campus "sex police," the policy aimed to prevent rape and sexual assault (Abrams & Herman, 1994). As one columnist put it, the policy forces us to acknowledge that the choice is not between regulation and freedom, but between implicit rules for sexual relationships and explicit rules (Fassin, 1993).

Violence Between Spouses

A form of intimate violence that has received substantially more attention than dating violence is that which takes place between spouses. Even so, the concealed and private nature of such violence—most of it occurs in seclusion, beyond the watchful eyes of relatives, neighbors, and strangers—makes exact statistics about its prevalence quite hard to calculate. Even with more stringent rules for police reporting of domestic calls, most incidents are never reported; others are dismissed as accidents. Furthermore, definitions of abuse and reporting practices vary from state to state.

The statistics on spouse abuse that do exist indicate that it is a widespread problem. According to one national survey of more than 8,000 families, approximately one out of every six married couples (or about 8.7 million couples) experiences at least one assault each year (Gelles & Straus, 1988). Most of these assaults are relatively minor (pushing, slapping, shoving, throwing things). If we look only at the more serious forms of violence (kicking, punching, biting, choking, and so on) we find that approximately 3.5 million couples experienced violence severe enough to put them at risk of serious injury or worse.

Contrary to popular belief, the rate of wife-to-husband violence is slightly higher than the rate of husband-to-wife violence. But because violence directed toward women tends to be more severe and more difficult to escape, women clearly are the disproportionate victims of dangerous or life-threatening domestic violence. In fact, violence in the household represents the single largest cause of injury to women in the United States today. Recent estimates indicate that between 2 and 4 million women are beaten in their homes each year (Roberts, 1996; Smolowe, 1994). Half of the victims are beaten three or more times a year (Straus, Gelles, & Steinmetz, 1980). In some areas of the country, domestic violence sends as many women to hospital emergency rooms as any other type of injury, illness, or assault.

Each year about 1,400 wives and girlfriends are killed by their husbands and boyfriends (cited in Gelles, 1995), accounting for more than 40 percent of female homicides in this country (Hyman, Schillinger, & Lo, 1995). Female homicide victims are nine times more likely to have been killed by a husband, ex-husband, or boyfriend than male homicide victims are to have been killed by a wife, ex-wife, or girlfriend (U.S. Bureau of Justice Statistics, 1995).

Given the shame and stigma associated with such violence, we can probably assume that these figures are *under*estimates of the actual incidence of spousal violence. However, we can safely say that many people—mostly women but also some men—face significant physical danger in their homes each day.

Spousal Violence Across Cultures

Like all family phenomena, spousal violence cannot be fully understood without considering the broader cultural context in which it takes place. When anthropologist Peggy Reeves Sanday (1981) examined violence against women in 156 tribal societies around the world, she found that 47 percent of them could be classified as "rape-free" cultures in which women command considerable respect and prestige both at work and at home. Eighteen percent were classified as "rape-prone" societies in which men use violence to ceremoniously punish or threaten women. Such acts are either culturally allowable or largely overlooked. The rest of the societies fell somewhere in between: Rape is not atypical but not completely condoned either.

Not everyone agrees, however, that a "rape-free" society is possible. Patricia Rozee (1993) examined a sample of thirty-five societies worldwide. She found that when the definition of sexual violence is broadened to include socially condoned rapes, such as the rape of a spouse, rape was found in all the societies studied. She concluded that such violence may be regulated in many societies but is rarely forbidden.

Indeed, when we examine *all* forms of family violence, it appears that most people around the world have either been the victim of, perpetrator of, or witness to violence within their families (Levinson, 1989). According to one study, wife beating is the most common form of family violence around the world, occurring at least occasionally in about 85 percent of the societies examined (Levinson, 1989). Husband beating is less common—occurring in about 27 percent of societies—and occurs less often than wife beating in those societies where both are present. Husband beating occurs only in those societies where wife beating also occurs. In those cultures where men's dominance is considered legitimate, husbands will control their wives and use violence to maintain that control when they believe it is necessary. They will, in fact, see the use of such violence as their right.

In South Korea, for instance, wife beating remains an integral part of family life. In one recent survey, 42 percent of South Korean women said they'd been beaten by their husbands at least once (cited in Kristof, 1996c). An old Korean saying declares, "Women should be beaten at least once every three days"; another says, "Dried fish and women both are better after they are beaten." Although things are changing—especially among young, better-educated couples in large cities—and most people say that beating is wrong, violence is still a "normal" part of Korean family life. One man, when asked if he had ever beaten his wife replied:

> I was married at 28 and I'm 52 now. How could I have been married all these years and not beaten my wife? For me it's better to release that anger and get it over with. Otherwise, I just get sick inside. . . . Of course, you have to apologize afterward. (quoted in Kristof, 1996c, p. A4)

Korean women's attitudes also support men's authority and right to beat their wives:

> Of course my husband beats me. But it was my fault because I scolded him. Maybe there are some cases where it's just the man's fault, but ultimately the woman is to blame, because if she won't argue with her husband, he probably won't beat her. I told [my daughter], "if he hits you, just sit back and take it." (quoted in Kristof, 1996c, p. A4)

In the Central American country of Belize, men have historically exercised almost complete economic and political power over women. In families, they have always exerted their authority and control through physical battering. Husbands frequently beat their wives with anything they can get hold of: guns, knives, crowbars, machetes, electric wire, bottles, mop handles, rocks, boards, rope, and so forth. These violent acts go unacknowledged by the community, go unreported to the police, and are rarely discussed among friends and families (McClaurin, 1996). Despite the fact that local papers periodically run stories of women mutilated, burned, and murdered by their husbands or partners, wife battering doesn't warrant any mention in the country's official crime documents.

▲ The relationship between gender and dependence is examined in Issue 5.

Women's dependence is so deep in Belize that they are usually willing to accept abuse and tolerate offensive behavior in exchange for economic security. ▲ Over the past decade, however, frustrated Belizean women have formed several women's groups and organizations aimed at increasing women's status, decreasing their dependence, and ending domestic violence. Their efforts came to fruition in 1993 with passage of the Domestic Violence Bill, which gives women the ability to acquire legal restraining orders against their husbands and grants police the power to make arrests in domestic disputes.

Worldwide, one of the most pernicious forms of spousal violence—known locally as "bride burning" or "dowry deaths"—takes place in India (Heise, 1989; Van Willigen & Channa, 1991). Dowry was traditionally a cultural institution in which a woman received money and gifts from her parents upon marriage. Even though it was officially banned in 1961, dowry is still an essential part of premarital negotiations and now refers to the wealth that the bride's family pays to the groom. In many cases it has become a get-rich-quick scheme for men and their families.

Young brides, who by custom live with their new husband's parents, are commonly subjected to severe abuse if the promised money is not paid. Sometimes dowry harassment ends in suicide or murder. In 1994, about 6,200 wives in India—or an average of 17 a day—were killed by their husbands for not providing adequate dowries ("Vital signs," 1995). Often the husband and his family try to disguise the murder as an accident by setting the wife on fire and then claiming she died in a kitchen mishap. In the city of Bombay, close to 20 percent of all deaths among women 15 to 44 years old are attributed to "accidental burns" (Heise, 1989).

Explanations of Spousal Violence

Trying to figure out why spousal violence occurs is not a simple task. It's tempting to see such violence in purely individualistic terms. Most often we simply assume that men who beat their wives are mean individuals who are incapable of controlling their rage or who gain some sort of pathological pleasure and feeling of power by inflicting pain on their spouses.

Alcohol abuse is often cited as a key culprit in spousal violence. To some researchers, the relationship between alcohol and family violence is undeniable: "Just as high alcohol intake leads to cirrhosis of the liver, brain damage, and heart failure, so does high alcohol intake lead to violence in the family" (Flanzer, 1993, p. 171). However, the contention that alcohol—as well as other drugs such as cocaine and crack—directly and inevitably produces violent and abusive behavior has little scientific support. Evidence from laboratory studies and blood tests of men arrested for wife beating indicates that although alcohol may be an immediate antecedent to some acts of violence, it is far from being a necessary or sufficient cause of domestic violence. Findings from a study of 5,159 couples nationwide revealed that alcohol is involved in only about 25 percent of instances of wife abuse (Kantor & Straus, 1990), which means the vast majority (75 percent) take place when neither person has been drinking. Furthermore, about 80 percent of men who are defined as heavy or binge drinkers *do not* beat their wives at all. Hence, although the stereotype of the violent, drunken husband has a kernal of truth, we cannot simply explain domestic violence as the result of alcohol.

Attributing spousal abuse to mentally defective or drunken husbands might be psychologically comforting to the public at large but we can only truly understand spousal violence as the complex product of psychological, interpersonal, societal, historical, and cultural forces. Each act of domestic violence brings these forces together. As one sociologist put it, "Compressed into one assault are our deepest human emotions, our sense of self, our power, and our hopes and fears about love and intimacy, as well as the social construction of marriage and its place within the larger society" (Yllo, 1993, p. 47). In short, spousal violence is best understood by going beyond individual-level explanations to an examination of the sociocultural environment in which it takes place.

The Social Organization of Families Families have several organizational characteristics that promote intimacy but at the same time increase the probability of conflict and violence. One such characteristic is the greater amount of time we usually spend with family members compared to the time we usually spend at work or with others. From a strictly quantitative perspective, we are at greater risk for violence at home because that's where we spend so much of our time (Gelles & Straus, 1988).

But what goes on during our time at home is much more important than the sheer number of hours we spend there. Not only are we with family members a lot, we also interact with them across a wide range of situations. The intimacy of these interactions is intense. Emotions run deep. It's ironic that the people who we can care about the most are also the ones who can make us the most angry. The anger we may feel toward a stranger or an acquaintance never approaches the intensity of the anger we feel toward a spouse—or for that matter toward a sibling or a child.

Moreover, we also know more about family members than we know about other individuals in our lives. We know their likes and dislikes, their fears and their desires. And they know these things about us too. If someone in your family insults you, you know immediately what you can say to get even. Married couples usually know the "buttons" they can push to hurt or infuriate each other. Arguments can escalate into violence when one partner focuses on the other's vulnerabilities and insecurities.

Long periods of intense contact with people you know virtually everything about can elevate even trivial matters into conflict situations. In many families, everyday decisions occur in a context of winning and losing. Hence, some of the most serious family conflicts occur over seemingly insignificant issues like what program to watch on television or what restaurant to go to for dinner.

Finally, family life contains endless sources of stress. For one thing, we expect a lot from our families: emotional and financial support, warmth, comfort, and intimacy. When these expectations aren't fulfilled, stress levels escalate. Moreover, the birth and raising of a child, financial problems, employment transitions (voluntary or involuntary), illness, old age, death, and so on are all events that potentially increase stress. ▲ Research indicates that the likelihood of domestic violence increases with the number of stressful events that a family experiences. Indeed, stressful life circumstances are the hallmark of violent families (Gelles & Straus, 1988).

Power and Family Inequality   Another important social factor related to spousal violence is the fact that family life is characterized by significant inequality. The more resources—whether personal, social, emotional, or financial—that a person controls, the more influence he or she has over the relationship. ▲

As conflict theory tells us, power, power confrontations, and perceived threats to dominance and authority are underlying issues in almost all acts of domestic violence (Gelles & Straus, 1988). And research has consistently shown that the balance of power within families has a noticeable effect on domestic violence. Sociologists Murray Straus, Richard Gelles, and Suzanne Steinmetz (1980), for instance, found that the level of violence against wives is lowest among couples who follow a pattern of egalitarian decision making. Fewer than 3 percent of these wives had suffered a severe violent attack within the previous year. In contrast, the rate of wife beating among couples in which the wife dominates is 7.1 percent, and where husbands dominate, the rate is 10 percent.

In male-dominated households, husbands turn to violence to maintain the subordination of their wives. But why is the rate of spouse abuse so high where *wives* tend to have the most say

▲ For more on the stresses of child rearing, read Chapter 5; for more on the stresses associated with caring for elderly parents and coping with death, read Chapter 8.

▲ Issue 5 examines how power is developed and maintained in families.

over decisions? Husbands in these families may be lashing out violently when they feel their masculinity is under attack. In other words, husbands may use violence as a final resource to gain control when other resources are insufficient or lacking (Goode, 1971). In an achievement-oriented society, husbands who lack the financial, occupational, and educational resources necessary to establish household dominance often turn to violence (Yllo & Straus, 1990).

A recent study of battered wives found that violence increased as the women's income approached or exceeded that of their husbands (McCloskey, 1996). However, researchers have found no such relationship between occupational prestige differences and violence, suggesting that the symbolic prestige of a wife's job represents less of a threat to male domination than her independent income does. Other research on this issue found that the wife's independent income is more of a threat in working-class families than in middle-class families, where violence may be seen as less legitimate (Allen & Straus, 1980).

Power and Structural Inequality   The forces of power operate at the societal level as well as the family level. In most societies, economic and social structures support male domination, which is revealed in the relatively low position women hold in the workplace, schools, politics, and other social institutions (Yllo & Straus, 1990). In many patriarchal societies, men blatantly classify and treat women as possessions. ▲

▲ Issue 5 further examines the relationship between patriarchy and family power.

Internationally, male dominance has a long history. Roman law, for instance, justified a husband's killing his wife for reasons such as adultery, wine drinking, and other so-called inappropriate behaviors (Steinmetz, Clavan, & Stein, 1990). The "rule of thumb" in English common law recognized a husband's right to beat his wife with a stick that was no bigger than the circumference of his thumb.

In the United States, too, male dominance is part of a centuries-old legacy of domestic violence. Early American law provided that upon marriage a husband acquired rights to his wife's person, the value of her paid and unpaid labor, and most property she brought into the marriage. The wife was obliged to obey and serve her husband. Her legal identity "merged" into his so that she was unable to enter into contracts without his approval. The husband, in turn, was responsible for his wife's conduct. As master of the household, he could subject her to corporal punishment or "chastisement" as long as he didn't inflict permanent injury (Siegel, 1996).

Prior to the Civil War, corporal punishment became the subject of widespread controversy, and campaigns against it began to develop. These movements coincided with early campaigns for women's rights. Over time the American legal system did respond. In 1871 an Alabama court declared that a husband no longer had the privilege of beating his wife:

> The wife is not to be considered as the husband's slave. And the privilege, ancient though it be, to beat her with a stick, to pull her hair, choke her, spit in her face or kick her about the floor, or to inflict upon her like indignities, is not now acknowledged by our law. (quoted in Siegel, 1996, pp. 2121–2122)

But because this privilege had such a long tradition in married life, it didn't die easily. The legal system continued to treat wife beating differently from other violent crimes, intervening only intermittently in cases of marital violence. In order to protect male authority and the privacy of families, courts granted most men formal or informal immunity from prosecution, implying that it was easier for a wife to forgive her husband's impulsive violence than for a husband to suffer the loss of authority entailed in having his behavior scrutinized by public authorities.

At the beginning of the twentieth century, judges, clergy, and social workers routinely urged couples to reconcile and preserve the marriage rather than punishing those who assaulted their partners. Battered wives were discouraged from filing charges against their husbands, urged to accept responsibility for their role in provoking the violence, and encouraged to remain in the relationship and rebuild it rather than separate or divorce (Pleck, 1987; Siegel, 1996). Physical violence in the home was not viewed as criminal conduct; it was viewed as an expression of emotions that, through counseling, needed to be rechanneled into the marriage. Such a "therapeutic" framework regulated marital violence for much of the twentieth century.

Not until the late 1970s did the feminist movement mount a significant challenge to male primacy and authority. Since then, many reforms have been secured, such as shelters for battered women and their children, new arrest procedures, and federal legislation that makes gender-motivated assaults a civil rights violation and prevents people convicted of domestic violence from purchasing handguns.

But the tradition of male dominance persists. For instance, the laws relating to rape in many states in this country, and in most countries around the world, include what is commonly known as "the marital rape exemption." These laws typically define rape as "the forcible penetration of the body of a woman, *not the wife of the perpetrator,*" making rape in marriage a legal impossibility (Russell, 1998, p. 71). In eight states, husbands cannot be prosecuted for raping their wives unless they are living apart or legally separated. In twenty-six other states, they can be prosecuted in some circumstances but are totally exempt in others—when, for example, the wife is unable to give consent because she is unconscious, drugged, asleep, or physically or mentally helpless in some other way (Russell, 1998). When the American Law Institute most recently revised the Model Penal Code provisions on rape, it decided to preserve language that exempted husbands from rape charges in hopes of protecting family privacy:

> The problem with abandoning the [marital] immunity in many . . . situations is that the law of rape, if applied to spouses, would thrust the prospect of criminal sanctions into the ongoing process of adjustment in the marital relationship. . . . Retaining the spousal exclusion avoids this unwarranted intrusion of the penal law into the life of the family. (quoted in Siegel, 1996, p. 2174)

Focusing on the patriarchal power structure of society enables us to see that the battering or rape of an individual wife by an individual husband—not to mention economic abuse, coercion, intimidation, and emotional abuse—is not simply a "family problem" isolated from the rest of society. It is the manifestation of a broad system of male domination and control that is built into the very structure of society.

Such explanations make intuitive sense. But, for the most part, they have not been tested empirically. Sociologists Kersti Yllo and Murray Straus (1990) overcame this limitation by examining the relationship between the structural inequality of women and wife beating. They ranked all fifty states in terms of women's status as a group relative to men's, taking into consideration four social institutions: economics, education, politics, and the law. For the economic dimension, they measured items such as the percentage of women in the labor force and in professional and managerial occupations, female unemployment rates relative to men's, and female median income relative to men's. For the educational dimension, they looked at women's high school graduation rates and rates of college enrollment relative to men. For the political dimension, they measured the percentage of female members of Congress, state senators, state representatives, and judges. And the legal dimension consisted of such factors as whether the state had equal-pay laws and mandated fair-employment practices, what kind of rape laws and divorce laws it had, and whether it had ratified the Equal Rights Amendment to the U.S. Constitution.

Yllo and Straus found that wife beating is highest in those states where economic, educational, political, and legal inequality are greatest. As the overall status of women improved, violence declined—but only to a point. Surprisingly, in those states where the status of women is highest, the rate of wife beating is also quite high. The researchers suggest that two different processes are at work. When social inequality is high, more coercion is needed to maintain the system. Thus force is used to keep wives "in their place" in those states where women have the lowest status. But rapid changes in sex roles and shifts in the balance of power between the sexes, found in states where women's status is high, may contribute to increased marital conflict because of the threat these changes pose to men.

Even though these forces provide a fertile social environment for violence, they don't make it inevitable. After all, most husbands who live in this violent, male-dominated society don't abuse their wives. Nevertheless, if some people do beat their partners because they feel that such behavior is appropriate given their position in society and in their families, then we would be wrong to conclude that abusers are simply psychotic, deranged, "sick" individuals. Rather, they are people who believe that dominance is their birthright.

Privacy and Spousal Violence Even though many Americans currently accept male dominance, most of us are horrified at the thought of a person beating or killing a spouse—or for that matter, a parent killing or beating his or her child. At the same time, we also dislike the thought of the state intervening in the private affairs of families. ▲ But the privacy of family life can be life threatening to certain members. An eminent anthropologist once observed that among the societies she had studied, violence between family members tended not to occur when families lived communally. Only when the walls of separate houses went up did the hitting start (cited in Gelles & Straus, 1988).

▲ You can see in Issue 3 that the ideal of family privacy and autonomy, although limited, defines the American way of life.

In this society, people who are socially isolated from neighbors and relatives are more likely to be violent against family members. For instance, cohabiting couples are more likely to be isolated from their network of kin than either dating couples or married couples. Not surprisingly, research indicates that much more, and more severe, violence takes place among cohabiting couples than among married or dating couples (Stets & Straus, 1990). Conversely, when families are well integrated into their communities and belong to groups and associations, violence becomes less likely (Gelles, 1995).

The relationship between family privacy and spousal violence is clear when we look at where and when such violence is most likely to take place. According to sociologists Richard Gelles and Murray Straus (1988), most domestic violence occurs in the kitchen, living room, or bedroom between 8 P.M. and midnight. As the evening wears on, family members have fewer places outside the home to escape to if problems arise. Similarly, weekends are the most violent time of the week for families because members are usually at home, away from school or work.

The cultural value of family privacy has also helped to reinforce a perception that spousal violence is somehow less bothersome and more tolerable than other types of violence. Even when violence between spouses occurs in public, it is often perceived as a private matter. Psychologists Lance Shotland and Margaret Straw (1976) performed an experiment that involved staging what appeared to be a heated altercation between a man and woman as they emerged from an elevator. The researchers set up two scenarios that were identical except for one important detail. In the first, the woman, who is the object of the man's verbal and physical threats, shouts, "Get away from me! I don't even know you!" In the second (with identical actors and identical behaviors), she says, "Get away from me! I don't know why I ever married you!" In the first situation, involving apparent strangers, 65 percent of the bystanders attempted to stop the fight. In the second situation, involving apparent spouses, bystanders intervened only 19 percent of the time. Clearly, the second case was defined by observers as a domestic dispute between spouses, conjuring up a set of norms that stopped them from "getting involved" in the private affairs of a married couple.

The family privacy so valued in the twentieth century has diminished the impact of neighborhoods, extended kin, and other informal networks in protecting people against violence from intimates. While more and more urban neighborhoods ban together to organize crime watch groups to prevent street crime or patrols to watch out for local teens who might get into trouble, such organizations rarely, if ever, address the violence that occurs off the streets, in their neighborhood homes (Mannon, 1997b).

The Escape from Abusive Relationships

One question that has captured the attention of many family researchers is: Why do victims stay in abusive relationships? During the 1960s the **masochism thesis**—that is, women derived pleasure from being humiliated and hurt—was the predominant reason offered by psychiatrists (Saul, 1972). Even today, many psychiatrists believe masochism, or **self-defeating personality disorder,** as it is now called, should be a "legitimate" medical explanation for women who stay in abusive relationships. Other contemporary explanations focus on the women's character flaws, such as weak will or abnormal emotional attachment.

A substantial proportion of the public subscribes to various stereotypes about battered women and the nature of domestic violence. In one study of 216 predominantly white registered voters, more than a third of those surveyed believed that a battered woman is at least partially responsible for the beatings she suffers and that if she remains in the relationship she must be either masochistic or emotionally disturbed. Nearly two-thirds believed that battered women can "simply leave" a relationship when it becomes abusive. Interestingly, women were more likely than men to subscribe to these stereotypes (Ewing & Aubrey, 1987).

These explanations and attitudes focus solely on the victim while paying little attention to her social situation. Many battered women end up staying in abusive relationships not because they are masochistic or weak willed but because they come to believe that there are worse things than being beaten. For instance, they might fear that if they are unsuccessful in escaping the relationship, the violence might get worse. In addition, they may be concerned for the well-being of children or possible retaliation against parents or other close relatives.

▲ In Chapter 2 you can see that the attractiveness and stability of a relationship depend on the presence or absence of viable alternatives.

According to social exchange theory, one of the most powerful reasons why women stay in abusive relationships is dependence. ▲ That is, an individual will be inclined to stay in a relationship—even a bad or abusive one—if she believes she has no other options. As one woman put it, "I had no place to go and no help. . . . I need to take care of my family" (quoted in Baker, 1997, p. 61). Women who are unemployed and cannot support themselves financially are significantly less likely to leave an abusive marriage than women who are employed and therefore have their own source of income (Strube & Barbour, 1983).

Some women in abusive relationships develop beliefs that help them accept the fact that they are staying in a situation generally condemned by society. Kathleen Ferraro and John Johnson (1983) were participant observers at a shelter for battered women in the Southwest. They gathered information from 120 women, ranging in age from 17 to 68, who came to the shelter over the span of a year. Some women had convinced themselves that they must endure the abuse while helping their "troubled" partners return to their "normal," nonabusive selves. Others claimed that their abusive partners were "sick" and that their actions were beyond their control; in other words, their partners were also victims. Finally, many women blamed themselves, taking the responsibility away from their spouses.

But the perception that battered women simply sit back and take the abuse, thinking they somehow deserve it, is inaccurate. One study of 1,000 battered and formerly battered women nationwide found that they tried a number of active strategies to end the violence directed against them (Bowker, 1993). They tried to talk men out of beating them, extracted promises that the men wouldn't batter them anymore, avoided their abuser physically or avoided certain volatile topics, hid or ran away, and even fought back physically. Many of these individual strategies had limited effectiveness, however, and so most of these battered women eventually turned to people outside the relationship for informal support, advice, and sheltering. From these informal sources, the women generally progressed to organizations in the community, such as police, social service and counseling agencies, women's groups, and battered women's shelters. Some of these women were able, eventually, to end the violence; others weren't. The study points out that most women actively try to end their victimization.

The Lack of Institutional Support One of the reasons why so many women are unable to get out of abusive relationships is that the social organizations and institutions that are designed to help battered women have traditionally been ineffective. In 1980 a bill was introduced in Congress that would have provided federally funded local community shelters for battered women and their children. Some religious groups vigorously—and successfully—opposed the bill, arguing that the shelters would become "anti-family indoctrination centers" (Scanzoni, 1983, p. 202). These groups didn't approve of violence, but they believed that such matters were best left to families.

Throughout the years, hospital personnel, police, and courts have been notoriously unsympathetic to the plight of battered women. As recently as 10 years ago, for instance, emergency room workers routinely interviewed battered women about their injuries with their husbands present. Police departments, in particular, have traditionally been reluctant to get too involved in domestic disputes. For instance, in the O. J. Simpson case, police were called to his home on at least nine occasions because of his physical abuse of his wife, Nicole. Some departments have arrest policies called "stitch rules," which specify how serious an injury a victim must sustain, measured by how many surgical stitches are required, to justify an arrest of the assailant (Gillespie, 1989). One study found that the majority of domestic disputes and family violence incidents reported to the police resulted in no arrest; either the police did nothing or the offender was referred to other agencies (Bell & Bell, 1991). Given this sort of response, we should not be surprised that only about 15 percent of battered women ever contact the police (Straus & Gelles, 1986).

The courts, too, have historically treated spousal violence less seriously than other crimes, making it even more difficult for women to seek help. In 1978, for instance, an Indiana prosecutor refused to prosecute for murder a man who beat and kicked his ex-wife to death in the presence of a witness and then raped her as she lay dying. Filing a manslaughter charge instead, the prosecutor said, "He didn't mean to kill her. He just meant to give her a good thumping" (quoted in Jones, 1980, p. 308).

Consider also the case of Kenneth Peacock. In February of 1994, Mr. Peacock, a long-distance truck driver, returned home unexpectedly and found his wife in bed, naked, with another man. He chased the man away at gunpoint. At about 4 A.M., after hours of arguing, he shot his wife in the head with a hunting rifle.

He pleaded guilty to voluntary manslaughter. The judge in the case sentenced him to 18 months in prison—a sentence half as long as the prosecution recommended—stating that he wished he didn't have to send him to prison at all because the feelings of anger the man had were understandable under the circumstances. The judge said, "I seriously wonder how many men married five, four years would have the strength to walk away without inflicting some corporal punishment" (quoted in Lewin, 1994b, p. A18).

For centuries, the law has either explicitly or implicitly recognized a "heat-of-passion" defense in domestic homicide cases. Under such considerations, killings may be treated less harshly if a reasonable person would have been so distraught as to be incapable of exercising proper judgment. In such cases—the most prototypical example being a man finding his wife in bed with someone else—prosecutors will allow the defendant to plead guilty to the lesser charge of voluntary manslaughter, knowing that a jury would be unlikely to hand down a murder conviction. In fact, as recently as the early 1970s killing an adulterous wife found in bed with another man was considered justifiable homicide.

Today, however, as a result of the battered women's movement and others who have worked hard to educate the public about domestic violence, the legal system has become somewhat more responsive to the needs of abuse victims. Many police departments around the country, for instance, have revised their unspoken "hands-off" policies toward domestic violence cases. In Indianapolis, for example, where the number of domestic violence cases doubled between 1990 and 1991, officers are now required to make an arrest even if they don't directly witness the assault. In addition, officers must have 30 hours of in-service domestic violence training each year. In other cities, domestic violence victims are prohibited from dropping assault charges once they are filed.

As a result, a cultural script has emerged that directs battered women to get away and stay away from their abusers. Those who stay with or return to abusive partners violate this new cultural expectation. Yet, many battered women find these expectations overly narrow and un-realistic. Consider, for example, recent reforms in the welfare system. As many as two-thirds of women who received welfare payments in the form of Aid to Families and Dependent Children (AFDC) had abuse in their backgrounds, suggesting that welfare may have been an escape route for many battered women with children (Gordon, 1997). Today, however, the inadequacy and unpredictability of the revised welfare system may force many of these women to stay in rela-tionships with men who abuse them or their children. ▲

▲ Recent welfare reforms are described in Issue 7.

Sometimes the resources in place to assist battered women are simply inadequate. In rural areas with no public transportation, shelters exist but may be inaccessible to women who live miles away and don't own a car. In small towns, confidentiality is virtually impossible. The fact that people tend to know one another can dissuade a woman from calling a local sheriff's office for help, because the person answering might be a friend or relative of her abusive partner.

The problem of inadequate resources is not limited to scarcely populated rural areas, how-ever. In New York City, for instance, the mayor recently launched a massive campaign against do-mestic violence. Most buses and subways now display posters encouraging battered women to come forward and seek help from city-supported shelters and other services. Every day sixty-five battered women who feel they're in danger call the Victim Services hotline requesting shel-ter. But every day about sixty of them are told no spaces are available (Sontag, 1997). Some of these women are so desperate that they agree to be bused hundreds of miles away to a place where shelter is available. This remedy may get them out of harm's way, but it may also wreck their work lives, endanger welfare checks, and disrupt their children's schooling.

In other cases, standard rules and regulations can work against women trying to escape their abusive situations. Here's how one woman who had been viciously brutalized by her hus-band describes the system failure that led to her decision to leave a shelter and return to him:

> He [her husband] would get my phone number and he would call me and call me and I'd have to pay $50 to get the number changed, and I'd tell the authorities, "Well, he called me and he called me," . . . They'd say, "Well, do you have proof or do you have it documented?" Well, how do you do that if you don't have a device on your phone that is gonna cost you. That's how he always got me to go back to him because he would just harass me until I would just be like "Fine, go meet him." (quoted in Baker, 1997, p. 59)

In sum, the decision to stay in an abusive relationship is the result not of irrationality or mental dysfunction but of rational choices women make in response to an array of conditions, including fear of and harassment by the abuser, the complex everyday realities of dependence, and the lack of institutional support (Baker, 1997). When we encourage battered women to leave abusive situations, we mean to be helpful, of course. However, without adequate institutional support often all we accomplish is making these women feel guilty about their already difficult and dangerous decision to stay.

Women Who Kill Their Abusers   There comes a time for some battered women when they re-alize they can't escape the situation, can't make the violence stop, and can no longer explain it away. So, seeing no way out, they resort to more drastic, violent measures. About 750 battered women kill their abusers each year (cited in Roberts, 1996). Most, as in the following case, are making a "last ditch" effort to get out of a situation that they perceive as life threatening and inescapable:

> Judy and Thomas Norman had been married for twenty-five years, since she was 14; he had beaten her for twenty years, "frequent assaults that included slapping, punching ... kicking ... striking her with various objects ... throwing glasses, beer bottles ... putting his cigarettes out on her, throwing hot coffee on her, breaking glass against her face and crushing food on her face. He forced her to make money by prostitution ... routinely called [her] 'dog,' 'bitch,' and 'whore,' ... made her eat pet food out of the pet's bowls and bark like a dog ... deprived her of food and refused to let her get food for the family." He threatened to cut off her breast and, increasingly frequently, to kill her. On a day when he made these threats continually, Judy Norman shot him as he took a nap." (quoted in Gordon, 1997, p. 25)

During Judy's trial in 1989 the court ruled that her attorney was not entitled to present her history of abuse as evidence. And because she shot him while he was asleep, she was unable to make a self-defense plea: There was no *imminent* threat to her life. She was convicted of manslaughter.

This case became a focal point for the frustration many victims, defense attorneys, and women's rights activists feel over the unsympathetic legal response and the high conviction rate of battered women who kill their abusive partners. The day after Kenneth Peacock was reluctantly sentenced to 18 months in prison for murdering his wife "in the heat of passion," another judge handed down a 3-year sentence to a woman who pleaded guilty to voluntary manslaughter for killing her husband after 11 years of abuse (Lewin, 1994b). Her sentence was *three times longer* than the sentence the prosecutors had sought.

Why have women who kill their abusive partners been treated so harshly by the courts? For several reasons, battered women have traditionally had trouble claiming self-defense. One study found that in over 70 percent of trials in which self-defense was raised, the defendant was still found guilty of some form of homicide (Ewing, 1987). First, a finding of self-defense requires that the defendant had reason to believe that death or grievous bodily injury was imminent at the time of the killing (Schuller & Vidmar, 1992). Battered women, however, often develop a keen ability to predict attack from a long history of observing their abuser's actions. Hence, many kill their abusive partners *before* the situation reaches the precise point at which the court could consider it life threatening. Furthermore, because of fear, women are likely to wait until a time when their partner is least dangerous and most vulnerable. One study found that in two-thirds of the cases reviewed, the woman had committed the killing outside of a direct confrontation, when no "imminent" threat seemed apparent to an outside observer. Commonly, the husband was walking away or asleep (Ewing, 1987).

Second, in some states self-defense stipulates that people in harmful situations first have a "duty to retreat." That is, as an alternative to using force, they must first attempt to escape from the situation. Only when no such opportunity exists can they legally use lethal force. With regard to domestic violence cases, the "duty to retreat" has become for many judges, attorneys, and juries a duty to leave a relationship in which violence has been occurring for a long time. During the course of the trial, prosecutors usually ask, "Why didn't the woman leave, if she was really being abused?" (Roberts, 1996). Such a question implies either that she hadn't really been beaten (therefore nullifying the self-defense claim) or, if she were being victimized, that she could have and should have "retreated," thereby putting an end to the violence.

Finally, self-defense requires that the victim respond with "proportional" force. For example, shooting someone you find rummaging through your garbage can is not usually considered self-defense. Historically, in domestic violence cases, courts have ruled that a woman cannot use lethal force against a man who slaps her around or is psychologically abusive. But because of the differences in physical strength between a woman and her male abuser, hitting back with proportional force would do a woman little good. Hence, the force she is likely to use will probably involve a deadly weapon.

Because of activism by feminists in the battered women's movement, things have changed in recent years. Since the 1980s, courts have increasingly allowed women to introduce a history of abuse as a legal defense against crimes they are accused of committing against their abusers. Courts now understand the **battered woman syndrome** as a state of mind that occurs when a woman's exposure to long-term physical and mental abuse makes her feel psychologically trapped in a relationship. This syndrome affects her judgment in such a way as to make her believe she is in imminent danger and that the use of force is the only way to escape.

The court's acceptance of the battered woman syndrome as a legitimate defense marked a turning point in the judicial treatment of battered women. It helped to shift the focus from the defendant to the person responsible for the victimization and helped overcome bias among the many judges who refused to recognize that self-defense laws apply to battered women. Now a long history of abuse could in itself constitute a reasonable expectation of attack.

Realizing that scores of women were in prison because of convictions that had occurred prior to these legal changes, the governor of Ohio in 1990 granted clemency to 26 women who were incarcerated for killing or assaulting their abusive partners. Since then, governors in twenty other states have freed more than 100 battered women who were in prison for similar crimes (cited in Gross, 1997).

The use of the battered woman's syndrome defense is not limited to cases in which women strike back at their abusers. It can also be used in cases of abused women who are accused of committing crimes against others, including their own children. In 1995 an Indiana woman was convicted of criminal neglect and sentenced to 20 years in prison for leaving her 4-year-old daughter in the care of a boyfriend, despite evidence of prior abuse and the fact that he threatened to kill them both. He eventually beat the girl to death. But 2 years later, her conviction was overturned because it was determined that the mother suffered from battered woman's syndrome and feared for her own life so much that she was incapable of protecting her daughter (McNeil, 1997).

Advocates for battered women say that these legal actions, and others like them, mark a positive shift in attitudes toward domestic violence. They are an indication that people are finally realizing that some women are trapped physically and emotionally in abusive situations and are unable to simply walk away.

Critics, however, argue that such legal actions send a very dangerous message to women. According to the president of the Ohio Prosecuting Attorney's Association, "The fact that you're battered does not give you license to kill. Now instead of going to the courts, or getting a divorce, these women will think, 'Maybe I'll kill him.'" Another Ohio prosecutor said, "Our concern is that in the future we're going to get a lot of women claiming to be battered. In our view, it is not a proper defense for murder" (quoted in Wilkerson, 1990, p. 11).

Others argue that the battered woman syndrome is a setback for the women's movement because it depicts battered women as psychologically impaired and helpless rather than as rational individuals responding to perceived danger (Bowker, 1993; Downs, 1996). They point to the most famous case—or infamous, depending on your perspective—involving the use of the battered woman syndrome defense, that of Lorena Bobbitt, who in 1993 was acquitted of charges that she maliciously wounded her husband John when she cut off his penis with a kitchen knife. The jury decided that Ms. Bobbitt was not responsible for her actions because a history of physical, psychological, and sexual abuse by her husband had rendered her temporarily insane. Instead of focusing public attention on the societywide problem of domestic violence, this case simply became a sensational news story about an individual woman who had "gone crazy" and was unable to control her actions.

Power and Violence in Gay and Lesbian Households

Although domestic violence between heterosexual spouses gets most of the attention, a growing number of researchers point out that domestic violence is also becoming more common in gay and lesbian relationships (Lockhart, White, Causby, & Isaac, 1994; Renzetti, 1992). The violence that takes place in homosexual relationships, according to recent research, is as prevalent as battering in heterosexual relationships (Coleman, 1996).

The causes of domestic violence are also much the same. For example, although most gay and lesbian couples promote and support the ideal of equal power in their relationships, a substantial minority of them—close to 40 percent in one study—report that power is unequally distributed (Renzetti, 1992). The power differences tend not to derive from the typical correlates of power found in heterosexual relationships: income, education, and sex. Instead it comes from things like who has primary responsibility for financial expenses and household chores (Kelly & Warshafsky, 1987). These power differences don't automatically generate violence. However, as we find in heterosexual relationships, they are associated with heightened levels of physical and psychological abuse (Elliot, 1996).

For the most part, homosexual domestic violence has remained invisible to the public, making it especially difficult for victims to get help. Battered gay men, for example, cannot get sympathy for being the victims of sexism and male dominance, as battered heterosexual women sometimes get. Indeed, many gay male victims themselves believe that battering is something that happens only to women and are extremely uncomfortable identifying themselves as battered (Letellier, 1996). A "real man"—regardless of sexual orientation—is supposed to be able to protect himself in any situation.

Many gay male victims of intimate violence do try to protect themselves when being beaten by striking back at their partners. Such retaliation—whether effective or futile—enables these men to characterize the violence as "mutual combat," an explanation which implies that both men are equally capable of and willing to commit violence. Unfortunately, such a characterization suggests that the violence is a "relationship problem" for which they are both equally responsible and not an act of aggression inflicted by one partner on the other.

Battered gay men and lesbians have an especially difficult time escaping the violence and getting help because of the denigration and animosity directed toward homosexuals in the larger society and the gay community's failure to acknowledge domestic violence as a serious problem. Consequently, battered homosexual partners are even less likely than battered heterosexual wives to tell anyone about the abuse and seek help, putting themselves at risk for more severe and more frequent violence. Resources available to assist them are almost nonexistent. For instance, half a million gay men or more are battered each year, yet only six agencies or organizations nationwide exist specifically to help them (Letellier, 1996).

Child Abuse

If we take violence to mean *any* act of physical aggression directed by one person toward another—including a parent spanking and slapping a child—then approximately nine out of every ten American children under the age of 3 have been the object of violence (Straus & Gelles, 1990). According to one national survey, if we look at the more abusive forms of violence (kicking, biting, punching, beating up, burning, hitting with an object, scalding, and threatening with a knife or a gun), approximately 6.9 million American children are physically abused by their parents or adult caretakers each year (Straus & Gelles, 1990). This figure is about sixteen times higher than the annual number of cases officially reported, suggesting that the vast majority of child abuse incidents remain hidden from the police and social service agencies. To make matters worse, a recent study by the Department of Health and Human Services confirmed that the number of child abuse cases has risen dramatically in the past decade—although it's not clear whether this rise represents an actual increase or better reporting of cases ("Child abuse," 1996). (See Demo•Graphic Essay, "Child Abuse and Maltreatment," at the end of the chapter.)

Child abuse is frequently fatal. Homicide is one of the five leading causes of death for children between 1 and 18 years of age in this country. More than 1,300 children are killed by their parents or caretakers each year (cited in Gelles, 1995). Parents and caretakers (including stepparents) are the most likely perpetrators of homicide of children younger than 5.

Child Abuse Across Cultures

Around the world, most acts of direct violence against children are carried out by their parents or by others with their parents' approval. Anthropologist David Levinson (1989) studied ninety small-scale and folk societies in all major cultural regions of the world to determine the extent to which violence against children is present in family life worldwide. About 74 percent of the societies he examined used physical punishment of children. Such punishment included slapping, spanking, hitting, beating, scalding, burning, pushing, pinching, and switching.

In most societies where physical punishment of children is used, it is used infrequently. But some, such as the Goajiro of Colombia, rely on physical punishment as their major method of child rearing:

There are punishments of various kinds. Some ... consist of striking the child, and these are the most frequent. They slap them on the mouth when they are insolent when given an order or when they give a sharp answer to the father or mother. They are punched and kicked or are whipped with lassos or riding whips, with twigs from woods or cudgels; but the mother generally beats them with a bunch of nettles when they commit any kind of naughtiness.... Another quite common form of punishment is to take the child and put him into a mesh bag of agave fiber, sling it on one of the high branches on [a bough-covered shelter] and rotate it until the child is nauseated and vomits, becoming unconscious. He is then lowered and left on the ground until he recovers. (quoted in Levinson, 1989, p. 28)

Ironically, the children most at risk for maltreatment worldwide are those who are most frail: the sick, malnourished, deformed, and unwanted. In many societies—such as the United States—stepchildren are also particularly vulnerable to physical abuse (Kobrin, 1991). On the other hand, children in extended-family households that contain many relatives are less likely to be physically punished than children in single-parent or nuclear family households (Levinson, 1989). When child rearing is shared within a supportive community, chances of maltreatment are diminished. Such networks not only scrutinize the actions of parents and enforce standards of child care, they provide assistance with child rearing tasks and responsibilities as well. Among rural Hawaiians, for instance, relatives don't hesitate to yell from one house to the next that a spanking has gone on long enough or is too severe for what the child did (Kobrin, 1991).

▲ Chapter 5 explains that different cultures have very different ideas about what constitutes appropriate child rearing and, therefore, have very different ideas about what constitutes child abuse.

It's important to remember that the abusive nature of a particular act of violence or punishment lies not in the nature of the act itself but in the way it is defined by a particular culture. ▲ What we in the United States consider to be the "healthy" practice of isolating small children in beds and rooms of their own at night would be considered abusive by members of societies in which parents form close bonds with their children by sleeping with them in the same bed. In Turkey, mothers routinely kiss and praise the genitals of their young children when they're playing or when their diapers are being changed, an act that would be considered sexual abuse in this country (Olson, 1981).

Even a phenomenon so universally disagreeable as a parent causing the death of a child can be understood quite differently in different cultures. In one region of northeastern Brazil, for example, mothers show such extreme neglect for some of their children that the infants eventually die. But when we look at the situation more closely, this apparently harsh treatment makes cultural sense (Scheper-Hughes, 1989). This area is extremely poor with a very high rate of infant and child mortality. Children are most often raised in single-parent households. Mothers commonly leave babies at home alone when they go to work.

The high expectancy of infant death has led to a pattern of nurturing in which infants are divided into two groups: those who are healthy and have a good chance of surviving and those who are sickly and have little chance of surviving. The latter designation is applied to children who are born weak, small, wasted, and passive. They suffer frequent respiratory infections and other common ailments of infancy. People in this region say that such children are born "wanting to die."

The children who are considered "survivors" are nurtured and cared for quite well. The others, however, are purposely neglected. If they develop acute symptoms like convulsions or very high fevers, food is withheld and they are simply left alone to die. Some die even before they have shown any life-threatening symptoms. Their death is seen as a way of letting nature take its course.

In this area of Brazil, learning to become a good mother means learning when to let go of a child who shows it "wants" to die. Although this emotional detachment contributes to the already high infant mortality rate, it is not seen as abusive within that culture. Instead, it is considered a practical recognition that not all of one's children can be expected to live. Under desperate economic conditions, selective neglect is a survival strategy that "weeds out" the weakest infants in order to enhance the life chances of healthier siblings and future children.

In Japan, child abuse and neglect—as we understand them in the West—do not constitute a serious social problem. Japanese parents rarely inflict physical punishment on their children. To Japanese mothers, who tend to spend a great deal of time with their children, the American practice of using babysitters so that parents can go out and do things on their own may very well suggest child neglect.

When Japanese parents do act aggressively toward their children, their violent acts take a different form from those commonly inflicted by American parents. Japanese parents, especially mothers, are more likely to abandon or even kill their children than to physically beat them. One study found that in a 1-year span, only 26 cases of child abuse were reported for the entire country. That same period, however, witnessed 139 cases of abandonment, 137 cases of abandonment that resulted in the child's death, 54 cases of murder or infanticide, and 67 cases of "joint suicide" in which the child was killed by the parents, who then killed themselves (Wagatsuma, 1981).

An explanation for this phenomenon lies in the traditional Japanese belief that the healthy and successful development of a child requires more than rearing by the biological parents. The child also needs the nurturing and protection of many other people in the community, who often become "ritual parents" for the child. Hence, when Japanese parents can't trust in or depend on others for the care of their children, they may kill or abandon them out of despair. Those who feel that they themselves have failed at providing for and properly raising their child may also take their own lives.

The Emergence of Child Abuse as a Social Problem

In the distant past, Roman law and English common law granted parents limitless power over their children, who had no legal right to protection against their parents. American parents in the eighteenth and nineteenth centuries had the right to impose any punishment deemed necessary for the child's upbringing. Terms like *child abuse, child battering,* and *child neglect* only appeared on the social scene within the past 3 decades or so (Johnson, 1995). Indeed, the country had no child abuse laws until the early 1960s (Pfohl, 1977).

In 1962 an article titled "The Battered-Child Syndrome" was published in the *Journal of the American Medical Association.* The article was accompanied by an official editorial asserting the grave nature of this new medical problem. The features of the **battered child syndrome** included traumatic head injuries and long bone fractures inflicted most commonly upon children under the age of 3. The media paid a great deal of attention to this article. By 1967 every state in the country had recognized the problem and quickly passed legislation calling for its control and punishment.

There had been several attempts to draw attention to the problem of child battering in the late nineteenth and early twentieth centuries, but none of these had the backing of groups powerful enough to convince the public that parents who purposely inflict injury upon their children should be punished and perhaps even lose custody of their children. Early efforts to fight child abuse generally resulted in institutionalizing beaten or neglected children rather than punishing violent parents.

The fact that the 1962 article had the backing of the powerful medical profession gave it credibility. However, according to sociologist Stephen Pfohl (1977), medical professionals—who would be the most likely people to see and report the devastating effects of parental violence—were actually unaware of the problem until they were forced to recognize it by a relatively obscure subspecialty: pediatric radiology (the interpretation of children's x-rays).

Pfohl suggests that physicians hadn't "seen" violence against children prior to 1962 for strong professional reasons. The medical profession itself was—and to some degree, still is—dominated by a concern for its power within the larger society. To formally diagnose willful abuse as the cause of a child's injuries would likely subordinate medicine to the interests of the legal profession. Doctors would have to become accessories in the courtroom domain of lawyers.

Moreover, doctors perceived parents as their real clients. After all, the parents, not the children, pay the bills. Diagnosing abuse, therefore, might threaten the physician-client relationship. Likewise, child abuse was not something doctors prior to the 1960s were trained to diagnose. Many of them, too, were parents. They simply bypassed the horrible implications of willful child abuse and saw, instead, a wide range of unusual physical problems. Where they could have seen evidence of deliberate beating, they saw accidents or bruises and fractures of "unspecified origins." According to Pfohl, such collective blindness did not involve bad motives, but instead reflected a *socially organized* lack of perception that kept doctors from coming into conflict with their own professional interests.

Pediatric radiologists broke through these perceptual barriers not because they were especially heroic but because they had more to gain than to lose by publicly recognizing the problem of child abuse. Radiologists were near the bottom of the medical prestige hierarchy. The discovery of the battered child syndrome allowed them to work in the higher-status domain of the more prestigious specialties. Furthermore, pediatric radiologists looked at children's x-rays, not the children themselves. The fact that they didn't see patients face-to-face freed them from the restraints of psychological denial and confidentiality that inhibited the diagnostic judgment of other medical professionals.

Pediatric radiologists were also able to avoid subordination to the legal profession by discovering a noncontroversial medical "syndrome," not a form of criminal behavior. Perpetrators were "sick," not bad. Child abuse, therefore, was something that should be "treated" rather than "punished."

But the medical profession didn't "discover" the problem of child abuse alone. Newspapers, magazines, and television also helped to proliferate the idea of abuse. By 1976, the issue had grown to encompass a much broader array of conditions that threatened the health and well-being of children (Best, 1993). The more general term, *child abuse and neglect,* replaced the narrower concept of the *battered child*. Maltreated children could be abused emotionally, verbally, psychologically, or nutritionally by their parents. Child abuse was now much more than a medical problem to be treated by physicians.

New state laws expanded the official domain of child abuse. As of 1994, all but five states had laws that, to varying degrees, require health practitioners to report cases of suspected domestic violence (Hyman, Schillinger, & Lo, 1995). Nurses, teachers, social workers, and law enforcement officers, in addition to physicians, are now obligated to report their suspicions. Child-protection workers have been granted extraordinary powers to investigate cases and separate children from their parents.

Needless to say, child abuse in recent years has become a well-established social problem. Between 1976 and 1987, reports of suspected child abuse and neglect increased from a little under 670,000 a year to well over 2 million (Besharov, 1993). Polls today consistently show that Americans rate child abuse as very serious. The term itself has become such a fundamental part of the culture that it is now used to describe a variety of problems and concerns, such as failure to pay child support, religious fervor, smoking in the presence of children, parental kidnapping, exposure to explicit rock lyrics, even circumcision (Best, 1993). And child abuse is no longer limited to parents and guardians; now other relatives, teachers, medical personnel, even other children are potential offenders.

Explanations of Child Abuse

▲ Chapter 4 provides a detailed examination of pronatalism.

Pronatalist ideals form the foundation of American family life. ▲ We simply assume, in this culture, that "normal" married couples will have children or at least want to have children. Why, then, in a social environment that idealizes children, would we find such a high rate of child abuse, maltreatment, and neglect?

Individual Factors Like popular theories of spousal violence, popular theories of child abuse tend to focus on characteristics of individual abusive parents. Many people, for instance, assume that parents who beat their children are alcohol or drug abusers or have some personality or psychiatric defect that renders them incapable of controlling their rage. Abusive parents are sometimes characterized as psychologically immature and unable to see their children as children. Therefore, the parents may expect more responsibility and control from their children than the parents themselves are capable of showing, leading to disappointment, anger, and violence. Most experts agree, however, that such characteristics actually account for only a very small percentage of child abuse cases.

A parent's socioeconomic condition would also seem to have something to do with child abuse. Existing data indicate that cases of child abuse are more likely to be reported among parents who have low income, low educational attainment, and long-term dependence on public assistance. In fact, any purported racial differences in domestic violence tend to disappear when parents' social-class standing is taken into consideration (Cazenave & Straus, 1990). ▲

▲ The influences of race and ethnicity on family life are discussed in Issue 6; the influences of social class are discussed in Issue 7.

But we must be cautious about drawing the conclusion that child abuse is confined to lower-class parents. Wealthier parents might very well be better able to hide abuse since they are more likely to live in private homes and are less likely to use public services for health care or transportation, where their actions can be scrutinized by others. Indeed, some studies have found that medical practitioners are more likely to label an injured child as "abused" if the parents are perceived as working class than if they're perceived as middle class (cited in Gelles & Straus, 1988).

Unemployment, often associated with other risk factors like low self-esteem, stress, and depression, is another factor frequently associated with child abuse. Unemployed people also spend more time at home, increasing their interactions with children. Certainly the resulting tension and frustration can increase the likelihood of child abuse as well as other forms of domestic violence. ▲

▲ Downward mobility can have a severe impact on parent-child relationships, as Issue 7 explains.

An individual-level factor that has become one of the most popular explanations of child abuse is the so-called **cycle of violence,** which refers to the tendency for people who are abused as children to grow up to be abusing parents and violent spouses themselves. Although this explanation is currently a popular one, childhood exposure to violence does not predetermine that people will become violent as adults. Empirical tests of this hypothesis find that roughly 30 percent of abusive adults were themselves abused as children. This figure is substantially higher than the rate of abuse found in the general population (between 2 percent and 4 percent), but it shows that most abusive adults (approximately 70 percent) were not battered as children (Gelles & Strauss, 1988).

In fact, children who *observe* their parents hitting each other, rather than being victims of violence themselves, may actually be more likely to become violent adults. According to Gelles and Straus (1988), seeing such violence teaches a child three things:

- Those who love you are also those who hit you, and those you love are people you can hit.
- Hitting those you love is "morally right."
- If other means of getting your way, dealing with stress, or expressing yourself don't work, violence is permissible.

Although these personal factors may explain the violent outbursts of some individual parents, they do little to explain why child abuse exists as a societal phenomenon and why it is so difficult to stop. To address these issues, we must turn to broader social and cultural conditions.

Parental Rights and State Intervention   On the night of April 18, 1993, Amanda Wallace and her two sons—3-year-old Joseph and 1-year-old Joshua—were visiting relatives. Ms. Wallace began raving that Joseph was nothing but trouble and threatened to kill him with a knife. The boy's grandmother offered to keep him overnight, but Ms. Wallace refused. At about 1:30 A.M. she stuffed a sock in Joseph's mouth and secured it with duct tape. She wrapped an extension cord around Joseph's neck several times. She carried him into the living room where she looped the cord around the metal crank arm over the door and, as he waved goodbye, hung him (Ingrassia & McCormick, 1994).

Amanda Wallace had been a ward of the state since the age of 8. Between 1976 and 1989, when Joseph was born, she had swallowed broken glass and batteries and had attempted to disembowel herself. When pregnant with Joseph she repeatedly stuck soda bottles into her vagina, claiming the baby wasn't hers. When Joseph was born, a psychiatrist who had examined Amanda warned that she "should never have custody of this or any other baby."

When Joseph was 11 months old, he was removed from his mother because of suspected child abuse. But an assistant public defender persuaded a juvenile-court judge to return Joseph to Amanda. Over the next 2 years, caseworkers removed Joseph from the home two more times following his mother's suicide attempts. A Department of Children and Family Services report recommended that he be sent back to his mother, citing the fact that she had gotten an apartment and had entered counseling. The last time Joseph was returned to his mother—2 months before his death—the judge ignored Amanda's turbulent history saying to her, "It sounds like you're doing O.K. Good luck."

Each time the state had determined that, in the interests of protecting the mother's parental rights to control her own affairs, it would be best if the child was returned to her. The sanctity of the family, state officials concluded, was paramount, no matter how undesirable the situation might appear to outside observers.

Most cases of child abuse aren't nearly as horrific as this one. Yet even here, where the evidence *against* placing this child with his mother would seem incontrovertible, the decision was still made to do so—on three separate occasions. According to the American Public Welfare Association, two-thirds of abused or neglected children who are placed in foster care are eventually reunited with their parents (cited in Ingrassia & McCormick, 1994).

Most modern child abuse laws are designed to uphold the family's integrity—that is, keep the family intact by giving abusive parents multiple opportunities to change their ways and retain custody—not to protect children. ▲ As these laws read, parents must be given every reasonable opportunity to resolve their problems before a child is removed permanently from the home. Children are not entitled to be free from all harm, just serious harm. Indeed, in 1989 the U.S. Supreme Court ruled that the state had no constitutional duty to protect abused children against violence at the hands of their parents ("Can't sue," 1989).

▲ This is a manifestation of our strong cultural bias toward family privacy, as Issue 3 explains.

However, the long-held premise that keeping families intact is the best policy is weakening. More and more parents are being arrested for child abuse and neglect, and many cities and states are beginning to favor child protection over family preservation (Swarns, 1997). Some child welfare and law enforcement officials across the country have been doing everything possible to delay or avoid returning children to potentially abusive or neglectful families.

But as a result, more children are spending longer periods of time in foster care. Since 1985 the population of foster children has nearly doubled—from 276,000 to 500,000. These children stay in foster homes for 3 years on average (cited in Kilborn, 1997a).

In 1997 President Clinton signed into law a bill that helps states take youngsters away from abusive parents. For instance, it requires states to seek the termination of parental rights for any child under 10 who has been in foster care for 15 of the previous 22 months and to seek termination immediately with evidence of severe abuse, including abandonment, torture or physical or sexual abuse, or of the death of a sibling at the hands of a parent. The new law also requires states to set up a permanent-placement plan for a child after 1 year of foster care, rather than 18 months, as previous rules stipulated (Seelye, 1997).

When we weigh the value of parental rights and the desire to keep families intact against the safety of individual family members, the solutions to the problem of domestic violence become complex. On one side are those situations—like the murder of Joseph Wallace—in which state intervention is considered *too slow* or insufficient to prevent serious harm to a child in danger. In these cases, if families are allowed to function as they see fit or if we hesitate about violating parental rights and family autonomy, some individual members will suffer.

On the other side are those situations in which state intervention is considered to be *too quick* or overzealous, causing unnecessary harm to the family. As you know, by its very nature, domestic violence thrives on privacy. So to encourage ordinary members of the community to report cases of suspected abuse, most states let the accusers remain anonymous. Even if the accusers do identify themselves to social workers, the state is required to keep their identities secret.

Research indicates that perhaps as many as two-thirds of anonymous child abuse reports are designated as "unfounded" (Best, 1993). Some false accusations are intentionally false; others may be based on honest mistakes or exaggerated concerns. Authorities in the field say that most baseless complaints come from warring family members, especially ex-spouses looking for revenge or seeking to gain custody of children.

Some states have tried (so far unsuccessfully) to bar social service officials from beginning a child abuse investigation based on an anonymous report. But many states across the nation have been successful in passing laws that make false reports of domestic violence a crime. Such attempts, designed to protect the rights of people falsely accused, will unfortunately have a chilling effect on well-meaning relatives. They might not come forward to report real abuse if the government doesn't shield their identities. Therefore, the cloak of privacy may drop over family violence once again.

Corporal Punishment

No one wants to see children hurt, abused, or killed. At the same time, though, the U.S. public generally approves of nonabusive, disciplinary violence: **corporal punishment** (see Exhibit 6.3).

▲ For more on the view that children are "little monsters" requiring stringent guidance, see Chapter 5.

In our country, hitting one's children "when necessary" is a cultural norm. ▲ "When necessary" is usually taken to mean when the child continually misbehaves after being told to stop or does something potentially dangerous. The most famous and popular baby advice book, Benjamin Spock's *Baby and Child Care,* doesn't advocate corporal punishment. However, it states that corporal punishment should be avoided "whenever possible," implying that sometimes it's not possible to avoid hitting children. Indeed, most advice books say that corporal punishment ought to be used under certain circumstances. Few, if any, argue unequivocally against it (Straus, 1994).

The distinction between abusive violence and "corporal punishment" is not always clear. The only formal difference between the two is that abuse is usually thought to cause perceptible

Exhibit 6.3

Necessity of
Sometimes
Spanking Children:
Survey of Adults

*United States:
1986–1996*

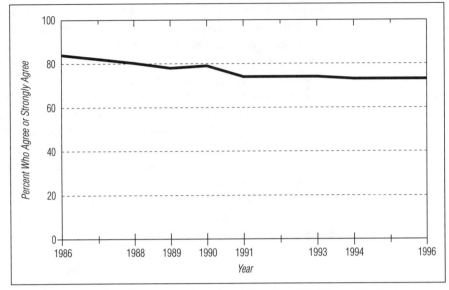

Source of data: National Opinion Research Center, University of Chicago, *General Social Survey, 1986–1996.*

injury while corporal punishment does not (or should not). No parent has the legal right to
"abuse" his or her child, but parents in all fifty states have the right to hit their children, provided
no serious injury results. About 90 percent of American parents are thought to hit their children
to punish them (Straus, 1994).

As widespread as corporal punishment is, it is an almost invisible part of American life.
Since most people spank or have been spanked, corporal punishment is so unremarkable and so
taken for granted that few people give it much thought (Straus, 1994). In fact, parents opposed to
the use of spanking are sometimes the ones who have to defend their child rearing philosophy to
skeptical friends and neighbors.

Despite its ubiquity, acceptability, and perceived harmlessness, 40 years of research indicate
that corporal punishment can have some of the same negative effects on children as child abuse:
physical aggression, delinquency, or both. The more violent parents are toward their children—
regardless of whether they use "ordinary" corporal punishment or more abusive forms of violence—the more violent these children are toward siblings, friends, and others (Straus, 1994).
When these children become adults, they are more likely to show elevated rates of child abuse
and spouse abuse than individuals who had never been hit as children. Of course, not all children who are physically punished become abusive adults. Nevertheless, such a finding has important social implications. To the extent that ordinary violence is linked to future child abuse
and wife beating, our efforts to reduce the incidence of family violence must include attention to
the less-extreme sorts of violence that are so typical of American families (Straus, 1990).

Concerns over the effects of corporal punishment have led several countries (Norway, Sweden, Denmark, Finland, and Austria) to criminalize spanking in recent years. These laws are
civil, not criminal. They provide no legal punishment for parents caught spanking their children.

Instead, these largely symbolic laws are meant to set national standards, educate and help parents, and make a cultural statement that hitting children is unacceptable. The Swedish law, for instance, realizes that parents need help now and then in dealing with their children, so many kinds of assistance are available. The law also focuses on teaching children in school and through the media that parents aren't allowed to hit them. As a result, public attitudes have changed. Today, 71 percent of Swedes favor managing children without corporal punishment.

Although most Americans would prefer to live in a nonviolent society, efforts to impose such antispanking laws here have been rare and futile. Our general cultural tolerance of violence, our extreme individualism, our fear of unwarranted government intervention in families, and our favorable attitudes toward punishment as a child rearing strategy present formidable obstacles to the passage of such laws. Hitting children is so common in this country that the idea that ending the practice will somehow benefit society is considered ridiculous by most people.

Indeed, the American public is reluctant to get involved in interactions between parents and their children. According to a survey by the National Committee for Prevention of Child Abuse, only 17 percent of its sample said they had "stopped someone they didn't know from hitting a child," a figure that is likely inflated by the vague wording of the question and the desire to report socially desirable actions (cited in Davis, 1991). Moreover, those who do get involved are often made to feel like busybodies who take an undue, even perverse, interest in the personal affairs of strangers.

Conclusion

Intimate violence is still defined differently than other forms of criminal violence. We (myself included) still use modifiers like "intimate," "date," "domestic," or "family" to separate the assaults, rapes, and murders that take place between people who are intimately involved with one another from those that take place between strangers. In so doing, we—perhaps unintentionally—perpetuate the myth that intimate violence is something other than criminal violence and that the relationship between perpetrator and victim is a key factor in determining the severity of a violent act.

Although it would be comforting to believe that intimate violence is rare and is committed only by "sick" boyfriends, parents, or spouses, you have seen in this chapter that it happens with alarming frequency and is likely to be committed by people we would otherwise consider normal. Dating violence, spouse abuse, child abuse, as well as other forms of family violence are found in every class, race, and religion. Most people in the world at some point in their lives either experience or witness violence between members of their families. Intimate violence is not an aberration; it is a fundamental characteristic of the way we relate to one another in intimate, family settings.

And so a complete understanding of domestic violence requires an acknowledgment of the social, historical, and cultural environment in which it is embedded. Wife abuse exists only in those societies where men learn that dominating women is appropriate, where gender inequality exists domestically and economically, and where aggression is encouraged by the culture. Child abuse exists only in those societies where physical punishment is tolerated and where parents are granted unquestioned power over their children. As one author puts it, "When the larger culture aggrandizes wife beaters . . . or nods approvingly at child slappers, the family gets a little more dangerous for everyone, and so, inevitably, does the larger world" (Ehrenreich, 1994, p. 62).

CHAPTER HIGHLIGHTS

- Outside of wars and riots, the home is the most violent location in American society. Family violence crosses lines of class, race, sexual orientation, and geography.

- Although domestic violence is still more likely to occur in private than in public, it no longer has the tacit approval and tolerance it once had from police, courts, and the public at large.

- According to recent research, most dating relationships may be marked by some form of coercion, violence, or sexual assault.

- Spouse abuse is a phenomenon that occurs worldwide. Instead of viewing it as a product of "sick" individuals, sociologists are likely to view it as the product of a culture that tolerates violence in a variety of situations, that traditionally grants men power and authority over women in families, and that values family privacy and autonomy over the well-being of individual members.

- Escape from abusive relationships is often hindered by a lack of institutional support from hospitals, police, and courts. Sometimes the resources in place to assist battered women are inadequate to deal with the problem.

- Men's traditional power over women is changing both in individual families and in the larger society, but the power parents exert over their children remains unquestioned. Around the world, most acts of direct violence against children are carried out by parents or by people who have the parents' approval. But the designation of a violent act against a child as abusive lies not in the nature of the act but in the way it's defined by a particular culture.

DEMO•GRAPHIC ESSAY

Child Abuse and Maltreatment

Between 1990 and 1995, the number of children involved in cases of reported child abuse or neglect rose from under 700,000 to approximately 1 million, an increase of approximately 50 percent (see Exhibit 6-A). Of particular interest, however, is that some forms of child abuse hardly increased at all (for example, emotional abuse), while "other" types of abuse almost tripled in number and "neglect" increased by half. It seems unlikely that these reported numbers accurately reflect actual behavior. Instead, there were very likely changes in the way social workers defined and substantiated abuse. Furthermore, as child abuse has received increasing attention from the popular media, it is likely that the kinds of cases that went unreported in 1990 were reported to authorities in 1995. The phenomenon of child abuse and neglect therefore is not a clearly defined behavior. Rather, it reflects cultural norms and values, in terms of both the actual behavior and the reporting of that behavior.

Exhibit 6-A

Child Abuse and Neglect Cases (by type of substantiated maltreatment)

United States: 1990 and 1995

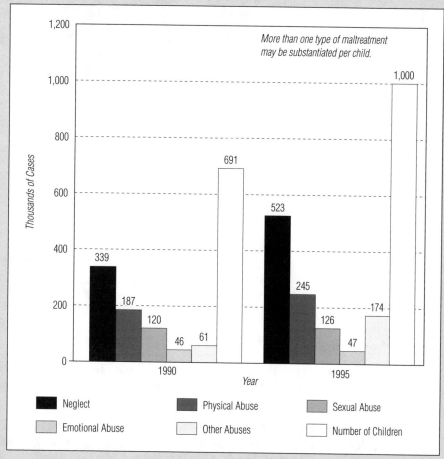

Source of data: U.S. Bureau of the Census, *Statistical Abstract of the United States: 1997* (117th edition). Washington, DC, 1997.

Exhibit 6-B

Child Abuse and
Neglect Cases
(by age of victim)

United States: 1995

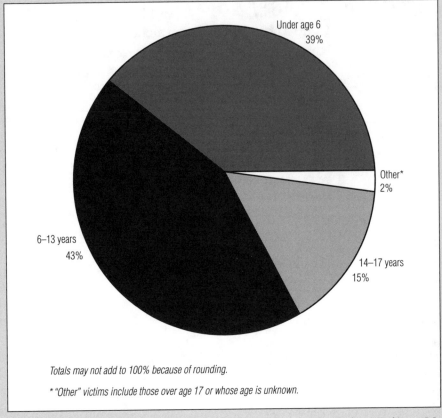

Under age 6
39%

Other*
2%

14–17 years
15%

6–13 years
43%

Totals may not add to 100% because of rounding.

* *"Other" victims include those over age 17 or whose age is unknown.*

Source of data: U.S. Bureau of the Census, *Statistical Abstract of the United States: 1997* (117th edition). Washington, DC, 1997.

Another variable to examine is the age of child abuse and neglect victims. Exhibit 6-B divides reported child abuse and neglect cases into four age groups: under age 6, ages 6 to 13, ages 14 to 17, and others. Contrast this graph with Exhibit 6-C, which shows the population of children in similar age groups in the United States in 1995.

Questions for Further Study

1. Suppose you had the opportunity to interview social workers who work with cases of child abuse and neglect. What questions would you ask based upon the information in Exhibit 6-A?

2. From Exhibits 6-B and 6-C, calculate the rate of child abuse and neglect for each age group (the percentage of child abuse victims in a given age group divided by the percentage of children in that approximate age group). Which age group of victims has the

Exhibit 6-C

Child Population

United States: 1995

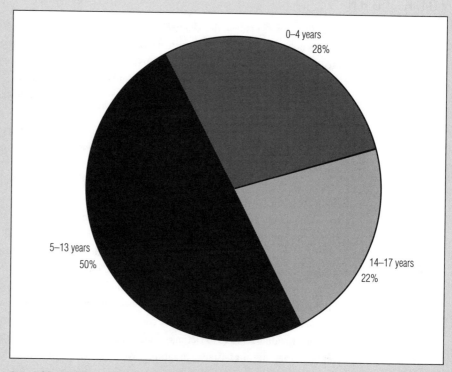

0–4 years
28%

5–13 years
50%

14–17 years
22%

Source of data: U.S. Bureau of the Census, *Statistical Abstract of the United States: 1997* (117th edition). Washington, DC, 1997.

highest rate of abuse? Which group has the lowest rate? What are some possible reasons for these differences by age? How do you suppose the types of abuse shown in Exhibit 6-A vary by age?

3. What variables other than age and type of abuse could you examine in order to understand more clearly reporting biases in child abuse and neglect?

YOUR TURN

One of the points made in this chapter is that the institutional support necessary to help people in violent home situations is often ineffective. What are the agencies or organizations in your area that deal with domestic violence? Consider shelters for battered women, foster care, individual counseling services, special units within hospitals or police departments, government agencies such as child protective services, support programs for batterers or abusive parents, and so on.

Try to interview a representative of each agency or program. Can the persons you interview provide a statistical breakdown of the people who are aided by their programs—for example, by age, race, social class, or marital status? Can each person identify a "typical" pattern of violence—for example, how the typical incident starts, how long it lasts, how frequent such incidents are in the life of a client?

What do the people you interview see as the primary goals of their programs (prevention, treatment, punishment)? How do they go about achieving these goals? What do they feel are the most serious impediments to their ability to provide services? Are these impediments more likely to stem from individual clients (such as the unwillingness of battered women to press charges against their assailants) or from institutions (such as not enough government or private funding to provide the services necessary to help victims leave abusive situations)?

Considering the information you've collected, what do you think the community's role ought to be in providing services to victims of domestic violence? Should the primary focus be on prevention programs or assistance programs? Would stricter laws and tighter enforcement make the problem better or worse?

CHAPTER 7

Divorce and Remarriage

I will never forget the day in second grade when my teacher stood at the front of the room after we pledged allegiance to the flag and briefly, nonchalantly announced to the class that Kim Hildebrandt, the girl who sat next to me, would from that point forward be called Kim Louise. That was all she said; she provided no explanation. Then she gave us that day's reading assignment.

I looked at Kim. She appeared slightly embarrassed, but any 8-year-old kid would look embarrassed if the teacher singled him or her out like that in front of the whole class. So I didn't think much of the teacher's announcement. I just figured her family probably changed their name because "Hildebrandt" was too hard to pronounce.

A few weeks later the teacher made another announcement: Billy Farrell—the dark-haired boy nobody liked because of his fondness for punching people in the arm—would now be called Billy Kuhns. Now I was puzzled. What was going on here? Why were all these kids' families changing their names? I put the question to Billy, who angrily and condescendingly replied, "My parents got a *divorce*, stupid!" and walked away. *Divorce*? I didn't know what a divorce was. I'd never heard the word before.

So that night, I asked my mother. She patiently explained to me that sometimes husbands and wives stop loving each other. When that happens, some of them decide to stop living together. She said that the kids in my class were changing their names because they were now living with their mothers, who had gone back to using their "maiden" names. I pressed on. "Do we know anyone who's divorced?" I asked.

"Are you kidding?" she replied incredulously. "Of course we do." She reminded me of my cousins who lived with their mother while their father lived across town with another woman and her two children. (All the time I thought that he lived where he did so he could be closer to his work.) She told me that the nice musician who lived alone across the street was divorced, as was the neighbor a few doors down whose children were only around on weekends and didn't go to my school. She reminded me that my friend, Mike, lived with his mother in a tiny apartment because his parents were divorced and his father lived in Cleveland.

The pathos in her voice as she told me about these people clearly signaled that divorce was not something good and that it should only be spoken of quietly, like cancer or institutionalized relatives. She told me not to tease those kids whose parents had divorced since they were "suffering enough already." The way she talked about the "tragedy" of divorce frightened me. I hoped I would never have to hear the word again. But, of course, I *would* hear the word again. Many times.

I don't think I was particularly naive as a child. But the fact that I had no idea what divorce was, even though so many people "had" one, showed how hidden and unpopular the topic was 30 years ago. Today things are quite different. You'd be hard-pressed to find an 8-year-old now who doesn't know what the word *divorce* means. Most children have witnessed the end of a marriage, either that of their parents' or of someone they are close to. Divorce has become a part of everyday life. It's in our movies, television shows, and novels. The children's sections of book stores stock picture books showing divorcing dinosaurs or Muppet babies worrying about the possibility of their parents divorcing. Hallmark has an entire line of greeting cards for parents whose children live elsewhere.

Thirty years ago a divorced politician didn't stand a chance of being elected. Today many of our most influential lawmakers are divorced. In the 1980s Ronald Reagan's divorce and remarriage didn't prevent him from being elected president twice. In the most recent presidential election, people barely mentioned candidate Bob Dole's divorce and remarriage. Most people now recognize that in some situations a divorce may be preferable to an unhappy marriage. In short, divorce is as much a part of American family life as, well, marriage.

This chapter examines divorce, single parenting, and remarriage at both the societal and the individual levels. These are profoundly emotional and often disorienting experiences for all involved. Yet, with such a high rate of divorce in our society, we must see it not just as a personal tragedy but as a social process with cultural and historical causes and consequences.

Children of Divorce

Although the divorce rate is quite high in American society, few couples contemplate divorce on their wedding day. With all the love and good cheer, all the toasts and vows, the possibility of divorce seems remote. Yet many couples do divorce, with sometimes painful consequences not only for themselves but for those who live within their circle.

As traumatic as it can sometimes be, divorce often brings siblings together to become each other's emotional anchor.

Divorce often places parents in unfamiliar and uncomfortable roles. Children may see their noncustodial parent only on alternating weekends, leading to awkwardness and even feelings of bitter resentment.

To ease the tension, noncustodial parents—sometimes with the help of grandparents—try to fill the time spent with their children with enjoyable activities such as baseball games.

Remarriage can bring a whole new set of difficulties as another family with its own unique personalities and traditions enters the mix. To a child used to being the "baby" of the family, a new gaggle of step-siblings can seem like an invasion.

Indeed, the child may feel left out of the picture entirely as the newly constituted family engages in the process of readjusting and redefining family roles. Because of such difficulties, many children of divorce find the companionship and nurturing they need from their friends.

Although most children eventually adapt to their new family circumstances, the process can be a rocky one.

Divorce in Cultural Context

Our preoccupation in this country with the frequency and consequences of divorce sometimes obscures the fact that divorce exists worldwide. Although it is more common and more acceptable in some places than in others, virtually all societies have provisions—legal, communal, or religious—for dissolving marriages (McKenry & Price, 1995).

Worldwide, divorce rates tend to be correlated with socioeconomic development. The underdeveloped or developing countries of Latin America (for example, Ecuador, Nicaragua, and Peru) and Asia (for example, Thailand, Malaysia, Sri Lanka) have substantially lower divorce rates than the developed countries of western Europe and North America (Trent & South, 1989). Practically every industrialized country in the world experienced an increase in its divorce rate between 1950 and 1990 (Goode, 1993).

China provides a good example of the influence of socioeconomic development on divorce patterns. Rapid economic and social changes in China over the past several years have brought a surge in the divorce rate. Between 1990 and 1994, the divorce rate in Beijing more than doubled. According to some observers, the increase reflects the Chinese people's new social and economic freedom and the rising expectations that women bring to their marriages. More than 70 percent of Chinese divorces are initiated by women (Faison, 1995). This trend is a far cry from past attitudes when, as one Chinese lawyer put it, "People would let a temple be destroyed before they would let a marriage fail" (quoted in Faison, 1995, pp. A1, A6). Now most Chinese people see divorce as an acceptable alternative to an unhappy marriage. Where divorces once took years to win approval, they now take 3 days if both spouses agree.

In societies where religion plays a dominant role in everyday life, the effects of socioeconomic development on divorce are tempered. In fact, even in some societies that we would consider modern and developed, powerful religious forces have kept divorce illegal until quite recently. Italians, for instance, have been able to legally divorce for only a little over a decade. In 1995 the Irish government began a campaign against the Catholic Church over the country's constitutional ban on divorce. The government estimated that at least 80,000 people were locked in broken marriages and that they deserved the right to remarry. But the Catholic bishops launched a massive advertising counterattack, arguing that even unhappily married people have an obligation to keep their marriages intact to provide a good example for society. The referendum was passed by a miniscule margin and in 1997, for the first time, people in Ireland had the right to legally divorce.

In many parts of the world, women have historically had limited access to divorce. In some patriarchal societies they have only recently been granted a say in the divorce process, even though men have traditionally been able to dissolve marriages very easily (McKenry & Price, 1995). ▲ In Egypt, for instance, men don't need a reason to divorce their wives. Women's rights to petition for divorce, on the other hand, are severely limited. Divorced women must wait 3 months before remarrying and are entitled to only 1 year of spousal support (McKenry & Price, 1995). In traditional Iran, women who are divorced are entitled to spousal support for only 3 months. To escape a bad marriage, many Iranian women have to forfeit all their possessions to their husbands. Men almost always retain custody of the children and continue to live in the

▲ Issue 5 describes other limits women face in patriarchal societies.

family home. Since Iranian culture discourages women from living by themselves, especially if they are young, they usually end up moving back home so they can be supported by their brothers and father.

In patriarchal societies, access to divorce is often seen as a civil rights issue, an important advancement in the personal freedoms and social status of women. In India, for instance, where arranged marriages are commonplace, divorce offers women an escape from the mistakes their families made in selecting a mate for them.

Yet even in those countries that actively and publicly oppose divorce—such as the Moslem countries of the Middle East or the Catholic countries of Europe—large numbers of people have always found ways, such as desertion or separation, to end marriages that don't work. For instance, in 1984—before divorce was permitted in Italy—about 400,000 married couples were living apart (Goode, 1993).

Some people might even view the trend toward rising divorce worldwide as a welcome end to suffering that people have had to endure under the highly restrictive divorce systems of the past. In China, many people think the increasing divorce rate is a sign of social advancement, a growing indication that people can control their own fates (Faison, 1995).

But despite the fact that the dissolution of marriage is virtually universal, no society places a positive value on divorce. In fact, in most societies, people who divorce are somehow penalized, either through formal controls like fines, prohibitions against remarriage, excommunication, and forced alimony and child support or through informal means such as censure, gossip, and stigmatization.

Divorce American Style

In the United States, divorce is common. In an average year, about 1.2 million divorces take place, a rate of roughly 20 divorces per 1,000 existing marriages (U.S. Bureau of the Census, 1997a). (See Exhibit 7.1.) Although this rate has more or less stabilized over the past decade or so, it is still more than twice the divorce rate of most other industrialized countries (Clark, 1996). (See Exhibit 7.2.)

Probably a little less than half of all marriages that begin this year will end in divorce at some point in the future. Divorce is no longer a rare and stigmatized occurrence; it is an inevitable risk of marriage. One can hardly begin a marriage these days without considering the possibility that it might not last.

Our relatively high divorce rate is often attributed to things like the decreasing influence of religion in people's lives, the liberalization of divorce laws, the rise of individualism, and women's increasing participation in the paid labor force. These changes have indeed created a cultural shift in the perception of marriage. ▲ Marriage has become a *voluntary contract* that can be ended at the discretion of either spouse. In the past, marriage was predominantly an economic agreement, representing the joining of the financial resources of two families. When economic needs—not to mention family expectations and religious norms—held couples together,

▲ This shift in perception is addressed in Issue 8.

Exhibit 7.1

Divorce Rate per
1,000 Marriages

*United States:
1920–1995*

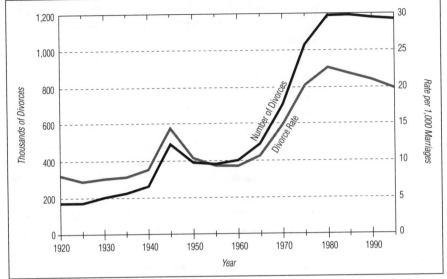

Sources of data: U.S. Bureau of the Census, *Historical Statistics of the United States: Colonial Times to 1970*. Washington, DC, 1975. U.S. Bureau of the Census, *Statistical Abstract of the United States: 1997* (117th edition). Washington, DC, 1997.

people "made do" with loveless, unsatisfying marriages because they had to. Now that these constraints are largely absent, people are less willing to make do (Skolnick, 1996). Today, marriage is seen primarily as an exchange of emotional gratification (Furstenberg & Cherlin, 1991). Hence, people are less inclined to stay in marriages that don't provide satisfaction and happiness.

Racial, Ethnic, and Religious Variation

▲ Issue 6 examines the historical roots of racial and ethnic differences in family experiences.

Divorce rates and perceptions of divorce can vary among racial, ethnic, and religious groups. ▲ For example, studies consistently show that African Americans are more likely than other groups to separate and divorce. But this difference has less to do with race than with socioeconomic status. Studies that compare whites and African Americans of similar socioeconomic status—that is, similar levels of education, income, occupational prestige, and unemployment—find similar rates of divorce (Cherlin, 1992). Thus, lower income, less education, and insecure employment place African-American families at significantly greater risk of marital disruption than other groups.

Ironically, because single-parent households are so common among African Americans, they tend to adjust better after divorce than people from other groups. Moreover because African-American women tend to have greater economic independence than white or Latina women, they are less likely to feel the need to remarry after a divorce. Single-parent status is more acceptable and therefore marriage is less central to their sense of personal well-being (McKenry & Price, 1995).

Exhibit 7.2

Divorce Rate per
1,000 Married
Women

*Selected Countries:
1970, 1980, and 1990*

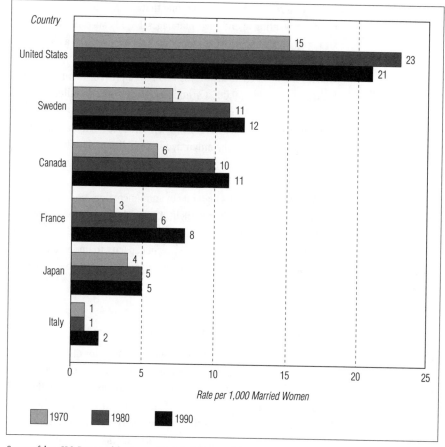

Source of data: U.S. Bureau of the Census, *Statistical Abstract of the United States: 1997* (117th edition). Washington, DC, 1997.

Conversely, the cultural emphasis on family in most Hispanic groups and the constraining role that the Catholic Church plays in their lives may explain their relatively low rate of divorce. Among Asian Americans, too, who have traditionally stressed the family unit over the individual, divorce still carries a significant stigma. Hence, the divorce rate among Asian Americans has consistently been lower than that of the population as a whole. For both Hispanic- and Asian-American groups, though, divorce rates are increasing among younger people, who are generally less influenced than older generations by traditional religious or ethnic values.

Prohibitions against divorce still exist among some American religious groups. Catholics, Jews, and fundamentalist Christians have historically been stricter about marital dissolution than mainstream Protestants. In addition, interfaith marriages tend to be less stable than marriages between people of the same religion. The divorce rate is also high among couples who are unaffiliated with any religious institution, since they are less bound by social conventions and face fewer sanctions than those actively involved with their faith (Glenn & Supancic, 1984).

But no religious group, even one that actively forbids divorce, is completely immune to members wanting to end their marriages. For instance, despite the Catholic Church's clear and strong opposition to divorce, practicing Catholics are just as likely as non-Catholics to divorce (cited in Coontz, 1997). Furthermore, means other than divorce exist to accommodate people whose religious beliefs are strong enough to prevent them from divorcing. Every year in the United States, over 50,000 Catholic marriages are annulled (cited in Woodward, Quade, & Kantrowitz, 1995). An **annulment** is a church declaration that a marriage was invalid from the beginning and therefore never existed in the eyes of God or the church. Since the church does not recognize divorce, the only way for Catholics to dissolve a marriage and be free to marry again in the church or to receive communion and other church sacraments is to have their marriage declared "null and invalid."

You will notice that a high rate of annulment does not challenge the sanctity of marriage as much as a high rate of divorce might. An annulment is not a statement that "the marriage didn't work." It is a statement that the marriage was established on faulty grounds to begin with or that one or both parties lacked sufficient capacity to understand what it means to *be* married. Therefore, individual inability and error are what create bad marriages, not the institution of marriage itself.

Historical Trends in Divorce

▲ Issue 8 provides a critical examination of the notion of family decline.

The current high divorce rate is an oft-cited indicator of the decline of American families. ▲ Such an argument is based on a popular notion that the divorce rate in this country was always very low until it accelerated with unprecedented speed during the 1960s and 1970s, and it has remained perilously high ever since. Some have attributed the rise in the divorce rate to the free-love movement of "swinging singles, open marriages, alternative lifestyles, and women's liberation" (Skolnick, 1991). True, this era was a revolutionary period in American history. Norms governing all aspects of social life were certainly changing. What these conclusions overlook, however, is the longer historical trend in American divorce. People have been comparing the high divorce rates of the 1960s, 1970s, and 1980s to the abnormally low rate of the 1950s.

Divorce has always been a feature of American society. Colonial records throughout the seventeenth and eighteenth centuries reveal a wealth of marital scandals, disruptions, and divorces. Even Puritan settlers condoned and practiced divorce. Indeed, when colonial and state governments attempted to restrict divorce, serious problems immediately became apparent: "Mates mistreated each other, were unfaithful, lived separately, abandoned one another, sought annulments for spurious reasons, obtained divorces in more permissive jurisdictions, and subverted the intent of restrained divorce laws by fabricating grounds that fell within legal limitations" (Riley, 1991, p. 183).

Such problems led to calls for the re-instatement of more liberal divorce laws (Clark, 1996). Shortly after achieving independence from England, many Americans began to believe that divorce was a citizen's right in a democratic country dedicated to the principles of personal freedom and happiness. Divorce was seen as a civil liberty, not a social ill.

Nor surprisingly, divorces began to proliferate. A French citizen touring the United States in the early 1800s noted that marriages were far more easily dissolved in America than in Europe (cited in Riley, 1991). In 1880, one in sixteen American marriages ended in divorce, a rate that was already the highest in the world. By the beginning of the twentieth century it was apparent that the United States had accepted divorce as a necessity.

After 1900 the divorce rate in this country increased steadily. It reached what many thought were calamitous levels in the 1920s, when one in four marriages was eventually ending in divorce. In fact, in 1927 the famous psychologist John Watson predicted that the institution of marriage would be obsolete within 50 years. Except for a brief decline during the Depression years, the divorce rate continued to rise. Then it increased sharply right after World War II, most likely because many couples hastily married just before the young men shipped out and realized when they reunited after the war that they were not compatible.

For a brief time during the 1950s, the rate dropped just as sharply as it had risen in the postwar years. ▲ But by the early 1960s, divorce began to rise again. The mid-1970s marked the first point in American history when marriages were as likely to end by divorce as by the death of one spouse. By the mid-1980s, the American divorce rate had reached its high plateau.

A historical analysis of divorce rates does show an increasing incidence overall, but this trend can be somewhat misleading. Comparatively low divorce rates do not necessarily signal a high proportion of happy, satisfying marriages. The rate of "hidden" marital separation a century ago was probably not that much less than the rate of "visible" separation today (Sennett, 1984). For financial or religious reasons, divorce was not an option for many people. A significant number of couples turned to the functional equivalents of divorce—desertion and abandonment—which have been around for centuries. Although the divorce rate may have been lower in the past, families found other ways to break up.

Furthermore, a comparison of divorce rates doesn't take into consideration how often marriages in the past were disrupted by the premature death of one or the other spouse. In fact, when we look at the total rate of marital dissolution—combining divorce and death—we find the level to be remarkably constant from the mid-nineteenth century to the late twentieth century (Bane, 1976). In short, marital disruption has been with us since the inception of the country, even though death made divorce less necessary and economic, legal, and religious barriers made it less available in the past.

▲ The anomalous 1950s have been used as a standard of comparison for many aspects of family life, as Issue 2 explains.

Changes in Divorce Laws

Today people involved in unsatisfying marriages can get a divorce more easily than ever. But as recently as 2 decades ago, before they would grant a divorce, the courts required evidence of wrongdoing, such as adultery, desertion, or cruelty. A person seeking a divorce had to sue his or her spouse.

The result was a veritable industry of sham divorces. In New York, for instance, where adultery was the only grounds for divorce for most of this century, people would hire a model and a photographer and stage a phony adulterous situation in a hotel room. If a judge wanted evidence of mental cruelty, a lawyer would advise a client to accuse the spouse of name-calling; if a judge wanted evidence of physical cruelty, the client would be advised to claim to have been slapped by a spouse. Thousands of other troubled couples avoided such schemes by traveling across the border to Mexico to take advantage of its less restrictive divorce laws.

But beginning with California in 1970, every state has adopted a form of **no-fault divorce**. These laws reduce the expense, acrimony, and fraud that typically accompanied divorce proceedings by eliminating the requirement that one partner be found guilty. Instead, marriages could be declared unworkable and simply terminated. In most states, one spouse can now obtain a divorce without the other's agreement and without hiring a lawyer.

No-fault divorce laws also redefined the responsibilities of husbands and wives. The husband is no longer automatically considered the head of the household, and the wife is no longer considered solely responsible for the care of the children. Financial awards—spousal support and child support—are based on each spouse's ability to work. If neither spouse is unable to work, courts usually assume that both are equally capable.

The Unforeseen Effects of No-Fault Divorce   This emphasis on equality in the divorce *process* has been a welcome change, but it has eclipsed any consideration of equality in divorce *outcomes.* While women tend to show better emotional adjustment than men after divorce, they suffer economically. Mothers retain custody of their children in the vast majority of divorces, but since the 1970s, many courts have had a tendency to reduce spousal and child-support payments for wives on the mistaken assumption that because more women are working, male-female economic equality had been reached. As a result, no-fault divorce has increased the number of divorced women and their children suffering economic hardship (Coltrane & Hickman, 1992).

In California, after no-fault divorce laws went into effect in the early 1970s, only 13 percent of mothers with preschool children received spousal support (cited in Tavris, 1992). The situation for divorced women, particularly older divorced women, was so bad that the California legislature had to pass the Displaced Homemakers Relief Act, which required judges to consider the future earning potential of each spouse before awarding a settlement.

It's not surprising that the economic effects of divorce hit men and women differently. In all racial groups and at all age levels, separation and divorce have more serious consequences for women than for men (Smock, 1994). For one thing, a divorced woman faces a world in which her earning capacity is significantly less than a man's. Women working full-time, year-round earn about 28 percent less than their male counterparts (U.S. Bureau of the Census, 1997a). ▲ Men experience an average 10 percent *increase* in their standard of living after a divorce because in many cases they no longer have a wife and children to support on a day-to-day basis; divorced women (and their children) experience, on average, a 27 percent *decrease* (Peterson, 1996). Divorce is the single most devastating economic event for American women today.

Custody of the children imposes further disadvantages on women's economic prospects. As one sociologist put it, after a divorce fathers become *single* and mothers become *single parents* (Weitzman, 1985). Child rearing responsibility restricts a woman's job opportunities by limiting her work schedule and job location, her availability to work overtime, and her freedom to take advantage of special training, travel, and other opportunities for advancement. So severe are these handicaps that 39 percent of divorced women with children live in poverty (Kurz, 1995). It takes, on average, 5 years for divorced women and their children to regain their predivorce standard of living. ▲

▲ The male-female wage gap is discussed further in Chapter 3.

▲ The debate over welfare, which is presented in Issue 7, is of special importance to poor divorced women.

Displaced homemakers, divorced women who didn't work outside the home during their marriage, are at even greater disadvantage than other women. They must deal with the toll those years off the career path have taken on their ability to earn a living. Research shows that these women are more likely to be impoverished by divorce than are women who have maintained jobs. Displaced homemakers eventually recover a far lower percentage of the family income they had during the marriage than women who worked prior to the divorce (Arendell, 1987).

Divorced women who experience dramatic economic changes require a redefinition of self. Their identity as members of a certain social class—and with it the core of their self-esteem—is suddenly shaken by the poverty that can result from divorce. Sociologist Christine Grella (1990) interviewed forty previously middle-class divorced women with at least one dependent child at home to explore how they defined their social class after divorce. On average, after divorce, their incomes were cut in half. Yet their assessments of their social class didn't follow neatly from this change in economic circumstances. The contradiction is apparent in the thoughts of a 40-year-old woman who moved to a poorer neighborhood following her divorce:

> I believe I have at least a middle-class and maybe an upper-middle-class mentality, my beliefs and convictions, the things I teach my children . . . are definitely a cut above much of what I see in the neighborhood I live in [and] the schools my kids go to. . . . Economically, I'm basically not a whole lot different from anybody in this neighborhood, and this is definitely not a middle-class neighborhood. (quoted in Grella, 1990, p. 46)

▲ For more on the effects of downward mobility on self-concept and family life, see Issue 7.

Notice that her values and beliefs were more important than economics in her class identity but they were being threatened by the reality of living in a poor neighborhood. ▲

In addition, cultural expectations of mothers contribute to women's disadvantage after divorce. A woman's need to work long hours to earn livable wages or her desire to educate herself to improve job prospects have typically been seen as detracting from her ability to perform her duties as a mother. For example, in 1994 a Michigan judge ordered a woman to give up custody of her 3-year-old daughter to the girl's father because the child was in day care 35 hours a week while the woman took college classes. The judge decided that the father wouldn't do such a thing and deserved custody. ("Day care costs mother," 1994). According to the judge, the mother was not providing the child with a feeling of security and permanence. She was granted visitation on alternate weekends and holidays.

The Movement to Make Divorce More Difficult   Many critics argue that no-fault divorce laws have not only imposed an unfair economic burden on women but have made divorce too easy and too quick. They believe that a majority of divorces occur because the spouses involved simply don't try hard enough to overcome their problems:

> Too many people feel that a bad marriage is like milk—once sour, it can never be made good and it smells up the refrigerator if you leave it there. But every relationship has its high and low points. The thing that distinguishes people in 50-year-old marriages isn't that they're scot-free of problems, but they've confronted those difficulties and persevered when others gave up. (quoted in Clark, 1996, p. 415)

Exhibit 7.3

Attitudes Toward
Obtaining Divorces:
Survey of Adults

*United States:
1974–1996*

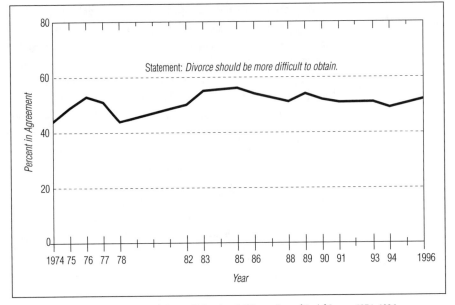

Source of data: National Opinion Research Center, University of Chicago, *General Social Survey, 1974–1996.*

The contention is that individuals are simply not trying hard enough to save marriages that, although not perfect, are "good enough." No-fault divorce has made it too easy for people to dissolve marriages that have not met expectations that were probably too high and unrealistic to begin with.

Public opinion does appear to be in favor of tightening the laws governing divorce. (see Exhibit 7.3). Several states—Iowa, Idaho, Georgia, and Pennsylvania, to name a few—have been debating bills that would toughen divorce laws. In Michigan, an extensive measure is being considered that would revoke the no-fault provision in cases where one spouse opposes the divorce. A divorce would not be granted unless the spouse seeking the divorce could prove that the partner had been abusive, had a problem with alcohol or drugs, had committed adultery, had deserted the home, or had been sentenced to prison. In addition, family therapy would be required for all parties in uncontested divorces and would be imposed at the court's discretion in contested divorces. The law would also provide an incentive—in the form of cheaper marriage licenses—for couples seeking premarital counseling (D. Johnson, 1996).

In 1997 the Louisiana State Legislature passed a measure forcing engaged couples to choose between a standard marriage contract, which permits no-fault divorce, and a "covenant marriage," which could be dissolved only by a mutually agreed-upon 2-year separation or proof of fault, chiefly adultery, abandonment, or abuse. The law requires couples who opt for a covenant marriage to receive counseling before the wedding and to seek it again if they experience marital difficulties. But to date only a tiny proportion of newlyweds have chosen the covenant option (Loe, 1997).

Some scholars (for example, Friedman, 1995; Galston, 1995) suggest that since the effects of divorce are most devastating to children, perhaps a two-tiered system of divorce might work better than the current divorce law. In such a system, adults without children would be free to divorce whenever they decided to, much as they do now. In the 1960s the famous anthropologist Margaret Mead made a similar argument, writing that American society might be better off codifying pre-children marriages as "trial marriages," which would last for a finite period. At the end of that period, the couple could decide if they want to "sign on" for another trial marriage, go their separate ways, or enter a more permanent state of matrimony signified by their desire to have children (Schupack, 1994).

Under these two-tiered systems, once children are present, the adults' legal identity would change from freely contracting individual to parent. Because society has a vested interest in making the breakup of a marriage with children difficult, parents with children under 18 would have to demonstrate that the children would be better off if the marriage broke up than if it remained intact. Unhappiness and incompatibility would no longer be compelling arguments for parents divorcing. ▲

▲ The conflict between individuals' well-being and their family obligations is examined in more detail in Issue 4.

▲ Concern over no-fault divorce is one element of the "family decline" perspective, which is critiqued in Issue 8.

Is the campaign against current divorce laws warranted? One of the arguments of those opposed to no-fault divorce laws is that too many people divorce in their selfish pursuit of individual happiness. ▲ Common cultural images of divorce depict lonely, neglected children and indifferent, selfish parents willing to break up a happy home (Stewart, Copeland, Chester, Malley, & Barenbaum, 1997). The research evidence, however, shows a different picture. In a study of 129 divorced mothers, only 19 percent of them cited "personal dissatisfaction" as the reason they divorced their husbands. The rest cited domestic violence, husband's alcohol or drug abuse, or the husband's involvement with another woman as the cause of the divorce (Kurz, 1995). Other researchers have shown that most women who stay in unsatisfactory marriages do so because they fear that life as a divorced woman will be exceedingly hard (Hochschild & Machung, 1989). In short, the assumption that most divorces consist of people frivolously "walking away" from satisfactory but less-than-perfect marriages simply because they're unhappy appears to be inaccurate.

The argument that no-fault divorce has dramatically increased the number of divorces is similarly flawed. In fact, the surge in divorce rates that began in the early 1960s occurred 15 years *before* no-fault laws became widespread. The implementation of these laws, then, was an adjustment by the legal process to a social trend that was already well under way (Clark, 1996). Furthermore, the observed increases in the divorce rate soon after the implementation of no-fault divorce may have actually reflected divorces that had long been "in the pipeline." In other words, many people were simply obtaining a formal declaration of divorce for marriages that had failed years earlier. Hence, we have no evidence that a repeal of no-fault divorce laws will reduce the divorce rate now.

▲ Chapter 6 describes the coping mechanisms of battered women.

In fact, the result of such a repeal may be an increase in contentious, expensive, potentially child-harming divorces. Imagine a woman living with an abusive husband. Without no-fault divorce, she would have to prove fault by spending a tremendous amount of time, money, and resolve to undertake what amounts to a civil prosecution for a violent crime (Whitehead, 1997). This can be a terrifying experience for a battered woman who wants to avoid her husband. ▲ Rather than do so, she may choose to endure him at home.

Being forced to find fault during divorce proceedings would also put a greater financial burden on those people who can least afford it. The process may require lawyers, therapists, private investigators, and expert witnesses. Such a costly undertaking would drain the pool of financial resources available to the children of divorce, further contributing to a decline in their standard of living.

Finally, repealing no-fault divorce would intensify the pain that children experience. A divorce can be emotionally draining enough. But forcing children to witness prolonged conflict as their parents go about blaming each other for the marriage's failure so that one can be the "winner" and the other the "loser," can only make matters worse. After such a battle, the chances of ex-spouses engaging in cooperative parenting, which increases the likelihood of a child adjusting well, would be nearly zero.

Some sociologists and social observers argue that instead of making divorce more difficult and more stigmatizing, we as a society ought to be thinking about ways to improve the quality of life *after* divorce. They argue that the most destructive aspect of divorce, one typically overlooked by reformers, is the poverty that usually ensues when children live with a low-wage-earning single mother. The solution would be to improve the award and enforcement of child-support payments and strengthen the safety net of supportive services, including child care, welfare, and Medicaid.

Uncoupling

Beyond economics, the "spoiling" of a marriage, or of any other long-term, intimate relationship, can create deep emotional wounds akin to those associated with the death of a loved one (McCall, 1982). Those who go through a breakup often experience a wide range of emotions, including anger, bitterness, sadness, self-pity, self-doubt, guilt, and shame. At the same time, as social exchange theory predicts, when a relationship ends, so do the interpersonal benefits that came with it. We lose the partner on whom we came to depend for important resources, and we lose contact with friends and acquaintances whom we came to know through that partner.

The Process of Breaking Up

According to the symbolic interactionist perspective, family experiences are created and given meaning within the context of social interaction. From this viewpoint, divorce can be understood not just as a discrete legal event that occurs when the legal papers are signed but as a definitional process that emerges over time (Ganong & Coleman, 1994). ▲ This "process" part of a divorce is the most significant element in shaping family dynamics and individual adjustment.

▲ A similar definitional process, mate selection, is described in Chapter 2.

The divorce process can last for months or even years. More often than not, it begins psychologically well before the two spouses consider separation and continues far beyond the time when the divorce becomes finalized. Here's how one sociologist, Diane Vaughan (1986), describes the slow evolution of divorce:

> I was married for twenty years. As I reflected on the relationship after our separation, the marriage seemed to have been coming slowly apart for the last ten. . . . I could retrospec-

tively pick out turning points—moments when the relationship changed, times when the distance between us increased.... Rather than an abrupt ending, ours appeared to have been a gradual transition. Long before we physically separated, we had been separating socially—developing separate friends, experiences, and futures. (pp. xiii–xv)

Using her own experience as a starting point, Vaughan set out to identify the process by which relationships come apart. She collected detailed interviews with 103 divorced or separated men and women. Although each person's experience with uncoupling is unique and the reasons for ending a relationship vary widely, she did find some common patterns. Keep in mind that Vaughan's findings can apply to any long-term intimate relationship, not just heterosexual marriage.

Harboring Secret Unhappiness   According to Vaughan, two partners rarely mutually and simultaneously arrive at the conclusion that they are unhappy and that their relationship needs to end. In most cases, uncoupling begins as a quiet, one-sided process. That is, one partner (whom she refers to as the "initiator") secretly mulls over his or her unhappiness.

This initial solitary reflection can unintentionally create an informational breach between two spouses. By being excluded, the other partner is not given the opportunity to understand the developing situation and act accordingly.

Making the Initial Disclosure   Eventually, the initiator begins to articulate his or her unhappiness. But these early disclosures are usually framed as complaints, attempts to correct the partner's perceived shortcomings in the hope that he or she will become a more suitable partner. The complaints may focus on specific annoying traits (hair, weight, conversational style, sexual technique, and so on).

These early verbal expressions of dissatisfaction tend to come across as attempts to improve the relationship rather than as a sign of the initiator's desire to end it. But behind the description of annoyances lies the real problem, which usually remains hidden. The other partner's awareness of the initiator's discomfort goes no deeper than these relatively minor complaints, which are all the initiator discloses.

Pursuing Outside Involvements   Sometimes changes in the relationship do occur as a result of these complaints. But even in these situations, the initiator's unhappiness is likely to remain. To avoid the unhappiness at home, the initiator may begin to devote more time and energy to things other than the relationship: children, work, friendships, recreational activities and hobbies, extramarital friendships, or even sexual affairs. By devoting time to these pursuits, the initiator creates a social world from which the partner is excluded. Since the partner's access to these experiences is limited, the breach between the two becomes wider.

In the process of engaging in other activities, the initiator often identifies alternative sources of satisfaction and pleasure. ▲ The probability of a relationship ending increases when the initiator begins to see it as less satisfying and less attractive than alternatives and when the costs of ending the relationship (for instance, community, religious, or family disapproval) are low (Cox, Wexler, Rusbult, & Gaines, 1997).

▲ Chapter 2 describes how, according to the social exchange perspective, the stability and attractiveness of a relationship are determined by comparisons to past relationships and present alternatives.

Few studies have attempted to measure the impact of partners' viable alternatives on their marriage. However, sociologists Scott South and Kim Lloyd (1995) examined the relationship between divorce rates and the supply of potential alternative partners in the local community. To estimate the number of potential partners in a particular geographic area, they counted people who were unmarried, not institutionalized, of the same race and ethnicity as their subjects, and in the same age range. In addition to considering the quantity of available potential mates, they also assessed their quality. Current or potential employment is believed to be particularly important to people, so the researchers computed the percentage of suitable men and women in each area who were employed or enrolled full-time in school.

They found that the risk of divorce is highest where wives or husbands encounter an abundance of available alternatives. They concluded that many people remain open to alternative relationships even while married and that the more attractive and available these alternatives are, the greater the chance that the spouses will leave their present marriage.

Vaughan points out that, up to this point in the uncoupling process, the initiator's creation of a life apart from the partner is not malicious. Rather, it occurs as the initiator attempts to ease his or her painful and disagreeable life situation. But the consequences are still serious. Even though no actual move toward ending the marriage has taken place, by creating this independent life and identity, the initiator has taken the first tentative step out of the relationship.

Accentuating the Negative Disillusioned by the inability to resolve unhappiness at home, the dissatisfied initiator begins to accentuate all the negative aspects of the relationship and to minimize the positive—precisely the opposite of what we tend to do when we initially fall in love with someone. The initiator may begin to redefine the entire history of the relationship. What once were a partner's endearing little rituals become annoying habits in retrospect. The good times get reinterpreted as bad; the bad times are seen as more typical and indicative of the deep problems in the relationship.

As discontent intensifies, it becomes more visible to the partner. The initiator's complaints start to reflect an attitude that the relationship is not only troubled but perhaps unsavable. The initiator may start telling others outside the relationship that all is not well or show his or her displeasure nonverbally in public settings. Since norms of privacy dictate that couples keep their problems to themselves and present a harmonious public image, such displays mark a public redefinition of the partner and of the relationship.

By focusing on the negative aspects of the partner and of the relationship, the initiator creates in his or her mind something that can and should be left behind. By defining the relationship as "bad," the initiator can justify his or her desire to end it.

Deciding to Separate For a while, the initiator lives in two worlds simultaneously. Not quite gone from the marriage, he or she still must participate from time to time in the old coupled world. The initiator tends to be uncomfortable in the old role he or she is attempting to shed and therefore simply "goes through the motions" of married life. The initiator may avoid any activity that would bind him or her to the partner for an extended period, such as having a baby, redecorating a room, buying season tickets, or taking out a loan. He or she may also express discomfort with being linked to the partner in public situations, where others still treat them as a couple. Especially troublesome are family gatherings or couple-confirming celebrations like weddings or anniversary parties.

Eventually the partner begins to notice the changes in the initiator's commitment to the relationship. The partner may realize that the initiator doesn't offer a kiss anymore when leaving or returning home, or that the initiator is undergoing a change in appearance (losing weight, growing a beard, buying new clothes, and so on). The partner may feel excluded but is still not likely to react to the initiator's behavior as a threat to the relationship. However, psychologically and emotionally, the initiator has already left.

How is it possible, you might be wondering, for one partner to slip so far away without the other person noticing? Often partners claim they were unaware that the relationship was deteriorating. Vaughan doesn't think this blindness is due to naivete, ignorance, or a "what you don't know won't hurt you" philosophy of avoidance. Instead, she attributes these contradictions to the way many married couples communicate:

> Unable to witness our partners' every activity or verify every nuance of meaning, we evolve a communication system based on trust. We gradually cease our attentive probing, relying instead on familiar cues and signals to stand as testament to the strength of the bond....
> As intimate relationships begin to deteriorate, this shorthand method ... tends to obscure change and can prevent the sending and receiving of new information. (Vaughan, 1986, p. 88)

The result is a sort of collaborative cover-up in which direct confrontation is avoided and facts are suppressed. Since the culture lacks useful guidelines for acknowledging problems and ending a relationship, routines continue and life goes on as usual. As Vaughan puts it, one "tells without telling; the other knows without knowing."

Eventually the "cover-up" breaks down, and the moment of separation arrives. Sometimes the initiator directly confronts the partner with his or her wish to end the relationship. Other times the initiator uses indirect methods, such as displaying so much discontent and misery that the partner is forced to confront the initiator. Although the initiator may want to be tactful, sensitive, and considerate, more often than not the opposite occurs:

> The truth is, we don't know how to tell our partners we no longer want to be with them. There is no good way, no kind way, no easy way to do it without hurting the other person. Often, we are in such pain ourselves as we consider taking our leave that we act out of frustration rather than rationality, hurting others despite our wish to be humane. (Vaughan, 1986, p. 296)

The actual decision to separate may be the result of discussion and planning, or it may occur spontaneously. It may be mutually agreed upon, but chances are it won't be. Disentangling a shared life into two separate ones is never easy. Normal living patterns are disrupted. Economic status, friendship networks, personal habits, sex life, relationships with children—all must be reorganized.

The Pain of Going Public

▲ Issue 3 explains why others are so uncomfortable when "backstage" issues become public.

The process of separation is particularly difficult when it comes time for the couple to tell others close to them that their marriage is ending. ▲ Friends, relatives, co-workers, and other interested parties typically want to know who to blame, who to help, and whose side to take (Gertsel, 1987). But the explanations offered by each partner will almost certainly be different because of their distinctive perspectives on the termination process (McCall, 1982).

Even though they may have noticed serious problems in the marriage, noninitiators are likely to oppose the divorce when their partners first bring it up. Hence, they are often able to use a moralistic tone when describing the breakup, talking about sacrifice, the sanctity of the marriage vows, and perseverance in their effort to make it work. When dealing with others, noninitiators may seek sympathy, perhaps even wanting to play the victim. At the same time, though, they don't want to advertise the fact that their "value" has plummeted in the former partner's eyes.

On the other hand, initiators are likely to face a "tough audience" (Vaughan, 1986). They may feel compelled to provide accounts that forestall any possibility that others will define them as the blameworthy party. Hence, they must frame the partner and the relationship in a way that justifies the termination. They may also begin to highlight the importance of individual needs over commitment or describe the divorce in terms of their emotional and practical needs going unfulfilled:

> I wanted to take care of me. And I knew as long as I stayed in the relationship that I would always take care of somebody else because that's just the way I was. It's probably stupid, but I felt that I couldn't grow and I couldn't be independent as long as I was in that position. (quoted in Hopper, 1993, p. 807)

Further complicating the process of going public is the social stigma associated with the termination of an intimate relationship. Like most things in our achievement-oriented society, relationships—especially marriages—tend to be viewed in success/failure terms. Although studies consistently show a clear decline in disapproval of divorce as a general category, disapproval of divorced *individuals* continues (Gertsel, 1987). Divorced families are still characterized as "broken," "weak," "fragile," "split," or "fragmented." Divorced individuals may come to feel rejected by married friends and experience diminishing self-esteem. Friends and family close to the couple can increase feelings of stigma by passing judgment and taking sides. As one divorced author describes it, "It's exhausting to be in the company of married people, with children or no. It forces me into a state of emergency alert, in which I have to rescue myself from interrogation and possible disgrace" (Rose, 1996, p. 82).

Our private, intimate relationships are never solely our possession. In a sense, they also belong to other people—friends and family—who have a vested interest in their continuation. When we marry someone, we "marry" an entire network of others who often incorporate our relationship into their own sphere of activity. For instance, when family members plan future events, like group vacations and holiday celebrations, they typically assume that our relationships will be intact and that we as a couple can be counted on to participate. Hence, a divorce requires the ending of associations with others who also have a strong investment in the relationship.

Divorce and Children

Although divorce is certainly difficult for the adults going through it, most adjust after a couple of years. However, about 65 percent of the divorces that occur each year involve couples with minor children (Clark, 1996), who have a more difficult time with divorce. Divorce sets a series of changes in motion with the potential to seriously disrupt children's lives.

To some people, the effect of divorce on children is so damaging that it has the potential of turning them into sociopaths. In her book *The Abolition of Marriage*, author Maggie Gallagher tells the story of an Iowa teenager named Michelle Jensen, a good kid who had fallen in with a bad crowd. One night she and six male friends left a party in her car. The boys wanted to rob a convenience store and told Michelle that they needed to use her car for the getaway. She refused. They forced her to stop the car on the side of the road. Michelle got out and began to walk away. One of the boys pulled out a sawed-off shotgun and told her to stop, but she continued walking. So he shot her in the head. The boys drove off in her car but decided against the robbery because the store was too crowded. Instead, they went to Hardee's for some burgers before heading back to the murder scene to prove to other friends that they had really killed someone. "For those who prefer to treat the collapse of marriages as a personal choice," Gallagher asserts, "or as somebody else's problem . . . Michelle's is a chilling story. . . . Five of the six [teenagers who murdered Michelle] came from what used to be called 'broken homes' " (Gallagher, 1996, p. 51). Clearly, Gallagher wants us to conclude that this murder wouldn't have happened if the parents of these boys had remained together.

Stories like this one are provocative. They inflame our passions. Yet it seems rather simple-minded to argue that divorce somehow causes murderous violence in children. Indeed, most criminologists discount the association between divorce and violent crime, claiming instead that family conflict and discord—as well as a multitude of factors outside the family—are more important determinants of criminal behavior (Siegel, 1995).

Nevertheless, we may still have reason to be greatly concerned over the long-term effects of divorce on children. Psychologists Judith Wallerstein and Sandra Blakeslee (1989) followed sixty mostly affluent divorced families and found the children, not to mention their fathers and mothers, to be seriously troubled years after the divorce. Many have criticized this study because it does not establish divorce as the cause of the children's difficulties: Wallerstein and Blakeslee had no information on their subjects prior to the divorces; they followed no control group of children from intact families; and didn't attempt to examine a matched set of spouses who faced similar marital problems and contemplated divorce but decided to stay married. In addition, the subjects in this study were referred to Wallerstein's clinic by lawyers, clergy, and the courts. Many of the parents suffered from emotional problems. So these conclusions must be viewed cautiously; they may not generalize to all divorces.

But other claims about the problems children suffer have received more support. A substantial body of research shows that regardless of race or education of parents, children raised in single-parent homes fare worse at every stage of life than children from two-parent families. They are more likely to do poorly in school or drop out, commit delinquent acts, and engage in drug and alcohol abuse. When they become adults, they get lower-paying jobs and are more likely to be unemployed or end up in jail. When they form relationships, they are more likely to marry young, have children early, and divorce (McLanahan & Booth, 1991; McLanahan & Sandefur, 1994).

Children's Adjustment to Divorce

Because of the possibility that children's lives will be permanently affected by divorce, researchers have devoted a great deal of energy to investigating the factors that determine how well children will adjust. If we could just figure out the answers, perhaps we could create programs or policies that would help minimize the damage. ▲ Maybe we should prevent parents from splitting up; maybe we should help custodial parents do a better job; maybe we shouldn't do anything at all. Unfortunately, the answers to these sensitive questions remain elusive.

▲ Issue 4 examines the pros and cons of using social policy to reinforce family obligations.

The research indicates that how well children adjust to their parents' divorce depends on a lot of things, such as the children's gender, age at the time of separation, duration of life in a single-parent household after the divorce, and so on. Furthermore, the way the children were raised, the economic resources available to them, their sense of emotional security, their enduring relationships with parents or other caring adults, and the amount of supervision they continue to receive can also influence their post-divorce adjustment. No one set of circumstances dooms children to a life of hardship or, for that matter, guarantees that they will come through the divorce experience trouble free.

In an attempt to bring some order to this confusion, sociologist Paul Amato (1993) has identified four perspectives from which pundits and policy makers seem to view the post-divorce adjustment of children:

1. The *parental loss perspective* assumes that a family with both parents living in the same household as the child is *always* a better environment for the child's development than a single-parent household. According to this perspective, both mothers and fathers are crucial sources of guidance, support, information, practical assistance, and supervision. The presence of two adults jointly conducting daily life helps children learn how to cooperate, negotiate, and compromise. Moreover, most children anticipate that they will grow up in homes with a mother and a father. They tend to see themselves as members of a family defined by who lives together (Seltzer, 1994). Most children of divorce are also assumed to suffer from the lack of contact with the noncustodial parent and from the reduction in contact with the custodial parent, whose need to work to support the household decreases the amount of time and energy devoted to the child. According to this perspective, anxiety, depression, and disruptive behavior are to be expected during children's short-term adjustment to divorce.

2. The *parental adjustment perspective* focuses on the importance of the psychological adjustment of the custodial parent. This perspective assumes that divorced parents who are supportive of their children and exert moderate control over them tend to enhance the development and well-being of their children. Stress, however, decreases a parent's ability to parent and may ultimately jeopardize the well-being of children. Some research has found that during the first year after a divorce, custodial mothers were more anxious, depressed, and angry than were married mothers (cited in Amato, 1993). Although the differences in stress between divorced and married women tend to diminish over time, they still remain significant 2 or 3 years after the divorce (Lorenz, Simons, Conger, Elder, Johnson, & Chao, 1997).

3. The *parental conflict perspective* suggests that children whose parents ultimately divorce are usually exposed to parents' conflict before separation, during the separation, and often afterwards. Children may react to their parents' conflict with fear, anger, and distress, or they may

be drawn into the conflict and forced to take sides. In some cases, children blame themselves for their parents' fighting. Parental conflict may also have indirect effects on children. Parents who are preoccupied with their own problems may be inattentive to their children's needs. During the divorce they may be unable to comfort their children because of their own pain and anger (Seltzer, 1994). Hence, from this perspective, conflict *and not parental separation* is assumed to have the most damaging effects on children. Conversely, children whose divorced parents get along well will do far better than children whose parents remain married but fight like cats and dogs.

4. The *economic hardship perspective* assumes that the monetary problems brought about by divorce are most responsible for the problems children face. Money may not buy happiness, but children cannot adjust very easily if they don't have enough to eat or a safe place to live following the divorce. Even if they're not poor, children whose parents separate and who live with their mothers experience, on average, about a 21 percent reduction in family income when their father moves out and sets up a second household (Seltzer, 1994). The economic hardships of divorce can affect children's health and nutrition and their access to books, toys, computers, and other things that can enhance school success. Limited financial resources may force single mothers and their children to live in poorer neighborhoods. Economic deprivation is also associated with frequent residential moves and tense emotional environments.

Amato found that the perspective with the strongest and most convincing support is the parental conflict model (3), although evidence exists to support all of them. He concludes that most of the behavioral problems that the children of divorce exhibit are caused not by the divorce itself but by exposure to conflict between ex-spouses. If we look at those kids whose married parents are unhappy or are frequently embroiled in conflict, we find just as many problems as in children of divorce (Furstenberg & Cherlin, 1991). In fact, children who grow up in intact families where conflict is frequent may actually have *more* problems, and those problems may last into adulthood.

Furthermore, divorce may only exacerbate some children's existing behavioral and emotional problems (Cherlin, Chase-Landale, & McRae, 1998). One study of children's lives repeatedly surveyed a panel of several thousand American and British children over 4 to 5 years (Cherlin, Furstenberg, Chase-Landale, Kiernan, Robins, Morrison, & Teitler, 1991). The researchers did find that the children whose parents separated or divorced showed more behavior problems and behaved worse in school than children whose parents remained married. However, when they looked back at the results from the beginning of their surveys, the researchers found that the children, particularly boys, whose parents were married at the beginning of the study but would later divorce were already showing behavioral problems *well before* the actual divorce occurred. In short, much of the effect of divorce on children can be predicted by conditions that exist before the parents actually separate.

When children maintain a good relationship with their parents after a divorce, the negative effects of the breakup can be minimized. A divorce that causes minimal disruption in a child's life is less harmful than an intact marriage that the child perceives as unhappy (Amato & Booth, 1991).

Custody Decisions

Custody decisions—determining where children will live and who will make the major decisions in their lives—are frequently the most painful and contentious issues in divorces in our society. But this isn't the case worldwide: The decision of who controls the child after a divorce is irrelevant in **patrilineal societies,** where children always belong to the husband and the husband's family, and in **matrilineal societies,** where they belong to the wife and her kin. However, in **bilateral descent systems,** such as ours, both sides of the family have an equal claim on the child. ▲ His or her well-being depends on the relationship between both parents.

▲ These kinship systems are discussed further in Issue 1.

Providing emotional and economic security for children is a significant challenge in bilateral, nuclear family systems. From the child's point of view, part of his or her extended family disappears when the marriage ends (Friedman, 1995). Certainly kin and even close non-kin remain deeply attached to children and make significant contributions to their well-being after the divorce. ▲ But there is nothing beyond affection to *compel* these contributions. It's ultimately the divorced parents who must guarantee the well-being of their children.

▲ Issue 1 explains the importance of kinship to our definitions of family.

So the most difficult problem in divorced families in the United States is determining which parent ought to have primary responsibility for the child and ensuring that both parents continue to contribute to the child's well-being after the divorce. Unfortunately, most children have relatively little contact with their noncustodial parents, typically fathers. Moreover, the majority of noncustodial parents don't pay the full amount of court-ordered child support. Even the parent who retains custody often reduces his or her contribution to the child after a divorce. Remarriage, for instance, involves time spent dating and courting, investing emotional energy in another adult who has no abiding incentive to contribute to the child, and perhaps even having additional children with the new partner. All of these things direct attention, time, and resources away from the child of the first marriage (Friedman, 1995).

Sole Custody When custody is granted solely to one or the other parent, it is typically granted to the parent who was the primary caretaker before the divorce. The logic of granting **sole custody** to the primary caretaker rests on two principles: (1) it provides continuity for children. The person who provided the most care during the marriage should do so after the marriage; (2) it fairly rewards the parent who has devoted the most to the child during the marriage.

Today, even though changes in divorce laws over the years have supposedly eliminated sex-based preferences in custody decisions, mothers end up with sole custody in about 90 percent of divorce cases (Fox & Kelly, 1995; Maccoby & Mnookin, 1992). It's important to note, though, that the majority of these cases are agreed to by both parents without any court intervention. In other words, the vast majority of fathers *don't seek* custody of their children.

▲ Chapter 4 discusses cultural presumptions about the mother role and the father role in American society.

The fact that fathers tend not to request custody of their children reflects a cultural presumption that, under normal circumstances, mothers are more crucial to their children's development than fathers (Friedman, 1995). ▲ Questions about child custody are usually posed as if the mother already has custody and therefore must be determined competent to keep it. In other words, at the time of divorce the court essentially decides whether children *will remain* in their mother's care and control or be taken from her, wholly or partially. In effect, custody "is hers to lose."

▲ For more about gay and lesbian parents, read Chapter 4.

Lesbian mothers present the one exception to this maternal custody assumption. ▲ Although some states have laws stipulating that sexual orientation should not be an issue in custody disputes, in other states parents who identify themselves as homosexual are automatically presumed to be unfit parents. In 1993 a 25-year-old Richmond, Virginia, woman lost custody of her son—to whom she gave birth while in a heterosexual marriage—when a judge ruled that homosexuality (the woman now lived with her lesbian partner) made her an unfit parent. The woman's mother (the child's grandmother) had sued for custody and won. In 1995 the Virginia Supreme Court upheld the judge's ruling, stating that "active lesbianism practiced in the home" could stigmatize the child and "inevitably afflict the child's relationships with its peers and with the community" ("Lesbian's appeal," 1995, p. 6). The court said that although lesbianism in and of itself didn't disqualify the mother, homosexual conduct is a felony under Virginia law and thus is an important factor in determining custody. The mother was given visitation rights, but the child is not allowed to go to her apartment and is not allowed to have any contact with the mother's partner.

The "Preference" for Maternal Custody   Maternal custody is such a dominant arrangement today that it seems inconceivable that mothers have not always been the preferred parent in divorce cases. Yet up until the early twentieth century, the law actually presumed *paternal custody*.

▲ See Chapter 5 for more on the concept of children as property.

Children were clearly defined as the property of their fathers. ▲ In fact, women were often considered legal dependents themselves and therefore couldn't even be awarded custody of children in the event of a husband's death.

But during a span of 40 years—roughly between 1880 and 1920—the presumption that divorced fathers should be granted custody of their children changed throughout the United States. The change was dramatic, as illustrated in the different language of these two custody decisions, the first from 1842 and the second from 1916:

> We are informed by the first elementary books we read, that the authority of the father is superior to that of the mother. . . . It is according to the revealed law, the law of nature, and it prevails even with the wandering savage, who has received none of the lights of civilization.

> Mother love is a dominant trait in even the weakest of women, and as a general thing surpasses the paternal affection for the common offspring, and, moreover, a child needs a mother's care even more than a father's. For these reasons courts are loathe to deprive the mother of the custody of her children, and will not do so unless it be shown clearly that she is so far an unfit and improper person to be intrusted with custody as to endanger the welfare of the children. (both quoted in Friedman, 1995, p. 18)

Sociologist Debra Friedman (1995) provides a provocative account of why such a dramatic change in child rearing philosophy occurred when it did. Up until the mid-1800s, when divorce was relatively infrequent, deciding whether a mother or a father should get custody of a child was rarely an issue. The vast majority of marriages ended when one or the other spouse died. If a mother died, the father obviously retained custody. Only if a father died without appointing a guardian for his children would the courts step in to determine where the child should live.

As divorce became more common, however, courts found themselves having to make child custody decisions between two living parents. At the time, it was assumed that fathers were responsible for raising and educating children. Fathers were simply called upon to continue honoring those obligations in the event of a divorce; hence, the presumption of paternal custody. Notice that these custody decisions were made not in the child's "best interest" but in terms of the father's legal obligation and *entitlement* to custody of his minor children.

Rising divorce rates at the turn of the century put pressure on these laws. New state laws enacted in the early twentieth century established the court's power to use its discretion in child custody matters. Depending on the state, the laws suggested that judges consider the age and sex of the child, the safety, well-being, happiness, comfort, and spiritual health of the child, or the character of the parents. Decisions were based on considerations of child welfare, not parents' rights or obligations. But what exactly constituted children's well-being? Did the benefits of mothers' nurturing outweigh the benefits of fathers' provision of material resources?

At this point, fathers and mothers had equal claims to custody. However, as the sphere of influence for women (especially middle-class women) became restricted to the home, and men's sphere of influence became the workplace, fathers began to have less contact with their children and mothers began to play a more active and exclusive role in raising them. ▲ At the same time, children were seen less as economic assets that men wanted to control and more as individuals who required significant care, emotional attention, and training to become useful and valuable adults (Friedman, 1995; Zelizer, 1985). Since most fathers were busy elsewhere, the task fell to mothers. So important was this task that motherhood was redefined from a "part-time job" to a "noble calling" (Ehrenreich & English, 1979).

▲ As you can see in Issue 2 and Chapter 4, this belief has not always been a part of American culture.

Hence, with regard to custody decisions, this new conception of motherhood and female domesticity led to a sense that some attention ought to be paid to mothers' claims to custody. If they were assumed to be the superior parent within marriage, they should also be considered the superior parent when the marriage ended. The irony, of course, is that women, even relatively privileged women, were finding that they had no way of supporting themselves financially, let alone supporting a child or several children.

The old laws favoring fathers made some sense: Fathers of that era were, after all, better able to provide financially for their children than mothers were. Without a paternal preference in custody decisions, however, fathers were no longer obligated to provide for their children. Thus a dilemma arose: If mothers were to be granted custody, how could fathers be compelled to pay for the care of their estranged children?

By 1930, all but four states had policies designed to address the economic plight of *widows* and their children. It would seem a short step to extend these financial benefits to *divorced mothers* and their children. However, widowhood was considered to be a state outside the control of women, whereas divorce was often associated with moral failure. Legislators were reluctant to tell taxpayers to subsidize what many considered to be an immoral act.

So most states focused on enforcing noncustodial fathers' obligation to provide financial support for their children and the mothers of their children after a divorce. When fathers were granted custody, they were obligated to provide only for their children; their ex-spouses were left to fend for themselves. Thus states had a clear economic rationale for presuming maternal custody. It prevented what could otherwise become a severe public burden: providing welfare to both divorced mothers and their children.

In sum, the change from paternal to maternal preference in custody cases did not occur because fathers had suddenly become unable or unwilling to fulfill their parental obligations or because mothers had suddenly become more deserving. Instead, maternal custody represented an effective solution to several societal problems:

- Maternal custody increased the probability that private individuals (that is, noncustodial fathers) and not society would pay to support two dependents rather than one.
- Maternal custody put off any efforts by women to claim they had a right to equal pay and employment opportunities. As long as divorced mothers had their estranged husbands to support them, they would have a weak argument for expanding their access to jobs.
- Maternal custody was favored by both conservatives and liberal feminists (Friedman, 1995): Conservatives favored it because it reduced the welfare obligations of the state; feminists because it lowered the cost of divorce for women by compelling ex-husbands to subsidize their support.

Joint Custody   Over the past few decades, the preference for sole maternal custody has been challenged. Popular child rearing ideologies now emphasize the importance of *both* parents in a child's life. More fathers than ever are actively seeking shared time with their children and joint decision making on issues such as religious upbringing, education, and health matters. At the same time, more mothers than ever are in the paid labor force and find themselves balancing the practical demands of work and home. Consequently, **joint custody** considerations are becoming more common (Hochman, 1997).

Joint custody policies vary from state to state. In certain states the judge can consider joint custody only when both parents request it; in others, judges can award it when only one parent has asked for it. In most states—thirty-five as of 1995—judges are required to consider joint custody as the *preferred* custody arrangement. In a few states, joint custody is mandated unless one or the other parent proves that this type of custody would be detrimental to the child (Flynn, 1991).

Joint custody takes two forms: legal and physical custody. **Joint legal custody** recognizes the rights of both parents to make major decisions affecting the child's life. Although a variety of living arrangements are possible under joint legal custody, children usually live with their mothers. Under **joint physical custody,** not only do parents share decision making, but they also share in the physical care of the child. Though the division of responsibilities need not be exactly equal, the child lives alternately for major periods of time with each parent.

Joint custody appears to be the equitable solution to the problem of a child's contact with one parent being curtailed after a divorce. Even when the actual physical custody of the child isn't shared, joint legal custody ensures that each parent maintains some interest in the child and some control over decisions that affect the child's well-being. With joint custody, neither parent needs to be considered a "winner" or a "loser." No one parent's rights are superior to the other's. The intent is to approximate an intact family as much as possible.

Proponents of joint custody believe that shared parenting negates the detrimental effects that the absence of one parent (usually the father) can have on the child. The child's deep sense of loss will be significantly lessened.

This position suggests, however, that parents whose antagonism and incompatibility were severe enough to end their marriage will suddenly be able to work together, in harmony, to decide the best path to raising their children. According to one study, only one out of four divorced couples who were granted joint custody were able to cooperate fully in raising the child (Maccoby & Mnookin, 1992). More commonly, parents continue to fight with one another or develop a pattern of "parallel parenting," wherein the child is shared but the parents don't cooperate at all with each other (Furstenberg & Nord, 1985).

Thus, opponents of joint custody argue that it undermines the continuity and stability that are essential to the child's adjustment. Shuffling back and forth between two parents and two households with different authority figures and different values can be confusing and unsettling.

In addition, the demands of joint custody may restrict the mobility of a parent. He or she may have to forgo a career advancement if it means moving to another city or involves changes that would otherwise interfere with the shared-parenting arrangement.

Research on the effects of joint custody is mixed. Mothers in joint custody arrangements tend to report better relationships with their former spouses, better interactions with them involving child rearing decisions, and greater levels of emotional support for parenting than mothers with sole custody (Arditti & Madden-Derdich, 1997). Mothers with sole custody tend to show greater parenting stress than joint custody mothers, even though they don't report feeling more burdened and are actually more satisfied with their custody arrangements. Their children might be a major source of stress, but they're also a source of happiness and satisfaction. Sole custody allows women to exercise greater control over child rearing and is also more consistent with society's traditional view of mother as primary caregiver. Perhaps because of those social norms, joint custody mothers may believe that their status somehow reflects negatively on their capabilities as a mother.

Some children in joint custody arrangements seem to appreciate the contact with both parents and the "change of pace" it allows. Others, however, report feeling "torn apart" by the arrangement, especially as they get older. In short, we have no evidence to suggest that joint custody is always best for children, but neither do we have evidence that it is more harmful than traditional sole custody.

Joint custody does tend to cause more problems for families when the arrangement is mandated by the state than when both parents agree that it would be the best situation for the child. Because of these problems, some states (for instance, California) have removed the legal preference for joint custody. It seems, then, that children and parents would be better served through policies that make joint custody an available option to those who want it rather than a legal presumption (Flynn, 1991).

The Father Role after Divorce

Despite the growing interest in joint custody, maternal custody continues to be the most common arrangement. Usually the father is required to pay child support and receives some visitation rights in return—typically the opportunity to take the children out of the mother's home for a few days each week or month. However, this arrangement seldom works well. Divorced mothers complain, with clear justification, that they do not receive the child-support payments mandated by the divorce courts. Noncustodial fathers often complain that their visitation rights are inadequate to begin with or are abused by the mother. Society as a whole, which is redefining the father's role in family life, frets that children of divorce growing up without a father's support and influence will suffer long-term harm. ▲ We therefore struggle to develop policies that will keep fathers involved—at least financially. But should we insist on fathers' obligations without also protecting some of their rights? Many divorced fathers don't think so.

▲ Fathers' changing role in American families is discussed further in Chapter 4.

Child-Support Policies As we've seen, women and children tend to be economically disadvantaged by divorce. One of the key reasons is the inadequacy of court-ordered child-support payments. Even more problematic is the failure on the part of many noncustodial parents to pay court-ordered child support. In a little over half of all divorces involving children, noncustodial fathers are required to pay child support. Of these, 51 percent pay the full amount, 24 percent pay a partial amount, and 25 percent pay nothing (U.S. Bureau of the Census, 1997a). About three-quarters of divorced mothers therefore don't receive any financial assistance at all. Award rates are especially low for African-American and Hispanic women, who suffer from a higher poverty rate to begin with (Klawitter, 1994).

One of the key problems seems to be the ineffectiveness or lack of enforcement procedures in child-support cases. The kinds of policies that were developed to "take care of" children in single-parent families focused originally on children of widows. In 1960 single-parent families consisted of almost as many widowed parents as divorced parents. But since then, the proportion of children living with a widowed parent has dropped considerably, while the proportion of children of divorced or never-married parents has increased (see Exhibit 7.4). The courts for the most part, have been ill-equipped to deal with these situations.

Up until the 1970s, most states left much discretion to judges and families in setting child-support standards, and they had virtually no strategies in place to enforce payment. In 1975 Congress created the federal Office of Child-Support Enforcement and required states to establish similar offices to assist in collecting support. However, these agencies had little enforcement power. So in 1984 Congress enacted the Child-Support Enforcement Amendment, which not only required states to set standards for support awards but also mandated such enforcement techniques as withholding money from fathers' paychecks after a history of nonpayment (Klawitter, 1994). This policy targeted unmarried parents as well as divorced parents. However, since determining the identity of the biological father in the case of nonmarital births is often difficult and frequently unsuccessful, these cases became a low priority.

Despite these governmental efforts, a recent report from the Department of Health and Human Services shows that delinquent parents still shirk court orders in four of every five cases (Clymer, 1997). Custodial parents still collect less than 20 percent of the child support they are owed. Thus, some legislators have proposed more dramatic solutions.

In 1996 the Department of Health and Human Services established a national databank of fathers who avoid paying court-imposed child support. Officials are now able to reach across state lines to seize "deadbeat" fathers' property (homes, cars, and so forth), garnish wages, and secure money directly from a checking account even if located in another state. In 1997 the federal government began operating a computer directory showing every person newly hired by

Exhibit 7.4

Children in Single-
Parent Household
of a Never-Married,
Widowed, Divorced
or Separated Parent

*United States:
1960–1994*

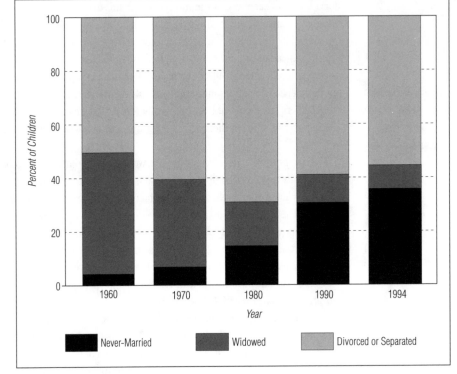

Source of data: Arlene Saluter, "Marital Status and Living Arrangements: March 1994." U.S. Bureau of the Census, *Current Population Report, Series P20-484.* Washington, DC, 1996.

every employer in the country so that investigators can track down noncustodial parents who move from state to state while owing money to their children. More than 30 percent of the 19 million child-support cases in this country are thought to involve parents who don't live in the same state as their children (Pear, 1997).

In addition, President Clinton recently directed the Department of Health and Human Services to require mothers to provide the names of their children's fathers and other identifying information before they can receive welfare benefits. Those who refuse will not receive payments, although the policy provides an exception for women who can't identify the father or who are afraid of physical abuse. The goal of the policy, according to the president, is not to punish mothers but to enforce fathers' responsibility to contribute to their children: "We're not going to just let you walk away from your children and stick the taxpayers with the tab. We have to make responsibility a way of life, not an option" (quoted in "President tells mothers," 1996, p. 27).

This approach may have a lot of appeal, but simply forcing noncustodial fathers to pay more child support may not be a perfect solution to the economic problems associated with divorce. Low-income custodial mothers tend to be associated with low-income noncustodial fathers, who may struggle to provide even for themselves. Indeed, the amount of child support awarded to low-income women is lower than that for other women and remains low relative to the costs of raising children (Klawitter, 1994). Stricter support policies may eventually narrow the differences in award rates for custodial mothers at various income levels, but they are unlikely to significantly alter the poverty rates of low-income women.

Absent Fathers   Financial support isn't the only thing missing from the lives of many children whose parents are divorced. In general, noncustodial fathers tend to play only a minor role in their children's everyday lives. One national study found that half of the children whose parents were divorced hadn't seen their fathers in the previous year, and only one out of six had regular, weekly contact with the noncustodial father. Children were most likely to see their fathers immediately after the separation. But after several years, contact dropped off sharply (Furstenberg & Nord, 1985). Another study found that 75 percent of noncustodial fathers never attend their child's school events, 85 percent never help them with homework, and 65 percent never take their children on vacations (Teachman, 1991).

Furthermore, fewer than one-third of divorced parents discuss their children with each other during a 12-month period, and just over 20 percent talk with each other weekly. Even among the estranged parents who do talk about their children, the level of fathers' participation in decision making is limited. Only about 17 percent have significant influence over health care matters, education, religion, and so forth (cited in Arendell, 1995).

What factors influence the frequency and nature of contact noncustodial fathers have with their children? One set of factors concerns events that occur *after* the divorce. For example, when fathers remarry, their contact tends to decrease because the new marriage is likely to impose new time constraints and added responsibilities. Divorced fathers are frequently more involved in the lives of their stepchildren than in the lives of their biological children (Stephens, 1996). The remarriage of custodial mothers may also diminish fathers' postdivorce contact because they may feel they've been replaced and view themselves as no longer needed by the children.

Another set of factors that may affect fathers' postdivorce contact with their children are socioeconomic factors. Better-educated fathers are more likely to be exposed to information emphasizing the importance of both parents in children's lives and therefore are likely to maintain significant, regular contact with their children after a divorce. Income may also be positively related to contact, since fathers cannot engage in costly activities (eating in restaurants, going to movies, going shopping, and so on) with their children during visitations if they don't have sufficient income. Noncustodial fathers must also have the financial resources to provide sufficient space (that is, an extra bedroom) and a duplicate set of child care equipment and toys for frequent contact to occur (Stephens, 1996).

But fathers' absence from their children's lives may also be a purposeful strategy designed to minimize discord with ex-spouses and, to some degree, the children themselves. Sociologist Terry Arendell (1992) interviewed seventy-five divorced men who had at least one minor child and had been divorced or separated for at least 18 months. She found that many fathers stay away from their children to avoid further conflicts and tensions with their ex-wives (Arendell, 1992). Confrontations are especially likely to occur if the end of the marriage was antagonistic. Even though visitation arrangements are legally determined, they are engulfed in ambiguity and are an ongoing source of dissatisfaction and conflict for many men. Most fathers in Arendell's study insisted that their former wives had hindered their access to their children: Scheduled visits were denied, telephone conversations interrupted, messages not conveyed, mail intercepted and not given to the child, and so on. Nearly half of the men Arendell interviewed had experienced going to pick up their child for a visit and finding no one at home.

So in order to avoid all of these conflicts, some men began to allow longer periods of time to lapse between contacts and visits. In fact, over half of the fathers who were fully absent from their children's lives became nonvisiting parents after a series of confrontations with their former wives.

Absence also served as a means of emotion management for Arendell's subjects. Fathers often felt the need to distance themselves from reminders of happier times and to limit their involvement in situations likely to evoke angry and hostile interactions and perhaps even outbursts of physical violence. Absence also served as a way to avoid unresolved feelings of loss and pain. One father indicated that his sporadic contacts with his son, as opposed to the routine daily contacts they had when the marriage was intact, produced feelings of such unbearable sorrow that he preferred not to see his son at all:

> Every time I pulled up to the driveway to let him off, it was like part of me was dying all over again. I could barely keep myself together long enough to give him a hug goodbye.... He would open the door, step out of the car, and I would feel as if I would never see him again. He would walk up the sidewalk and a sense of grief would utterly overcome me. It would take me several days to pull myself together enough to even function at work. I'd have to keep his bedroom door closed; I couldn't bear to see his empty room. I had to break it off totally just to survive; the visits themselves were terrible because I had this constant unease, knowing what was coming. (quoted in Arendell, 1992, p. 577)

Since seeing their children was usually defined as a "visit," and not as a routine part of everyday life, many noncustodial fathers in Arendell's study found their time with their children to be awkward and uncomfortable. Some sought primarily to entertain their children, with little attempt to establish a routine. Others were extremely anxious and uncertain about how to deal with their children without a mother present. These men probably had little experience dealing with their children during the marriage and were therefore confronted with a kind of on-the-job training with few guidelines. They were not familiar with how to negotiate parent-child interactions. As one father put it:

> I found that I really couldn't control my boys except by getting angry. They just argued and fought when they were around. Every visit was incredibly tense; we were like coiled rattlesnakes just waiting to strike. I'd end up losing my temper which just made it worse because they treated me like I had no right to punish them. (quoted in Arendell, 1992, p. 577)

For their part, the children could also indirectly make contact with their fathers uncomfortable. Some younger children actively resisted leaving their homes or their mothers, often crying and physically fighting against being taken by their fathers. Some fathers felt unappreciated or were blatantly rejected by their older children. Many of these children directed resentment over the change in their standard of living caused by the divorce toward their fathers. Others behaved "too formally" or "too well," as if they were "guests" during the visits. Fathers interpreted such behavior as the child's way of denying the parent-child relationship. Because many of the fathers were unwilling or uncertain about how to talk to their children about these problems, the tensions and feelings of rejection increased over time, making absence an even more viable response.

Most of the men in Arendell's study felt that their former wives could help make the visits less strained and less awkward by intervening with the children. Arendell points out that this expectation is an extension of the traditional marital division of labor, in which women are expected to be the emotional caretakers in the family. Men perceived former wives who refused to intervene as misusing their power to deliberately undermine postdivorce relationships with the children.

Contrary to popular images of absent fathers happy to be free from child rearing responsibilities they were disinclined to adopt in the first place, the majority of absent fathers in Arendell's study were emotionally upset by the quality of their relationships with and absence from their children. They felt extremely isolated and were unable or unwilling to express their feelings about their children to others. Even men who had remarried felt reluctant to reveal the scope of their feelings about their children from a prior marriage to their present wives. Their sense of isolation and the gamut of emotions they experienced led many noncustodial fathers to believe that *they* were the unrecognized emotional victims of divorce.

The Fathers' Rights Movement Many divorced men who feel they are victimized have begun to fight against what they perceive to be a gender-biased system that discriminates against them during divorce. Lost in the divorce proceedings, they argue, are their rights to fatherhood, discretionary control of their earnings, the exercise of family authority, and the ability to control and handle their own futures (Arendell, 1995).

What's come to be known as the **fathers' rights movement** borrows the language of the women's movement, arguing that sole maternal custody is sexist and discriminatory, a denial of fathers' equal rights (Williams & Williams, 1995). The names of fathers' rights groups—such as Human Equality Action Resource Team (HEART), Fathers for Justice, and In Search of Justice—convey the belief that fathers are being treated unfairly by the legal system. Noncustodial father characters in movies like *Kramer vs. Kramer* and *Mrs. Doubtfire* have become symbols of the downtrodden, victimized divorced father whose love for his children is squashed at every turn by a gender-biased system unsympathetic to his situation. Many men report feeling a significant lack of control over the divorce settlement process, leading to greater feelings of dissatisfaction and inequity than women experience (Sheets & Braver, 1996).

The fathers' rights movement identifies several issues as sources of discrimination. One obvious issue is the maternal preference in custody. What fathers' rights groups don't acknowledge is that in most cases *both* parents agree that the mothers ought to have sole custody. And they ignore the fact that when fathers formally petition for custody, they have a good chance of receiving it.

However, when pressed, the majority of fathers admit that they don't want sole custody but want liberal, unrestricted access to their children. Few want to have responsibility for their children's everyday care but essentially want to continue the traditional parenting role they held prior to the divorce. In fact, one father went so far as to say that taking on 1 percent of the child care responsibilities would constitute "shared parenting" (Bertoia & Drakich, 1993).

Another issue that concerns the fathers' rights movement is mothers' power to control their children's activities after divorce. Even in cases of joint legal custody, mothers usually decide what schools children attend, what events they participate in, and what doctors, friends, and relatives they see. The loss of control fathers feel is reinforced by their limited access to their children. The change may be very distressing, particularly for men who were either used to exerting power in the family setting or deeply involved in their children's lives before the divorce.

Finally, the fathers' rights movement claims that mothers have often been awarded unjust child-support payments. Fathers who pay support resent that they have no way of monitoring how the money is spent. For lower-class fathers in particular, the payments may be a real financial burden, severely affecting a lifestyle that was never particularly comfortable even when they were married. Fathers paying support feel especially victimized when their physical access to their children is limited.

▲ For more on how movements and counter-movements affect social change, read Chapter 9.

The fathers' rights movement has been somewhat successful in addressing the complaints of noncustodial fathers. ▲ As we've seen, in most states, joint custody is becoming the preferred option in divorce settlements. And although single-parent families headed by men are still relatively uncommon, the proportion of such families has doubled over the past 3 decades (Meyer & Garasky, 1993). In some states, judges are forbidding custodial mothers to move out of the state if relocation would make it harder for fathers to see their children. Mothers who fail to produce children for scheduled visits may now face criminal charges or lose custody outright to the father. In other states, fathers who are willing to spend extra time caring for their children—which may include setting up separate bedrooms in their homes, paying for meals, buying them clothes, and taking them to the movies—may be able to reduce their child-support payments (Hoffman, 1995). In 1995 the New Jersey Commission to Study the Law of Divorce recommended laws to ensure that parents without custody see their children more often and have a greater say in how they are raised. For instance, it recommended that noncustodial parents have access to children's medical and school records and that a parent who prevents the other from seeing the children be fined.

Women's groups counter that such sanctions are not evenhanded. No similar effort is being made against fathers who don't show up for scheduled visits, and no state restricts a noncustodial father from moving away from his children. Furthermore, they argue that increasing noncustodial fathers' access to children has the potential for creating more strife between ex-spouses. In fact, some cynically note that the fathers' rights movement is less interested in keeping divorced fathers involved in their children's lives than in reducing their support payments.

Remarriage and Stepfamilies

The contentious issues surrounding divorce and custody can become even more difficult when former spouses remarry and start new families. Half of all marriages today involve at least one partner who was previously married (Bumpass, Sweet, & Castro Martin, 1990). Overall, four out of every five divorced individuals in this country are likely to remarry (Norton, 1987). These statistics suggest that although people are quite willing to escape a bad marriage, they have not necessarily given up on the concept of marriage. But the divorce rate for second marriages is actually higher than the divorce rate for first marriages. Thirty-seven percent of remarriages collapse within the first 10 years, compared to 30 percent of first marriages (Sweet & Bumpass, 1987).

Until the 1960s, the divorce rate and the remarriage rate in the United States rose and fell in tandem. In the 1960s, 75 percent of divorced women and about 80 percent of divorced men remarried. Today, only about 67 percent of divorced women and 75 percent of divorced men remarry (Cherlin & Furstenberg, 1994). But this decline in remarriage is deceptive. At the same time that remarriage rates have decreased, the number of cohabiting couples has increased. Many previously married individuals are not abandoning their desire to live with someone. Instead, many have substituted cohabitation for remarriage. (The Demo•Graphic Essay at the end of this chapter examines the effect of age on statistical trends in divorce and remarriage.)

The Complexities of "Blended" Families

One in five families today is a **blended family** or stepfamily, and one in four children will spend some time in a such a family (Furstenberg & Cherlin, 1991). Furthermore, 15 percent of all children in divorced families may see the parent they live with remarry and redivorce before they reach 18 (cited in Chira, 1995). This figure is conservative since it doesn't include couples who live together instead of remarrying. It also doesn't include the nearly one-third of American children who are born to unmarried mothers, many of whom will see their families form, split, reform, and split again and again.

Remarriage has been described as an "incomplete institution," meaning that it lacks the guiding norms, values, and role expectations that first marriages typically have. We have no set of common expectations for relationships between former and current spouses, between stepparents and stepchildren, between step- and half-siblings, and with extended kin following remarriage (Ahrons & Rodgers, 1987). Laws and customs have been slow to catch up. For instance, do stepchildren have legal claims to their stepparents' property? Do incest rules apply to step-siblings?

Remarriage creates ties that cross traditional household boundaries. The kinship relationships that it produces can be complex and confusing since they involve original parents (biological or adoptive), stepparents, biological siblings, step-siblings, half-siblings, multiple grandparents, and a seemingly infinite number of aunts, uncles, and cousins. Family alliances can become improvised and unpredictable when remarriage, redivorce, and cohabitation are blended into the mix. If you asked the individuals in a blended family who they considered to be in their family, you'd likely get a different response from every one of them. One-third of children in stepfamilies don't mention their stepparent as part of their family; 10 percent don't mention a biological parent (Furstenberg & Cherlin, 1991).

Step-Siblings

Much of the tension in blended families comes from the relationship between step-siblings, who may be asked to share bedrooms or other possessions. If one part of the blended family is moving into the home of the other, such sharing may be perceived as an intrusion. Furthermore, children may have a difficult time overcoming the tendency to divide the family into "us" and "them." They often see their connection to their biological parent as giving them a larger claim to that parent's affection and resources. Such situations can create feelings of rejection and envy (Beer, 1988).

Children's place in the family hierarchy may also be altered upon remarriage. A teenager may have gotten used to the responsibilities and privileges of being the "oldest child," only to see that role disappear with the entry of an older step-sibling. Likewise, the "baby of the family" may suddenly have younger siblings to contend with. Such changes can create tension in blended families.

Despite these formidable problems, most step-siblings adjust well and form close relationships. The bonds that develop between step-siblings occur most quickly when the children are similar in age, sex, and life experience. In addition, most step-siblings do keep in touch with one another when they become adults, although not as closely or as frequently as blood siblings do (White & Riedmann, 1992).

Relationships Between Stepparents and Stepchildren

In American society, the mere existence of a blood tie doesn't necessarily make two people think of themselves as family (Cherlin & Furstenberg, 1994). We typically consider kinship to be achieved by establishing a relationship with a person and making repeated connections. ▲ So to be considered a relative, you must do the work of creating and maintaining kinship. Among parents and children, this work usually happens automatically. But among stepparents and stepchildren, it can be problematic.

▲ Issue 1 discusses the importance of the relationship, versus blood ties, in defining a family's boundaries.

For one thing, a stepparent who enters a family after a divorce doesn't *replace* a stepchild's nonresident parent, as is the case when remarriage follows the death of a parent. Instead, the stepparent—not to mention all the members of the stepparent's family—is added to the child's stock of potential kin. If both biological parents are involved in the child's life, the stepparent's role remains unclear. Step-relatives are more like in-laws than kin. In fact, in France the same term—*beau-parent*—means both stepparent and "parent-in-law."

The guidelines and norms are much less clear for stepparents than they are for parents. One obvious illustration of this lack of clarity has to do with how children refer to their stepparents. "Step-dad" sounds too awkward and indeed is quite rare. Some children use the term *dad,* but many others use the first name, which suggests a relationship somewhere between parent and stranger. Not using the term *dad* or *mom* for a stepparent implies that children aren't granting stepparents the rights and obligations typically associated with parenthood.

▲ The symbolic interactionist perspective, explained in Chapter 1, focuses on how members construct the definition of their family.

After a divorce, single parents and their children establish, usually with some difficulty, new rules, routines, and schedules. They create a system with shared histories, intensive relationships, and agreed-upon roles. ▲ When a stepparent enters the former single-parent family, the entire system may be thrown out of balance. He or she may be seen as an outsider, or worse, as an intruder. Rules and habits have to change, and for a time, confusion, resentment, and hostility may be the norm. Although conflict is common in all types of families, issues like favoritism, divided loyalties, the right to discipline, and financial responsibility are particularly likely to occur in stepfamilies.

The friction and disruption found in stepfamilies decrease the odds of building durable, intimate bonds. Many studies show that the well-being of children in stepfamilies isn't all that much better than that of children in single-parent households (Cherlin & Furstenberg, 1994). In fact, some people who counsel children of multiple divorce say that the trauma of forming a new stepfamily, with a stranger intruding on their time with their parent, can be harder on children than a prior or subsequent breakup (Chira, 1995).

Remarriage can, however, improve the financial well-being of children whose parents had divorced. One national study found that 8 percent of children in mother-stepfather households live below the poverty line compared to 49 percent of children in single-mother households (cited in Cherlin & Furstenberg, 1994). In addition, a stepparent adds a second adult to the household who can interact with the child, serve as a role model for the child, and take some of the burden off the custodial parent.

Many stepparents manage to build strong, durable, and loving relationships with their partner's children. The majority of stepparents and children in a recent national survey described their households as "relaxed" and "close." And most children in stepfamilies are doing quite well psychologically (cited in Coontz, 1997). In fact, the biggest source of problems for kids in stepfamilies may actually be parental conflict left over from the first marriage (Rutter, 1997).

The "success" of remarriages and stepfamilies, then, depends in large part on the nature of the divorce itself. Adults and children who welcomed a divorce or defined it as basically a "good thing" are more likely to anticipate remarriage with eagerness and to see it as a chance for a new start than those who defined the divorce as a "bad thing" or something that should have been avoided.

But, ironically, what works well for divorced spouses may not always work so well for stepfamilies. Ex-spouses who continue to have mutual respect for one another as people and parents, who remain close friends, and who continue to be a significant presence in their children's lives provide a healthy postdivorce environment for their children. But such a situation can be difficult for a stepparent, who might feel threatened by the continuing intimacy maintained by the divorced couple. The open boundaries maintained by the harmonious divorced couple after the breakup (for instance, having and using their key to the ex-spouse's house) can feel like an invasion of privacy to the new spouse. Likewise, changes in routines initiated by the stepparent may be resented by the children.

Thus, the most conducive postdivorce environment for a stepfamily may be a total lack of contact between former spouses. With no ex-spouses present, stepparents can more easily adopt stepchildren. Defining parental roles is less of a problem because the noncustodial biological parent is out of the picture, and the stepparent can serve as a replacement or substitute parent. Thus, the newly formed family can more closely approximate a nuclear family.

However, stepfamilies can never function quite like first-marriage nuclear families. Family relationships and, as a result, the emotional life of the family are both more complicated (Rutter, 1997). The extensive kin connections established in first marriages cannot be overlooked or ignored. Hence, stepfamilies have to remain more flexible and open than nuclear families (Ganong & Coleman, 1994).

As you can see, the high divorce rate of remarriages and the high levels of conflict within some stepfamilies are not simply an outgrowth of the spouses' psychological inability to sustain intimate relationships, as some analysts have claimed. The fact that remarriages are not fully institutionalized is what makes them susceptible to failure. The lack of clear role definitions, the absence of established societal norms, and the increased complexity of the family structure all increase the likelihood of tension and turmoil. But perhaps in the future, our culture will develop standard ways of defining and coping with remarriage.

Conclusion

Throughout history, some couples have always sought escape from bad marriages. But as long as the community was able to cite the flaws of the individuals involved as the source of the marital problems—one or the other partner was abusive; one or the other partner was unfaithful; one or the other was incapable of sustaining emotional commitment; or, in later years, these two people were simply incompatible—the sanctity of marriage remained intact.

But even though divorce is a tragic personal experience, it is not solely a personal matter. If the only causes of divorce were private unhappiness and mistreatment, we wouldn't see differences in *rates* of divorce over time, between groups, or across cultures. Divorce rates, then, are the product of long-term social and economic changes, not a breakdown of personal values.

Legal restrictions or moral warnings are not likely to alter historical trends that have been building for so long. As long as we live in a society that grants individuals the freedom to choose whom to marry, people will from time to time make bad choices. Perhaps, then, the solution to the "divorce problem" lies not so much in increasing legal and economic sanctions against it, "restigmatizing" it, or restricting access to it but in helping people to have more realistic expectations and to learn better methods for dealing with conflict before and during their marriages.

Or, even more radically, maybe the answer lies in not perceiving divorce as a problem in the first place. Our society would have to acknowledge that, although a long-lasting marriage is something all couples should strive for, a certain proportion of marriages will always end in divorce. Instead of punishing divorced people and making their lives—and their children's lives—more difficult, we might consider aiding parents in their transition from marriage to singlehood, and children in their transition from two live-in parents to one.

CHAPTER HIGHLIGHTS

- Although divorce is more common and acceptable in some societies than in others, virtually all societies have provisions for dissolving marriages. Nevertheless, no society places a positive value on divorce.
- In the United States, the prevalence of divorce varies among racial, ethnic, and religious groups.
- Changes in divorce laws over the past 2 decades have made it easier for people in unsatisfying marriages to end them. However, no-fault divorce laws have had disastrous effects on some women and children, who are likely to suffer financially as a result of divorce. Thus, some states have attempted to make divorces more difficult to obtain.

- The individual experience of divorce is a process that can extend for months, even years, beginning well before the actual separation and continuing far beyond the time when the divorce becomes final.

- Most of the societal concern over high divorce rates focuses on the impact on children. However, the bulk of research suggests that the problems children experience after a divorce are caused not by the breakup but by the conflict between the parents. In fact, children who grow up in intact but conflict-ridden families may suffer more than children whose parents divorce but maintain a friendly relationship.

- Although mothers still retain custody of children in the vast majority of divorce cases, joint custody and paternal custody are becoming more common. But child-support policies remain inadequate to meet the economic needs of children in single-parent families.

- The large number of remarriages and stepfamilies challenges traditional notions of what a family is. These blended families create complex roles, alliances, and loyalties, which can make adjustment difficult, especially for children.

DEMO•GRAPHIC ESSAY

Trends in Divorce and Remarriage

As we saw in this chapter, the U.S. divorce rate—the number of divorces in a given year divided by the total population that year—is beginning to level off after a period of steady increase. However, the divorce rate is simply a measure of new divorces. The prevalence of divorce may be better measured by including persons who have been divorced for many years. Exhibit 7-A shows how the status of being divorced has increased in the United States over the past quarter century, from fewer than 4 percent of men and women in 1970 to more than 10 percent of all adult women and approximately 7 percent of all adult men in 1995. By this measure, divorce is continuing to become more prevalent.

One way to understand the discrepancy between the two measures of divorce is to look at how it varies by age. Exhibit 7-B shows that for both men and women, the prevalence of divorce increases from ages 20–24 up to ages 45–54, then begins to decrease. To understand the reasons for this age-related trend, we must interpret age in two different ways. First, age can be thought of as a kind of exposure variable. As persons age, they become more susceptible to the risk of being divorced. They are more likely to have been married

Exhibit 7-A

Divorce Among Adults 18 Years and Older

United States: 1970–1995

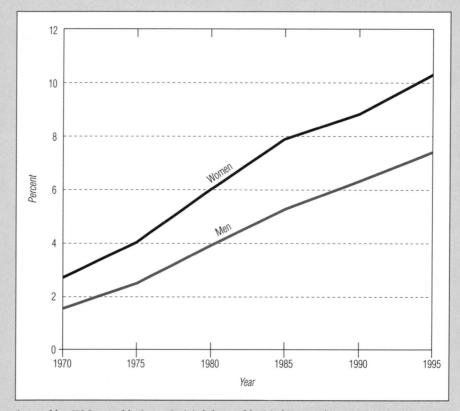

Sources of data: U.S. Bureau of the Census, *Statistical Abstract of the United States.* Washington, DC, 1984, 1990, 1997.

in the first place, which makes them "eligible" to get divorced. Then, as they age, they will have been married longer and been exposed to the risk of divorce for a longer time. Quite possibly, however, someone can leave the status of being divorced by getting married again. And a person could get divorced again after remarrying. So the age-related increase in the percent of the population who are divorced makes some sense. But what about the decrease after ages 45–54? One explanation might be that people who stay married until their mid-50s have passed a point when divorce is a relevant option. Finally, married persons are susceptible not only to the risk of divorce but also to the risk of widowhood, and with age comes an increasing risk of widowhood.

These explanations consider age to be a kind of exposure to the risk of divorce, remarriage, and widowhood. Age can also represent the birth cohort to which individuals belong, such as the baby boom cohort. Cohorts born earlier in this century experienced the lower divorce rates that were in effect when they were in the prime ages for divorce (young to middle age), so proportionately fewer of them are divorced today than are people from later, more divorce-prone cohorts. Often, looking at how a social phenomenon varies by age can give clues about the reasons for the phenomenon itself as well as a better of understanding of its variations.

Patterns of remarriage also can clarify divorce trends. Between 1970 and 1990, remarriage rates (remarriages per 1,000 divorced persons) declined steadily (see Exhibit 7-C). Note also that, in each year, men were more likely than women to remarry. A reasonable conclusion is that the increasing prevalence of divorce reflects both a rising divorce rate (at least until very recently) and a decreasing remarriage rate.

Exhibit 7-B

Divorced Persons (by age)

United States: 1996

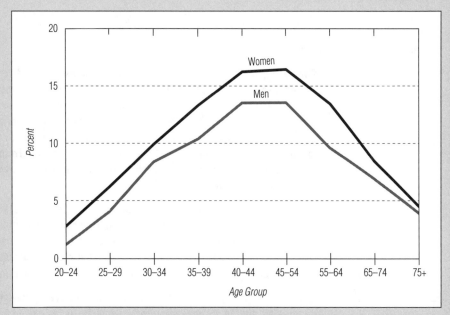

Source of data: U.S. Bureau of the Census, *Statistical Abstract of the United States: 1997* (117th edition). Washington, DC, 1997.

Exhibit 7-C

Remarriage Rates
for Divorced
Persons Ages 15
and Older

*United States:
1970–1990*

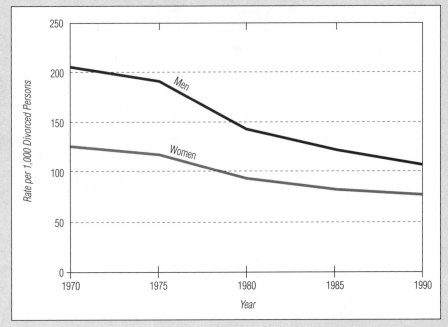

Source of data: U.S. Bureau of the Census, *Statistical Abstract of the United States: 1997* (117th edition). Washington, DC, 1997.

Questions for Further Study

1. One trend that has persisted across time is that there are more divorced women than divorced men in the United States. Do the statistics mean that women are more likely than men to get divorced? What other reason might account for the greater extent of divorce among women? What are some additional sociological variables (in addition to age and gender) that might be related to divorce? Consider both variables that can affect the likelihood of someone getting divorced (and staying divorced) as well as variables that divorce itself can affect. How might divorced persons behave differently than never-married persons or widowed persons?

2. *The Statistical Abstract of the United States* provides not only data on the proportion of adults who are divorced, but also on the proportion of adults in other marital statuses (married, never married, widowed, separated). Given the information in this chapter, what do you hypothesize has happened to the other marital statuses over the past 20 or so years? See if your hypotheses are confirmed by data from the *Statistical Abstract.*

3. Compare remarriage trends with trends for marriage overall (check *The Statistical Abstract of the United States*). Is the trend for remarriages part of an overall pattern for marriage in general, or are remarriage trends peculiar? How might you explain the relationship between the two trends?

YOUR TURN

We've seen in this chapter that divorce and remarriage are becoming a common part of everyday family life in this society. Nevertheless, blended families face many unique dilemmas and challenges.

Interview a variety of people who live in stepfamilies. Try to speak to both stepmothers and stepfathers, stepsons and stepdaughters—although they need not be from the same family. See if you can also talk to people from various social class, racial, and religious backgrounds. Try to talk to children who still live at home as well as grown children who live on their own.

First, get some background information. When did the divorce occur? How long ago did remarriage take place? How long was the respondent in a single-parent arrangement? Are there any step-siblings or half-siblings? If so, what are their sexes and ages? How did the respondent's living arrangements change upon remarriage? Did he or she move into someone else's home, or did both sides of the family move into a "neutral" home?

What happened when the respondent first met the new members of the family? Did the situation confirm or contradict expectations? In the new family, what term do the children use to refer to their stepparent? Are they comfortable calling this person Dad or Mom?

Try to get a sense of how certain issues are handled in the blended family, such as parental discipline, everyday financial support, leisure time, and so on. What about issues of favoritism between biological and step-relations? Does the respondent feel any confusion, resentment, hostility?

After you complete your interviews, analyze whether parents or children seem to have more problems adjusting to blended families. Considering just the children, compare responses for:

- Those whose stepparent is of the same sex and those whose stepparent is of the opposite sex
- Those who were young and those who were older when remarriage took place

What can you conclude from your interviews about the nature of blended families and their place in the larger society?

CHAPTER 8

Family Transitions in Adulthood

My relationship with my father was fairly typical. We argued sometimes and annoyed one another sometimes, but clearly we always loved each other deeply. Like most fathers in the 1960s and 70s, he took his breadwinner role seriously and spent a lot of time at work. He'd leave early in the morning, often before I had awakened, and he'd return, usually exhausted, close to dinner time.

Like most children, I created some psychological distance from my father as I became a know-it-all teenager and came to depend less and less on his help and advice. As time passed, I went off to college, got married, and started my own family. My father and I were living separate lives. We'd talk once a week on the phone and see each other two or three times a year. I knew he was proud that I was studying for a Ph.D., and I knew he loved being a grandfather, even if he didn't see his grandson very often. I didn't need him that much, but I just figured he'd be around if I ever did.

Shortly before Thanksgiving in 1987—my last year of graduate school—I received a call from my sister telling me that my father was gravely ill and in the intensive care unit of his local hospital. As far back as I can remember, my father had had health problems of one sort or another. But this time was different. Two days after Thanksgiving my sister called again, saying that I had better get there right away. I caught the next flight and sped directly to the hospital from the airport.

As I approached his room, I saw my sister, brother, and sister-in-law in the hallway, waiting to tell me that my father was hooked up to several machines and was floating in and out of consciousness. They warned me that he looked very different from the way he looked the last time I had seen him.

As I walked into the room, my mother met me with a tearful embrace. I tentatively looked toward the person lying in the bed. For a split second I thought everyone had made a big mistake. That man wasn't my father, I thought. My father was a big, robust man; the fellow in the bed was skinny and frail. His skin was a faint yellow, not the tanned brown my father sported. My father's face was happy and chubby; this man's face had the hollow eyes and sunken cheeks of a skull. But of course it wasn't a mistake. It was my father.

He opened his eyes and looked at me and slightly smiled. He mumbled something, but I couldn't make out what it was. We all stayed there for about 45 minutes making small talk while my father lay there motionless and unaware. "How was your flight?" "How's school going?" "How's the baby?" "How's your job?" As we left I told my father I'd see him first thing in the morning. He didn't respond.

At about 1:30 the following morning the phone rang. It was the hospital. The nurse said my father had "taken a turn for the worse." We all got in the car and rushed to the hospital. A nurse met us in the hallway. Her simple, direct words to us sound as clear in my head today as they did over a decade ago: "I'm sorry, he's gone."

My father was dead. The man who had supported me and loved me unconditionally—even when I didn't deserve it—was dead. Like a character out of some sappy made-for-television movie, I thought of all the things I should have told him but didn't. I had had countless opportunities to tell this man how much he meant to me, but I never did. I had spent far too much time criticizing him and focusing on his flaws and embarrassing habits.

But aside from the guilt, I also came to a frightening realization: My life, from that day forward, would never again be the same. I had experienced a turning point and was now a different person. My family had been transformed. My mother was a widow. What was her life going to be like now? My baby son would never know his grandfather. I missed my father, the person. But even though I was a grown man, I also missed *having* a father. The transformation had occurred to my family in an instant, but we would feel its effects forever.

Family life is never static. It is punctuated by transformative events. Some are joyous—a graduation, a wedding, the birth of a child. Others, like the death of a parent, rank as the most painful experiences a person can endure. Some are unexpected; others are anticipated for years. Some take place suddenly; others are gradual changes with ill-defined beginnings and endings.

As we grow, we move from a high degree of dependence on others to greater independence. Our values change. Our tastes change. If you have younger brothers or sisters you know that, right around the time you became a teenager, you discovered that your interests no longer matched those of your siblings. The games you once played together now seemed embarrassingly childish.

Nothing is more certain about family life than the fact that it is constantly changing. It is a continuous string of transitions: from baby to toddler, from child to adolescent, from adolescent to adult, from single to coupled, from nonparent to parent, from middle age to old age, from employed to retired, from healthy to frail, and so on. We grow up, change physically, leave home, sometimes return home, form relationships, end relationships, have children, raise children, watch children leave, watch family members die, and eventually die ourselves.

This chapter looks at some of the important family changes and life transformations that most of us have experienced or will at some point experience. In particular, I will focus on the transitions that occur in adulthood, middle age, old age, and death. You'll see that while most of these transformations are somehow related to biological changes associated with aging, they are all influenced by powerful historical, cultural, and demographic forces.

Generations of Family Across Time

The generation born during the Great Depression has reached old age, and in their lifetimes they have come to know wealth and consumption beyond the wildest dreams they formed during their early years of hardship.

The baby boomers, those Americans born between 1945 and the early 1960s, were in many ways the first generation to define the culture while in their youth. Growing up within the relative economic prosperity of the 1950s and 1960s, this generation demanded the gratification of their various desires and loudly protested when their wishes were denied. Realizing they could make a difference, they created the counterculture of the "sixties" and helped bring an end to the Vietnam War through their protests. Many of these rebellious boomers have now become parents themselves. Their immense desires have been transferred to their children, and the most affluent have given their children the greatest opportunities affordable—from elite, private nursery schools to every type of toy imaginable.

Children born in the 1970s—those caught between the boomers and Generation X—have had to grapple with global economic insecurities, rapid social change, and continual technological development. For many this has meant the delay of adulthood. Some still live at home well into their late 20s and retain the party attitude of their early college days; many others will not marry until well into their 30s, if at all.

Today's teens and 20-somethings are the first generation to grow up in the computer age. Like their grandparents and sometimes great-grandparents, who were the first to grow up with TV, their generation marks an important social transformation. What implications do you think this technological exposure will have on the way they go about creating their own families?

Since the beginning of television, family ideals have shifted from *Leave It to Beaver* to *Beavis and Butthead,* reflecting broader cultural changes.

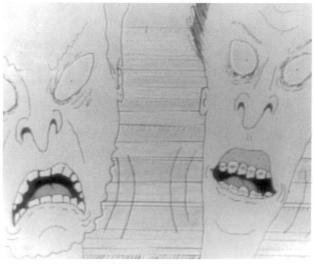

Family forms are also shifting as a result of the movements of people across continents.

Demographers predict that by the year 2020, Hispanics will no longer be a minority in several major cities. How will this trend change Hispanic family structure? Do you think more families will adopt the Euro-American norms of smaller family size, as this family of five has done, or will they work to maintain their ethnic heritage?

Many recent immigrants from Korea and Vietnam maintain a small family size and show higher degrees of solidarity than do white Americans. Mother, father, and children can be found working long hours together to ensure a successful family business.

More and more people these days are marrying across racial and ethnic lines. What impact do you think this will have on family structures, transitions, and race relations in the future?

The Influence of Birth Cohorts

A key factor that affects the way we experience family transformations is our **birth cohort**—the set of people who were born during the same period and who therefore face similar societal circumstances. Each cohort has distinctive properties—such as its initial size, ethnic composition, age-specific birthrates, and average life expectancies—that set it apart from other cohorts.

You've no doubt asked yourself questions like: What career will I pursue? Where will I live? Will I be able to afford a house? Will I have children? The answers to these questions are obviously influenced by your personal desires, traits, values, ambitions, and abilities, not to mention your social class, gender, race, religion, and ethnicity. But the shape of your birth cohort and its position and size relative to other cohorts will also determine your responses to these questions. For instance, the sheer number of people graduating from college in a given year will affect the availability of high-paying jobs,

Birth cohorts influence the everyday lives of individuals in two fundamental ways (Riley, 1971):

1. People born during the same era tend to experience life course events or social rites of passage—including puberty, marriage, childbearing, graduation, entrance into the workforce, retirement, and death—at roughly the same time. Sociologists call this life course dimension **cohort effects**. Think of it as the collective experience of aging.
2. People born during the same era also share a common history. A cohort's place in time tells us a lot about the opportunities and constraints placed on its members. Historical events and major social trends, called **period effects,** contribute to the unique shape and outlook of each cohort.

Cohort and period effects combine to profoundly affect the lives of individual people. Cohort members experience the same major societal or world circumstances at about the same stage in their lives.

To better understand the combined influence of cohort effects and period effects, consider the research of social historian Tamara Hareven (1994). Hareven studied two cohorts of adult children of immigrants in the industrial community of Manchester, New Hampshire. She found significant differences in the attitudes and practices of these two cohorts that could be attributed to their earlier historical experiences. Members of the earlier cohort (born between 1910 and 1919), toughened by the Depression they experienced as teenagers and young adults, were primarily concerned with keeping the entire family afloat economically. They pooled resources, doubled up on housing when possible, scrimped and saved, and supported their aging parents and needy relatives. They held on to traditional beliefs about relying on kin rather than public agencies in time of need.

In contrast, members of the more recent cohort (born between 1920 and 1929) were very small children during the Depression. They took advantage of the economic recovery brought about by World War II and were eager to develop middle-class lifestyles upon becoming adults. They devoted themselves to improving their own lives and their children's future. They were more likely to live separately from their kin. They were more prepared to accept government help and were more willing to place their elderly parents in nursing homes if necessary.

▲ The degree to which people feel obligated to their families also varies by race, ethnicity, gender, and culture, as explained in Issue 4.

The earlier cohort was clearly more committed to collectivist family values. ▲ Many had actually gone through the experience of caring for elderly parents in their homes or had sacrificed their own marriage to care for a parent. But they had felt significant ambivalence, doubt, and bitterness. The nagging fear that the care they gave their elderly parents had robbed them of the opportunity to start their own families increased the threat that old age would be troublesome for them. They took the posture of resignation to family norms and acceptance of "fate" over free choice. Members of the more recent cohort, on the other hand, who followed the more individualistic path, were often racked by guilt over the way in which they relinquished responsibility for supporting their aging parents to others.

The very different outlooks of these two cohorts reflect a historical process: increasing separation between the **family of origin** (parents, grandparents, siblings, and so on) and the **family of procreation** (spouses and children), combined with the privatization of family life and the disappearance of norms emphasizing mutual assistance among kin. As these changes have become more pronounced, so have the feelings of insecurity and isolation of successive cohorts (Hareven, 1994).

Different cohorts develop and mature in what amounts to fundamentally different societal environments. The very nature of society—the size of the population, its age distribution, and its racial or ethnic proportions—varies from cohort to cohort. We start our lives in one historical period, which has its own distinct pattern of behavior for people of different ages and its own set of social norms, and we end our lives in another. As we grow older, we develop and change in a society that itself is developing and changing.

The social, cultural, and environmental changes to which a cohort is exposed as it moves through the life course can even affect the way people experience the biological process of aging. People are living longer than ever before thanks to advancements in nutrition, education, sanitation, and other areas. As a result, cohorts experience the physical consequences of aging in different ways (Riley, Foner, & Waring, 1988). For instance, the average age of menarche (a girl's first menstrual period) has gradually lowered from about 14 a century ago to 12.5 today (Darton, 1991; Skolnick, 1991). In addition, better health and a longer life span have led to an increase in babies born to middle-aged people. ▲ When combined with changing social norms, values, and cultural beliefs, such changes will inevitably speed up the point at which young people become sexually curious and explorative and delay the point at which people decide they are "too old" to have children.

▲ Chapter 9 explores the effect this trend will have on future families.

Certain cohorts are so distinctive that they get pinned with a label. One example is the baby boom generation, consisting of people born between 1948 and 1964. ▲ A more recent cohort of interest is **Generation X,** which consists of roughly 48 million people who are now in their 20s. The birth rate during the late 1970s, when these individuals were born, was about half as high as it was during the post–World War II years of the baby boomers.

▲ A historical examination of the baby boom years appears in Issue 2; the relationship between this cohort and large-scale social change is explored in Chapter 9.

People in the Generation X cohort are less likely to get married than older generations and more likely to delay marriage if they do. In 1970, 55 percent of men and 36 percent of women between the ages of 20 and 24 had never married. In 1996 the figures were 81 percent of young men and 68 percent of young women (U.S. Bureau of the Census, 1997a). Furthermore, the high divorce rate over the past several decades has had a direct and lasting impact on this cohort. Roughly 40 percent of people in their 20s today are children of divorce. Even more of them were so-called latchkey children, the first generation of children to experience the effects of two work-ing parents. For many of them, childhood was marked by dependence on secondary relation-ships—teachers, friends, day care teachers, and so on.

Many members of Generation X are disillusioned over the variety of gargantuan crises they have inherited from previous generations, from the national debt and the likely cutbacks in their Social Security benefits to the degradation of the natural environment and growing urban decay. Resentful of the excesses of their elders, they are experiencing great apprehension about their own futures. Many sense they are destined to become society's sacrificial "clean-up crew."

But rather than evoke sympathy from other cohorts, they have instead become to many a symbol of a culture in decline. From the perspective of older generations, Generation X—with its hard-edged and sometimes threatening language, fashion, music, and recreational pursuits—has become the embodiment of uncontrollable change and fear for our collective future (Howe & Strauss, 1992). However, the members of Generation X have a bold style of confronting the world that is having a significant impact on everything from TV advertising to employee recruiting. As they form their own families, that aspect of life is also likely to see the impact of their style.

The Transitions of Adulthood

▲ Chapter 5 describes the social construction of adolescence.

The presence of a socially accepted but vaguely defined stage of life like adolescence makes it difficult to pinpoint the exact threshold to adulthood. ▲ Depending on how you define "adult-hood," a person can be considered an adult anywhere between age 13 and 25. You might consider adulthood to begin at the age at which a person can procreate, drive a car, vote, be drafted for military service, legally drink or purchase alcohol, get married, have an abortion without paren-tal consent, or support him- or herself financially

Sometimes the age at which one is thought to be an adult in one situation contradicts such an age in another situation. In 1990, for example, 50,000 teenagers got married before they turned 18, thereby obtaining the legal right to have sex before they were allowed to watch sexual activity in an X-rated movie (Mogelonsky, 1996). Americans can purchase cars before they are legally allowed to drive them, and they can do both of these things long before they're eligible to rent cars.

Identifying when adulthood begins became particularly problematic in 1971, when the Twenty-sixth Amendment to the U.S. Constitution was adopted. This amendment reduced the age at which citizens could vote from 21 to 18. The amendment was passed at a time when 18-year-olds were being drafted in record numbers to fight in the Vietnam War. Many people sup-ported the amendment because they thought it was hypocritical that they be old enough to fight and die but not old enough to vote for the people who made the decisions to send them to war in the first place.

Delayed Adulthood

Since World War II, we have had a strong cultural expectation that adulthood means college at-tendance away from home, postgraduate or professional training away from home, and entry-level positions in a career that will lead to sufficient income to provide independence. We have

Exhibit 8.1

Adults Who Believe
That Living Apart
from In-Laws
Is Very Important
for a Successful
Marriage

*World Values Survey:
1990–1993*

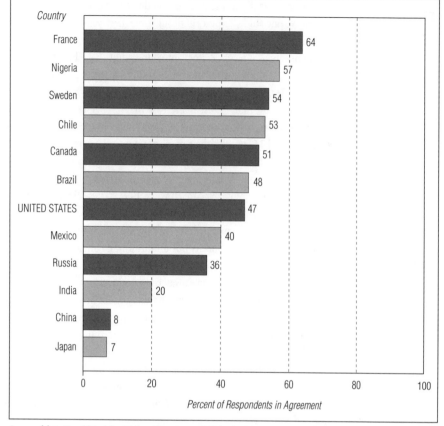

Country

Country	Percent of Respondents in Agreement
France	64
Nigeria	57
Sweden	54
Chile	53
Canada	51
Brazil	48
UNITED STATES	47
Mexico	40
Russia	36
India	20
China	8
Japan	7

Percent of Respondents in Agreement

Source of data: Ronald Inglehart, Miguel Basañez, and Alejandro Moreno, *Human Values and Beliefs: A Cross-Cultural Sourcebook.* Ann Arbor: University of Michigan, 1998.

expected children to live in dorms, fraternity or sorority houses, or apartments while in college and to establish their own households after they graduate. We have expected them to marry early and have children, all within the context of a union that we expected to be permanent. We may think it's appropriate for young married couples to live with one set of parents (see Exhibit 8.1), but we don't expect children to remain dependent on their parents their entire lives. Our definitions of adulthood are often based on cultural ideas about appropriate living arrangements (see Demo•Graphic Essay at the end of this chapter).

Today, many young adults are having a tough time with the transition to adulthood. More and more people are choosing to remain single, delaying marriage, or, if married, deciding not to have children. ▲ Buying a home is beyond the means of most young adults, and periodic downswings in the economy can make getting a good job exceedingly difficult, even for college graduates. In short, the traditional indicators of adulthood have become more difficult to attain.

Thus, a new pattern of entry into adulthood has developed among young people, which includes interrupted, delayed, or postponed college attendance; erratic job patterns with no assurance of an income high enough for self-sufficiency; and postponement of marriage and/or

▲ See Issue 8 for a
more detailed discussion
of these topics.

childbearing. Many young people who do attend college live at home and commute daily. According to one study, 25 percent of full-time, first-year college students live at home while they attend school (cited in Mogelonsky, 1996).

Consequently, recent cohorts of young adults have been slower to leave the nest and more likely to return home after they have tried to leave than older cohorts were (Goldscheider & Goldscheider, 1994). The percentage of young adults who live with their parents has increased steadily since the mid-1970s, an increase that has been more dramatic for men than for women. According to statistics from the U.S. Census Bureau, 15 percent of American men between the ages of 25 and 34 live with their parents, up from 10 percent in 1970. Eight percent of women in this age bracket live with their parents, up from 7 percent in 1970 (U.S. Bureau of the Census, 1997a). Approximately 10 percent of all unmarried middle-aged individuals are still living at home with their parents (Speare & Avery, 1993). These figures include children who have never left and those who have left and returned, perhaps more than once.

Although today's young adults are slower to leave home than young adults of the baby boom generation, their experience is not unique among all cohorts this century. In the 1930s, when their great-grandparents were in their late teens and early 20s, few people went to college. For the most part, they didn't move away from home until they'd found a steady job or got married. But today's young adults are unique in that they are more likely than any other previous generation to *return* home after moving out. Young women are less likely to return home after leaving than young men, a difference almost entirely accounted for by the fact that women are more likely leave home initially because of marriage (White, 1994).

The prevailing cultural image is that adults who live with their parents are either slackers who lack the drive to become independent or immature "Peter Pans" who don't want to grow up. But according to sociologists Allan Schnaiberg and Sheldon Goldenberg (1989), neither is the case. They believe that lack of economic opportunity is the major reason why today's young adults are more likely to remain at home. Between 1976 and 1996, the average per capita income (measured in 1996 dollars) of people between the ages of 25 and 34 dropped from $23,123 to $20,305 (U.S. Bureau of the Census, 1998).

Money makes it easier to set up a new household, and a sudden reversal of economic fortunes can easily force a return to the parents' home. Furthermore, the money spent on short-term living expenses—rent, food, utilities, and so on—might take away from money spent for schooling or a "nest egg" for marriage. Thus, many young adults conclude that they should postpone residential independence in order to have a more secure financial future.

Another factor associated with the delay in leaving home is the rise in the age at which young people first marry. Between 1970 and 1995, the median age at first marriage rose from 23.2 to 26.9 for men and from 20.8 to 24.5 for women (U.S. Bureau of the Census, 1997a). The marriage delay affords young adults more time to live with their parents. But we should note that it also increases the number of young adults who live alone or who cohabitate. In short, people in their 20s are less likely to be married than they were in the recent past, leading to an increase in all sorts of other living arrangements, including living with their parents.

Most adults would rather not have to live with their parents. Since we still tend to take independent living as the most important indicator of being adult in this culture, adults who live with their parents—even if they're working and saving money for a family or going to school to enhance their future earning capabilities—feel that others see them as not-quite-adults

(Schnaiberg & Goldenberg, 1989). For better or worse, they are deviating from the cultural expectation that they will physically separate from their parents during young adulthood.

Parents, too, may feel anxiety over their adult children still living at home. Periodically, conflict can erupt over the organization of household labor and the allocation of family resources (Schnaiberg & Goldenberg, 1989). Families may argue over whether the child ought to pay rent or contribute to household utilities. Some parents may feel they've somehow failed to adequately prepare their children for adulthood. Since expectations of college and career are most pervasive in upper-middle-class families, the anxieties over delayed adulthood are likely to be most pronounced among this segment of the population.

The Empty Nest

Even though the proportion of young adults remaining or returning home has been increasing in recent years, the vast majority eventually do leave, for good. Most parents, therefore, are likely to face a time when they no longer have children living with them at home. Because more Americans than ever live to be middle aged and beyond, more and more couples experience an unprecedented length of time together after the children have grown and left home. This extended postparental period—referred to as the *empty nest*—can pose many challenges.

▲ Chapter 5 examines historical variations in conceptions of children's roles in families.

A century or so ago, the leaving of a child marked the loss of a valued contributor to the household income for most families. On farms, children were an important source of labor. ▲ In cities, their earnings helped keep the home together. When all their children had moved out, couples had to face the problem of replacing children's economic contributions. Rural couples often had to hire farm laborers, and urban couples often took in boarders and lodgers to compensate for the child's absence. Hence, the postparental period in the last century meant less privacy and more uncertainty (Treas & Bengtson, 1982).

Perhaps because of this history, American culture has a pervasive belief that middle-aged parents—particularly stay-at-home mothers—suffer severe emotional crises when all their children grow up and leave home. The idea is that so much energy has been spent raising children that when they are longer there, parents face the frightening question of what to do with the rest of their lives. They become depressed and aimless, responding to their children's departure as if they were grieving and mourning. This experience has been dubbed the **empty nest syndrome**. Some psychiatrists believe this syndrome to be a clinically diagnosable condition, and medical journals have run full-page advertisements for antidepressants that can be prescribed as treatment (Harkins, 1978).

▲ The cultural emphasis on motherhood is examined in Chapter 4.

Such a contention makes intuitive sense. The roles we occupy provide us with meaning and behavioral guidance in our lives. Historically, women have found obstacles to developing professional identities outside the home. They have, therefore, devoted a significant portion of their lives to raising children. ▲ Consequently, we'd expect them to suffer when their children leave, because a key element of the all-important mother role has gone.

▲ The influence of maternal employment on family relations is examined in Issue 8 and Chapter 3.

But such an explanation operates on some dubious assumptions. First, it assumes that being a parent is the individual's only pertinent social role; that when the children are gone, parents—especially mothers—are essentially stripped of their identity. But as you know, we all take on multiple roles. Mothers today are likely to have other pursuits, including work, and therefore don't depend totally on mothering activities to determine their self-worth. ▲

Second, this explanation also assumes that when children leave home, parenting abruptly stops. But as you know, your parents don't stop being your parents once you leave home. They may not provide you with daily meals or chauffeur you from place to place anymore, but they certainly retain their identity as your parents. In fact, some "empty nest" parents are surprised to learn how much their nonresident children still need them. Listen to how one mother describes her relationship with her son in college:

> My son Josh called me collect from junior college during his first year away from home. "Mom . . . I need your opinion on how [my paper] sounds. I want an A in speech." I could have answered, "C'mon Josh . . . you're 19 . . . you're independent . . . I don't need to worry about your schoolwork anymore, especially on my long-distance phone bill." Instead . . . I gave the needed advice, the strokes of support—to a young man, my son, striving toward adulthood. When I had my babies in the 60s I didn't realize that I would still be parenting in the late 80s. I thought my mother role would end when my children reached 16; they would get their drivers' licenses and speed away toward total independence. I was wrong. . . . I have discovered that parenting is a 25-year commitment. I never suspected that it would last quite this long. (Dardick, 1993, pp. 62–63)

Contrary to popular belief, research on the "empty nest syndrome" suggests that, for most parents, the departure of grown-up children from home is actually a happy event. When the nest empties, the parents find freedom, relief from responsibilities, and time for themselves. A national study of 402 parents over a period of 4 years found that the "empty nest" is associated with significant *improvements* in marital happiness and life satisfaction (White & Edwards, 1990). The day-to-day pressures of taking care of children end, and couples can look forward to more intimacy with each other. They can also pursue interests that they have set aside in favor of their children's needs.

Still, parents don't want to be completely isolated from their adult children. Parents tend to experience greater improvement in life satisfaction when children maintain frequent contact after they move out. In other words, continuation of the parental role—albeit at a distance—appears to be important to well-being in middle age.

Sociologist Lillian Rubin (1992) interviewed 160 middle-aged women from varied backgrounds whose children had left home to go to college, get married, or start a career. She too found that the stereotype of the painful empty nest is largely a myth. Almost all the women she spoke with responded to the departure of their children with a decided sense of relief. Consider these comments from women whose adult children had recently moved out:

> I can't tell you what a relief it was to find myself with an empty nest. Oh sure, when the last child went away to school, for the first day or so there was a kind of a throb, but believe me, it was only a day or two.

> When the youngest one was ready to move out of the house, I was right there helping him pack. We love having the children live in the area, and we love seeing them and the grandchildren, but I don't need for any of them to live in this house ever again. *I've had as much as I ever need or want of being tied down with children* [emphasis in original]. (quoted in Rubin, 1992, p. 263)

Even divorced single mothers, whom you might expect would have trouble with the departure of their children, seemed relieved to be freed of the responsibilities of mothering. They may have felt lonely and depressed as a result of the divorce, but having the children at home didn't seem to do anything to alleviate those feelings. As one woman said, "Why should it make a difference if the kids are home or not? They don't warm up the bed" (quoted in Rubin, 1992, p. 264).

Interestingly, many of the women Rubin interviewed seemed guilty about feeling happy that their children were out of the house, even though the majority felt this way. Such guilt illustrates the pervasiveness of gender-based expectations in parenting and the lingering belief that women are supposed to be sad when their children leave:

> To tell you the truth, most of the time it's a big relief to be free of them, finally. I suppose that's awful to say. But you know that, most of the women I know feel the same way. It's just that they're uncomfortable saying it because there's all this talk about how sad mothers are supposed to be when the kids leave home. (quoted in Rubin, 1992, p. 266)

The women feared that such expressions of relief might be interpreted as a lack of commitment to parenting or a lack of love for their children.

Rubin did notice some important class differences in the way mothers respond to the leaving of their children. Most middle-class parents know exactly when their children will fly from the nest: the day they leave home for college. Thus, middle-class parents have plenty of time to prepare. These mothers frequently reported that the child's senior year in high school served as a time when much of the emotional separation could be done.

In working-class families, however, college attendance is not so easily taken for granted. Children might even be expected to live at home until they marry. Even working-class children who attend college are more likely to attend more affordable campuses close to home, which allows them to continue to live with their parents. The unpredictability of the "departure date" makes preparation for the empty nest more difficult. Nevertheless, the difficulty is usually brief and in no way approaches anything that could rightfully be called "depression."

In sum, parents tend to see the departure of their children not with sadness but with a feeling of accomplishment that they've done their "job" well. For those who do suffer disappointment, the relief can be mixed with painful feelings of failure. Yet none of the women Rubin interviewed yearned for another chance. For better or worse, they were glad the job was done and were ready to move on to the next stage of life.

Menopause

▲ The role of culture in the experience of menopause reminds us of culture's influence on sexuality in general, as discussed in Chapter 2.

Similar cultural misconceptions exist regarding **menopause**, the cessation of menstruation that typically occurs in women's 50s. Since it is associated with the end of fertility, it too can have a direct effect on women's identity in a culture that values motherhood.

The personal experience of menopause is determined as much by the culture as it is by biology. ▲ Despite the fact that menopause is a natural phase of a woman's life, Western doctors have historically defined it as a destructive, abnormal force. In the nineteenth century, physicians believed that, at menopause, women entered a period of irritability, depression, hysteria, and even insanity. Doctors well into the twentieth century likened menopause to death: "[At menopause a] woman has ended her existence as a bearer of future life and has reached her natural end—her partial death—as a servant of the species" (Deutsch, 1945, p. 458). The message was clear: If you can no longer bear children, you might as well be dead. Here's how another doctor described its effects:

> The vagina begins to shrivel, the breasts atrophy, sexual desire disappears.... Increased facial hair, deepening voice, obesity ... coarsened features, enlargement of the clitoris, and gradual baldness complete the tragic picture. Not really a man but no longer a functional woman. (quoted in Fausto-Sterling, 1985, pp. 110–111)

In the 1960s doctors labeled menopause a "disease" and began treating it with hormone replacement therapy. By 1975, some 6 million women had started taking Premarin—a brand name for the female hormone estrogen—making it the fourth or fifth most popular drug in the country at the time. In 1981 the World Health Organization formally defined menopause as an estrogen-deficiency disease.

Today, hormone replacement therapy is commonly recommended for menopausal and postmenopausal women. And even more drastic "cures" are frequently performed. In 1994 about 556,000 women underwent hysterectomies (the removal of the uterus and ovaries) (U.S. Bureau of the Census, 1997a); 40 percent of all American women may eventually have this operation. The vast majority of hysterectomies, however, are medically unnecessary. Only about 10 percent are performed because of cancer or other life-threatening diseases (Tavris, 1992). Nevertheless, the view that nonreproductive uteruses are unnecessary has led some gynecologists to recommend the removal of the uterus and ovaries in *all* women around the age of 40 (Payer, 1987). Ironically, while the removal of essentially healthy—albeit nonfunctioning reproductive organs—continues to be a popular and lucrative medical procedure, there is growing evidence that the removal of the uterus and ovaries increases the risk of breast cancer and heart disease (Payer, 1987).

In a culture like ours, which values youth and fertility, we should not be surprised that menopausal women are often depicted as emotional and physical wrecks. However, the notion that menopause necessarily brings about catastrophic changes may be exaggerated. A study of 2,500 menopausal women found that apart from a few bothersome symptoms, such as hot flashes and vaginal dryness, most of them said that menopause was "no big deal" (McKinlay, McKinlay, & Brambilla, 1987). In fact, the vast majority characterized it as a relief and a pleasure since they no longer had to worry about pregnancy or menstrual periods. Only 3 percent regretted reaching menopause because it signaled an end to their fertility. Even those who were depressed could not attribute their depression solely to menopause. They had a variety of other problems that could explain their depression, including job pressures, ailing husbands, and aging parents.

Other cultures have a very different conception of menopause. For instance, among the Hadza, a small group of Tanzanian hunter-gatherers who subsist on fruits, honey, tubers, and game, the most industrious and invaluable members of this group are postmenopausal women in their 50s, 60s, and 70s. They are out in the woods 8 hours a day, gathering more food than any other group members. When a woman is burdened with a nursing infant and cannot gather food for her family, she turns not to her mate but to an older female relative, typically a grandmother. These postmenopausal helpers are essential for the group's survival (Angier, 1997).

Grandparenthood

For most parents who make it through the minefields of the empty nest and menopause, grandparenthood awaits. Historically, the image of the grandparent has been one of a gray-haired, elderly person. However, most people become grandparents while in midlife, when they are married, when they are fully employed, and, with increasing frequency, when their own parents are still alive. For most of the past century, the age at which Americans become grandparents has been in their 40s or 50s. Even today, grandparenting is not a role that people begin in old age. Contemporary grandparents are more likely to be healthy, relatively well-off financially, and have a living spouse than was the case 40 years ago (Aldous, 1995).

Falling birthrates have had an impact on grandparenting too. In the late 1800s, for instance, American women gave birth to more than four children, on average (Cherlin & Furstenberg, 1987). Many parents found themselves raising young children after older children had left home, married, and started their own families. So parenting and grandparenting often overlapped. It's certainly likely that the responsibilities of raising children who were still at home took precedence over the responsibilities of tending to grandchildren. Hence, most grandparents in the past tended to be somewhat uninvolved in their grandchildren's lives.

In contrast, the birthrate today is lower, and people are getting married and starting families later. Hence, parents are more likely to be finished raising their own children before any grandchildren are born. So now when a person becomes a grandparent, fewer family roles are likely to be competing for his or her time and energy. Grandparenting has become a separate identity and a separate stage of family life. With advances in travel and communications, grandparents today have an easier time seeing and talking to their grandchildren, even if they don't live close by. In addition, 40-hour workweeks and an increase in available leisure time mean that grandparents today have more time to spend with grandchildren than they did a century ago. Contemporary grandparents also have more money to spend on grandchildren than ever before.

Other social changes, however, have made contemporary grandparenthood more difficult. One such change is the high rate of divorce. Often grandparents don't find out that their grown children are getting a divorce until it happens. And they are rarely, if ever, consulted about custody and visitation arrangements for the grandchildren. Since mothers generally receive custody of the children after a divorce, maternal grandparents are more likely to be able to continue their relationship with the grandchildren than paternal grandparents, who can experience a sudden loss of contact and have no clear legal rights to visitation. ▲ Some states have laws protecting visitation rights of grandparents, but others have ruled that grandparents have no such legal rights.

▲ Chapter 7 provides a detailed examination of child custody.

In general, the degree to which grandparents are incorporated into the lives of their children and grandchildren is far stronger in other cultures than in ours. Listen to how one American couple describes the relationships among grandparents, parents, and children in recent Russian immigrant families:

We have quite a few Russian friends. Now these friends, invariably the mothers are living with the sons, the daughters, with grandchildren—they're all together.... The grandchildren have great reverence for the grandparents; they live together. When they go on vacation they take the grandparents with them! I'm just shocked! When they go out eating, they take the grandparents with them! ... And this is such a new experience because we don't go eating with our children. They go their way, we go our way.... The [Russian] grandparents are very much involved with the families of their children.... We know a woman who was a famous surgeon in Russia, she's here in America, and she has that same feeling that she has to take care of her grandchild if the mother goes away. She's always obligated to that little girl. Now you wouldn't find the same thing in America. (quoted in Cherlin & Furstenberg, 1997, pp. 361–362)

But although they speak fondly of these family relationships, few elderly Americans desire such an arrangement. Like most Americans, they want intimate, satisfying, stable family ties, but at the same time they want to retain their independence from kin. They want affection and respect from their children and grandchildren but don't want to be obligated to them and don't want to be a burden to them (Cherlin & Furstenberg, 1997). As in the case of these Russian immigrants, the price paid for strong family ties is a significant loss of autonomy—a price most American grandparents are unwilling to pay. Consider this comment from an American grandparent who believes that he and his wife have worked hard to raise their children and now deserve to have their own pleasures:

When we were raising children, we figured when the children got married and moved to their own locales, we'd be free to do as we please. All our lives, we've worked for the kids, to make sure they had an education and everything else. Then we find out when we're grandparents they say, "Uh, Mom, Pop, how about babysitting? We're going away for a couple of days." ... Once in a while is fine, but we wouldn't want to be tied down to that like three or four times a year. (quoted in Cherlin & Furstenberg, 1997, p. 363)

Types of Grandparents   According to sociologists Andrew Cherlin and Frank Furstenberg (1987), who interviewed 510 grandparents nationwide, several types of grandparent styles exist in American society:

- *Companionate grandparents*. Most of the grandparents the researchers studied (55 percent) characterized their relationships with their grandchildren using terms like closeness, affection, companionship, and play. Companionate grandparents are likely to live close to their grandchildren and to have regular, intimate contact with them. These grandparents don't see themselves in any sort of parentlike disciplinary role. Their purpose is to be friends to their grandchildren and have fun with them.
- *Remote grandparents*. Remote grandparents (about 30 percent of the sample) are not intimately or closely involved in the lives of their grandchildren. They may have periodic contact, but their grandchildren are not a sustained presence in their lives. They are not necessarily cold-hearted people. The lack of involvement in their grandchildren's lives is more likely to be a result of living far away than of making the choice not to be involved.

■ *Involved grandparents.* Unlike companionate grandparents, involved grandparents (16 percent of those surveyed) assume parentlike roles and responsibilities. They set and enforce rules and discipline their grandchildren. Their involvement often emerges in difficult situations, such as when the mother is an unmarried teenager or a divorced mother who has to work.

Ethnic Variation in Grandparenting   Grandparenting styles can vary among different ethnic groups. ▲ In African-American families, for instance, grandmothers frequently play critical, involved roles in child rearing and parental support (Hunter, 1997). In fact, African-American children are much more likely to have been "raised" by their grandmothers than other children. Over 12 percent of African-American children live with their grandparents, and close to 40 percent of those have neither of their parents living with them in the household (cited in Morgan & Kunkel, 1998). Most of the literature on the role of African-American grandparents points to crisis situations, such as poverty and single parenthood, as the reason for their involvement.

▲ The impact of race and ethnicity on family life is explored in Issue 6.

However, involved grandmothering can also be seen as a time-tested family strategy with roots in black cultural traditions and the economic and social realities of black life. Research shows that African-American grandmothers rarely show a passive style of grandparenting. Their style is frequently described as "authoritative" or "influential," involving high levels of support and parentlike behaviors (Hunter, 1997). Black children tend to see grandmothers not simply as a fill-in authority figure but as an important teacher of lessons about life, morality, the importance of education, and religious faith (Strom, Collinsworth, Strom, & Griswold, 1992–1993).

To be sure, reliance on grandmothers in raising African-American children is more likely among young single mothers with inadequate financial resources who depend on kin networks for support and survival. But, in addition, mothers perceive that they can count on grandmothers for parenting support (Hunter, 1997). The extent to which young parents are willing to depend on grandmothers reflects not only a response to urgent problems but also a way of thinking about and organizing family relationships.

▲ Issue 6 addresses the issue of family similarity and difference between and within racial and/or ethnic groups.

However, we must be careful not to overgeneralize. Not all families within a particular racial or ethnic group are alike. ▲ African-American families vary significantly in the role of grandparents. For instance, one study found that 31 percent of black single mothers with children under the age of 5 received no parental assistance of any kind—compared to only 23 percent of their white counterparts (Eggebeen & Hogan, 1990). Nevertheless, in general, African-American grandparents—especially grandmothers—play a more important, involved role than white grandparents.

Many Native-American grandparents may also have the responsibility for raising grandchildren who have been left without a father, mother, or both. Indeed, depending on grandmothers as primary caretakers of grandchildren is a long-established Native-American child rearing strategy. However, Native-American grandparents play family roles that are somewhat different from those found among other groups.

Historically, grandparenting roles in Native-American families have been shaped by practical division-of-labor issues and the need to free up younger women so they can participate more fully in the economics of the tribal community; the high value placed on the nurturing of small children so the tribe can continue as a social entity; and the belief that old age represents the culmination of cultural experience. Elders are believed to be the best equipped to transmit culture across generations, thus helping to ensure the cultural integrity of the tribe (Weibel-Orlando, 1997).

Consequently, many Native-American grandparents actively solicit their children to allow the grandchildren to live with them. The express purpose is to expose the grandchildren to the American Indian way of life (Weibel-Orlando, 1997). Grandparents may be annoyed by the disdain their own urbanized and assimilated children show for this way of life and may feel that the grandchildren are the only hope for the future of the tribe. As one Sioux grandmother puts it:

> The second- or third-generation Indian children out in [Los Angeles], most of them never get to see anything like ... a sun dance or a memorial feast or giveaway or just stuff that Indians do back home. I wanted my own children to be involved in them and know what it's all about. So that's the reason that I always try to keep my grandchildren whenever I can. ... I'm building memories for them. (quoted in Weibel-Orlando, 1997, pp. 385–386).

Having grandchildren in their home and under their absolute custody for extended periods of time is one way Native-American grandparents can fulfill their culture's expectations of properly traditional elders. Their grandparenting is not just for the benefit of the grandchildren themselves, but for all future generations.

Old Age

Unless we die prematurely, all of us will at some point enter old age. But just what is meant by "old" is unclear. Different people "become elderly" at different ages. Some people experience serious deficits in cognitive and physical functioning in their 50s; others remain active and energetic well into their 90s.

The degree to which people can accumulate social and economic resources in their youth and middle age can shape the impact old age will have on their lives (Stoller & Gibson, 1994). Having fewer financial resources before old age means that people of color as well as working-class and poor individuals may face greater financial and health problems in old age than will middle-class whites. Competency and vitality may last a long time for middle-class and upper-class people, but not so long for the poor and the socially isolated on whose life span the deficiencies in the health care system and the environment may take a toll. A friend of mine recently returned from a trip to Hungary, where economic and environmental devastation have made adults look 20 or 30 years older than they are. Hungarians consistently estimated his age to be in the mid-20s (he's actually in his mid-40s). One person said to him, "You Americans wear your affluence on your faces."

Culture and the Elderly

Becoming elderly is not determined simply by the number of years a person has lived but by the trajectory of his or her life accomplishments, family relationships, and social circumstances. Larger cultural definitions of and attitudes toward the elderly can also shape the experience of aging. In some cultures, the elderly are highly respected; in others they are either ignored or treated with contempt.

The Elderly in Japan and Korea The population of Japan is aging faster than any on earth. By 2025, one-quarter of the Japanese population will be 65 or older (Dentzer, 1991). Government programs for the elderly in Japan are significantly less generous and universal than programs in the United States (Pampel, 1998). However, unlike Americans, the Japanese have traditionally maintained a relatively high level of respect for elders (called **filial piety**), integrating them into work and family (Palmore, 1975). The most common word for the aged in Japanese is *otoshiyori,* which means "honorable elders."

Although gone are the days when elderly people were assumed to be superior simply because they were old, rules of etiquette still give elders priority in most social settings, such as public seating arrangements and serving order at meals. Japan even has a national holiday called Respect for Elders Day. People use the age of 61 as an occasion for celebration, much like the American tradition of celebrating the age of 21. Japan's 1963 National Law for the Welfare of the Elders states: "The elders shall be loved and respected as those who have for many years contributed toward the development of society, and a wholesome and peaceful life shall be guaranteed to them" (quoted in Kart, 1990, p. 203).

Over 55 percent of Japan's elderly live with their children or in extended families, compared with less than 20 percent in the United States (Kristof, 1997). The majority of Japanese men over 65 are in the paid labor force. Although most Japanese industries have a mandatory retirement age, which was raised to age 65 in 1986, almost all provide some kind of employment for older workers even after they retire. The employer may extend the old job, create a new one not subject to compulsory retirement, or offer a part-time or lower-paying job (Kart, 1990). Voluntary organizations called Silver Human Resource Centers assist older workers in finding part-time or temporary work, like supervising parking lots or cleaning parks (Martin, 1989). Those who are not employed remain useful with housekeeping, child care, shopping, gardening, and other household tasks (Palmore, 1975).

Why do the Japanese attach such high social value to their aged citizens? Japanese society is "vertically" structured, meaning that most relationships are hierarchical rather than egalitarian. Age is the most important dimension for determining who is above and who is below. In addition, religious principles of filial piety dating back to Confucius suggest that respect for one's parents is one of the most important virtues an individual can possess. Family patriarchs or matriarchs were once seen as virtual divinities in the house. In the past, schoolchildren were rigorously taught moral stories of filial piety, such as the tale of the couple who decided, after running out of food, to kill their child so they would have more to feed their parents. They were rewarded when they dug the child's grave and found a treasure (Kristof, 1997).

So revered are the elderly in some rural areas of Japan that even when they die they remain a respected, everyday presence in the household (Kristof, 1996d). Dead elders are regularly consulted by family members on important matters. People may give them a rundown on the local news; present them daily with tea, rice, and water; and even include a place for them at family meals.

But the venerated position of the elderly in Japan is changing. In recent years—especially in modern, urban areas—attitudes toward the elderly have become more negative, particularly among the young. The belief that children are obligated to care for their aging parents has weakened (Ogawa & Retherford, 1993). Even though over half of people over 65 live with their children, that proportion has dropped from 80 percent in 1970. And the number of elderly living alone has doubled over the past 25 years as well (Kristof, 1997). In 1963, 80 percent of Japanese in a national survey said that caring for elderly parents was either a "good custom" or a "natural duty." By 1990, the figure had dropped to 50 percent.

Traditionally, wives bore the responsibility of taking care of aged parents and in-laws. However, since more Japanese women are now working outside the home, they are less inclined to take on this duty. A survey of Japanese women shows that the proportion who plan to depend on their children in old age has declined from 65 percent in 1950 to 18 percent in 1990 (Ogawa & Retherford, 1993).

Many Japanese elders have grown fearful of young people and are reluctant to move in with their children because they know they wouldn't occupy the traditional position of respect in the household. Instead, they feel they would be treated as guests, staying by the grace of their children.

Before 1945 it was exclusively the family that ensured the care for the elderly. In those days, institutional care was considered a disgrace and a sign of unsuccessful family life (Hashimoto & Takahashi, 1995). It violated the duty-oriented idea that family members should take care of each other. But shrinking family size, the aging of the Japanese population, and economic difficulties have made family care of the elderly more burdensome and have increased the proportion of Japanese elderly who are placed under institutional care—although that percentage is still rather small. About 2 percent of the 14 million elderly in Japan live in nursing homes or in similar institutions. In the United States, 5 percent of the elderly live in such institutions (Kristof, 1997).

Similarly, in Korea, forms of respect for the aged have slowly been changing in recent years as the female labor market expands, multigenerational households decrease, and younger generations emphasize a more individualistic lifestyle (Sung, 1993). But respect for the aged has strong roots in Korean culture, and values based on filial piety have not yet been completely undermined. Over 80 percent of elderly Korean parents still live with their children.

To promote children's respect for their elders, the Korean government in 1973 established the annual Filial Piety Prize, which is awarded during Respect for the Elderly Week. Between 150 and 380 persons nationwide—overwhelmingly women—are awarded the prize each year for the respect and responsibility they show their elderly parents. Respect is demonstrated by treating the parent with courtesy and deference; showing exceptional, earnest, and sincere consideration for the parent; and showing extraordinary honor and esteem for the parent. Responsibility is shown by delaying marriage and education or withdrawing from social activities to be fully devoted to parental care, giving care to a parent-in-law after the death of one's spouse or to a mother after the death of a father, and supporting a large family in addition to an aged parent. The prizewinners are individuals who have endured physical, financial, and social sacrifices for their parents. ▲ They have disregarded their own comfort and given up the good life, have paid for their parents' medicine or for other forms of care, and may even have quit their jobs to care for their parent.

▲ Korea is a good example of a "collectivist" culture, described in Issue 4.

The high level of sacrifice necessary to be worthy of the Filial Piety Prize is indicated by the fact that the majority of winners are low-income people. More affluent sons and daughters may show just as much respect and take on just as much responsibility, but their acts are not so publicly praiseworthy. They have the financial means to provide care without much personal sacrifice.

The Elderly in Immigrant Families Cultural values regarding the elderly can cause problems when families migrate from one society to another. Latin-American immigrants, for instance, bring with them traditional values which emphasize respect for elders (Stanford, Peddecord, & Lockery, 1990). Women are the assumed caregivers of older relatives. Such traditions become difficult to sustain when immigrants are faced with the financial uncertainties and cultural contradictions of living in a new country.

▲ The difficulties faced by immigrant Vietnamese families are discussed further in Issue 4.

The difficulties that elderly people in Southeast Asian refugee families face are particularly acute. ▲ The experience of aging in America is far different from what they had expected for the later phases of their lives in their native countries (Yee, 1992). They must cope with rapidly acculturating children and grandchildren while taking on different roles, under a different set of expectations, in a foreign culture.

For one thing, many Southeast Asian refugee elders find that they aren't considered elderly by American standards. For example, in the traditional Hmong culture, one becomes elderly when one becomes a grandparent, which could happen at age 35. With grandparent status, these elder Hmong can retire and expect their children to take financial responsibility for the family. But I doubt you'd find many Americans retiring at the age of 35 so that their children can take care of them.

In addition, as is true of the Japanese and Korean societies discussed earlier, filial piety is a strong value in Southeast Asian families. Elders are considered crucial sources of wisdom. But because refugee elders lack knowledge of American culture, their credibility in advising young people on important decisions is diminished considerably. As younger people become more Americanized, they are more likely to reject the teachings of the traditional culture.

In fact, young people tend to be the family members most proficient in the English language, and therefore they act as important mediators between their families and American institutions. Older refugees find themselves increasingly dependent on their children and grandchildren, rather than the reverse. Hence, elders lose many of their leadership roles in the eyes of the family and the larger community (Yee, 1992). Such role reversal can be a source of considerable conflict and shame in refugee families.

Refugee elders also find their socioeconomic status diminished. They may still provide child care assistance and perform household duties, but they can no longer offer financial support, land, or other material goods, as they would have in their homeland. The refugee process strips away these resources and, simultaneously, elders' control of inheritance in the family.

Culture and Old Age in the United States In this culture we tend to see old age for the losses that accompany it, not the gains it provides. For many of us, the elderly represent precisely what we spend most of our lives trying to deny: our own mortality. Old people symbolize disease, disability, and death (Butler, 1975). Rather than venerate their years and seek their wisdom, we tend to segregate them in housing designed for their "special needs" (Fausto-Sterling, 1985). As a result, they are one of the most excluded age groups in American society today.

Common stereotypes about the elderly—that they're sick, slow-witted, senile, mean, depressed, and dangerous behind the wheel of a car—reinforce the public perception that they are socially worthless (Neugarten, 1980). Television commercials that advertise products for the elderly portray them as arthritic, constipated, incontinent, wrinkled, and toothless.

Like other forms of prejudice, these perceptions are usually translated into action—that is, overt discrimination. Although the Age Discrimination in Employment Act of 1967 prohibits hiring, firing, or determining wages or other privileges and conditions of employment on the basis of age, age discrimination in employment practices still exists today. Mandatory retirement policies in some businesses operate on the assumption that all people experience a decrease in mental and physical capabilities when they reach a certain age. As long as the elderly are perceived to be rigid, unhealthy, unhappy, and unemployable, discriminatory treatment will seem justified.

While the elderly tend to be a devalued segment of the American population, they are more likely than any other age group to benefit from social policies. Many federal programs are designed to assist the elderly in areas such as retirement, health care, housing, transportation, and other social services. The elderly have been the principal beneficiaries of the federal government's involvement in ensuring health care for high-risk populations (Medicare and Medicaid) and guaranteeing minimum income (Social Security). Thus, the proportion of elderly people

▲ Chapter 7 provides a more thorough portrait of poor families.

who fall below the poverty line has *decreased* over the past 2 decades, even though the proportion of poor young people has *increased*. ▲

The "Graying" of America

Ironically, although Americans tend to devalue old age, we're collectively becoming an older society (see Exhibit 8.2). Two hundred years ago, the median age for Americans was 16. Today it is about 34.6 and is expected to be over 38 by the middle of the next century (U.S. Bureau of the Census, 1997a).

Two developments that began in the 1960s and 1970s have changed the age structure of the United States in dramatic ways (Preston, 1984). The first has been a decrease in the number of children being born. In 1960 there were approximately 24 births per 1,000 people in the population. By 1994 the rate had dropped to 15 per 1,000. Between 1980 and 1996, the proportion of the population under 15 decreased from 23 percent to 22 percent (U.S. Bureau of the Census, 1997a), and it will continue to drop for decades to come.

The second factor has been an increase in the number of people surviving to old age. Several centuries ago, death was an ever-present possibility from the day a person was born. Mortality rates were several times higher than they are today. A white baby girl born today has a greater chance of living to the age of 60 than a white baby girl born in 1870 had of reaching her first birthday (Skolnick, 1991). Young people commonly died of tuberculosis, pneumonia, or one of a host of other infectious diseases.

In the past, old age was a stage of life available only to those segments of the population that had access to adequate health care and nutrition. But technological advances in medicine and

Exhibit 8.2

Population Ages 65 and Older

United States: 1870–2000

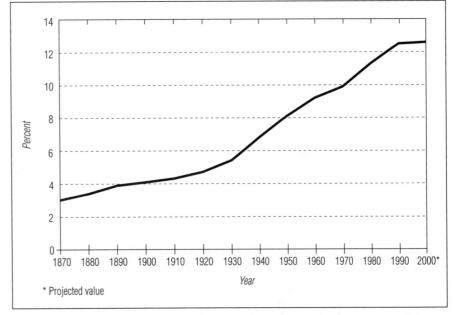

* Projected value

Sources of data: U.S. Bureau of the Census, *Historical Statistics of the United States: Colonial Times to 1970.* Washington, DC, 1975. U.S. Bureau of the Census, *Statistical Abstract of the United States: 1997* (117th edition). Washington, DC, 1997.

nutrition have extended the lives of countless Americans who would have routinely died several decades ago. Old age is now available to a broader cross section of the population, rather than a select few (Treas & Bengtson, 1982).

Overall, life expectancy at birth has risen dramatically from 1970 to 1995: from 67.1 to 72.6 for males and from 74.0 to 78.9 for females (U.S. Bureau of the Census, 1997a). By 2020, the American population under the age of 25 is projected to grow by 19.8 percent; the population over 65 is projected to grow by close to 65 percent (Morgan & Kunkel, 1998). The number of people over 85 will grow fastest of all, doubling to 6.5 million by 2020 and soaring to 17.7 million by 2050 (Angier, 1995). Currently people over 85 make up 1.4 percent of the population; by 2050 they will account for 4.6 percent (Seelye, 1997a). Close to a million people will be over the age of 100 by then as well (cited in Rimer, 1998b).

Why should we be concerned about this "graying" of the American population? The answer is that a society with an aging population will inevitably experience increased demands for pensions, health care, and other social services catering to the needs of the elderly. For instance, 1 percent of people between the ages of 65 and 74 require nursing home care. But that figure increases to 22 percent for those over 85 and almost 50 percent for those over 95 (cited in Rimer, 1998b). Moreover, aging populations change the assumptions we make about our economy, such as the size and composition of the labor force, productivity, and patterns of saving, spending, and consuming (Morgan & Kunkel, 1998).

The Effects of "Graying" on Families

The continuing growth of the elderly population will undoubtedly have an enormous impact on American families. Increased life expectancy encourages stronger emotional bonds between parents and children, lengthens the duration of marriage and parent-child relationships, makes grandparenthood an expectable stage of life, and increases the number of grandparents or even great-grandparents a child will actually know (Skolnick, 1991).

In the distant past it was quite rare for a child to know, let alone grow up with, his or her grandparents. Today's children commonly grow into adulthood without experiencing the loss of a grandparent. Most children today have four grandparents alive at one time—more than that if step-grandparents are counted. And over half of all people over 65 have great-grandchildren (Baca-Zinn & Eitzen, 1996).

Prolonged Marriage   One important familial consequence of increasing longevity is prolonged marriage. When life expectancy was lower, the average marriage ended as a result of the death of one of the spouses after only 25 or so years of marriage. At the turn of the century the median age at marriage was 21.2 for women and 24.6 for men. Life expectancy was about 51 years for women and 48 for men, 35 and 32.5 for African-American men and women (Morgan & Kunkel, 1998). More than half of all marriages were ended by the death of one spouse before the last child had left home (Kart, 1990). So you can see that many people were widowed well before their children were grown.

Today, the average couple could live 30 years or more after the last child has left home. So married couples have more time to compile extensive common experiences and share broad historical changes. But they also have more time to get on each other's nerves (Preston, 1976). Between 1980 and 1996, the percentage of divorced people over the age of 65 increased from 3.5 percent to 6.4 percent (U.S. Bureau of the Census, 1997a). Now, in a sense, more and more people are "outliving" their marriages.

Prolonged Parent-Child Relationships   Increased longevity also extends the amount of time parents spend with their children. In the near future a significant number of parents and children could spend 60 or more years together, of which only 18 or so would be in the traditional parent-child relationship (Riley, 1983). A government study found that one or both parents are still alive for 44 percent of people between the ages of 58 and 66 (Kolata, 1993). Certainly such longevity increases the number of important experiences that parents and children can share.

However, the lengthening of parent-child relationships also increases the financial and emotional burdens on the children when they reach adulthood. The likelihood that one's parents will live well into their 80s means that, for many people, their role as someone's child and the accompanying responsibilities will long overlap their roles as someone's spouse and parent.

Generational Obligations

In contemporary American society, relationships between adult children and their parents are characterized by two seemingly contradictory sets of norms: obligation and independence (Aldous, 1995). Norms concerning obligation specify that adult children and parents should assist and care for each other over the course of their lives. On the other hand, norms of independence specify that adult children must at some point assume responsibility for their own wellbeing and that nuclear families should maintain themselves, independent of wider kin networks (Lye, 1996). Relations between adult children and their elderly parents sit precariously between these two ideals.

The History of Generational Obligation The feelings of obligation that cross generations are molded not only by individual and familial experiences but by specific historical circumstances. The adaptation of individuals and their families to the social and economic conditions they face in the later years of life is determined by the pathways they took to old age. Wars, migration, depressions, and the decline of local economies can affect patterns of support and expectations for receiving and providing assistance in old age (Hareven, 1994).

▲ Other inaccurate images of past American families are examined in Issue 2.

Contrary to popular images, early American households were nuclear in their structure. ▲ Older generations lived in households separate from their married children but nearby, often on the same land. Opportunities for contact and cooperation were numerous. But even though adult children were expected to care for aging parents, such responsibility was voluntary. No laws required children to care for their elderly parents. Even in the colonial period, elderly people were insecure in their family supports, though they were given more respect and higher status than they are given today (Hareven, 1994). In fact, aging parents had to enter into legal contracts with their inheriting sons in order to secure support in old age. The presence of such contracts indicates that many elderly parents had a great deal of anxiety about what would happen to them when they became too frail to support themselves.

Similarly, in the nineteenth and early twentieth centuries, elderly parents usually didn't live with their adult children and weren't guaranteed support from them in old age. In fact, only about 12 percent to 18 percent of all urban households in the later nineteenth and early twentieth centuries contained any relatives other than members of the nuclear family. Today's preferred mode of generational interaction—dubbed "intimacy from a distance"—has persisted since the earliest days of the country, characterizing rural as well as urban families (Hareven, 1994).

Nevertheless, American families have always been willing to expand their households to include other kin in times of need. When elderly parents and especially widowed mothers were unable to maintain themselves in a separate household, they would live with their adult children. These arrangements were typically for limited periods, and usually the children moved into the parents' home to care for them rather than vice versa.

▲ The tension between personal interests and family obligation is the topic of Issue 4.

Care for Elderly Parents In recent decades, norms of obligation have weakened somewhat and become rather uncertain, while norms of independence have strengthened (Lye, 1996). ▲ A nationwide study of over 13,000 American adults found that half of them didn't routinely give or receive assistance from their aging parents (Hogan, Eggebeen, & Clogg, 1993). Higher living standards among the elderly may have reduced adult children's feelings of obligation. In addition, high rates of divorce and remarriage, and the complicated family structures that result, can also increase uncertainty about obligations to parents.

Nevertheless, many people do maintain close ties with their aging parents, even when they don't necessarily feel a deep sense of obligation to provide direct assistance. Research indicates that relationships between elderly parents and adult children today can be quite close, characterized by frequent visits, telephone calls, and letters. A recent national survey found that over half of adult children live within a 1-hour drive of their parents. Close to 70 percent have weekly contact with their mothers, and 20 percent have daily contact (cited in Lye, 1996).

The closeness of relationships between adult children and elderly parents varies along ethnic lines (Raley, 1995). For instance, by long tradition in the African-American community, adults are expected to care for their parents and grandparents. This tradition arose to address the harsh economic realities of life: limited access to medical care, public support, and good jobs, the sorts of things that would guarantee a secure old age. According to one recent study, older blacks are twice as likely as whites to receive care and assistance from family members when their health deteriorates (cited in Rimer, 1998a). However, the toll that such caregiving expectations can exact on a family—in terms of stress, lost wages, postponed or missed employment and educational opportunities, and so on—is often quite high. Some experts fear that in coming generations, as African-American families become increasingly mobile, fewer people will be able to take on the traditional caregiving role.

As for Hispanics, within the next 60 years they are expected to grow from 4 percent to 12 percent of the elderly population (Miranda, 1992). Hispanic families are usually close-knit. Around 80 percent of Mexican-American elderly, for instance, have frequent contact with their children, because they either live with them or live within a few minutes of their home. Compared with Anglo Americans, on average, Mexican Americans show significantly higher levels of devotion to their families, more collectivist attitudes, and more helping behavior in relationships with their elderly parents (Freeberg & Stein, 1996). They feel significantly more obligated to avoid conflict and provide assistance. In general, Mexican Americans tend to feel a deeper pride in their families and stress group goals over individual goals. But some studies show relatively few Mexican-American families actually *help* aging family members. Despite frequent contact, fewer than 20 percent of the elderly respondents in one survey reported receiving assistance with meal preparation, financial matters, shopping, transportation, light housework, or everyday activities like bathing, dressing, eating, and so on (Dietz, 1995).

In general, however, against a backdrop of uncertainty about family obligations, close to three-quarters of all Americans continue to believe that adult children *should* provide financial assistance to their parents (cited in Lye, 1996), and close to half agree that adult children should let their parents live with them when they can no longer care for themselves (see Exhibit 8.3). People are a little less certain, though, about parents' obligations to their adult children. For instance, less than half agree that parents ought to provide financial assistance to their adult children, and slightly more than a third agree that parents should let their adult children live with them (cited in Lye, 1996).

Beneath these statistics is a disapproval of the kind of intergenerational support that creates dependence between family members. People are concerned about creating feelings of dependence in the recipient, and that concern is stronger among the elderly than among their adult children. The elderly are less in favor of the idea of living with their grown children than younger people are. The elderly worry about lifestyle differences, struggles over authority and the household division of labor, and the chaos caused by grandchildren as potential areas of conflict. With adequate financial, housing, and social resources, most older Americans would prefer to live in-

Exhibit 8.3

Adults Who Believe It Is a Good Idea for Older Persons to Share a Home with Their Grown Children

United States: 1973–1996

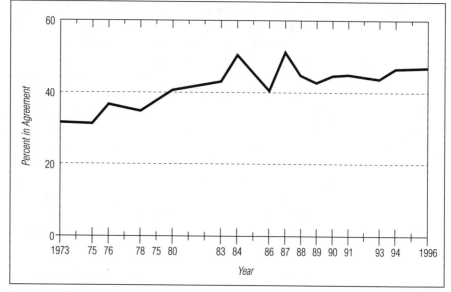

Source of data: National Opinion Research Center, University of Chicago, *General Social Survey, 1973–1996.*

dependently of their adult children, although in reasonably close proximity. Hence, many elderly people perceive living with their children as a last resort prior to institutionalization.

Nevertheless, more and more adult children are having to cope with the burden of caring for elderly parents in addition to the usual demands of work and family. More than 6 million elderly Americans now need help with such everyday basics as getting out of bed, eating, dressing, bathing, and using the bathroom (Beck, 1990). Given the high cost of nursing homes, many elderly parents do end up moving in with their children.

Gender and Elder Care Both men and women claim a high acceptance of responsibility for aged parents, but women are more likely to be called upon to act on those responsibilities. Even in eras and among ethnic groups in which individuals were deeply dependent on relations with extended kin, the day-to-day involvement with and responsibility for caring for elderly parents fell primarily to adult daughters (Hareven, 1994). In fact, prior to World War II, norms dictated that a younger daughter would delay or forgo marriage in order to care for her parents until their death (Morgan & Kunkel, 1998). Although such expectations have diminished over the years, we still may expect adult female children to support and assist an older parent or parents should they require it.

Men tend to perform managerial and maintenance tasks and provide financial support for their parents; women predominantly perform the daily hands-on caregiving. Outside of a spouse, adult female children are the most common caretakers of the frail elderly (Stone, Cafferata, & Sangl, 1987). Middle-aged daughters provide the bulk of care for functionally impaired parents in the United States, performing between 80 and 90 percent of the medical and everyday care these older people receive (cited in Albert, 1990).

One survey found that about one out of every five female employees over the age of 30 provides some sort of care to an elderly parent (cited in Lewin, 1989). With increases in life expectancy, these caretaking responsibilities can last 10 years or more.

Meeting these obligations often comes at the expense of other family roles. Many women who provide care to elderly parents are forced to spend less time with their husbands and children, leading to resentment and frustration and ultimately threatening the structure of family life. Women's occupational roles and financial well-being may also suffer. At a time when most families depend on two incomes for survival, some women have had to switch to part-time work, pass up promotions, or quit their jobs altogether. A study by the American Association of Retired Persons estimated that 14 percent of all part-time adult female workers had left their full-time jobs because of caregiving responsibilities. Of those not employed but who once had jobs, 27 percent had taken early retirement or simply quit (cited in Lewin, 1989).

With these conflicting responsibilities come feelings of guilt, inadequacy, and anger. One woman, who had quit her job to care for her mother, who had developed Alzheimer's disease, echoed the thoughts of many:

> I felt like I was going under. I couldn't do my job because I was pretty much in pieces. I was furious at my brother who didn't help at all. My 15-year-old daughter is mad at me because I am so engaged with my mother. My son has stopped visiting me. And the friends who had been wonderful and supportive through the birth of my babies and my divorce just faded away now that I need them the most. I am alternately so sad about my mother's decline that I can't stop crying and so enraged that my life is being messed up that I want to dump her. I used to think I was good at crises, but this just goes on and on, and I'm falling apart. (quoted in Lewin, 1989, p. 13)

Although the adverse effects of caring for elderly parents on women's well-being are well documented, the experience apparently isn't always so bad. A national study of married persons found that changes in family responsibilities had little effect on female caregivers' well-being, even among those women who worked full-time (Loomis & Booth, 1995). The authors offered several possible explanations for why caregiving responsibilities for children and elderly parents don't develop into particularly difficult situations for these women:

■ *The caregiver knows the individual needing care quite well.* Hence, what that person requires is seldom a mystery or a surprise.

■ *The people who take on the added responsibilities may be the ones most capable of doing so.* The people with the stronger marriages were more likely to assume multigenerational caregiving responsibilities than people in weak or unstable marriages. So those who take on additional responsibilities may be the ones who are best equipped to balance family, work, and personal needs.

■ *The individuals who take on these responsibilities may value caring for others.* Hence, meeting familial obligations may be a source of fulfillment that offsets any negative effects that may be experienced. Many women come to view the care of their elderly parents as a sort of "payback" for the care they received growing up.

The changing economic status of women will have a significant impact on the availability of family caregivers in the future, however. The mass entrance of women into the workforce, changing attitudes concerning "gender appropriate" roles, and the growing necessity for two incomes in a family have already reduced the number of women who are able to care for elderly parents. Hence, caring for elderly parents is likely to remain a potentially stressful dilemma for adult daughters in the future.

▲ Child abuse and spouse abuse are the focus of Chapter 6.

Elder Abuse The 1960s and 1970s saw a dramatic increase in the amount of attention paid to child abuse. In the 1980s and early 1990s, spouse abuse gained the cultural spotlight. ▲ But as these other social problems were receiving their rightful attention, the problem of elder abuse has remained relatively unnoticed.

As more and more adult children find themselves assuming a caretaker role, more and more elders will be abused by their children. When an older person becomes dependent, the "normal" parent-child relationship is reversed, placing unexpected stress on caregiving adult children.

Adult children can perpetrate several types of abuse on their parents (Boudreau, 1993):

- *Physical abuse*: hitting, slapping, using physical restraints, and withholding personal care, such as food, medicine, and medical attention
- *Psychological abuse*: using verbal assaults and insults, threats, fear, and isolation to control the dependent person
- *Drug abuse*: encouraging elders to take too many drugs so that they are kept sedated and more manageable
- *Financial abuse*: stealing, embezzling, or misusing money and other personal property of the elderly
- *Violation of rights*: forcing a parent into a nursing home or reducing personal freedom and autonomy

▲ Many cases of domestic violence go unreported because of the private nature of families, as explained in Issue 3 and Chapter 6.

Accurately gauging the extent of elderly abuse, or any other form of domestic abuse, is difficult. ▲ Estimates of older people being abused range from 3 to 10 percent, meaning that anywhere from 700,000 to 1.5 million are abused nationally. One government study revealed that 11 percent of all murder victims over the age of 60 were killed by a son or daughter (Dawson & Langan, 1994).

The experiences of abused elders can, indeed, be tragic. Listen to how this 79-year-old woman describes the abusive treatment she received from her daughter:

> My daughter locked me in the garage and left me for more than an hour. She always parked the car behind mine in the garage so I could not get my car out except by her permission. . . . Whenever I tried to cook a meal she would appear and turn the gas off and remove the grills so that the only way I could cook would be to hold the pan the right distance over the flame. Also, if she found me using the electric toaster oven, my food was thrown on the floor and the toaster oven was removed and hidden for several days. . . . [My daughter was] always hurting me physically and mentally; kicking me, pushing me, grappling with me, telling me to get out, at one time throwing a drawer down the stairs at

me, calling me names, telling me I belonged in a nursing home and why didn't I go to one. (quoted in Steinmetz, Claven, & Stein, 1990, p. 472)

Elder abuse seems to be most common in situations where adult children are overwhelmed by the costs, responsibility, frustration, and stress of taking care of a parent or parents. Caretakers may resent the extra work, the intrusions on privacy, and the excessive demands on time that result from the elder's presence. As the elderly parents get older and more frail, the care they need can become even more taxing.

To make matters worse, typical family roles can become confused or reversed. The elderly parents may continue to treat their adult children like children by trying to retain their traditional authority over decision making. At the same time, though, the elderly parents occupy a childlike role, depending completely on their adult children to take care of them. ▲ Hostility can increase when the adult children feel they have been forced into taking responsibility for their elderly parent or parents.

▲ The social exchange perspective, outlined in Chapter 1, highlights the role of dependence in family life.

You will notice that such an explanation of elder abuse tends to place the blame on the elderly themselves. But focusing on the stress and strain that the elderly cause runs the risk of normalizing the problem, of relieving abusers of much of the blame for their behavior toward a parent who is demanding, difficult, and unpleasant (Pillemer, 1993). We should not relieve abusers of responsibility, but we should acknowledge the larger structural factors that make elder abuse more likely to occur. Without condoning the behavior, we must realize that stress and tension have economic and demographic sources that go beyond the individuals involved.

Elderly victims have a particularly difficult time reporting abuse. Victims often refuse to report the abuse for fear of retaliation, lack of alternative shelter, and shame associated with having to admit that a child they raised is treating them so poorly. Often the adult child is providing financial and other resources necessary for survival, which makes it nearly impossible for the elderly victim to leave the situation.

Death and Families

The most devastating transition that a family can experience is the death of one of its members. Like aging, death is a biological event. But also like aging, death is shaped by culture. In preindustrial societies, sick people were taken care of at home and they died at home. Since life was relatively short, most people could expect to see the death of a sibling or parent during their childhood.

In some cultures today, death remains a part of everyday life. In Mexico, for instance, November 1 and 2 are known as *los dias de todos muertos*, or "days of the dead." Representations of death pervade every aspect of life during these 2 days. Children eat sugar skulls and candy coffins and play with skeleton puppets. They eat picnic lunches in graveyards and gamble and play board games on the tombstones there. In some areas of Mexico, special bread—called *pan de los muertos* or "bread of the dead"—is baked and eaten only on these days. Families decorate their homes with symbols of funerals (tombs, coffins, and pallbearers) and the afterlife (ghosts, angels, and devils). They build altars and prepare food, which they offer to the spirits of dead relatives (Green, 1995).

The inclusion of children in all these rituals reinforces the cultural belief that there is no need to hide death from children. It is an event with which children are intimately familiar because, like birth, it takes place at home with the family.

In American society, industrialization and the advent of modern medicine have made dying a distant event managed by professionals in hospitals. As a result, many Americans have never personally seen someone die—although, ironically, most of us have witnessed thousands of fictionalized deaths on television and in film by the time we reach adulthood. Dying has become a remote occurrence disconnected from everyday life. Most Americans die alone, in institutional medical settings, surrounded by doctors, nurses, and attendants.

Not surprisingly, then, dying is a strange and fearful process to Americans, something to be hidden or perhaps even denied. We have developed an elaborate vocabulary of euphemisms so that we can refer to death without using the word itself. People aren't dead, they're *gone* or *no longer with us*. They don't die, they *pass away* or *expire*. Our pets aren't killed, they're *put to sleep*.

Widowhood

Barring a divorce, virtually all marriages end with the death of one or the other spouse. But gender differences in life expectancy mean that widows far outnumber widowers in this country. In 1996, 2.7 percent of men were widowers, compared to 11 percent of women (U.S. Bureau of the Census, 1997a).

Despite its ubiquity, the death of a spouse can be one of the most severe social and personal crises we experience. Widowhood is associated with impaired social and psychological functioning as well as an increased risk of sickness and death for the surviving spouse. Depression is a particularly common response to widowhood, especially during the first year or two after the death (Umberson, Wortman, & Kessler, 1992). Of course, a number of factors influence people's response to the death of a spouse, such as how close the couple's relationship was prior to the death and whether the death was the anticipated result of a long-term illness or the unanticipated result of an accident, an acute medical episode, or suicide.

People's response to widowhood is, to some degree, influenced by perceptions of gender within the larger culture. In traditional India, for instance, Hindu women had no identity outside of being a wife. Hence, many widows used to commit suicide by ceremoniously throwing themselves on the funeral pyres of their dead husbands. Those who didn't kill themselves were outcasts in the community. Widows are still considered bad luck in India and are often referred to by the pronoun *it*. In Japan, the word for widow, *mibojin*, means "a person who has not yet died."

In this society, the status of widow or widower is likely to be pitied rather than stigmatized. Interestingly, even though men occupy a more advantaged position in the larger society, evidence suggests that they experience widowhood as a more emotionally distressing event than women (Umberson et al., 1992). Since women are more likely than men to have close, confiding relationships with others outside the marriage, widowhood is more likely to leave men socially and emotionally isolated. This lack of emotional support and social contact may leave them more vulnerable to depression during widowhood. Furthermore, since women are more likely to handle the bulk of day-to-day household tasks, the death of a wife constitutes an important source of strain for the surviving husband, who may be ill equipped to deal with cooking, cleaning, laundry, and so on.

Women are by no means unaffected by the death of a spouse. But the source of difficulty is different than that for men. For one thing, women in traditional marriages can experience severe psychological problems because widowhood takes away a key element in their self-identity: being a wife. In addition, since men earn, on average, substantially more than women, widowhood can lead to greater financial strain for women than it does for men. According to one study, the average standard of living of widows drops 18 percent after a husband's death (Bound, Duncan, Laren, & Oleinick, 1991). African-American and Latina women are especially prone to poverty after the death of a spouse.

The Death of a Parent

Because of medical and nutritional advances that have increased life expectancy, only one in ten children today has lost a parent by the age of 25. By the age of 54, however, half of Americans have lost both parents (Umberson & Chen, 1994).

Although the death of a parent is a common event in adulthood, it can nonetheless adversely affect the physical and psychological well-being of adult children. To them, the death of a parent signifies the loss of a significant part of their living historical record. To lose a parent is to lose one of the few people who has known you your whole life. Furthermore, as we've already seen, parental influence continues to be important throughout adulthood, even in the absence of physical proximity. Finally, because the duration of the parent-child relationship is longer than ever before, the symbolic importance of parent-child relationships may also be greater now than in the past.

Not every adult has a strong relationship with his or her parents. Individuals for whom relationships with parents are more salient have a more difficult time adjusting to their death than adult children for whom relationships with parents are an insignificant part of their lives (Umberson & Chen, 1994).

The Death of a Child

Most of us assume that we will outlive our parents and will therefore have to deal with their death. The death of a child, however, is something few parents assume will happen to them.

In the past, however, the loss of a child was an expected part of family life. High infant-mortality rates meant that parents were likely to experience the death of one, some, or even all of their children. ▲ In 1900 half of all American parents experienced the death of a child under the age of 15, compared to less than 5 percent today (Uhlenberg, 1980).

▲ Chapter 5 explains how high infant-mortality rates in the past affected definitions of childhood.

Today, the death of a child is always untimely and unnatural. Often it is sudden and unexpected: the result of an accident, an injury, or a medical emergency. Less frequently it is caused by a progressive disease, which affords parents the opportunity to begin the grieving process before their child actually dies (Raphael, 1995).

Parents experience grief over the loss of a child differently depending on when the child dies. Miscarriages, abortions, stillbirths, and deaths in infancy can all be crushing blows to parents, who may mourn the lost opportunity to establish a history and a relationship with the child. The death of a child in childhood or adolescence takes on added significance. This child is known and related to as a real person. Parents who lose a young child or adolescent often plague themselves with thoughts of what could have been done differently. They may become angry and locked into an "if only" state of mind. In some cases parents exhibit little overt grief, just restless, agitated distress. Sadness and depression can persist, unabated, for many years.

Parents who lose their adult children experience intense grief as well. What makes the grieving process especially complex in these situations is the fact that the adult child had probably established his or her own separate life. Hence, the grieving process is likely to include a variety of others—a surviving spouse, children, in-laws, and so on—each with his or her own perspective on the loss and own sense of entitlement to sympathy.

The AIDS epidemic has had a particularly transformative effect on the way parents deal with the illness and death of their grown children. Families may unite in support of an infected member, but often conflict erupts, especially if the family focuses on how the disease was transmitted. Families must face social stigma and isolation, fear of contagion and infection, as well as guilt, anger, and grief (Dane, 1991; Macklin, 1988). Most people with AIDS have at least one family member who has ceased contact with them after learning of the illness.

The difficulties may be particularly acute for gay people with AIDS. Even those whose families in the past appeared to accept their lifestyle may be rejected once the diagnosis is known. The diagnosis of AIDS forces parents to recognize that their children aren't simply gay in some abstract way but have been engaged in activities the parents may find distasteful. Relationships can become strained, formal, and awkward (Dane, 1991).

Families can heighten the sense of stigma by adopting extreme, medically unwarranted anticontagion precautions. A family in one study brought their own sheets when visiting their ill son's home; others refused to allow their infected children to touch any food, share their bathrooms, or come closer than an arm's-length away (Weitz, 1990).

For parents who reject their sick children, death brings many conflicting emotions. They may still experience tremendous grief and sadness over the loss of a beloved child, even though that child pursued a life they either felt uncomfortable with or actively and openly renounced.

In sum, the death of a child not only affects parents and other family members as individuals, it affects the structure of the family as well. A process of reorganization must occur within the family after the death of a child. One common dilemma surviving members face is how to now define their families (Brabant, Forsyth, & McFarlain, 1994). We have terms in this society to describe some of the many changes that families experience. "Empty nest," for instance, implies that the children are grown and gone. "Blended family" refers to families resulting from second marriages. But we have no term to describe the family that has lost a child. Some families grieve the loss and no longer include the deceased child as part of the family; others continue to count their deceased children as part of the family.

Conclusion

We all have reached (or will reach) a point in our lives when we disengage from the protection of our parents and become self-reliant adults. We will all reach a point in our lives when others address us "Sir" or "Ma'am," stop asking us for identification when we purchase alcohol, and see us as too old and out of touch to know what life is all about. Many of us will raise children and someday watch them leave the nest to begin their own families. Many of us will someday find ourselves responsible for the care of our own parents, and barring some unforeseen illness or accident, we will all experience the death of our parents. We have all experienced the physical changes brought about by the aging process and will all someday know what it's like to be defined as elderly. We will all die.

Most of these changes and transitions are inevitable. They come whether we want them to or not. Nevertheless, a multibillion dollar industry exists to help us try to ward off the aging process. We can buy products that dye our hair when it becomes too gray or smooth our skin when it becomes too wrinkled. Surgery can help us firm up what has begun to sag. We can spend a lot of money trying to avoid old age, but in the end we will always, always fail.

Yet despite the inevitability of these transformations, their social meaning is far from inevitable. We've seen in this chapter that every life-changing event we experience is shaped and influenced by larger cultural, historical, and institutional forces. We can't understand what it's like to enter adulthood without knowing something about the economic and demographic forces that can impede or enhance such a transition. We can't understand the aging experience without understanding the value of the aged in that particular society. We can't understand the role of death in families without understanding how death is perceived by the dominant culture.

Furthermore, recent social changes mean that the timing of some transformative events will be different for younger cohorts than they were for their parents or grandparents. People are leaving home later, marrying later, having children later, launching their children later, and living longer than earlier cohorts. These changes will, no doubt, have an enormous impact on people's personal family experiences, on cultural definitions of family, and on political, economic, and other social institutions in society.

CHAPTER HIGHLIGHTS

- The way people experience family transformations in adulthood is influenced by their birth cohort. People born roughly at the same time experience personal life course events (graduation, marriage, childbearing, entry into the paid labor force, retirement, death, and so on) at roughly the same point in history, and they experience major historical events at around the same age.

- We have a pervasive belief in American culture that middle-aged parents—particularly stay-at-home mothers—suffer severe emotional crises when all their children grow up and leave home. However, for most parents, the departure of grown children from home actually provides them with freedom, relief from responsibilities, and time for themselves.

- We usually think of grandparents as elderly and retired. But most people become grandparents while in mid-life, when they are married, when they are fully employed, and, with increasing frequency, when their own parents are still alive.

- Different cultures and different racial and ethnic groups within this culture vary in the degree to which grandparents are incorporated into the daily lives of families.

■ Cultural definitions of and attitudes toward old age can shape the experience of becoming elderly. In some cultures, the elderly are highly respected; in others they are either ignored or treated with contempt.

■ Decreasing birthrates and increasing life expectancy mean that the American population is getting progressively older. An aging population changes the assumptions we make about families. It prolongs marriage, prolongs relationships between parents and children, and increases caretaking demands on adult children.

■ In American society today, death is something that has become disconnected and remote. Most Americans die alone, in institutional medical settings, surrounded by doctors, nurses, and attendants.

DEMO•GRAPHIC ESSAY

Family Transitions and Living Arrangements

Events that mark family transitions are usually associated with changes in living arrangements. Traditionally, a wedding—the transition from being single to being married—signified the time when it became appropriate for the couple to begin living together. The end of a marriage, either by divorce, separation, or widowhood can also result in a change in living arrangements.

An important transition, both for families and for individuals, is the transition to adulthood, for it means a change not only for the child but also for the parents, and can affect other family members, too. When does an individual become an adult? Legally speaking, significant ages for becoming an adult are either 18 (minimum age to vote) or 21 (minimum age to purchase alcohol). The transition to adulthood can begin even earlier, for example, age 13, in some religious communities. In many states, individuals can get a driver's license at age 16, which gives them many "adult" freedoms. Finishing school and working full-time, as well as marriage and parenthood, are also important indicators of adulthood. Possibly the most significant indicator of adulthood, however, is living on one's own, away from the parental household.

Exhibit 8-A shows the percent of young adults (ages 18–24) in four types of living arrangements. For both men and women, by far the most common living arrangement is with parents—"child of householder." In this data set, college students living in dorms are considered to be living with their parents. The next most common living arrangement for young women is to be a "family householder or spouse" of the householder.

Exhibit 8-A

Living Arrangements for Persons Ages 18–24

United States: 1994

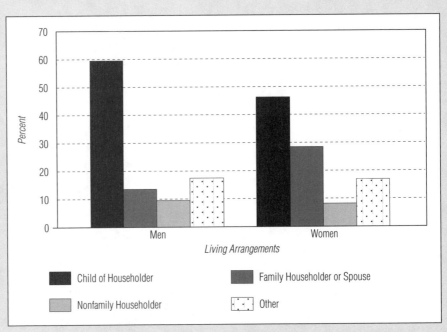

Source of data: U.S. Bureau of the Census, *Statistical Abstract of the United States: 1997* (117th edition). Washington, DC, 1997.

Young men are much less likely than young women to head a family, which makes sense, since men tend to marry at older ages than women do. "Nonfamily householders" include persons who live alone in their own households and those persons who are designated the head of the household and live with roommates. "Other" living arrangements include living as a roommate with someone else who is designated the head of the household or living in group quarters, such as in the military. Between the ages of 18 and 24 is the time when individuals experience the events that mark the transition to adulthood, and their living arrangements reflect these phenomena.

Older persons also make significant family transitions, such as the transition from spouse to widow. In addition, older persons who experience a decline in health may need to move from living independently, either alone or with a spouse, to living with others. Exhibit 8-B shows the distribution of living arrangements for men and women ages 65 and older. Because women tend to marry men who are older than they are and, furthermore, live longer than men, a much greater proportion of older women live alone. Older men, not surprisingly, are much more likely than women to live with a spouse. Living with relatives other than one's spouse is a more likely living arrangement for older women than for older men.

When discussing families, we often think of persons living alone either as not having a family or being in transition between families. Young adults who live alone are in transition between their families of origin and their families of procreation. Middle-aged and older adults who live alone may be widowed or divorced, or may have never married or formed domestic partnerships. Because of the wide variations in possibilities,

Exhibit 8-B

Living Arrangements for Persons Ages 65 and Older

United States: 1994

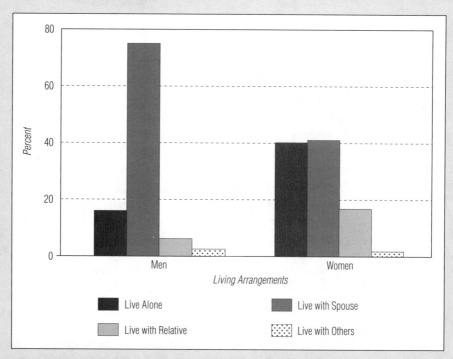

Source of data: Frank Hobbs with Bonnie Damon, "65+ in the U.S." In U.S. Bureau of the Census, *Current Population Reports P23-190.* Washington, DC, 1996.

Exhibit 8-C

Age and Gender of
Persons Living
Alone

United States: 1996

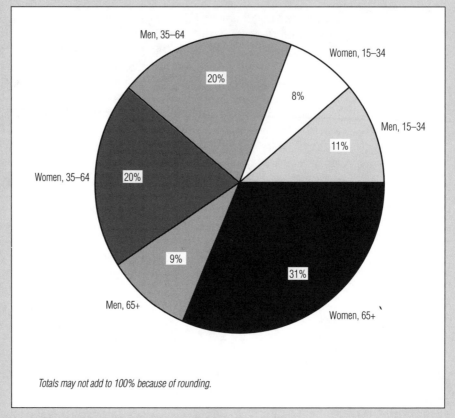

Totals may not add to 100% because of rounding.

Source of data: U.S. Bureau of the Census, *Statistical Abstract of the United States: 1997* (117th edition). Washington, DC, 1997.

it may be difficult to develop a "profile" describing someone who lives alone. Exhibit 8-C presents the age and gender composition of persons living alone. While some people may conjure up an image of a young, carefree bachelor as a typical person who lives alone, the data in Exhibit 8-C show that the largest single category consists of older women, many of whom are likely to be widowed. The next largest groups among the population living alone are men ages 35–64 and women ages 35–64—working-age adults. Young men and young women (ages 15–34) comprise relatively small proportions of the population living alone. For economic reasons they may be living with parents or roommates. Many may also be recently married and possibly have children living at home, unlike the middle-aged adults who are more likely to be divorced or to have an "empty nest."

Questions for Further Study

1. **Exhibit 8-A presents a "snapshot" of the living arrangements of young adults ages 18–24. Between those ages, however, individuals may make more than a few changes in living arrangements. Interview five to ten persons in their mid-20s and ask them to de-**

scribe each of their living arrangements since age 18. Try to estimate the proportion of time that they spent in each of the living arrangements shown in Exhibit 8-A. How are your findings similar to those in Exhibit 8-A? For example, have your interviewees spent most of their young adult years living with parents? Are there significant differences between men and women?

2. Try to find out about the living arrangements of older members of your extended family. See if you can discover what events led to changes in living arrangements. Are there differences for men and women in your family?

3. Some researchers and policy makers believe that living alone is a problem; that those who live alone are lacking something. Suppose you could compare older persons who live alone with older persons who live with others. What kinds of information would you want to know about each group to decide whether those who live alone are worse off than those who live with others?

YOUR TURN

Getting older is not simply a matter of adding an extra year to your age. It is intricately tied to the unique culture and historical era in which you live. Hence, the personal experience of aging can differ dramatically in different cultures and even among different ethnic groups within the same culture. Nowhere is this diversity more apparent than when we examine differences in the roles older people play in their own families.

To get a sense of these differences, see if you can interview grandparents from several different groups (white, African American, Asian American, Latino/a, Native American, recent immigrants, and so on). Try also to interview grandparents from different social classes and different religious groups.

Ask all grandparents a similar set of questions: How old were they when they became grandparents? How often do they see their grandchildren? Do they consider their relationship "close"? Are they satisfied with the amount and quality of time they spend with them? If not, what are the reasons for their dissatisfaction? Do they have any responsibility for raising their grandchildren other than occasional visits? How did their relationship with their children change when they became grandparents? Is being a grandparent any different from what they expected? What sort of support (financial, emotional, practical, and so on) do they receive from their children? What kind of support, if any, do they *provide* to their children?

Pool your findings with those of classmates, and from all the responses see if you can detect any systematic differences across groups. For instance, are grandparents in some ethnic groups more involved in the lives of their grandchildren than others? What do these differences tell us about the broader value of older people in the various groups represented? Are some grandparents more or less likely than others to feel like valued members of the family? Were grandmothers and grandfathers any different in this regard? How do the experiences of recent immigrants compare to those of grandparents who have lived in this country all their lives?

CHAPTER 9

Changing American Families

Margaret Atwood's best-selling 1985 novel, *The Handmaid's Tale*, takes place in the not-too-distant future society of "Gilead," ruled by a brutal fundamentalist regime. All universities have been closed. "Enemies" of the state—homosexuals, religious "heretics," people who speak freely, doctors who've performed abortions, and others—are routinely executed, their bodies displayed on walls in town squares for all to see. People's lives are completely controlled by the Guardians, Gilead's regular police force, and a secret organization of faceless spies called the Eyes who use sophisticated surveillance techniques to monitor citizens' activities.

Women have been systematically deprived of any power and autonomy. Many have been fired from their jobs and forbidden access to their credit cards or bank accounts. Following an environmental disaster that has left most women sterile, those few who still have "viable ovaries" and are capable of reproducing are rounded up and assigned to government and military officials for breeding purposes. These women—known as Handmaids—have become faceless reproducers, wearing long red cloaks, red gloves, and white winged hats that hide their bodies and faces. Poor women who cannot bear children have either become Marthas (domestic servants) or "unwomen," who are shipped to some far-off place called the Colonies. Sterile women lucky enough to be married to powerful men—known as Commander's Wives—retain their position as upper-class housewives.

Handmaids occupy a curiously paradoxical role in Gilead. Since there are so few fertile women, the future of the entire society lies in their ability to reproduce. Others are supposed to show them respect because of the vital nature of their service. But their ostensible high status is purely symbolic. They have no authority in the household or in society. They are forbidden to marry. They are treated exclusively as reproductive "machines" with no human feelings or identity. For instance, the story's narrator is a Handmaid named Offred, or "of Fred," meaning she belongs to a Commander named Fred.

Not only are Handmaids not allowed to use their given names, but their everyday lives are completely controlled by their Commanders and Commanders' wives. They may leave the home of the Commander and his wife once a day to walk to food markets, whose signs are now pictures instead of words because women are no longer allowed to read. The sexual intercourse they are required to endure with their Commanders once a month is devoid of any emotion or pleasure. It is a state-controlled procreative necessity. The Commander's wife is present during the act, which is euphemistically referred to as The Ceremony:

> What's going on in this room . . . is not exciting. It has nothing to do with passion or love or romance or any of those other notions we used to titilate ourselves with. It has nothing to do with sexual desire. . . . Arousal and orgasm are no longer thought necessary; they would be a symptom of frivolity . . . : superfluous distractions for the light-minded. Outdated. It seems odd that women once spent such time and energy reading about such things, thinking about them, worrying about them, writing about them. They are so obviously recreational. This is not recreation, even for the Commander. This is serious business. The Commander, too, is doing his duty. (Atwood, 1985, p. 122)

After a child is born, it is immediately given over to the Commander's wife, who is praised by others as if she had given birth to the child. After a few months of breastfeeding, the Handmaid is transferred to another household to become impregnated by a different Commander, thereby maximizing genetic variety as much as possible. Handmaids have no parental rights, no legally or socially recognized relationship to the child they've borne. They are not considered part of any family. Nor are they considered sexual beings. They are merely reproductive vessels.

Atwood's futuristic portrayal of family and parenthood is chilling. Gilead is a society in which intimacy and emotional commitment, the cornerstones of contemporary families, no longer exist. Unlike some other fictional portrayals of future family life—which simply place traditional family structures in a high-tech futuristic setting of carplanes, fully automated appliances, interplanetary civilizations, and robot servants—Atwood's family of the future is dark and alarming. Indeed, the institution of family as we know it has been destroyed.

The book is not meant to be a realistic *prediction* of the future. Instead, it is speculative fiction, meant as a cautionary tale of what would be the most extreme outcome if current trends—particularly those regarding societal attitudes about women's place in families and in society—are allowed to continue.

I have used *The Handmaid's Tale* to introduce this final chapter not because I have a dismal, pessimistic view of future families but to show you that the future is never completely separate from the past or the present. It is a continuation and an extension of the events and trends that precede it. Shortly after Atwood's book was published, she told an interviewer, "It's not science fiction. There are no spaceships, no Martians, nothing like that. There is nothing in *The Handmaid's Tale*, with the exception of maybe one scene, that has not happened at some point in history . . . I didn't invent a lot" (quoted in Davidson, 1986, p. 24).

Of course, trying to predict the events and trends that will impact people's family experiences 10, 50, or 100 years from now is quite difficult. Although the future is always, to some degree, an extension of the past, simply knowing what happened in the past is *never* sufficient to predict the future. We have no way of knowing which as-yet-unknown events or forces will shape our social worlds and leave their mark on our family lives. A sudden downturn in the economy, a lethal epidemic, a dramatic shift in the political leadership, or a presidential sex scandal, for instance, could wreak unanticipated havoc on people's family lives.

Underlying any discussion of future families—especially as they relate to the past—is the notion of change. What is the nature of social and family change? How do these changes come about? After addressing these questions, I will offer some tentative predictions about what families may look like in the twenty-first century and discuss society's role in influencing these changes through public policy.

What Will This Family Be Like?

Below are images of newly formed or recently changed families along with their demographic profile. What do you think the future holds for each of these families? How will social factors affect each family? How might each change the assumptions we make about "American families"?

Middle-class, African-American family of four. Mother recently died in a car crash. Father works as bank loan officer and has hired a housekeeper and babysitter to care for the children while he is at work. The two girls want to be attorneys, whereas the young boy is having difficulties coping with the loss of his mother.

White, mid-20s, middle-class, college-educated, gay couple. The partner on the right is an industrial engineer, and the partner on the left is a graphic designer. They were together 3 years before "marrying" and, in addition to the dog, plan on adopting a child within the next 5 years.

Upper-middle-class, white male and his new bride. She is a lower-middle class, Latina mother of a 3-year-old. The man, a cardiologist, will adopt the boy and hopes to have more children of his own. They share the Catholic faith, but relatives have not been supportive of the marriage.

Unwed teen parents with baby girl. Fifteen-year-old mother has dropped out of school to care for the child. Twenty-year-old father is trying to complete the GED after quitting school to join a gang. They live with her parents in a Brooklyn, New York, housing project.

Middle-class, suburban family at last child's college graduation ceremony. Daughter plans to move to New York City to pursue her career. The mother once worked as a typist but stayed at home to raise her four children, who have all moved to different parts of America. The father will be retiring from his executive position in 2 years.

This Vietnamese family immigrated from Vietnam in the early 1990s. Until 1995 they were housed by a Lutheran church congregation that sponsored them. Since that time, the oldest children have begun college and both parents started working—he works in a factory; she works as a hotel maid. They are barely able to afford a three-bedroom apartment on their two incomes.

Social Change

Part of the difficulty in talking about families in the future is that the present is so fleeting. Change is the preeminent characteristic of modern human societies, whether it occurs in our personal relationships, in our cultural norms and values, or in our social institutions. I have no doubt that the world in which you are living at this precise moment is, in many ways, different from the one I experienced when I wrote this book. On several occasions I have had to revise or update examples or statistics at the last minute because some things have changed so abruptly.

Over the past 3 decades, we've seen divorce rates skyrocket, then stabilize. People are waiting longer to get married, and once they do, they are having fewer children. Cultural concerns over gender equality have altered the way men and women relate to one another inside and outside the home. Social and sexual rules that once seemed permanent have disintegrated: Unmarried couples can live openly together, unmarried women can have and keep their babies, remaining single and remaining childless have become acceptable lifestyle options (Skolnick & Skolnick, 1992). The traditional breadwinner/housewife family with children represents a small—and shrinking—minority of families. Most families today are either dual-earner, single-parent, "blended," or "empty-nest." Children spend less time with their parents than they did 30 years ago, forcing them to depend on secondary relationships: paid caregivers, friends, teachers. In short, today's American family bears little resemblance to the cultural ideal that existed just a generation ago. ▲

▲ Issue 2 offers a historical examination of cultural images of families.

Sources of Social Change

Families don't suddenly change on their own. Changes that occur in other areas of society transform family life, often disrupting traditional roles. Demographic shifts in the population, technological innovation, and economic, cultural, and institutional trends often force families to alter the way they do things.

Population Pressures   The shifting size and shape of a population can create change in society. For instance, the passing of the massive baby boom cohort through the life course has been described metaphorically as "a pig in a python." ▲ If you've ever seen one of those *National Geographic* films of snakes digesting small animals, you know how apt the metaphor is. As this cohort ages, it stretches the parameters of the relevant social institutions at each successive stage of their lives. Baby boomers packed hospital nurseries as infants; school classrooms as children; and college campuses, employment lines, and the housing markets as young adults (Light, 1988).

▲ Chapter 8 provides more information on how birth cohorts influence family transitions.

When this massive generation reached childbearing age, it continued to leave its mark on society. Throughout the 1990s, school districts around the country have had to deal with overcrowded classrooms, as the offspring of all those baby boomers—sometimes called the "baby boomlet"—entered the educational system. Political pressure from this large group of parents has led to the building of new schools, increased scrutiny of television programs for children, and heightened concern over the effect of advertising on children.

As the baby boomers reach old age, those institutions concerned with later life—pension plans, Social Security, medical and social care—will be seriously stressed, leading one gerontologist to call the baby boomers a "generation at risk" (Butler, 1989). By the year 2030, one out of every three Americans will be over 65. At that time, there will be over 50 million retirees, about twice the number there are today. Some have even predicted a huge surge in business for the funeral industry by then as this generation reaches the end of its collective life cycle (Schodolski, 1993).

Because of its size, the baby boom cohort has left a particularly influential mark on families. That generation was the first to redefine families to include a variety of living arrangements like cohabitation, domestic partnerships, and never-married women with dependent children (Wattenberg, 1986). It was also the first to expect paid work to be a central feature of women's lives. And it was the first to grow up with effective birth control, making delayed childbearing and voluntary childlessness possible.

Technological Innovation   Sometimes change is spurred by scientific discoveries and technological inventions. The discovery of fire and electricity changed the nature of human lives and cultures for all time. The invention of the internal combustion engine, television, telecommunications, and the microchip have been instrumental in determining the course of history in the twentieth century. Scientific developments like improved knowledge of disease processes, medical care, nutrition, and water quality have all helped to reduce illness and therefore increase life expectancy.

▲ This trend is also examined in Issue 2 and in Chapter 3.

We've already seen a prime example of how technological change influences family life. By separating economic production from home life, industrialization in the nineteenth century had a powerful effect on family dynamics and gender roles. ▲ Along with these trends came other important changes: Both men and women began acquiring more formal education as access to schools increased and new labor force skills became necessary. Industrialization created greater access to wealth and thereby increased the size of the middle class. Members of the middle class also gained more leisure time, which could be devoted to pursuits such as volunteer work. Birthrates declined, in part because the large number of children who were useful and necessary in a farm-based economy became an economic burden in an industrial one (Staggenborg, 1998; Zelizer, 1985).

Technological innovations can also increase the moral choices families must make. Sophisticated techniques in genetic engineering, for instance, may eventually allow parents to choose the characteristics of their offspring. Many parents will face situations in which they must decide whether or not to abort a child who has a characteristic that is perceived to be undesirable. Indeed, recent advances in cloning technology have raised the possibility that adults may someday be able to create genetic replicas of themselves.

Technology has also raised moral issues regarding the end of life. With the help of respirators and other advanced life-support equipment, a person can now be kept alive long after the brain has ceased functioning. Perhaps sometime in the distant future, death from disease will always be a matter of choice.

Society can sometimes be slow to adjust to the changes brought about by scientific and technological innovation. Artificial insemination, in vitro fertilization, surrogate motherhood,

▲ Chapter 4 examines the social implications of infertility.

and other medical advances in the area of infertility have increased the number of infertile couples who can now have children. ▲ Yet these technological developments were changing the face of parenthood well before society began to recognize and address the ethical, moral, and legal issues they raised. For instance, since surrogacy technology may involve three "mothers"—the gestational mother, the genetic mother, and the social mother—legal parenthood is unclear. In divorce cases, legal battles rage over which partner is entitled to custody of frozen embryos conceived in a laboratory.

Electronic and telecommunications advances also have undeniable consequences for family life. Telephones, personal computers, TVs, and VCRs rob families of time they once spent interacting with one another (see Exhibit 9.1). One-quarter of American households now own pagers; more than one-third use cellular phones; and over 7 million people regularly check their work-related electronic mail from outside the office (Harmon, 1997). These gadgets blur the

▲ Chapter 3 examines the tension between work and family.

boundaries between work time and family time to a degree unknown just a decade ago. ▲

Some argue that these changes are good for families. Traditionally, working has meant being physically away from home. Now people can do much of their work while in the presence of their loved ones. Some futurists even point out that homes may once again become workplaces and schools, healing the split between men and women and the split between parents and children that began over 100 years ago (Skolnick, 1996).

Others, however, are not so optimistic. The urge to electronically "stay in touch" with the workplace is robbing families of uninterrupted time with one another. Family vacations, at one time a near-sacred ritual of withdrawal from the demands of everyday life, are no longer respites from work responsibilities. Many rural resort towns now have cybercafes where hikers

Exhibit 9.1

Households with Selected Electronic Media

United States: 1970–1995

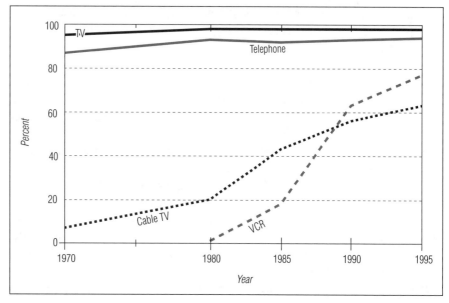

Source of data: U.S. Bureau of the Census, *Statistical Abstract of the United States: 1997* (117th edition). Washington, DC, 1997.

and tourists can check their E-mail for important messages. Simply being hundreds of miles away from the office is no longer enough to keep work at bay (Harmon, 1997). With today's technology, there's no excuse for being away from work.

In sum, many of the most difficult family issues we face today derive from technologies that provide benefits few people are willing to part with: longer, healthier lives; the ability to choose when and how many children to have; quicker access to information; and so on. Technology has forced us to face conditions that were unknown to previous generations. And we are unlikely to reverse the changes that have occurred. Therefore, there is little good to be derived from the nostalgic belief that family difficulties could be solved by returning to a simpler, less technologically sophisticated time.

Cultural Diffusion   Another source of social change that affects families is **cultural diffusion**: the process by which beliefs, customs, and other cultural items are spread from one group or society to another. Most of the taken-for-granted aspects of our everyday lives originally came from somewhere else. For instance, pajamas, clocks, toilets, glass, coins, newspapers, soap, even our alphabet and language were once imported from other cultures (Linton, 1937). Japanese innovations in microelectronics have dramatically altered the patterns of communication, transportation, and personal entertainment in American society. At the same time, American culture, as expressed in fashion, art, music, and food, is being incorporated into the lives of many young Japanese. The changing value of the elderly in Japan and other collectivist societies, is, in part, traceable to the influx of Western ideals and values into these cultures.

▲ Immigrant families also sometimes find it difficult to retain their traditional customs in their new countries, as you can see in Issue 6.

The diffusion process is not always friendly. When one society's territory is taken over by another society, people may be required to adapt to new customs and beliefs. ▲ When the Europeans conquered the New World, Native-American peoples were forced to abandon their traditional ways of family life and become more "civilized." Hundreds of thousands of Indians died in the process, not only from warfare but also from new diseases inadvertently brought over by their conquerors.

Institutional Diffusion   Changes that occur in one social institution usually create changes in other institutions, a phenomenon known as **institutional diffusion**. A slow-growing or stagnant economy, for instance, encourages people to maintain close networks with other relatives and may discourage young people from moving out of their parents' home. On the other hand, a booming economy leads to higher rates of employment, which encourage earlier entry into independent living and moves to new areas.

▲ Issue 7 and Chapter 3 examine the interplay between economic forces and family life.

Outside of the small percentage of families who are independently wealthy, families need two secure, well-paying jobs to ensure that they remain financially secure. If good jobs become more scarce and continue to be replaced by low-paying and sporadic employment, even two earners may not be enough to safeguard many families from poverty. ▲ Furthermore, women and minorities are disproportionately affected by economic trends that produce low wages and underemployment.

At the same time, changes in the institution of family extend to the law, politics, workplace policy, and schools. One cannot be a teacher these days without understanding the psychological aspects of divorce and remarriage that many students experience. Some school districts bend residency rules to accommodate children in joint-custody situations, hold separate teacher conferences for divorced parents, and make duplicate copies of students' papers, assignments, and report cards to send to both parents (Keller, 1997). As more and more families find themselves unable to adequately cope with the social problems their children face, schools are being called on to provide students with services that were once the sole province of families. They teach moral values and technological "literacy," provide adequate nutrition, and administer programs to help students avoid drug and alcohol abuse, teen pregnancy, and AIDS.

Social Movements

But social change is not just something that *happens* to society or families. Sometimes change is brought about purposefully by individuals or groups of individuals. These changes, then, are not a by-product of population pressures, technological innovation, or cultural and institutional diffusion. Rather, they are the result of a concerted effort on the part of people who feel that things aren't they way they ought to be.

Social movements are sustained attempts by groups of people with common goals and bonds of solidarity to bring about change through collective action targeted at the government or other opponents (Staggenborg, 1998). People who participate in social movements take part in a variety of actions—such as engaging in violent protest, demonstrating peacefully, lobbying politicians, signing petitions, donating money, or simply wearing the symbols of the movement on their clothing. Underlying all social movements is change: the desire to enact it, stop it, or reverse it.

Family life may seem far removed from these concerted efforts to change society, but in fact some of the most persistent and far-reaching social movements in this century have had a profound impact on families. The labor movement, the movement to protect workplace safety, the women's movement, the environmental movement, the civil rights movement, the abortion rights and anti-abortion movements, the gay and lesbian rights movement, and the religious right movement have all directly or indirectly affected people's ability to create, sustain, and direct their family lives.

Ideology   To be effective, a social movement must have an **ideology,** a coherent system of beliefs, values, and ideas that justifies its existence (Turner & Killian, 1987; Zurcher & Snow, 1981). People are almost never neutral about family matters that lie at the heart of religious, political, and philosophical belief systems. Issues like welfare, homosexual rights, abortion, sex education, and divorce often divide people into clear ideological camps.

With regard to social movements that involve the institution of family, we can talk about two broad ideologies. A **traditionalist family ideology** rests on the assumption that "the American family" is in serious decline. ▲ To traditionalists, the primary cause of family problems is the disappearance of "family values" and the prevalence of moral decay among people who are either selfish (such as women who would rather work than stay at home to raise their children) or behaviorally corrupt (such as people who have premarital or extramarital sex). In addition, traditionalists believe that the family rests primarily on duty and obligation. People have a duty to be chaste before legal marriage and monogamous afterward, to have children only within a legal

▲ For more on the issue of family decline, see Issue 8.

marriage, to live for children and not do anything that might impact negatively on them, and to maintain a permanent marriage "for the children's sake" (Scanzoni, 1991). These are the arrangements and expectations that traditionalists consider "normal" and highly desirable. Hence, they favor movements seeking to reverse the trend toward quick and easy divorce and mothers' participation in the paid labor force; to prevent homosexuals from legally marrying; and to restrict easy access to welfare, abortion, and sex education in schools.

A good example of a traditionalist movement is the antiabortion, or "pro-life," movement. Its ideology rests on several assumptions about the nature of childhood and motherhood (Luker, 1984): Each conception is an act of God, and so abortion violates God's will; life begins at conception; the fetus is an individual who has a constitutional right to life; and every human life should be valued (Michener, DeLamater, & Schwartz, 1986). The antiabortion movement subscribes to the belief that everyone can "make room for one more," reinforcing the view that abortion is not only evil but self-indulgent (Luker, 1984). Anyone who favors continued legal abortion is automatically branded as immoral.

Although abortion remains legal in this country and most adults support the availability of abortion (see Exhibit 9.2), the antiabortion movement has achieved some success. Since 1996, for instance, virtually every state has enacted some sort of restriction on abortion. In addition, fewer and fewer medical schools now teach their students how to perform abortions, a trend that will significantly reduce the number of abortion providers in the future.

In contrast, the foundational theme of a **progressive family ideology** is that families are not declining but instead are caught up in the continual evolution and transition that has been

Exhibit 9.2

Attitudes Toward Availability of Abortion: Survey of Adults

United States: 1977–1996

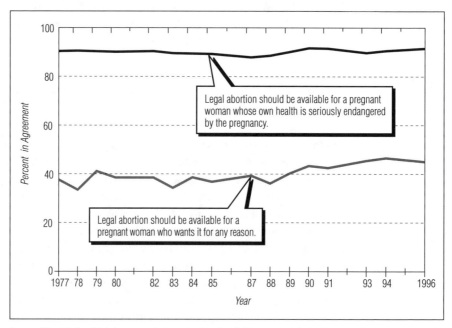

Source of data: National Opinion Research Center, University of Chicago, *General Social Survey, 1973–1996.*

occurring since the founding of this country. While progressives agree with traditionalists that the family is a vital social institution, they also believe it is a social construction—a product of the attitudes and behaviors of the people touched by it—not a universal form that exists for all times and all societies. The stresses and strains that people experience in their families do not result from forsaking a traditionalist vision but instead emerge from the curious paradox of adhering to traditional norms while at the same time behaving in distinctly nontraditional ways. For progressives, the view that a shift away from traditional values has caused the breakdown of families is wrong:

> The [traditionalists] have it backward when they argue that the collapse of traditional family values is at the heart of our social decay. The losses in real earnings and in breadwinner jobs, the persistence of low-wage work for women and the corporate greed that has accompanied global economic restructuring have wreaked far more havoc on [families] than have the combined effects of feminism, sexual revolution, gay liberation . . . and every other value flip of the past half-century. (Stacey, 1994, pp. 120–121).

Rather than issuing inflexible rules, progressives seek to discover what works and what doesn't work for families across a variety of circumstances (Scanzoni, 1991).

Progressive family ideology pays a lot of attention to the place of women in society. It makes little sense to speak of the well-being of families until gender makes no difference with regard to adult economic security, until men become more involved in household tasks and child rearing, and until we become a nation committed to high-quality early childhood enrichment (Scanzoni, 1991). For instance, progressives argue that, since both women's employment and day care are here to stay, social movements must aim to reduce their costs and maximize their benefits for *both* adults and children. If the economic well-being of women is enhanced, kids will ultimately be better off. If children participate in high-quality day care programs, women (not to mention men) will be better off.

Ironically, partisan politics and the needs of special interests often blur the boundaries between traditionalist and progressive ideologies. The Family and Medical Leave Act of 1993 granted full-time workers leaves of absence for childbirth, adoption, and family emergencies. Although such a bill would seem to fit a traditionalist ideology, which stresses the interests of children, many traditionalist lawmakers were initially opposed to the bill because they felt the policy would impose undue hardships on businesses. These legislators were successful in diluting the original bill, reducing the amount of time workers could take off and eliminating many workers from coverage. As a result, this law has had little effect on the lives of the working families it was intended to help (Marks, 1997).

Moreover, activists may be forced to engage in behaviors that conflict with the ideological tenets of the movement. For instance, during the early stages of the religiously conservative, antifeminist movement of the 1980s, it became clear that to succeed it would have to enlist high-profile women to campaign against feminist policies. These women had to abandon their families, travel the country to make speeches, and display independent strength—characteristics that were anything but the ideal models of passive womanhood they were publicly promoting. Phyllis Schlafly, a woman who has vehemently argued that a woman's natural role is that of a wife and mother in a household supported by her husband, is a Harvard-educated lawyer, an author of nine books, and a two-time congressional candidate (Faludi, 1991).

Clearly, dividing ideologies into broad "traditionalist" and "progressive" categories is an oversimplification. We cannot assume that everyone fits neatly into one category or the other. Indeed, the same person may be rather "traditional" on some issues but "progressive" on others. Yet we must remember that fundamental ideological and practical conflicts do separate these two positions and can therefore influence the sorts of changes society experiences.

Movements and Countermovements   Social movements are usually responses to social problems. For instance, the progressive responses to sexual inequality and oppression were the women's movements of the late nineteenth century and the mid-twentieth century. The main focus of the women's movement at the turn of the century was women's right to divorce, to retain custody of children after a divorce, to retain property, to work and keep their wages, and to vote.

Beginning in the 1960s, women—particularly white, middle-class, well-educated women—were becoming increasingly aware of the gap between their capabilities and the limiting domestic roles they were consigned to. Women began to realize that the best way to improve their lives was to organize and fight to increase their economic and social opportunities. Through organizations like the National Organization for Women and the National Abortion and Reproductive Rights Action League, women gained the political clout to have their voices heard.

Some women of color and working-class women have found today's women's movement irrelevant to their immediate needs and concerns. And the major goal of full equality has not yet been met, as evidenced by the failure of the Equal Rights Amendment to be ratified in 1982. Nevertheless, the movement has been quite successful in securing important economic, political, legal, and familial changes in society. The vast majority of women today believe that the women's movement has improved their lives (Wallis, 1989). And more than two-thirds of women believe that the United States continues to need a strong women's movement to enact changes that would further benefit women (Belkin, 1989).

But because such social movements seek to alter some aspect of existing social arrangements, there will always be people and groups opposed to such changes. Hence, movements for social reform typically spawn organized **countermovements**, which aim to prevent or reverse the changes sought or accomplished by an earlier movement. Countermovements are most likely to emerge when the reform movements against which they are reacting become large and effective in pursuing their goals and therefore come to be seen as threats to personal and social interests (Chafetz & Dworkin, 1987; Mottl, 1980).

The emergence of the religious New Right in the 1980s and 1990s was provoked by a growing perception that the women's movement of the 1960s and 1970s had created enormous social upheaval, breaking down traditional roles and values and challenging the institution of family (Klatch, 1991). Its positions as pro-family, pro-motherhood, and anti–equal rights for women were clearly designed to turn back the feminist agenda, which was perceived as an ideological attack on the family. Indeed, the leaders of the New Right were the first to articulate the notion that gender equality was responsible for women's unhappiness and the weakening of American families (Faludi, 1991). The rising divorce rate and the increased number of working mothers were seen as eroding the moral bases of family life (Klatch, 1991). As one New Right minister said, "We're not here to get into politics. We're here to turn the clock back to 1954 in this country" (quoted in Faludi, 1991, p. 230).

Through organizations such as the Moral Majority, the Heritage Foundation, the Eagle Forum, the Christian Coalition, the Family Research Council, and many smaller religious groups around the United States, the New Right has sought to restore the faith, morality, and decency they feel American families have lost in recent years. By 1995, the Christian Coalition had 1,100 chapters all across the country and over a million members. The New Right makes effective use of the media through 1,200 full-time Christian radio stations and cable television networks that reach 57 million households (Baca Zinn & Eitzen, 1996).

Over the past 2 decades, the New Right has been successful in shifting the political and social mood of the country. It first gained legitimacy in 1980, when Ronald Reagan and several Senate candidates supported by the New Right won election; it reaffirmed its influence in 1994 with the Republican takeover of Congress. Many of its most notable triumphs have been at the state and local levels, where it has succeeded in determining school curricula, in placing limits on divorce, and in passing anti-abortion and anti–gay rights legislation.

Future Family Trends

Knowing something about the nature of social change and the dynamics and structure of social movements allows us to explain how the institution of family has changed and is changing. Now we must turn our gaze to the future, a far more risky and uncertain endeavor. But we can extrapolate from some current trends to get a glimpse of what family life *might* look like as we enter the next century (see Demo•Graphic Essay, "Families in the Twenty-First Century," at the end of this chapter).

Risks of Sexual Freedom

Despite energetic attempts to convince young people of the virtues of sexual abstinence, sexuality for most people will continue to be a matter of personal choice not bound to marriage and childbearing. The old double standard—female virginity and male sexual experience at the time of marriage—is fading. Some, perhaps many, young people in the future will decide to "wait" until they marry to begin an active sexual life, but such a decision will undoubtedly be theirs to make.

Advances in medical technology may also have an effect on future sexuality. No disease has had as powerful an impact on people's lives over the last 2 decades as AIDS. By 1995, close to 500,000 AIDS cases had been reported and over 300,000 Americans had died of the disease (U.S. Bureau of the Census, 1996). AIDS remains the leading cause of death among men between the ages of 25 and 44 in close to 40 percent of America's large cities. By 1996, three times as many young Americans had died of AIDS as died in the entire Vietnam War.

However, over the last few years, an array of new drugs have been introduced, creating some guarded optimism that eventually infection with the HIV virus that causes AIDS will no longer mean inevitable death (A. Sullivan, 1996). Indeed, between 1995 and 1996 the estimated number of AIDS-related deaths dropped by 19 percent (Altman, 1997).

The incidence of new AIDS cases has also slowed dramatically in recent years. At the height of the epidemic in the mid-1980s, the number of new cases from year to year increased as much as 85 percent. In 1996, the increase in AIDS cases over the previous year was only 2 percent (Altman, 1997).

Although it is premature to declare the epidemic over, the optimistic projection that AIDS can be treated will no doubt have an impact on American sexuality in the near future. But a re-turn to uninhibited and unprotected sexuality is not likely, especially since many other sexually transmitted diseases are still "out there." Recent statistics indicating a drop in the proportion of American teens who've had sexual intercourse and an increase in contraceptive use among those who are sexually active ("Sexual activity," 1997) suggest that many young people have come to recognize that freedom of choice requires responsibility. ▲

▲ For more information on teen sexuality, read Chapter 5.

Will the stigma of homosexuality fade if the disease originally so closely identified with gay sex becomes less ominous? It's hard to say. However, with a smaller and smaller percentage of gay men becoming infected with HIV, the isolation of those who already are infected may actu-ally increase, and those with full-blown AIDS could feel more intensely alone than ever before (A. Sullivan, 1996).

We must also realize that medical breakthroughs in the treatment of AIDS are highly limited in scope. Although each day seems to bring an announcement of some new treatment or pos-sible progress toward a cure, no cure has yet been found. In fact, researchers at the 1998 World AIDS Conference indicated that the newest drugs are somewhat less effective than previously thought, dashing hopes that the discovery of a cure was imminent. Furthermore, the vast major-ity of HIV-positive people around the world don't have access to the very expensive drug treat-ments that are now available. Thus, worldwide, AIDS cases and AIDS deaths are *increasing* dra-matically.

Even in this country, the prevalence of AIDS and the availability of effective treatment vary by race and gender. Each year, African Americans and Hispanics constitute a larger and larger proportion of the AIDS population. Before 1986, African Americans accounted for 25 percent and Hispanics 13 percent of all American AIDS cases. Today the figures are 45 percent African Ameri-can and 16 percent Hispanic. Women are experiencing a similar trend. Prior to 1986, women con-stituted 7 percent of American AIDS cases; today, they make up over 18 percent (Stolberg, 1998; U.S. Bureau of the Census, 1996). The decrease in AIDS deaths has been most dramatic for men (22 percent) and whites (28 percent). Female deaths decreased by only 7 percent, black deaths by only 10 percent, and Hispanic deaths by only 16 percent (Altman, 1997). AIDS is now the third leading cause of death for American women between the ages of 25 and 44 and *the* leading cause of death among African-American women in this age group (Stolberg, 1997).

In short, we must be tremendously cautious in how we interpret encouraging statistics re-garding the AIDS epidemic. Although there is some reason for optimism, it's probably too early to be thinking about a massive societal shift toward carefree sexual behavior.

Increasing Life Expectancy

Medical advances in other areas—like the treatment of heart disease and cancer—will likely contribute to a continued decline in mortality rates and an increase in life expectancy (see Ex-hibit 9.3). Low death rates coupled with low birthrates will result in a larger proportion of the

Exhibit 9.3

Life Expectancy
at Birth for Males
and Females

United States:
1900–2010

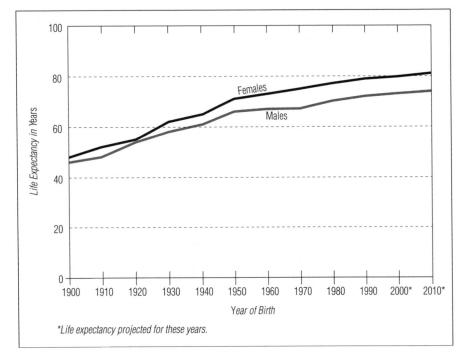

Life expectancy projected for these years.

Sources of data: U.S. Bureau of the Census, *Historical Statistics of the United States: Colonial Times to 1970.* Washington, DC, 1975. U.S. Bureau of the Census, *Statistical Abstract of the United States: 1997* (117th edition). Washington, DC, 1997.

▲ Chapter 8 provides
an analysis of the
aging of the American
population.

population being over 75. ▲ In fact, people over 85 will become the fastest-growing age group by the middle of the next century (Seelye, 1997a). It used to be the case that only the most durable and healthiest people lived to this age. However, improved medical care has increased the proportion of frail people who reach old age (Pampel, 1998). Hence, the demands of a growing elderly population in need of care will be felt more strongly by society in the foreseeable future.

The aging of the American population will have serious implications for the way people live their lives within families. The financial responsibility for the care of elderly family members, as well as demands for emotional and social support, will likely still fall on families. Certain issues heretofore unknown to the majority of families will become more common. What, for instance, will be the role of great-grandparents in family life? How will they be incorporated into the kinship structure? Will they be regarded as an obstacle to younger generations' independence, as a "social problem" for family members and for the community, or as valued members of a vastly extended family? What about five-generation families in which a grandparent can also be a grandchild? Such structures will surely require adjustments in patterns of family life (Riley, 1983).

Marriage, Divorce, and Remarriage

In the distant past, spouses didn't require much of one another to make a marriage work. Marriages were primarily economic arrangements. If two partners found that they could tolerate each other's company and were mildly compatible, that was enough. Today, people expect a lot more from their marriages; they want deep intimacy, sexual compatibility, and self-fulfillment.

The increased intensity of marriage and the heightened expectations that accompany it have made it all the more difficult for people to keep their marriages together when they are less than perfect. Furthermore, in the face of increased economic opportunities for women outside the home, their financial incentives to be married have decreased. Hence, although the divorce rate has stabilized and even dipped a little recently, all indications are that it will remain high into the foreseeable future. ▲

▲ The various facets of divorce are examined in Chapter 7.

Along with the high level of divorce, cohabitation and voluntary singlehood have become more commonplace and acceptable. People are also waiting longer to get married. In short, marriage as an institution is being challenged like never before.

So what will become of marriage in the future? Some people have gone so far as to suggest that we should rethink our long-standing tradition of organizing society around married couples. For instance, feminist scholar Martha Fineman (1995) has proposed that marriage, as a legal category, ought to be abolished. People would still be allowed to engage in ceremonial marriage, but such an event would have no *legal* (that is, court-enforceable) consequences. The decision to define the relationship as a "marriage" would be left to the individuals involved, who may or may not seek religious ratification.

Fineman imagines a future in which no special legal rules would govern the relationship between husband and wife or define the consequences of marriage. Instead, the interactions of married people would be governed by the same rules that regulate all other interactions in society, namely, those of property, contract, and criminal law. Equality between adults would be asserted and assumed. No special legal or economic privileges would be granted to husbands over wives or to married couples over unmarried couples.

Fineman believes that one benefit of abolishing marriage as a legal category is that the state's interest in bolstering the institution of marriage and stigmatizing other types of relationships would be dissolved. Voluntary, adult sexual interactions would be of no interest to the state, because it would no longer have a preferred model of family intimacy to protect. "All such sexual relationships would be permitted—nothing prohibited, nothing preferred" (Fineman, 1995, pp. 229–230).

Under this legal system, the treatment of children would no longer be based on the marital status of their parents. They would be protected by the same laws that apply to all citizens. So parents would no longer have the right to hit their children. The category of "illegitimate" children would also disappear and, with it, the stigma attached to being born "out of wedlock."

In this proposed legal scheme, a new definition of family would focus on the relationship between dependents and the people who care for them, regardless of their blood or marital ties. The caregiving family would become a privileged and protected entity, entitled to special, preferred treatment by the state. Government-conferred benefits currently reserved for married couples would instead be allocated as rewards for behavior that contributes to social stability. Tax breaks would be awarded, regardless of marital status, to stable lower- and middle-income households financially responsible for children, the elderly, or the handicapped. The motivation behind these changes would be not to eliminate marriage entirely but to encourage and sustain stable caregiving households (F. Johnson, 1996).

This radical suggestion is unlikely to be implemented any time soon because marriage still occupies a hallowed place in our national psyche. Rates of marriage will continue to be high into the foreseeable future. The vast majority of the adult population will continue to marry—at least 90 percent, the U.S. Census Bureau estimates (Coltrane, 1996a). Marriage, for all its problems and pitfalls, is here to stay.

This fact, coupled with consistently high rates of divorce, means that a growing proportion of the population in the twenty-first century will marry more than once. Families and stepfamilies will continue to grow in complexity. Consequently, the culture will no doubt have to develop standard, institutionalized ways of defining and supporting stepfamily relationships.

Complexities of Gender Equity

We've seen throughout this book that American men and women are slowly moving toward a blending of gender and family roles and away from traditional notions of wives and husbands, mothers and fathers. ▲ Each year Americans show more accepting attitudes toward women's increasing independence and influence over family decision making, work, and child care arrangements. Attitudes about men are changing too. Surveys of high school students over the years show that a growing proportion believe that husbands should take on more household and child care responsibilities. The vast majority believe that wives should expect their husbands to participate fully. Most adolescent boys expect that when they get married their wives will work, and more and more of them indicate that they intend to take time off from work after having a baby (Coltrane, 1996a).

▲ Issue 5, Chapter 3, and Chapter 4 all deal with various aspects of this trend.

There also seems to be a growing recognition in this society that the best way to ensure that families with or without children will not suffer is to increase economic opportunities for women as well as men. As dual-earner or dual-career couples become the norm, employers will have more and more trouble ignoring the importance of their employees' need to balance their work and family lives. Hence, we may see the slow disappearance of the 40-hour workweek, an acknowledgment of how employees' needs change through the life course, and a more flexible and less gender-specific definition of what it means to be a good worker.

As dual-earner families become more common, fewer people will publicly condemn working mothers as negligent parents. Most people today already say that they believe, at least in principle, in the ideal of equal opportunities for men and women. And if current trends continue, more people will endorse such a belief in the future.

▲ The complexities of this trend are explored in Chapter 4.

With regard to the household division of labor, sociologist Scott Coltrane (1996b) argues that changes in the gender-based division of labor will propel us toward equality between men and women at home. When men take on more of the mundane domestic tasks, the balance of power in the household begins to shift. When fathers take on more child care responsibilities, they begin to develop the sort of nurturant sensitivities traditionally associated with mothers. ▲ When parents share responsibilities, children thrive intellectually and emotionally and grow up holding less-rigid gender stereotypes.

Some fathers are already becoming more involved in child care and are more likely to desire an active role in raising their children. We can expect that men in the future will place even more value on spending time with their children. Of course, not everyone's attitudes will conform to this ideal. Nevertheless, Coltrane predicts that household tasks will become less tied to gender in the future.

These changes in the home and the workplace have the potential to transform the meaning of gender in future generations and reduce inequality and discrimination against women in the present generation (Coltrane, 1996a). As men take on more responsibility for housework and child care, traditional distinctions between men's work and women's work could begin to blur.

But the road toward gender equity in the future will not be completely free of potholes. Most jobs are still based on the assumption that an employee can and should work long hours without worrying about child care and other household needs. Most employed women continue to work in traditionally "female" occupations and still earn substantially lower wages than men. And the vast majority of women are still responsible for the vast majority of housework and child care.

Furthermore, work is still structured around a male model of 20 years of schooling, followed by 40 years of employment and then retirement (Skolnick, 1996). This model doesn't work for many women, who must combine work and domestic responsibilities. They often have to step out of the paid labor force to raise a family and return to it later when the children are grown.

Some sociologists predict that despite changing attitudes and the growth of well-intentioned "family friendly" workplace policies, family status (married, single, childless), rather than gender, may become the most potent discriminating characteristic among workers in the future. They predict that without a fundamental change in the workplace, the social and economic gap between "career-oriented" families (those couples who forgo children in pursuit of career advancement) and "child-oriented" families (those couples who forgo careers in the interests of their families) will inevitably widen. They fear that employers interested in productivity will favor career-oriented workers over child-oriented workers, whether they're male or female (Hunt & Hunt, 1990). If future work environments fail to part with the assumption that the most committed employees are those who are unfettered by family demands (that is, single and childless), neither women nor men who openly express a desire to spend more time with their families will be able to advance in their careers.

The Science of Childbearing

Advances in reproductive technology will continue to expand the boundaries of biological parenthood. One issue that will become especially controversial in the years to come is who should be eligible for infertility treatments. For instance, more and more gay male couples are choosing to become parents with the help of female surrogates and egg donors. These couples are not infertile in the standard medical sense, but they are using these procedures to satisfy their desire to have children with whom they share some biological connection. Such trends will further alter our cultural definition of family.

▲ Chapter 4 provides more detail on the social implications of reproductive technology.

Advances in reproductive technology will also combine with increased longevity to shatter what were once thought to be impenetrable boundaries of biological parenthood. ▲ In 1997 a 63-year-old Los Angeles woman gave birth to a normal baby girl who was created from her husband's sperm and an anonymous donor's egg. She became the oldest woman on record to give birth. Although the number of women over 50 who have given birth is small—worldwide fewer than 100 have been reported (Kalb, 1997)—the possibility that someone could become a mother at a time when most women are thinking about becoming grandmothers raises difficult questions about parent-child relationships and, indeed, the assumptions underlying family. What, for instance, would prevent a couple from waiting until they retire to have children? If they are in good health, they can expect to live over 20 years in retirement. Moreover, with no job to take their time and energy, they wouldn't have to worry about balancing the demands of work and family as so many younger parents have to.

Critics, however, argue that older parents place excessive strains on themselves and their children. They may be unable to keep up with the demands of teenagers; and children may worry that their parents may die at any moment. Raising children under such circumstances thus seems selfish.

It should be noted that becoming a parent at age 60 or 70 has always been a biological option for men, especially well-to-do men. The actor Tony Randall and his wife had their first baby in 1996. She was 26; he was going on 77. So-called *start-over dads* have always been commonplace, and their parenthood has never raised the sorts of ethical questions raised by postmenopausal women bearing children.

Another technology with significant ramifications for childbearing is genetic engineering. Our understanding of genetic disease will no doubt become more exact in the twenty-first century. Will parents then be able to precisely engineer offspring who are completely free of genetic anomaly? Probably not. But our understanding of the genetics of human disease and defect will transform medical practice as we now know it. Imagine what a prenatal doctor's visit might look like a hundred years from now:

> The patient, let's call her Baby K, has her first checkup when she is an 8-week-old fetus. A technician removes a few fetal cells. Several days later, interviews with the doctor and a genetic counselor provide a detailed picture: a 250-page printout sums up information about the DNA at 50,000 regions of the fetal chromosomes—all those regions whose functions in human development are at last understood. (Kitcher, 1996, p. 124)

With all this information, genetic counselors in the future will be able to provide the expecting parents with reasonably accurate predictions about Baby K's susceptibility to the major diseases that develop later in life, the strength of her immune system, and perhaps even her future behavioral tendencies:

> The probability that Baby K will develop a particular personality trait might vary quite widely. But, thanks in part to advances made in neurochemistry . . . Mr. and Mrs. K can learn a few things about their daughter . . . : there is no reason to think she will have less than average intelligence; she is not very likely to be hyperactive or suffer from an attention deficit, and she displays no abnormal propensity for depression. (pp. 124–125)

What will parents do with such knowledge in the future? Although it seems technologically as well as ethically and morally unlikely that parents will be able to order a baby engineered to their specifications, they will be able to decide what kinds of children they will carry to term, provided they are prepared to abort fetuses with characteristics they don't like or don't want. The likelihood of genetic prejudice and discrimination is high. Will some parents choose to terminate a pregnancy when the fetal genes indicate a possibility of homosexuality or bisexuality, a risk for heart attack in middle age, a propensity toward obesity or shortness, or a disease that can only be treated at great expense?

The prospect is not all that futuristic. Recently, an American couple was advised that their fetus had a rare extra chromosome that was *potentially* linked to tall stature, severe acne, and aggressive behavior. The couple responded by aborting the child (Shenk, 1997). Thousands, perhaps millions, of women in other parts of the world are already aborting female fetuses or killing infant girls because they believe that their daughters, growing up in cultures heavily biased toward men, will not lead happy and healthy lives. "Intense competition and social inequality already drive middle-class parents to register newborn infants for elite schools, to select the 'right' preschool enrichment programs. Tomorrow, the struggle for advancement may begin in the womb" (Kitcher, 1996, p. 126).

Unless prospective parents can rely on tolerance and respect for those who are different, unless they can be assured that their community will do what it can to aid people with disabilities, then the pressure to view reproduction as a process in which the "right" products have the societal stamp of approval and the "wrong" ones are discarded will be irresistible. Parents always want what is best for their child. In the future, will they do all they can to produce a "perfect" baby? Even today, infertile couples can "adopt" frozen embryos custom made by doctors from donor sperm and eggs to approximate the couple's physical appearance, ethnic background, and in some cases educational level (Kolata, 1997b).

In this future vision of childbearing is also the continuing impact of social class. As long as we assign social and economic status to those who succeed by society's prevailing standards, many middle-class parents will feel compelled to have only children who satisfy genetic requirements for success. At the other end will be those people whose genetic shortcomings doom them to unemployment. They are the people with disabilities whose lives are inadequately supported and whose limited insurance coverage or minimal education denies them access to new preventive medicine. Hence, some genetic disabilities virtually eliminated in the middle class will persist with relatively great frequency in the lower classes. Given today's social attitudes and the persistent gap between the rich and poor, it is not far-fetched to predict that socioeconomic inequality could help to create a true genetic underclass in the future.

The Disappearance of Childhood

One of the major family concerns over the past decade has to do with the problems children are being forced to face. Recent studies have unearthed some startling findings:

- One in six children between the ages of 10 and 17 has seen someone shot or knows someone who has been shot.
- One in twelve high school students has attempted suicide and one in four has seriously considered it.
- One in eight high school students carries a weapon to school, and one in nine stays away from school because of fear.
- One in three 13-year-olds uses drugs.

■ The number of children under 18 arrested for violent crimes has more than doubled since 1970; the number arrested for weapons violations has tripled.

Kids today worry about everything from contracting AIDS to drive-by shootings to not being able to find a good job when they grow up (Adler, 1994; Applebome, 1996a; Kantrowitz, 1993). Many parents have stopped trying to shield their children from the world's woes and instead focus on preparing them for the dangers that inevitably await them (Stryker, 1997).

Some social critics have argued that childhood as a distinct stage of life has all but disappeared. ▲ Psychologists estimate that children today are about 2 to 3 years ahead of children their age 25 years ago:

▲ Shifting definitions of childhood are explored in Chapter 5.

> The idea of childhood as a sheltered time, free from adult anxieties, is becoming a nostalgic luxury in a world where young people die of AIDS and TV newscasts are filled with stories of child-pornography rings, kidnappings and the sorrowful faces of abused children. (Darton, 1991, p. 62)

From all indications, the duration of childhood will continue to shrink. Children will continue to be exposed to even more events, devices, and ideas that would have been inconceivable to their parents when they were children. Death, illness, violence, and sexuality will continue to be revealed to children in their homes, in their schools, in their neighborhoods, on their computers, and on television.

Ethnic Diversity

The ethnic composition of the American population has been steadily changing over the past several decades and will continue to do so well into the twenty-first century. The proportion of Americans who trace their ancestry to Europe will grow smaller in the coming years. The U.S. Census Bureau recently predicted that by the year 2050, close to half the population will consist of people of Hispanic, Asian, Native-American, and African-American heritage. And by the year 2005, Hispanic Americans will surpass African Americans as the nation's largest minority (cited in Seelye, 1997a).

How will these trends affect family life? Certainly the notion that something called "American culture" or "the American family" exists will be noticeably less tenable in the future. Making broad general statements about American families will become increasingly more difficult, because no single family type is likely to dominate as the Euro-American family does today.

I think most of us want a society in which racial division and animosity are no longer such potent elements in everyday life. However, for those groups who have historically been ignored, or worse, treated with outright hostility, the unique ethnic elements of family life are a rich and important source of pride and identity. But in the end, the move toward a less white, less European-American society may matter little. Important economic, political, and cultural forces will continue to affect *all* families, no matter what their ethnic backgrounds.

Whether American families in the future become more similar to one another or more diverse depends on whether the formation of families across racial, religious, or social class lines becomes more common than it is today. As rates of intermarriage and the number of multiethnic children continue to increase, traditional ethnic and racial boundaries will begin to blur. In fact, if this trend continues, ethnic differences in family structure may someday become less noticeable than class differences.

The Influence of Globalization

As global influences on everyday life grow stronger, the dynamics of family lives will inevitably be affected. Consider, for instance, how the competitive pressures of the international capitalist marketplace have forced many employers to make greater use of so-called disposable workers— those who work part-time or on temporary contract. These jobs offer no benefits and no security and thus create instability in family life (Kilborn, 1993; Uchitelle, 1993). More and more companies cut costs by relocating their manufacturing facilities to other countries, where they can pay lower wages. Over 1,000 U.S.-owned manufacturing plants, including plants run by Ford, General Motors, RCA, and Zenith, are now located in northern Mexico alone (Baca Zinn & Eitzen, 1996). These companies obviously benefit financially, but the displaced American workers and their families do not.

▲ Issue 7 contains a detailed discussion of the role of economic inequality and poverty in family life.

At a deeper level, we are also being forced to understand family problems in a global context. For many poor American families, each and every day is filled with suffering and despair. ▲ In a global context, however, even the poorest of Americans live relatively privileged lives compared to the millions of extremely impoverished people worldwide. The houses, food, clothing, health care, and transportation that poor Americans have access to may be inadequate to sustain respectable lives here, but they are well beyond the dreams of a majority of families around the world. In short, even poor people in a wealthy country have certain privileges.

I'm not suggesting that poor American families don't suffer or that they should feel content with what they have. Instead, I'm arguing that global economic inequality will affect all of us in the future. It's precisely the fact that even poor American families are in better shape than poor families in most other countries that brings large numbers of immigrants—legal and otherwise—into this country each year. They come to escape abject poverty as well as other massive problems, like overcrowding, political unrest, and repressive discrimination. We are all touched, in both positive and negative ways, when waves of immigrants leave their countries to seek a better life here for themselves and their families. Hence, the long-term future of American family life will be linked to the solution of social problems worldwide.

Expanded Definitions of Family

▲ Issue 1 examines this trend in detail.

In recent years the American definition of family has expanded beyond the traditional form. ▲ While nuclear families will continue to be important, I suspect the term *family* will be used with increasing looseness in the future. In part, the liberal use of the word is a testament to its profound cultural and personal importance. To metaphorically refer to a sports team or a work group as a family is to symbolically reinforce the power that family holds over our lives. Yet, aside from such usage of the term, the trend toward including various nontraditional relationships under the legal rubric of *family* will be at the forefront of emotional debates for years to come.

For instance, each year more and more major corporations are granting financial benefits to unmarried domestic partners. Huge multinational corporations don't make such policies frivolously, and I suspect few are interested in making some sort of political statement about the acceptability of certain lifestyles. Instead, these companies have apparently concluded that such policies make good financial sense because they increase workers' motivation and, hence, their productivity and retention. To the extent that using an inclusive definition of *family* continues to make good business sense, the list of economically and socially "legitimate" types of families will continue to expand.

Family Policy

With all the heated political rhetoric we hear these days about the state of "the family," you'd expect that the United States government would have an identified set of family-related objectives and specific measures to achieve them. But, unlike most Western industrialized countries, we have no formal family policy to guide us in the future (Zimmerman, 1992).

Certainly, at one level, all of our government policies—on taxes, education, welfare, health care, and so on—affect families, even if they're not designed specifically to do so. However, the U.S. government and state governments have no systematic and developed plan regarding families. Instead, we have a mishmash of state laws and regulations that lack coherence.

In contrast, most European countries have an extensive policy structure for families, which includes national health insurance or services, cash benefits for families based on the number and age of children, guaranteed minimum child-support payments, and sometimes housing subsidies for low- and middle-income families (Kamerman & Kahn, 1995). Although specific services and philosophies vary from country to country, the common goal is to support families at home and in the community:

> The French want not only to protect the economic well-being of children in vulnerable families but also to ensure that women continue to have children even while entering the labor force in ever-increasing numbers. The Germans and Austrians want to acknowledge and affirm the value of children and of "family work." The Finns . . . see their policies as supporting the values of parental choice and family work. . . . The Italians stress maternal protection and support for child well-being. The Swedes, and to a lesser degree the Danes, have sought to promote gender equity, child well-being, responsiveness to labor market demands, and support for a strong work ethic. (Kamerman & Kahn, 1995, p. 25)

The differences between Europe and the United States are noteworthy because European family policies tend to be associated with the enhanced well-being of children. Infant mortality rates are lower in Europe than in the United States, fewer babies are born underweight, childhood immunization rates are higher, and, therefore, the rates of certain childhood diseases are lower. In most but not all European countries, school learning is more successful, and schools have fewer problems with disruptive students than do schools in the United States. Later on, fewer European adolescents have babies or abortions than do adolescents in the United States (Kamerman & Kahn, 1995).

In the United States, much of the government support for families is limited to programs that serve children with behavioral problems, poor children, or children from deprived groups. Such programs provide safety-net income or remedial services. However, U.S. policies don't offer basic preventive and development services that can enhance socialization and avert future problems.

One reason for the lack of a coherent family policy in the United States is the powerful cultural belief in individualism and family privacy (Moen & Schorr, 1987). ▲ Thus, policies have traditionally been directed toward individuals rather than families. To some people, the very notion of a government plan regarding families is disturbing because it implies state intrusion into family life. Anything that seems to violate families' right to think, judge, and act for themselves is tantamount to sacrilege.

▲ Issue 3 provides a detailed examination of family privacy. Issue 4 looks at the role of individualism in family life.

Also inhibiting the development of a family policy in the United States is the diverse nature of families themselves. Regional, state, racial, religious, ethnic, and generational variation in values have precluded agreement on what families are, not to mention what the government should be doing for them.

Despite the lack of a formal family policy, federal and state governments are perpetually considering family-related legislation on such issues as abortion, parental responsibility, family leave, welfare, and tax benefits for families (Schneider, 1996). Decisions made over the next few years will likely determine the nation's course into the next century.

Consequently, the long-term fate of American families will depend on how family scholars and politicians define certain social trends. If trends like the increase in dual-earner and single-parent families are labeled as harmful to family life, then social policies will probably oppose family diversity and discourage "nontraditional" households. If, on the other hand, such developments are viewed as inevitable—and perhaps even beneficial—then social policies will likely support the needs of new and diverse family forms (Gerson, 1998).

At the forefront of the political debate over these issues will be fundamental questions, such as the following, about government's role in family life:

■ *Should we emphasize "traditional" family values?* One direction the government might take is to promote and support traditional views on family issues like marriage, sexual activity outside marriage, maternal child care at home, and so on. Public policies, including taxes, would give preference to married couples and discourage or place restrictions on divorce, illegitimacy, and single and gay parenting. Schools would teach children that sex outside of marriage is wrong; the government would cease subsidizing abortion and states would repeal no-fault divorce laws. However, at a time when the country is becoming more diverse, a return to the "traditional family" at the expense of "nontraditional" families seems unlikely.

■ *Should we promote parental responsibility?* This policy approach would make family planning and sex education a national priority, discouraging people who aren't prepared financially or emotionally from becoming parents unexpectedly. It would strictly enforce existing laws that hold parents responsible for raising children and accountable for their children's legal transgressions. Failure to pay child support, for instance, would be considered a form of child neglect. Divorce and custody arrangements would make the financial well-being of children—not the financial wherewithal of parents—the highest priority. But the problem with this perspective is that it would further complicate the decision to bear and raise children at a time when many people are already struggling to meet the demands of family and work.

- *Should we expand the government's responsibility for helping families raise children?* We have programs designed to help the elderly (Social Security, Medicare), so why not make similar provisions for parents and children? Following models that exist in other industrialized countries, the government could take any steps necessary to lift all children out of poverty. The government would subsidize child care, preschool, health care, and paid parental leave when babies are born. It would also require employers to pay women the same wages that men earn in similar jobs. However, such a policy would require a more pronounced government role in people's lives at a time when a majority of Americans favor limiting government and reducing public spending.

Regardless of which direction government policy ultimately takes, many specific legal issues will be debated well into the next millennium (Minow & Shanley, 1996). These include:

- *The place of biology in reproduction, custody, and access.* What, if any, claims should those people with biological ties to a child have regarding the conception, gestation, birth, and custody of that child? Should grandparents have legally protected access to their grandchildren in the event of a divorce?
- *Sexual orientation.* What relations between adult homosexual partners, and among homosexual parents and minor children, should the state permit or promote?
- *The preference or privilege accorded to legal families compared to families formed informally.* Should those in legally executed marriages and adoptions receive benefits denied those in informal, legally unrecognized arrangements?
- *The role of the economic marketplace in forming family relationships.* Should people be able to contract for the conception or generation of a child? For a child available for adoption? For sexual services? For a spouse?
- *The role of government money in providing support for families.* Should the government subsidize child care, care of ill or disabled family members, or nursing homes for *all* working Americans? Should the government subsidize greater choice in children's education, in the form of charter schools or school voucher systems?
- *The relationship between the workplace and family life.* Should workplaces be structured to favor or support one family type over others? Should workloads in the paid labor force be made more flexible to accommodate the demands of caring for children or elderly relatives or of performing other family duties?
- *The relative power of family members in family-related decision making.* What is the legal or philosophical basis for granting greater power to one member of an adult partnership over the other, as in decisions over abortion and child custody? Should children have as much say as parents in custody decisions? In medical treatment decisions, how should the views of all involved—patients, spouses, and other relatives—be collected and given force?
- *Racial and religious identities.* Should the state rely on racial or religious identity as a basis for deciding disputes over child custody or regulating foster care, adoption, marriage, divorce, and medical treatment?

■ *Dependency, disability, and illness.* Who is responsible for the daily care and financial support of such dependents as children, elderly people, and people with severe disabilities or illnesses? What degree of family relationship establishes such responsibilities?

Each of these questions (many of which have been examined at length in this book) has arisen because of new technologies, changing social practices, and normative or ethical conflict. Their resolution will not be easy because family life is the result of a complex interplay among human agency, institutional structure, cultural values, and conscious political choices.

Final Word

I hope that reading this book has motivated you to take a closer, more sociologically informed look at your own family experiences. In families, we have a topic about which everyone has some expertise. It is tempting, therefore, to assume that we can know everything that needs to be known about families by simply looking at our own lives. But, of course, such a subjective view can never be sufficient. Assuming that something that happens in my family happens in all families is a little like saying, "Because my older brother likes M & M's, everyone's older brother likes M & M's."

At the same time, though, you have seen in this book that many, if not most, families have certain patterns and features in common. I hope that occasionally you've read something here and felt that I must have been writing about *your* family. It's the patterns and commonalities that are intriguing to sociologists, because they suggest a much larger reality than the private experience of individual families.

Furthermore, families, private and unique though they be, are tightly intertwined with larger political, historical, economic, cultural, and environmental forces. We can never understand our own families without understanding the social structure within which our families are situated.

Will families exist in the future? Yes. But we must always keep certain important points in mind:

■ It has never been and never will be possible to think of "the family" or "the American family." Family diversity has always characterized family life and will continue to do so in the next century.

■ The experiences that individuals have within their own families will always be filtered by their race, social class, gender, sexual orientation, religion, and other social characteristics.

■ None of the shifts in family life can be understood in isolation. Each change takes place within a particular cultural and historical context. Furthermore, each aspect of family life touches on others. We can't begin to understand parent-child relationships, for instance, without understanding something about marriage, gender, demography, culture, domestic and global economics, work, even biology.

As I wrap up this book, I feel a curious combination of failure and success. On the one hand, I think that I have provided few, if any, ironclad answers to the crucial questions that drive discussions and debates over families in American society. People can't agree on what a family is or what the relative importance of biology and culture are in forming family experiences. No one knows for sure what the perfect balance of family privacy and public accountability should be or whether individual rights or family responsibilities should be granted more importance in society. People still argue vehemently over whether American families are declining or merely adapting to changing social circumstances and whether or not divorce or having two working parents hurts children.

But the lack of consensus on these issues is not based on my ignorance or stupidity. It's the nature of the beast. None of these important questions have clear, simple answers. Sociological research can provide invaluable information on general tendencies and truths as they apply to the majority of the population, but it can never and will never be able to predict the family experiences of every single person. Sure, some kids are hurt by the divorce of their parents, but others aren't. Some kids with homosexual parents thrive, while others don't. Yes, the cultural value of family privacy creates serious and dangerous problems, but it also prevents other problems from occurring. Black families and white families, rich families and poor families are indeed different; but they're also similar in a lot of ways.

So maybe the lack of clear, unequivocal answers isn't a failure after all. Maybe what I've done is succeed in showing you that *no* family issue has an easy explanation. While sociological theory and research are invaluable tools in understanding the nature of these issues, no two people experience their families in exactly the same way; and no two families deal with economic, political, religious, cultural, and educational institutions in the same way. There's an important lesson here: Be wary and skeptical of commentators, critics, politicians, and fellow citizens bearing simple answers to complex family questions. Instead, appreciate families—your family, friends' families, and families in general—for what they truly are: familiar and confusing, painful and wonderful, frightening and exciting.

Conclusion

All right, let's be honest. The question you really want answered after spending an entire semester with this book is: What can I expect in my own family life in the next decade or so? Maybe that's why you took this course on "family" in the first place. I don't blame you. Intimate, family relationships, as we've seen throughout this book, occupy such a crucial position in our lives that we all have a powerful desire to know what's in store for us.

But after spending most of this chapter offering my speculative thoughts about what families may look like in the future, I can be 100 percent certain of only two things:

■ Families will be the same as they've always been.
■ Families will never be the same again.

I'm only being mildly facetious in making these apparently contradictory predictions. In some not-yet-known ways, families in the twenty-first century will be nearly unrecognizable to contemporary observers. No doubt we will encounter some new, frightening things that we haven't yet had to deal with. In other ways, though, families will be much the same as they are today.

People will still worry about the same things they've always worried about and criticize families on the same grounds upon which they've always criticized them.

Consider this account of a family event that, although it took place recently, is likely to become a common, unremarkable occurrence in the future:

> At the recent wedding of my stepson, my husband sat companionably between his former wife (the mother of the groom) and me. The groom, in his toast, warmly acknowledged the bride's ex-husband (the father of her son), who was there with his long-time partner, who sat next to the lesbian couple with their new baby. The new husband of my husband's ex-wife introduced us to the daughters of his two previous marriages, one of whom described the difficulties of living with your ex-husband in the apartment right above you. All in all, a typical post-modern family—one typical of Republicans as well as Democrats, conservatives as well as liberals, rich as well as poor. (Tavris, 1996, p. 27)

The scene is humorously bizarre and confusing. Complicated step-relationships and "nontraditional" living arrangements abound. But notice also that age-old things like long-term, committed relationships and child rearing remain important aspects of family life. In short, even though the structure of people's family relationships may look quite different than they do today, people will always have a need for intimacy and commitment and a desire to produce offspring and therefore will always have a need to construct some sort of family—whatever it may look like.

Barring some cataclysmic fascist revolution like that depicted in *The Handmaid's Tale,* people in the future will continue to face choices about the things people currently contemplate: whom to date, whether to marry, whether to have children, whether to have an abortion, whether to remain married. The growing racial, ethnic, cultural, and sexual diversity of the population will create substantial variation in the ways people make these choices in the future. But the fundamental needs of human intimacy will always remain, even though people are going to find new and interesting ways of satisfying those needs.

CHAPTER HIGHLIGHTS

- When massive social changes occur in a society, their effects are often strongly felt in families. Sometimes these changes occur as the result of major demographic shifts or technological innovations; other times they are brought about purposefully by individuals or groups of individuals who feel that some aspect of society isn't functioning the way it should.

- Unlike other industrialized countries, the United States lacks a national family policy. Ironically, some of our most cherished "family values" (for instance, family privacy and autonomy) prevent the establishment of a coherent state policy.

- At the forefront of political debate over future family trends will be the government's role in family life.

- Although future families will face some issues very different from those faced today, they will also, in many ways, struggle with the same questions and dilemmas families have always struggled with.

DEMO•GRAPHIC ESSAY:

Families in the Twenty-First Century

During the twentieth century, American families have diversified beyond the stereotypical "nuclear" family of mother, father, and children. Other kinds of families have emerged, families that meet the emotional and physical needs of their members even if they don't look like "traditional" families. Proportionately fewer families consist of a mother, father, and small children; more families consist of single parents with children. One of the most significant trends over this past century has been the increase in households consisting of persons living alone, single-person households.

As we turn the corner on the next millennium, demographers project that single-person households will continue to increase, both in numbers and as a proportion of all households (see Exhibit 9-A). This increase will contribute to an increase in the numbers of households overall by the year 2010. Single-person households make up the majority of nonfamily households—households composed of one or more individuals who are not related. The most common type of family household is one headed by a married couple. Although they do not make up the majority of households, families headed by a married couple (both with and without children) will still be the predominant type of household in the year 2010. Other types of family households, such as single-parent households, will become more numerous but will still be a much smaller segment of all households than married-couple households are.

Exhibit 9-A

Growth of
Households

*United States:
1990, 2000, 2010*

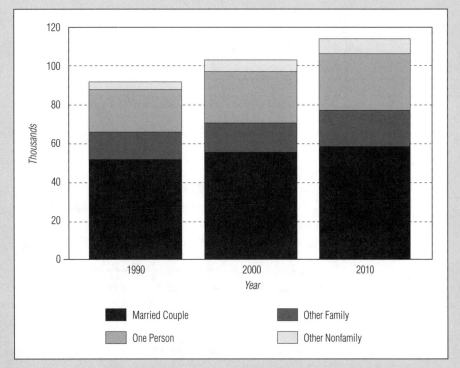

Source of data: U.S. Bureau of the Census, *Statistical Abstract of the United States: 1997* (117th edition). Washington, DC, 1997.

Exhibit 9-B

Population
Projections
by Ethnicity

*United States:
1990–2025*

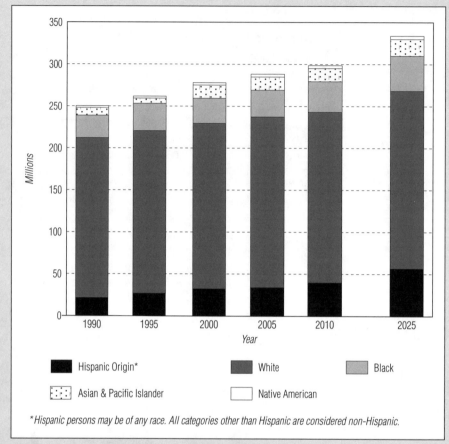

Source of data: U.S. Bureau of the Census, *Statistical Abstract of the United States: 1997* (117th edition). Washington, DC, 1997.

That isn't the only change likely. Since its inception, the United States has experienced numerous changes in ethnic composition. The changes experienced in the latter half of the twentieth century will continue into the first quarter of the next century. Exhibit 9-B shows population projections by ethnicity to the year 2025. Even though the non-Hispanic white population will continue to be the largest major ethnic group, Hispanic and Asian populations are projected to increase much more rapidly.

Exhibit 9-C compares projected population growth for five ethnic groups in the United States between the years 2000 and 2025. Non-Hispanic Asians and Pacific Islanders are expected to almost double, as are persons of Hispanic origin. The non-Hispanic blacks and non-Hispanic Native Americans are projected to increase much less than the two former populations, yet they are expected to increase more rapidly than the non-Hispanic white population.

What are some of the implications of this changing ethnicity for families? Family customs, values, behaviors, and rituals are loosely linked to ethnicity. So, with increased interaction among individuals from various ethnic groups, we can expect to see changes in "American" family culture overall, as well as changes

Exhibit 9-C

Projected Growth
of Ethnic Groups

*United States:
2000–2025*

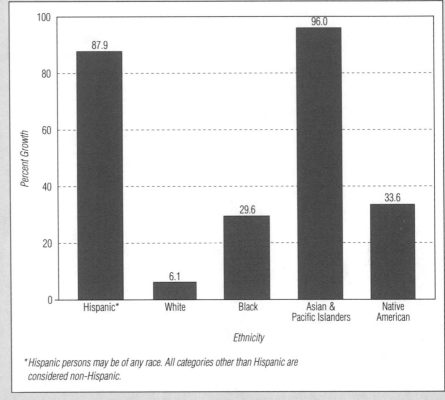

*Hispanic persons may be of any race. All categories other than Hispanic are
considered non-Hispanic.

Source of data: U.S. Bureau of the Census, *Statistical Abstract of the United States: 1997* (117th edition). Washington, DC,
1997.

in the family cultures specific to each ethnic group. Also, increasing numbers of marriages between persons
of different ethnic groups has resulted in more individuals who consider themselves to have more than one
ethnic identity. When people identify with more than one ethnic group, their values, norms, and behaviors
very likely reflect more than one ethnic culture.

Because of the growing numbers of "biracial" or "multi-ethnic" individuals, the U.S. Census is changing the way it determines ethnicity. (See Issue 6.) For the first time, the U.S. Census in the year 2000 will allow individuals to mark more than one ethnicity. Projections such as the ones in Exhibits 9-B and 9-C may
need to be modified, therefore, to take account of persons with multiple ethnic identities. Furthermore, the
United States equates the ethnic identity of a household with the ethnic identity of the householder. This
practice may also need to be modified as more and more households consist of persons with different
ethnicities.

Questions for Further Study

1. **One significant trend in the U.S. population is the aging of the baby boom cohort (persons born between 1946 and 1964). How will the growing numbers of middle-aged and**

older persons in the beginning of the next century affect changes in the composition of households, as shown in Exhibit 9-A?

2. The growing ethnic diversity of the American population is likely to increase the incidence of intermarriage between persons of different races or ethnicities. In what ways do multi-ethnic families incorporate customs from both the mother's family and the father's family? Consider your own experience or that of someone you know who has grown up in a multi-ethnic family.

YOUR TURN

One of the key themes of this concluding chapter has been that change is a permanent characteristic of the institution of family. Such change is sometimes the by-product of changes that occur in other areas of society. Other times, the change comes from the purposeful actions of groups of individuals.

Most communities contain people who are active in a major movement for social change that has at its core concern over family roles and responsibilities: the pro-choice movement, the pro-life movement, the women's movement, the welfare reform movement, and so on. Find a few people who are involved in one such movement. Ask them to describe their experiences. What was their motive for joining the movement? What sorts of activities do they participate in? What are the goals they want to accomplish? How does the movement reflect their image of what a family ought to be? Do they feel the movement has been effective in accomplishing its goals? If not, why not? What else needs to be done? What do they feel they've personally accomplished?

Try to attend a gathering in which a movement addressing family needs is involved. It might be an organizational meeting, a town council meeting, a protest march, or a demonstration. What happened at the gathering? What seemed to be the overall atmosphere? Was it festive? solemn? angry? businesslike? Was any opposition present?

What do such movements tell us about the nature of families and their relationship to broader elements of social change?

BIBLIOGRAPHY

Abbey, A., Ross, L. T., McDuffie, D., & McAuslan, P. 1996. "Alcohol and dating risk factors for sexual assault among college women." *Psychology of Women Quarterly, 20,* 147–169.

Abell, E., Clawson, M., Washington, W. N., Bost, K. K., & Vaughn, B. E. 1996. "Parenting values, attitudes, behaviors and goals of African American mothers from a low-income population in relation to social and societal contexts." *Journal of Family Issues, 17,* 593–613.

Abrams, A., & Herman, K. 1994. "Antioch is not legislating 'sexual correctness.'" *Chronicle of Higher Education,* January 26.

Acker, J. 1978. "Issues in the sociological study of women's work." In A. H. Stromberg & S. Harkees (Eds.), *Women working.* Palo Alto, CA: Mayfield.

Acock, A. C., & Demo, D. H. 1994. *Family diversity and well-being.* Thousand Oaks, CA: Sage.

Adamec, C., & Pierce, W. L. 1991. *The encyclopedia of adoption.* New York. Facts on File.

Adams, B. 1968. *Kinship in an urban setting.* Chicago: Markham Publishing.

Adelson, J. 1996. "Splitting up." *Commentary,* September, 63–66.

Adler, J. 1994. "Kids growing up scared." *Newsweek,* January 10.

Ahlburg, D. A., & De Vita, C. J. 1992. "New realities of the American family." *Population Bulletin, 47,* 2–42.

Ahrons, C. R., & Rodgers, R. H. 1987. *Divorced families: A multidisciplinary developmental view.* New York: Norton.

Albert, S. M. 1990. "Caregiving as a cultural system: Conceptions of filial obligation and parental dependency in urban America." *American Anthropologist, 92,* 319–331.

Aldous, J. 1995. "New views of grandparents in intergenerational context." *Journal of Family Issues, 16,* 104–122.

Aldous, J., & Dumon, W. 1990. "Family policy in the 1980's: Controversy and consensus." *Journal of Marriage and the Family, 52,* 1136–1151.

Alksnis, C., Desmarais, S., & Wood, E. 1996. "Gender differences in scripts for different types of dates." *Sex Roles, 34,* 321–336.

Allen, A. L. 1988. *Uneasy access: Privacy for women in a free society.* Totowa, NJ: Rowman & Littlefield.

Allen, C. M., & Straus, M. A. 1980. "Resources, power and husband-wife violence." In M. A. Straus & G. T. Hotaling (Eds.), *The social causes of husband-wife violence.* Minneapolis: University of Minnesota Press.

Allen, J. 1993. "Boys: Hanging with the Spur Posse." *Rolling Stone,* July 8–22.

Allen, K. R., & Demo, D. H. 1995. "The families of lesbians and gay men: A new frontier in family research." *Journal of Marriage and the Family, 57,* 111–127.

Allen, W. 1978. "The search for applicable theories of black family life." *Journal of Marriage and the Family, 40,* 111–129.

Altman, D. 1979. *Coming out in the seventies.* Sydney, Australia: Wild & Wooley.

Altman, D., & Ginat, J. 1996. *Polygamous families in contemporary society.* New York: Cambridge University Press.

Altman, I., & Taylor, D. A. 1973. *Social penetration: The development of interpersonal relationships.* New York: Holt, Rinehart & Winston.

Altman, L. K. 1997. "AIDS deaths drop 19% in U.S., continuing a heartening trend." *New York Times,* July 15.

Alvarez, L. 1997. "House passes bill to replace system of public housing." *New York Times,* May 5.

Amato, P. R. 1987. "Family processes in one-parent, stepparent, and intact families: The child's point of view." *Journal of Marriage and the Family, 48,* 327–337.

———. 1993. "Children's adjustment to divorce: Theories, hypotheses and empirical support." *Journal of Marriage and the Family, 55,* 22–54.

Amato, P. R., & Booth, A. 1991. "Consequences of parental divorce and marital unhappiness for adult well-being." *Social Forces, 69,* 895–914.

"America's poor showing." 1993. *Newsweek,* October 18.

Ammerman, N. T. 1987. *Bible believers: Fundamentalists in the modern world.* New Brunswick, NJ: Rutgers University Press.

Anderson, E. A., & Koblinsky, S. A. 1995. "Homeless policy: The need to speak to families." *Family Relations, 44,* 13–18.

Anderson, E. A., & Spruill, J. W. 1993. "The dual-career commuter family: A lifestyle on the move." *Marriage and Family Review, 19,* 131–147.

Anderson, L. 1988. "Property rights of same-sex couples: Toward a new definition of family." *Journal of Family Law, 26,* 357–372.

Angier, N. 1995. "If you're really ancient, you may be better off." *New York Times,* March 27.

———. 1997(a). "Sexual identity not pliable after all, report says." *New York Times,* March 14.

———. 1997(b). "New debate over surgery on genitals." *New York Times,* May 13.

———. 1997(c). "Theorists see evolutionary advantages in menopause." *New York Times,* September 16.

Antill, J. K., Goodnow, J. J., Russell, G., & Cotton, S. 1996. "The influence of parents and family context on children's involvement in household tasks." *Sex Roles, 34,* 215–236.

Appell, L. W. R. 1988. "Menstruation among the Rungus of Borneo: An unmarked category." In T. Buckley & A. Gottlieb (Eds.), *Blood magic: The anthropology of menstruation.* Berkeley: University of California Press.

Applebaum, R. P., & Chambliss, W. J. 1995. *Sociology.* New York: HarperCollins.

Applebome, P. 1996(a). "Holding parents legally responsible for the misbehavior of their children." *New York Times,* April 10.

———. 1996(b). "A carrot and stick for parenthood." *New York Times,* June 16.

Arbuthnot, J. 1990. "Fathers' rights." *Dad, 1,* 41.

Archer, D. 1985. "Social deviance." In G. Lindzey & E. Aronson (Eds.), *Handbook of social psychology* (3rd ed., Vol. 2). New York: Random House.

Arditti, J. A., & Madden-Derdich, D. 1997. "Joint and sole custody mothers: Implications for research and practice." *Families in Society, 78,* 36–45.

Arendell, T. 1987. "Women and the economics of divorce in the contemporary United States." *Signs, 13,* 121–135.

———. 1992. "After divorce: Investigations into father absence." *Gender and Society, 6,* 562–586.

———. 1995. *Fathers and divorce.* Thousand Oaks, CA: Sage.

Aries, P. 1962. *Centuries of childhood.* New York: Vintage.

Arras, J. D. 1991. "Beyond Cruzan: Individual rights, family autocracy and the persistent vegetative state." *Journal of the American Geriatrics Society, 39,* 1018–1024.

Atwood, M. 1985. *The handmaid's tale.* New York: Fawcett.

Aulette, J. R. 1994. *Changing families.* Belmont, CA: Wadsworth.

Ayres, B. D. 1996. "Marriage advised in some youth pregnancies." *New York Times,* September 9.

Babbie, E. 1992. *The practice of social research.* Belmont, CA: Wadsworth.

Baca Zinn, M. 1980. "Employment and education of Mexican American women: The interplay of modernity and ethnicity in eight families." *Harvard Educational Review, 50,* 47–62.

———. 1997. "Family, race and poverty." In A. S. Skolnick & J. H. Skolnick (Eds.), *Family in transition* (9th ed.). New York: Longman.

Baca Zinn, M., & Eitzen, D. S. 1996. *Diversity in families.* New York: HarperCollins.

Bailey, B. L. 1988. *From front porch to back seat.* Baltimore: Johns Hopkins University Press.

Baker, P. L. 1997. "And I went back: Battered women's negotiation of choice." *Journal of Contemporary Ethnography, 26,* 55–74.

Ballard, C. 1987. "A humanist sociology approach to teaching social research." *Teaching Sociology, 15,* 7–14.

Balswick, J. O., & Balswick, J. K. 1995. "Gender relations and marital power." In B. B. Ingoldsby & S. Smith (Eds.), *Families in multicultural perspective.* New York: Guilford.

Baltzell, E. D. 1958. *Philadelphia gentleman: The making of a national upper class.* Glencoe, IL: Free Press.

Bane, M. J. 1976. *Here to stay.* New York: Basic Books.

Bane, M. J., & Ellwood, D. 1989. "One fifth of the nation's children: Why are they poor?" *Science, 245,* 1047–1053.

Barich, R. R., & Bielby, D. D. 1996. "Rethinking marriage: Change and stability in expectations, 1967–1994." *Journal of Family Issues, 17,* 136–169.

Barker, K. 1993. "Changing assumptions and contingent solutions: The costs and benefits of women working full- and part-time." *Sex Roles, 28,* 47–71.

Barnett, R. C., & Rivers, C. 1992. "The myth of the miserable working women." *Working Woman,* February.

Barone, C., Ickoviis, J. R., Ayers, T. S., Katz, S. M., Voyce, C. K., & Weissberg, R. P. 1996. "High-risk sexual behavior among young urban students." *Family Planning Perspectives, 28,* 69–74.

Barrett, N. 1987. "Women and the economy." In S. E. Rix (Ed.), *The American woman, 1987–88.* New York: Norton.

Barry, J. B. 1993. "Daddytrack." *Utne Reader,* May/June, 70–73.

Bartholet, E. 1993(a). *Family bonds.* Boston: Houghton Mifflin.

———. 1993(b). "Where do black children belong? The politics of race matching in adoption." In M. Minow (Ed.), *Family matters.* New York: New Press.

Bassuk, E. L., Rubin, L., & Lauriat, A. S. 1986. "Characteristics of sheltered homeless families." *American Journal of Public Health, 76,* 1079–1101.

Beal, C. R. 1994. *Boys and girls: The development of gender roles.* New York: McGraw-Hill.

Bean, F. D., & Tienda, M. 1987. *The Hispanic population in the United States.* New York: Russell Sage.

Becerra, R. N. 1992. "Mexican American families." In J. M. Heuslin (Ed.), *Marriage and family in a changing society.* New York: Free Press.

Beck, M. 1990. "Be nice to your kids." *Newsweek,* March 12.

Becker, G. S. 1981. *A treatise on the family.* Cambridge, MA: Harvard University Press.

Beckett, J. O. 1976. "Working wives: A racial comparison." *Social Work, 21,* 463–471.

Beekman, D. 1977. *The mechanical baby: A popular history of the theory and practice of child raising.* Westport, CT: Lawrence Hill.

Beer, W. R. 1988. *Relative strangers: Studies of stepfamily processes.* Totowa, NJ: Rowan & Littlefield.

Belkin, L. 1989. "Bars to equality of sexes seen as eroding, slowly." *New York Times,* August 20.

Bell, D. J., & Bell, S. L. 1991. "The victim-offender relationship as a determinant factor in police dispositions of family violence incidents: A replication study." *Policing and Society, 1,* 225–234.

Bellah, R. N. 1995. "The quest for self." In A. Etzioni (Ed.), *Rights and the common good.* New York: St. Martin's Press.

Bellah, R. N., Madsen, R., Sullivan, W. M., Swidler, A., & Tipton, S. M. 1985. *Habits of the heart.* New York: Harper & Row.

Belluck, P. 1998. "Heartache frequently visits parents with multiple births." *New York Times,* January 3.

Belsky, J. 1988. "The effects of infant day care reconsidered." *Early Childhood Research Quarterly, 3,* 235–272.

———. 1990. "Infant day care, child development, and family policy." *Society,* July/August, 10–12.

Belsky, J., & Kelly, J. 1994. *The transition to parenthood: How a first child changes a marriage; Why some couples grow closer and others apart.* New York: Delacorte.

Bem, S. L. 1974. "The measurement of psychological androgyny." *Journal of Consulting and Clinical Psychology, 42,* 155–162.

Bennett, N. G., Bloom, D. E., & Craig, P. H. 1986. *Black and white marriage patterns: Why so different?* (Discussion paper No. 500). New Haven, CT: Economic Growth Center, Yale University.

Benokraitis, N. V., & Fegin, J. R. 1993. "Sex discrimination: Subtle and covert." In J. Henslin (Ed.), *Down-to-earth sociology.* New York: Free Press.

Berger, P. L., & Kellner, H. 1964. "Marriage and the construction of reality: An exercise in the microsociology of knowledge." *Diogenes, 46,* 1–23.

Bernard, J. 1981. "The good provider role: Its rise and fall." *American Psychologist, 36,* 1–12.

———. 1982. *The future of marriage.* New York: Bantam.

Bernhardt, A., Morris, M., & Handcock, M. S. 1995. "Women's gains or men's losses? A closer look at the shrinking gender gap in earnings." *American Journal of Sociology, 101,* 302–328.

Bertoia, C., & Drakich, J. 1993. "The father's rights movement." *Journal of Family Issues, 14,* 592–615.

Besharov, D. J. 1993. "Overreporting and underreporting are twin problems." In R. J. Gelles & D. R. Loeske (Eds.), *Current controversies on family violence.* Newbury Park, CA: Sage.

Best, J. 1993. *Threatened children.* Chicago: University of Chicago Press.

Beutler, I. F., Burr, W. R., Bahr, K. S., & Herrin, D. A. 1989. "The family realm: Theoretical contributions for understanding its uniqueness." *Journal of Marriage and the Family, 51,* 805–815.

Bianchi, S. M., & Spain, D. 1986. *American women in transition.* New York: Russell Sage.

———. 1996. "Women, work and family in America." *Population Bulletin, 51,* 2–47.

Biernat, M., & Wortman, C. B. 1991. "Sharing of home responsibilities between professionally employed women and their husbands." *Journal of Personality and Social Psychology, 60,* 844–860.

Birchler, G. R., Weiss, R. L., & Vincent, J. P. 1975. "Multimethod analysis of social reinforcement exchange between maritally distressed and non-distressed spouse and stranger dyads." *Journal of Personality and Social Psychology, 31,* 349–360.

"Black or white." 1994. *The Economist,* May 14.

Blackwell, J. E. 1985. *The black community: Diversity and unity.* New York: Harper & Row.

Blakeslee, S. 1991. "The male link to birth defects figures." *American Health,* April.

Blank, R. H. 1993. "Reproductive technology: Pregnant women, the fetus and the courts." *Women and Politics, 13,* 1–17.

Blankenhorn, D. 1990. "The family in transition." In D. Blankenhorn, S. Bayne, & J. B. Elshtain (Eds.), *Rebuilding the nest: A new commitment to the American family.* Milwaukee, WI: Family Service America.

Blau, P. M. 1964. *Exchange and power is social life.* New York: Wiley.

Blau, P. M., & Duncan, O. D. 1967. *The American occupational structure.* New York: Wiley.

Blood, R. O., & Wolfe, D. M. 1960. *Husbands and wives.* New York: Free Press.

Blumberg, R. L., & Coleman, M. T. 1989. "A theoretical look at the gender balance of power in the American couple." *Journal of Family Issues, 10,* 225–250.

Blumstein, P., & Kollock, P. 1988. "Personal relationships." *Annual Review of Sociology, 14,* 467–490.

Blumstein, P., & Schwartz, P. 1983. *American couples.* New York: Morrow.

"The body counters." 1993. *People Weekly,* April 12, 34–37.

Boudreau, F. A. 1993. "Elder abuse." In R. L. Hampton et al. (Eds.), *Family violence: Prevention and treatment.* Newbury Park, CA: Sage.

Boulding, E. 1976. "Familial constraint on women's work roles." *Signs, 1,* 95–118.

Bound, J., Duncan, G., Laren, D., & Oleinick, L. 1991. "Poverty dynamics in widowhood." *Journal of Gerontology, 46,* 115–124.

Bowker, L. H. 1993. "A battered woman's problems are social, not psychological." In R. J. Gelles & D. R. Loeske (Eds.), *Current controversies on family violence.* Newbury Park, CA: Sage.

Boxer, S. 1997. "One casualty of the women's movement: Feminism." *New York Times,* December 14.

Brabant, S., Forsyth, C. J., McFarlain, G. 1994. "Defining the family after the death of a child." *Death Studies, 18,* 197–206.

Bradsher, K. 1995(a). "Gap in wealth in U.S. called widest in west." *New York Times,* April 17.

———. 1995(b). "Sluggish income figures show modest gains for some groups." *New York Times,* July 22.

———. 1996. "Rich control more of U.S. wealth, study says, as debt grows for poor." *New York Times,* June 22.

Brehm, S. 1992. *Intimate relationships.* New York: McGraw-Hill.

Breslau, K. 1990. "Overplanned parenthood." *Newsweek,* January 22.

Brewer, R. M. 1988. "Black women in poverty: Some comments on female-headed households." *Signs, 13,* 331–339.

Brines, J. 1994. "Economic dependency, gender and the division of labor at home." *American Journal of Sociology, 100,* 652–688.

Brody, J. E. 1991. "Children of divorce: Actions to help, can hurt, study finds." *New York Times,* July 11.

Bronner, E. 1998. "U.S. 12th graders rank poorly in math and science, study says." *New York Times,* February 25.

Brown, D., & Bryant, J. 1990. "Effects of television on family values and selected attitudes and behaviors." In J. Bryant (Ed.), *Television and the American family.* Hillsdale, NJ: Lawrence Erlbaum.

Brown, R. 1986. *Social psychology.* New York: Free Press.

Browne, A. 1993. "Family violence and homelessness: The relevance of trauma histories in the lives of homeless women." *American Journal of Orthopsychiatry, 63,* 370–384.

Buckley, T., & Gottlieb, A. 1988. "A critical appraisal of theories of menstrual symbolism." In T. Buckley & A. Gottlieb (Eds.), *Blood magic: The anthropology of menstruation.* Berkeley: University of California Press.

Bumiller, E. 1992. "First comes marriage—then maybe love." In J. M. Henslin (Ed.), *Marriage and family in a changing society.* New York: Free Press.

Bumpass, L. 1990. "What's happening to the family? Interactions between demographic and institutional change." *Demography, 27,* 483–498.

Bumpass, L., Sweet, J., & Castro Martin, T. 1990. "Changing patterns of remarriage." *Journal of Marriage and the Family, 52,* 747–756.

Burnham, M. 1993. "An impossible marriage: Slave law and family law." In M. Minow (Ed.), *Family matters: Readings on family lives and the law.* New York: New Press.

Burtt, S. 1994. "Reproductive responsibilities: Rethinking the fetal rights debate." *Policy Sciences, 27,* 179–196.

Buss, D. M. 1994. *The evolution of desire: Strategies of human mating.* New York: Basic Books.

Bussell, D. A. 1994. "Ethical issues in observational family research." *Family Process, 33,* 361–376.

Butler, A. 1996. "The effect of welfare benefit levels on poverty among single-parent families." *Social Problems, 43,* 94–115.

Butler, R. 1975. *Why survive? Being old in America.* New York: Harper & Row.

———. 1989. "A generation at risk: When the baby boomers reach Golden Pond." In W. Feigelman (Ed.), *Sociology full circle.* New York: Holt, Rinehart & Winston.

Butterfield, F. 1997. "1995 data show sharp drop in reported rapes." *New York Times,* February 3.

Cancian, F. 1986. "The femininity of love." *Signs, 11,* 692–709.

———. 1987. *Love in America.* Cambridge, MA: Cambridge University Press.

———. 1993. "Gender politics: Love and power in the private and public spheres." In B. J. Fox (Ed.), *Family patterns: Gender relations.* Toronto: Oxford University Press.

Cancian, F., & Gordon, S. C. 1988. "Changing emotion norms in marriage: Love and anger in U.S. women's magazines since 1900." *Gender and Society, 2,* 308–342.

"Can't sue negligent officials in abuse cases, court rules." 1989. *Los Angeles Times,* February 22.

Cantor, M. G. 1991. "The American family on television: From Molly Goldberg to Bill Cosby." *Journal of Comparative Family Studies, 22,* 205–216.

Carlson, B. E. 1996. "Dating violence: Student beliefs about consequences." *Journal of Interpersonal Violence, 11,* 3–18.

Carr, B. J. 1988. *Crisis in intimacy.* Pacific Grove, CA: Brooks/Cole.

Carter, H., & Glick, P. C. 1976. *Marriage and divorce: A social and economic study.* Cambridge, MA: Harvard University Press.

Cavalli-Sforza, L. 1994. *The history and geography of human genes.* Princeton, NJ: Princeton University Press.

Cazenave, N. A., & Straus, M. A. 1990. "Race, class, network embeddedness, and family violence: A search for potent support systems." In M. A. Straus & R. J. Gelles (Eds.), *Physical violence in American families.* New Brunswick, NJ: Transaction.

Chafetz, J. S. 1978. *A primer on the construction and testing of theories in sociology.* Itasca, IL: Peacock.

Chafetz, J. S., & Dworkin, A. G. 1987. "In the face of threat: Organized anti-feminism in comparative perspective." *Gender and Society, 1,* 33–60.

Charon, J. 1992. *Ten questions: A sociological perspective.* Belmont, CA: Wadsworth.

Chasnoff, I. J. 1989. "Cocaine, pregnancy and the neonate." *Women and Health, 15,* 23–25.

Chasnoff, I. J., Landress, H. J., & Barrett, M. E. 1990. "The prevalence of illicit drug or alcohol use during pregnancy and discrepancies in mandatory reporting in Pinellas County, Florida." *New England Journal of Medicine, 332,* 1202–1206.

Cherlin, A. J. 1990. "The strange career of the 'Harvard-Yale study.'" *Public Opinion Quarterly, 54,* 117–124.

———. 1992. *Marriage, divorce, remarriage.* Cambridge, MA: Harvard University Press.

Cherlin, A. J., Chase-Landale, P. L., & McRae, C. 1998. "Effects of parental divorce on mental health throughout the life course." *American Sociological Review, 63,* 239–249.

Cherlin, A. J., & Furstenberg, F. F. 1987. *The new American grandparent: A place in the family, a life apart.* New York: Basic Books.

———. 1994. "Stepfamilies in the United States: A reconsideration." *Annual Review of Sociology, 20,* 359–381.

———. 1997. "The future of grandparenthood." In M. Hutter (Ed.) *The family experience.* Boston: Allyn & Bacon.

Cherlin, A. J., Furstenberg, F. F., Chase-Landale, P. L., Kiernan, K. E., Robins, P. K., Morrison, D. R., & Teitler, J. O. 1991. "Longitudinal studies of effects of divorce on children in Great Britain and the United States." *Science, 252,* 1386–1389.

"Child abuse a growing problem, report says." 1996. *CNN On-line,* September 18. (www.CNN.com).

"Child care caste system." 1998. *New York Times Magazine,* April 5.

Chilman, C. S. 1995. "Hispanic families in the United States: Research perspectives." In M. R. Rank & E. L. Kain (Eds.), *Diversity and change in families: Patterns, prospects and policies.* Englewood Cliffs, NJ: Prentice-Hall.

Chira, S. 1993. "Census data show rise in child care by fathers." *New York Times,* September 22.

———. 1995. "Struggling to find stability when divorce is a pattern." *New York Times,* March 19.

Chodorow, N. 1986. "Family structure and feminine personality." In L. Richardson, & V. Taylor (Eds.), *Feminist frontiers II: Rethinking sex, gender and society.* New York: Random House.

Christensen, B. J. 1990. *Utopia against the family.* San Francisco: Ignatius Press.

Ciancanelli, P., & Berch, B. 1987. "Gender and the GNP." In B. B. Hess & M. M. Ferree (Eds.), *Analyzing gender: A handbook of social science research.* Newbury Park, CA: Sage.

Cicirelli, V. G. 1983. "Adult children and their elderly parents." In T. H. Brubaker (Ed.), *Family relationships in later life.* Beverly Hills, CA: Sage.

Clark, C. S. 1996. "Marriage and divorce." *CQ Researcher,* May 10.

Clark, K. B., & Clark, M. P. 1947. "Racial identification and preference in Negro children." In T. M. Newcomb & E. L. Hartley (Eds.), *Readings in social psychology.* New York: Holt.

Clymer, A. 1997. "Child-support collection net usually fails." *New York Times,* July 17.

Colapinto, J. 1997. "The true story of John/Joan." *Rolling Stone,* December 11.

Coleman, V. E. 1996. "Lesbian battering: The relationship between personality and the perpetration of violence." In L. K. Hamberger & C. Renzetti (Eds.), *Domestic partner abuse.* New York: Springer.

Collins, R. 1985. "Women and men in the class structure." *Journal of Family Issues, 9,* 27–50.

———. 1992. *Sociological insight: An introduction to non-obvious sociology.* New York: Oxford University Press.

Collins, R., & Coltrane, S. 1995. *Sociology of marriage and the family.* Chicago: Nelson-Hall.

Coltrane, S. 1989. "Household labor and the routine production of gender." *Social Problems, 36,* 473–490.

———. 1996(a). *Gender and families.* Thousand Oaks, CA: Pine Forge Press.

———. 1996(b). *Family man.* New York: Oxford University Press.

Coltrane, S., & Hickman, N. 1992. "The rhetoric of rights and needs: Moral discourse in the reform of child custody and child support laws." *Social Problems, 39,* 400–420.

Comer, J. P., & Poussaint, A. F. 1992. *Raising black children.* New York: Plume.

Cook, S. L. 1995. "Acceptance and expectation of sexual aggression in college students." *Psychology of Women Quarterly, 19,* 181–194.

Coontz, S. 1992. *The way we never were.* New York: Basic Books.

———. 1996. "Where are the good old days?" *Modern Maturity,* May/June.

———. 1997. *The way we really are.* New York: Basic Books.

Corsaro, W. A. 1997. *The sociology of childhood.* Thousand Oaks, CA: Pine Forge Press.

Cose, E. 1995. "Black men and black women." *Newsweek,* June 5.

Cowan, C. P., & Cowan, P. A. 1992. *When partners become parents.* New York: Basic Books.

Cowan, R. S. 1987. "Women's work, housework and history: The historical roots of inequality in work-force participation." In N. Gertsel & H. E. Gross (Eds.), *Families and work.* Philadelphia: Temple University Press.

———. 1991. "More work for mother: The postwar years." In L. Kramer (Ed.), *The sociology of gender.* New York: St. Martin's Press.

Cowley, G. 1997. "Gender limbo." *Newsweek,* May 19.

Cox, C. L., Wexler, M. O., Rusbult, C. E., & Gaines, S. O. 1997. "Prescriptive support and commitment processes in close relationships." *Social Psychology Quarterly, 60,* 79–90.

Crossette, B. 1995. "Female genital mutilation by immigrants is becoming cause for concern in U.S." *New York Times,* December 10.

Cunningham, J. A., Strassberg, D. S., & Haan, B. 1986. "Effects of intimacy and sex-role congruency on self-disclosure." *Journal of Social and Clinical Psychology, 4,* 393–401.

Dalley, G. 1988. *Ideologies of caring.* London: Macmillan.

Dane, B. O. 1991. "Anticipatory mourning of middle-aged parents of adult children with AIDS." *Families in Society, 72,* 108–115.

Daniels, C. R. 1993. *At women's expense: State power and the politics of fetal rights.* Cambridge, MA: Harvard University Press.

D'Antonio, W. V. 1983. "Family life, religion and societal values and structures." In W. V. D'Antonio & J. Aldous (Eds.), *Families and religion: Conflict and change in modern society.* Newbury Park, CA: Sage.

Dardick, G. 1993. "The long haul." *Utne Reader,* May/June.

Darity, W. A., & Meyers, S. L. 1984. "Does welfare dependency cause female hardship? The case of the black family." *Journal of Marriage and the Family, 46,* 765–779.

Darton, N. 1991. "The end of innocence." *Newsweek* [special summer issue].

Davidson, C. N. 1986. "A feminist '1984.'" *Ms. Magazine,* February.

Davis, F. J. 1991. *Who is black?* University Park: Pennsylvania State University Press.

Davis, P. W. 1991. "Stranger intervention into child punishment in public places." *Social Problems, 38,* 227–246.

Dawson, J. M., & Langan, P. A. 1994. "Murder in families." *Bureau of Justice Statistics Special Report, July.* Washington, DC: Government Printing Office.

"Day care costs mother custody of daughter, 3." 1994. *New York Times,* July 27.

Deal, J. E. 1995. "Utilizing data from multiple family members: A within-family approach." *Journal of Marriage and the Family, 57,* 1109–1121.

Della Fave, L. R. 1980. "The meek shall not inherit the earth: Self-evaluation and the legitimacy of stratification." *American Sociological Review, 45,* 955–971.

DeMaris, A., & Longmore, M. A. 1996. "Ideology, power and equity: Testing competing explanations for the perception of fairness in household labor." *Social Forces, 74,* 1043–1071.

DeMaris, A., & Rao, V. 1992. "Pre-marital cohabitation and subsequent marital stability in the United States: A reassessment." *Journal of Marriage and the Family, 55,* 399–407.

deMause, L. 1975. "Our forebears made childhood a nightmare." *Psychology Today, 8,* 85–88.

Demick, B. 1996. "Albanian 'virgins.'" *Indianapolis Star,* August 25.

D'Emilio, J., & Freedman, E. B. 1988. *Intimate matters: A history of sexuality in America.* New York: Harper & Row.

Demo, D. H., & Acock, A. C. 1993. "Family diversity and the division of domestic labor: How much have things really changed?" *Family Relations, 42,* 323–333.

Democratic National Committee. 1996. *Convention transcripts,* Official DNC website: www.DNC96.org, August 27.

Demos, J. 1970. *A little commonwealth.* New York: Oxford University Press.

———. 1986. *Past, present and personal: The family and life course in American history.* New York: Oxford University Press.

Denny, E. 1994. "Liberation or oppression? Radical feminism and in vitro fertilization." *Sociology of Health and Illness, 16,* 62–80.

Dentzer, S. 1991. "The graying of Japan." *U.S. News and World Report,* September 30.

DeParle, J. 1990. "In debate over who is poor, fairness becomes the issue." *New York Times,* September 3.

———. 1996. "Slamming the door." *New York Times Magazine,* October 20.

———. 1997(a). "Learning poverty first hand." *New York Times Magazine,* April 27.

———. 1997(b). "U.S. welfare system dies as state programs emerge." *New York Times,* June 30.

Derlega, V. J., Harris, M. S., & Chaikin, A. L. 1973. "Self-disclosure reciprocity, liking and the deviant." *Journal of Experimental Social Psychology, 9,* 277–284.

Deutsch, H. 1945. *The psychology of women.* New York: Grune & Stratton.

De Vita, C. J. 1996. "The United States at mid-decade." *Population Bulletin, 50,* 2–44.

De Witt, K. 1992. "Quayle contends homosexuality is a matter of choice, not biology." *New York Times,* September 14.

Diamond, D. 1996. "Keeping tabs on teens." *USA Weekend,* August 30–September 1.

Diamond, J. 1994. "Race without color." *Discover,* November, 82–89.

Dickson, L. 1993. "The future of marriage and family in black America." *Journal of Black Studies, 23,* 472–491.

Dietz, T. L. 1995. "Patterns of intergenerational assistance within the Mexican American family: Is the family taking care of the older generation's needs?" *Journal of Family Issues, 16,* 344–356.

Dill, B. T. 1995. "Our mothers' grief: Racial ethnic women and the maintenance of families." In M. L. Anderson

& P. H. Collins (Eds.), *Race, class, and gender: An anthology.* Belmont, CA: Wadsworth.

Dill, B. T., Baca Zinn, M., & Patton, S. 1994. "Feminism, race and the politics of family values." Report from the *Institute for Philosophy and Public Policy, 13,* 13–18.

DiMaggio, P. J., & Powell, W. W. 1991. "Introduction." In W. W. Powell & P. J. DiMaggio (Eds.). *The new institutionalism in organizational analysis.* Chicago: University of Chicago Press.

DiNitto, D. M., & Dye, T. R. 1987. *Some welfare politics and public policy.* Englewood Cliffs, NJ: Prentice-Hall.

Dion, K. K., & Dion, K. L. 1996. "Cultural perspectives on romantic love." *Personal Relationships, 3,* 5–17.

Domhoff, G. W. 1983. *Who rules America now?* Englewood Cliffs, NJ: Prentice-Hall.

Dornbusch, S. M., Herman, M. R., & Chun Lin, I. 1996. "Single parenthood." *Society,* July/August, 30–32.

Douglas, W., & Olsen, B. M. 1996. "Subversion of the American family? An examination of children and parents in television families." *Communication Research, 23,* 73–99.

Dowd, M. 1983. "Many women in poll value jobs as much as family life." *New York Times,* December 4.

Downs, D. A. 1996. *More than victims: Battered women, the syndrome society, and the law.* Chicago: University of Chicago Press.

Dugger, C. W. 1996(a). "African ritual pain: Genital cutting." *New York Times,* October 5.

———. 1996(b). "Immigrant cultures raising issues of child punishment." *New York Times,* February 29.

Dujon, D., Gradford, J., & Stevens, D. 1995. "Reports from the front: Welfare mothers up in arms." In M. L. Anderson & P. H. Collins (Eds.), *Race, class, and gender: An anthology.* Belmont, CA: Wadsworth.

Duncan, G. J., Brooks-Gunn, J., & Klebanov, P. K. 1994. "Economic deprivation and early childhood development." *Child Development, 65,* 296–318.

Durkheim, E. 1965. *The elementary forms of the religious life.* Trans. by J. W. Swain. New York: Free Press.

Dyssegaard, E. K. 1997. "The Danes call it fresh air." *New York Times,* May 17.

Edin, K., & Jencks, C. 1992. "Reforming welfare." In C. Jencks (Ed.), *Rethinking social policy: Race, poverty and the underclass.* Cambridge, MA: Harvard University Press.

Edin, K., & Lein, L. 1996. "Work, welfare, and single mothers' economic survival strategies." *American Sociological Review, 61,* 253–266.

Edwards, J. N. 1987. "Changing family structure and youthful well-being." *Journal of Family Issues, 8,* 355–372.

Egan, T. 1993. "A cultural gap may swallow a child." *New York Times,* October 12.

———. 1996. "Mail-order marriage, immigrant dreams and death." *New York Times,* May 26.

Eggebeen, D. J., & Hogan, D. P. 1990. "Giving between generations in American families." *Human Nature, 1,* 211–232.

Eggebeen, D. J., & Lichter, D. T. 1991. "Race, family structure, and changing poverty among African American children." *American Sociological Review, 56,* 801–817.

Eggebeen, D. J., Snyder, A. R., & Manning, W. D. 1996. "Children in single-father families in demographic perspective." *Journal of Family Issues, 17,* 441–465.

Ehrenreich, B. 1983. *The hearts of men: American dreams and the flight from commitment.* New York: Anchor.

———. 1990. *Fear of falling.* New York: Harper Perennial.

———. 1994. "Oh, those family values." *Time,* July 8.

———. 1996. "In defense of splitting up." *Time,* April 8.

Ehrenreich, B., & English, D. 1979. *For her own good: 150 years of experts' advice to women.* Garden City, NY: Anchor.

Eitzen, D. S., & Baca Zinn, M. 1991. *In conflict and order: Understanding society.* Boston: Allyn & Bacon.

Elkind, D. 1994. *Ties that stress: The new family imbalance.* Cambridge, MA: Harvard University Press.

Elliot, P. 1996. "Shattering illusions: Same-sex domestic violence." *Journal of Gay and Lesbian Social Services, 4,* 1–8.

Emerson, R. 1962. "Power-dependence relations." *American Sociological Review, 27,* 31–41.

Epstein, C. F. 1988. *Deceptive distinctions: Sex, gender and the social order.* New Haven, CT: Yale University Press.

Ettelbrick, P. L. 1992. "Since when is marriage a path to liberation?" In S. Sherman (Ed.), *Lesbian and gay marriage.* Philadelphia: Temple University Press.

Etzioni, A. 1993. "How to make marriage matter." *Time,* September 6.

———. 1994. *The spirit of community: The reinvention of American society.* New York: Touchstone.

Evans-Pritchard, E. E. 1951. *Kinship and marriage among the Nuer.* Oxford, England: Oxford University Press.

Ewing, C. P. 1987. *Battered women who kill: Psychological self-defense as legal justification.* Lexington, MA: Heath.

Ewing, C. P., & Aubrey, M. 1987. "Battered women and public opinion: Some realities about myths." *Journal of Family Violence, 2,* 257–264.

Ewing, W. 1992. "The civic advocacy of violence." In M. S. Kimmel & M. A. Messner (Eds.), *Men's lives.* New York: Macmillan.

"Excerpt from the Antioch College sexual-offensive policy." 1995. In A. M. Stan (Ed.), *Debating sexual correctness.* New York: Delta.

Fadiman, A. 1997. *The spirit catches you and you fall down.* New York: Farrar, Straus & Giroux.

Faison, S. 1995. "In China, rapid social changes bring a surge in the divorce rate." *New York Times,* August 22.

"Faith healers sentenced in daughter's death." 1997. *New York Times,* June 11.

Faludi, S. 1991. *Backlash: The undeclared war against American women.* New York: Crown.

"Family wins right to end their son's ordeal." 1994. *New York Times,* October 18.

Fan, P. 1996. "Indian brothers marry same women for economic gain." *CNN On-line,* September 16. (www.CNN.com).

Farber, B. 1987. "The future of the American family: A dialectical account." *Journal of Family Issues, 8,* 431–433.

Farhi, P. 1992. "Number of millionaires soars." *Washington Post,* July 11.

Farley, R. 1996. *The new American reality: Who we are, how we got here, where we are going.* New York: Russell Sage.

Farley, R., & Bianchi, S. 1991. "The growing racial differences in marriage and family patterns." In R. Staples (Ed.), *The black family: Essays and studies.* Belmont, CA: Wadsworth.

Farnsworth, C. H. 1997. "Facing pain of Aborigines wrested from families, many Australians shrug." *New York Times,* June 8.

Fassin, E. 1993. "Playing by the Antioch rules." *New York Times,* December 26.

Fausto-Sterling, A. 1985. *Myths of gender.* New York: Basic Books.

———. 1993. "How many sexes are there?" *New York Times,* March 12.

Feigelman, W., & Silverman, A. B. 1984. "The long-term effects of transracial adoption." *Social Service Review, 58,* 588–602.

Fein, E. B. 1998. "For lost pregnancies, new rites of mourning." *New York Times,* January 25.

Felmlee, D., Sprecher, S., & Bassin, E. 1990. "The dissolution of intimate relationships: A hazard model." *Social Psychology Quarterly, 53,* 13–30.

Ferraro, K. J., & Johnson, J. M. 1983. "How women experience battering: The process of victimization." *Social Problems, 30,* 325–339.

Ferree, M. M. 1991. "Gender, conflict and change: Family roles in biographical perspective." In W. Heinz (Ed.), *Theoretical advances in life course research.* Weinheim, Germany: Deutscher Studien Verlag.

Feshbach, S., & Feshbach, N. D. 1978. "Child advocacy and family privacy." *Journal of Social Issues, 34,* 168–178.

Fiene, J. I. 1995. "Battered women: Keeping the secret." *Affilia, 10,* 179–193.

Finder, A. 1998. "Evidence is scant that workfare leads to full-time jobs." *New York Times,* April 12.

Fineman, M. A. 1995. *The neutered mother, the sexual family, and other twentieth century tragedies.* New York: Routledge.

Flanzer, J. P. 1993. "Alcohol and other drugs are key causal agents of violence." In R. J. Gelles & D. R. Loeske (Eds.), *Current controversies on family violence.* Newbury Park, CA: Sage.

Flynn, C. P. 1991. "Rethinking joint custody policy: Option or prescription." In E. A. Anderson & R. C. Hula (Eds.), *The reconstruction of family policy.* Westport, CT: Greenwood.

Foote, D. 1998. "And baby makes one." *Newsweek,* February 2.

Foster, D. 1994. "The disease is adolescence." *Utne Reader,* July/August.

Foucault, M. 1990. *The history of sexuality.* New York: Vintage.

Fowlkes, M. 1987. "The myth of merit and male professional careers: The role of wives." In N. Gerstel & H. Gross (Eds.), *Families and work.* Philadelphia: Temple University Press.

Fox, G. L., & Kelly, R. F. 1995. "Determinants of child custody arrangements at divorce." *Journal of Marriage and the Family, 57,* 693–708.

Frank, M., Ziebarth, M., & Field, C. 1982. *The life and times of Rosie the Riveter.* Emeryville, CA: Clarity Educational Productions.

Frankel, M. 1996. "Mom and Pop test for drugs." *The Nation,* January 29.

Franklin, C. W. 1988. *Men and society.* Chicago: Nelson-Hall.

Fraser, J. 1987. "The community, the private, and the individual." *The Sociological Review, 35,* 795–818.

Freeberg, A. L., & Stein, C. H. 1996. "Felt obligation towards parents in Mexican-American and Anglo-American young adults." *Journal of Social and Personal Relationships, 13,* 457–471.

Friedan, B. 1963. *The feminine mystique.* New York: Norton.

Friedman, D. 1995. *Towards a structure of indifference: The social origins of maternal custody.* New York: Aldine de Gryter.

Frisbie, W. P., & Bean, F. D. 1995. "The Latino family in comparative perspective: Trends and current conditions." In C. K. Jacobson (Ed.), *American families: Issues in race and ethnicity.* New York: Garland.

Frye, M. 1992. *Willful virgin: Essays on feminism.* Freedom, CA: Crossing Press.

Furstenberg, F. F. 1997. "Good dads—bad dads: Two faces of fatherhood." In A. S. Skolnick & J. H. Skolnick (Eds.), *Family in transition* (9th ed.). New York: Longman.

Furstenberg, F. F., & Cherlin, A. J. 1991. *Divided families.* Cambridge, MA: Harvard University Press.

Furstenberg, F., & Nord, C. 1985. "Parenting apart: Patterns of childrearing after marital disruption." *Journal of Marriage and the Family, 47,* 893–904.

Gabriel, T. 1996. "High-tech pregnancies test hope's limit." *New York Times,* January 7.

Galambos, N. L., & Maggs, J. L. 1991. "Children in self-care: Figures, facts and fictions." In J. V. Lerner & N. L. Galambos (Eds.), *Employed mothers and their children.* New York: Garland.

Gallagher, M. 1996. *The abolition of marriage.* Washington, DC: Regnery.

Galston, W. A. 1995(a). "A liberal-democratic case for the two-parent family." In A. Etzioni (Ed.), *Rights and the common good.* New York: St. Martin's Press.

———. 1995(b). "Needed: A not-so-fast divorce law." *New York Times,* December 27.

Ganong, L. H., & Coleman, M. 1994. *Remarried family relationships.* Thousand Oaks, CA: Sage.

Gans, H. J. 1995. *The war against the poor.* New York: Basic Books.

Gartrell, N., Hamilton, J., Banks, A., Mosbacher, D., Reed, N., Sparks, C. H., & Bishop, H. 1996. "The national lesbian family study." *American Journal of Orthopsychiatry, 66,* 272–281.

Gelles, R. J. 1987. *Family violence.* Thousand Oaks, CA: Sage.

———. 1995. *Contemporary families: A sociological view.* Thousand Oaks, CA: Sage.

Gelles, R. J., & Straus, M. A. 1988. *Intimate violence.* New York: Touchstone.

Gellott, L. 1985. "Staking claim to the family." *Commonweal, 20,* 488–492.

Genevie, L., & Margolies, E. 1987. *The motherhood report: How women feel about being mothers.* New York: Macmillan.

Gerbner, G., Gross, L., Morgan, M., & Signorielli, N. 1980. *Media and the family: Images and impact.* Washington, DC: White House Conference on the Family, National Research Forum on Family Issues.

Gerson, K. 1985. *Hard choices: How women decide about work, career and motherhood.* Berkeley: University of California Press.

———. 1993. *No man's land: Men's changing commitments to family and work.* New York: Basic Books.

———. 1998. "Dismantling the 'gendered family': Breadwinning, gender, and the family values debate." *Contemporary Sociology, 27,* 228–230.

Gertsel, N. 1987. "Divorce and stigma." *Social Problems, 34,* 172–186.

Gertsel, N., & Gross, H. 1984. *Commuter marriage: A study of work and family.* New York: Guilford Press.

———. 1987. "Commuter marriage: A microcosm of career and family conflict." In N. Gertsel and H. Gross (Eds.), *Commuter marriage: A study of work and family.* New York: Guilford Press.

Gibbs, N. R. 1993(a). "How should we teach our children about SEX?" *Time,* May 24.

———. 1993(b). "Bringing up father." *Time,* June 28.

Gies, F., & Gies, J. 1989. *Marriage and the family in the middle ages.* New York: Harper & Row.

Gill, R. T. 1991. "Family breakdown as family policy." *Public Interest, 110,* 84–91.

Gillespie, C. K. 1989. *Justifiable homicide.* Columbus: Ohio State University Press.

Gillings, A. 1996. "Sleeping with the enemy?" *Village Voice,* July 2.

Gillis, J. R. 1996. *A world of their own making: Myth, ritual and the quest for family values.* New York: Basic Books.

Gladwell, M. 1996. "Black like them." *The New Yorker,* April 29 & May 6.

Gleick, J. 1996. "Big brother is us." *New York Times Magazine,* September 29.

Glenn, E. N., & Yap, S. G. H. 1994. "Chinese American families." In R. L. Taylor (Ed.), *Minority families in the United States.* Englewood Cliffs, NJ: Prentice-Hall.

Glenn, N. 1982. "Interreligious marriage in the United States: Patterns and recent trends." *Journal of Marriage and the Family, 44,* 555–566.

Glenn, N. D., & Supancic, M. 1984. "The social and demographic correlates of divorce and separation in the United States: An update and reconsideration." *Journal of Marriage and the Family, 46,* 563–575.

Glenn, N. D., & Weaver, C. N. 1988. "The changing relationship of marital status to reported happiness." *Journal of Marriage and the Family, 50,* 317–324.

Glick, P. C., & Norton, A. J. 1977. "Marrying, divorcing, and living together in the U.S. today." *Population Bulletin, 32.*

Goffman, E. 1959. *Presentation of self in everyday life.* Garden City, NY: Doubleday.

Goldberg, C. 1997. "Hispanic households struggle as poorest of the poor in United States." *New York Times,* February 2.

Goldberg, S., & Lewis, M. 1969. "Play behavior in the year-old infant: Early sex differences." *Child Development, 40,* 21–31.

Goldscheider, F. K., & Goldscheider, C. 1994. "Leaving and returning home in twentieth-century America." *Population Bulletin, 48,* 1–35.

Goldscheider, F. K., & Waite, L. J. 1991. *New families, no families?* Berkeley: University of California Press.

Golombok, S., Spencer, A., & Rutter, M. 1983. "Children in lesbian and single-parent households: Psychosexual and psychiatric appraisal." *Journal of Child Psychology and Psychiatry, 24,* 551–572.

Golombok, S., & Tasker, F. 1996. "Do parents influence the sexual orientation of their children? Findings from a longitudinal study of lesbian families." *Developmental Psychology, 32,* 3–11.

Golub, S. 1992. *Periods: From menarche to menopause.* Newbury Park, CA: Sage.

Goodchilds, J., Zellman, G., Johnson, P., & Giarusso, R. 1988. "Adolescents and the perceptions of sexual interaction outcomes." In A. W. Burgess (Ed.), *Sexual assault.* New York: Garland.

Goode, E. 1996. "Gender and courtship entitlement: Responses to personal ads." *Sex Roles, 34,* 141–169.

Goode, W. J. 1959. "The theoretical importance of love." *American Sociological Review, 24,* 38–47.

–––. 1963. *World revolution and family patterns.* New York: Free Press.

–––. 1971. "Force and violence in the family." *Journal of Marriage and the Family, 33,* 624–636.

–––. 1981. "Why men resist." In B. Thorne & M. Yalom (Eds.), *Rethinking the family: Some feminist questions.* New York: Longman.

–––. 1993. *World changes in divorce patterns.* New Haven, CT: Yale University Press.

Goodstein, L., & Connelly, M. 1998. "Teen-age poll finds support for tradition." *New York Times,* April 30.

Gordon, L. 1988. *Heroes of their own lives.* New York: Viking.

–––. 1994. *Pitied but not entitled: Single mothers and the history of welfare: 1800–1935.* New York: Free Press.

–––. 1997. "Killing in self-defense." *The Nation,* March 24, 25–28.

Gordon, M. 1964. *Assimilation in American life.* New York: Oxford University Press.

Gordon, M. 1981. "Was Waller ever right? The rating and dating complex reconsidered." *Journal of Marriage and the Family, 43,* 67–76.

Gose, B. 1996. "Public debate over a private choice." *Chronicle of Higher Education,* May 10.

Gottfried, A. E. 1991. "Maternal employment in the family setting: Developmental and environmental issues." In J. V. Lerner & N. L. Galambos (Eds.), *Employed mothers and their children.* New York: Garland.

Gottman, J. S. 1990. "Children of gay and lesbian parents." In F. W. Bozett & M. B. Sussman (Eds.), *Homosexuality and family relations.* New York: Harrington Park Press.

Gough, K. 1971. "The origin of the family." *Journal of Marriage and the Family, 33,* 760–770.

Gove, W., Style, C. B., & Hughes, M. 1990. "The effect of marriage on the well-being of adults." *Journal of Family Issues, 11,* 4–35.

Graham, L. O. 1995. *Member of the club.* New York: HarperCollins.

Green, J. S. 1995. "The days of the dead in Oaxaca, Mexico: An historical inquiry." In J. B. Williamson & E. S. Schneidman (Eds.), *Death: Current perspectives.* Mountain View, CA: Mayfield.

Greene, R., Mandel, J. B., Hotvedt, M. E., Gray, J., & Smith, L. 1986. "Lesbian mothers and their children: A comparison with solo parent heterosexual mothers and their children." *Archives of Sexual Behavior, 15,* 167–183.

Greenhouse, L. 1996. "Christian Scientists rebuffed in ruling by Supreme Court." *New York Times,* January 23.

Greenstein, T. N. 1995. "Are the 'most advantaged' children truly disadvantaged by early maternal employment?" *Journal of Family Issues, 16,* 149–169.

———. 1996(a). "Husbands' participation in domestic labor: Interactive effects of wives' and husbands' gender ideologies." *Journal of Marriage and the Family, 58,* 585–595.

———. 1996(b). "Gender ideology and perceptions of the fairness of the division of labor: Effects on marital quality." *Social Forces, 24,* 1029–1042.

Greil, A. L. 1991. *Not yet pregnant: Infertile couples in contemporary America.* New Brunswick, NJ: Rutgers University Press.

Grella, C. E. 1990. "Irreconcilable differences: Women defining class after divorce and downward mobility." *Gender and Society, 4,* 41–55.

Griffin, J. L. 1993. "Domestic partners getting benefits." *Indianapolis Star,* November 28.

Griffin, S. 1989. "Rape: The all-American crime." In L. Richardson & V. Taylor (Eds.), *Feminist frontiers II.* New York: Random House.

Gringlas, M., & Weinraub, M. 1995. "The more things change . . . single parenting revisited." *Journal of Family Issues, 16,* 194–211.

Griswold, R. L. 1993. *Fatherhood in America: A history.* New York: Basic Books.

Griswold del Castillo, R. 1979. *The Los Angeles Barrio: 1850–1890.* Los Angeles: University of California Press.

Gross, J. 1997. "A new life opens, after prison and battering." *New York Times,* February 18.

Gubrium, J. F., & Holstein, J. A. 1987. "The private image: Experimental location and methods in family studies." *Journal of Marriage and the Family, 49,* 773–786.

———. 1990. *What is family?* Mountain View, CA: Mayfield.

Gutman, H. G. 1978. "Persistent myths about the Afro-American family." In M. Gordon (Ed.), *The American family in social-historical perspective.* New York: St. Martin's Press.

Haas, L. L. 1986. "Wives' orientation toward bread winning: Sweden and the United States." *Journal of Family Issues, 7,* 358–381.

———. 1995. "Household division of labor in industrial societies." In B. B. Ingoldsby & S. Smith (Eds.), *Families in multicultural perspective.* New York: Guilford.

Hacker, A. 1992. *Two nations: Black and white, separate, hostile, unequal.* New York: Charles Scribner's Sons.

Hamer, D., & Coupland, P. 1994. *The science of desire.* New York: Simon & Schuster.

Hareven, T. K. 1978. *Transitions: The family and the life course in historical perspective.* New York: Academic Press.

———. 1992. "American families in transition: Historical perspectives on change." In A. S. Skolnick & J. H. Skolnick (Eds.), *Family in transition* (7th ed.). New York: HarperCollins.

———. 1994. "Aging and generational relations: A historical and life course perspective." *Annual Review of Sociology, 20,* 437–461.

Harkins, E. 1978. "Effects of empty nest transition on self-report of psychological and physical well-being." *Journal of Marriage and the Family, 40,* 549–556.

Harmon, A. 1997. "High-technology: Bliss or bust on vacation?" *New York Times,* July 13.

"Harper's index." 1997. *Harper's Magazine,* February, 13.

Harris, J. R. 1998. *The nurture assumption.* New York: Free Press.

Harris, K. M. 1996(a). "Life after welfare: Women, work, and repeat dependency." *American Sociological Review, 61,* 407–426.

———. 1996(b). "The reforms will hurt, not help, poor women and children." *Chronicle of Higher Education,* October 4.

Harris, K. M., & Marmer, J. K. 1996. "Poverty, parental involvement, and adolescent well-being." *Journal of Family Issues, 17,* 614–640.

Harris, M. 1964. *Patterns of race in the Americas.* New York: Norton.

Harry, J. 1983. "Gay male and lesbian relationships." In E. D. Macklin & R. H. Rubin (Eds.), *Contemporary families and alternative lifestyles: Handbook on theory and research.* Newbury Park, CA: Sage.

Hartman, A. 1994. "Ideological themes in family policy." *Families in Society, 76,* 182–192.

Hartocollis, A. 1997. "The big test comes early." *New York Times,* December 15.

Hashimoto, R., & Takahashi, M. 1995. "Between family obligation and social care: The significance of institutional care for the elderly in Japan." *Journal of Sociology and Social Welfare, 22,* 47–62.

Hatchett, S., & Jackson, J. 1993. "African American extended kin systems." In H. McAdoo (Ed.), *Family ethnicity: Strength in diversity.* Newbury Park, CA: Sage.

Hatchett, S., Veroff, J., & Douvan, E. 1995. "Marital instability among black and white couples in early marriage." In M. B. Tucker & C. Mitchell-Kernen (Eds.), *The decline in marriage among African Americans.* New York: Russell Sage.

Hatfield, E., & Rapson, R. L. 1993. "Historical and cross-cultural perspectives on passionate love and sexual desire." *Annual Review of Sex Research, 4,* 67–97.

Hatfield, E., Traupmann, J., Sprecher, S., Utne, M., & Hay, J. 1985. "Equity and intimate relations: Recent research." In W. Ickes (Ed.), *Compatible and incompatible relationships.* New York: Springer-Verlag.

Hatfield, E., Walster, G. W., & Traupmann, J. 1978. "Equity and premarital sex." *Journal of Personality and Social Psychology, 37,* 82–92.

Hausman, B., & Hammen, C. 1993. "Parenting in homeless families: The double crisis." *American Journal of Orthopsychiatry, 63,* 358–369.

Hays, C. L. 1995. "Increasing shift work challenges child care." *New York Times,* June 8.

Hays, S. 1996. *The cultural contradictions of motherhood.* New Haven, CT: Yale University Press.

Heise, L. 1989. "The global war against women." *Washington Post Magazine,* April 9.

Hendrick, S. S. 1981. "Self-disclosure and marital satisfaction." *Journal of Personality and Social Psychology, 40,* 1150–1159.

Henton, J., Cate, R., Koval, J. E., Lloyd, S. A., & Scott, C.F. 1983. "Romance and violence in dating relationships." *Journal of Family Issues, 4,* 467–482.

Hertz, R. 1986. *More equal than others: Women and men in dual-career marriages.* Berkeley: University of California Press.

Hess, R. D., & Handel, G. 1985. "The family as a psychosocial organization." In G. Handel (Ed.), *The psychosocial interior of the family.* New York: Aldine.

Hessler, P. 1997. "Into the past at China's edge." *New York Times,* May 11.

Hewlett, S. A. 1991. *When the bough breaks: The cost of neglecting our children.* New York: Basic Books.

Hines, P. M., Garcia-Preto, N., McGoldrick, M., Almeida, R., & Weltman, S. 1997. "Intergenerational relationships across cultures." In A. S. Skolnick & J. H. Skolnick (Eds.), *Family in transition* (9th ed.). New York: Longman.

Hitchcock, J. T., & Minturn, L. 1963. "The Rajputs of Khalapur." In B. Whiting (Ed.), *Six cultures: Studying child rearing.* New York: John Wiley & Sons.

Hochman, N. K. S. 1997. "Fathers play larger roles in custody." *New York Times,* April 20.

Hochschild, A. R. 1983. "Attending to codifying and managing feelings: Sex differences in love." In L. Richardson & V. Taylor (Eds.), *Feminist frontiers.* Reading, MA: Addison-Wesley.

———. 1997(a). "The economy of gratitude." In M. Hutter (Ed.), *The family experience: A reader in cultural diversity.* Boston: Allyn & Bacon.

———. 1997(b). *The time bind: When work becomes home and home becomes work.* New York: Metropolitan Books.

Hochschild, A. R., & Machung, A. 1989. *The second shift: Working parents and the revolution at home.* New York: Viking.

Hofferth, S. 1983. *Updating children's life course.* Bethesda, MD: Center for Population Research, National Institute for Child Health and Human Development.

Hoffman, J. 1990. "Pregnant, addicted—and guilty?" *New York Times Magazine,* August 19.

———. 1995. "Divorced fathers make gains in battles to increase rights." *New York Times,* April 26.

Hofstede, G. 1984. *Culture's consequences: International differences in work-related values.* Beverly Hills, CA: Sage.

Hogan, D. P., Eggebeen, D. J., & Clogg, C. C. 1993. "The structure of intergenerational exchanges in American families." *American Journal of Sociology, 98,* 1428–1458.

Hollander, D. 1996. "Nonmarital childbearing in the United States: A government report." *Family Planning Perspectives, 28,* 29–32.

Hollway, W. 1993. "Heterosexual sex: Power and desire for the other." In B. J. Fox (Ed.), *Family patterns, gender relations.* Toronto: Oxford University Press.

Holmes, S. A. 1995. "Bitter racial dispute rages over adoption." *New York Times,* April 13.

———. 1996(a). "Is this what women want?" *New York Times,* December 15.

———. 1996(b). "U.S. reports drop in rate of births to unwed women." *New York Times,* October 5.

———. 1996(c). "Quality of life is up for many blacks." *New York Times,* November 18.

———. 1997(a). "Few back multiracial label, survey by census reaffirms." *New York Times,* May 16.

———. 1997(b). "People can claim more than 1 race on federal forms." *New York Times,* November 30.

Holtzworth-Munroe, A., & Jacobson, N. S. 1985. "Causal attributions of married couples: When do they search for causes? What do they conclude when they do?" *Journal of Personality and Social Psychology, 48,* 1398–1412.

Homans, G. 1961. *Social behavior: Its elementary forms.* New York: Harcourt Brace Jovanovich.

"Home sweet home." 1995. *The Economist,* September, 25–33.

Hood, J. 1983. *Becoming a two-job family.* New York: Praeger.

Hopper, J. 1993. "The rhetoric of motives in divorce." *Journal of Marriage and the Family, 55,* 801–813.

Horowitz, R. 1997. "The expanded family and family honor." In M. Hutter (Ed.), *The family experience: A reader in cultural diversity.* Boston: Allyn & Bacon.

Horton, R. 1995. "Is homosexuality inherited?" *New York Review of Books,* July 13, 36–41.

Houseknecht, S., & Sastry, J. 1996. "Family decline and child well-being: A comparative assessment." *Journal of Marriage and the Family, 58,* 726–739.

Howard, J. A., & Hollander, J. 1997. *Gendered situations, gendered selves.* Newbury Park, CA: Sage.

Howe, N., & Strauss, W. 1992. "The new generation gap." *Atlantic Monthly,* December.

Howes, C. 1990. "Can the age of entry into child care and the quality of child care predict adjustment in kindergarten?" *Developmental Psychology, 29,* 292–303.

Humphreys, L. 1970. *The tearoom trade.* Chicago: Aldine.

Hunt, J. G., & Hunt, L. L. 1987. "Male resistance to role symmetry in dual earner households: Three alternative explanations." In N. Gertsel & H. E. Gross (Eds.), *Families and work.* Philadelphia: Temple University Press.

———. 1990. "The dualities of careers and families: New integrations or new polarizations?" In C. Carlson (Ed.), *Perspectives on the family: History, class and feminism.* Belmont, CA: Wadsworth.

Hunter, A. G. 1997. "Counting on grandmothers: Black mothers' and fathers' reliance on grandmothers for parenting support." *Journal of Family Issues, 18,* 251–269.

Hunter, J. 1991. *Culture wars: The struggle to define America.* New York: Basic Books.

Hyde, J. S. 1984. "How large are gender differences in aggression? A developmental meta-analysis." *Developmental Psychology, 20,* 722–736.

Hyman, A., Schillinger, D., & Lo, B. 1995. "Laws mandating reporting of domestic violence." *Journal of the American Medical Association, 273,* 1781–1787.

Ignatius, A. 1988. "China's birthrate is out of control again as one-child policy fails in rural areas." *Wall Street Journal,* July 14.

"Impact of the family and medical leave law." 1997. *World Almanac.* Mahwah, NJ: World Almanac Books.

Ingrassia, M. 1994. "Virgin cool." *Newsweek,* October 17.

Ingrassia, M., & McCormick, J. 1994. "Why leave children with bad parents?" *Newsweek,* April 25.

Ingrassia, M., & Wingert, P. 1995. "The new providers." *Newsweek,* May 22.

Ishii-Kuntz, M. 1989. "Collectivism or individualism? Changing patterns of Japanese attitudes." *Sociology and Social Research, 73,* 174–179.

Jankowiak, W. R., & Fischer, E. F. 1992. "A cross-cultural perspective on romantic love." *Ethnology, 31,* 149–155.

Janoff-Bulman, R. 1979. "Characterological versus behavioral self-blame: Inquiries into depression and rape." *Journal of Personality and Social Psychology, 37,* 1798–1809.

Jencks, C., & Edin, K. 1995. "Do poor women have a right to bear children?" *American Prospect,* Winter.

John, D., Shelton, B. A., Luschen, K. 1995. "Race, ethnicity, gender and perceptions of fairness." *Journal of Family Issues, 16,* 357–379.

Johnson, A. M. 1992. "Sexual lifestyles and HIV risks." *Nature,* December 3, 400–412.

Johnson, D. 1991. "Polygamists emerge from secrecy, seeking not just peace but respect." *New York Times,* April 9.

———. 1992. "Survey shows number of rapes far higher than official figures." *New York Times,* April 24.

———. 1993. "Pair who left children home alone are freed." *New York Times,* January 1.

———. 1996. "No-fault divorce is under attack." *New York Times,* April 27.

Johnson, F. 1996. "Wedded to an illusion." *Harper's Magazine,* November.

Johnson, J. M. 1995. "Horror stories and the construction of child abuse." In J. Best (Ed.), *Images of issues.* New York: Aldine de Gryter.

Jones, A. 1980. *Women who kill.* New York: Fawcett Columbine.

Julian, T. W., McKenry, P. C., & McKelvey, M. W. 1994. "Cultural variations in parenting: Perceptions of Caucasian, African-American, Hispanic, and Asian-American parents." *Family Relations, 43,* 30–37.

Kagan, J. 1976. *Raising children in modern America: Problems and prospective solutions.* Boston: Little, Brown.

Kagay, M. R., & Elder, J. 1992. "Numbers are no problem for pollsters. Words are." *New York Times,* August 9.

Kain, E. 1990. *The myth of family decline.* Lexington, MA: Lexington Books.

Kalb, C. 1997. "How old is too old?" *Newsweek,* May 5.

Kallgren, C. A., & Caudill, P. J. 1993. "Current transracial adoption practices: Racial dissonance and racial awareness." *Psychological Reports, 72,* 551–558.

Kalmijn, M. 1991(a). "Shifting boundaries: Trends in religious and educational homogamy." *American Sociological Review, 56,* 786–800.

———. 1991(b). "Status homogamy in the United States." *American Journal of Sociology, 97,* 496–523.

———. 1994. "Assortive mating by cultural and economic occupational status." *American Journal of Sociology, 100,* 422–452.

Kamerman, S. B. 1985. "Time out for babies." *Working Mother, 4,* 80–82.

Kamerman, S. B., & Kahn, A. J. 1995. *Starting right: How America neglects its youngest children and what we can do about it.* New York: Oxford University Press.

Kanter, G. K., & Straus, M. A. 1990. "The 'drunken bum' theory of wife beating." In M. A. Straus & R. J. Gelles (Eds.), *Physical violence in American families.* New Brunswick, NJ: Transaction.

Kanter, R. M. 1986 . "Wives." In J. Cole (Ed.), *All-American women: Lines that divide, ties that bind.* New York: Free Press.

Kantrowitz, B. 1993. "Wild in the streets." *Newsweek,* August 2.

Karney, B. R., Davila, J., Cohan, C. L., Sullivan, K. T., Johnson, M. D., & Bradbury, T. N. 1995. "An empirical investigation of sampling strategies in marital research." *Journal of Marriage and the Family, 57,* 909–920.

Karraker, K. H., Vogel, D. A., & Lake, M. A. 1995. "Parents' gender-stereotyped perceptions of newborns: The eye of the beholder revisited." *Sex Roles, 33,* 687–701.

Kart, C. S. 1990. *The realities of aging.* Boston: Allyn & Bacon.

Katz, P. A. 1986. "Modification of children's gender-stereotyped behavior: General issues and research considerations." *Sex Roles, 14,* 591–602.

Kearl, M. C. 1989. *Endings: A sociology of death and dying.* New York: Oxford University Press.

Keller, B. 1997. "Divorce increasingly puts schools in the middle of family conflicts." *Education Week,* April 9.

Kelly, C. E., & Warshafsky, L. 1987. *Partner abuse in gay male and lesbian couples.* Paper presented at the Third National Conference for Family Violence Researchers, July, Durham, NC.

Kennedy, P. 1993. *Preparing for the 21st century.* New York: Random House.

Kerckhoff, A., & Davis, K. E. 1962. "Value consensus and need complementarity in mate selection." *American Sociological Review, 27,* 295–303.

Kershner, R. 1996. "Adolescent attitudes about rape." *Adolescence, 31,* 29–33.

Kessler, S. J., & McKenna, W. 1978. *Gender: An ethnomethodological approach.* Chicago: University of Chicago Press.

Kessler-Harris, A. 1982. *Out to work: A history of wage-earning women in the United States.* New York: Oxford University Press.

Kibria, N. 1994(a). "Vietnamese families in the United States." In R. L. Taylor (Ed.), *Minority families in the United States.* Englewood Cliffs, NJ: Prentice-Hall.

———. 1994(b). "Household structure and family ideologies: The dynamics of immigrant economic adaptation among Vietnamese refugees." *Social Problems, 41,* 81–96.

Kilborn, P. T. 1993, "New jobs lack the old security in time of 'disposable workers.'" *New York Times,* March 15.

———. 1997(a). "Priority on safety is keeping more children in foster care." *New York Times,* April 29.

———. 1997(b). "Child-care solutions in a new world of welfare." *New York Times,* June 1.

———. 1997(c). "Illness is turning into financial catastrophe for more of the uninsured." *New York Times,* August 1.

Kingston, P. W., & Nock, S. L. 1987. "Time together among dual-earner couples." *American Sociological Review, 52,* 391–400.

Kirschner, D. 1992. "Understanding adoptees who kill: Dissociation, patricide and the psychodynamics of adoption." *International Journal of Offender Therapy and Comparative Criminology, 36,* 323–333.

Kitano, H. L. 1976. *Japanese Americans: The evolution of a subculture.* Englewood Cliffs, NJ: Prentice-Hall.

Kitano, H. L., & Daniels, R. 1988. *Asian Americans: Emerging minorities.* Englewood Cliffs, NJ: Prentice-Hall.

Kitano, H. L., Yeung, W., Chai, L., & Hatanaka, H. 1984. "Asian American interracial marriage." *Journal of Marriage and the Family, 46,* 179–190.

Kitcher, P. 1996. "Junior comes out perfect." *New York Times Magazine,* September 29.

Klaff, V. Z. 1995. "The changing Jewish family: Issues of continuity." In C. K. Jacobson (Ed.), *American families: Issues in race and ethnicity.* New York: Garland Press.

Klatch, R. 1991. "Complexities of conservatism: How conservatives understand the world." In A. Wolfe (Ed.), *America at century's end.* Berkeley: University of California Press.

Klawitter, M. M. 1994. "Who gains, who loses from changing U.S. child support policies?" *Policy Sciences, 27,* 197–219.

Klein, D. M., & White, J. M. 1996. *Family theories.* Thousand Oaks, CA: Sage.

Kobrin, J. E. 1991. "Cross-cultural perspectives and research directions for the twenty-first century." *Child Abuse and Neglect, 15,* 67–77.

Kohlberg, L. A. 1966. "A cognitive-developmental analysis of children's sex-role concepts and attitudes." In E. Maccoby (Ed.), *The development of sex differences.* Stanford, CA: Stanford University Press.

Kohn, M. 1979. "The effects of social class on parental values and practices." In D. Reiss & H. A. Hoffman (Eds.), *The American family: Dying or developing.* New York: Plenum.

Kolata, G. 1993. "Strong family aid to elderly is found." *New York Times,* May 3.

———. 1997(a). "A record and big questions as woman gives birth at sixty-three." *New York Times,* April 24.

———. 1997(b). "Clinics enter a new world of embryo 'adoption.' " *New York Times,* November 23.

Kollock, P., & Blumstein, P. 1988. "Personal relationships." *Annual Review of Sociology, 14,* 467–490.

Komarovsky, M. 1962. *Blue-collar marriage.* New Haven, CT: Vintage.

Komter, A. 1989. "Hidden power in marriage." *Gender & Society, 3,* 187–216.

Kondratas, S. A. 1991. "Ending homelessness: Policy challenges." *American Psychologist, 46,* 1226–1231.

Koss, M. P., Gidycz, C. A., & Wisniewski, N. 1987. "The scope of rape: Incidence and prevalence of sexual aggression and victimization in a national sample of higher education students." *Journal of Consulting and Clinical Psychology, 55,* 162–170.

Kranichfeld, M. L. 1987. "Rethinking family power." *Journal of Family Issues, 8,* 42–56.

Kristof, N. D. 1993(a). "China's crackdown on births: A stunning and harsh success." *New York Times,* April 25.

———. 1993(b). "Peasants of China discover new way to weed out girls." *New York Times,* July 21.

———. 1996(a). "Japan is a woman's world, once the front door is shut." *New York Times,* June 19.

———. 1996(b). "Who needs love! In Japan, many couples don't." *New York Times,* February 11.

———. 1996(c). "Do Korean men still beat their wives? Definitely." *New York Times,* December 5.

———. 1996(d). "For rural Japanese, death doesn't break family ties." *New York Times,* September 29.

———. 1997. "Once prized, Japan's elderly feel dishonored and fearful." *New York Times,* August 4.

Kurdek, L. A. 1993. "The allocation of household labor in gay, lesbian, and heterosexual married couples." *Journal of Social Issues, 49,* 127–139.

Kurz, D. 1995. *For richer, for poorer: Mothers confront divorce.* New York: Routledge.

Ladner, J. 1978. *Mixed families: Adopting across racial boundaries.* Garden City, NY: Anchor Press.

Lakoff, R. 1973. "Language and women's place." *Language and Society, 2,* 45–80.

Lamb, M. E. 1987. "Introduction: The emergent American father." In M. E. Lamb (Ed.), *The father's role: Cross-cultural perspectives.* Hillsdale, NJ: Lawrence Erlbaum.

Lamp, F. 1988. "Heavenly bodies: Menses, moon, and rituals of license among the Temne of Sierra Leone." In T. Buckley & A. Gottlieb (Eds.), *Blood magic: The anthropology of menstruation.* Berkeley: University of California Press.

Landis-Kleine, C., Foley, L. A., Nall, L., Padgett, P., & Walters-Palmer, L. 1995. "Attitudes toward marriage and divorce held by young adults." *Journal of Divorce and Remarriage, 23,* 63–73.

Laner, M. R. 1989. *Dating: Delights, discontents and dilemmas.* Salem, WI: Sheffield.

Langman, L. 1988. "Social stratification" In M. B. Sussman & S. K. Steinmetz (Eds.), *Handbook of marriage and the family.* New York: Plenum.

Langston, D. 1992. "Tired of playing monopoly?" In M. L. Anderson & P. H. Collins (Eds.), *Race, class and gender: An anthology.* Belmont, CA: Wadsworth.

LaRossa, R. 1992. "Fatherhood and social change." In M. S. Kimmel & M. A. Messner (Eds.), *Men's lives.* New York: Macmillan.

Larson, M. S. 1996. "Sex roles and soap operas: What adolescents learn about single motherhood." *Sex Roles, 35,* 97–110.

Larzelere, R. E., & Klein, D. M. 1987. "Methodology." In M. B. Sussman & S. K. Steinmetz (Eds.), *Handbook of marriage and the family.* New York: Plenum.

Lasch, C. 1977. *Haven in a heartless world: The family besieged.* New York: Norton.

Laslett, B. 1973. "The family as a public and private institution." *Journal of Marriage and the Family, 35,* 480–492.

Laumann, E. O., Gagnon, J. H., Michael, R. T., & Michaels, S. 1994. *The social organization of sexuality.* Chicago: University of Chicago Press.

Lawson, C. 1991. "A bedtime story that's different." *New York Times,* April 4.

———. 1992. "Who believes in make-believe? Not these new toys." *New York Times,* February 6.

———. 1993. "Stereotypes unravel, but not too quickly, in new toys for 1993." *New York Times,* February 11.

Lee, G. R., & Stone, L. H. 1980. "Mate-selection systems and criteria: Variation according to family structure." *Journal of Marriage and the Family, 42,* 319–326.

Lee, J. A. 1982. "Three paradigms of childhood." *Canadian Review of Sociology and Anthropology, 19,* 591–608.

Lee, S. M., & Yamanaka, K. 1990. "Patterns of Asian American intermarriage and marital assimilation." *Journal of Comparative Family Studies, 21,* 287–305.

Leichter, H. L., Ahmed, D., Barrios, L., Bryce, J., Larsen, E., & Moe, L. 1985. "Family contexts of television." *Educational Communication and Technology Journal, 33,* 26–40.

Leidner, R. 1991. "Serving hamburgers and selling insurance: Gender work and identity in interactive service jobs." *Gender and Society, 5,* 154–177.

Lekachman, R. 1991. "The specter of full employment." In J. H. Skolnick & E. Currie (Eds.), *Crisis in American institutions.* New York: HarperCollins.

Leland, J., & Beals, G. 1997. "In living colors." *Newsweek,* May 5.

Lennon, M. C., & Rosenfield, S. 1994. "Relative fairness and the division of housework: The importance of options." *American Journal of Sociology, 100,* 506–531.

"Lesbian's appeal for custody of son rejected." 1995. *New York Times,* April 22.

Letellier, P. 1996. "Gay and bisexual male domestic violence victimization." In L. K. Hamberger & C. Renzetti (Eds.), *Domestic partner abuse.* New York: Springer.

Levant, R. F., Slatter, S. C., & Loiselle, J. E. 1987. "Fathers' involvement in housework and child care with school-age daughters." *Family Relations, 36,* 152–157.

LeVay, S. 1991. "A difference in hypothalmic structure between heterosexual and homosexual men." *Science,* August 30, 1034–1037.

———. 1996. *Queer science.* Cambridge, MA: MIT Press.

Levine, E. M. 1981. "Middle-class family decline." *Society,* January/February, 72–78.

Levine, G. N., & Rhodes, C. 1981. *The Japanese-American community: A three generation study.* New York: Praeger.

LeVine, R. A., & White, M. 1992. "The social transformation of childhood." In A. S. Skolnick & J. H. Skolnick (Eds.), *Family in transition* (7th ed.). New York: HarperCollins.

Levine, R. V. 1993. "Is love a luxury?" *American Demographies,* February, 27–29.

Levinson, D. 1989. *Family violence in cross-cultural perspective.* Newbury Park, CA: Sage.

Levinson, R. M. 1975. "Sex discrimination and employment practices: An experiment with unconventional job inquiries." *Social Problems, 22,* 533–543.

Levy, B. 1991. *Dating violence: Young women in danger.* Seattle, WA: Seal Press.

Lewin, T. 1989. "Aging parents: Women's burden grows." *New York Times,* November 14.

———. 1990. "Suit over death benefits asks, what is a family?" *New York Times,* September 21.

———. 1991. "Jobless pay for mother." *New York Times,* March 13.

———. 1994(a). "Men whose wives work earn less, studies show." *New York Times,* October 12.

———. 1994(b). "Outrage over 18 months for man who killed his wife in 'heat of passion.'" *New York Times,* October 21.

———. 1995(a). "The decay of families is global, study says." *New York Times,* May 31.

———. 1995(b). "Workers of both sexes make trade-offs for family, study shows." *New York Times,* October 29.

———. 1997(a). "Detention of pregnant women for drug use is struck down." *New York Times,* April 23.

———. 1997(b). "Abuse laws cover fetus, a high court rules." *New York Times,* October 30.

———. 1997(c). "U.S. is divided on adoption, survey of attitudes asserts." *New York Times,* November 9.

———. 1998(a). "Schools are moving to police students' off-campus lives." *New York Times,* February 6.

———. 1998(b). "Study finds that youngest U.S. children are poorest." *New York Times,* March 15.

———. 1998(c). "Birth rates for teen-agers declined sharply in the 90's." *New York Times,* May 1.

———. 1998(d). "From welfare roll to child care worker." *New York Times,* April 29.

Lichter, D. T., Anderson, R. N., & Hayward, M. D. 1995. "Marriage markets and marital choice." *Journal of Family Issues, 16,* 412–431.

Lichter, D. T., & Costanzo, J. A. 1987. "How do demographic changes affect labor force participation of women?" *Monthly Labor Review, 110,* 23–25.

Lichter, D. T., LeClere, F. B., & McLaughlin, D. K. 1991. "Local marriage markets and the marital behavior of black and white women." *American Journal of Sociology, 96,* 843–867.

Lifton, B. J. 1994. *Journey of the adopted self: A quest for wholeness.* New York: Basic Books.

Light, P. 1988. *Baby boomers.* New York: Norton.

Linden, D. W., & Machan, D. 1997. "The disinheritors." *Forbes Magazine,* May 19.

Lindsey, K. 1981. *Friends as family.* Boston: Beacon Press.

Lindsey, L. L. 1997. *Gender roles: A sociological perspective.* Upper Saddle River, NJ: Prentice-Hall.

Linton, R. 1937. "One hundred percent American." *The American Mercury, 40,* 427–429.

Lipman-Blumen, J. 1984. *Gender roles and power.* Englewood Cliffs, NJ: Prentice-Hall.

Lips, H. M. 1993. *Sex and gender: An introduction.* Mountain View, CA: Mayfield.

Lockhart, L. L., White, B. W., Causby, V., & Isaac, A. 1994. "Letting out the secret: Violence in lesbian relationships." *Journal of Interpersonal Violence, 9,* 469–492.

Loe, V. 1997. "New nuptial license gets cool reception." *Indianapolis Star,* September 21.

Loomis, L. S., & Booth, A. 1995. "Multigenerational caregiving and well-being: The myth of the beleaguered sandwich generation." *Journal of Family Issues, 16,* 131–148.

LoPresto, C., Sherman, M., & Sherman, N. 1985. "The effects of a masturbation sermon on high school males' attitudes, false beliefs, guilt, and behavior." *Journal of Sex Research, 21,* 142–156.

Lorber, J. 1989. "Dismantling Noah's Ark." In B. J. Risman & P. Schwartz (Eds.), *Gender in intimate relationships: A microstructural approach.* Belmont, CA: Wadsworth.

———. 1994. *Paradoxes of gender.* New Haven, CT: Yale University Press.

Lorenz, F. O., Simons, R. L., Conger, R. D., Elder, G. H., Johnson, C., & Chao, W. 1997. "Married and recently divorced mothers' stressful events and distress: Tracing change across time." *Journal of Marriage and the Family, 59,* 219–232.

Lubeck, S., & Garrett, P. 1990. "Child care 2000: Policy options for the future." In C. Carlson (Ed.), *Perspectives on the family.* Belmont, CA: Wadsworth.

Ludtke, M. 1997. *On our own: Unmarried motherhood in America.* New York: Random House.

Luker, K. 1984. *Abortion and the politics of motherhood.* Berkeley: University of California Press.

———. 1994. "Dubious conceptions: The controversy over teen pregnancy." In A. S. Skolnick & J. H. Skolnick (Eds.), *Family in transition* (8th ed.). New York: HarperCollins.

———. 1997. "World views of pro-life and pro-choice activists." In D. Newman (Ed.), *Sociology: Exploring the architecture of everyday life.* Thousand Oaks, CA: Pine Forge Press.

Lye, D. N. 1996. "Adult child-parent relationships." *Annual Review of Sociology, 22,* 79–102.

Lynch, M. 1982. "Forgotten fathers." In E. Jackson & S. Persky (Eds.), *Flaunting it! A decade of gay journalism from the body politic.* Vancouver: New Star Books.

Lytton, H., & Romney, D. M. 1991. "Parents' differential socialization of boys and girls: A meta-analysis." *Psychology Bulletin, 109,* 267–296.

Maccoby, E., & Mnookin, R. H. 1992. *Dividing the child: Social and legal dilemmas of custody.* Cambridge, MA: Harvard University Press.

MacDonald, K., & Parke, R. D. 1986. "Parent-child physical play: The effects of sex and age on children and parents." *Sex Roles, 15,* 367–378.

Macklin, E. 1980. "Nonmarital heterosexual cohabitation." In A. S. Skolnick & J. H. Skolnick (Eds.), *Family in transition* (3rd ed.). Boston: Little, Brown.

———. 1988. "AIDS: Implications for families." *Family Relations, 37,* 141–149.

Major, B. 1993. "Gender, entitlement and the distribution of family labor." *Journal of Social Issues, 49,* 141–159.

Mannon, J. M. 1997(a). *Measuring up: The performance ethic in American culture.* Boulder, CO: Westview.

———. 1997(b). "Domestic and intimate violence: An application of routine activity theory." *Aggression and Violent Behavior, 2,* 9–24.

Mantsios, G. 1995. "Class in America: Myths and realities." In P. S. Rothenberg (Ed.), *Race, class, and gender in the United States.* New York: St. Martin's Press.

Maranto, G. 1995. "Delayed childbearing." *The Atlantic Monthly,* June, 55–66.

Marciano, T. D. 1988. "Families wider than kin or marriage." *Family Science Review, 1,* 115–124.

Margolick, D. 1990. "Death and faith, law and Christian Science." *New York Times,* August 6.

Marks, M. R. 1997. "Party politics and family policy: The case of the Family and Medical Leave Act." *Journal of Family Issues, 18,* 55–70.

Marmor, J. 1996. "Blurring the lines." *Columns,* December.

"Marriage and divorce." 1996. *CQ Researcher,* May 10.

Martin, A. 1996. "Why get married?" *Utne Reader,* January/February.

Martin, L. 1989. "The graying of Japan." *Population Bulletin, 44,* 1–43.

Martin, M. K., & Voorhies, B. 1975. *Female of the species.* New York: Columbia University Press.

Marzollo, J. 1981. "Confessions of a (sort of) grown-up." *Parents,* July 3.

Masnick, G., & Bane, M. J. 1980. *The nation's families: 1960–1990.* Boston: Auburn House.

Mathews, L. 1996. "More than identity rides on new racial category." *New York Times,* July 6.

Mattox, W. R. 1985. "The parent trap." *Policy Review, 5,* 6–13.

McAdoo, H. P. 1998. "African-American families." In C. H. Mindel, R. W. Habeastein, & R. Wright (Eds.), *Ethnic families in America: Patterns and variations.* Upper Saddle River, NJ: Prentice-Hall.

McBride, J. 1996. "Adopting across the color line." *New York Times,* June 3.

McCall, G. J. 1982. "Becoming unrelated: The management of bond dissolution." In S. Duck (Ed.), *Personal relationships #4: Dissolving personal relationships.* London: Academic Press.

McClaurin, I. 1996. *Women of Belize: Gender and change in Central America.* New Brunswick, NJ: Rutgers University Press.

McCloskey, L. A. 1996. "Socioeconomic and coercive power within the family." *Gender and Society, 10,* 449–463.

McCoy, E. 1981. "Childhood through the ages." *Parents Magazine,* January, 60–65.

McCrate, E., & Smith, J. 1998. "When work doesn't work: The failure of current welfare reform." *Gender and Society, 12,* 61–80.

McKenry, P. C., & Price, S. J. 1995. "Divorce: A comparative perspective." In B. B. Ingoldsby & S. Smith (Eds.), *Families in multicultural perspective.* New York: Guilford Press.

McKinlay, J. B., McKinlay, S. M., & Brambilla, D. 1987. "The relative contributions of endocrine changes and social circumstances to depression in middle-aged women." *Journal of Health and Social Behavior, 28,* 345–363.

McLanahan, S., & Booth, K. 1991. "Mother-only families." In A. Booth (Ed.), *Contemporary families: Looking forward, looking back.* Minneapolis: National Council on Family Relations.

McLanahan, S. S., & Sandefur, G. 1994. *Growing up with a single parent.* Cambridge, MA: Harvard University Press.

McNeil, M. 1997. "Neglect conviction of mom overruled by appeals court." *Indianapolis Star,* January 1.

McRoy, R. G., & Zurcher, L. A. 1983. *Transracial and inracial adoptees: The adolescent years.* Springfield, IL: Charles C Thomas.

McWhirter, D. P., & Mattison, A. M. 1984. *The male couple: How relationships develop.* Englewood Cliffs, NJ: Prentice-Hall.

Mead, M. 1963. *Sex and temperment in three primitive societies.* New York: William Morrow.

———. 1978. "The American family: An endangered species?" *TV Guide,* December 30.

Mellot, K. 1997. "Faith-healers get the max." *Tribune-Democrat* (Johnstown, PA).

Meyer, D. R., & Garasky, S. 1993. "Custodial fathers: Myths, realities, and child support policy." *Journal of Marriage and the Family, 55,* 73–89.

Meyrowitz, J. 1984. "The adultlike child and the childlike adult: Socialization in an electronic age." *Daedalus, 113,* 19–48.

Miall, C. E. 1989. "The stigma of involuntary childlessness." In A. S. Skolnick & J. H. Skolnick (Eds.), *Family in transition* (6th ed.). Boston: Little, Brown.

Michael, R. T., Gagnon, J. H., Laumann, E. O., & Kolata, G. 1994. *Sex in America: A definitive survey.* Boston: Little, Brown.

Michener, H. A., DeLamater, J. D., & Schwartz, S. H. 1986. *Social psychology.* San Diego: Harcourt Brace Jovanovich.

Miller, C. L. 1987. "Qualitative differences among gender-stereotyped toys: Implications for cognitive and social development." *Sex Roles, 16,* 473–488.

Miller, J. A., Jacobsen, R. B., & Bigner, J. J. 1981. "The child's home environment for lesbian vs. heterosexual mothers: A neglected area of research." *Journal of Homosexuality, 7,* 49–56.

Miller, R. 1987. "Trends in marital happiness in Provo, Utah: 1955–1983." *Sociology and Social Research, 71,* 294–297.

Millman, M. 1991. *Warm hearts and cold cash: The ultimate dynamics of families and money.* New York: Free Press.

Mills, C. W. 1959. *The sociological imagination.* New York: Oxford University Press.

Minow, M. 1993. "Definitions of family: Who's in, who's out and who decides." In M. Minow (Ed.), *Family matters: Readings on family lives and the law.* New York: Free Press.

Minow, M., & Shanley, M. L. 1996. "Relational rights and responsibilities: Revisioning the family in liberal political theory and law." *Hypatia, 11,* 4–29.

Mintz, S. 1989. "Regulating the American family." *Journal of Family History, 14,* 387–408.

Mintz, S., & Kellogg, S. 1988. *Domestic revolutions.* New York: Free Press.

Miranda, M. R. 1992. "Quality of life and the elderly: The continuing disparity between whites and minorities." *Perspectives on Aging, 21,* 4–10.

Mitford, J. 1993. *The American way of birth.* New York: Plume.

Moen, P., & Schorr, A. L. 1987. "Families and social policy." In M. B. Sussman & S. K. Steinmetz (Eds.), *Handbook of marriage and the family.* New York: Plenum.

Mogelonsky, M. 1996. "The rocky road to adulthood." *American Demographics,* May, 26–34.

Molloy, B. L., & Herzberger, S. D. 1998. "Body image and self-esteem: A comparison of African-American and Caucasian women." *Sex Roles, 38,* 631–643.

"Mom's market value." 1998. *Utne Reader,* March/April.

Moore, M. L. 1992. "The family as portrayed on prime-time television, 1947–1990: Structure and characteristics." *Sex Roles, 26,* 41–61.

Moorman, J. E. 1987. "The history and future of the relationship between education and first marriage." Unpublished paper. Washington, DC: U.S. Bureau of the Census.

Morgan, L., & Kunkel, S. 1998. *Aging and society.* Thousand Oaks, CA: Pine Forge Press.

Mottl, T. L. 1980. "The analysis of countermovements." *Social Problems, 27,* 620–635.

Moynihan, D. P. 1965. *The Negro family: The case for national action.* Washington, DC: Office of Planning and Research, Department of Labor.

Murdock, G. P. 1949. *Social structure.* New York: Free Press.

———. 1957. "World ethnography sample." *American Anthropologist, 59,* 664–687.

Murray, C. 1994. "Does welfare bring more babies?" *American Enterprise, 5,* 53–59.

Nack, W., & Munson, L. 1995. "Sports' dirty secret." *Sports Illustrated,* July 31.

Nanda, S. 1990. *Neither man nor woman: The hijras of India.* Belmont, CA: Wadsworth.

———. 1994. *Cultural anthropology.* Belmont, CA: Wadsworth.

National Committee on Pay Equity. 1995. "The wage gap: Myths and facts." In P. S. Rothenberg (Ed.), *Race, class and gender in the United States*. New York: St. Martin's Press.

Navarro, V. 1992. "The middle class—a useful myth." *The Nation*, March 23.

Neal, A. G., Groat, H. T., & Wicks, J. W. 1989. "Attitudes about having children: A study of 600 couples in the early years of marriage." *Journal of Marriage and the Family, 59*, 313–328.

Nelkin, D., & Lindee, M. S. 1995. *The DNA mystique: The gene as a cultural icon*. New York: Freeman.

Nemy, E. 1995. "No children, and no apologies." *New York Times*, April 6.

Neugarten, B. L. 1980. "Grow old along with me! The best is yet to be." In B. Hess (Ed.), *Growing old in America*. New Brunswick, NJ: Transaction Books.

"New kit can help parents detect their kids' drug use." 1995. *JET Magazine*, April 17.

"The new 'parental rights' crusade." 1996. *The Humanist*, March/April.

Newman, K. 1988. *Falling from grace: The experience of downward mobility in the American middle class*. New York: Free Press.

———. 1993. *Declining Fortunes*. New York: Basic Books.

Niebuhr, G. 1996. "An interfaith-marriage vote has reform Judaism divided." *New York Times*, December 14.

———. 1998. "Southern Baptist vote puts men first." *Indianapolis Star*, June 10.

Nock, S. L. 1987. "The symbolic meaning of child bearing." *Journal of Family Issues, 8*, 373–393.

———. 1995. "A comparison of marriages and cohabiting relationships." *Journal of Family Issues, 16*, 53–76.

———. 1998. "Too much privacy?" *Journal of Family Issues, 19*, 101–118.

Nock, S. L., & Kingston, P. W. 1988. "Time with children: The impact of couples' work-time commitments." *Social Forces, 67*, 59–85.

Norton, J. A. 1987. "Families and children in the year 2000." *Children Today*, July/August, 6–9.

Oaks, D. H. 1995. "Rights and responsibilities." In A. Etzioni (Ed.), *Rights and the common good*. New York: St. Martin's Press.

O'Brien, M., & Huston, A. C. 1985. "Development of sex-typed play behavior in toddlers." *Developmental Psychology, 21*, 866–871.

Ogawa, N., & Retherford, R. D. 1993. "Care of the elderly in Japan: Changing norms and expectations." *Journal of Marriage and the Family, 55*, 585–597.

Ojito, M. 1997. "Culture clash: Foreign parents, American child rearing." *New York Times*, June 29.

Okin, S. M. 1989. *Justice, gender and the family*. New York: Basic Books.

Oliker, S. J. 1995. "Work commitment and constraint among mothers on welfare." *Journal of Contemporary Ethnography, 24*, 165–194.

Olsen, F. 1993. "The myth of state intervention in the family." In M. Minow (Ed.), *Family matters*. New York: New Press.

Olson, E. 1981. "Socioeconomic and psychocultural contexts of child abuse and neglect in Turkey." In J. Kobrin (Ed.), *Child abuse and neglect: Cross-cultural perspectives*. Berkeley: University of California Press.

———. 1998. "U.N. surveys paid leave for mothers." *New York Times*, February 16.

Orenstein, P. 1994. *School girls: Young women, self-esteem, and the confidence gap*. New York: Anchor.

Orthner, D. K. 1990. "The family in transition." In D. Blankenhorn, S. Bayne, & J. B. Elshtain (Eds.), *Rebuilding the nest: A new commitment to the American family*. Milwaukee, WI: Family Service America.

Ostrander, S. 1984. *Women of the upper class*. Philadelphia: Temple University Press.

Pader, E. 1997. "Redefining the home." *New York Times*, May 7.

Palmore, E. 1975. *The honorable elders: A cross-cultural analysis of aging in Japan*. Durham, NC: Duke University Press.

Pampel, F. C. 1998. *Aging, social inequality, and public policy*. Thousand Oaks, CA: Pine Forge Press.

Parcel, T. L., & Menaghan, E. G., 1990. "Maternal working conditions and children's verbal facility: Studying the intergenerational transmission of inequality from mothers to young children." *Social Psychology Quarterly, 53*, 132–147.

———. 1994. "Early parental work, family social capital, and early childhood outcomes." *American Journal of Sociology, 99*, 972–1009.

Parsons, T., & Bales, R. F. 1955. *Family socialization and interaction process*. Glencoe, IL: Free Press.

Patterson, C. J. 1992. "Children of lesbian and gay parents." *Child Development, 63*, 1025–1042.

———. 1994. "Children of the lesbian baby boom: Behavioral adjustment, self-concepts and sex-role identity." In B. Greene & G. M. Herek (Eds.), *Lesbian and gay psychology: Theory, research and clinical applications.* Thousand Oaks, CA: Sage.

Patton, W., & Mannison, M. 1995. "Sexual coercion in high school dating." *Sex Roles, 33,* 447–457.

Payer, L. 1987. *How to avoid a hysterectomy.* New York: Pantheon.

Pear, R. 1992. "New look at the U.S. in 2050: Bigger, older and less white." *New York Times,* December 4.

———. 1993. "Wide health gap, linked to income, is reported in the U.S." *New York Times,* July 8.

———. 1997. "U.S. inaugurating a vast database of all new hires." *New York Times,* September 22.

———. 1998. "Number on welfare dips below 10 million." *New York Times,* January 21.

Penner, D. 1995. "Aid recipients defy stereotypes, seek a better way." *Indianapolis Star,* April 16.

"Perfect boyfriend is sold in a box for $14.95." 1997. *Indianapolis Star,* February 16.

Perkins, H. W., & DeMeis, D. K. 1996. "Gender and family effects on the 'second shift' domestic activities of college-educated young adults." *Gender and Society, 10,* 78–93.

Peterson, I. 1992. "For absent fathers, a ray of hope." *New York Times,* September 29.

Peterson, J., & Kim, P. 1991. *The day America told the truth.* New York: Prentice-Hall.

Peterson, R. R. 1996. "A re-evaluation of the economic consequences of divorce." *American Sociological Review, 61,* 528–536.

Peterson, W. C. 1994. *The silent depression: The fate of the American dream.* New York: Norton.

Pfohl, S. J. 1977. "The discovery of child abuse." *Social Problems, 24,* 310–323.

Pillemer, K. A. 1993. "Abuse is caused by the deviance and dependence of abusive caregivers." In R. J. Gelbs & D. R. Loeske (Eds.), *Current controversies in family violence.* Newbury Park, CA: Sage.

Pittman, J. F., & Blanchard, D. 1996. "The effects of work history and timing of marriage on the division of household labor: A life-course perspective." *Journal of Marriage and the Family, 58,* 78–90.

Pleck, E. 1987. *Domestic tyranny.* New York: Oxford University Press.

Pollard, K. M. 1996. "One third of U.S. children in poverty live in working-poor families." *Population Today, 24,* 4–5.

Pollitt, K. 1991. "Fetal rights: A new assault on feminism." In J. H. Skolnick & E. Currie (Eds.), *Crisis in American institutions.* New York: HarperCollins.

Popenoe, D. 1988. *Disturbing the nest.* New York: Aldine de Gryter.

———. 1993. "American family decline, 1960–1990: A review and appraisal." *Journal of Marriage and the Family, 55,* 527–555.

———. 1995. "Family values: A communitarian position." In D. Sciulli (Ed.), *Macro-socioeconomics: From theory to activism.* Armonk, NY: M. E. Sharpe.

———. 1996. "Where's Papa?" *Utne Reader,* September/October, 63–66.

Potuchek, J. L. 1997. *Who supports the family? Gender and breadwinning in dual-earner marriages.* Stanford, CA: Stanford University Press.

Powell-Hopson, D., & Hopson, D. S. 1988. "Implications of doll color preferences among black preschool children and white preschool children." *Journal of Black Psychology, 14,* 57–63.

"Prenatal drug use is ruled child abuse." 1996. *New York Times,* July 17.

"President tells mothers to either name fathers or lose welfare." 1996. *Jet,* July 8.

Presser, H. 1994. "Employment schedules among dual-earner spouses and the division of household labor by gender." *American Sociological Review, 59,* 348–364.

Preston, S. H. 1976. *Mortality patterns in national population: With special references to recorded causes of death.* New York: Academic Press.

———. 1984. "Children and the elderly in the U.S." *Scientific American,* December, 44–49.

"The Promise Keepettes." 1997. *New York Times Magazine,* April 27.

Pyke, K. 1994. "Women's employment as a gift or burden? Marital power across marriage, divorce, and remarriage." *Gender and Society, 8,* 73–91.

———. 1996. "Class-based masculinities: The interdependence of gender, class, and interpersonal power." *Gender and Society, 10,* 527–549.

Quayle, D. 1992. "Restoring basic values: Strengthening the family." *Vital Speeches of the Day, 58,* 517–520.

Queen, S. A., & Habenstein, R. W. 1974. *The family in various cultures.* Philadelphia: Lippincott.

Quindlen, A. 1992. "Digging a divide." *New York Times,* June 14.

Rafferty, Y., & Rollins, N. 1989. *Learning in limbo: The educational deprivation of homeless children.* New York: Advocates for Children.

Raley, R. K. 1995. "Black-white differences in kin contact and exchange among never married adults." *Journal of Family Issues, 16,* 77–103.

———. 1996. "A shortage of marriagable men? A note on the role of cohabitation in black-white differences in marriage rates." *American Sociological Review, 61,* 973–983.

Rank, M. 1994. *Life on the edge: The realities of welfare in America.* New York: Columbia University Press.

Raphael, B. 1995. "The death of a child." In J. B. Williamson & E. S. Schneidman (Eds.), *Death: Current perspectives.* Mountain View, CA: Mayfield.

Raymond, J. G. 1993. *Women as wombs.* San Francisco: Harper.

Reich, R. B. 1996. "My family leave act." *New York Times,* November 8.

Reiman, J. 1998. *The rich get richer and the poor get prison.* New York: Macmillan.

Reinharz, S. 1992. *Feminist methods in social research.* New York: Oxford University Press.

Reinholtz, R. K., Muehlenhard, C. L., Phelps, J. L., & Satterfield, A. T. 1995. "Sexual discourse and sexual intercourse: How the way we communicate affects the way we think about sexual coercion." In P. J. Kalfleisch & M. J. Cody (Eds.), *Gender, power and communication in human relationships.* Hillsdale, NJ: Lawrence Erlbaum Associates.

Reiss, I. L. 1960. "Toward a sociology of the heterosexual love relationship." *Marriage and Family Living, 22,* 139–145.

Reiss, I. L., & Lee, G. R. 1988. *Family systems in America.* New York: Holt, Rinehart & Winston.

Renzetti, C. 1992. *Violent betrayal: Partner abuse in lesbian relationships.* Newbury Park, CA: Sage.

Renzetti, C., & Curran, D. J. 1989. *Women, men and society: The sociology of gender.* Boston: Allyn & Bacon.

Reskin, B., & Hartmann, H. 1986. *Women's work, men's work: Sex segregation on the job.* Washington, DC: National Academy Press.

Reskin, B., & Padavic, I. 1994. *Women and men at work.* Thousand Oaks, CA: Pine Forge Press.

Ribbens, J. 1994. *Mothers and their children.* London: Sage.

Rico, B. R., & Mano, S. 1991. *American mosaic: Multicultural readings in context.* Boston: Houghton Mifflin.

Ridgeway, C. L. 1997. "Interaction and the conservation of gender inequality: Considering employment." *American Sociological Review, 62,* 218–235.

Riley, G. 1991. *Divorce: An American tradition.* New York: Oxford University Press.

Riley, M. W. 1971. "Social gerontology and the age stratification of society." *The Gerontologist, 11,* 79–87.

———. 1983. "The family in an aging society: A matrix of latent relationships." *Journal of Family Issues, 4,* 439–454.

Riley, M. W., Foner, A., & Waring, J. 1988. "Sociology of age." In N. J. Smelser (Ed.), *Handbook of sociology.* Newbury Park, CA: Sage.

Rimer, S. 1998(a). "Tradition of care thrives in Black families." *New York Times,* March 15.

———. 1998(b). "As centenarians thrive, 'old' is redefined." *New York Times,* June 22.

Risman, B. J. 1989. "Can men mother? Life as a single father." In B. J. Risman & P. Schwartz (Eds.), *Gender in intimate relationships.* Belmont, CA: Wadsworth.

Roberts, A. R. 1996. "Battered women who kill: A comparative study of incarcerated participants with a community sample of battered women." *Journal of Family Violence, 11,* 291–304.

Roberts, D. E. 1991. "Punishing drug addicts who have babies: Women of color, equality and the right of privacy." *Harvard Law Review, 104,* 1419–1482.

Robinson, C. 1993. "Surrogate motherhood: Implications for the mother-fetus relationship." *Women and Politics, 13,* 203–224.

Robinson, J., & Godbey, G. 1995. *Time for life.* University Park: Pennsylvania State Press.

Rodman, H., Pratto, D. J., & Nelson, R. S. 1985. "Child care arrangements and children's functioning: A comparison of self-care and adult care children." *Developmental Psychology, 21,* 413–418.

Roland, A. 1988. *In search of self in India and Japan.* Princeton, NJ: Princeton University Press.

Rose, A. 1996. "How I became a single woman." *The New Yorker,* April 8.

Rosellini, L. 1992. "Sexual desire." *U.S. News and World Report,* July 6, 60–66.

Rosen, J. 1997. "Abraham's drifting children." *New York Times Book Review,* March 30.

Rosenblatt, P. C., Karis, T. A., & Powell, R. D. 1995. *Multiracial couples.* Thousand Oaks, CA: Sage.

Ross, C. E., & Van Willigen, M. 1996. "Gender, parenthood, and anger." *Journal of Marriage and the Family, 58,* 572–584.

Rossi, A. 1968. "Transition to parenthood." *Journal of Marriage and the Family, 30,* 26–39.

———. 1977. "A bio-social perspective on parenting." *Daedalus, 106,* 1–31.

Roth, R. 1993. "At women's expense: The costs of fetal rights." *Women and Politics, 13,* 117–135.

Rothman, B. K. 1987. "Reproduction." In B. B. Hess & M. M. Ferree (Eds.), *Analyzing gender: A handbook of social science research.* Newbury Park, CA: Sage.

Rotundo, E. A. 1985. "American fatherhood: A historical perspective." *American Behavioral Scientist, 29,* 7–25.

Rowland, R. 1990. "Technology and motherhood: Reproductive choice reconsidered." In C. Carlson (Ed.), *Perspectives on the family: History, class and feminism.* Belmont, CA: Wadsworth.

Rozee, P. D. 1993. "Forbidden or forgiven? Rape in cross-cultural perspective." *Psychology of Women Quarterly, 17,* 499–514.

Rubin, J. Z., Provenzano, F. J., & Luria, Z. 1974. "The eye of the beholder: Parents' views on sex of newborns." *American Journal of Orthopsychiatry, 44,* 512–519.

Rubin, L. 1976. *Worlds of pain.* New York: Basic Books.

———. 1990. *Erotic wars: What happened to the sexual revolution?* New York: Harper Perennial.

———. 1992. "The empty nest." In J. M. Heaslin (Ed.), *Marriage and family in a changing society.* New York: Free Press.

———. 1995. *Families on the fault line.* New York: Harper Perennial.

Rubin, Z. 1973. *Liking and loving.* New York: Holt, Rinehart & Winston.

Rusbult, C. E. 1983. "A longitudinal test of the investment model: The development (and deterioration) of satisfaction and commitment in heterosexual involvement." *Journal of Personality and Social Psychology, 45,* 101–117.

Russell, D. E. H. 1998. "Wife rape and the law." In M. E. Odem & J. Clay-Warner (Eds.), *Confronting rape and sexual assault.* Wilmington, DE: SR Books.

Rutter, V. 1995. "Adolescence: Whose hell is it?" *Psychology Today,* January/February.

———. 1997. "Lessons from stepfamilies." In K. R. Gilbert (Ed.), *Annual editions: Marriage and family 97/98.* Guilford, CT: Dushkin.

Ryun, J., & Ryun, A. 1997. "A date with the family." *Harpers Magazine,* January.

Saenz, R., Hwang, S. S., Aguirre, B. E., & Anderson, R. N. 1995. "Persistence and change in Asian identity among children of intermarried couples." *Sociological Perspectives, 38,* 175–194.

Safilios-Rothschild, C. 1976. "A macro- and micro-examination of family power and love: An exchange model." *Journal of Marriage and the Family, 38,* 355–362.

Safire, W. 1995. "News about Jews." *New York Times,* July 17.

Salholz, E. 1986. "Too late for Prince Charming?" *Newsweek,* June 2.

Sanchez, L. 1994. "Gender, labor allocations, and the psychology of entitlement within the home." *Social Forces, 73,* 533–553.

Sanday, P. R. 1981. "The socio-cultural context of rape: A cross-cultural study." *Journal of Social Issues, 37,* 5–27.

Sandefur, G. 1996. "Welfare doesn't cause illegitimacy and single parenthood." *Chronicle of Higher Education,* October 4.

Sanger, D. E. 1997. "The last liberal (almost) leaves town." *New York Times,* January 9.

Saul, L. 1972. "Personal and social psychopathology and the primary prevention of violence." *American Journal of Psychiatry, 128,* 1578–1581.

Scanzoni, J. 1983. *Shaping tomorrow's family: Theory and policy for the twenty-first century.* Newbury Park, CA: Sage.

———. 1991. "Balancing the policy interests of children and adults." In E. A. Anderson & R. C. Hula (Eds.), *The reconstruction of family policy.* Westport, CT: Greenwood Press.

Scanzoni, J., & Marsiglio, W. 1991. "Wider families as primary relationships." In T. Marciano & M. B. Sussman (Eds.), *Wider families: New traditional family forms.* New York: Haworth Press.

Scheper-Hughes, N. 1989. "Lifeboat ethics: Mother love and child death in northeast Brazil." *National History, 98,* 8–16.

Schmitt, E. 1996. "Adoption bill facing battle over a provision on Indians." *New York Times,* May 8.

———. 1998. "Day-care quandary: A nation at war with itself." *New York Times,* January 11.

Schnaiberg, A., & Goldenberg, S. 1989. "From empty nest to crowded nest: The dynamics of incompletely launched young adults." *Social Problems, 36,* 251–269.

Schneider, D. M. 1980. *American kinship: A cultural account.* Chicago: University of Chicago Press.

Schneider, M. B. 1996. "A campaign truth: Values matter." *Indianapolis Star,* September 29.

Schodolski, V. J. 1993. "Funeral industry, pitching videos, 2-for-1 specials to baby boomers." *Indianapolis Star,* December 26.

Schuller, R. A., & Vidmar, N. 1992. "Battered woman syndrome evidence in the courtroom." *Law and Human Behavior, 16,* 273–291.

Schupack, D. 1994. " 'Starter' marriages: So early, so brief." *New York Times,* July 7.

Schur, E. 1988. *The Americanization of sex.* Philadelphia: Temple University Press.

Schwartz, F. N. 1989. "Management women and the new facts of life." *Harvard Business Review, 67,* 65–76.

Schwartz, P. 1987. "The family as a changed institution." *Journal of Family Issues, 8,* 455–459.

———. 1994. *Love between equals.* New York: Free Press.

Schwartz, P., & Rutter, V. 1997. *Sex and society.* Thousand Oaks, CA: Sage.

Sciolino, E. 1997. "The Chanel under the chador." *New York Times Magazine,* May 4.

Scott-Jones, D. 1997. "Adolescent childbearing." In K. R. Gilbert (Ed.), *Annual editions: Marriage and family 97/98.* Guilford, CT: Dushkin.

Scritchfield, S. A. 1995. "The social construction of infertility: From private matter to social concern." In J. Best (Ed.), *Images of issues: Typifying contemporary social problems.* New York: Aldine de Gryter.

Scull, A., & Favreau, D. 1986. "A chance to cut is a chance to cure: Sexual surgery for psychosis in three nineteenth century societies." In S. Spitzer & A. T. Scull (Eds.), *Research in law, deviance and social control* (Vol. 8). Greenwich, CT: JAI Press.

Sedney, M. A. 1987. "Development of androgyny: Parental influences." *Psychology of Women Quarterly, 11,* 311–326.

Seelye, K. Q. 1997(a). "Future U.S.: Grayer and more Hispanic." *New York Times,* March 27.

———. 1997(b). "President is set to approve sweeping shift in adoption." *New York Times,* November 17.

Seltser, B. J., & Miller, D. E. 1993. *Homeless families: The struggle for dignity.* Urbana: University of Illinois Press.

Seltzer, J. A. 1994. "Consequences of marital dissolution for children." *Annual Review of Sociology, 20,* 235–266.

Sennett, R. 1984. *Families against the city: Middle-class homes in industrial Chicago.* Cambridge, MA: Harvard University Press.

Sennett, R., & Cobb, J. 1972. *Hidden injuries of class.* New York: Vintage.

Settles, B. H. 1987. "A perspective on tomorrow's families." In M. B. Sussman & S. K. Steinmetz (Eds.), *Handbook of marriage and the family.* New York: Plenum.

Sexton, J. 1997. "For some, work may not mean self-sufficiency." *New York Times,* April 21.

"Sexual activity among U.S. youths is declining, a report shows." 1997. *New York Times,* May 2.

Shakin, M., Shakin, D., & Sternglanz, S. H. 1985. "Infant clothing: Sex labeling for strangers." *Sex Roles, 12,* 955–964.

Shalala, D. 1996. "Welfare reform: We must all assume responsibility." *Chronicle of Higher Education,* October 4.

Shanker, A. 1990. "The Family Medical Leave Act." *New York Times,* June 24.

Sheets, V. L., & Braver, S. L. 1996. "Gender differences in satisfaction with divorce settlements." *Family Relations, 45,* 336–342.

Sheffield, C. J. 1987. "Sexual terrorism: The social control of women." In B. B. Hess & M. M. Ferree (Eds.), *Analyzing gender: A handbook of social science research.* Newbury Park, CA: Sage.

Shelton, B. A. 1992. *Women, men, time.* New York: Greenwood.

Shelton, B. A., & John, D. 1993. "Ethnicity, race, and difference: A comparison of white, black, and Hispanic men's household labor time." In J. C. Hood (Ed.), *Men, work, and family.* Newbury Park, CA: Sage.

———. 1996. "The division of household labor." *Annual Review of Sociology, 22,* 299–322.

Shenk, D. 1997. "Biocapitalism: What price the genetic revolution?" *Harper's Magazine,* December.

Shenon, P. 1995. "Bitter aborigines are suing for stolen childhoods." *New York Times,* July 20.

Sherman, S. 1992. *Lesbian and gay marriage: Private commitments, public ceremonies.* Philadelphia: Temple University Press.

Sherman, S. R., Ward, R. A., & LaGory, M. 1988. "Women as caregivers of the elderly: Instrumental and expressive support." *Social Work,* March/April, 164–167.

Shireman, J. F., & Johnson, P. R. 1986. "A longitudinal study of black adoptions: Single parent, transracial and traditional." *Social Work, 31,* 172–176.

Shorter, E. 1975. *The making of the modern family.* New York: Basic Books.

Shotland, R. L., & Straw, M. K. 1976. "Bystander response to an assault: When a man attacks a woman." *Journal of Personality and Social Psychology, 34,* 990–999.

Shweder, R. A. 1997. "It's called poor health for a reason." *New York Times,* March 9.

Sidel, R. 1986. *Women and children last.* New York: Penguin.

———. 1990. *On her own: Growing up in the shadow of the American dream.* New York: Penguin.

Siegel, J. M. 1995. "Looking for Mr. Right? Older single women who become mothers." *Journal of Family Issues, 16,* 194–211.

Siegel, L. J. 1995. *Criminology: Theories, patterns and typologies.* Minneapolis: West.

Siegel, R. B. 1996. "The rule of love: Wife beating as prerogative and privacy." *Yale Law Journal, 105,* 2116–2207.

Simon, R., Alstein, H., & Melli, M. S. 1994. *The case for transracial adoption.* Washington, DC: American University Press.

Simon, R. W., Eder, D., & Evans, C. 1992. "The development of feeling norms underlying romantic love among adolescent females." *Social Psychology Quarterly, 55,* 29–46.

Sims, C. 1997. "Justice in Peru: Rape victim is pressed to marry attacker." *New York Times,* March 12.

———. 1998. "Using gifts as bait, Peru sterilizes poor women." *New York Times,* February 15.

Singleton, R., Straits, B. C., & Straits, M. M. 1993. *Approaches to social research.* New York: Oxford University Press.

Sjoberg, G., Williams, N., Gill, E., & Himmel, K. F. 1995. "Family life and racial and ethnic diversity: An assessment of communitarianism, liberalism, and conservatism." *Journal of Family Issues, 16,* 246–274.

Skolnick, A. S. 1979. "Public images, private realities: The American family in popular culture and social science." In V. Tufte & B. Myerhoff (Eds.), *Changing images of the family.* New Haven, CT: Yale University Press.

———. 1987. *The intimate environment: Exploring marriage and the family* (4th ed.). Boston: Little, Brown.

———. 1991. *Embattled paradise.* New York: Basic Books.

———. 1996. *The intimate environment: Exploring marriage and the family* (6th ed.). New York: HarperCollins.

Skolnick, A. S., & Skolnick, J. H. 1992. *Family in transition* (7th ed.). New York: HarperCollins.

Smeeding, T., Torrey, B. B., & Rein, M. 1988. "Patterns of income and poverty: The economic status of children and the elderly in eight countries." In T. Smeeding, J. L. Palmer, & B. B. Torrey (Eds.), *The vulnerable.* Washington, DC: Urban Institute Press.

Smith, A. 1996. "Making unpaid labor count." *Ms. Magazine,* September/October.

Smith, D. 1997. "Study looks at portrayal of women in media." *New York Times,* May 1.

Smock, P. J. 1994. "Gender and the short-run economic consequences of marital disruption." *Social Forces, 73,* 243–262.

Smolowe, J. 1994. "When violence hits home." *Time,* July 4.

Snow, E. A. 1997. *Inside Bruegel: The play of images in children's games.* San Francisco: North Point Press.

Somers, M. D. 1993. "A comparison of voluntarily childfree adults and parents." *Journal of Marriage and the Family, 55,* 643–650.

Sontag, D. 1997. "For some battered women, aid is only a promise." *New York Times,* February 14.

South, S. J., & Lloyd, K. M. 1992. "Marriage opportunities and family formation: Further implications of imbalanced sex ratios." *Journal of Marriage and the Family, 54,* 440–451.

———. 1995. "Spousal alternatives and marital dissolution." *American Sociological Review, 60,* 21–35.

South, S. J., & Spitze, G. D. 1994. "Housework in marital and nonmarital households." *American Sociological Review, 59,* 327–347.

Spanier, G. B., Lewis, R. A., & Cole, C. L. 1975. "Marital adjustment over the family life cycle: The issue of curvilinearity." *Journal of Marriage and the Family, 37,* 263–275.

Speare, A., & R. Avery. 1993. "Who helps whom in older parent-child families?" *Journal of Gerontology, 48,* 564–573.

Spickard, P. R. 1989. *Mixed blood: Intermarriage and ethnic identity in twentieth century America.* Madison: University of Wisconsin Press.

Spigel, L. 1992. *Make room for TV: Television and the family ideal in postwar America.* Chicago: University of Chicago Press.

Spitze, G. 1988. "Women's employment and family relations: A review." *Journal of Marriage and the Family, 50,* 595–618.

Stacey, J. 1993. "Good riddance to 'the family': A response to David Popenoe." *Journal of Marriage and the Family, 55,* 545–547.

———. 1994. "Dan Quayle's revenge: The new family values crusaders." *The Nation,* July 25/August 1, 119–122.

———. 1996(a). *In the name of the family.* Boston: Beacon Press.

———. 1996(b). "The father fixation." *Utne Reader,* September/October, 72–73.

Stack, C. 1974. *All our kin: Strategies for survival in a black community.* New York: Harper & Row.

Staggenborg, S. 1998. *Gender, family and social movements.* Thousand Oaks, CA: Pine Forge Press.

Stanford, E. P., Peddecord, M., & Lockery, S. 1990. "Variations among the elderly in black, Hispanic and white families." In T. Brubaker (Ed.), *Family relations in later life.* Newbury Park, CA: Sage.

Staples, R. 1992. "African American families." In J. M. Henslin (Ed.), *Marriage and family in a changing society.* New York: Free Press.

Steinberg, S. R., & Kincheloe, J. L. 1997. "Introduction: No more secrets—Kinderculture information saturation and the postmodern childhood." In S. R. Steinberg & J. L. Kincheloe (Eds.), *Kinderculture: The corporate construction of childhood.* Boulder, CO: Westview.

Steinhauer, J. 1995. "No marriage, no apologies." *New York Times,* July 6.

Steinmetz, S. K., Clavan, S., & Stein, K. F. 1990. *Marriage and family realities: Historical and contemporary perspectives.* New York: Harper & Row.

Stephan, C. W., & Stephan, W. G. 1989. "After intermarriage: Ethnic identity among mixed-heritage Japanese-Americans and Hispanics." *Journal of Marriage and the Family, 51,* 507–519.

Stephens, L. S. 1996. "Will Johnny see Daddy this week? An empirical test of three theoretical perspectives on post-divorce contact." *Journal of Family Issues, 17,* 466–494.

Stephens, W. N. 1963. *The family in cross-cultural perspective.* New York: University Press of America.

Stets, J. 1992. "Interactive processes in dating aggression: A national study." *Journal of Marriage and the Family, 54,* 165–177.

Stets, J., & Straus, M. A. 1990. "The marriage license as a hitting license: A comparison of assaults in dating, cohabiting, and married couples." In M. A. Straus & R. J. Gelles (Eds.), *Physical violence in American families.* New Brunswick, NJ: Transaction.

Stewart, A. J., Copeland, A. P., Chester, A. L., Malley, J. E., & Barenbaum, N. B. 1997. *Separating together: How divorce transforms families.* New York: Guilford Press.

Stoddard, T. B. 1992. "Why gay people should seek the right to marry." In S. Sherman (Ed.), *Lesbian and gay marriage.* Philadelphia: Temple University Press.

Stolberg, S. G. 1997. "The better half got the worse end." *New York Times,* July 20.

———. 1998. "Eyes shut, black America is being ravaged by AIDS." *New York Times,* June 29.

Stoller, E. P., & Gibson, R. C. 1994. *Worlds of difference: Inequality in the aging experience.* Thousand Oaks, CA: Pine Forge Press.

Stone, L. 1979. *The family, sex and marriage in England 1500–1800.* New York: Harper Torch Books.

Stone, R., Cafferata, G., & Sangl, J. 1987. "Caregivers of the frail elderly: A national profile." *The Gerontologist, 27,* 616–626.

"The strange world of JonBenet." 1997. *Newsweek,* January 20.

Straus, M. A. 1990. "Ordinary violence, child abuse, and wife beating: What do they have in common?" In M. A. Straus & R. J. Gelles (Eds.), *Physical violence in American families.* New Brunswick, NJ: Transaction.

———. 1991. "Physical violence in American families: Incidence, rates, causes, and trends." In D. Knudsen & J. Miller (Eds.), *Abused and battered.* New York: Aldine.

———. 1994. *Beating the devil out of them.* New York: Lexington Books.

Straus, M. A., & Gelles, R. J. 1986. "Societal change in family violence from 1975 to 1985 as revealed by two national surveys." *Journal of Marriage and the Family, 48,* 465–479.

———. 1990. "How violent are American families? Estimates from the National Family Violence Resurvey and other studies." In M. A. Straus & R. J. Gelles (Eds.), *Physical violence in American families.* New Brunswick, NJ: Transaction.

Straus, M. A., Gelles, R. J., & Steinmetz, S. K. 1980. *Behind closed doors: Violence in the American family.* New York: Doubleday/Anchor.

Strom, R., Collinsworth, P., Strom, P., & Griswold, D. 1992–1993. "Strengths and needs of black grandparents." *International Journal of Aging and Human Development, 36,* 255–268.

Strong, B., & DeVault, C. 1992. *The marriage and family experience.* St. Paul, MN: West.

Strube, M. J., & Barbour, L. S. 1983. "The decision to leave an abusive relationship: Economic dependence and psychological commitment." *Journal of Marriage and the Family, 45,* 785–793.

Stryker, J. 1997. "The age of innocence isn't what it once was." *New York Times,* July 13.

"Study of poor children shows powerful choice: Heat over food." 1992. *New York Times,* September 9.

Suarez, Z. 1998. "The Cuban-American family." In C. H. Mindel, R. W. Habeastein, & R. Wright (Eds.), *Ethnic families in America: Patterns and variations.* Upper Saddle River, NJ: Prentice-Hall.

Sullivan, A. 1996. "When plagues end: Notes on the twilight of an epidemic." *New York Times Magazine,* November 10.

Sullivan, M. 1996. "Rozzie and Harriet? Gender and family patterns of lesbian coparents." *Gender and Society, 10,* 747–767.

Sullivan, O. 1997. "The division of housework among 're-married' couples." *Journal of Family Issues, 18,* 205–223.

Sung, K. 1993. "Filial piety and care of the old in Korea." In L. Tepperman & S. J. Wilson (Eds.), *Next of kin.* Englewood Cliffs, NJ: Prentice-Hall.

Swarns, R. L. 1997. "In a policy shift, more parents are arrested for child neglect." *New York Times,* October 25.

Sweet, J. A., & Bumpass, L. L. 1987. *American families and households.* New York: Russell Sage.

Szinovacz, M. E., & Egley, L. C. 1995. "Comparing one-partner and couple data on sensitive marital behaviors: The case of marital violence." *Journal of Marriage and the Family, 57,* 995–1010.

Takagi, D. Y. 1994. "Japanese American families." In R. L. Taylor (Ed.), *Minority families in the United States.* Englewood Cliffs, NJ: Prentice-Hall.

Talbot, M. 1997. "Dial-a-wife." *The New Yorker,* October 20 & 27.

Tauber, M. A. 1979. "Parental socialization techniques and sex differences in children's play." *Child Development, 50,* 225–234.

Tavris, C. 1992. *Mismeasure of women.* New York: Touchstone.

———. 1996. "Goodbye, Ozzie and Harriet." *New York Times Book Review,* September 22.

Taylor, R. J., Chatters, L. M., Tucker, M. B., & Lewis, E. 1990. "Developments in research on black families: A decade review." *Journal of Marriage and the Family, 52,* 993–1014.

Taylor Haizlip, S. 1995. "Passing." *American Heritage,* February/March, 46–54.

Teachman, J. D. 1991. "Contributions to children by divorced fathers." *Social Problems, 38,* 358–371.

"Ten facts about women workers." 1997. *World Almanac.* Mahwah, NJ: World Almanac Books.

Terman, L. 1938. *Psychological factors in marital happiness.* New York: McGraw-Hill.

Terry, D. 1996. "In Wisconsin, a rarity of a fetal-harm case." *New York Times,* August 17.

Testa, M., & Krogh, M. 1995. "The effect of employment on marriage among black males in inner-city Chicago." In M. B. Tucker & C. Mitchell-Kernan (Eds.), *The decline in marriage among African Americans.* New York: Russell Sage.

Thibaut, J., & Kelley, H. 1959. *The social psychology of groups.* New York: Wiley.

Thompson, L., & Walker, A. J. 1989. "Gender in families: Women and men in marriage, work, and parenthood." *Journal of Marriage and the Family, 51,* 845–871.

Thoresen, J. H. 1991. "Sociolegal definitions of family." *Clinical Sociology Review, 9,* 59–70.

Thorne, B., & Yalom, M. 1982. *Rethinking the family: Some feminist questions.* New York: Longman.

Thornton, A. 1989. "Changing attitudes toward family issues in the United States." *Journal of Marriage and the Family, 51*, 873–893.

Thurow, L. 1995. "Companies merge, families break up." *New York Times,* September 3.

Tiano, S. 1987. "Gender, work and world capitalism: Third world women's role in development." In B. B. Hess & M. M. Ferree (Eds.), *Analyzing gender: A handbook of social science research.* Newbury Park, CA: Sage.

"Tough love index." 1996. *New York Times,* December 8.

Tran, T. V. 1998. "The Vietnamese-American family." In C. H. Mindel, R. W. Habeastein, & R. Wright (Eds.), *Ethnic families in America: Patterns and variations.* Upper Saddle River, NJ: Prentice-Hall.

Treas, J., & Bengston, V. L. 1982. "The demography of mid- and late-life transitions." *Annals of the American Academy of Political and Social Science, 464,* 11–21.

Trent, K., & South, S. J. 1989. "Structural determinant of the divorce rate: A cross-societal analysis." *Journal of Marriage and the Family, 51,* 391–404.

Trost, J. 1988. "Conceptualising the family." *International Sociology, 3,* 301–308.

Tucker, M. B., & Mitchell-Kernan, C. 1990. "New trends in Black American interracial marriage: The social structural context." *Journal of Marriage and the Family, 46,* 279–290.

———. 1995. "Trends in African American family formation: A theoretical and statistical overview." In M. B. Tucker and C. Mitchell-Kernan (Eds.), *The decline in marriage among African Americans.* New York: Russell Sage.

"Tune in to adoption myths." 1988. *Psychology Today,* November, p. 12.

Turner, R. W., & Killian, L. M. 1987. *Collective behavior.* Englewood Cliffs, NJ: Prentice-Hall.

Tuttle, W. 1993. *Daddy's gone to war: The Second World War in the lives of America's children.* New York: Oxford University Press.

Uchitelle, L. 1993. "Use of temporary workers is on rise in manufacturing." *New York Times,* July 6.

———. 1997. "Welfare recipients taking jobs often held by the working poor." *New York Times,* April 1.

Uhlenberg, P. 1980. "Death and the family." *Journal of Family History, 5,* 313–320.

Uhlenberg, P., & Myers, M. A. 1981. "Divorce and the elderly." *The Gerontologist, 21,* 276–282.

Ulrich, L. T. 1990. *A midwife's tale: The life of Martha Ballard, based on her diary, 1785–1812.* New York: Knopf.

Umberson, D., & Chen, M. D. 1994. "Effects of a parent's death on adult children: Relationship salience and reaction to loss." *American Sociological Review, 59,* 152–168.

Umberson, D., Chen, M. D., House, J. S., Hopkins, K., & Slaten, E. 1996. "The effect of social relationships on psychological well-being: Are men and women really so different?" *American Sociological Review, 61,* 837–857.

Umberson, D., Wortman, C. B., & Kessler, R. C. 1992. "Widowhood and depression: Explaining long-term gender differences in vulnerability." *Journal of Health and Social Behavior, 33,* 10–24.

United States Bureau of the Census. 1991. *Statistical abstract of the United States.* Washington, DC: U.S. Government Printing Office.

———. 1992. *Statistical abstract of the United States.* Washington, DC: U.S. Government Printing Office.

———. 1993. *We the American . . . Asians.* Washington, DC: U.S. Government Printing Office.

———. 1994. *Statistical abstract of the United States.* Washington, DC: U.S. Government Printing Office.

———. 1995. *Statistical abstract of the United States.* Washington, DC: U.S. Government Printing Office.

———. 1996. *Census and you,* April, p. 4.

———. 1997(a). *Statistical abstract of the United States.* Washington, DC: U.S. Government Printing Office.

———. 1997(b). *Census and you,* May, p. 8.

———. 1997(c). *Poverty in the United States: 1995, series p. 60–194.* Washington, DC: U.S. Government Printing Office.

———. 1998. *All persons 15 years old and over by median and mean income and sex: 1974–1996.* Table P–9. U.S. Census Bureau Web Site (www.census.gov).

United States Bureau of Justice Statistics. 1995. *Violence against women: Estimates from the redesigned survey.* Washington, DC: U.S. Government Printing Office.

Usdansky, M. L. 1996. "Single motherhood: Stereotypes vs. statistics." *New York Times,* February 11.

Utne, M. K., Hatfield, E., Traupmann, J., & Greenberger, D. 1984. "Equity, marital satisfaction, and stability." *Journal of Social and Personal Relationships, 1,* 323–332.

van den Berghe, P. 1979. *Human family systems.* New York: Elsevier.

Vanek, J. 1980. "Work, leisure and family roles: Farm households in the United States: 1920–1955." *Journal of Family History, 5,* 422–431.

Van Willigen, J., & Channa, V. C. 1991. "Law, custom and crimes against women: The problem of dowry death in India." *Human Organization, 50,* 369–377.

Vaughan, D. 1986. *Uncoupling.* New York: Vintage.

Veevers, J. 1980. *Childless by choice.* Toronto: Butterworth.

Vincent, J. P., Weiss, R. L., & Birchler, G. R. 1975. "Dyadic problem solving behavior as a function of marital distress and spousal vs. stranger interactions." *Behavior Therapy, 6,* 475–487.

"Vital signs." 1995. *The Nation,* September 11.

Vobejda, B. 1996. "Study rebuts 'danger' of day care." *Indianapolis Star,* April 21.

Voyandoff, P. 1990. "Economic distress and family relations: A review of the eighties." *Journal of Marriage and the Family, 52,* 1099–1115.

Vroegh, K. S. 1997. "Transracial adoptees: Developmental status after 17 years." *American Journal of Orthopsychiatry, 67,* 568–575.

Wagatsuma, H. 1981. "Child abandonment and infanticide: A Japanese case." In J. E. Korbin (Ed.), *Child abuse and neglect: Cross-cultural perspectives.* Berkeley: University of California Press.

Waite, L. J. 1995. "Does marriage matter?" *Demography, 32,* 483–507.

Waldfogel, J. 1997. "The effect of children on women's wages." *American Sociological Review, 62,* 209–217.

Walker, A., & Parmar, P. 1993. *Warrior marks: Female genital mutilation and the sexual blinding of women.* New York: Harcourt Brace.

Waller, W. 1937. "The rating and dating complex." *American Sociological Review, 2,* 727–737.

Wallerstein, J., & Blakeslee, S. 1989. *Second chances: Men, women and children a decade after divorce.* New York: Ticknor & Fields.

Wallis, C. 1989. "Onward, women!" *Time,* December 4.

Walsh, A., & Gordon, R. A. 1995. *Biosociology: An emerging paradigm.* Westport, CT: Praeger.

Walters, L. H. 1982. "Are families different from other groups?" *Journal of Marriage and the Family, 44,* 841–850.

Walton, J. 1990. *Sociology and critical inquiry.* Belmont, CA: Wadsworth.

Warren, C. A. B. 1987. *Madwives: Schizophrenic women in the 1950's.* New Brunswick, NJ: Rutgers University Press.

Wattenberg, E. 1986. "The fate of baby boomers and their children." *Social Work, 31,* 20–28.

Weibel-Orlando, J. 1997. "Grandparenting styles: Native American perspectives." In M. Hutter (Ed.), *The family experience.* Boston: Allyn & Bacon.

Weitz, R. 1990. "Living with the stigma of AIDS." *Qualitative Sociology, 13,* 23–38.

Weitzman, L. 1985. *The divorce revolution: The unexpected consequences for women and children in America.* New York: Free Press.

West, C., & Zimmerman, D. H. 1991. "Doing gender." In J. Lorber & S. A. Farrell (Eds.), *The social construction of gender.* Newbury Park, CA: Sage.

Westin, A. 1984. "The origins of modern claims to privacy." In F. D. Schoeman (Ed.), *Philosophical dimensions of privacy: An anthology.* New York: Cambridge University Press.

Westman, J. C. 1996. "The rationale and feasibility of licensing parents." *Society, 34,* 46–52.

Weston, K. 1991. *Families we choose: Lesbians, gays and kinship.* New York: Columbia University Press.

White, J. E. 1997. "Multiracialism: The melding of America." *Time,* May 5.

White, L. 1987. "Freedom versus constraint: The new synthesis." *Journal of Family Issues, 8,* 468–470.

———. 1994. "Coresidence and leaving home: Young adults and their parents." *Annual Review of Sociology, 20,* 81–102.

White, L., & Brinkerhoff, D. 1981. "The sexual division of labor: Evidence from childhood." *Social Forces, 60,* 170–181.

White, L., & Edwards, J. N. 1990. "Emptying the nest and parental well-being: An analysis of national panel data." *American Sociological Review, 55,* 235-242.

White, L., & Keith, B. 1990. "The effect of shift work on the quality and stability of marital relations." *Journal of Marriage and the Family, 52,* 453–462.

White, L., & Riedmann, A. 1992. "When the Brady Bunch grows up: Step/half- and fullsibling relationships in adulthood." *Journal of Marriage and the Family, 54,* 197–208.

Whiteford, L. M., & Gonzalez, L. 1995. "Stigma: The hidden burden of infertility." *Social Science and Medicine, 40,* 27–36.

Whitehead, B. D. 1993(a). "Dan Quayle was right." *The Atlantic Monthly,* April, 47–84.

———. 1993(b). "The new family values." *Utne Reader,* May/June, 61–66.

———. 1997. *The divorce culture.* New York: Knopf.

"Why law firms cannot afford to maintain the mommy track." 1996. *Harvard Law Review, 109,* 1375–1392.

Whyte, M. K. 1990. *Dating, mating and marriage.* New York: Aldine de Gryter.

———. 1992. "Choosing mates—the American way." *Society,* March/April, 71–77.

Wiederman, M. W., & Allgeier, E. R. 1992. "Gender differences in mate selection criteria: Sociobiological or socioeconomic explanation." *Ethnology and Sociobiology, 13,* 115–124.

Wilkerson, I. 1990. "Clemency granted to 25 women convicted for assault or murder." *New York Times,* December 22.

———. 1991. "As interracial marriage rises, acceptance lags." *New York Times,* December 12.

Will, J., Self, P., & Datan, N. 1976. "Maternal behavior and perceived sex of infant." *American Journal of Ortho Psychiatry, 46,* 135–139.

Williams, G. H. 1995. *Life on the color line: The true story of a white boy who discovered he was black.* New York: Dutton.

Williams, G. I., & Williams, R. H. 1995. " 'All we want is equality': Rhetorical framing in the fathers' rights movement." In J. Best (Ed.), *Images of issues.* New York: Aldine de Gryter.

Williams, L. 1991. "In a 90's quest for black identity, intense doubts and disagreements." *New York Times,* November 30.

Willie, C. V. 1981. *A new look at the black family.* Bayside, NY: General Hall.

Wilson, W. J. 1987. *The truly disadvantaged: The inner city, the underclass and public policy.* Chicago: University of Chicago Press.

Winston, N. A. 1988. "Sex-bias response to telephoned job inquiries, Tampa, 1987." *Sociology and Social Research, 72,* 121–124.

Winton, C. A. 1995. *Frameworks for studying families.* Guilford, CT: Dushkin.

Wolfe, A. 1991. *America at century's end.* Berkeley: University of California Press.

Wong, M. G. 1998. "The Chinese-American family." In C. H. Mindel, R. W. Habeastein, & R. Wright (Eds.), *Ethnic families in America: Patterns and variations.* Upper Saddle River, NJ: Prentice-Hall.

Wood, P. L. 1975. "The victim in a forcible rape case: A feminist view." In L. G. Schultz (Ed.), *Rape victimology.* Springfield, IL: Charles C Thomas.

Woodward, K. L., Quade, V., & Kantrowitz, B. 1995. "Q: When is a marriage not a marriage?" *Newsweek,* March 13.

"Working women's woes." 1994. *US News and World Report,* October 24.

"Workplace experts say more men are taking time off to care for children." 1997. *CNN On-line,* June 13. (www.CNN.com)

Wright, E. O., Costello, C., Hachen, D., & Sprague, J. 1982. "The American class structure." *American Sociological Review, 47,* 709–726.

Wright, E. O., Shire, K., Hwang, S. L., Dolan, M., & Baxter, J. 1992. "The non-effects of class on the gendered division of labor in the home: A comparative study of Sweden and the United States." *Gender and Society, 6,* 252–282.

WuDunn, S. 1995. "In Japan, still getting tea and no sympathy." *New York Times,* August 27.

———. 1996. "A taboo creates a land of Romeos and Juliets." *New York Times,* September 11.

Ybarra, L. 1982. "When wives work: The impact on the Chicano family." *Journal of Marriage and the Family, 44,* 169–178.

Yee, B. W. K. 1992. "Elders in Southeast Asian refugee families." *Generations,* Summer, 24–27.

Yllo, K. 1993. "Through a feminist lens: Gender, power and violence." In R. J. Gelles & D. R. Loeske (Eds.), *Current controversies on family violence.* Newbury Park, CA: Sage.

Yllo, K., & Straus, M. A. 1990. "Patriarchy and violence against wives: The impact of structural and normative factors." In M. A. Straus & R. J. Gelles (Eds.), *Physical violence in American families.* New Brunswick, NJ: Transaction.

Yoest, C. C. 1997. "Fountain of youth, spring of wealth." In H. A. Widdison (Ed.), *Social problems 1997/1998.* Guilford, CT: Dushkin/McGraw-Hill.

Yogev, S. 1981. "Do professional women have egalitarian marital relationships?" *Journal of Marriage and the Family, 43,* 865–871.

Yorburg, B. 1993. *Family relationships.* New York: St. Martin's Press.

Young, M. E. 1995. "Reproductive technologies and the law: Norplant and the bad mother." *Marriage and the Family Review, 21,* 259–281.

Zastrow, C. 1977. *Outcome of black children–white parents transracial adoptions.* San Francisco: R & E Research Associates.

Zelizer, V. 1985. *Pricing the priceless child.* New York: Basic Books.

Zhang, S. D., & Odenwald, W. F. 1995. "Misexpression of the white gene triggers male-male courtship in Drosphilia." *Proceedings of the National Academy of Sciences, 92,* 5525–5529.

Zimmerman, S. L. 1992. *Family policies and family well-being: The role of political culture.* Newbury Park, CA: Sage.

Zinsmeister, K. 1990. "Raising Hiroko: The child-centered culture of Japan." *The American Enterprise, 1,* 52–59.

Zurcher, L. A., & Snow, D. A. 1981. "Collective behavior: Social movements." In M. Rosenberg & R. H. Turner (Eds.), *Social psychology: Sociological perspectives.* New York: Basic Books.

Zvonkovic, A. M., Greaves, K. M., Schmiege, C. J., & Hall, L. D. 1996. "The marital construction of gender through work and family decisions: A qualitative analysis." *Journal of Marriage and the Family, 58,* 91–100.

GLOSSARY/INDEX

P

Pakistan, 166
parental adjustment perspective, 394
parental conflict perspective, 394–395
parental investment The relative contribution parents make to the biological creation of offspring, 187
parental loss perspective, 394
parenthood, 246–282
  adoptive, 252–253
  blended families and, 408–410
  childbearing process and, 262–264
  child-support policies and, 401–403
  custody decisions and, 396–400
  dating rights of children and, 180–181
  divorce and, 384–385, 394–396, 400–406
  empty nest syndrome and, 429–431
  gender differences in, 248–250, 266–276
  grandparenting and, 433–436
  homosexuality and, 262, 318
  postponement of, 258, 260
  poverty and, 261
  privacy rights and, 44–45, 109
  pronatalism and, 251–262
  social changes and, 116–117
  study assignment on, 282
  summary points on, 277
  transition to, 264–265
  trends in motherhood and, 278–281
  See also child rearing; fathers; mothers
parents
  absent, 403–405
  abusive, 356–365
  death of, 450
  elderly, 59, 437–439, 442–448
  gay and lesbian couples as, 262
  homeless, 108–109
  privacy rights of, 44–45, 109, 361–363
  sexual orientation of, 318
  single, 123, 380, 384–385
  stepparents, 408–410
paternal custody, 397
paternity, 270
Paterno, Joe, 335
patrilineal society A society in which children's kin are traced only

through the father's side of the family, 10, 396
Peacock, Kenneth, 351, 353
peer groups Reference groups that consist of people with similar attributes, such as age, education, activities, preferences, and so on, 301–302
period effects Historical events or major social trends that contribute to the unique shape and outlook of a birth cohort, 424
Pfohl, Stephen, 359
politics
  gay marriage and, 13–15
  symbolism of family and, 15–16
  See also social policy
polygamy, 9–10
population pressures, 465–466
poverty, 102–109
  debate over welfare and, 103–107
  divorced women and, 384–385
  housing issues related to, 107–108
  pronatalism and, 261
  race/ethnicity and, 323
power
  consequences of, 74–75
  contemporary changes in, 75–76
  family inequality and, 345–346
  family relations and, 64–76
  gender differences and, 66–70
  homosexual households and, 355–356
  marital dynamics and, 70–74
  orchestration vs. implementation, 74–75
  societal inequality and, 346–348
powerlessness bias, 151
pregnancy
  fetal rights and, 271–274
  infertility treatments and, 255–257
  teenage, 302–304
  See also childbearing; human reproduction
prejudice, 30. *See also* discrimination
premature ejaculation, 172
principle of least interest A situation in which the less-dependent partner in a relationship—that is, the one who has more alternatives outside the relationship—has the

greatest power in it because that person can more easily abandon the relationship, 193
privacy
  cultural variations in, 46–47
  family rights to, 37–42
  history of, 40–42
  intimate violence and, 38, 348–349
  location of, 38–40
  paradox of, 42–43
  parents' rights to, 44–45
  research ethics and, 151–153
private culture A couple's own unique way of dealing with the demands of everyday married life; a consistent pattern of interaction—a set of habits, rules, and shared reality that develops in families, 208
progressive family ideology A system of beliefs that families are not declining but instead are caught up in continual evolution and transition; a belief that family is a social construction—a product of the attitudes and behaviors of the people touched by it—not a universal form that exists for all times and all societies, 470–472
pronatalist society A society in which it is believed that all married couples should reproduce or should want to reproduce; having children is portrayed as essential to self-fulfillment and necessary for the future survival of the society, 251–262
  adopted children in, 252–253
  infertility in, 254–259
  public policy in, 260–262
  voluntary childlessness in, 259–260
property, children as, 296–297
protective incarceration, 273
puberty The maturing of the genital organs and the development of secondary sex characteristics (for example, breasts and hips in girls; facial hair and deepening of the voice in boys), 297–298. *See also* adolescence
public policy. *See* social policy